BIOFEEDBACK

CLINICAL
APPLICATIONS
IN BEHAVIORAL
MEDICINE

David S. Olton

*The Johns Hopkins University
and Medical School*

Aaron R. Noonberg

Kent State University

Prentice-Hall, Inc., Englewood Cliffs, New Jersey 07632

Library of Congress Cataloging in Publication Data

OLTON, DAVID S
    Biofeedback: clinical applications in behavioral
medicine.

    Bibliography: p. 385
    Includes index.
    1. Medicine, Psychosomatic. 2. Biofeedback
training. I. Noonberg, Aaron R., joint author.
II. Title.
RC49.04 1980   616.08   80–366
ISBN 0–13–076315–2

A. R. N. dedicates his efforts to his most understanding parents,
Herman and Edith Noonberg

Editorial/production supervision and interior design by Dianne Poonarian
Cover design by Jerry Pfeifer
Manufacturing buyers: Harry P. Baisley and Edmund W. Leone

Printed in the United States of America

10 9 8 7 6 5 4 3

PRENTICE-HALL INTERNATIONAL, INC., *London*
PRENTICE-HALL OF AUSTRALIA PTY. LIMITED, *Sydney*
PRENTICE-HALL OF CANADA, LTD., *Toronto*
PRENTICE-HALL OF INDIA PRIVATE LIMITED, *New Delhi*
PRENTICE-HALL OF JAPAN, INC., *Tokyo*
PRENTICE-HALL OF SOUTHEAST ASIA PTE. LTD., *Singapore*
WHITEHALL BOOKS LIMITED, WELLINGTON, *New Zealand*

CONTENTS

Preface, ix

I THE NATURE OF BIOFEEDBACK   1

Biofeedback as Behavioral Medicine, 3   **1**

Feedback and Control Systems, 9   **2**

> Control Systems and Biofeedback, 10
> Types of Feedback, 14
> Feedback and Knowledge of Results, 15
> Negative Feedback and Homeostasis, 17
> Control Systems and the Central Nervous System, 19
> Biofeedback and the Mechanisms of Mediation, 21

Learning and Performance, 23   **3**

> Operant Conditioning, 24   Classical Conditioning, 34

The Biological Bases of Behavior, 41   **4**

> Nerve Cells, 42   Autonomic Nervous System, 47
> Functional Organization of the Nervous System, 50
> Muscles, 53

II PROCESS AND PROCEDURES 55

5 Visceral Control and Mediation, 57

Voluntary Control, 58
Direct and Indirect Mediation, 60
Control or Conditioning, 67

6 Psychophysiology, 70

Signals, 72   Muscle Activity, 74   Blood Pressure, 80
Heartbeat, 81   Brain Waves, 82
Blood Flow and Skin Temperature, 84
Suppliers of Biofeedback Equipment, 85

7 Clinical Procedures, 89

Initial Sessions, 90   Middle Sessions, 100
Terminal and Follow-up Sessions, 111

III CLINICAL APPLICATIONS OF BIOFEEDBACK 113

8 Tension Headaches, 116

Introduction, 118   Symptoms, 119
Mechanism, 123   Treatment, 138
Clinical Program, 152   Research Considerations, 155

9 Migraine Headaches, 157

Introduction, 158   Symptoms, 160
Mechanism, 164   Treatment, 179
Clinical Program, 189   Research Considerations, 197

Peripheral Vascular Disorders: Raynaud's Disease, 201 **10**

*Introduction, 202   Symptoms, 204   Mechanism, 208
Treatment, 211   Clinical Program, 214*

Asthma, 220 **11**

*Introduction, 221   Symptoms, 223   Mechanism, 232
Treatment, 236   Clinical Program, 245
Research Considerations, 250*

Epilepsy, 252 **12**

*Introduction, 253   Symptoms, 254   Mechanism, 259
Treatment, 260   Clinical Program, 273
Research Considerations, 282*

Neuromuscular Reeducation, 284 **13**

INTRODUCTION, 285

MUSCLES OF THE LIMBS AND TRUNK, 287

*Paralysis and Paresis, 287
Peripheral Nerve Injury, 292   Cerebral Palsy, 293
Foot Drop Following Cerebral Stroke, 296*

MUSCLES OF THE HEAD AND NECK, 299

*Spasmodic Torticollis, 299   Bell's Palsy, 303
Facial Paralysis Following Traumatic Damage to the
Facial Nerve, 305
Temporomandibular Joint Syndrome, 306
Blepharospasm, 310
Excessive Contraction of Throat Muscles, 311
Parkinson's Disease, 312*

CLINICAL PROGRAM, 313

Gastrointestinal Disorders, 322 **14**

INTRODUCTION, 323

Peptic Ulcers, 323   Fecal Incontinence, 331

OTHER GASTROINTESTINAL DISORDERS, 337

Functional Diarrhea, 337
Urinary Retention and Incontinence, 338

CLINICAL PROGRAM, 339

Cardiovascular Disorders, 343 **15**

INTRODUCTION, 344

HYPERTENSION, 344

CARDIAC ARRHYTHMIAS, 357

Wolff-Parkinson-White Syndrome, 358
Premature Ventricular Contractions, 359
Tachycardia and Fibrillation, 364

OTHER CARDIAC ABNORMALITIES, 365

Postural Hypotension, 365

CLINICAL PROGRAM, 373

Glossary, 375

References, 385

Author Index, 417

Subject Index, 424

PREFACE

This book is written primarily for those who are interested in the practical application of biofeedback in a clinical or research setting. Consequently our emphasis has been on a set of psychophysiological disorders (Chapters 8 through 15), the way in which biofeedback has been used to treat them, and a suggested treatment program. The list of problems to which biofeedback has been applied is impressive—tension headaches, migraine headaches, peripheral vascular problems producing cold hands or feet, epilepsy, asthma, ulcers, fecal incontinence, neuromuscular difficulties such as paralysis and spasticity, and cardiovascular disorders such as hypertension and abnormal heart beats. The success of biofeedback in each of these areas has varied. In some cases, it is ready to be used as a routine treatment procedure with the expectation of a very high cure rate in a relatively short period of time. In other cases, evidence is encouraging but biofeedback must be used more cautiously and in an exploratory manner. There is little question in our minds, however, that biofeedback has matured to the point where it should become a major component in the treatment program of every psychophysiological disorder.

The format of each clinical chapter is the same. The final goal, of course, is a treatment program and at the end of each chapter we have provided such an outline. Read in conjunction with Chapter 7 describing general clinical procedures, it should provide sufficient information necessary to understand and initiate biofeedback treatment. The rest of the chapter is devoted to a review of the disorder being considered. First is a brief introduction to the topic, describing the disorder and the approaches taken by biofeedback treatment. Next is a discussion of the symptoms as experienced by the patient, and the physiological mechanism that is responsible for these symptoms. The treatment sections begin with a short overview, describing the general procedures for biofeedback treatment. Wherever possible, this is followed by one or more case reports, describing in detail the procedures and progress of a particular individual. A summary of treatment reports follows, with particular emphasis on issues such as the overall effectiveness of biofeedback when used as the only treatment, the ability of biofeedback to treat problems that are severe and of long duration, the general format of clinical procedures, and the long-term success as indicated by follow-up information. Knowing how to use biofeedback is one issue; knowing whether it is justified or not is another. The purpose of this section is to provide information necessary to decide the costs and benefits of biofeedback treatment.

People who wish to use biofeedback come from a variety of fields—psychology, medicine, engineering, and social work, to name just a few. To meet the needs of students and workers in these fields who wish to become involved with clinical and/or experimental biofeedback, we have offered a course at Hopkins during the past four years, and the book was developed in this course. Students typically have expertise in one or more related fields and wish to understand biofeedback with the ultimate goal of critically evaluating the field and subsequently improving it. Because many of the readers of this book may be in a similar position, that is, expert in a related field but lacking a thorough background in all areas relevant to biofeedback, we have organized the book into three sections. The first two provide a quick overview of the relevant bodies of knowledge and their application to biofeedback treatment. The rest of the book can be read without reference to these chapters, but where further details are necessary, they will be of help. We have also provided a glossary at the end which defines the technical terms used here.

While the book has a strong applied emphasis, we have also tried to maintain high scholarly standards. As one step toward this goal, we have included only material that is published or should be published soon. This restriction ensures that the data we discuss have been through an editorial review and that they are available for the reader to pursue in more detail if desired. Our reviews of biofeedback treatment have been extensive, and we have summarized the reports in a table near the end of each treatment chapter. Finding one miraculous cure by almost any method is not difficult. Consequently, the emphasis is on the overall success seen in the field as a whole.

We have also made a great deal of effort to be accurate throughout the book. For example, a common complaint is the number of errors that appear in references. To avoid these, we have personally taken the final list of references and rechecked them again with the original sources to make certain the citations are accurate. Another common difficulty is the lack of critical pieces of information about either the procedures or results of published reports. In our reviews of the literature, we have provided as many of the relevant details as possible, but occasionally these were missing from the original sources so they had to be omitted here. In spite of our efforts, there will undoubtedly be a few errors that appear in the book, and we would appreciate hearing about them so they can be corrected. If we have overlooked some relevant information, we apologize, and would like to be told about that as well.

We have done our best to help the reader use this book efficiently, and there are four aids to finding material. The Table of Contents gives the overall organization of the book. The first page of each chapter provides the major topics and the order in which they are discussed. The Subject Index, which is as extensive and as thoroughly cross-referenced as we could make it, can be used to find particular subjects and the other topics related to them. The Author Index provides an alphabetical listing of authors, irrespective of the order of the names on a publication; it can be used to find all citations to a given individual. The Glossary provides a list of technical terms which may be unfamiliar, gives their definitions, and indicates the pages where we first discuss them. We hope that these aids will enable you to find all the material you need rapidly and accurately.

We gratefully thank the following for their help: Dr. Paul McHugh, the Chairman of the Department of Psychiatry and Behavioral Sciences, and Dr. Michael Cataldo, the Director of the Behavioral Medicine Clinic, for allowing us to use the facilities of the Behavioral Medicine Clinic for treatment and research; Drs. David Anderson, Fred Berlin, Bruce Bird, Joe Brady, Tom Cayton, Henry Emurian, Bernie Engel, Alan Harris, Rudolf Hoehn-Saric, Bruce Masek, Lynn Parker, Alex Perski, Dennis Russo, Ed Taub, Jim Varney, and Bill Whitehead, all members of the Behavioral Medicine Center who provided examples of the right way to do research and treatment and constantly helped improve our ideas about biofeedback; Mss. Peggy Holden, Eileen Kelmartin, Barbara Kerr, Joan Krach, Carol Mangini, and Mary Richardson, who patiently typed and retyped the manuscript and corrected our writing errors; the many students in our course, Biofeedback and Self Control, during the past four years who have patiently worked through earlier versions of this manuscript, improved our ideas, and most especially helped us learn how to communicate them effectively; Mss. Penny Schwind and Libby Olton and Dr. James Becker who read the initial manuscript and provided us with valuable suggestions for revisions; Drs. Al Chapanis, James Deese, Robert

Hogan, and Julian Stanley who taught us to use rather than abuse the English language; Ms. Dianne Poonarian, who was forever patient, pleasant, and efficient while taking care of the apparently endless details of the production of this book; Mr. Ted Jursek, who answered more questions than we thought we could ask, set inhuman deadlines for the production of the book, and then was slightly forgiving when we failed to meet them; our friends who rarely saw us as we worked and heard us discuss little else besides the book when we did get together with them; the many publishers who freely gave us permission to reproduce their material.

THE NATURE OF BIOFEEDBACK

I

The chapters in this section review some of the basic concepts that are relevant to the application of biofeedback, and the ways these concepts are used to design a treatment program. The first chapter considers biofeedback as a component of behavioral medicine, indicates the ways in which it can be incorporated into any treatment program, and evaluates both its benefits and its limitations. The second chapter describes the idea of feedback. The effectiveness of biofeedback lies in its ability to teach a person to control a biological system. Thus an understanding of the nature of control systems and the ways in which they can be made to function most accurately is important in the design of any biofeedback program. The next chapter relates the topics of learning and performance to biofeedback. These areas of psychology have described the variables that influence behavior and the procedures that can produce the most rapid and most substantial changes in behavior as a result of experience. Biofeedback seeks to change behavior by applying the principles of learning to a particular individual and a particular biological system; the success of treatment should be enhanced by optimizing the parameters which lead to effective learning. The last chapter in this section reviews briefly the organization of the nervous system as it pertains to biofeedback. Of particular interest is the autonomic nervous system because this is the nervous system involved in so many psychophysiological disorders.

1

BIOFEEDBACK
AS BEHAVIORAL
MEDICINE

1

Biofeedback has developed from a curiosity to a well-established treatment for a variety of medical problems. Yet the scientific basis for its success and the procedures for using it are not widely known. As a result, biofeedback is not used as often as it should be, and a powerful therapeutic tool is omitted from treatment. By placing our discussion of biofeedback in the context of behavioral medicine, we will emphasize its role as a treatment for medical illness and describe the ways in which it can be most appropriately incorporated into a clinical program.

Biofeedback may be defined as any technique which increases the ability of a person to control voluntarily physiological activities by providing information about those activities. As discussed in further detail in the next chapter, feedback is information and *bio*feedback is information about the state of biological processes. In the context of this book, biofeedback is discussed as a means to treat a variety of medical illnesses. As such, it incorporates information from many different disciplines. The field of medicine describes the mechanisms which are responsible for the symptoms and the ways in which biofeedback alters these mechanisms. Biomedical engineering provides the concepts of control systems and the techniques which can be used to record and provide feedback about biological activities. Psychiatry, particularly psychosomatic medicine, has documented the role of behavioral factors both in the development of illness and in the alleviation of it. Psychology describes the ways in which treatment programs can be organized to teach self-control most rapidly and produce the highest level of performance. This brief review indicates that biofeedback is truly an interdisciplinary enterprise, and for those who may be unfamiliar with any of the relevant areas, the remaining chapters in these first two sections should provide the information necessary to understand the clinical applications discussed in the final section of the book.

The medical illnesses to which biofeedback has been applied are extensive (Fotopoulus & Sunderland 1978). They include some that are commonly associated with stress—tension and migraine headaches, ulcers, and asthma. They also include some that arise from obvious organic injury—fecal incontinence following damage to the nerves that control defecation, and paralysis and paresis following cerebral strokes or damage to the motor nerves. An important point in the application of biofeedback is the assumption that self-control can reduce the symptoms of the illness, *regardless of the reason why the illness occurred in the first place.* This statement is not meant to imply that biofeedback "cures" the illness in the sense that it restores the body parts destroyed by the injury. But as long as the damaged system has some function, biofeedback can train the individual to use the system more effectively. The general idea of control systems analyses is discussed further in the next chapter which points out that the aim of biofeedback is to improve the person's self-control with whatever resources are available. Obviously, the less the organic damage, the more successful the client can be. But even when the symptoms follow severe physical destruction, as in cerebral palsy and strokes, biofeedback can still improve function.

Behavioral medicine has emphasized the importance of having the client actively participate in the treatment program. The field is indeed part of medicine, because the problems it treats are medical ones. But it emphasizes the contribution of the person's behavior, both to the development of the medical illness and to its alleviation (Shapiro & Surwit 1976). Biofeedback is clearly a type of behavioral medicine (Miller 1978). First, the problems it treats are medical ones, as can be seen by a quick glance through the topics covered in Section III discussing the clinical applications of biofeedback. Second, the client is an important component in the treatment. The therapist can tell the client how to use the feedback equipment, but only the patient can actually produce the desired changes through compliance with the instructions and regular practice.

Placing the responsibility for the cure with the patient has both advantages and disadvantages. Once self-control is learned, the patient should be able to be independent of any other form of treatment. The very word *self-control* says it all: the patient has the capacity to alleviate the symptoms through his or her own behavior, and this independence is clearly a major advantage of this type of treatment. But independence has disadvantages too. Success will be obtained if and only if the patient is willing to take the considerable amount of time necessary to learn the self-control skills and then practice them conscientiously as needed. The therapist may have designed the perfect treatment program, but unless the patient follows it, no benefit will result.

The association of behavioral variables with illness has been known for many years. Indeed, the whole field of psychosomatic medicine developed documenting the ways in which people's behavior influenced the course of their diseases (Lipowski, Lipsitt, & Whybrow 1977). More recently, experimental studies have provided strong evidence of the relationship between people's experiences and their health. Of particular importance has been quantitative measures of stress and the effects they produce. One approach has ranked events in terms of *life change units.* Each change in a person's life is assumed to require some type of readjustment, and the magnitude of this readjustment can be measured in terms of the number of life change units on a Social Readjustment Scale (Holmes & Rahe 1967; Rahe 1975). The scale was originally established by having people rank order events in terms of the amount of readjustment that was required and rate each event with life change units ranging from 0 to 100. At the top of the list with 100 LCUs (life change units) was death of a spouse. Marriage received 50 units, minor violations of the law—11 units, and death of a close friend—37 units. All events required some readjustment, even events that were pleasant, such as an outstanding personal achievement (26 LCUs), completing school (26 LCUs), and vacations (13 LCUs). The importance of the number of LCUs accumulated during the course of several years was demonstrated by correlating the number of LCUs experienced by an individual with the likelihood of a major illness. As the number of LCUs in a year increased from less than 150 to over 300, the probability of an illness steadily increased until more than 85% of the people with scores greater than 300 experienced some serious health problem.

Biofeedback acknowledges the relationship between behavioral variables and illness, but it emphasizes the ways in which behavior can be used to alleviate the illness rather than to induce it. Much of the excitement about biofeedback and behavioral medicine is this optimistic outlook; whatever the person's problem, it can probably be made better through appropriate use of behavioral treatments.

As evidence accumulated that biofeedback was therapeutically effective, the next question to be answered was the component of biofeedback responsible for success. Many of the initial reports were case studies describing the results of relatively uncontrolled procedures. This type of approach has its merits (Blanchard & Young 1974), especially as a field begins to develop. But once a procedure has shown its therapeutic potential, well designed studies are necessary to determine what aspects of the treatment program are being effective. For example, the expectations of the client (Stroebel & Glueck 1973), the impressiveness of the electronic equipment associated with biofeedback, the enthusiasm of the therapist—these and many other factors not associated with the biofeedback itself may have been responsible for success. However, the results of subsequent experiments comparing the effectiveness of different types of feedback do not support these explanations and show that the critical component for therapeutic success is learning to control the biological function using feedback.

The studies addressing this issue have used two types of feedback. One is *correct* feedback. Here the information the person receives about the biological function accurately reflects the state of that function and is therapeutically appropriate. As a result the person can use the feedback to learn to control the biological function in the way necessary to eliminate the symptoms. The other type of feedback is *incorrect* so that the person cannot learn the necessary control. With *uncorrelated* incorrect feedback, the information the person receives does not reflect the state of the biological system. For example, feedback indicating that skin temperature has risen may be given both when the skin temperature has risen and when it has fallen. Because the feedback is not correlated with the state of the biological function, the person cannot learn to control the function and the changes required for successful therapy do not take place. With *therapeutically inappropriate* incorrect feedback, the information given to the person accurately reflects the state of the biological function, but the person is trained to change the system in a direction opposite to that which will reduce the symptoms. Again the person does not learn to control the function in the correct way and the changes required for successful therapy do not take place.

The results of studies incorporating these three different feedback procedures consistently demonstrate that only the correct feedback procedure is clinically effective. With either type of incorrect feedback, clients continue to have symptoms that are unchanged or actually somewhat worse. An important point in these comparisons is that *all* aspects of the treatment procedure in the different conditions are the same with the single exception of the type of feedback: the clients are told that the treatment should be successful, they come to the clinic for the same number of treatment sessions of the same duration, and so on. The only difference is the type of feedback, and this must be the component responsible for the therapeutic success.

Although biofeedback's success is now well documented, the field is by no means closed. Indeed, the successes pose as many questions as they answer and challenge some of the fundamental ideas about the nature of an "illness" and the definition of a "cure." Biofeedback is at that exciting stage where its therapeutic usefulness has been clearly demonstrated, but the ways in which this usefulness can be maximized are not yet fully understood. This lack of understanding in no way compromises the clinical effectiveness of the treatment. Rather it provides the challenge for the future.

FEEDBACK AND CONTROL SYSTEMS

2

Control Systems and Biofeedback

Types of Feedback

Feedback and Knowledge of Results

Negative Feedback and Homeostasis

Control Systems and the Central Nervous System

Biofeedback and the Mechanisms of Mediation

At the core of biofeedback is, naturally enough, feedback. Indeed, bio-feedback can be thought of as a specialized application of feedback; the controller of the system is a person, and the system from which feedback is obtained is a biological one in that person. An understanding of feedback, and particularly the way in which it is used to assist the development of control, is critical to many aspects of biofeedback treatment, ranging from the design of effective clinical procedures to the description of the neurological and psychological mechanisms underlying performance. This chapter will provide a brief review of control systems analysis as applied to biofeedback, and indicate how this analysis is an effective means of integrating many of the diverse aspects of biofeedback discussed earlier in Chapter 1.

CONTROL SYSTEMS AND BIOFEEDBACK

In the context of biofeedback, feedback may be described as (a) information about the effects of a response (b) that is given to the person making that response (c) in order to improve control over that response. This description incorporates the basic meaning of feedback as it is used in a more general sense (Anliker 1977; Weiner 1948), but makes it directly applicable to biofeedback. Consider, for example, a procedure used to train patients who have abnormal heart beats to control their heart rate (Engel 1973). The patient lies down on a bed. Electrodes which record the electrical activity of the heart are put on the person's chest. The electrical signal from these is taken through amplifiers and then to a computer that calculates the heart rate by determining the time interval between each pair of heart beats. A box with three lights on it provides instructions to the person and indicates whether these instructions are being successfully carried out. Two lights indicate the direction in which heart rate should be changed. When the top (green) light is illuminated, heart rate should be increased; when the bottom (red) light is illuminated, heart rate should be decreased. The third (yellow) light in the middle tells the person whether heart rate has changed in the appropriate direction. When this light is on, heart rate has changed in the direction indicated by the instruction light; when the light is off, heart rate is either unchanged or moving in the wrong direction. The patient's goal is to keep the yellow light illuminated as long as possible.

The heart rate control procedure described here has all three characteristics of feedback described above. First, information is obtained about the heart rate response by the electrodes on the chest. Second, this information is provided to the person by means of the yellow light which tells him whether he has produced the desired change or not. Third, the goal of the procedure is to improve control over heart rate so that the person can increase it when the green light is on and decrease it when the red light is on. Finally, of course, the feedback is about a biological function so that the whole procedure is an example of *bio*feedback.

This heart rate biofeedback procedure can be summarized by a control system diagram as illustrated in Figure 2–1. The elements in the procedure are indicated by either a square (the instruction lights, the heart rate) or a circle (the patient). The relationship between each pair of elements is indicated by a line with an arrow showing the direction of this relationship. The diagram summarizes succinctly what took a paragraph to describe earlier. The patient (one element) is attempting to control heart rate (a second element) through the control relationship (upper line) while information about the state of the heart rate is being provided by the feedback relationship (lower line).

The symbol for the patient is a circle rather than a square to empha-

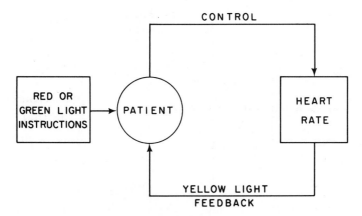

FIGURE 2–1   Biofeedback Training to Alter Heart Rate Presented as a Control Systems Diagram.
The red and green lights tell the client to decrease and increase heart rate, respectively. The yellow light provides feedback about success.

size the fact that the patient receives two pieces of information which must be compared: the red and green lights which provide the instruction about the type of response desired and the yellow light which indicates whether this response is being achieved. In actuality, of course, the patient could produce the correct response without having the red or green instruction lights by alternately trying to raise or lower heart rate and determining which response produced the yellow light. Such a procedure would be less efficient than providing the correct instructions, however, and in most control systems some indication of the desired state is provided by instructions which may be called the *set point* or *reference input.*

The whole feedback process makes a loop because all the arrows of the relationships point in a clockwise direction, emphasizing the continuous nature of the feedback process (Anliker 1977). The patient attempts to control heart rate, heart rate changes in some fashion, information about the actual heart rate change is provided by the yellow light, the patient evaluates the outcome, makes changes in his attempt to control heart rate, observes the subsequent results, makes further changes, and so on. In a more general sense, the person compares the instructions received with the actual response produced and seeks to reduce any discrepancy between these two (Anliker 1977).

This control loop can be drawn in a more general form as in Figure 2–2. This diagram incorporates all the aspects of biofeedback and self-control just discussed in the definition of biofeedback. Information about the state of a biological function is given to the person who then attempts

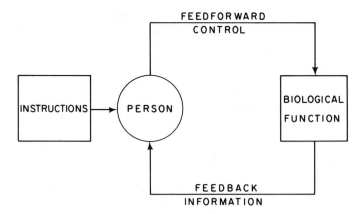

FIGURE 2–2   Biofeedback Indicated as a General Control Process.
The diagram emphasizes both the biofeedback and the self-control aspects of biofeedback treatment.

to control the function. Here the term *feedforward* has been introduced as another word to describe control. Although it is often used to indicate the takeover of a subordinate system by a superordinate system (Anliker 1977), such is not the case here, and it is used in its more mundane sense indicating simply a controlling relationship.

The parallels between feedback and feedforward emphasize their roles in this loop. The excitement about biofeedback arises not from the notion of feedback but rather from the use of this feedback to gain control over a feedforward mechanism (Mulholland 1977). Thus ironically the feedback in biofeedback is not really the important focus; the feedforward is. But in order to obtain accurate feedforward, the person needs to have feedback.

In some cases, feedback is readily available and feedforward control is relatively easy. Many of our behaviors, especially those in sports and motor skills, can be illustrated with the basic diagram of Figure 2–2. One example is an archer trying to put an arrow in the gold center of a target. The archer aims at the gold, releases the arrow, sees that it hits below the target, aims higher for the next shot, sees that the arrow hits just above the target, aims just slightly lower, and puts an arrow into dead center. There are two elements (archer and target) and two relationships (feedback about the location of the arrow, feedforward about the aim). This example fits the characteristics of feedback described in Figure 2–2, and is clearly one of biofeedback as well because the mechanism used to alter the aim of the bow and arrow is the skeletal muscle system. In this sense, the arrow's position in the target is an indicator of the success of the control over the biological function of the muscles just as the yellow light was an indicator of control over the biological function of the heart in the example described earlier.

Viewed in this way, biofeedback is not particularly new or startling. We have all been engaging in it probably since the very first days of life when we stuck our hands out in front of our face and looked to see where they went and what they did. This analysis points out that at a general descriptive level, biofeedback as practiced today may share many similarities with other types of motor performance and may be influenced by the same variables that influence motor skills (Bilodeau 1969; Johnston 1977). The interest in biofeedback lies not in the general notion of feedback loops, but rather in the specific application of these loops to biological functions that were once thought to be beyond voluntary control. Unlike movements of the arms and legs, which provide many sources of accurate feedback through sight and kinesthesis, changes in the activity of other biological functions may yield little feedback or else feedback that is so degraded as to be of little use. For example, consider trying to increase your heart rate and assume that you don't have a watch available. How sensitive are you to changes in your heart rate? By placing your finger on one of your arteries, you can feel your pulse. Certainly you can tell the difference between, say, 70 beats per minute (bpm) and 100 bpm. But what about 70 bpm and 75 bpm, or perhaps just 70 bpm and 72 bpm? As will be discussed in Chapter 3, learning to make the proper response often requires a substantial period of shaping during which feedback is provided for very slight changes in behavior. Indeed, Miller (1969) has suggested that early biofeedback experiments failed primarily because they did not use an adequate shaping procedure. Furthermore, the aim of the feedback experiment is to provide control; feedback is a means, not an end. The means are important because they make it possible to obtain ends that are not readily achieved without it. Thus the interest in biofeedback lies not in the ideas of feedback and control systems, but rather in the application of these ideas to biological function in general and to psychophysiological disorders in particular.

Two descriptions of biofeedback, when combined, capture the essense of this argument very nicely. Birk (1973, p. 2) describes biofeedback as ". . . the use of monitoring instruments (usually electrical) to detect and amplify internal physiologic processes within the body, in order to make this ordinarily unavailable information available to the individual and literally to feed it back to him in some form." [1] Schwartz and Beatty (1977, p. 1) describe biofeedback as ". . . a group of experimental procedures in which an external sensor is used to provide the organism with an indication of the state of bodily process usually in an attempt to effect a change in the measured quantity." These definitions, as well as the control systems diagrams presented here, emphasize the role of feedback as a means to obtain control of biological functions.

TYPES OF FEEDBACK

Feedback comes in many different forms. It differs in the sensory modality used and the particular stimuli in that modality. Most common in biofeedback is auditory or visual feedback. Auditory feedback is usually a tone which varies in pitch. Visual feedback may be a numerical display, with the numbers providing quantitative information about the state of the biological function being recorded, or may be a series of lights, each of which has a specific meaning, as described earlier in the example of heart rate control. Other sensory modalities could be used, but for practical reasons they generally are not.

An important consideration is the amount of information provided by the feedback. The distinction between *binary* and *analogue* feedback

[1] Lee Birk, Biofeedback—furor therapeutics. In Lee Birk, ed., *Biofeedback: Behavioral Medicine*. New York: Grune & Stratton, Inc., 1973. Used by permission.

illustrates this point. Consider an experiment in which a person is being asked to raise skin temperature. The pitch of a tone provides feedback. One way of arranging the feedback is to have the tone change pitch only once at a predetermined criterion level, say 30°C. If skin temperature is below this level, a low tone is heard; if skin temperature is above this level, a high tone is heard. This type of feedback is called *binary* because there are only two states of the feedback stimulus. The change from one state to the other takes place when skin temperature crosses the criterion. Thus the pitch of the tone tells the person whether or not skin temperature is above or below criterion but provides no information about the extent to which it deviates from this level.

A second way of arranging the feedback procedure is to have the tone change in pitch through a whole range of skin temperatures. For example, 28° might be 1,000 cycles per second (cps), 28.1° might be 1,100 cps, and so on. Here, each pitch is associated with a single temperature, and the pitch increases as the skin temperature increases. This arrangement is called *analogue* feedback because there is a ratio between the pitch of the tone and the temperature of the skin. Analogue feedback provides much more information to the person than binary feedback; every 1/10th of a degree change in skin temperature is reflected by a change in the pitch of the tone.

The difference between analogue and binary feedback is illustrated in Figure 2–3. In both cases, the pitch of the tone (on the vertical axis) changes with skin temperature (on the horizontal axis). For binary feedback, indicated by the dashed line, there is only one change in pitch, occurring at the criterion of 30°. For the analogue feedback, indicated by the solid line, there are many changes in pitch.

FEEDBACK AND KNOWLEDGE OF RESULTS

When used in the context of motor skills learning, feedback is often described as knowledge of results, or *KR*. Accurate learning is assisted by feedback that is rapid, consistent, and precise. *Rapid* feedback is important to determine what action produced the observed response. Consider again the archer shooting arrows at the target. If the archer can follow the flight of the arrow and learn the position of the arrow in the target immediately after every shot, then the steps taken to make that shot can be easily remembered. If, however, the archer is prevented from seeing the path of the arrow and/or the place it struck the target, the memory will gradually fade. The longer the delay between the shot and the feedback, the less accurately the archer will be able to remember the actions taken to make that shot, and the less useful the feedback will be in directing subsequent shots. The rapidity of feedback also places a limit

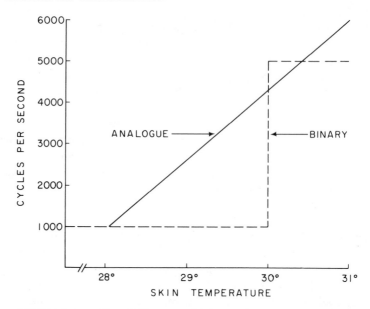

FIGURE 2–3   The Difference Between Binary and Analogue Feedback.

In both cases, the pitch of the tone changes with skin temperature. In binary feedback, there is only one change, at 30°, resulting in only two different pitches of the tone; hence the name *binary*. For analogue feedback, the pitch of the tone changes gradually with the skin temperature. (In reality, analogue feedback would not be this smooth. Commonly, each one-tenth of a degree in skin temperature produces a perceptible change in pitch so that the analogue curve is really composed of a series of steps, rather than a straight line. Thus the analogue line represents an ideal case and emphasizes the difference between the two procedures.)

on the accuracy of control. A deviation from the desired state cannot be corrected until it is detected, and the longer the interval between the deviation and the detection, the longer the period of time the undesired state can remain.

Control improves with *consistent* feedback, for obvious reasons. Consider a person who is being trained to raise skin temperature using the pitch of a tone as feedback. If the pitch decreases, the person assumes that the response made just prior to that decrease was incorrect and should not be made again. Thus a decrease in the pitch of the tone when skin temperature actually increased (due to equipment failure or some other reason) may cause the person to abandon the correct response and seek other less effective alternatives. *Precise* feedback is also important, particularly in the initial stages of learning. During the first few training sessions, information about very slight changes in the desired direction can be very influential in identifying the general category of desired responses. The precision of the feedback limits the accuracy of control, too, in the same way that the precision of a ruler used by a machinist limits the accuracy with which material can be measured.

These considerations point out the critical role of instruments to measure biological functions and provide feedback. Without instruments, most of the functions that people are trained to control through bio-feedback do not provide information that is rapid, consistent, and precise. To the extent that feedback is needed to learn control initially, the lack of control in the absence of appropriate feedback should not be surprising. The assumptions behind the emphasis on instrumentation are two. First, feedback is necessary to obtain control. Second, the characteristics of feedback necessary for control can be enhanced through appropriate instruments. One of the major contributions of biofeedback, then, is to take the concepts of feedback and control systems, add the technological advances from biomedical engineering, and combine these into appropriate treatment procedures to teach people self-control.

Most of the data demonstrating the importance of feedback on motor-skills learning has dealt with control systems in which a specific point of control was desired. In contrast, most biofeedback applications have emphasized directional control only. The goal usually is not to maintain skin temperature at a specific point, such as 32.1°C, but rather to increase it as much as possible. Considerations of point control may not always be applicable to cases of directional control, and the extent to which the detailed analyses of motor skills apply to biofeedback remain to be determined (Johnston 1977). None the less, the general considerations of feedback presented here are undoubtedly important in designing treatment programs and developing instrumentation.

NEGATIVE FEEDBACK AND HOMEOSTASIS

The previous examples of feedback have considered feedback as information about a response to be used by the person to control that response. But there is another type of feedback which is particularly important and contributes to the process of homeostasis. A *homeostatic mechanism* maintains the same state, a point of equilibrium. A common example is a heating-cooling system in a building. A thermostat is used to provide the set point, the temperature that is desired. A temperature measuring device determines the actual temperature which is compared to the set point. If the actual temperature is too low, the heating system raises the building's temperature to that of the set point. If the actual temperature is too high, the cooling system lowers the building's temperature to that of the set point. Thus any fluctuation in the building's temperature is corrected by the heating-cooling system to maintain homeostasis, a relatively constant temperature.

In a homeostatic mechanism, the feedback always returns the system to the steady state condition indicated by the set point. When feedback is used in this way, it is referred to as *negative feedback* because the influence of the feedback on the controlling mechanism is always negative; the difference between the current state of the system and the state set by the instructions or reference input is subtracted from the output of the system (Anliker 1977). In short, negative feedback functions as a governor attempting to minimize any fluctuation in the system. Inherent in the definition of negative feedback is the direction in which the system is being changed, an implication not present in the definition of feedback offered earlier.

The body has many of these negative feedback, homeostatic mechanisms because they are required to keep functioning within the physiological limits that can be tolerated. Consider heart rate again. If heart rate is too slow, the body will not get enough oxygen, and cells will begin to die. If heart rate is too fast, the pumping mechanism will be ineffective in moving blood, and again the body will not get enough oxygen. Internal homeostatic mechanisms are found almost everywhere in the body. If the core temperature of the body increases, the blood vessels come to the surface of the skin, and we perspire to lose heat. If the core temperature decreases, the blood vessels move away from the skin, we shiver to produce heat and develop goose bumps trying to raise what little hair we have to insulate ourselves from the cold. Likewise, our water balance is under homeostatic control. When we don't drink enough liquid, a hormone (antidiuretic hormone) is produced in greater quantities so that we conserve water, urinate very little, and what urine we do pass is very concentrated. When we drink too much, the amount of this hormone decreases, we urinate a great deal, and the urine is very dilute. Other examples could be given until a long list was formed. But the important point is that the biological functions a patient attempts to control through feedforward are almost inevitably influenced by homeostatic mechanisms, and these should be incorporated into the control system diagram, as in Figure 2–4.

The inclusion of the negative feedback system in Figure 2–4 has an important implication for biofeedback. Because homeostatic mechanisms are so prevalent, they may counteract just the type of control that the patient is trying to learn through biofeedback. Thus any attempt to increase heart rate in the feedforward system may be counteracted and reduced by the homeostatic mechanism. Certainly these homeostatic mechanisms will provide limits to the extent of control possible through the feedforward system, and they may make the desired type of control more difficult even within the attainable limits.

This particular figure also illustrates a major advantage of diagraming control systems; it forces a clear statement of assumptions that might

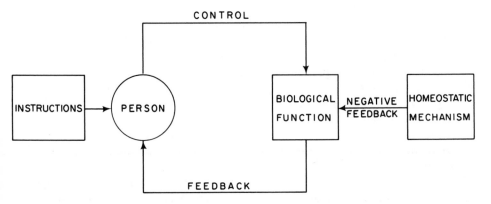

FIGURE 2–4   A Homeostatic Mechanism and Negative Feedback Incorporated Into the Basic Feedback System.
Negative feedback will always attempt to return the system to its original state and may counteract the efforts made by the person to manipulate the biological function through the control mechanism.

otherwise go unnoticed. For example, the diagram indicates that the influence from the feedforward line goes directly to heart rate, independently of the influence from the homeostatic mechanism. Such an organization is reasonable, of course. But there are other alternatives as well. For example, the feedforward mechanism may actually work directly on the homeostatic mechanism so that the feedforward line ought to be drawn directly to the homeostatic mechanism. If such were the case, then there would be only a single control line to the biological function and that would come from the homeostatic mechanism. Likewise, the diagram assumes that the person has no direct information (feedback) from the homeostatic mechanism itself, so that feedback always comes from the biological function. Again, this assumption is reasonable, but may not be correct. Thus diagrams are useful for two reasons. First, they provide in a highly summarized form a great deal of information about the control system. Second, they force the person who draws the diagram to make explicit the assumptions about how the mechanism works. Thus they can be useful in developing hypotheses about the ways in which the system might function and the ways in which biofeedback can alter this function.

CONTROL SYSTEMS AND
THE CENTRAL NERVOUS SYSTEM

The control systems illustrated earlier in terms of general processes can also be presented more concretely in terms of the components of the nervous system. After all, the general concepts of control have to be turned into action somehow, and this is through the nervous system. A full discussion of biological mechanisms will be postponed until later (see Chapter 4) but a rudimentary framework, especially in terms of control loops, is appropriate here. In this model, the self is seen as the brain or the central nervous system. The brain exerts control by means of *efferent* nerves, nerves that carry impulses from the brain to the *effectors,* which are the muscles or glands which in turn control the biological function. The feedback system is composed of *receptors,* cells which are sensitive to the state of the biological function and code this state into nervous impulses which flow through the *afferent* nerves to the brain.

In order for this control system to function effectively, each component must be in good physiological order. Malfunction of any of the nervous system components may cause biofeedback to fail (Engel 1973). For example, if the efferent nerves are destroyed, the brain may have knowledge of the state of the biological function through feedback and send out the appropriate commands, but these commands will never reach the effectors and cannot change the biological function. Failure of the effectors, perhaps through disease, will also prevent control because the efferent nerves will be unable to produce a change in the biological function. Receptors and afferent nerves must be intact in order to provide the brain the necessary information about the state of the biological function, and finally the brain must be functioning adequately to provide motivation and learning. Thus for biofeedback to be effective,

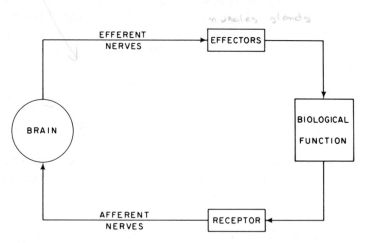

FIGURE 2–5   The Nervous System Components Underlying Biofeedback.

Efferent neurons take information from the brain to effectors, which change the biological function while receptors register changes in the biological function and send this information through afferent nerves to the brain.

the person must have certain physiological prerequisites, and the absence of any of these can make biofeedback training difficult or impossible.

As knowledge about the nervous system components underlying voluntary control of biological functions grows, further specification of nervous pathways can be made. Some information has already been obtained. For example, drug experiments with patients controlling heart rate have provided information about which of two nerves were used to change heart rate (Bleecker & Engel 1973a). Each of the nerves uses a different neurotransmitter, and drugs are available which selectively alter the activity of one of the neurotransmitters but not the other. Consequently, these drugs can be used to manipulate activity in one nerve independently of the other, and the effects of these manipulations on heart rate allow the experimenter to determine which nervous pathway is actually being used by the person to control heart rate. In other cases, information about the general organization of the brain can be used to make intelligent guesses at the nervous pathways underlying control. For example, considerable information is available about the components of the brain which have direct and indirect influences on the control of skeletal muscles and about the nerves which bring sensory information into the brain. Basic diagrams of biofeedback experiments for neuromuscular control can be created which must be correct in their general outlines (Wolf 1979), even though there is little direct information available to prove that the specific organization suggested is the one which actually occurs. Considerable progress has been made in understanding the relationship between brain mechanisms and many behaviors, and the application of those techniques to biofeedback should enable us to describe in detail the way in which the brain mediates control in biofeedback procedures as well.

BIOFEEDBACK AND
THE MECHANISMS OF MEDIATION

Several people are trained to decrease their heart rate and do so successfully. They are then asked how they accomplished this goal. One person replies that she imagined a peaceful, relaxing scene. She pictured herself sitting on a beach in the warm sunlight, in a secluded cove on a Pacific island with the wind blowing gently through her hair and the waves washing lightly up on the sand. Another person replies that he just concentrated on the feedback light and tried to turn it on; he had no images and focused his thoughts on making his heart beat slower and turning the light on. A third person says that he felt a particular emotion, but the emotion was not associated with any visual image. He developed a feeling of being relaxed, peaceful, at ease with the world, satisfied with his role in life.

Have all three of these people really been in the same experiment? The answer is yes, and the wide divergence in their answers illustrates a core question for biofeedback, namely, the psychological mechanisms by which people generate the feedforward control. The term *voluntary control* has often been described as the goal of biofeedback. By this is usually meant that an individual, when instructed to do so, can produce the desired changes in biological function (see Chapter 5). But this description is one of the relationships between a stimulus (the instructions) and the response (the heart rate increase) and says nothing about the steps that mediate this interrelationship. Several possibilities exist, three of which were given in the examples above. The first person generated an *image*; the second person, a *thought*; and the third person, a *feeling*. These are common responses from individuals tested in biofeedback experiments and illustrate some of the many different sensations associated with successful biofeedback control.

There are many issues that remain to be resolved concerning the role of these sensations in biofeedback performance. Are they necessary for successful control, or are they just a byproduct of an active mind? What do they imply about the physiological mechanisms of biofeedback control? Answers to these questions may influence both the design of biofeedback experiments in the research laboratory and the course of biofeedback treatment in the clinic.

LEARNING
AND PERFORMANCE

3

Operant Conditioning

Classical Conditioning

OPERANT CONDITIONING

Biofeedback teaches a person to develop voluntary control over some biological process. In this respect, it is a form of learning, differing from other forms mainly in the types of responses that are controlled. In almost all cases, the clinician is interested in teaching the client to develop the maximum control in the minimum amount of time. There are three steps to this process: identifying the reinforcers and making them contingent upon behavior in the appropriate way, establishing quantitative measures of learning and performance, and arranging the parameters of the training procedure to maximize the rate of learning and the final level of performance. Each of these steps will be discussed in turn.

Reinforcers and Contingencies

After an interview with a client, the therapist decides that the most appropriate biofeedback treatment is teaching her to raise the temperature of her hands. A training session is begun with the biofeedback equipment. There are two possible outcomes. Either skin temperature increases, or it doesn't. What now? What can the therapist do to increase the likelihood that she will be able to raise skin temperature successfully at the next opportunity? An answer to this question is found in a consideration of reinforcers, and the relationship between reinforcers and the responses that precede them.

Reinforcers are events which follow a response and influence the probability of that response being made on a subsequent occasion. Some reinforcers are desirable; examples of these *positive reinforcers* are money, praise, and food, at least when hungry. These are all items that people will work to obtain, and if they occur after a response is made, the probability of that response being made again will increase. Other reinforcers are undesirable; examples of these *negative reinforcers* are physical pain, traffic fines, and verbal scolding. These are all items that people will work to avoid, and if they occur after a response is made, the probability of that response being made again will decrease.

To be effective in controlling behavior, reinforcers must be made *contingent* upon behavior. Although there are many types of contingencies, resulting in complicated schedules of reinforcement (Ferster & Skinner 1957; Honig & Staddon 1977), only two are of major interest to the biofeedback therapist. One of them was described above in the definition of positive and negative reinforcers. In both those examples, the reinforcer is generally unavailable to the person and is presented contingent upon a response. If the appropriate response is made, the reinforcer is given to the person; if that response is not made, the reinforcer is kept away. Thus, the person receives the reinforcer if and only if the correct response occurs. An alternative procedure is to make the reinforcer generally available to the person and remove it contingent upon a response. If the appropriate response is made, the reinforcer is taken away; if that response is not made, the reinforcer remains. Here the person receives the reinforcer if and only if the response in question does not occur.

At the end of a biofeedback trial, then, the therapist has four alternatives, resulting from the combination of the two types of reinforcers and the two types of contingencies. Table 3–1 summarizes these, presenting the types of reinforcer on the left side and the type of contingency along the top. In each quadrant of the table is the name of the process and a description of its effect on the responses that precede it. For example, in the upper left hand quadrant a positive reinforcer is presented after the response occurs. This process is known as *positive reinforcement* and should increase the probability of that response occurring again. The therapist wants to increase the probability of the correct response and decrease the probability of the incorrect response; successful performance should be followed by either positive or negative reinforcement, and failure should be followed by punishment.

Considerable debate has taken place about the effectiveness and/or morality of using punishment to control behavior (Campbell & Church

TABLE 3–1   A Summary of the Way in Which the Two Different Types of Reinforcers Can Be Made Contingent upon Responses

		Type of Contingency	
		Presentation	*Removal*
	Positive	Positive reinforcement Response strength increases	Punishment Response strength decreases
Type of Reinforcer	*Negative*	Punishment Response strength decreases	Negative reinforcement Response strength increases

Note: The terms in the center of the Table describe each process (on the first line) and indicate the way in which the process affects the strength of the response that preceded it (on the second line).

1969; Mikulas 1974). However, punishment is really an inappropriate focus because punishment by definition is unavoidable any time reinforcers are made contingent upon responses. Consider positive reinforcers: if these are presented to a person if and only if the correct response is made (positive reinforcement), then they must be removed if that response is not made (punishment). A fundamental assumption of reinforcement theories is that in order for reinforcers to be effective in controlling behavior, they must be differentially available, following some responses but not others. Punishment is an inevitable result of any differential reinforcement program.

The decision of most concern to the biofeedback therapist is the use of negative reinforcers. These are by definition unpleasant, and people will work to escape or avoid them. This unpleasant or noxious quality of negative reinforcers may produce physiological and psychological responses, both of which may be counterproductive. The physiological changes are substantial and are similar to those produced by activation of the sympathetic nervous system, the same part of the nervous system that is involved in the development of many psychosomatic diseases. The psychological effects may also be damaging. Anticipating a negative reinforcer can produce anxiety, and receiving it can produce fear or anger. In short, negative reinforcers can reproduce the pattern of physiological and psychological responses that makes disease states worse and is exactly the opposite of the states the therapist wishes the client to obtain. In spite of these drawbacks, negative reinforcement can be used effectively to train both animals and people. But the possible liabilities of negative reinforcers are substantially greater than those of positive reinforcers, and care must be taken to counteract these liabilities (Mikulas 1974). In most cases, then, the therapist will be using positive reinforcers, presenting them when the client succeeds and withholding them when the client fails.

One other distinction between the types of reinforcers should be made, and that is between a primary reinforcer and a secondary reinforcer. *Primary reinforcers* have their influence over behavior because their desirable or undesirable characteristics are inherent in their nature. For example, food is considered to be a primary reinforcer because no particular training is necessary for food to be effective in modifying response probabilities in a hungry person. Likewise, shock is a primary reinforcer because its aversive nature seems to be an inherent property. But some stimuli develop their reinforcing properties only through association with primary reinforcers, usually through the process of classical conditioning discussed later in this chapter. A classic example of a *secondary reinforcer* for people is money. Money is certainly a strong positive reinforcer, as indicated by its remarkable influence on all measures of response strength. But the piece of metal or paper by itself is actually of little use for food, clothing, or shelter. Rather, its effectiveness as a reinforcer lies in its association with primary reinforcers. Another example of a secondary reinforcer is the whistle that animal trainers use to give the animal information that the act has been performed correctly and that food is soon to follow.

In biofeedback procedures, the feedback given to the patient functions as a secondary reinforcer. The stimuli used for feedback have little intrinsic value so that their significance arises from their relationship to the successful reduction of the symptoms which brought the client to the clinic. Maintaining this relationship is important because secondary reinforcers control behavior only to the extent that they are associated with primary reinforcers, a point considered in further detail in the discussion of classical conditioning (and in Chapter 7).

Response Strength

"If you can't measure it, you can't talk about it." This statement is just as true for biofeedback and conditioning as it is for any other branch of science. If learning takes place as a result of biofeedback, you ought to be able to identify it and measure how much actually occurred. This latter point is particularly important when the effectiveness of different types of training procedures is being compared. Here the notion of response strength is useful. It is a general concept used as an intervening variable (MacCorquodale & Meehl 1948) which reflects the extent to which a particular response has been learned.

Consider a person who is learning to raise skin temperature. On the first few trials, skin temperature may not change at all. On subsequent trials, it may increase by a few tenths of a degree, but this change doesn't begin for about five minutes and then it proceeds slowly, taking another five minutes to be completed. By the end of training, performance has improved substantially. Skin temperature increases on every trial. Furthermore, these increases are at least five degrees, begin as soon as the trial is started, and are completed within just a few minutes. This improvement in the ability to control skin temperature can be quantified with four measures of response strength:

1. The probability that the correct response occurs
2. The latency required for the response to begin
3. The magnitude of the response when it occurs
4. The speed with which the response is completed

Response measures may be grouped into two classes (Hulse and others 1975). The first describes the likelihood that the response will appear during a given test interval. One measure in this class is the *probability* of a response, the number of trials in which the response appears divided by the total number of trials given. At the beginning of training, the probability of the correct response is small and may be close to zero. During training, the probability gradually increases so that at the end, it may be close to 1.0, indicating that the person is successful on every test. Thus one measure of increased response strength is increased response probability. A second measure is the *frequency* or *rate* of response. Here the question is how often the correct response occurs during a test, indicated by the number of correct responses divided by the time available to produce those responses. This measure is most appropriate for discrete responses of short duration which are to be repeated many times, and thus is not useful in biofeedback procedures that seek to produce large magnitude responses of long duration.

A second class of response measures includes those which describe the characteristics of the response when it does occur. One is response *latency*, the length of time between the beginning of a trial and the occurrence of a response. At the beginning of learning, response latency is usually substantial, but with continued practice it decreases. Thus an increase in response strength is indicated by a decrease in response latency. Another measure in this class is response *speed*, the rapidity with which a response can be completed once it is begun. Response speed, like response latency, measures time, but the period of time is different. Whereas latency reflects the interval between the start of a trial and the initiation of the response, speed reflects the interval between the initiation of the response and its completion. An increase in response strength is reflected by an increase in response speed. The third measure is response *magnitude*, which is simply the largest response that occurs during the test interval. An increase in response strength is reflected by an increase in response magnitude.

This discussion of response measures has three implications for biofeedback treatments. First, there are many different measures of response strength. In some cases, such as the hand-warming experiment described previously, the different measures are highly correlated with each other so that any one will provide the same picture of the learning process. But such is not always the case, and the lack of correlation among different response measures (Kimble 1961, p. 111) has often led psychologists to question whether learning can be described as a single process (Mikulas 1974). When response measures do not correlate highly, the conclusions drawn at the end of an experiment may differ substantially depending on the measure chosen. For example, headache pain may be assessed by the frequency, intensity, or duration of headaches. With some patients, biofeedback completely alleviates headaches so that all three response measures go to zero. In other cases, however, the frequency of headaches may remain about the same, but their intensity and duration may be markedly reduced. The frequency measure suggests that biofeedback treatment was a failure while the other two measures suggest it was a success. The truth, of course, lies somewhere in between; the patient experiences less pain than before, but the pain occurs just as frequently. At the present time, there is no single "best" measure of response strength, and the implications of the above discussion are clear. Multiple measures are desirable whenever possible, and conclusions about the effectiveness of a treatment must be qualified by stating the measures that are being taken as an indication of response strength.

A second implication of the above discussion is the importance of a baseline condition. Learning is usually defined as a relatively permanent change in behavior as a function of experience. The interest here is in the *change* in response strength as a function of the treatment. Change, of course, can only be measured if there is an initial point to which present performance can be compared. Many biofeedback procedures, both in research laboratories and in treatment clinics, are concerned with this aspect of response strength. By obtaining baseline measurements before treatment begins, the therapist can determine the normal level of function. This information allows better assessment of the effect of treatment in producing the desired changes in behavior.

Finally, the need for quantitative data is apparent. At first, the question about biofeedback was whether it had any use at all—for any disease in any person at any time. Now we know that biofeedback is effective at least for some diseases in some people at some times. The current issue, then, is a comparison of the relative effectiveness of biofeedback and other treatments with respect to the rapidity and ultimate level of relief, and the costs of treatment. Because many different treatments have similar qualitative effects, the issue can be addressed only by a quantitative analysis of the relevant variables.

Variables Affecting Response Strength

When describing the treatment used in a clinic, the therapist outlines the following considerations which are incorporated into every treatment protocol.

1. Each client is first trained to make very small changes in the state of the biological function, even though these may be too small to be of therapeutic value.
2. There is a short interview to determine why the client wants to learn biofeedback and the extent to which the client is willing to expend the energy and time necessary to learn the procedures.

3. The therapist always provides explicit praise when the client succeeds at biofeedback.
4. The biofeedback apparatus is arranged so that the client has immediate knowledge about the results of any attempt to change biological function.
5. There are many opportunities for the individual to practice.
6. These opportunities are separated by intervals of time so that the client can rest in between them.

Each of these procedures increases the rate of learning and/or the final level of performance attained by the client. The rationale for each of them will be discussed in turn below.

Shaping.   Consider a patient suffering from Raynaud's disease in which the hands are painfully cold, 17°C. The goal of therapy is to increase skin temperature to a normal range of about 33°C. But the patient is unlikely to be able to produce a skin temperature increase this large at the first attempt so that if a positive reinforcer is contingent upon this magnitude of response, the patient will probably never receive it. Indeed, one of the important benefits of the biofeedback instrumentation is being able to measure very small changes in biological function so that these can be used for shaping. On the first few trials tnen, the patient might be rewarded for increasing skin temperature by just one tenth of a degree. Such a change will have little clinical effect, but it is an important step in being able to learn to produce the changes of the desired magnitude that will lead to effective clinical results. With more trials, the criterion for successful performance is gradually increased—first to a few tenths of a degree, then to several degrees, and finally up to the goal of 33°C.

Shaping refers to the gradual development of the correct response from initial attempts in the same way a pot is molded out of a clump of clay. In order to teach the person to produce the ultimately desired response, reinforcement must be provided for the first tentative steps in the right direction, even though these may not be sufficient for reinforcement at some later time. Shaping is a critical step in the establishment of almost any behavior, and the training phase here may be long and difficult. Indeed, shaping is probably the greatest challenge for the therapist because here the client receives the first instructions about how to perform correctly. The importance of shaping in biofeedback has been emphasized by Miller (1969), who suggested that the failure to pay adequate attention to shaping was responsible for many of the difficulties in first demonstrating control through biofeedback.

Motivation.   Intuitively, you might think that the greater the level of motivation, the faster learning will take place. But such is probably not the case (Kimble 1961; Murray 1967). If the level of motivation is sufficient to make the reinforcer effective, further increases in motivation will probably have little effect on the rate of learning. However, motivation does have a significant effect on performance. The relationship between the level of motivation and performance is a complicated one and looks like an inverted *U*, at least on complex tasks. With no motivation, of course, there is little performance. From this point, as the level of motivation increases, performance increases. But there comes a point when further increases in motivation are actually debilitating and tend to lower performance. Most of us have "clutched" at a crucial moment—the motivation to perform well was so great that it actually interfered with our ability. Thus, optimal performance does not necessarily come with the highest level of motivation, but usually at some intermediate level, a finding often referred to as the *Yerkes-Dodson law* (Broadhurst 1957).

An extrapolation of the Yerkes-Dodson law to the patient's expectations about the success of treatment has been made by Stroebel and Glueck (1973) who discuss a PATI model. The initials stand for *Placebo-Active Therapeutic Index*. The model describes the effects of different levels of expectation on therapeutic success, and as to be expected there is a curve that looks very similar to the inverted *U*. Patients with very low expectations performed poorly, presumably because they were unwilling to expend the effort necessary to see if biofeedback would help their condition. Patients with very high expectations also performed poorly, but for a different reason. Because these patients often expected to obtain rapid and miraculous changes through biofeedback, they became discouraged when the expected changes were not forthcoming. This problem was particularly acute for those patients who had these high expectations coupled with only moderate ability. Optimum performance was obtained by patients who had an intermediate level of expectation matched to an intermediate level of ability.

The Stroebel and Glueck (1973) analysis, in conjunction with the data supporting the Yerkes-Dodson law, indicate that in biofeedback the motivation of the person should be kept in careful balance. On the one hand, too little motivation may result in the individual not being willing to expend the effort to perform appropriately. This lack of motivation may result from a number of causes ranging from a general lack of belief that the treatment will be a success (Stroebel & Glueck 1973) to ambivalence about getting rid of the psychosomatic symptoms (for example, Weiss & Engel 1973, p. 97). On the other hand, too much motivation or too high an expectation about the outcome can result in failure for a number of reasons. The tenseness and excitement associated with high motivation can be deleterious in learning many biofeedback techniques, especially the ones having to do with relaxation (Brown 1977, p.

7). Learning to relax may be difficult, and an important component of relaxation is giving up the striving, anxious type of feeling associated with high motivation and adopting a more passive attitude (Benson 1975). Failure to relax can come from the incompatibility of the state associated with relaxation and that associated with high motivation. Thus the therapist should maintain a sensitive balance of motivation for the client. Enough motivation must be provided to have the person actively participate, but excessive motivation must be avoided in order to avoid false expectations and anxiety.

Reinforcer Magnitude. Another way of influencing performance is through changes in the magnitude of the reinforcer. This is actually a process that is complementary to the level of motivation. It enhances the influence of the reinforcer and will generally produce an increase in the level of performance, at least up to some point. By magnitude is meant not only quantity, but also quality. In most biofeedback procedures there has been little attempt to explicitly manipulate the magnitude of reward. Indeed, the therapist usually assumes that the feedback itself acts as an effective reinforcer because the person associates the feedback with alleviation of disease. As described earlier, there are problems with this assumption, particularly at the beginning of training. Thus providing explicit reinforcers for success may improve performance. In one biofeedback experiment, the amount of positive reinforcement varied for people participating in an alpha-conditioning experiment (Brolund & Schallow 1976). Two groups of subjects were instructed to increase the amount of alpha activity above a certain level and put in the same general experimental procedure. One of the groups was given the usual set of instructions only, leaving the motivation to perform largely in the hands of the person participating in the experiment. Another group was given the same set of instructions but was offered extra rewards for performing well. This latter group performed significantly better than the group without explicit rewards, demonstrating that the additional reward enhanced performance. Other examples of explicit reinforcements are given in Chapter 7.

Delay of Reinforcement. The period of time between performance of the correct response and the receipt of reinforcement is particularly important. The general rule is that the longer this interval, the worse the performance. Two explanations have been offered for this effect. One is a rather cognitive approach and deals with the information value of reinforcement, treating it in the same way as feedback or knowledge of results described in Chapter 2. According to this idea, the sooner the person knows the results of an intended response, the more effectively he can change that response to match the desired one. The second explanation of the effect of delay of reinforcement is a more mechanistic one and deals with the notion of response strength as measured by any of the variables previously discussed. According to this explanation, reinforcement changes the strength of the response that preceded it, whatever that response might be. If the client produces the correct response but doesn't receive praise for it until a week later, the association of the praise with that response will be weaker than if the positive reinforcer occurred immediately after the response, and the increase in response strength will be smaller. Both these explanations suggest that the best performance will come with the shortest delay of reinforcement.

Number of Trials. This effect is obvious from the previous discussion of the measures of learning. As the number of trials increases, so does performance, at least to some asymptote.

Distribution of Trials. There is another variable which has to do with the arrangement of trials in time. For example, consider a client who is to get 30 training trials. How should these trials be arranged? At one extreme, all 30 could take place in a single session, a procedure known as *massed practice.* Alternatively, they might be spread out over six sessions with five trials in each session, a procedure called *spaced practice.* In both cases there are the same number of trials and the question is which procedure will give better performance at the end of these trials. The answer to that question is probably spaced practice. True, a substantial amount of learning will take place with the massed procedure, but the fatigue that develops will suppress performance substantially. Whether the temporal distribution of trials also affects learning is a matter of debate (Deese & Hulse 1967, p. 117).

The preceding discussion is summarized in Table 3–2 describing the optimal arrangement of variables to increase the rate of learning and the level of performance. The learning-performance distinction is a complicated one, but worth making. *Learning* generally refers to information obtained by the individual, *performance* to the expression of this learning in behavior. Performance usually doesn't occur without learning, but learning may not be reflected in performance, a sad tale often told by students who perform poorly on examinations. Looked at another way, learning limits performance, setting the upper bounds. The extent to which performance actually attains these upper bounds depends on a number of short-term, usually reversible factors, such as fatigue and motivation. In most instances of application to biofeedback, the learning-

TABLE 3–2   A Summary of the Optimal Arrangement of Different Variables to Obtain the Maximum Rate of Learning and the Highest Level of Performance

Variable	Rate of Learning	Level of Performance
Reward contingency	Shaping	(see Table 3–1)
Level of Motivation	?	Moderate
Magnitude of Reinforcement	?	Moderate
Delay of Reinforcement	Small	Small
Number of trials	Large	Large
Distribution of trials	?	Spaced

Note: A question mark in the table indicates that the optimal setting of the variable is not clear, and that a moderate level is appropriate.

performance distinction is not critical. But as indicated by Table 3–2, there are a few cases in which a variable affects either learning or performance without influencing the other to a very great extent.

Extinction and Partial Reinforcement

The increases in response strength just described resulted from a contingency between the response and the reinforcement. Eliminating this contingency, so that the response is no longer followed by reinforcement, can reduce response strength, a process called extinction. Extinction is a useful way of eliminating unwanted responses, as long as the contingency between the response and the reinforcement is permanently broken. Responses that are sometimes, but not always, followed by reinforcement are remarkably resistant to extinction, even more so than responses that are always followed by reinforcement. This phenomenon is often referred to as the *partial reinforcement extinction effect*, reflecting the fact that an animal given an intermittent schedule of reinforcement in which reinforcement follows some responses, but not all of them, will continue to respond for prolonged periods of time when reinforcement is removed permanently. Thus consistency during extinction is critical to eliminate the undesired response, and no reinforcement should be given for any response.

CLASSICAL CONDITIONING

Another form of learning, called *classical* or *Pavlovian* conditioning, can play a role in biofeedback therapies, especially those designed to treat phobias or anxiety states through desensitization and cued relaxation (discussed at the end of this chapter). This section will discuss the procedures used for classical conditioning and describe the ways in which these-procedures are incorporated into biofeedback treatment.

In classical conditioning, one stimulus is associated with a second stimulus so that the first one comes to stand for, predict, or signify the second. The important result of this association is that the first stimulus is then able to elicit the same response as the second stimulus. Classical conditioning differs from instrumental conditioning because there is no contingency between the occurrence of a response and the presentation or withdrawal of the reinforcers. Consequently, the individual has no control over the occurrence of the reinforcers. This distinction is an operational one, based on procedural differences, and does not necessarily imply that the learning involved in the two types of conditioning is different (Kimble 1961; Rescorla & Solomon 1967). At the start of an experiment one of the two stimuli elicits an obvious response. Because this stimulus-response relationship was not developed through conditioning (at least in this experiment), this stimulus is called an *unconditioned stimulus* (UCS) and the response it produces is called an *unconditioned response* (UCR). The second stimulus does not produce a response, or at least not one similar to that produced by the UCS. If this second stimulus is always presented just prior to the UCS, it will eventually produce a response very similar to the UCR. The new stimulus is called the *conditioned stimulus* (CS) because it attained the ability to produce the *conditioned response* (CR) through conditioning.

To make this process clear, consider a typical procedure used by Pavlov (Anrep 1960) to train his dogs. A dog was brought into the laboratory and placed in a harness which supported and restrained him. A tube was placed in the dog's mouth to measure the amount of saliva. A small amount of meat powder was presented to the dog for a few seconds so that he could see and smell the powder but couldn't eat it. In response to the food powder, the dog salivated, and the saliva was collected in the tube. Then a second stimulus, a bell, was presented by itself. As to be expected, there was little if any salivation to the bell. Thus one stimulus (the food powder UCS) elicited a response (salivation UCR) while the second stimulus (the bell CS) did not.

The experiment continued so that whenever the bell was sounded, food powder was presented immediately after it. After a few pairings of the bell and food powder, only the bell was presented; some salivation occurred, but not as much as in response to the food powder. The bell and food powder were presented together for more trials and then just the bell again. As the number of trials increased, the amount of salivation in response to the bell alone increased until the bell produced almost as much salivation by itself as the food powder had at the beginning of the experiment. As a result of the association between the bell and the food powder, the bell became able to produce a response that initially was elicited only by the food powder.

Classical conditioning procedures may be described as appetitive or aversive based on the characteristics of the unconditioned stimulus. In the salivation procedure, the food powder was desirable (at least from the dog's point of view) and if used in an instrumental procedure would function as a positive reinforcer, increasing the probability of any response that preceded it. This type of classical conditioning is called *appetitive*. The UCS may be undesirable, as for example an electric shock. If used in an instrumental procedure, this stimulus would function as a negative reinforcer, decreasing the probability of any response that preceded it. Classical conditioning using a negative reinforcer for the UCS is called *aversive*.

Aversive conditioning procedures are parallel to appetitive ones, differing only in the characteristics of the UCS. Pavlov used a procedure in which the UCS was a mild electric shock to the leg. The UCR of the dog was to lift that leg. At the beginning of the experiment, a bell was sounded; the dog did not lift his leg. Then the bell and shock were paired together so that immediately after the bell was sounded, the leg was shocked. At the end of many trials the bell alone produced the leg lift.

Comparing the reactions of dogs trained in an appetitive procedure with those of ones trained in an aversive procedure emphasizes the point that through conditioning a stimulus may come to have markedly different effects on behavior. In both the examples above, the same stimulus (a bell) was used for the CS. Yet for dogs in the appetitive procedure, the bell meant that food would follow and the dogs salivated, while for dogs in the aversive procedure, it meant that shock would follow and the dogs lifted their legs. The general behavior of the dogs usually reflected the differing significance of the tone. Dogs in appetitive procedures looked alert, wagged their tails, and held their heads up. Dogs in aversive procedures cowered, let their tails hang down, and lowered their ears against their heads. These behavior patterns indicate substantially different emotional reactions (Darwin 1965) which were obviously not due to the properties of the bell itself, but rather to the associations between the bell and the UCS established through classical conditioning.

Generalization

During classical conditioning, associations are built up not only between the CS and the UCS, but also among all similar stimuli. The degree of association is a function of the similarity of the stimuli, and the process is known as *generalization*. An experiment to illustrate this process might begin with several dogs, each of which was trained to salivate to a tone with a pitch of 1,000 cycles per second (cps). This tone was paired with food powder until the dog produced ten drops of saliva in response to the tone. Each dog was given a transfer test in which a tone of a different pitch was presented. One dog was given 800 cps; nine drops of saliva appeared. A second dog was given 600 cps; six drops of saliva appeared. A third was given 400 cps; only one drop appeared. Obviously the amount of saliva was a function of the similarity between the pitch of the tone presented on the transfer test and the pitch of the tone during initial learning. As illustrated in Figure 3–1, the amount of saliva, indicated on the vertical axis, decreased steadily as the pitch of the tone on the transfer test differed from the pitch of the initial tone, as indicated on the horizontal axis. A line connecting these points is called a *generalization gradient*. As indicated by the generalization gradient, conditioning in response to one stimulus has implications not only for that stimulus, but for many others as well.

Extinction

Responses established through classical conditioning can be eliminated through *extinction*. The procedures and the results are similar to those described for instrumental conditioning. The CS is presented as

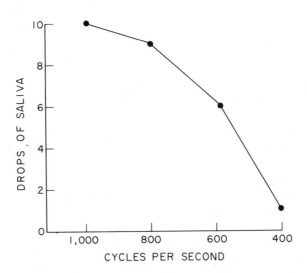

FIGURE 3–1   A Generalization Gradient from a Hypothetical Classical Conditioning Experiment.
The dog initially learned that food followed a tone of 1,000 Hz. Subsequent testing with tones of different frequencies showed that as the tones became more different from the original one, the amount of salivation decreased.

usual, but it is not followed by the UCS. As a result, the magnitude of the conditioned response gradually decreases until the response no longer appears at all. In most classical conditioning procedures, extinction is very rapid, especially if a partial reinforcement schedule has been used during acquisition. This rapidity contrasts with the prolonged responding found after equivalent schedules in operant procedures and complicates the explanation of phobias in terms of classical conditioning, a point that will be further discussed below.

Development and Maintenance of Phobias

Formally, a phobia can be viewed as a specialized case of classical conditioning. Consider the fear of snakes. The snake may be viewed as a CS, and the anxiety response as a CR. The question, of course, is how did the anxiety become conditioned to the snake? People with phobias are sometimes able to describe a traumatic event that was associated with the stimulus, suggesting that the phobia developed as a result of this experience (Blanchard & Abel 1976; Dekker & Groen 1956; Javel & Denholtz 1975). Attempts to produce psychosomatic reactions in people through classical conditioning have had mixed results (Dekker, Pelser, & Goren 1957), questioning the role of classical conditioning in the initial development of the phobia. One well-known success was an experiment by Watson & Rayner (1920). A young boy was shown a white rat and gave no evidence of being afraid. Then every time the white rat was presented to the boy, he was frightened by a loud noise (UCS). After several pairings of the white rat (CS) and the noise (UCS), he was afraid of the rat and cried when it was presented. As to be expected, his fear generalized to other white furry objects.

Although the development of a phobia may be formally similar to the process of classical conditioning, some difficulties still remain for this interpretation. The most important points concern the strength of the association between the anxiety response and the stimulus of the phobia as compared to the relative weakness of the association between the CS and CR in laboratory procedures. Phobias usually develop more quickly than most classically conditioned responses, and they are remarkably resistant to extinction. The person who is afraid of snakes probably sees many snakes without being hurt by them. None the less, the phobia remains. The strength of a phobia may be due in part to its traumatic nature. When the shock used in avoidance conditioning is severe, learning takes place very quickly and may be remarkably resistant to extinction (Solomon & Wynne 1954). Even so, interpreting the development and maintenance of phobias in terms of classical conditioning clearly needs further experimental support.

Treatment of Phobias

Successful treatment of phobias with behavioral medicine relies heavily on the use of classical conditioning. The object is to extinguish the anxiety response elicited by the stimulus and substitute a more normal relaxed state. This process may be referred to as *desensitization,* reflecting the reduction of anxiety, or it may be called *counterconditioning,* emphasizing the establishment of a relaxed state. The general procedure is the same irrespective of the name (see Eysenck & Beech 1971, for a detailed review). First the person is trained to relax. Then stimuli which originally elicited anxiety are paired with this relaxation. A critical step in counterconditioning is the use of a *stimulus hierarchy,* similar to the generalization gradient described earlier. The anxiety associated with a phobia is usually so great that it will completely overwhelm any state of relaxation, at least initially. Thus the therapist establishes a hierarchy of stimuli, all of which are similar to the *target stimulus* (the one which evokes the greatest anxiety) but sufficiently different from it that they produce less of a response. One means of establishing a hierarchy is to vary the distance between the person and the target stimulus or the length of time before which the person must interact with the target stimulus. These spatial and temporal gradients form the hierarchy; as the distance/time between the individual and the target stimulus increases, the amount of anxiety decreases.

After the stimulus hierarchy is established, relaxation is conditioned to stimuli farthest away from the target stimulus. This relaxation generalizes to all the other stimuli in the hierarchy, lowering the amount of anxiety produced by them and making it easier for the patient to relax in the presence of them. Relaxation is then paired with the next stimulus in the hierarchy until the anxiety response to it disappears. This procedure is continued until the person is able to relax in the presence of the target stimulus itself.

The counterconditioning procedure, and the role of biofeedback in it, is illustrated by two case reports. In the first one, a female law student, 26 years old, came for treatment because of a very strong fear of spiders (Javel & Denoltz 1975). When confronted with a spider, she would often scream and run, and she spent inordinate amounts of time checking her environment to make certain that no spiders were present. She also reported being afraid of crawling insects, bats, snakes, and even the printed word "spider." The development of this phobia seemed to be related to a single traumatic instance in her childhood. She had an upsetting visit with relatives, and her emotional upset became associated with spiders through a nightmare.

In treatment, the galvanic skin resistance (GSR) was recorded. The

GSR provides an indication of anxiety, and increases in the GSR are associated with increased relaxation. She was given feedback about the state of the GSR by a tone and was trained to turn off the tone by relaxing and increasing the GSR. When she had learned this control through biofeedback, a stimulus hierarchy was established. Live spiders were enclosed in jars which were placed at different distances from her. The GSR was recorded during the presentations of the spiders, and whenever the tone occurred, she was instructed to relax and turn it off. When a spider could be presented at a certain distance with no change in GSR as indicated by the tone remaining off, the spider was moved closer. She was given practice sessions in the clinic which lasted about one hour each day, for eight days. At the end of this treatment, she could touch a jar with a spider in it and even catch a loose spider and place it in a jar. All three aspects of her emotional reaction had changed. Behaviorally, she no longer ran away from spiders but treated them as any other stimulus in her environment. Physiologically, she no longer had the marked decrease in GSR. Psychologically, she reported being relaxed and no longer being upset by spiders.

Another application of biofeedback in counterconditioning treated three patients who had a fear of flying (Reeves & Mealiea 1975). The activity of the muscles in the forehead was recorded. A tone provided feedback, and the patients were instructed to decrease the pitch of the tone as much as possible by relaxing the muscle. Five biofeedback sessions, each 20 minutes long, were used to teach relaxation. Each person was told to say the word "relax" and then make the pitch of the tone go as low as possible, enabling them to use the word as a cue to induce relaxation. With training, all three patients were able to reduce the amount of activity in the forehead muscles and learned to do so even without the tone, which was gradually eliminated by a fading process in which the volume was steadily decreased until the tone was no longer audible. For each person, a stimulus hierarchy was established ranging from reading an article about flying to landing in rough weather. Relaxation was first paired with the stimulus producing the least anxiety and then with each successive stimulus in the hierarchy. Following treatment the participants all took commercial flights and reported no unusual discomfort.

Another example of biofeedback used in conjunction with counterconditioning treated a musician who had trouble with excessive contraction of the throat muscles when performing (Levee, Cohen, & Rickles 1976). This treatment is reviewed as case study A, Excessive Contraction of Throat Muscles, in Chapter 14. Biofeedback and counterconditioning also alleviated cardiovascular problems associated with a rape (Blanchard & Abel 1976; see Chapter 15).

THE BIOLOGICAL
BASES OF BEHAVIOR

4

Nerve Cells

Autonomic Nervous System

Functional Organization of the Nervous System

Muscles

Biofeedback is information about the biological functions of the body. Successful performance requires an intact nervous system which is able to carry out all of the necessary steps in the control loop, as explained in Chapter 2. This loop is composed of the brain, efferent nerves, effectors, the biological system, receptors, and afferent nerves (see Figure 2–5). A purely behavioral analysis of biofeedback may ignore the underlying physiological processes, but any attempt to understand the mechanisms by which biofeedback works must consider them. This chapter briefly reviews some of the areas that are most relevant to biofeedback applications—nerve cells, the autonomic nervous system, the functional organization of the nervous system, and muscles.

NERVE CELLS

A nerve cell, or *neuron,* is the functional unit of the nervous system. Each nerve cell is physically and metabolically independent of all others. By being organized into networks, they allow us to behave in a coordinated fashion. This discussion will focus on three aspects of the nerve cell: function, structure, and process. Function describes the role of the activity in the nervous system; structure describes the part of the neuron which carries out that function; and process describes the physiological mechanism which occurs in that structure. A diagram of a nerve cell with a summary of the following discussion is presented in Figure 4–1.

Transmission

One of the most important functions of a neuron is transmission from one place to another. Our bodies are extensive, and there must be some way of making certain that one area of the body knows what another is doing in order to get all the myriad activities integrated together. The *axon* of a nerve cell is a long thin extension which is specialized for transmission. Axons vary in length. Although some are just a few millimeters long, others may run through almost the entire body.

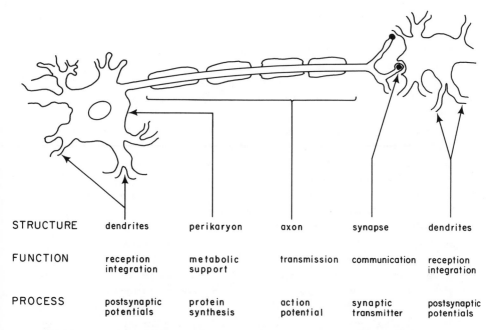

STRUCTURE	dendrites	perikaryon	axon	synapse	dendrites
FUNCTION	reception integration	metabolic support	transmission	communication	reception integration
PROCESS	postsynaptic potentials	protein synthesis	action potential	synaptic transmitter	postsynaptic potentials

FIGURE 4–1   A Diagram of a "Typical" Neuron Relating Function, Structure and Process.
These are discussed in detail in the text.

For example, there is a neuron which brings us information about pressure on the big toe. The axon of this neuron runs from the big toe, up the leg, into the bottom part of the spinal cord, and up the spinal cord to terminate finally in an area of the brain at the level of our neck. All mammals have this neuron, even the giraffe, in which case it is approximately 10 meters long! Similar long axons are associated with motor control. It is through these axons that one area of the body is able to communicate with another—obtaining information about activities in other areas through afferent neurons and changing activities in those areas through efferent neurons.

Axons are nicely designed to carry out faithful transmission, in spite of their small size. The axon which runs from our big toe to our neck is only about 1 micron in diameter and thus has an incredible length to width ratio. At a more understandable macroscopic level, an equivalent length to width ratio could be obtained by taking a piece of kite string and stretching it out for five miles. The axon has solved the problem of how to transmit a signal for such a long distance over such a small path by incorporating a process that regenerates the signal at every step along the way, in much the same way that a fuse carries along the spark by providing material to be burned all along its length.

~ The signal in the axon is called an *action potential*. It is a brief event; the major portion of the action potential takes place in just a few milliseconds, and the entire event is completed in about 10 milliseconds. During an action potential, the membrane potential of the cell is changed from its resting level of about −70 millivolts (mV) to +30 mV, to −75 mV, and then back to the resting level again. This change in voltage is accomplished by first increasing the permeability of the membrane to sodium ions which move into the axon, making the inside more positive, and then increasing the permeability of the membrane to potassium ions, which move out of the axon, making the inside less positive.

An action potential is triggered by rapidly decreasing the membrane potential from its resting level to a threshold at about −50 mV. When the axon reaches this threshold, an action potential occurs. The action potential in any given area of the axon will decrease the membrane potential in the area of the axon adjacent to it, producing an action potential in that area. In this fashion, the action potential is actively propagated from along the entire length of the axon. Because the sodium and potassium ions are present in the necessary concentrations along the entire axon, every bit of the axon has the capability of producing an action potential by itself. In fact, the metabolic machinery of the cell can be stopped by a poison, and an axon will continue to conduct action potentials for some period of time.

As a result of this regenerating process, the action potential that arrives at the far end of an axon is identical to the one that initially started the process. Unlike a passive process, which would allow the potential to decay due to the resistance of the conducting medium, this active process continually renews the action potential at each point. Thus an important characteristic of an action potential is that it is an "all-or-none" process. If the potential of the membrane reaches the threshold, an action potential will occur which will be maintained identically throughout the axon (unless, of course, the axon has been injured in some way or the concentration of sodium and potassium ions altered).

Communication

In order to have any influence on the rest of the body, an action potential must alter the activity of some other cell, and a second function of a neuron is communication. Although each nerve cell is independent of other nerve cells, it needs to communicate with them, and it does so through a *synapse*, which is a small gap, about .02 microns wide, between two neurons. A single axon usually divides into many branches. Each of these branches forms a synapse, and the branches may go to many different cells. Likewise, any given cell has axons from many other cells terminating on it. This divergence and convergence, respectively, means that action potentials in any given axon are communicated to many other neurons, and any given neuron is influenced by action potentials from many other axons. Thus the diagram in Figure 2–1 is highly simplified; it helps to highlight the operational distinctions being made here but doesn't accurately reflect the complexity of nervous networks as they actually exist in the brain.

The action potential itself is unable to move across the synapse, and the electrical potential is so small that it has little direct effect on the subsequent cell (with the exception of some specialized neuron cells which have direct electrical coupling). Thus the process of communication across the synapse takes place with a *synaptic transmitter*. This chemical substance is stored in the presynaptic membrane, the termination of the axon at the synapse. An action potential in the axon releases the synaptic transmitter from the presynaptic membrane. The transmitter diffuses across the gap of the synaptic cleft and then combines with receptors on the postsynaptic membrane of the other cell.

Integration

The receptors in the postsynaptic membrane are located most often on dendrites, although occasionally they appear on the cell body or the axon itself. The dendrites are responsible for receiving information from other cells and for integrating this information. As discussed earlier, action potentials are excellent for getting information from one place to another, but their all-or-none characteristic does not allow them any modification. Intelligent behavior requires modification—integration of many different types of information and changes in behavior as a result of experience. This integration takes place in the form of two different types of potentials which occur in the postsynaptic membrane when the synaptic transmitter substance combines with the receptor. Unlike action potentials which are all-or-none and cannot be added together, the postsynaptic potentials vary in size and can summate.

One of the potentials, an *excitatory postsynaptic potential* or EPSP, makes the cell more likely to produce an action potential. An EPSP takes about 10 milliseconds and moves the membrane potential from the resting level toward the threshold for an action potential. EPSPs vary in size, depending on the amount of transmitter released and the time period during which it is released. They can also summate together. If one EPSP begins and another follows it within a few milliseconds, the potentials will add together to produce a combined EPSP that is larger than either one would be alone. If enough EPSPs are added together in a short enough period of time, they can move the membrane potential of the neuron above the threshold and generate an action potential in the axon.

The second type of postsynaptic potential is an *inhibitory postsynaptic potential*, or IPSP. IPSPs inhibit the cell and make it less likely to produce an action potential. They last for up to 100 milliseconds and make the membrane potential more negative, moving it away from the threshold for an action potential. Like EPSPs, they are graded in size and can summate together; two IPSPs will make the membrane potential more negative than a single IPSP.

Integration takes place because EPSPs and IPSPs can summate, not only with themselves, but also with each other. Thus the two types of potentials can counteract each other and produce the necessary integration of nervous activity. Consider a neuron which has just received 20 EPSPs simultaneously (one EPSP from one action potential in each of 20 different axons, for example). Summated together, these would move the membrane potential above the threshold and produce an action potential in the axon. But if at the same time 15 IPSPs arrived, these could counteract the EPSPs, keep the membrane potential below the threshold, and prevent an action potential.

A commonly used example of this type of integration is the case of a person who picks up a tea cup which is both incredibly hot and incredibly valuable. The pain from the heat excites the neurons in the spinal cord which stimulate the extensor muscles to make the fingers release the cup. The knowledge that the cup is valuable and the consequences of letting it go send down a barrage of impulses from the brain which have exactly the opposite effect—they inhibit the neurons in the spinal cord that stimulate the extensor muscles preventing the fingers from releasing the cup. (A complementary state of affairs is taking place at the flexor muscles, of course.) The critical neurons in the spinal cord receive both EPSPs and IPSPs, and the fate of the cup lies in the balance between these; if EPSPs to the neurons which contract the extensor muscles predominate, there are no blisters and a broken tea cup; if IPSPs predominate, there are lots of blisters, but the tea cup remains intact.

Metabolic Support

A neuron must keep itself alive, too, and support all of the activities just discussed. It carries out this function in the cell body or *perikaryon* using the normal cell processes of protein synthesis. These are common to all cells and do not differentiate between neurons and other types of cells.

AUTONOMIC NERVOUS SYSTEM

In contrast to the skeletal nervous system, which influences the activity of striated muscles that move the bones in the skeleton, the autonomic nervous system influences the activity of smooth muscles and glands. The autonomic nervous system is important in biofeedback. Many of the psychophysiological disorders which bring clients to treatment are influenced by autonomic nervous system activity. Biofeedback treatment often teaches people to gain control over autonomic activities, and one of the major controversies concerning the mechanism of voluntary control has dealt with the interactions between the autonomic and skeletal nervous systems (see Chapter 5).

The autonomic nervous system can be divided into two major components, as illustrated in Figure 4–2. Both of them influence many different visceral activities, but they differ in the pathways taken, the transmitter substances used, and the direction of their influence. The *parasympathetic* portion of the autonomic nervous system leaves the central nervous system at two places. One of them is at the base of the brain, particularly through the tenth cranial nerve or the vagus nerve. This nerve travels through the body innervating organs ranging from the heart to the large intestine. The second origin of the sympathetic nervous system is the very ventral portions of the spinal cord. Axons from here go through the pelvic nerve to the rectum, kidney, bladder, and genital organs. The *sympathetic* portion of the autonomic nervous system leaves the middle portions of the spinal cord. Axons go to a series of chain ganglia next to the spinal cord, form a synapse, and then proceed to visceral organs.

The sympathetic and parasympathetic portions of the nervous systems use different transmitter substances in the final synapse at the target organ. The transmitter substance of the parasympathetic system is acetylcholine while that of the sympathetic system is epinephrine or adrenalin. This pharmacological division allows independent manipulation of these two systems through appropriate drugs, providing information about the ways in which people control these visceral activities (Bleecker & Engel 1973a,b).

The effects of activity in the sympathetic and parasympathetic systems differ also. The sympathetic system has often been described as one that is involved in "fight or flight" or ergotrophic processes. As illustrated in Figure 4–3, stimulation of the sympathetic nervous system increases the diameter of the bronchioles in the lungs, raises blood pressure and heart rate, causes the hair on the skin to become erect, and decreases digestive processes. In contrast, the parasympathetic nervous system has been described as one that is involved in relaxation or trophotropic processes.

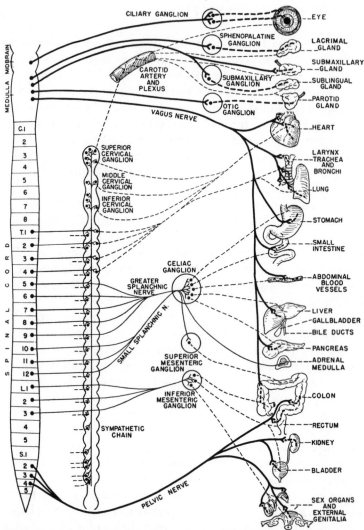

FIGURE 4–2   A Diagram of the Autonomic Nervous System.
The parasympathetic portion originates from the top of the drawing in the medulla and midbrain and at the bottom of the drawing from the lower levels of the spinal cord. The sympathetic portion originates from the middle portions of the spinal cord and has its first synapse in the sympathetic chain ganglia. (From W. B. Youmans, *Fundamentals of Physiology for Students in the Medical Sciences.* Chicago: Year Book Medical Publishers, 1957. By permission.)

Activity in this system reduces blood pressure and heart rate and increases digestive processes.

Because of the different patterns of visceral activity produced by stimulation of the sympathetic and parasympathetic portions of the autonomic nervous system, they are often regarded as mutually exclusive

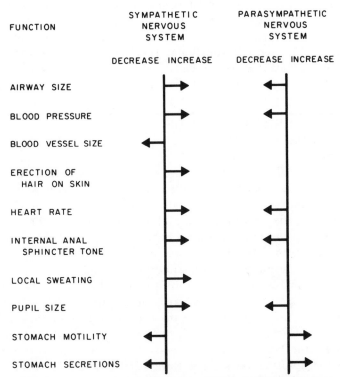

FIGURE 4–3   An Illustration of the Effects of the Sympathetic (Middle Column) and the Parasympathetic (Right Column) Stimulation on Different Autonomic Functions (Left Column).

systems underlying the states of anxiety and relaxation, respectively. Almost all the relaxation techniques take as physiological indications of relaxation increased parasympathetic activity and decreased sympathetic activity. The correlations between a dominance of parasympathetic activity and the state of relaxation are substantial. But two points need to be kept in mind. First, some organs are innervated by only one of these two systems. Erection of the hair (piloerection) is produced by sympathetic activity but not inhibited by parasympathetic activity because the parasympathetic system does not have any axons going to the mechanism that raises the hair. A similar case exists in terms of the diameter of the veins in the skin; sympathetic stimulation produces constriction and reduces the blood flow, but parasympathetic activity has no effect because there are no parasympathetic axons going to the blood vessels (or if there are, they have only a minimal effect). Thus the sympathetic and parasympathetic systems do not always influence the same organ in opposite ways.

A second point to remember is that there is probably not ". . . a physiologic rationale for the discharge of the parasympathetic system as a whole. Simultaneous dilation of the pupil, salivation, slowing of the heart, increased activity of the gut, defecation, urination, and erection of the penis have no sensible functional association. . . . The components of the parasympathetic system behave independently, participating in specific reflexes or well-integrated reactions" (Koizumi and Brooks 1974).[1]

FUNCTIONAL ORGANIZATION OF THE NERVOUS SYSTEM

People in biofeedback treatments are often able to control the biological function as requested but unable to explain verbally how they do it. Such an outcome is not unique to biofeedback and reflects the functional organization of the nervous system. This point can be made clearer by examining other *dissociations*—cases in which people are able to perform one activity appropriately but not another.

Dissociations result from a fundamental principle called *localization of function*. Some areas of the brain are specialized to carry out some behavioral functions while other areas of the brain are specialized to carry out other functions. This organization is seen most clearly at sensory and motor levels. For example, the pathways from the retina of the eye through the lateral geniculate body to the occipital cortex handle mainly visual information while pathways from the basilar membrane in the ear through the medial geniculate to the temporal lobe handle mainly auditory information. Thus destruction in the retina—lateral geniculate—occipital cortex system will produce an impairment in vision but not have much of an effect on hearing, while destruction in the basilar membrane—medial geniculate—temporal lobe system will produce an impairment in hearing but not have much of an effect on vision.

A similar organization is found in other brain areas. Axons from afferent nerves enter the spinal cord through the dorsal root while axons from efferent nerves leave the spinal cord through the ventral roots. Thus stimulation or destruction in the dorsal root will directly alter sensory processes while stimulation or destruction in the ventral root will directly alter motor processes. Localization of function takes place at levels further removed from sensory and motor processes, although it is harder to demonstrate there. Thus different areas of the brain are primarily involved in regulating sleep and wakefulness, controlling body temperature, directing aggression, producing speech, and so on.

The phrase *localization of function* does not imply that a single func-

1 From Koizumi, Kiyomi, and Brooks, Chandler McC.: The autonomic nervous system and its role in controlling visceral activities. In Mountcastle, Vernon B., ed., *Medical Physiology*, ed. 13, St. Louis, 1974, The C.V. Mosby Co.

tion is located in a single area of the brain. To make that strong statement we would need to know much more about both functions and brains than we do now. But the statement does mean that brain areas are not equipotential so that they can be interchanged with each other; some brain areas handle some functions better than other functions and handle those better than other brain areas handle the same functions.

There are many examples of dissociations supporting the concept of localization of function. One of the most dramatic comes from epileptics who have received an operation cutting the corpus callosum, a bundle of fibers that normally interconnects the two hemispheres of the brain. These people had been suffering from severe seizures that medication was unable to control; the corpus callosum was cut in the hope of reducing the seizures. The results of these experiments showed that the brain area allowing the person to talk about a stimulus was located primarily in the left hemisphere, and that cutting the corpus callosum had produced a set of disconnections (Geschwind 1965a, b; Horel & Keating 1969; Mishkin 1958, 1966) so that the person was able to talk about some stimuli but not others.

These experiments used the fact that the nervous systems involved in vision, touch, and motor control all have crossed projections. A stimulus in the left visual field stimulates receptors in the eye which project impulses only to the right hemisphere. Likewise, a stimulus in the left hand stimulates receptors that project only to the right hemisphere, and motor control of the left hand is coordinated primarily by the left hemisphere. Similarly, the nervous pathways for vision, touch, and motor control for the right side project to the left hemisphere of the brain.

Because of these selective projections, a stimulus can be presented so that information goes only to a single hemisphere, and a response can be required that is controlled mainly by one hemisphere. The experimenters found that without the corpus callosum, one hemisphere was unable to communicate with the other, but that different areas within each hemisphere were able to communicate with each other. Stimuli were presented in either the left or right visual fields and to either the left or right hand. The person was asked to identify the stimulus by naming it or by picking up a matching object (without seeing it) with one hand. When the picture of the object was presented in the right visual field, the person could name the object, and could pick up a matching object with the right hand, but not with the left hand. When the stimulus was presented in the left visual field, the person could not name the object or pick up a matching object with the right hand, but could pick it up with his left hand.

These dissociations can be understood simply by tracing the required stimulus and response pathways through the nervous system and determining if they need to cross the corpus callosum. If they do, the person is unable to produce the correct response; if they don't, the person is able to produce the correct response. For example, the picture of an object in the right visual field is projected to the left hemisphere, and the response of naming it is carried out in the left hemisphere; consequently, the correct response is given. If the same stimulus is presented in the same visual field, but a response is requested from the left hand, interhemispheric communication is required because the stimulus is projected to the left hemisphere, but the response is controlled by the right hemisphere. Because the corpus callosum is severed, the two hemispheres cannot communicate with each other, and the person cannot give the correct response.

A similar line of logic holds for stimuli presented in the left visual field. These are projected to the right hemisphere. Because the response of naming and the response of picking up a matching stimulus with the right hand are carried out by the left hemisphere, these responses require interhemispheric communication and fail. Because the response of picking up a matching object with the left hand is carried out by the right hemisphere (the same one that received information about the stimulus), this response proceeds correctly.

The results of these experiments demonstrate localization of function and provide examples of dissociations in which the person can identify the stimulus correctly with one response mechanism, but not another. The major point is that the nervous system is organized in such a way that different behavioral functions take place in different areas of the

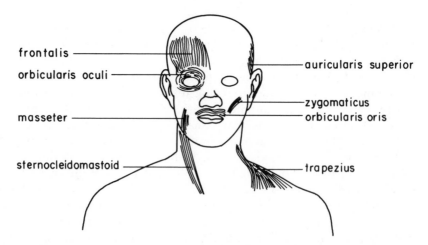

FIGURE 4–4   A Drawing of Some of the Major Muscles of the Head and Neck that are Mentioned in Later Chapters Discussing Clinical Applications of Biofeedback.

(Adapted from Stedman's Medical Dictionary, plate 1. Copyright © 1976 by The Williams & Wilkins Co., Baltimore. Reprinted by permission.)

brain, and unless these areas of the brain are able to communicate with each other, these functions cannot be integrated together (see also Geschwind 1965a, b; Horel & Keating 1969; Mishkin 1972).

MUSCLES

Biofeedback has recorded from a number of different muscles in the body. Some of these treatments are directly for the muscle itself (as in

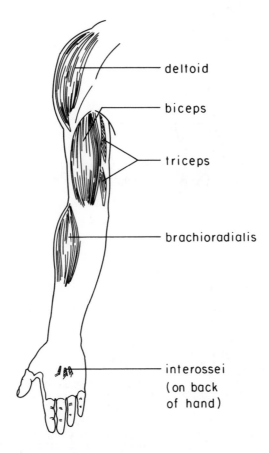

deltoid

biceps

triceps

brachioradialis

interossei
(on back
of hand)

RIGHT   ARM

FIGURE 4–5   A Drawing of Some of the Major Muscles of the Arm that are Mentioned in Later Chapters Discussing Clinical Applications of Biofeedback.
(Adapted from Stedman's Medical Dictionary, *plate 4. Copyright © 1976 by The Williams & Wilkins Co., Baltimore. Reprinted by permission.)*

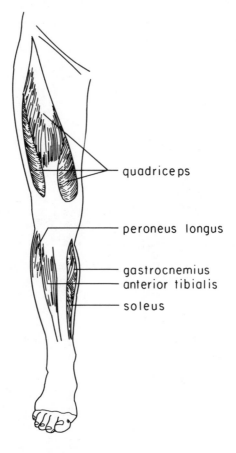

quadriceps

peroneus longus

gastrocnemius
anterior tibialis

soleus

RIGHT LEG

FIGURE 4–6   A Drawing of Some of the Major Muscles of the Leg that are Mentioned in Later Chapters Discussing Clinical Applications of Biofeedback.
(Adapted from Stedman's Medical Dictionary, *page 6. Copyright © 1976 by The Williams & Wilkins Co., Baltimore. Reprinted by permission.)*

neuromuscular reeducation); other treatments are for an indirect effect that accompanies control of the muscle (as in the treatment of asthma or tension headaches). The muscles are discussed in many places throughout the book, and we provide the diagrams in Figures 4–4, 4–5, and 4–6 for those who may be unfamiliar with them.

PROCESS
AND PROCEDURES

II

The three chapters in this section discuss what actually happens during biofeedback treatment. The success of biofeedback challenged some fundamental beliefs about the organization of the nervous system and the ways in which people control their behavior. In response to this challenge, a series of experiments and debates examined biofeedback and asked how it differs from other types of voluntary behavior. The issue focuses primarily on the processes through which people learn voluntary control, the topic that is considered in Chapter 5. The next two chapters discuss procedures used in biofeedback applications. The first one (Chapter 6) describes the physiological recording techniques used to obtain information about the state of the biological system. As pointed out earlier, one of the strengths of biofeedback is its ability to obtain rapid, precise, and accurate information about biological functions, a step that requires appropriate techniques to obtain this information. We describe briefly the ways in which the biological systems produce the signals which are of interest and the subsequent procedures for recording these signals. The next chapter (Chapter 7) discusses clinical procedures. It provides an outline for the procedure used to treat any psychophysiological disorder and points out the many different factors that the therapist should consider when designing the most effective treatment.

We have placed the details of the recording procedures and the treatment program in separate chapters in this section in order to avoid having to constantly repeat the information in each clinical chapter. Thus the topics covered in these three chapters are relevant to all the clinical chapters that follow in the subsequent section. For example, when the treatment of migraine headaches discusses raising skin temperature,

Chapter 6 should be consulted for further information on the way in which this is accomplished. Likewise when a clinical program outlines a procedure for treatment, further information about the details of that program should be obtained from Chapter 7.

VISCERAL CONTROL
AND MEDIATION

5

Voluntary Control

Direct and Indirect Mediation

Control or Conditioning

For the first half of this century, instrumental conditioning procedures examined mainly those responses mediated by the skeletal nervous system. For reasons that are not entirely clear, the custom of studying instrumental conditioning with only skeletal responses gradually developed into a belief that operant and classical conditioning could be distinguished on the basis of the nervous system used by them (Kimble 1961). Direct control of the autonomic nervous system through operant procedures was thought to be impossible (Kimmel 1967; Miller 1969), and few investigators attempted the experiments necessary to challenge this idea. With the advent of biofeedback, this belief (which grew up without any systematic body of data to support it) has been discarded, and now there is no question that autonomic responses can be influenced by operant procedures. But the question still remains as to how this influence takes place, and the answer to that question requires a description of the processes mediating feedforward control.

The question is very simple. How does an individual voluntarily control biological activities in his own body? Or in terms of the control loop diagrams outlined in Chapter 2, what are the physiological and psychological processes represented by the control line interconnecting the person and biological function being controlled? Although there are no definitive answers to these questions yet, the debates have forced all the participants to think clearly and be very specific in describing their proposals. As a result, ideas that were once vague have become crystallized and can be subjected to experimental test. The resulting hypotheses are of interest because they provide us with alternative descriptions of how visceral control might take place and suggest ways in which both the clinical therapist and the research scientist can improve biofeedback procedures.

VOLUNTARY CONTROL

Biofeedback has shown that many biological systems can be voluntarily controlled by an individual. What does the word voluntary mean in this context? Many people who are successful in biofeedback procedures are unable to communicate to another person the manner in which they achieved success. Thus the term voluntary should not imply conscious control or the ability to verbalize the process. Furthermore, animals can be trained to control visceral activities so that the term voluntary should not be defined in such a way that it applies only to humans.

One of the most useful operational definitions of voluntary is presented by Brener (1977, p. 30): ". . . a voluntary response is one that is systematically influenced by verbal instructions." Thus, if an individual is able to raise heart rate when told to do so, the response of increased heart rate is said to be a voluntary one. To be more generally applicable, the above definition should be amended to two ways. First, the instructions need to be given by an individual other than the one who is to carry them out (Brener 1977). If the instructions come from the person doing the control, that individual can wait until the response is ready to begin for some other reason and then give himself the instructions. The second extension of Brener's definition is the need for deleting the word "verbal." First, it is unnecessary; a person can be trained in a task without any verbal communication at all. Second, it prevents the application of this definition to animals because of the difficulty of communicating directly with words.

When these changes are made, the modified definition of voluntary becomes: a *voluntary response* is one that is systematically influenced by instructions from an individual other than the one making the response. This definition is useful because it allows us to set up an experimental procedure to test whether or not any given response can be placed under voluntary control. The individual is given a set of instructions describing the desired response. Then the experimenter tells the individual when to produce that response. If the response appears after those instructions (and not in the absence of them), then the response is voluntary. Note that this definition does not indicate the psychological or physiological characteristics of the control, nor does it provide a resolution to the philosophical and epistemological issues about the relationship of the term voluntary to other terms such as consciousness, free will, and awareness.

The importance of the ability to follow instructions has already been acknowledged in the discussion of feedback in Chapter 2. Figure 2–1, describing the basic biofeedback experiment, showed the person as receiving two pieces of information, one from the feedback and one from the instructions which determined the set point to be maintained. The person must compare the two sources of information and match the feedback, describing the actual state of the biological function to the instructions, describing the desired state of the biological function. If this match can be accomplished, then the person has voluntary control of the biological function.

DIRECT AND INDIRECT MEDIATION

The word *mediation* has two meanings (Webster's 1973), both of which are relevant to biofeedback. In one of them, mediation simply implies that the control process lies between the person doing the controlling and the biological function being controlled so that the person has a direct influence on the biological function. In the other, mediation implies that the control process acts through an intervening step so that the person can influence the biological function only in an indirect way and must change the mediating process before altering the biological function. To keep these two meanings distinct in the following discussion, we will use different words for each one.

Direct mediation will refer to the first type in which the mediating mechanism occupies a middle position between the controller and the function being controlled. *Indirect mediation* will refer to the second type in which the mediation takes place through intermediate, indirect steps. In those cases where the distinction between these two forms of mediation is unnecessary, no preliminary adjective will be used.

The difference between direct and indirect mediation is illustrated in Figure 5–1. The first example is one that you have already seen; control occupies a middle position between the person and the biological function being controlled. This diagram implies that the relationship between the person and the function is direct and that no intervening agencies are needed. The second example is one in which a new element, the *mediating process,* has been introduced. Now the relationship between the person and the biological function is an indirect one because the function can be controlled only by first activating the mediating device.

Two general categories of indirect mediators have been proposed. One of them is biological and attempts to describe the neuroanatomical systems through which control takes place, emphasizing the relative roles of the skeletal and autonomic nervous systems in providing feedforward control. The second is psychological and attempts to detail the cognitive processes through which a person manipulates biological function, the relative roles of imagery, thoughts, and feelings.

Biological Mediation

As outlined in Chapter 4, there is substantial localization of function within the nervous system. Although definitions of both structure and function are somewhat fuzzy and complex, none the less there is still general agreement that some parts of the brain are better at carrying out certain functions and other parts of the brain are better at carrying out

DIRECT MEDIATION

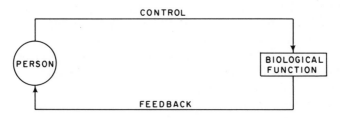

INDIRECT MEDIATION

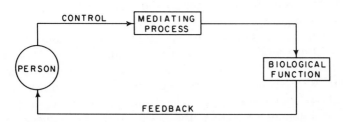

FIGURE 5–1   The Difference Between Direct and Indirect Mediation.

With direct mediation, represented at the top of the diagram, control of the biological function is accomplished without any intervening mechanisms. With indirect mediation, represented at the bottom of the diagram, the person has control only of the mediating process. By altering this mediating process, the person can produce changes in the biological function, but changes in the biological function cannot occur directly, that is, without going through the mediating step.

other functions. In light of this general principle, some of the areas of the brain are undoubtedly more involved in visceral control than others; identifying these areas can help us understand how the brain goes about the process of visceral control.

Although the issue may seem somewhat esoteric, it actually has several practical implications. One has to do with understanding how control over bodily activities actually takes place. The better we understand the basic mechanisms, the better we should be able to design biofeedback procedures to be maximally effective in using this mechanism. A second has to do with developing alternative modes of treatment. For example a patient might come to the clinic with damage to some part of the nervous system. If this damage is placed to interfere with the control loop usually effective in treatment (see Chapter 2), the traditional approach will probably fail. But if a second means of gaining control using a different component of the nervous system can be established, this alternative approach may be successful even though the original was not.

Attention has been focused on two major subsystems in the body, the autonomic nervous system and the skeletal nervous system. As outlined in Chapter 4, the autonomic nervous system (ANS) is composed of nerves that terminate on visceral organs such as the heart, veins, stomach, and sweat glands. The skeletal nervous system (SNS) is composed of nerves that terminate on skeletal muscles, the muscles that move the bones in our body. There are many different ways in which the ANS and SNS may be interrelated through feedforward and feedback loops (see Brener and others 1974). For the moment, we will be concerned with only three of them as outlined by Black (1967) and presented by Katkin (1971).

In the first example, at the top of the Figure 5–2, the actions of the ANS and SNS are independent of each other, arising from different origins in the brain. The area of the brain doing the controlling of the autonomic function has direct access to autonomic nerve fibers, resulting in direct control of the function. The second example, in the middle of the figure, is clearly one of indirect mediation. The brain has access only to the nerves that control the skeletal muscles. In order to produce a change in autonomic function, the brain must first influence the SNS which will in turn produce changes in the autonomic function through various reflex pathways. In the final diagram, presented at the bottom of the figure, the SNS and ANS arise from the same axons of the brain (in contrast to the situation presented in the first diagram). If the nervous system is organized in this fashion, then independent control of the ANS and the SNS is not possible because every time an action potential goes down the axons to the ANS it also goes down their branches to the SNS.

Three different research strategies have been used to investigate the relationship between ANS and SNS activity during biofeedback experiments (Black 1974). The *correlational experiment* trains control of an autonomic function while monitoring the activity of skeletal muscles at the same time. The question is whether ANS activity changes independently of SNS activity. Although the correlational experiment can describe whether SNS activity does accompany ANS activity, it cannot determine whether the skeletal muscle activity is necessary for the autonomic changes to take place. To answer this latter question, some type of *intervention procedure* must be used in which the experimenter forces a separation between the activity of the two systems (Schwartz 1977) to determine if skeletal activity must take place during autonomic condi-

DIRECT MEDIATION THROUGH
THE AUTONOMIC NERVOUS SYSTEM

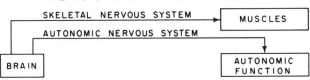

INDIRECT MEDIATION THROUGH
THE SKELETAL NERVOUS SYSTEM

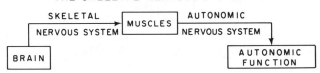

CORRELATED OR PARALLEL
NERVOUS ACTIVITY

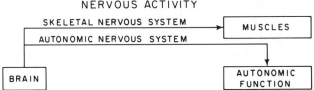

FIGURE 5–2   Three Different Possible Relationships Between the Skeletal Nervous System (SNS) and the Autonomic Nervous System (ANS).

In the top diagram, the SNS and the ANS function independently of each other because they originate from independent parts of the nervous system. In the middle diagram, the SNS is a mediating process between the person and the ANS. Curare blocks nervous system transmission at the junction between the SNS and the muscles and prevents muscle movement. In the bottom diagram, the SNS and ANS inevitably function together because the axons that control them come from the same neurons in the brain.

tioning. Two types of interventions have been used. One is with the drug curare. At appropriate doses, this drug produces paralysis by blocking synaptic transmission between the fibers of the skeletal nervous system and the muscles they stimulate (Koelle 1975) so that action potentials in these nerves are unable to produce muscle contraction and the individual is effectively paralyzed. Curare has little effect on transmission in other parts of the nervous system; sensory and cognitive systems are functionally intact so that the individual is sensitive to stimuli and can think and reason as usual. Autonomic systems are unaffected by curare, at least in low doses (Black 1974).

Experiments with curare can determine whether indirect mediation via the skeletal nervous system (the second diagram in Figure 5–2) is necessary for autonomic control. Curare acts at the junction between the SNS and the muscles and prevents activity in the SNS from stimulating muscle contraction. If the pathway in this diagram is the only way through which the individual has voluntary control over autonomic functions, then blocking this pathway must lead to failure in the ability to produce control. The curare experiment is not adequate to provide a distinction between direct mediation via the ANS (top diagram in Figure 5–2) and correlated parallel activity in both the ANS and SNS (bottom diagram in Figure 5–2). In each case there is a direct connection between the brain and the ANS, and curare should have no effect on the ability to control ANS activity (Black 1967; Katkin 1971).

The second type of intervention experiment is called *dissociative conditioning* (Black 1974) or *differentiation* (Schwartz 1972). Here the individual is given two discrimination tasks to perform simultaneously. One requires control of an autonomic function, such as heart rate. The other requires control of the system thought to do the mediating. If the hypothesis is that increases in heart rate occur only if the muscles are contracted, then the individual might be required simultaneously to increase heart rate and decrease muscle contraction. Success at performing this task would indicate that activity in the autonomic and skeletal nervous systems can be uncoupled, thus disproving the second and third diagrams in Figure 5–2. Another way to address the issue is by requiring the individual to generate patterns of activities in autonomic functions (Schwartz 1977). The experiment might demand changes in both heart rate and blood pressure in all four possible combinations: heart rate increase, blood pressure increase; heart rate increase, blood pressure decrease; heart rate decrease, blood pressure increase; heart rate decrease, blood pressure decrease. This particular design does not address directly the role of the SNS in ANS conditioning because it is possible that for each pattern of heart rate and blood pressure, the individual develops a specific pattern of skeletal movements. The likelihood of such an outcome seems very low however. (In addition, of course, success at the heart rate–blood pressure patterning would indicate that neither of these is a necessary indirect mediator for the other.)

Much of the original excitement about visceral control came from a series of experiments in which rats were trained to alter a number of visceral activities while under the influence of curare (see Miller 1969). These experiments were elegantly designed. Unfortunately, their results were unreplicable, both in the original laboratory and in other laboratories (see Dworkin & Miller 1977; Miller & Dworkin 1974). Thus, the curare experiments are currently unable to provide information about the importance of the SNS in control of autonomic functions.

The ability of people to learn to control patterns of autonomic activities has been reviewed by Schwartz (1974, 1977). The most relevant experiments are those in which people have been asked to produce selective control of heart rate and blood pressure simultaneously. In one case (Schwartz and others 1972) systolic blood pressure and heart rate were the functions to be controlled. All four possible conditions were used. The two groups instructed to change heart rate and blood pressure in the same direction (either up or down) did so in a convincing manner. The two groups instructed to change them in opposite directions had great difficulty in doing so. In another experiment (Schwartz 1972), people were trained in the same four conditions for systolic blood pressure and heart rate. Again a similar pattern was found; the groups asked to change the functions in the same direction performed better than those asked to change them in different directions. The failure to find strong evidence for successful control in the groups instructed to produce opposite changes in heart rate and blood pressure demonstrates that these two functions are closely coupled together. They can be separated in other types of procedures (Anderson & Brady 1971; Harris & Brady 1977), so that part of the failure here may have been due to the limited training received by each person.

At the present, we do not know the extent to which different biological functions can be independently controlled; this is one question that future research will most certainly address. The important points of this discussion, then, are the ways in which indirect mediation might take place, and the experimental designs that can be used to distinguish among them.

Psychological Mediation

The question of the processes intervening between the person doing the controlling and the autonomic function being controlled can also be addressed at the psychological level. The ways in which psychological processes mediate biofeedback and produce various kinds of biological changes can provide a powerful tool for the therapist. Individuals often have strong predispositions to behave in certain ways. For example, some feel at home with all the electronic equipment in biofeedback procedures and have no difficulty in using it. Others, however, are put off by the instrumentation. For these individuals, imagery, thoughts, emotions, or actions may constitute an effective alternative means of producing the intended result. Even for people who are comfortable with the electronic procedures, these mediating strategies may provide assistance in developing control. If there are consistent patterns of physiological changes in response to various psychological states, the person may be told that generating these ideas (which is relatively easy to do) may assist in learning the required biological control (which may be relatively difficult to do).

One discussion of indirect mediators (Katkin 1971) has emphasized an analysis in terms of classical conditioning, as discussed in the latter part of Chapter 3. The four alternatives were based on a combination of the source of stimulation (external or internal) and the nature of the response (unconditioned or conditioned). Consider first stimuli that are inside the person. The autonomic response might be an unconditioned response produced by these stimuli. For example, increasing muscle contraction can raise blood pressure, and changing respiration can alter heart rate. Both of these activities are carried out by changing activity in the SNS, and the changes in the ANS happen through normal reflex pathways, making this an example of indirect mediation as described earlier. Alternatively, the autonomic response might be a conditioned response to internal stimuli. Thoughts and ideas often have associated emotional states. Thinking about an arousing experience should activate the sympathetic nervous system, while thinking about a peaceful scene should activate the parasympathetic nervous system. By using these thoughts and ideas as indirect mediators, the person might be able to produce the desired autonomic response.

The effective stimuli may also be external to the person, even though this possibility is unlikely in most biofeedback applications. The autonomic response might be an unconditioned response to that stimulus. The individual might pinch his skin or listen to a loud noise, stimuli which should produce reflexive autonomic changes not established through conditioning. Alternatively the autonomic response might be a conditioned response. As a result of learning, the person might be excited by certain pictures or colors and by looking at these produce a change in the autonomic nervous system. In both these examples, the external stimulus always functions as an indirect mediator, the only difference being whether or not the autonomic response produced by the stimulus occurs as a result of conditioning.

Each of the above four processes might function as a mediator, but what evidence is there that these processes actually do function as mediators? The most relevant data come from experiments dealing with relaxation techniques. One commonly used procedure is the progressive muscle relaxation technique of Jacobson (1929, 1938, 1978). Here the person is told how to relax muscles only; no instructions about imagery, thoughts, or feelings are provided. Training is carried out by the therapist until the person can eliminate all signs of tension in the muscles that control the limbs and those in the face. Accompanying this muscular relaxation is usually a significant psychological relaxation as well. The person reports being calm, quiet, at ease, and relaxed. Another relaxation technique is Autogenic Training (Schultz & Luthe 1969). Here the person is given training with a series of word phrases emphasizing changes in the body (such as warmth or heaviness in the limbs) or various images (such as patterns of colors). The concentration on these phrases produces a marked state of psychological relaxation.

More idiosyncratic methods may also work. Few people are probably willing to poke themselves with a pin in order to generate physiological changes, but at least one person has tried a similar strategy (Lynch 1973). The individual in question was being trained to generate brain waves of the alpha rhythm. For a few trials, there was no success. Almost at once, however, the person gained very strong control of alpha activity and produced more alpha in a shorter time than anyone else in the experiment. The experimenters were delighted with this success until they asked him how he did it, and he told them he pinched his cheek. This strategy was developed by accident, but it proved to be very effective in producing the desired biological change (although it did have a few undesirable side effects in terms of the condition of the cheek).

CONTROL OR CONDITIONING

One debate argued the relative merits of using the term *control* or the term *conditioning* (Crider and others 1969; Katkin & Murray 1968; Katkin and others 1969). The discussion was concerned not with experimental data, but with their interpretation. There was general agreement that control of autonomic activities had been demonstrated because both people and animals were able to alter autonomic processes in the appropriate direction when given instructions by the experimenter. The debate was whether this control was an example of conditioning or not. At a superficial level, of course, this dilemma can easily be resolved by providing a technical definition of each of the terms, comparing the definitions, and then deciding if they are the same. Indeed, this epistemological exercise was one resolution of the debate. At a deeper level, there is a more profound question about the mechanisms of mediation. The term control may imply an unspecified relationship between the individual doing the controlling and the function being controlled. The term conditioning may imply a direct relationship with no intervening processes, and one that is learned. When phrased in this way, the debate strikes at the core of the problem discussed in this chapter.

The question is whether the observed changes in the biological function are due to *associative* factors as a result of learning, or whether they are due to *nonassociative* ones such as arousal, fatigue, and so on. The best examples of this distinction come from animal experiments, but the general issue is still relevant to clinical applications. For example, a dog is trained to increase heart rate when a bright light is presented by giving him food when the heart rate exceeds a criterion. This behavioral change may have been due to learning, but it may have resulted from nonassociative factors as well. The dog may simply have become excited when he learned that he was to get food during the experiment, and this excitement in itself may have been sufficient to produce the heart rate increase. Heart rate changes reflexively in response to many different stimuli (Clifton 1974), and if the dog really learned only about food being in the box and not about how to change his heart rate, the the results would have few implications for clinical treatment. If the heart rate response of the dog was a reaction to getting fed in the box, then every time the dog wished to raise his heart rate, he would have to go to the box and get fed there. Few humans would be interested in controlling heart rate through this type of procedure.

Can nonassociative variables have an influence on visceral activities? Certainly there is ample reason to assume that they might. The individual will be relatively more or less successful. Success is often accompanied by arousal and excitement; failure, by anger and frustration. Any of these states have substantial autonomic correlates. Furthermore, the rewards and punishments themselves might be expected to have autonomic correlates.

One of the strongest experimental designs to demonstrate control through associative learning is called the *bidirectional discriminated control* design (Miller 1969; Black 1974). As to be expected from the name, this design has two components to it. The first is a requirement that the autonomic function be changed in two directions, both increased and decreased. The second is that these changes be under discriminative control, occurring in the presence of the discriminative stimulus, but not in its absence. Applied to the heart rate conditioning experiment in dogs just described, this experimental design includes two groups and two conditions for each group, as illustrated in Table 5–1. One group is trained to increase heart rate, but only when the discriminative stimulus is presented. The other group is trained to decrease heart rate, again only when the discriminative stimulus is presented.

Now let's go back and consider the two different explanations of the

| | | Discriminative Stimulus | |
		Present	Absent
	Increase Heart Rate	Heart rate increases	Baseline A
Condition			
	Decrease Heart Rate	Heart rate decreases	Baseline B

Note: The entries in the table show the changes that are necessary if an individual really has obtained bidirectional control. For example, consider the condition in which heart rate is to be increased (the top line). When the discriminative stimulus is present telling the individual to increase heart rate (top left quadrant), heart rate should increase relative to Baseline A (top right quadrant). Likewise in the condition in which heart rate should be decreased (the bottom line); when the discriminative stimulus is present telling the individual to decrease heart rate (bottom left quadrant), heart rate should decrease relative to Baseline B (bottom right quadrant).

dog's heart rate change in the first experiment. One said that the change was due, not to direct control of heart rate, but rather to an indirect response of excitement about being fed. If that explanation is correct, dogs should be unable to decrease heart rate in the second part of the bidirectional experiment because all conditions in both the increase and decrease conditions are the same except the contingency between the response and the reinforcement. In one case reinforcement is given only for increases in heart rate; in the other case it is given only for decreases in heart rate. If the dog learns to perform correctly in both conditions, the only reasonable explanation is that he has learned the contingency between the response and reinforcement.

The bidirectional discriminated control experiment provides further information about the relative ability to learn the two procedures. In one experiment, one group of rats was trained to increase heart rate; the other, to decrease it (Black, Cott, & Pavloski 1977). These two groups differed in mean heart rate during the presence of the discriminative stimulus indicating that something had been learned about the response-reinforcement contingency. But what learning had taken place was entirely in the group trained to increase heart rate. Only for this group was heart rate during the discriminative stimulus significantly different than that during baseline conditions when the discriminative stimulus was absent.

A second reason for using this experimental design is due to the fact that the baseline of the group may gradually change in the direction provided by reward. For example, Miller and DiCara (1967) used a bidirectional discriminated control design to train rats to increase or decrease their heart rates. When the discriminative stimulus was present, rats trained to decrease heart rate had lower heart rates than when the discriminative stimulus was absent, and rats trained to increase heart rate had higher heart rates than when the discriminative stimulus was absent. These results indicate that the rats had learned the association between changes in heart rate and reinforcement. In addition, however, the general baseline of these two groups of rats diverged substantially. Even when the discriminative stimulus was absent, rats in the group trained to increase heart rate had higher heart rates than rats in the group trained to decrease heart rate. These data indicate that in addition to the change in heart rate specific to the presence or absence of the discriminative stimulus, there was also a general heart rate change in response to the overall experimental procedure.

In summary, both associative and nonassociative variables can influence visceral conditioning. For the research scientist, separating the behavioral changes due to each of these is critical to obtain the appropriate interpretation of the data. The clinical therapist should also be concerned about them too because visceral changes produced as a result of nonassociative variables may not be as therapeutically effective as those produced by associative ones, and because the strategies used to produce associative changes differ from those used to produce nonassociative ones.

PSYCHOPHYSIOLOGY

6

Signals

Muscle Activity

Blood Pressure

Heartbeat

Brain Waves

Blood Flow and Skin Temperature

Suppliers of Biofeedback Equipment

Learning to control a biological system is helped by feedback about the state of that system (see Chapter 2). This chapter describes how that information is obtained. We provide only the basic details necessary to understand the instruments most commonly used in biofeedback training, and the physiological basis for the signal they record. For more detailed discussions of psychophysiological instrumentation and procedures see Brown (1967), Greenfield and Sternbach (1972), or Venables and Martin (1967). The first sections consider the ways in which the *signal*, the desired piece of information, is obtained from the biological system, amplified and filtered, and then presented to the client in a feedback display. The subsequent sections consider each of the most widely used applications of biofeedback. Each one is organized to describe the way in which the biological function produces the signal, the transducers which are used to record the signal, and the equipment which subsequently processes it.

SIGNALS

Detection

The biological signal is detected with either invasive and/or noninvasive techniques. *Invasive* procedures require surgery to place the measuring device near the physiological system being monitored. *Noninvasive* procedures do not require surgery and apply the measuring device to the skin over the system to be monitored. Both of these procedures have their respective advantages and disadvantages. The invasive procedures can gather more detailed information about the physiological function being recorded, but they have the risks and difficulties associated with surgery. Noninvasive procedures gather less detailed information, but can be easily used in a clinical setting. In most cases, the information obtained by noninvasive procedures is adequate for successful biofeedback training, and their convenience and minimum risk make them the most common procedure.

Processing

There are two major components to the information obtained by a monitoring device. One is the *signal*, the information about the biological function. The second is *noise*, electrical activity produced by deficiencies in the recording equipment or by interference from other biological functions or other electronic equipment. In many cases the noise is more predominant than the desired biological signal so that the *signal-to-noise ratio* must be increased. The signal-to-noise ratio is usually specified as a decibel or db level. Higher db levels indicate higher signal-to-noise ratios (Peffer 1979) which should be as large as possible (Cohen 1979). For most biofeedback applications, band-pass filters with filter roll-offs are built into the equipment. A high band-pass filter passes only those signals which are above a selected frequency; a low band-pass filter passes only those signals which are below a selected frequency. Setting a high band-pass filter at 30 Hz (cycles per second) and a low band-pass filter at 1,000 Hz will result in the processing of only those signals with frequencies between 30 and 1,000 Hz. Filter roll-offs, expressed in dbs per octave, attenuate (suppress) signals just beyond the band-pass filter regions at a designated rate. A filter roll-off of six db per octave in our example above will attenuate frequencies below 30 Hz and above 1,000 Hz at a rate of six db per octave. Higher roll-off rates provide better attenuation. A filter roll-off of six db per octave is adequate for most biofeedback training. Where a particular frequency such as 60 Hz activity interferes with the desired signal, a filter roll-off of about 30 db may be necessary.

The goal of filtering, then, is to determine which frequencies contribute needed information and which do not. Undesired ones are eliminated by setting the filters to suppress them. However, restricting the range of acceptable frequencies is not the only answer to the problem of maximizing the signal-to-noise ratio. Smaller ranges may pass less noise, but they may also reduce the signal and result in a lower signal-to-noise ratio. The decision concerning the frequency to be recorded and the characteristics of the filtering apparatus must be based upon the particular biological function recorded and information about the types and frequencies of interference specific to a given location. Some signals, such as those from the heart, are relatively strong and can be recorded with relative ease. Others, such as brain waves, may require special filtering apparatus because they are relatively weak.

Display

After the signal reflecting the state of the biological system has been obtained, it must be given as feedback. Some considerations about the types of feedback have already been discussed (see Chapter 2). Of particular relevance here is the decision to use binary feedback or analogue feedback. The various advantages and disadvantages of each of these have been discussed in Chapter 2 and will not be repeated here.

A second decision about the signal display is the general form it should take. Although feedback could be presented in any sensory modality, vision and audition are the two most commonly used. Although we know of no controlled studies documenting the effectiveness of one over the other, clients often have strong preferences (or aversions) to one of them. Furthermore, different treatments may require one or the other. For example, relaxation-meditation procedures may use biofeedback as an aid to provide information about the client's success. Most relaxation procedures are carried out with the eyes closed, making visual feedback inappropriate. Thus both visual and auditory feedback should be available.

Biofeedback applications have varied in the extent to which they process the information before it is given to the client, and the degree to which the client understands the physiological significance of the feedback. In some applications, the client is simply told to produce changes in the signal and is not provided much information about its meaning. In others, the client sees the information in a relatively unprocessed form which is described in detail. This later approach has typically been used by Engel in the treatment of both cardiac arrhythmias (see Chapter 15) and fecal incontinence (see Chapter 14). In both cases the patients were provided with polygraph records which were described extensively. For the fecal incontinence treatment, the polygraph records were used for feedback during treatment. Engel typically encouraged patients to ask questions, understand the biofeedback process, and obtain as much information as they desired. The consistent success of his treatment programs suggests that this care in explanation may be an important component in treatment.

MUSCLE ACTIVITY

Electromyographic or EMG feedback is one of the most common and successful types of biofeedback. EMG feedback training is used to increase the contraction of inadequately functioning muscles and decrease activity in hyperactive ones. The EMG measures the amount of electrical discharge in the muscle fibers. Electrical activity increases as muscle contraction increases.

Physiological Basis

A single muscle is composed of a group of motor units, each of which is composed in turn of many muscle fibers bound together, acting as a group. Each muscle fiber is about 1/10 mm in diameter and may be as long as 310 mm (Basmajian 1978). The fibers in a motor unit contract together because they are stimulated by the axon of a single neuron in the brain or spinal cord. Figure 6–1 illustrates a motor unit with its muscle fibers and the axon coming from the spinal cord. The number of muscle fibers which are functionally grouped together into a motor unit varies depending upon the muscle type. Muscles which have discrete movements (such as those in the fingers) may contain fewer than 20 muscle fibers in a single motor unit, while muscles responsible for large adjustments to body position (such as those in the back) may contain well over 2,000 fibers in a motor unit. When innervated by nerve impulses, muscle fibers contract and decrease in length by as much as 50% of their resting length (Eccles 1959; Galambos 1962; Haines 1932, 1934; Katz 1966; Woodbury 1965). Contraction of the muscle is accompanied by electrical current recorded as the EMG (Goldstein 1972). Under certain conditions of relative inactivity, a linear relationship may be observed between the actual force exerted by a muscle and the EMG (Goldstein 1972).

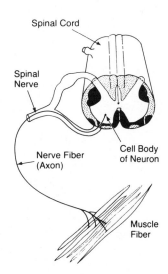

Spinal Cord

Spinal Nerve

Nerve Fiber (Axon)

Cell Body of Neuron

Muscle Fiber

FIGURE 6–1   A Diagram of a Motor Unit and Its Innervation by a Motoneuron in the Spinal Cord.
At the top is a representation of the spinal cord. In the bottom portion is a neuron. The axon from the neuron leaves the spinal cord, divides, and connects to several different muscle fibers in the muscle. Because an action potential in the neuron will go down all the branches of the axon, all the muscle fibers that are innervated by the axon contract at the same time. *(From James Hassett, A Primer of Psychophysiology. Copyright © 1978 by W. H. Freeman and Company. Reprinted by permission.)*

Signal Detection and Processing

The potentials associated with muscular contraction are measured by electrodes which determine the difference in potential between two locations. There are many types of electrodes, but in most biofeedback training only two general types are used: (1) *in-dwelling,* those which are inserted through the skin and into the muscle and (2) *surface,* those which record from the surface of the skin the activity of underlying muscles. The choice of which type of electrode to use is based upon the degree of activity of the muscle, how deep in the body the muscle lies, and whether the muscle has been separated from the skin surface.

The use of either in-dwelling or surface electrodes has both advantages and disadvantages. In-dwelling electrodes record a clearer and larger electrical signal which contains less electrical activity from neighboring muscles. Two types of in-dwelling electrodes, bipolar fine-wire and concentric needle, are displayed in Figure 6–2. Because these must be inserted through the skin, they carry the risks of invasive procedures. In-dwelling electrodes are often necessary for a person to learn initial control of a muscle which is very inactive following a stroke or damage

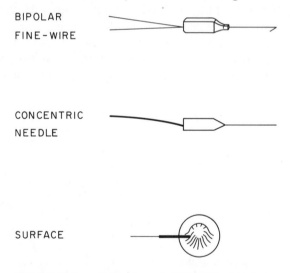

BIPOLAR
FINE-WIRE

CONCENTRIC
NEEDLE

SURFACE

FIGURE 6–2   Examples of Electrodes Used for EMG Biofeedback.
The top two electrodes are used in invasive procedures. *A* is a bipolar fine wire electrode placed inside of a hypodermic needle which provides the strength necessary to insert it through the skin. *B* is a concentric needle electrode. At the bottom in *C* are examples of surface electrodes. *From S. Wolf, 1978. In* Physical Therapy, 58 *(1978), p. 26. Reprinted by permission of the American Physical Therapy Association.*

to the peripheral nerves innervating it. In most other applications, surface electrodes are sufficient.

Surface electrodes range in size and are selected according to the needs of each application. For most biofeedback treatments, electrodes with recording surface diameters between 4 and 13 mm should be suitable. The advantage of using larger electrodes is that they generally have lower impedance (resistance). Large electrodes are inappropriate, however, when the curvature of the body prevents their usage or if they record from too many muscles. In most instances, proper preparation of the skin in conjunction with the use of readily available high-power, low-noise amplifiers will enable the use of smaller surface electrodes.

An important point is that any electrode records all the electrical activity present at the recording site, irrespective of the origin of this activity. This fact is particularly relevant when using large surface electrodes. The potentials recorded from these electrodes come not only from the muscle directly underneath the electrodes, but also from neighboring muscles and organs, as well as sources outside the person. The relative contribution of any given muscle depends on its distance from the site of the recording electrode, its size, and its activity. Thus the term *frontalis EMG* indicates that the surface electrodes were placed on the skin over the frontalis muscle, and does *not* imply that the frontalis muscle was the only one contributing to the EMG record (Basmajian 1976).

For optimal recordings with surface electrodes, the skin over the muscle area should be carefully cleansed, abraded, and dried before the electrodes are applied. This removes oils, sweat, and dead skin which might otherwise raise the impedance (resistance) to the flow of electrical current and attenuate the EMG signal. Failure to carefully prepare the skin may also reduce adhesion between electrode collars and the skin when individual electrodes are used. A gauze pad soaked in alcohol and then moistened with electrode paste or gel may be used to abrade the skin. Another suitable technique is to clean the area with alcohol and then rub the area with a gel containing quartz crystals. In either case the skin should be thoroughly cleansed, frequently until it turns pink, and then allowed to dry completely before attaching the electrodes. Other means for abrading the skin have been incorporated into commercially-available agents. Some investigators have even used sandpaper to prepare the skin (Swann, van Wieringen, & Fokkema 1974).

Once the skin is prepared the electrodes may be applied. The electrodes may be individual ones or they may be mounted in a rubber or elastic headband stretched around the head. Individual electrodes weigh very little and may be less disturbing to the client. However, they fall off if moved only slightly. Electrodes mounted in a headband have the advantage of ease of application but may be less comfortable for the client. The headbands may slide on the skin if disturbed and this causes the feedback to include more activity from neighboring muscles. A few minutes spent adjusting the headband will usually enable the therapist to attach the band tightly enough to prevent sliding across the skin while at the same time leaving it loose enough to keep the client comfortable.

The first step when using individual electrodes is to attach the electrode collar to the electrode. The collar has an adhesive surface on both sides, one of which is covered by a protective shield. Collars are specially designed for each size electrode so that the diameter of the opening in the center of the collar is the same size as the diameter of the recording surface in the center of the electrode. Care should be taken, therefore, to fit the collar onto the electrode so that the entire recording surface of the electrode is exposed. Electrode paste or gel should then be applied to the electrode to serve as a conducting medium. The paste or gel should come up to the edge of the electrode cup in order to make only light contact with the skin. When electrodes are mounted in a headband, the collars are unnecessary. The paste or gel is applied into the electrode cup in the same manner as with individual electrodes. If too much paste or gel is applied it will be forced out of the electrode cup and under the adhesive collar of an individual electrode, or out of the cup of headband electrodes and onto the forehead. In either case the EMG signal may be reduced or distorted.

Individual electrodes are applied by removing the protective cover over the adhesive surface of the electrode collar and gently pressing the collar on the skin, taking care not to push down on the back of the electrode itself. When electrodes are mounted in a headband, the cups are filled with paste or gel and then strapped over the skin.

Three electrodes should be used, two for recording and one for a ground. Most bands have these three electrodes mounted in line, the center one being used for the ground. Individual electrodes are usually placed at three sites over the muscle, with the ground electrode in the middle.

The placement of electrodes on the skin requires careful choice of the amount of spacing between them because electrodes will measure activity both from muscles under them and from neighboring muscles as well (Basmajian 1976). Muscles nearest the electrodes will make a larger contribution to the EMG than those farther away (Goldstein 1972). Wide spacing of three centimeters or more between the electrodes produces a larger signal because more muscles contribute activity to the recording. However, the recording from many muscles makes discrete muscle training difficult. In most biofeedback use, electrodes spaced one to two centimeters apart will record a signal with a sufficient amplitude (Goodgold &

Eberstein 1972, pp. 32–40) and also allow discrete muscle training. In general, electrodes should be spaced farther apart with spastic muscles but closer together with very weak ones. The type of electrodes and their spacing should be kept constant across sessions wherever possible to provide comparable readings. If electrode positions are changed, the meaning of the feedback will change and may confuse the patient.

The electrical activity of muscle potentials is produced over a broad range of frequencies and the most desirable range may differ for each biofeedback application. Further discussions of the most appropriate EMG frequencies can be found in Basmajian (1978), J. F. Davis (1959), R. C. Davis (1942), Goodgold and Eberstein (1972), Schwartz and others (1949a,b), and Whitfield (1953). In general, high-powered amplifiers with adjustable filters are desirable.

As Figure 6–3 indicates, the raw EMG signal (traces one and three) presents a limited amount of information and is difficult to interpret as feedback. Consequently, the raw EMG is usually transformed into more meaningful information through the use of integration techniques. One of the easiest ways to quantify the EMG is to measure the largest voltage which occurs in a given period of time, say one second. A second way to quantify the EMG is to count the total number of potentials exceeding specified criterion levels during specified periods of time. This second

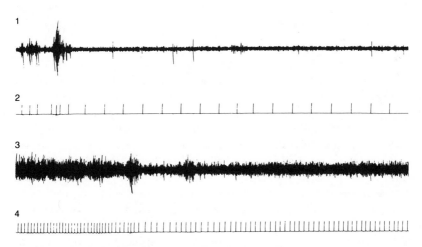

FIGURE 6–3   An Example of Different Types of EMG Records.

Traces 1 and 3 are the recordings of muscle potentials. Traces 2 and 4 are the associated outputs of an integrator which cumulatively adds the muscle potentials and provides a pulse when the amount of activity reaches a certain level. Note that when the muscle contracts at the beginning of trace 3, the rate of the pulses from the integrator in trace 4 increases too. *(From James Hassett, A Primer of Psychophysiology. Copyright © 1978 by W. H. Freeman and Company. Reprinted by permission.)*

method provides information about a broader spectrum of EMG activity than the first.

Integration techniques provide a measure which more closely approximates the actual EMG activity across time (see Shaw 1967). Figure 6–3 contains a sample output of an integrator (lines two and four). The integrator stores and sums EMG activity cumulatively until a predetermined level when it produces a pulse indicating that the level has been reached. Note that the pulses are spaced close together in the left part of line four reflecting the greater EMG activity during that time.

BLOOD PRESSURE

Physiological Basis

Blood pressure reflects the force with which blood travels through the arteries. Pressure is highest during *systole* when the heart contracts and is lowest during *diastole* when the heart relaxes between beats. Blood pressure is recorded at these two points as *systolic* or maximum pressure, and *diastolic* or minimum pressure, respectively. The different blood pressures are measured in millimeters of mercury (mm Hg) and are expressed as the ratio of systolic over diastolic (for example 140/90 mm Hg).

Signal Detection and Processing

The most accurate way to determine blood pressure is to implant a catheter directly into an artery to measure the force of blood flowing through it. Because this procedure is impractical in most biofeedback training, blood pressure is determined by techniques which permit non-invasive recording from the skin. The most commonly used technique is to wrap an inflatable pressure cuff around the upper part of the client's arm between the brachialis and coracobrachialis muscles. The pressure cuff is connected to an air pump. Inflation of the cuff to a level above the systolic blood pressure prevents the blood from flowing through the limb. As air is released from the cuff, blood flow resumes, marking the level of systolic pressure. The first pulse travelling through the previously occluded artery generates a *Korotkoff sound* which can be heard through a microphone or stethoscope, and recorded as a spike on polygraph paper. These sounds continue until diastolic pressure is reached when they disappear. This method is one of the most reliable means for external determination of blood pressure although it may slightly underestimate both systolic and diastolic levels (Tursky 1974) and vary from one measurement to another. For this reason, several readings should be obtained.

The most widely used technique for recording blood pressure during biofeedback training is the *constant cuff* method (Shapiro and others 1969; Tursky and others 1972; Tursky 1974) which uses a pressure cuff and an automated air inflation system. A microphone in a pressure cuff which is wrapped around the patient's upper arm is placed to lie above the brachial artery. The pressure cuff is inflated to the point at which about half of the heartbeats are followed by a Korotkoff sound, marking the median systolic pressure. The cuff pressure is then held constant during a trial lasting about 60 to 90 seconds. The patient is provided with feedback of increases or decreases in median pressure with each beat of the heart. This is accomplished by determining whether a Korotkoff sound did or did not follow each R wave of the heartbeat (see below). The presence of a Korotkoff sound following a heartbeat indicates that blood pressure rose above the constant cuff pressure; the absence of a Korotkoff sound indicates that the blood pressure decreased below the constant cuff pressure. A sliding criterion is used to set the level of cuff pressure on each trial. The trials are separated by rests of at least 30 seconds to allow the blood to recirculate through the arm. Failure to allow sufficient rests could result in ischemic pain and other complications and should therefore be avoided.

An indirect measure of blood pressure may be obtained from pulse wave velocity. Two measurements are necessary. These may be obtained from two different points on an artery, or they may be obtained from the R wave of the EKG and a single point on an artery. In either case, the length of time required for the blood to travel down the artery, divided by the distance between the two recording sites, gives pulse wave velocity. Blood pressure and pulse wave velocity are inversely correlated (Gribbin and others 1976; Steptoe and others 1976; Obrist and others 1979).

HEARTBEAT

Physiological Basis

The beat of the heart is maintained by pacemaker cells in the sinoatrial node. These cells undergo periodic, spontaneous excitation (Adolph 1967), sending impulses through the atrium to the atrioventricular node from which they are transmitted to the ventricles. These impulses excite first the atrial and then the ventricular muscles which contract and propogate the impulses responsible for the recorded electrocardiogram. Blood is pumped from the ventricles, the two lower chambers of the heart and returns to the atria, the two upper chambers. The heart is influenced by nerve impulses from sympathetic and parasympathetic systems which counteract each other (Adolph 1967) as they innervate the sinoatrial and atrioventricular nodes. Increased sympathetic activity accelerates the heart rate by increasing the rate of firing at the sinoatrial node while increased parasympathetic activity reduces the heart rate by decreasing the firing rate.

Signal Detection and Processing

The electrocardiogram is a recording of the electrical activity accompanying the muscular contraction of the heart. The electrical signal is very strong and can easily be detected by electrodes placed on the surface of the skin. Figure 6–4 illustrates a typical recording of two successive heartbeats. The *PQRST complex* represents a complete cycle from the intake to the expulsion of blood by the heart. As the figure shows, the R wave is the clearest and most striking signal and is therefore used most frequently in procedures that count the number of heart contractions during a specified time interval. Heart rate is generally measured in beats per minute, a measure of the rate at which ventricular contractions occur and of the number of times the heart moves through the PQRST cycle each minute.

Electronic determination of heart rate is accomplished through analysis of the time between two successive R waves, the *interbeat interval* as illustrated in Figure 6–4. For example, if one second elapsed between two successive R waves, then 60 such intervals would occur in one minute, indicating a heart rate of 60 bpm. Commercially available devices can be connected to a polygraph to obtain the EKG signal similar to the one in Figure 6–4.

BRAIN WAVES

Physiological Basis

When nerve cells discharge, they create electrical activity (see Chapter 4). Although the precise nature of the EEG is still open to debate

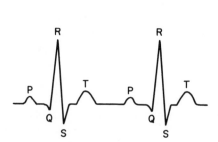

FIGURE 6–4   A Diagram of an Electrocardiogram (EKG) Showing Two Typical Heart Beats.

The QRS complex is associated with the contraction of the ventricles. The *R* peak is the largest potential, and the interbeat interval is usually calculated between successive *R* waves. Heart rate in beats per minute can be calculated by dividing 60 by the interbeat interval.

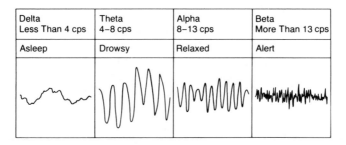

Delta Less Than 4 cps	Theta 4–8 cps	Alpha 8–13 cps	Beta More Than 13 cps
Asleep	Drowsy	Relaxed	Alert

FIGURE 6–5   An Illustration of Four Rhythms Commonly Seen in the EEG.
The top of the figure describes in order the name of the wave, the number of cycles per second in it, and the behavioral state during which it is most prevalent. The bottom part of the figure gives an example of an EEG tracing of the wave. *(From James Hassett, A Primer of Psychophysiology. Copyright © 1978 by W. H. Freeman and Company, Reprinted by permission.)*

Brazier 1958; Whitteridge & Walsh 1963), several general characteristics can be described with confidence. The EEG reflects the activity of many nerve cells, probably hundreds of thousands, and maybe more. Consequently, it can provide only a very crude picture of the functioning in individual parts of the brain and primarily reflects activity in cerebral cortex. The EEG changes substantially as a function of the behavior of the person and reflects some general changes in psychological state.

Identification and classification of brain waves reflects both their frequency and amplitude which generally vary inversely with each other. The amplitude of the brain wave indicates the magnitude of the electrical change and is measured in microvolts (millionths of a volt), abbreviated as uV. The frequency of the brain waves is measured in cycles per second (Hz). The relationship between brain wave frequency and amplitude, along with one of the more common classifications of brain wave activity, is presented in Figure 6–5. These waves represent a common, although relatively arbitrary, grouping of EEG frequencies, rather than a clear physiological distinction.

Signal Detection and Processing

Brain activity is usually recorded with disk electrodes placed in standard positions on the scalp (Jasper 1958). The hair may be shaved to obtain better contact. Because scalp oils and fine hair movement may lead to poor electrode contact and signal interference, they should be reduced as far as possible (see discussion of EMG recording). In addition, care must be taken to detect and eliminate muscle artifact produced by blinking and movement of scalp muscles.

Brain waves do not appear as a distinct frequency, changing into other clearly distinguishable frequencies. Rather, they are complex waveforms that simultaneously contain more than one frequency. For this reason, waves are typically defined in terms of both frequency and amplitude. The EEG should be processed by band-pass filters that eliminate frequencies which are not of interest. Alternatively, a spectral analysis may be carried out providing information about the relative amount of activity in each frequency range. An example of an EEG recording procedure is presented in Figure 12–5.

BLOOD FLOW AND SKIN TEMPERATURE

Physiological Basis

The amount of blood flowing to an area of the body, say a hand, determines to a large extent the temperature of the skin over that area (Hertzman 1953). Hence peripheral blood flow and peripheral skin temperature generally change together; peripheral blood flow and skin temperature decrease with reductions in external temperature and increase with elevations in external temperature. This thermoregulatory response allows the body to hold constant the temperature of the internal organs and adjust to changes in environmental temperature. Blood flow and skin temperature are also affected by a range of dietary, biochemical, environmental, psychological, and nervous system factors which operate in isolation and in combination. *Vasodilation* is the condition in which blood vessels increase in size and allow greater blood flow, which is followed by higher skin temperatures. *Vasoconstriction* is the condition in which blood vessels decrease in size and restrict blood flow, which is followed by lower skin temperature.

Signal Detection and Processing

The thermistor and the photoplethysmograph are the two most common means for determining relative changes in the volume of blood flowing to the periphery. A *thermistor* is a small transducer which detects changes in the temperature of the skin where it is attached. A *photoplethysmograph* measures changes in the volume of an area by transmitting a light through it to a photocell as illustrated in Figure 6–6. While there exists no one-to-one correspondence between the amount of blood flow detected by a photoplethysmograph and the skin temperature measured by a thermistor, the two measures are positively correlated with each other (Surwit and others 1976).

Commercially available photoplethysmographs generally come with a connector cable to be plugged into a polygraph. In addition to recording

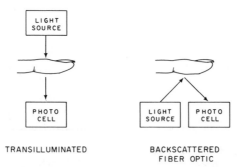

TRANSILLUMINATED

BACKSCATTERED
FIBER OPTIC

FIGURE 6–6   The Two Ways in Which a
Photoplethysmograph functions.
In all cases, light produced by the light source
is measured by a photocell. As the volume of
the finger changes, the amount of light reaching
the photocell changes, which in turn is reflected
in a difference in voltage. The positions of the
light source and the photocell may vary, as
indicated in the figure.

changes in blood volume, the photoplethysmograph can easily record
heart rate. Measurement of skin temperature can be accomplished with
commercially available devices which usually include a power source,
one or more thermistors, and auditory and/or visual feedback signals. In
many cases, no additional equipment is needed.

SUPPLIERS OF BIOFEEDBACK EQUIPMENT

Advanced Electro Labs, Inc.
P. O. Box 2386
Pomona, CA 91766

Advanced Health Systems, Inc.
881 Dover Drive, Suite 20
Newport Beach, CA 92663

Aleph One Ltd.
P. O. Box 72
Cambridge CB3 ONX
ENGLAND

APL, Inc.
2814 Metropolitan Place
Pomona, CA 91767

Aquarius Electronics
P. O. Box 96
Albion, CA 95410

Autogenic Systems, Inc.
809 Allston Way
Berkeley, CA 94701

Biobehavioral Instruments
1663 Denver Ave.
Claremont, CA 91711

Biocybernautic Institute
3526 Randolph Avenue
Oakland, CA 94602

Biofeedback Computers, Inc.
420 Laurel Avenue
Cheltenham, PA 19012

Biofeedback Electronics, Inc.
147 Eldorado Street
Monterey, CA 93940

Biofeedback Instrument Co.
255 West 98th Street
New York, NY 10025

Biofeedback Instruments Inc.
213 West Plain Street
Wayland, MA 01778

Biofeedback International, Inc.
2155 Buchanan St. #2
San Francisco, CA 94115

Biofeedback Research Institute, Inc.
6325 Wilshire Blvd.
Los Angeles, CA 90048

Biofeedback Systems, Inc.
2736 47th Street
Boulder, CO 80301

Bio-Feedback Systems Inc.
(Karlan Industries)
881 Dover Drive, #20
Newport Beach, CA 92663

Biofeedback Systems, Ltd.
6 Lower Ormond Street
Manchester 1, England

Bio-Feedback Tech. Inc.
10612A Trask Avenue
Garden Grove, CA 92643

Biofeedback Training Inst., Inc.
1800 N. Highland Ave. Suite 500
Hollywood, CA 90028

Bio-Medical Instruments
P. O. Box 248
Warren, MI 48090

BioMonitoring Applications, Inc.
270 Madison Ave.
New York, NY 10016

Bio-My-Products
P. O. Box 154
Fallbrook, CA 92028

Bio-Temp Products, Inc.
3266 N. Meridian Street #703
Indianapolis, IN 46208

BMA Audio Cassette Programs
270 Madison Avenue
New York, NY 10016

BRS/LVE
5301 Holland Drive
Beltsville, MD 20705

Clark International, Inc.
6050 W. Beloit Road
Milwaukee, WI 53219

Coherent Communications
13733 Glenoaks Blvd.
Sylmar, CA 91342

Coulbourn Instruments, Inc.
P.O. Box 2551
Lehigh Valley, PA 18001

Cybersystems
4306 Governors Drive
Huntsville, AL 35805
Chuck Gibb

Cyborg Corporation
342 Western Avenue
Boston, MA 02135

Dektor
5508 Port Royal
Springfield, VA 22151

EDCO Scientific, Inc.
P. O. Box 64
Sherborn, MA 01770

Edmund Scientific Company
EDS Corp. Building
Barrington, NJ 08007

EKEG Electronics Co., Ltd.
P. O. Box 46199
Station G
Vancouver 8, BC, Canada

Electro Labs
P. O. Box 2386
Pomona, CA 91766

Enting Instruments
VIJFTIG Bunderweg 1
Dorst, The Netherlands

Extended Digital Concepts
P. O. Box 9161
Berkeley, CA 94709

Farrell Instruments
P. O. Box 1037
Grand Island, NE 68801

G & W Applied Science Labs
335 Bear Hill Road
Waltham, MA 02154

J & J Enterprises
22797 Holgar Ct., N.E.
Poulsbo, WA 98370

John Chaney Instrument Co.
965 Wells St (PO Box 72)
Lake Geneva, WI 53147

Karlin Industries
738 W. Algonquin Road
Arlington Heights, IL 60005

Lafayette Instrument Co.
P. O. Box 1279
Lafayette, IN 47902

Lawson Electronics
P. O. Box 711
Poteet, TX 78065

Linear Instruments
17282 Eastment Ave.
Irvine, CA 92714

LVB Corporation
P. O. Box 2221
Lehigh Valley, PA 18001

Marietta Apparatus Co.
118 Maple Street
Marietta, OH 45750

Med Associates Inc.
P. O. Box 47
E. Fairfield, VT 05448

Med General
10800 Lyndale Avenue, So.
Minneapolis, MN 55420
Chuck Lennon

Medical Device Corporation
1555 N. Bellefontaine St.
Indianapolis, IN 46202

Medical Devices, Inc.
833 3rd Street, S.W.
St. Paul, MN 55112

Medlab
P. O. Box 31035
San Francisco, CA 94131

Medrad
4084 Mt. Royal Blvd.
Allison Park, PA 15101

M.O.E.
Department 6
P. O. Box 2693
Santa Cruz, CA 95063

Motion Control, Inc.
1005 S. 300 West
Salt Lake City, UT 84101

Narco Bio-Systems, Inc.
P. O. Box 12511
Houston, TX 77017

Neuro Feedback Instruments
6901 Katherine Avenue
Van Nuys, CA 91405

Neuronics, Inc.
104 East Oak
Chicago, IL 60611

Nicolet Inst. Company
5225 Verona Road
Madison, WI 53711

Ortech Inc.
Life Science Products
100 Medland Road
Oak Ridge, TN 37830

Ouroboros Instruments
212 Bryn Mawr, N.E.
Albuquerque, NM 87106

Para Medical Instrument Co.
2350 Lafayette Ave.
Bronx, NY 10473

Quartec
1662 Doone Road
Columbus, OH 43221

Remco Tape Products
5547 Vineland
North Hollywood, CA 91601

Royer-Anderson
763 La Para Avenue
Palo Alto, CA 94306

Sandweiss Biofeedback Inst.
P. O. Box 38474
Los Angeles, CA 90038

Self-Control Systems
P. O. Box 6462
San Diego, CA 92106

Semantodontics
Box 15668
Phoenix, AZ 85060

Somatronics, Inc.
399 Buena Vista East
Suite 323
San Francisco, CA 94117

Spectrum/Intronix, Inc.
303 N. Broadway
Fresno, CA 93701

Staodynamics, Inc.
601 S. Bowen
Longmont, CO 80501

Stoelting Company
1350 S. Kostner Avenue
Chicago, IL 60623

Systec, Inc.
500 Locust Street
Lawrence, KS 66044

Terrasyn, Inc.
P. O. Box 975
Longmont, CO 80501

Thought Technology, Ltd.
2193 Clifton Avenue
Montreal, Quebec H4A 2N5
Canada

Note: We have attempted to be as accurate as possible in this information, but we can't be certain that it will remain correct. Inclusion of a supplier on this list does not imply any evaluation of the quality of the product.

CLINICAL PROCEDURES

7

Initial Sessions

Middle Sessions

Terminal and Follow-up Sessions

This chapter discusses general clinical procedures in biofeedback treatment, presenting an outline of the course of treatment and the considerations that go into almost any biofeedback program. By focusing our attention on biofeedback treatment rather than clinical practice in general, we do not mean to imply that other variables are not important. They undoubtedly are, and factors such as therapist warmth, good rapport between the client and therapist, appropriate scheduling of treatments, setting of fees, and so on should be considered as well. But these are common to all types of treatment and are not unique to biofeedback. Thus, we have omitted discussion of them here. This chapter, read in conjunction with the section describing clinical programs at the end of each clinical chapter, should provide enough information to develop a treatment program for each of the disorders discussed here.

INITIAL SESSIONS

Goals

The initial sessions begin by obtaining the necessary background information from the client and end with the proposing of a specific treatment program. In between, a number of different points are covered, as summarized in the list that follows. These will be discussed in order below.

Goals of the Initial Sessions

1. Description of the client's problem
2. Medical and psychological history
3. Discussion of the rationale and procedure used for biofeedback treatment
4. Demonstration and/or practice of the biofeedback techniques to be used
5. Psychophysiological profile of the client when stressed
6. Psychophysiological profile of the client when relaxed

7. Establishment of procedures for recording symptoms and other data
8. Specific treatment program for this client, with the procedures to be followed and an outline of the results to be sought

With some clients, all of these goals may be met in a single one-hour session. This is reasonable if the therapist already has access to much of the history and the psychophysiological profiles of the client, the client knows about the disorder and biofeedback treatments for it, and the treatment procedure has already been established in the clinic. If none of the above information is available before the first visit, more than one visit will probably be necessary for this part of treatment. A logical place to stop the first session is before the design of the specific treatment program. This allows the therapist to gather additional information from other health care providers who have seen the client and to set up a detailed program. Such a division is appropriate if the case is complicated or requires a great deal of individual attention.

Description of Client's Complaint

We first ask the client why he has come to the biofeedback clinic. The client's initial statement may be informative, and we record it as accurately as possible. Our subsequent discussion then takes two forms. The first is relatively unstructured. We request a thorough description of the symptoms, ask leading questions, and do not restrict the types of answers. The object here is to determine the most salient features of the symptoms as the client sees them, providing us with points that need to be considered when measuring symptom severity, choosing target symptoms for treatment, examining types of stress, and so on.

The second part of the discussion is highly structured, based on the type of problem. For each of the disorders considered, the client is provided with a checklist of adjectives that people use to describe the symptoms. We seek information about the subjective characteristics of the symptoms, where they are located in the body, their frequency, intensity, and duration, and the effects that they have on the individual's behavior. This component of the discussion helps to determine the extent to which the person's complaint falls into a particular diagnostic category (which has implications for the most appropriate type of biofeedback treatment) and also obtains more structured and quantified information about the complaint. Examples of checklists and questionnaires are provided in some of the clinical treatment chapters. Recent studies of the reliability of symptom questionnaires indicate that they can, if properly designed, be reliable reports of those symptoms (Thompson & Collins 1979).

Medical and Psychological History

The usual procedures for taking both medical and psychological histories can be followed, and information should be obtained from other health care professionals in the usual manner. Because the problems treated by biofeedback are medical ones, a complete examination by a physician is always appropriate. Particular attention should be given to some points, however, which are relevant to the biofeedback treatment. An aid in obtaining this information may be a form such as that illustrated in the following list. A symptom history which is objective, extensive, and quantified is the ultimate goal. Retrospective data always suffer from problems of distortion due to memory failure and to other passive and active influences, but some information is better than no information at all. Notes can be taken to indicate how accurate the person thinks the information is, and these notes can be used to temper conclusions where appropriate.

Data on Symptom History

When did the symptoms first appear?
In the past two months (or other more appropriate unit of time):
 How many times did the symptoms occur?
 How long did they last?
 How severe were the symptoms?
 What did you do about them?
 What were the behavioral effects of the symptoms?
  What medication did you take?
  What activities in which you might have participated if you didn't have the symptoms did you miss because you had them?
  How well did you carry out the activities which you did pursue?
 What patterns or cycles appear in your attacks?
  With respect to time (season of year, days of week, hours of day, and so on)?
  With respect to events (vacations, jobs, and so on)?
  With respect to people (spouse, parents, employer, acquaintances, and so on)?

There are several ways in which this information can be useful in biofeedback treatment. First, it provides the initial symptom history against which the effectiveness of biofeedback can be compared. Second, it may identify the variables that trigger attacks of the disorder, indicating parts of the person's life which should be explored further. Finally, it begins to introduce the patient to the types of information that are necessary in recording the symptom history and that will be used during treatment to record progress.

Rationale for Biofeedback

To many people, biofeedback is still a mysterious process more similar to psychic phenomena than to real science. Finding out how much the client knows about biofeedback and the physiological bases of his particular problem will help to determine the level at which the therapist should begin the discussion. Many points are important in developing the rationale for biofeedback. Our explanation runs along the following (abbreviated) lines, with details added as appropriate for each problem.

Psychological and behavioral events can have a strong effect on bodily activities. These can be maladaptive, as in stress related disorders, but they can also be adaptive, as in biofeedback. We have obvious control over some parts of our body, as in movements of the muscles in our hand. One of the characteristics of these muscles is that we can get feedback, information about the effect of our intended action. For example, if we intend to raise our right hand off the table, we can look at our hand and see the result of our intention. There are many other activities in the body which may not provide us with any obvious feedback. For example, we have difficulty knowing about muscles that control the diameter of the blood vessels (and thus influence our skin temperature), the muscles in our stomach, and sometimes even muscles just under our skin, such as those in the forehead. We can make some distinctions about the relative levels of activity in these muscles, but these judgments are not very accurate and are certainly not as fine as those we can make about the movements of the muscles in our hand.

One of the important components in learning is feedback. With feedback, learning may proceed rapidly, while without feedback, learning may not proceed at all. For example, consider two people shooting arrows at a target in an indoor target range. For one person, the range is set up as you would expect and is well illuminated. The target is visible, and the archer can watch the flight of the arrow from the bow to determine where it hits. For the other person, however, the range is lit only by a very dim light bulb. The target itself is barely visible, and an arrow in the target cannot be seen. Thus, the only information this person has about whether or not the arrow hit the target is the sound of the arrow entering the target with a "slap" or silently embedding itself into the bales of hay behind the target when it reaches the end of the alley.

For many of your bodily activities, you are like the person in the shooting range with the dim light—you have only limited feedback about the results of your intended actions. The equipment associated with biofeedback obtains very discrete information about the state of your biological processes and gives you very accurate information about even small changes in function. This feedback allows you to learn to gain control. Once you have this control, feedback is usually not required. After you have learned the skills here in the clinic with the biofeedback equipment, you can practice your skills outside the clinic without further need of the equipment.

After this general introduction, we provide a description of the symptoms, mechanism, and general treatment procedures for the client's problem. This information is a summary from the appropriate clinical treatment chapter in Section Three and is used to explain the medical and psychological characteristics of the disorder and its treatment through biofeedback.

Demonstration of Biofeedback

Most of the procedures for biofeedback are not inherently appealing. The preparations for measuring the biological process are often messy or complicated, and being hooked up with a set of cables to a mysterious piece of equipment may be unsettling. Consequently, we generally demonstrate the biofeedback procedure to the client ourselves using EMG from the forehead. Our procedure usually goes as follows.

After discussing the rationale for biofeedback, we introduce the client to the biofeedback equipment in general, describing the way in which the general processes discussed in the rationale for treatment become operationalized in our particular clinic. We choose EMG for the demonstration because it easily illustrates the principles, procedures, and general equipment function and can be controlled with little training. As we prepare ourselves and turn the equipment on, we explain each step: preparation of the skin, use of electrode paste, placement of the electrodes on the skin, amplification, and feedback. Then we demonstrate the relationship between what we do with our muscles (increasing or decreasing activity) and what happens with the feedback (increasing or decreasing numbers on the display panel, changing the pitch of the tone, and so on). Questions are answered during this process, and we attempt to put the client at ease. After this brief demonstration, we then offer the client the opportunity to try the feedback and provide a few minutes to practice with the equipment.

Psychophysiological Profile
When Relaxed

As will be described in each of the chapters on biofeedback treatments, people with psychophysiological disorders often have an abnormal level of physiological function, even when not experiencing subjective pain. For example, a person who suffers from frequent and severe tension headaches may have elevated activity in the muscles of the head during periods when there is no headache. Obtaining data during a period of rest provides a baseline against which future changes as a result of bio-feedback treatment can be compared. Control of the biological function is desirable, not only during periods of feedback, but also during every-day activities. The resting profile should provide some indication of the extent to which the biological function is abnormal. In some disorders, such as Bell's palsy or fecal incontinence, the question will probably not be whether function is normal, but whether there is any function at all. In others, the initial measurements will provide some indication of the client's position relative to other individuals. To the extent that a func-tion is abnormal, the likelihood that the function in question is involved in the mechanism of the disorder increases and provides further ra-tionale for biofeedback treatment.

To obtain the resting psychophysiological profile, the therapist should be certain that the client is indeed resting and at ease with the pro-cedure. Demonstrating the procedure and answering questions about it will help relax the client. Conversation prior to obtaining the data should be neutral, neither emphasizing the client's difficulties nor making an excessive attempt to produce relaxation. Then the client can be asked to sit quietly for about five minutes without feedback of any kind, doing whatever is commonly done to relax. Measurements may be taken every minute to determine if changes take place during this period. Whenever possible, a stable baseline should be sought, that is, a time period during which there are no obvious trends towards increased or decreased physiological activity.

Psychophysiological Profile
When Stressed

Most, if not all, of the psychophysiological disorders discussed here are exacerbated when the person is under stress. This relationship is apparent to many people who can identify the types of situations which make the disorder worse. Even if the client is not aware of a possible re-lationship, exploring the reactions of the individual to stress will provide some information about the lability of the client's physiology (Lacey and others 1953) and the tendency of it to react to stressful events. Further-more, just the simple demonstration of this relationship may be useful to illustrate the importance of controlling the reactivity of the person dur-ing stress.

A simple means of inducing stress is to use the procedures outlined by Wolff (1968) in his book, *Stress and Disease*. Each client is asked to describe an event or dilemma which produced anxiety, stress, fear, or upset. Then the client is asked to relive this event in as much detail as possible. This is a much different type of procedure than experimental stresses, such as mental arithmetic or task-oriented performance where the stress is placed on the individual by the therapist in a relatively artificial situation. In Wolff's procedure, the attempt was to get the person to experience a stress that was familiar to them. Individuals differ in their ability to follow this request, depending on a variety of factors such as their imagination, their willingness to follow the therapist's instructions, and so on. Five to 10 minutes is usually sufficient to determine what effects the procedure will have. During this time the therapist should have continuous feedback so that the reactions of the client to the questions can be clearly seen. Furthermore, large changes in physiological function may be indicative of areas of the person's life which may be explored to determine what types of stresses are most important, as well as how the person reacts to particular stresses.

When this period is over, the client should be encouraged to relax and the effects of the procedure should be discussed. If there is a large change, the therapist may take this opportunity to discuss in some detail the relationship between stress and the physiological changes, answer questions about this relationship, and describe further the rationale for biofeedback. The relationship between stress and the onset of psychophysiological disorders may also be pursued at this time.

Two pieces of information are relevant. One is the extent to which the individual is responsive to outside influences. Presumably, the greater the variability in response, the easier it is to produce changes in that response. Also of interest is the specific reactivity of the person to stress, and this can be useful in explaining the disorder and describing the rationale for biofeedback. Often this simple demonstration can remove skepticism about the role of psychological events influencing physiological ones and provide motivation to practice biofeedback.

Record Keeping

Record keeping is needed to document progress and design appropriate treatment procedures. Symptoms are commonly recorded on a 24-hour graph, as illustrated in Figure 7-1. In this case, the horizontal axis is divided into the 24 hours of each day, and one graph is used for each day. The vertical axis is divided into a scale with six divisions, numbered from 0 to 5. Each division is given an explicit meaning which may be provided by the therapist or established jointly by the client and therapist. For headaches, we have used the definitions illustrated in Table 7-1.

The numbers 0 to 5 provide a quantitative estimate of headache intensity. This intensity is subjectively determined by the client and re-

Name _____

Date _____

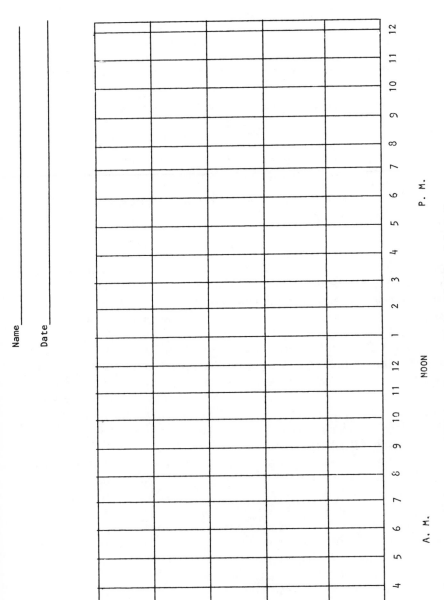

FIGURE 7–1 An Example of a Graph for Daily Recording of Symptoms and Other Information.
The definitions of the numbers for intensity are given in Table 7–3.

TABLE 7-1   Definitions of Numbers for Headache Intensity Scale on Headache Chart

Number	Definition
5	Intense, incapacitating headache prevented me from starting or continuing activities
4	Severe headache made concentration difficult; I could start or continue some activities but not others
3	Painful headache, but I could start or continue daily activities as usual
2	Painful headache, but the pain was low enough to ignore at times while it bothered me at other times
1	Slight headache, but I was only aware of it when I thought about it
0	No headache at all

ported to the therapist, who has no objective means of verifying the accuracy of the self-report. Thus the number scale does not make the ratings of headache intensity any more objective; they are still introspective, subjective, self-reports. The numbers do, however, provide a quantitative means for accurately and quickly summarizing symptom activity. Typically, at least three measures are obtained: intensity (maximum level), duration (number of hours with symptoms), and frequency (number of times symptoms reappear after having returned to baseline). These are sometimes combined into an overall index which considers all three measures in an interactive way. The information from these charts can be placed on a master chart (see for example, Figure 9-2 in the chapter on migraine headaches) to provide a summary of progress.

The numbering system provides an explicit frame of reference. One difficulty with most adjectives is that they change their meaning depending on the context. The word "cool" in a weather report can mean 70°F in August and 30°F in March. Likewise, the client's statement "I had a difficult week" may mean constant symptoms of intensity 3 or more when the person first comes to the clinic, and transient symptoms of intensity 2 for a few hours at the end of treatment. By providing the numerical framework and explicit definitions, the charting helps to maintain the reference point for each intensity.

Charting can gather other information. Clients are often instructed to practice at home, and these times can be placed on the chart so that the therapist can examine the compliance (or at least the stated compliance). The amount and kind of medication consumed is an index of symptomatology, and the number of pills and their type can be recorded as another indication of the subjective pain caused by the symptoms. Most of the psychophysiological disorders treated by biofeedback are provoked by psychological stress. If there are events that happen at particular times of the day or week, and these tend to be the triggers for the symptoms, then cyclical patterns of symptoms ought to appear. Not all stressful events are nicely correlated with the hands of the clock, of course, and these will not produce a temporal pattern. We often ask clients to keep a record of important events on the bottom of the charts. These are informal and unstructured but very informative. They help identify the events that the client thinks are most important and provide a permanent, contemporary record which is highly preferable to an attempt to remember what happened at some later time.

When clients are first introduced to the record-keeping scheme, they are often skeptical, commenting on the number of definitions or the difficulties of keeping records, and so on. Clear explanation and encouragement are important at this time. After a few weeks, however, there is usually enthusiastic acceptance. The client becomes interested in the cycles of symptoms and makes an effort to provide an informative, accurate record. Conversations in the clinic tend more to numbers than words. Therapist: "How was your week?" Client: "Good, I had only 3 attacks, these were of grade 2 intensity, and they disappeared within a few hours." The amount of information in that sentence is substantial, due largely to the numbers. Some of the more avid clients eventually complain that they have symptoms of intermediate intensities (say, 3.4) and want to know why we don't have more divisions! We suggest they put data points not just on the division lines, but also in between, if they wish.

Goals and Contracts

Behavioral therapies commonly set explicit goals and make specific contracts between the therapist and the client (see for example Gambrill 1977, pp. 143–150). The overall aim of biofeedback is to produce the psychophysiological changes desired. This aim may be formalized by a written contract stating what the therapist intends to do (keep appointments, teach a certain psychophysiological procedure, provide counseling, and so on) and what the client is supposed to do (keep records of symptoms, practice at home twice a day, participate in an assertiveness program, and so on).

The long-term goal (eliminating tension headaches) may seem almost insurmountable to a client, particularly if the problem is severe and of long duration. Furthermore, this ultimate goal is best achieved through small incremental steps. Consequently, intermediate goals are set throughout the course of treatment, and the concepts of shaping are fundamental to attaining the desired goal. To keep progress orderly and clear, intermediate goals may be set for each week and even for each treatment session. These are usually not as formalized as the written contract but none the less indicate an explicit agreement between the therapist and client with respect to the goal that is to be sought and the means of reaching that goal. Because positive reinforcement is more desirable than punishment (see Chapter 3), these goals should be set so that they can almost always be obtained by the client. A record of the goals, and the success in obtaining them, can be kept to provide an indication of therapeutic progress. Relating success at the intermediate goals to the overall aim of biofeedback treatment can help provide the motivation to continue and a feeling of accomplishment at having already made progress.

A client almost always asks whether biofeedback will be effective and if so, how long treatment will have to be continued. Predicting the outcome for any given individual is difficult, but we do try to provide a history of people in our own clinic and in the literature at large. Here the review of treatment reports can be particularly valuable in providing the general range of outcomes and the length of time it took to achieve them. This information can be used to provide guidelines for the expected results of treatment, both in terms of its ultimate outcome and its time course.

MIDDLE SESSIONS

After a specific treatment program has been designed and initiated, subsequent sessions are concerned with the practice and evaluation of this program. The goals for these sessions are summarized in the list that follows and will be discussed in order below.

Goals of the Middle Sessions

1. Review of symptom records
2. Practice of biofeedback
3. Evaluation of home practice
4. Evaluation of treatment program in general

Review of Records

The client's records can be one of the most important sources of information for therapy. Reviewing them with the client is advantageous because it demonstrates the therapist's interest in them, helping to provide the motivation for the client to continue and keep them accurate. Several points are important in these records, especially in relation to those provided for previous weeks. One overall question is whether there are regular changes in the intensity, frequency, or duration of symptoms. To the extent that these changes have taken place, the previously established procedures are having their desired effect, and new goals can be set. To the extent that changes in symptomatology have not taken place, the therapist should evaluate the appropriateness of the training program and institute new procedures as required.

A second question to be addressed in the records is the pattern of symptoms, their relationship to time (such as the time of day, day of the week, and so on), and to specific events (such as the interactions with people at work, obligations on weekends, and so on). Any apparent correlation between events and symptoms may be pursued to determine the client's reaction to discussion of this topic. Physiological recordings during this time can be helpful also, especially if the client reacted to the stress test performed during the initial sessions.

Where appropriate, encouragement and praise should be offered to the client for success. The records can provide a perspective that is often lost without them, and even small changes in the frequency, intensity, or duration of symptoms can be used to point out progress. Compliance with treatment programs is rarely complete, and by selectively rewarding appropriate behavior with praise and emphasizing the need to follow a regular regimen, the therapist can help the client follow the treatment program more rigorously.

Practice of Biofeedback

One of the most important reasons for clinical visits is to have the client practice biofeedback skills and develop more physiological control. Here, the discussion of operant conditioning presented previously (Chapter 3) will be useful in establishing general guidelines, and the review of the treatment reports in each clinical treatment chapter will provide more specific information on the structure of each treatment session. In the section below, we emphasize some of the more important questions that must be addressed in establishing a treatment procedure.

These training sessions are the focus of biofeedback therapy and should be carefully planned. The optimal arrangement of practice periods and rest periods depends on the task being used. Because biofeedback requires effort, the sessions should be relatively short, allowing the person an opportunity to have sufficient rest breaks. Two criteria can be used to judge the appropriate length of a session. The first is the client's statement about how long he can practice successfully. The second is the record of success; if performance begins to deteriorate after 15 minutes so that the psychophysiological changes are less than desired, then there is little sense in prolonging the practice. In general, individuals will have more difficulty at first, and initial sessions may be shorter than subsequent ones.

Each session should begin with an explicit statement of the goal. The goal should be determined by previous success and should be set so that it challenges the client to perform but allows success. After the session is completed, an evaluation of performance should be offered, questions answered about performance, and guidance offered to help the individual perform better.

Feedback Environment. A quiet, comfortable environment, free from as many distractions as possible, is important in biofeedback therapy. The ideal environment is one which by itself gives the client a feeling of being insulated from the outside world. Such variables as lighting, seating, soundproofing, room temperature, and room decor may help clients relax and concentrate on the feedback. The placement of the equipment should also be considered. Some clients may feel comfortable around equipment while others may become anxious. Removing as much of the equipment as possible from the treatment room should minimize the chances of generating anxiety.

Shaping. Shaping refers to the gradual development of the final form of the desired behavior from the first rudimentary approximations to it. Its importance has been emphasized in the discussion of operant procedures in Chapter 3, and it will continue to be highlighted throughout the following chapters dealing with specific biofeedback treatments. The need for shaping follows logically from the basic principles of operant conditioning; to increase the frequency of a desired behavior, the therapist should provide a positive reinforcer each time the desired response occurs. But reinforcement can be given only if the behavior occurs. The long term goal of therapy (for an epileptic, say) may be to eliminate all EEG abnormalities and associated behavioral seizures, but if reinforcement is first made contingent on this final goal, it may never be achieved. Shaping is an orderly progression to the desired behavior which requires that the person doing the shaping have designed a logical sequence of steps, each of which builds upon the previous ones and comes closer to the desired goal. There is an art in knowing when to terminate one step and go on to the next, more difficult one. Proceeding too rapidly may produce failure and frustration. Proceeding too slowly may prolong the course of treatment and cause the individual to fixate at a certain level of performance, rather than remain flexible and continue to strive for further improvement.

Reinforcement. As discussed in Chapter 3, the probability of a response is markedly influenced by the type of reinforcement that follows it, and the larger the magnitude of the reinforcer, the greater the change in response strength. Feedback itself functions as a secondary reinforcer, and successful performance of the biofeedback skill may, by itself, be sufficient reinforcement for the person. However, the major goal of therapy is the elimination of symptoms, and if the relationship between success at biofeedback and symptom reduction is not clear, success at biofeedback may provide inadequate reinforcement to sustain the desired level of practice. Two steps may be taken to overcome this potential problem. One is to increase the reinforcing value of success at biofeedback by emphasizing the relationship between it and therapeutic gains. Such a step is particularly important at the beginning of training because initial control of the biological function may not be sufficient to produce noticeable reductions in symptoms. A second step is to provide explicit reinforcers following success. One example has already been presented in Chapter 3. Other examples occur throughout the discussion of the biofeedback treatments in the following chapters and include money (Kohlenberg 1973; Scott and others 1973), felt tip pens (Engel, Nickoomanesh, & Schuster 1974), photographic slides (Benson and others 1971), and praise (Elder and others 1973). This latter reinforcer is easily given and can have pronounced effects. In our treatment, we always provide praise following success, and the magnitude of this praise depends on the magnitude of the success. Thus the therapist should determine what events function as reinforcers for the patient, and make these events contingent on the patient's performance.

Generalization. The client must learn to make the appropriate physiological and/or behavioral changes, not just in the clinic, but also in the "real world," whatever that may be for the client. In essence, generalization is just another form of shaping and is the logical extension of it. Clients often find biofeedback in the clinic relatively easy; they have set the time aside for themselves and have taken both á physical and psychological step to insulate themselves from their normal routine. In these conditions, the probability of success is enhanced. Several clients have told us that when they come to the clinic and sit down in the chair used for biofeedback, they automatically relax and have relatively little difficulty achieving success. Such a step is an important one and indicates that the shaping procedures used earlier have made it possible for the person to produce the desired physiological changes under at least one set of stimulus conditions. The next step, of course, is to transfer this physiological control to other stimulus conditions and generalize the training so that it can take place at any time or place the patient desires. Again, this process may have to take place in small steps. Particularly helpful is setting aside regular times and places that are not associated with any particular stress to practice. When success is achieved here, then steps can be taken towards more stressful conditions.

There are often moments when people are forced to wait; lines seem to exist everywhere in this world. These waiting periods offer an excellent opportunity for the person to practice the biofeedback skills. Most relaxation procedures can be carried out rather inconspicuously, and practicing these while waiting has two benefits. First, there is little else that can be done, so the person is not losing anything by practicing. Second, waiting in lines often produces tension or irritation, which may enhance the person's symptoms, and practicing relaxation (or other techniques learned through biofeedback) may help relax the client.

Criteria for Successful Performance. Some goal always has to be set for any biofeedback session; otherwise, there is no way to evaluate the success of the effort. In some cases binary feedback may be given, specifying whether current performance is above or below a certain level. Here, of course, the criterion for success must be explicitly established before the biofeedback session is begun. In other cases, analogue feedback may be given. Yet, there still has to be some goal for the patient, either limited ("try to raise your skin temperature above 89°F") or more general ("try to raise your skin temperature as high as possible"). The goal set by the therapist should be high enough to motivate the individual to perform as well as possible but low enough to be certain that there is a high probability of success. Consequently, the goal should be altered on the basis of past performance; increased when the performance is excellent, held constant when performance is adequate, and decreased when performance is poor. A number of different *sliding criteria* have been used. They usually specify an increase in the criterion when performance is successful more than about 70% of the time, a decrease in the criterion when performance is above criterion less than 30% of the time, and no change in the criterion when performance lies between 30% and 70%. In this way, the client is generally successful but is constantly challenged to perform better than the current level. Even if analogue feedback is used, the therapist can make a quick calculation of the appropriate criterion level for any particular session and suggest it as an explicit goal for the client. Explicit goals when reached ought to produce a feeling of accomplishment, and a record of performance with respect to the goals can provide an evaluation of the progress of treatment.

Criteria for Terminating a Trial. Flexibility and experimentation will dictate the number and length of trials within a session, which may change as a function of training. In some biofeedback applications, such as blood pressure biofeedback using the constant-cuff method, the trial length must be short because blood is occluded from the limb and must return within approximately 50 heartbeats. In other applications, as for epilepsy or skeletal muscle training, a trial might be as long as an hour. The clinician must consider the individual's needs, particularly with regard to fatigue, the stage in training, the type of training, and the response pattern of the client when deciding on the length and number of trials within a session. Each of our clinical chapters provides an indication of the average length and ranges of lengths which have proven successful.

Biofeedback sessions have ranged from a few minutes up to more than an hour, and various systems have been used to intersperse biofeedback trials with rest periods. At the present time, there is no consensus on the optimal time period to practice, and to some extent this can be dictated by the client's performance. There are several ways in which to terminate a trial. One is on the basis of time, irrespective of performance; another is on the basis of performance, irrespective of time; a third might be on the basis of some combination of the two—say at least 10 but not more than 20 minutes, and until there is no change in performance for two consecutive minutes. In general, extended trials are probably inappropriate because clients report that they become fatigued and are unable to concentrate. At first, this point might be reached after only a few minutes. With more practice, it might not occur for much longer periods of time. As stated earlier, therapy should generally be designed to produce continued success; thus extending trials when performance is improving and terminating trials when performance is deteriorating is a reasonable strategy.

Failure. Occasionally, a client will be unable to perform well during an entire session or after a period of time with good performance. This failure usually produces a feeling of frustration and a psychophysiological state exactly the opposite of the one desired. When this occurs, the frustration is punishment enough, and further punishment by the therapist is hardly needed. In our experience, the failures can provide important opportunities to explore some of the behavioral and/or psychological variables surrounding the psychophysiological symptoms, encouraging the client to consider the reasons why failure might have occurred. This discussion encourages the client to examine the broader setting in which the psychophysiological difficulties occur, and the therapist may be able to conclude positively by emphasizing what has been learned from the session and what should be done on the basis of this information.

Elimination of Feedback. One of the goals is to enable the individual to produce changes in psychophysiological function without the need of the machine or the feedback. This "weaning" allows the person freedom of control and may actually improve performance, at least after the client knows how to make the response. In two studies (Engel, Nikoomanesh, & Schuster 1974; Goldstein, Ross, & Brady 1977), the participants were first taught to perform the response and learned to do so successfully. Then when feedback was removed, the people performed even better, apparently because they didn't know whether or not they had achieved the goal. Obviously, such an endeavor can be attempted only when the person knows the response. The results suggest that with feedback, people may sometimes produce only as much control as demanded by the experimenter, while without feedback, they may strive to produce the greatest change possible.

The client should develop confidence that the control can be carried out without feedback. This is a difficult concept. If feedback was necessary to learn the response in the first place, why isn't it necessary to perform the response subsequently? The distinction between learning and performance must be made clear to the person, and the reason for the truth of both of these statements made clear. The person should develop an ability to assess the outcome of voluntary control without immediate feedback from the machine. In other words, internal feedback from the person should be substituted for the external feedback from the equipment. The major goal is to provide the person with independence from feedback. Indeed, as pointed out in the introduction, the goal of feedback is to provide control, and once this control has been obtained, if feedback can be eliminated, then there is no need for it.

Practice without feedback can be introduced by alternating periods of feedback with no feedback during a training session. The client can be told that the feedback may be eliminated at some times, and these times will be indicated by the experimenter. (In an analogue procedure, this is not difficult because during feedback there is some type of signal, and without feedback there is no signal. With binary feedback, it may be difficult if the feedback is the presence or absence of a tone. If such is the case, then the therapist must make clear when the absence of the tone is part of the binary feedback and thus provides information, and when the absence of the tone is due to removal of the feedback contingency and reflects no information at all.) At the end of these sessions without feedback, clients may be asked to report how successful they were during the session and then be given information about the course of feedback during that period of time in order to validate their opinion.

As training progresses, the periods without feedback can be gradually increased. Some time during each practice session ought to be given to providing the person feedback, in order to help learning. But as the person becomes better and obtains more voluntary control, less and less feedback can be given. The ultimate purpose, of course, is to have the person be able to institute control without feedback whenever desired.

Initially, the no-feedback sessions might be only a few minutes long. Subsequently, they can be the entire training session. The length of time which this training requires will depend on the success of the client.

Home Practice

Home practice gives the client an opportunity to develop the skill of voluntary control learned in the clinic, and generalize that skill to other environments. The procedures most commonly used for home practice are

(1) practice of the biofeedback skill as learned in the clinic,
(2) autogenic training (Schultz & Luthe 1969),
(3) progressive relaxation (Jacobson 1929, 1938),
(4) the relaxation response (Benson 1975).

Clients typically practice for about 10 to 30 minutes twice a day. These practice sessions should be explicitly incorporated into the client's schedule for two reasons. First, scheduling will make the client more likely to carry out the practice, rather than skip it because of too many commitments. Second, practice requires a relatively quiet environment, which in turn requires planning. The four different types of home practice discussed above and the types of physiological changes expected from them are summarized in Table 7–2.

Practice of the Skill Learned in the Clinic. In many types of biofeedback training the client is told to practice at home the strategy learned

TABLE 7–2   Summary of Home Practice Procedures

Practice	*Technique*	*Type of Change*
Response learned in the clinic	Practice the skill learned in the clinic at home for 10 to 30 minutes, once or twice daily	Varies; specifically what is learned in the laboratory
Autogenic Training	Repetition of specific phrases	Muscle relaxation, and overall relaxation
Progressive Relaxation	Alternately contracting and relaxing skeletal muscles	Deep relaxation of the skeletal muscles
Relaxation Response	Silent repetition of mental device for about 20 minutes once or twice daily	General reduction in metabolic activity, overall relaxation

in the clinic. Although unable to verbalize the precise strategy which results in the desired physiological change, the person can still produce these changes without feedback. Where biofeedback equipment is available for home use (for example, portable trainers), the client may practice with the aid of such equipment. As described earlier, some means of reducing the client's dependence on equipment is desirable and should be implemented as soon as is practical.

Autogenic Training. Autogenic training (Schultz & Luthe 1969) produces relaxation by having the person concentrate on verbal cues which are repeated silently or aloud. The program includes six basic exercises (groups of statements) and a series of advanced ones. The basic exercises and their goals are summarized in Table 7–3. The exercises start with attempts to induce muscular relaxation and then focus on increases in peripheral blood flow, lowering of heart rate, lowering of respiration rate, relaxation of the upper abdominal cavity, and general sedation and drowsiness. Clients move sequentially from one exercise to the next as they learn to produce the desired physiological changes in each exercise. Each of the statements in the six exercises are repeated silently by the client or aloud by the therapist. The statements are repeated and then "held mentally" for 30 to 60 seconds (the first exercises) or 60 to 90 seconds (the later exercises). The exercises are practiced for about five minutes after lunch, after supper, and before going to sleep. A new exercise is typically introduced each week.

Progressive Relaxation. Progressive relaxation (Jacobson 1929, 1938) reduces excess muscle tension and produces relaxation. There are two steps to the process: (1) learning to recognize excessive activity in certain muscles and (2) learning to reduce that activity. The client begins learning how to relax larger muscles because their activity is more easily sensed than the activity of smaller ones. First the muscle is contracted and held tense for a moment so that the client can learn to recognize the tension. Then the client is told to relax the muscle, to keep doing so past the point at which the muscle feels perfectly relaxed, and to continue doing the action done at the beginning of relaxation. The procedure is repeated with various other muscle groups large and small. The relaxation training lasts from three minutes to 60 minutes, three to seven times each week. The client may sit or lie down and should have the eyes closed.

The Relaxation Response. The relaxation response (Benson 1975) is a variant of meditation and Yoga in which the client is instructed to silently repeat a word while concentrating on it. Ideally, the word will

TABLE 7-3 The Six Basic Autogenic Exercises along with the Statements
Which Induce Specific Physiological States

Exercises	Statements	Goals
One: Heaviness in the extremities	My right arm is heavy. My left arm is heavy. Both arms are heavy. My right leg is heavy. My left leg is heavy. Both legs are heavy. My right side is heavy. Everything is heavy.	Muscular relaxation
Two: Warmth in the extremities	My right arm is warm. My left arm is warm. Both arms are warm. My right leg is warm. My left leg is warm. Both legs are warm. My arms and legs are heavy and warm.	Vasodilation
Three: Cardiac Regulation	Heartbeat calm and regular	Heart rate reduction
Four: Respiration	Breathing calm and regular; it breathes me.	Deep, calm, and regular breathing
Five: Abdominal warmth	My solar plexus is warm.	Muscular and central nervous system relaxation
Six: Cooling of the forehead	My forehead is cool.	Sedation, drowsiness, and calming

Each statement is repeated about three times and the client is instructed to keep the statement in mind for 30 to 180 seconds. (*From J. H. Schultz and W. Luthe, 1969.* Autogenic Therapy. *Vol. 1,* Autogenic Methods. *Used by permission of Grune & Stratton, Inc.*)

capture the person's consciousness, and no other distracting thoughts will enter it. The word is silently repeated each time the person exhales. With practice the person should be able to decrease all metabolic activity, a condition referred to as a wakeful hypometabolic state (Beary & Benson 1974). The person should be seated, not lying down, and should say the word silently, not aloud. No therapist is necessary to present instructions during the practice. The relaxation is practiced for 10 to 20 minutes, two times a day. The person is instructed not to practice within two hours after eating or immediately before going to sleep.

The details of the procedure as outlined by Benson (1975) are summarized in the list that follows. The person is instructed to sit in a comfortable position in an environment which is quiet and which will not interrupt the relaxation. The mental device may be any sonorous word; the word "one" is sufficient. The word should be said quietly while the person exhales. Breathing should be relaxed, quiet, and regular, but no attempt should be made to control it. The final ingredient is a passive attitude, one which is characterized by the person just waiting to see what happens. This attitude is probably the most difficult component of the relaxation response. Most clients are eager to see how well they can perform, and this competitiveness often interferes with the relaxation that is being sought. Particular emphasis may be necessary to convince the client that there is no race to be won here and that quite the opposite state of mind is the objective of the procedure.

Components of the Relaxation Response

1. A quiet environment
2. A comfortable position
3. A mental device
4. A passive attitude

Evaluation of Home Practice

In most biofeedback therapies, the client is asked to practice certain skills at home. These may be the same ones learned in the clinic during biofeedback, or they may be some form of relaxation. In any case, knowing the physiological effects of this practice is important in evaluating its success. Because there is usually no feedback to the patient at home, results are typically monitored in the clinic. Consequently, some portion of each session is usually devoted to this practice. No feedback is given to the client, who is encouraged to practice exactly what is done at home.

Following this practice, the similarity of its subjective effects to those experienced at home is discussed in order to determine how similar the period was to those usually experienced. Then information about the physiological effects of the session is provided from the biofeedback equipment. Questions are answered about the way in which the client should pursue the practice and suggestions and changes made as they are appropriate.

Evaluation of Treatment Program in General. The advantage of terminating each session with a set of explicit conclusions has been emphasized by Gaarder and Montgomery (1977). Here the purpose is to review briefly all the changes that have taken place during treatment, to emphasize the approaches that have been successful, to encourage the client to continue pursuing them, and to make a statement about the immediate and long-term goals of the training program. At all times, the therapist and client must both evaluate the appropriateness of the current procedures, whether they should be followed as currently planned or altered in some way. Thus, this closing component of each session becomes important for making decisions about the future course of therapy and for providing the client with the objectives for the next period of time as well as the motivation to pursue them.

TERMINAL AND FOLLOW-UP SESSIONS

The client can decide to terminate treatment at any time, but if therapy has progressed well, the termination will come as a joint decision between the therapist and client. The ultimate goal of biofeedback is to eliminate the need for the equipment so that the client has complete control. Gradually decreasing the frequency of clinical biofeedback sessions is a way to obtain this independence while at the same time monitoring symptoms to determine that there is no loss in effectiveness. The client is usually encouraged to practice at home without feedback, and the physiological effectiveness of this practice should be checked in the clinic by monitoring physiological functions without immediate feedback. Clinical visits can be spaced farther and farther apart as long as the client continues to demonstrate good physiological control without feedback and has no reappearance of symptoms.

Generally, one-week and one-month follow-ups should be sufficient to determine any immediate changes in the patient's psychophysiological profile as a result of the termination of treatment. Thereafter, three-month follow-ups to determine the enduring effects of the feedback treatment as well as seasonal or periodic fluctuations in the client's psychophysiological profile should be sufficient. The actual procedure within the follow-up might vary from a telephone conversation to see if the symptoms have remained under control to a psychophysiological profile and feedback sessions. The client's individual needs along with the clinician's judgment will determine precisely when and how to conduct the follow-up sessions.

CLINICAL
APPLICATIONS
OF BIOFEEDBACK

III

This section of the book describes the biofeedback treatment for each of a series of psychophysiological disorders. All the chapters are organized along the same framework and understanding that framework will help the reader to make the most efficient use of the information presented there.

Following a brief introduction, the first major segment of each chapter presents the symptoms of the disorder. Accurate diagnosis of the client's problem is important in designing the appropriate treatment. In some cases, the diagnosis may be straightforward, as for example with motor difficulties following a stroke. In other cases, the diagnosis is complicated and a full consideration of the symptoms presented by the patient is necessary. Both the whole range of symptoms that may be described by the client and the ways in which these symptoms are usually grouped together are discussed.

The second segment of each chapter describes the mechanism thought to be responsible for the symptoms. We chose the word *mechanism* (rather than *cause*) to emphasize the description of the physiological way in which the symptoms come to be expressed in the individual. Thus, the mechanism may be thought of as the final common path through which the various causal events come to express themselves in the symptoms presented by the client. Both the interpretation of the symptoms presented by the client and the development of the appropriate biofeedback treatment require an understanding of the intervening mechanism.

The third segment of each chapter continues this development into treatment. A general outline of the usual treatment procedures is given to provide an overview of the material that follows. Then one or more case studies are presented in detail. The case studies are given to provide a feeling for the actual course of treatment, a feeling that is often lost in group reports. The psychophysiological and clinical procedures are described only briefly because they have been presented in detail in Chapters 6 and 7, respectively.

The treatment section continues with a comprehensive review of the published treatment reports. This restriction to published reports was made for the reasons outlined in the preface. The material is presented in two ways. The treatments are first organized by a set of issues that we saw as the most important ones in the field. The organization around critical issues helps to evaluate the usefulness of biofeedback treatment and to determine its current strengths and weaknesses. Then the treatments are summarized in a table. The entries in the table are organized alphabetically by the first author's last name and provide a summary of the most critical features of the study: client population, method of treatment, and results, both psychological and physiological. Here the reader can get a quick overview of the available literature and formulate whatever conclusions are appropriate without any editorializing by us.

As a means of summarizing the previously presented material and making a general statement about the "state of the art," we have closed each chapter with two sections. The Clinical Program describes what we think is the most effective treatment for that disorder. Again, the intention of this section is not to specify a rigid set of procedures that ought to be followed in all cases, but to give the therapist a quick summary of the most appropriate courses of action. Furthermore, biofeedback is a young and rapidly developing field. Both the individual therapist doing work in the field and the researcher investigating the efficacy of different treatment procedures will undoubtedly provide information to modify the suggestions that we have made. But at the present time, the procedures described appear to be the most effective. These Clinical Programs should be read in conjunction with the relevant parts of Chapter 6 discussing psychophysiological procedures and Chapter 7 discussing clinical procedure.

The final section in each chapter is Research Considerations. Here we raise some of the questions about the more basic characteristics of biofeedback. Even in cases where the effectiveness of biofeedback is well documented, the relationship among the symptoms, mechanisms, and treatments remains unclear. There are a number of puzzles raised by the therapeutic value of biofeedback, and the Research Considerations point out some of these and the ways in which they might be solved.

The discussions of symptoms and mechanism have been explicitly separated because they are logically independent of each other. Furthermore, the symptoms describe behaviors that are readily reported by the patient or observed by the therapist, while the mechanism describes a putative pathological process that is usually difficult to examine directly and is often not investigated at all in the clinical setting. This distinction has been nicely emphasized by DeMyer (1977, p. 1234) in the context of spasmodic torticollis (see further discussion in Chapter 13). He says:

Spasmodic torticollis is an intermittent, more or less sustained deviation of the head, often with superimposed jerking movements. This statement is a descriptive definition of the clinical abnormality. *Spasmodic torticollis is regarded as a hyperkinesis based on involuntary neck-muscle contractions due to abnormal innervation patterns originating in or mediated through the extrapyramidal centers.* The second statement interprets the disorder in terms of current pathophysiological theories. Because most definitions are indiscriminate blends of observation and interpretation (fact or fancy), our understanding of neurology in general and of involuntary movements in particular has been immeasurably impeded. The reader will find he must critically discriminate between descriptive-operational definitions as contrasted to interpretational ones.

This issue appears most dramatically in the context of headaches (Chapters 8 and 9). The definitions offered by the Ad Hoc Committee (1962) defined both tension headaches and migraine headaches in terms of both their symptoms and their mechanisms. This joint definition has created substantial difficulty for those seeking to describe accurately the types of headaches experienced by their patients, and has probably slowed the development of a more reasonable diagnostic outline, a point also raised by DeMyer (1977) in the context of spasmodic torticollis.

TENSION HEADACHES

8

Introduction

Symptoms

Mechanism

Treatment

Clinical Program

Research Considerations

INTRODUCTION

A person facing a perplexing problem may often say, "It's giving me a headache" and mean that in both the literal and figurative sense. Almost all of us have experienced some type of headache in our life, and the beginning of the headache is often linked to psychological stress. Waters (1970) reports that 65% of the males and 79% of the females surveyed had suffered from at least one headache in the previous year. Similar estimates from a survey of a large general practice in London were obtained by Philips (1977a). The economic costs of headaches are substantial: sick pay for missed work, reduced performance on the job, and an estimated 400 million dollars for medicine each year (Rachman & Philips 1975). Headache is common in clinical practice and it is the major complaint of about half of the people who seek help from a physician (Friedman & Merritt 1959).

The word "tension" has been used to describe three different aspects of tension headaches:

1. The subjectively experienced symptoms of head pain reported by the patient
2. The contracted state of the involved head muscles
3. The personality characteristics and/or life style of the person experiencing the headache

Such usage obviously complicates the discussion of headaches because the reader may not always know the writer's intention and consequently may make the wrong interpretation. In order to avoid these problems, we will refer to the painful symptoms as *head pain* and the state of the muscles as *muscle contraction* or *muscle activity*. The word *tension* will be used only as an adjective in *tension headaches* to describe a diagnostic category. We have chosen the terms tension headache rather than muscle contraction headache (Ad Hoc Committee 1962) to provide a definition based on the clinical description of the symptoms of head pain without reference to putative pathophysiological mechanisms. The rationale for this approach was presented in the introduction to Section III (see also DeMeyer 1977).

Tension headaches are associated with increased contraction of the head muscles, particularly the frontalis muscle, the muscle in the forehead (see Chapter 4). Biofeedback treatments have recorded the electromyogram (EMG) from the frontalis muscle and trained people to reduce the level of contraction of this muscle. This procedure has been highly successful, substantially reducing or eliminating headache symptoms in about 80% of the people receiving treatment.

SYMPTOMS

A variety of adjectives have been used to describe the head pain associated with tension headaches. Most common are statements including the words "tight band," "tightness," "pressure," or "soreness." The pain may be centered at the back of the head and neck but can appear in almost any portion of the head, neck, and shoulders, ranging from a small circumscribed area to the entire head-neck region. In most cases it is bilateral. A summary of the adjectives used to describe the head pain of tension headaches is presented in Table 8–1. The table includes both the

TABLE 8–1   Adjectives Used to Describe the Head Pain of Tension Headaches

Adjective	Ad Hoc Committee 1962, p. 718	Budzynski, Stoyva, Adler & Mullaney 1973, p. 38	Dalessio, 1972, pp. 533–535	Tunis & Wolff, 1954, p. 425	Wolff, 1948, pp. 606–607
aching					X
any region of the head					X
bandlike		X	X	X	X
constriction	X				
bilateral		X		X	
cramp				X	X
drawing			X	X	X
dull pain		X			
long duration		X		X	
pressure	X		X	X	X
sore			X	X	X
steady, nonpulsating			X	X	
stiff cap					
suboccipital tenderness	X				X
tightness	X		X	X	
unilateral				X	X
viselike			X		X
weight			X	X	

four words mentioned above and other adjectives suggesting tension or constriction.

Noticeably absent from the table are three characteristics: (1) accompanied by nausea and/or vomiting, (2) preceded by a prodrome with signs of sensory or motor abnormalities, and (3) prevented by vasoconstricting drugs, particularly ergotamine. The absence of these characteristics is important because their presence is often used to classify a headache as migraine rather than tension. Unilateral head pain may be used in the same way, as a symptom indicating a migraine rather than a tension headache.

Although there is general agreement that people use the adjectives listed in Table 8–1 to describe their head pain, there is considerable disagreement as to whether or not there is a discrete class of headaches characterized by one or more of these symptoms. Two major viewpoints have been expressed. The first suggests that there is a specific category of tension headaches that can be differentiated from other categories (such as migraine) on the basis of the type of head pain, the physiological mechanism of the headache, and the most effective means of treatment (Ad Hoc Committee 1962; Friedman and others 1953; Wolff 1963). According to these sources, tension headaches are described by a specific subset of adjectives, caused by increases in the contraction of muscles in the head, and treated most effectively with analgesic and/or sedative drugs. Furthermore, tension headaches are distinct from other headache syndromes which have different types of head pain, different physiological causes, and/or different effective treatments.

An alternative viewpoint suggests that there is a continuum of head pain and that the distinction between tension headaches and other types is not clear-cut. Although a particular set of adjectives may be used to describe head pain, this set of symptoms is not qualitatively distinct from other sets of head pain symptoms (Bakal & Kaganov 1977; Cohen 1978; Philips 1977b, 1978).

The data relevant to this issue come from a variety of sources. In all cases, the question is the extent to which different types of head pain symptoms are grouped together and independent of other symptoms. If there is a distinct tension headache syndrome, then (a) the head pain symptoms of tension headaches ought to be highly correlated with each other, and (b) this cluster of symptoms ought to be relatively independent of other clusters of symptoms characterizing other headaches. If, on the other hand, there is not a distinct tension headache syndrome, this clustering of head pain symptoms might not appear. As will be seen in the review below, the data generally support this latter position, suggesting that the symptoms associated with tension headaches are not clearly separated from the symptoms associated with other classes of headaches. Other literature reviews have also reached this conclusion (Philips 1978).

Data from 2,000 people with migraine or tension headaches were summarized by Friedman and others (1954; see also Friedman and others 1953; Friedman & von Storch 1953). The patients were presumably those appearing for treatment in a private practice. The types of symptoms reported by each of the patients were recorded and included three of the ones thought to differentiate between tension headaches and migraine headaches: unilateral head pain, preceded by a prodrome, and accompanied by nausea and/or vomiting. The results of the study are summarized in Table 8–2. Few of the symptoms provided a clear differentiation between the two types of headaches. The best ones were the three commonly associated with migraines; at least 50% of the patients with migraine headaches experienced these symptoms while at most 10% of those with tension headaches did. Thus a tension headache might be described as head pain in the absence of a prodrome, unilateral pain, and nausea and/or vomiting. This diagnosis by exclusion is not unusual (see Philips 1978) but is far from satisfying. By this procedure, headaches that are not due to any other demonstrable cause get classified as tension headaches with the result that this category becomes the residual, receiving all the headaches that don't fit somewhere else.

A questionnaire survey from a general practice in London of 597 patients with head pain examined the relationship among nausea and/or vomiting, prodromes, and the laterality of head pain (Philips 1977a). Patients were divided into two groups on the basis of the type of head pain. Bilateral head pain is generally associated with the tension headache diagnosis, while unilateral head pain is one of the defining characteristics of migraine headaches. If the symptoms of prodromes and nausea and/or

TABLE 8–2   Comparison of the Symptoms of Patients Diagnosed as Having Tension Headaches and Those Having Migraine Headaches

Measure	Type of Headache	
	Tension	Migraine
Positive family history	40	65
First headache occurred		
when less than 20 years old	30	55
Prodrome present	10	60
Frequency		
constant or daily	20	0
less than once per week	15	60
Duration		
constant or daily	20	0
from one to three days	10	35
Throbbing	30	80
Unilateral	10	80
Associated with vomiting	10	50

Note: The numbers are the percentage of patients reporting the indicated characteristic. (From Friedman, von Storch, & Merritt 1954.)

vomiting are selectively associated with the migraine diagnosis, they should appear mainly in patients with unilateral, but not bilateral, head pain. Such was not the case, however. The percentage of patients who experienced nausea and/or vomiting, prodromes, or both was basically the same in the group having bilateral head pain as in the group having unilateral head pain. The patients also rated the severity of their headaches on a scale from 0 to 6, with 0 indicating a very mild headache and 6 indicating a very severe one. As headache severity increased, so did the probability of it being accompanied by nausea, vomiting, and visual prodromes, and the likelihood that it was diagnosed as a migraine, rather than a tension, headache. These results suggest that there may be a continuum of headache intensity, with tension headaches lying at one end and migraine headaches at the other, rather than two discrete categories.

There are two potential difficulties with the Philips (1977a) study. The first is the diagnosis of tension headache, made on the basis of head pain accompanied by, at most, one of the three migraine symptoms. Thus, patients might have been included in the tension headache group without having any of the symptoms thought to be diagnostic of tension headaches. In addition, the data analysis did not differentiate between symptoms appearing successively during different headaches. None the less, the results provided no support for the idea that the symptoms of tension headaches are clearly distinguishable from the symptoms of other types of headaches.

Similar results were found with a group of patients diagnosed by neurologists following the guidelines of the Ad Hoc Committee (1962); 25 patients had migraine headaches only; 20 patients had tension headaches only (Bakal & Kaganov 1977). The characteristics of these headaches were compared particularly with respect to the three variables used to differentiate between tension headaches and migraine headaches. The location of the pain was determined by asking patients to sketch the appropriate areas on drawings of a human head. The results of this survey are summarized in Table 8–3. Of all the variables examined, only the presence of nausea and/or vomiting was significantly different for the two groups of patients, and even for this characteristic the distinction between the two groups was not clear-cut; about one-quarter of the migraine patients did not report nausea and/or vomiting, and about one-third of the tension headache patients did. In this carefully conducted study, there were virtually no differences in the symptoms of those patients diagnosed as having tension headaches and those diagnosed as having migraines, even when questions about prodromes and the laterality of the head pain were included.

In summary, then, there are a set of adjectives used by patients to

TABLE 8–3   Comparison of Head Pain Characteristics of Patients Diagnosed
as Having Migraine Headaches or Tension Headaches

Measure	Type of Headache	
	Tension	Migraine
Visual disturbance preceding headache	52	52
Family history of headache	48	44
Nausea and vomiting	36	72
Location of pain		
bilateral neck	38	28
bilateral forehead	38	28
unilateral side of head and eye	26	21
unilateral forehead	26	31
bilateral side of head and eyes	48	42

Note: The numbers are the percentages of patients in the sample reporting the indicated symptoms. *(From Bakal & Kaganov 1977.)*

describe the head pain associated with their headaches. The diagnosis of tension headache has commonly used the presence of the symptoms suggested by the Ad Hoc Committee (1962) in conjunction with the absence of migraine symptoms, (unilateral head pain, preceded by a prodrome, accompanied by nausea and/or vomiting). Certainly some people coming to a clinic for treatment have tension headaches as defined in this way, but the data reviewed above question the general usefulness of this diagnostic scheme because overall, the symptoms supposedly diagnostic of tension headaches are not highly correlated with each other, nor are they strongly independent of the symptoms thought to be diagnostic of other types of headaches. The actual distribution of head pain symptoms, and the appropriate categories of head pain remain to be determined (see Melzak & Torgerson 1971), and the diagnostic criteria of tension headache clearly need further documentation (see Swets and others 1979 for a discussion of medical diagnoses). For the present, however, the appearance of the types of head pain described in Table 8–1 is sufficient to indicate that biofeedback training to reduce the level of activity in the head muscles is appropriate.

MECHANISM

Head Pain Caused by Muscle Contraction

To address the causal relation between elevated muscle activity and head pain, the experimenter must first increase muscle contraction (the independent variable) and then measure any resulting pain (the dependent variable). If the head pain of tension headaches is caused by excessive muscle contraction, manipulations that produce increases in muscle contraction should lead to increases in head pain.

The most relevant data come from a series of experiments (Simons and others 1943; see also Wolff 1963, pp. 496–509; Dalessio 1972, pp. 525–535), all of which relied on the same general design. First the experimenters induced localized head pain by some means. Then they monitored the contraction of muscles in other areas of the head and neck and asked the person to report the location of any subsequent head pain. The initial head pain and any associated muscle contraction in that area are not relevant to the question here because the experimental manipulation may have produced both head pain and muscle contraction simultaneously; the initial head pain is important only as a stimulus producing subsequent muscle contractions in other areas. The result of interest is whether the initial head pain produced subsequent muscle contraction in other areas, and if so, whether this muscle contraction led to head pain in the area surrounding it.

In two experiments, the initial head pain was very brief. It was produced by an injection of histamine (three people) or removal of cerebrospinal fluid from the spinal cord (two people). In both cases, the neck muscles contracted, and following spinal drainage, the frontalis and other muscles contracted also. The contractions lasted from four to twenty minutes but were not followed by additional head pain. Wolff (1963, p. 498) concluded that muscle contractions taking place for a short period of time were not the sources of head pain.

In other experiments, the initially induced pain was of longer duration, and it in turn produced muscle contractions of longer duration. Again, the question was whether the muscle contractions induced in other areas would lead to pain in those areas. Four procedures were used. Hypertonic saline (6% saline) was injected into the right temporalis muscle of one individual. As to be expected, muscle contraction and pain occurred in the temporal muscle. Within one minute following the injections, muscles in the neck contracted. Six minutes later, a pain arose in the neck. Both the muscle contraction and the pain were maintained throughout the 50-minute test period.

In a second experiment, ethylmorphine hydrochloride (a local irritant) was placed in the right eye of two subjects while they looked at a 100 watt light bulb four feet away. The injection produced immediate pain and muscle contraction on the right side of the face. At the same time, the neck muscles increased their contraction, and ten minutes later pain in the neck region occurred. The neck muscle contraction and the neck pain lasted longer than the pain in the eye induced by the injection.

Another experiment was carried out with three people. A distorting lens was placed in front of the dominant eye of each of them. In order to focus normally, the muscles of the dominant eye had to be contracted more than usual. The results of this experiment were ambiguous. Pain occurred around the dominant eye in two individuals. In one person, the neck muscles gradually increased their contraction when the lens was put over the eye; 20 minutes later pain began. In a second person, muscle contractions took place in the neck on the side of the head where the lens had been placed, but no head pain occurred. The results from the third person were not clear.

Three other people were tested with a screw clamp instrument which looked like a medieval torture device. It was placed around the head and the screws were tightened to produce gentle pressure. Muscle contraction and pain occurred where the device touched the head. Within a few minutes, the muscles of the neck began to contract; pain in the neck followed.

This series of experiments demonstrates that localized head pain can induce muscle contractions in other areas and that these contractions may be followed by pain in those areas. But these results are not directly related to the normal course of tension headaches. First, the manipulations were extreme. In all cases they were events unlikely to be encountered in the course of everyday life, and in some instances the resulting pain was excruciating. Second, the muscle contractions and pain that were induced were all located in the neck, not in the muscles at the side, front, or back of the head.

As can be seen by the above qualifications, the hypothesis that independently produced increases in the contraction of head muscles can produce head pain characteristic of tension headaches has virtually no support in experimental data. The hypothesis has intuitive appeal, but its apparent reasonableness is no substitute for real data. This caution is particularly important in light of the data indicating that there may be a causal relationship in the opposite direction so that head pain may produce an increased level of muscle contraction. The experiments by Simons and others (1943) just reviewed are relevant to this question. In almost all cases, production of pain in one location in the head induced muscle contraction in other areas. Furthermore, trauma to the head can often produce both muscle contractions and head pain (Simons & Wolff 1946). Thus, the presence of pain in the head can cause reflexive muscle contraction.

Muscle Activity in the Same Person
With and Without Headaches

If the head pain of tension headaches is caused by increases in muscle contraction, then in any given person the level of muscle activity should be greater when a headache is present than when it is absent. In general, the relevant studies demonstrate that muscle activity is two to ten times greater during headaches, although there are some exceptions to this rule.

Several studies have provided dramatic demonstrations of a correlation between the onset of a headache and an increase in muscle tension. The results of one of them (Sainsbury & Gibson 1954) are summarized in Figure 8–1. EMG records were taken from the frontalis muscle and the left forearm extensor muscles. During seven minutes of relaxation, as indicated in the left hand portion of the figure, the EMG from both muscles was about 20 counts (arbitrary units) per minute. Ten minutes after the interview began, the activity of the frontalis muscle increased to about 100 counts per minute. This increase took place during a period of about five minutes (minutes 16 to 20 in the figure) and was accompanied

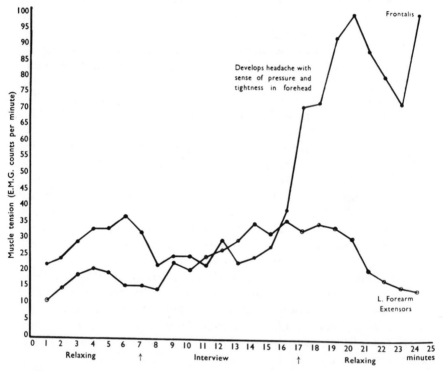

FIGURE 8–1   A Correlation Between the Onset of a Headache and an Increase in Muscle Activity in the Frontalis Muscle.

During the interview, in which the patient discussed stressful topics, the activity in the frontalis muscle rose dramatically from its level in the relaxation period before the interview. EMG in the extensor muscles of the forearm did not change substantially during the interview, indicating a specificity in the muscle changes. (From P. Sainsbury and J. F. Gibson, 1954. In Journal of Neurology, Neurosurgery, and Psychiatry, 17 (1954), p. 22. Reprinted by permission.)

by a headache with ". . . a sense of pressure and tightness in the forehead" (Sainsbury & Gibson 1954, p. 222). The EMG from the forearm muscle did not change markedly, demonstrating some specificity of the changes in muscle tension.

Two cases show the amount of contraction in the right temporal muscle before, during, and after a headache (Tunis & Wolff 1954, pp. 431–432). The EMG results are presented as a polygraph trace with the amplitude in arbitrary units. Prior to the headache, there was relatively little EMG activity as indicated by the small amplitude of the polygraph trace. During a headache the level of the EMG increased to about 10 times that seen previously. After the headache had gone, the EMG returned to the level found before the headache began.

Results of other studies also support the idea that the level of muscle contraction during a headache is greater than the level of muscle contraction when no headache is present. One group of people was composed of 21 college students with tension headaches (Haynes and others 1975). The headaches were severe enough that 19 of the participants had consulted a physician about them. The data are from an unspecified number of these 19 individuals during the pretreatment baseline periods of biofeedback sessions. EMG was recorded from the forehead. No information was provided about the intensity of the headaches experienced at the time of recording. When the people did not have a headache, the EMG was 4.2 uV/min (microvolts/minute); when they did have a headache, the EMG was 5.4 uV/min. The authors say that although the group as a whole demonstrated an increase in EMG during headaches, for some individuals the muscle activity with a headache was lower than the muscle activity without a headache.

Other data showing a correlation between EMG levels and headache activity come from the studies treating tension headaches with biofeedback. As discussed later in the chapter, these treatments have produced a reduction in both EMG levels and headache activity. The two case studies illustrate how closely these two changes may be associated with each other, and Budzynski, Stoyva, Adler, and Mullaney (1973) report a .90 correlation between headache activity and frontalis EMG levels. In successful biofeedback treatment, then, the reduction in headache activity is almost always accompanied by a reduction in the EMG recorded from the forehead, although there are exceptions (Chesney & Shelton 1976).

One description of the typical tension headache patient emphasized the global nature of the syndrome, in addition to increased muscle activity. "Observation of the patient should yield these findings: dilated pupils, stress in facial expression, guard in the neck and shoulders, moist or cold hands, rapid or variable pulse and high chest breathing. The combination of visceral, somatic, and feeling tone disturbances gives the picture of one ready for battle or take off" (Dixon & Dickel 1967, p. 817). Furthermore, the EMG indicates ". . . rapid high frequency firing of neck muscles and often of temporal and supra-orbital muscles" (Dixon & Dickel 1967, p. 818).

An exception to the picture of generally elevated levels of muscle contraction during headache is the report of Philips (1978). The patients came from a questionnaire survey of a general practice, said that their head pain was not associated with nausea and/or vomiting, and had at most one of the following two symptoms: unilateral head pain or a prodrome. Cases of obvious organic pathology were excluded from the sample. Surface electrodes were used to obtain EMG from the frontalis, temporalis, neck and trapezium muscles. Recordings were taken during a headache (of unspecified intensity) and when no headache was present. When a headache was present, the level of activity in each of the four muscles decreased slightly. Thus not only was there no sign of an increase in muscle contraction, the change in activity was in the opposite direction. The reasons for this discrepancy are not immediately apparent. One possible reason is that the diagnosis of tension headache apparently did not include the presence of any of the symptoms of tightness or pressure around the head. Consequently, these patients may have had head pain not really characteristic of tension headaches.

No correlation between frontal EMG and head pain was found for 33 females who had been referred by a physician for possible biofeedback treatment of tension headaches (Harper & Steger 1978). The mean duration of the symptoms in this group was 9.1 years. EMG was recorded from the frontalis muscle in two sessions, separated by a week. Two ratings of headache pain were obtained, one during the EMG recording session and the second during the week separating the two recording sessions. The correlations between these two variables were low (.10 to .22) and statistically insignificant. The failure to find substantial correlations between head pain and EMG levels could be due to a small range of either EMG or headache pain during the experiment. However, the absolute levels of EMG and head pain were not reported so the data necessary to test this idea are unavailable.

In summary, this set of correlational studies demonstrates that muscle activity when a person has a headache is generally greater than muscle activity when that same person does not have a headache. These results are consistent with (but do not prove) the hypothesis that increased muscle activity is the mechanism of head pain in tension headaches. However, three important qualifications should be kept in mind with respect to this summary. First, the body of relevant information is small and obviously needs replication with much larger samples, both from clinical and nonclinical populations. Second, there are specific exceptions to the overall positive correlation. Third, the amount of muscle activity varies considerably so that there is a substantial overlap between the levels of muscle contraction found when headaches are present and the levels found when headaches are absent, indicating that variables other than just muscle contraction must be having a substantial influence on the appearance of head pain.

Muscle Activity from People with Frequent and/or Severe Headaches Compared with Muscle Activity from People Who Rarely Have Headaches

The previous section examined the levels of muscle activity in the same individual when having a headache and when not having a headache. In contrast, the present section looks at the levels of muscle activity in different individuals, those having frequent and/or severe headaches and those having few or no headaches. Arguments can be made for any one of three different results, including increases, decreases, or no change in the level of muscle activity for people who have abnormally high headache activity. Fortunately, the data are not as complicated as the predictions. They generally indicate that even when free of head pain, people who have frequent and/or severe headaches have a resting level of muscle contraction greater than that found in people who do not have these headaches. These results have been supported with data from people as diverse as college students, adults with long histories of tension headaches, and psychiatric patients on a psychiatric ward. The results of the relevant studies are summarized in Table 8–4.

A marked elevation in the resting level of muscle activity of people who had frequent and severe tension headaches was found in 18 individuals who were recruited through a newspaper advertisement (Budzynski and others 1973). Patients with neurologic and organic disorders were excluded from the sample, and confirmation of the tension headache diagnosis was made through a questionnaire. "Typically, this type of headache is characterized by a dull 'band like' pain located bilaterally in the occipital region, although it is often felt in the forehead region as well. It is gradual in onset and may last for hours, weeks, even months" (Budzynski and others 1973 p. 38). EMG recordings were taken with surface electrodes over the frontalis muscle. Data are provided for 12 individuals, six in each of two groups. During two baseline sessions, the mean frontalis EMG was about 10 uV, a value that was ". . . at least double those shown by young normal subjects in our laboratory" (Budzynski and others 1973 p. 42). As pointed out by Philips (1978), these clients were using a substantial amount of medication to treat their headaches, ranging from aspirin and Anacin to Librium and Valium. This

TABLE 8–4   The EMG Activity of People with Mild and/or Infrequent Headaches
Compared to the EMG Activity of People with Severe and/or Frequent Headaches

Study	*Participants with Infrequent and/or Mild Headaches*		*Participants with Frequent and/or Severe Headaches*	
	Description	*EMG*	*Description*	*EMG*
Budzynski, Stoyva, Adler, & Mullaney, 1973	"young normal subjects"	at most one-half the value for the headache group frontal	12 carefully selected people who had experienced severe tension headaches for a mean of 8 years	10 uV frontal
Haynes, Griffin, Mooney, & Parise, 1975	college students with a high frequency of tension headaches	3.4 uV frontal	college students with a low frequency of tension headaches.	5.3 uV frontal
Malmo, Wallerstein & Shagass, 1953	31 psychiatric patients not complaining of head pain	9.4 uV during the prestimulus baseline of an experiment neck¹	29 psychiatric patients with a major complaint about sensations in the head and neck	12.6 uV during the prestimulus baseline of an experiment neck
Philips, 1978	20 "no headache controls" from a questionnaire survey of a private practice	3.4 uV frontal 3.9 uV temporal 2.7 uV neck 2.1 uV trapezium	17 patients who had head pain not accompanied by nausea and/or vomiting, and not associated with both unilateral onset and visual prodromes	5.0 uV frontal 5.2 uV temporal 3.0 uV neck 3.4 uV trapezium
Vaughn, Pall & Haynes, 1977	9 people from a college community with 2 or fewer headaches per month	5.9 uV/min during the prestimulus baseline of an experiment	8 people from a college community with at least 3 headaches per week	7.2 uV/min during the prestimulus baseline of an experiment

drug use might reflect a general bias towards psychiatric difficulties, or it might reflect the general severity of the headaches. In any case, the high incidence of drug use may indicate that these individuals were not a representative sample of those who suffer from tension headaches.

Studies which have included presumably more normal populations, however, have obtained similar results. One experiment examined a group of college students responding to an advertisement (Vaughn and others 1977). All individuals had head pain that was bilateral, did not experience an aura prior to the headache, and did not have a family history of migraine. Two groups were formed. One group was composed of people who had headaches relatively infrequently, no more than twice per month. The second group was composed of people who often had headaches, at least three per week. EMG from the frontalis was recorded by surface electrodes while the participants relaxed for 15 minutes with their eyes closed. For people who rarely had headaches the EMG was 5.9 uV/min while for those who often had headaches it was 7.2 uV/min. Furthermore, the EMG for the low frequency group decreased to 5.2 uV/min during the last three sessions, while the EMG for the high frequency group remained at the same level, ending with an EMG of 7.2 uV/min.

Similar results were reported from an unspecified number of college students (Haynes and others 1975). The group that had frequent tension headaches had a frontal EMG of 5.3 uV/min while the group that had few tension headaches had a frontal EMG of 3.4 uV/min. The authors say there were major exceptions to this general picture; some individuals had extremely high EMGs but did not experience headaches, while others had relatively low EMGs but did experience headaches. Thus although EMG levels were generally elevated in the group with frequent headaches, other variables influenced headache activity as well.

Complaints of head or neck pain in psychiatric patients were associated with slight elevations of activity in neck muscles (Malmo and others 1953). One group of 31 patients did not have a major complaint concerning the head or neck. A second group of 29 patients complained of head and neck problems: feelings of tightness, pressure, or heaviness. The data come from an experiment measuring the reactions of the individuals to a thermal stress. Recordings were taken during an interval prior to the application of the stress. During this period the patients without head complaints had an EMG of 9.4 uV/min; those with head complaints had a slightly higher level of 12.6 uV/min.

Muscle activity may be elevated in individuals who do not have a major complaint of head pain, but who are chronically anxious or tense (Sainsbury & Gibson 1954). In this experiment, one group was composed of 30 healthy soldiers. The other group was composed of 26 patients who were diagnosed as having an anxiety state on the basis of a questionnaire and clinical observations. The patients described themselves as being tense and anxious in terms of bodily sensations, particularly cramps and stiffness in muscles. Eighty percent of the patients attributed these sensations to excessive muscle contraction. EMG was recorded from the frontalis muscle with surface electrodes while the participants reclined on a hospital bed. The healthy soldiers had a mean EMG of 5.2 counts (arbitrary units) per minute while the anxious patients had a mean level of 9.6 counts per minute.

One set of data (Sainsbury & Gibson 1954) doesn't fit into either the within-subjects analysis of the previous section or the between-subjects analysis of the current section, but it is relevant to the issue of the relationship between muscle activity and head pain. The participants were 30 patients: 28 were diagnosed as having an anxiety or tension state, and 2 were obsessional neurotics with a marked anxiety state. EMG records were obtained from the frontalis, arm, and neck muscles, and the patients were asked to specify the areas of their body that were accompanied by pain at the time of the EMG recording. The frontalis EMG of the seven patients who said they had a headache at the time of the interview was 31.3 counts per minute, while the frontalis EMG of the other 23 patients (who said they did not have a headache at the time of the interview) was 11.8. There was also some specificity of the relationship between the area of pain and the area of increased muscle tension. Generally the increased muscle contraction was only in that area of the body perceived as painful.

Taken together, these studies provide a consistent picture of elevated muscle activity in people who suffer from chronic tension headaches, even when they are not experiencing a headache at the time of the measurement. The magnitude of the increase may be influenced by factors other than just the headache. For example, individuals with a general anxiety state and individuals whose drug taking behavior suggests more general problems may have muscle activity greater than that of a presumably more normal population. Thus an increased level of activity in the frontalis muscle when headaches are absent may be more useful in confirming the diagnosis of tension headache and indicating the use of biofeedback than a normal level is in refuting the diagnosis or suggesting that biofeedback is not appropriate.

Levels of Muscle Activity in Relation to Stress

Discussions of tension headaches usually assume that most, if not all, headaches occur in response to stressful events in a person's life. If such is the case and an increase in muscle contraction produces the head pain of tension headaches, then the muscle activity of people who have problems with head pain ought to be greater when they are under stress than the muscle activity of people who do not have problems with head pain. The studies reviewed below, many of which deal with a general category of head pain rather than a specific category of tension headaches, support this idea.

A detailed case study presents data from a 45-year-old female with a 30 year history of tensional symptoms and tension headache (Malmo and others 1950). The EMG was recorded from the frontalis muscle during 12 different interviews. Two of the interviews were stressful. During both of these, the mean EMG was elevated from the preceding and subsequent interviews. In the first instance, the mean EMG was 63 uV, up from 54 uV in the session before and 53 uV in the session following. In the second instance, the mean EMG was 76 uV, up from 30 uV in both of the adjacent sessions. The EMG of the arm changed in a similar fashion, suggesting a diffuse reaction, rather than a specific increase in just the head muscles.

Psychiatric patients with complaints of head and neck pain had a greater muscle activity in response to a thermal stimulus than did a group of control patients (Malmo & Shagass 1949b). The participants were divided into two groups. One group of 47 patients said they had headaches or feelings of tightness in the head and neck. A second group of 27 patients did not complain about these types of head pains. A standard test procedure was established in which a 500 watt light bulb was periodically focused on the forehead for three seconds (Malmo & Shagass 1949a). The EMG was recorded from the left side of the neck and was scored positive or negative for the appearance of a clear burst of muscle activity during the three seconds of thermal stimulation and during the 17 seconds following the stimulus. The mean score for the group who had head complaints was 13.8 units, while the mean score for those who did not have such complaints was 9.2 units. This difference was found for all patients who had head complaints, whether they were headache, head tightness and numbness, neck tension, or a combination of these. For a subset of the above patients, the EMG from the left neck muscle was calculated. Twelve patients who did not have head complaints had a mean EMG of 207 uV/sec, while 20 patients who did have head complaints had a mean EMG of 369 uV/sec.

A similar result was reported for two groups of psychiatric patients (Malmo and others 1953). One group of 29 had major complaints of heaviness, tightness, or fullness in the head. The second group of 31 did not have a major complaint of headache. The EMG from the neck and from the arm was recorded in reaction to the thermal stress applied separately to the forehead and the arm. As indicated previously, the group with head pain complaints had a generally elevated EMG even before the thermal stimulus was presented. During the stimulus, however, the difference increased even more; the patients with head complaints had a mean EMG of 16.6 (an increase of 4 units from the prestimulus baseline), while those with no head complaints had an EMG of 11.1 (an increase of 2.7 units from the baseline). A similar effect was found in the response of the arm EMG when the stimulus was applied to the arm.

An exception to this pattern of results is reported by Vaughn, Pall, and Haynes (1977). Details of the participants in the experiment and the baseline data were presented in the previous section. During the first 15 minutes of the experiment, the EMG from the frontalis muscle was recorded while the individuals relaxed with their eyes closed. The stress was one minute of serially subtracting the number 13 from 300; that is, 287, 274, 261, and so on. The experimenters encouraged each person to do this as rapidly and accurately as possible, but they did not measure compliance with this instruction or success at the task. Then the EMG was recorded for an additional 11-minute period of relaxation. The group with a low frequency of headaches had a marked reaction to the stress and showed a substantial increase in EMG during the mental arithmetic. Immediately following the stress, however, the EMG decreased, and at the end of the session, even further reductions were seen. Thus, although there was a reaction to the stress, it was brief and terminated as soon as the stress ended. The group with a high frequency of headaches began with a higher baseline EMG, but the EMG did not change significantly either during or after the stress.

Elevated muscle tension may be found in patients who do not have a major complaint of head pain. Psychiatric patients who were anxious, tense, depressed, hysterical, or schizophrenic all had elevated muscle activity in the neck (Malmo & Shagass 1949a; Malmo & Smith 1954; Wallerstein & Shagass 1953). All three of these studies indicate that an elevated EMG in the head or neck may be associated with symptoms other than tension headaches.

In summary, these studies indicate that people who have tension headaches or other head complaints are more likely to have elevated levels of muscle activity during or immediately after stress than people who do not have these complaints. The magnitude of the increase from prestress baselines is slightly larger than in control groups, and coupled with the generally elevated baselines, these changes result in an enhanced level during the stress. Detailed psychophysical studies are necessary to accurately pinpoint the stimulus-response function, but the present data suggest that the power of this function is greater than normal for people with tension headaches so that any given increment in stress produces a greater increment in muscle contraction than would occur in people who do not have headaches.

Vascular Changes and Tension Headaches

According to the Ad Hoc Committee (1962), excessive muscle contraction is the primary mechanism of tension headaches; involvement of the vascular system leads to head pain characteristic of migraine, not tension headaches. Both direct and indirect data suggest that this point of view is incorrect.

One series of experiments demonstrates that reductions in blood flow to a working muscle have a marked influence on reports of pain resulting from the muscle contractions (Dorpat & Holmes 1955; Lewis 1942, p. 158; Lewis and others 1931; Rodbard 1975). Each person was asked to repeatedly contract and relax a given set of muscles, usually by grasping and releasing an object with one hand. Blood flow to the muscles controlling the hand was manipulated by a blood pressure cuff applied between the muscles and the heart. The experimenters measured the number of contractions required before the person reported pain and/or was unable to continue hand movements because the pain was so great.

Reduction of blood flow in conjunction with exercise had a marked effect on the appearance of pain; the less the blood flow, the fewer contractions that were made before the person reported pain and had to stop because of the pain. The pain was described as deep, radiating, viselike, drawing, and burning; it was continuous and independent of individual muscle contractions (Robard 1975, p. 183). Parametric manipulations demonstrated that the pain was a function of the product of (a) the number of contractions, (b) the square root of the load on the muscles, and (c) the cube root of the duration of each contraction. Reduction of blood flow in the absence of muscle activity had no effect on pain: if no muscle activity had taken place, stopping blood flow did not produce pain, and if muscle activity had taken place but pain had not yet occurred, stopping blood flow did not induce pain if muscle activity ceased. Thus, reduction of blood flow by itself was not sufficient to produce pain.

These experiments were all carried out with normal people who presumably did not have an increased incidence of tension headaches. Furthermore, the muscles examined were in the hand and not the head. None the less, the data provide convincing evidence that reports of pain following muscle contractions are a function not only of muscle activity, but also of the state of the vascular system providing blood to those muscles. Evidence for this interaction is important because it suggests that the vascular system plays a role in the generation of tension headaches as well as migraine headaches, and that the head pain of tension headaches arises from a conjoint disturbance of the muscular and the vascular system.

Direct evidence for the role of vasoconstriction in the pain of headaches was obtained from 20 patients with normal blood pressure and diagnosed as having tension headaches (Tunis & Wolff 1954). The EMG of three head muscles was recorded and the state of the arteries supplying these areas was determined by a pulsewave analysis. Only data from the right temporal muscle and the right temporal artery were reported; the authors state that the results from the other muscles and arteries were the same as from these. The mean pulse wave amplitude in the temporal artery during the systolic phase of the heart beat was 4.6 mm when the patients were having headaches, and 8.3 mm when they were not. Thus, the presence of head pain was associated with a decrease in pulse wave amplitude, indicating vasoconstriction. An unspecified control group of patients without headaches had a mean pulse wave amplitude of 12.0 mm, suggesting that the tension headache patients had a chronic vaso-constriction of the temporal artery even when not having a headache.

Illustrations from individual cases showed the results of increased muscle activity without temporal artery constriction and temporal artery constriction without increased muscle activity. In both instances, no head pain occurred if the changes took place for a short period of time. Tunis and Wolff (1954, p. 431) say that persistent increases in muscle activity produced "disagreeable head sensations or even headache," but provide no data to evaluate this statement. They also say (without supporting data) that injections of a vasoconstricting drug such as ergota-mine may increase the head pain of tension headaches. In general, the data support the idea that vasoconstriction can lower the threshold for pain and/or increase the amount of pain resulting from a given magnitude of muscle contraction. "It is inferred that head pain arose from sustained contraction of ischemic muscle" (Tunis & Wolff 1954, p. 430).

A case study of the relationship among vasoconstriction, muscle contraction, and head pain is presented in Figure 8–2 (Tunis & Wolff 1954). For the first ten minutes of the study (left side of Figure 8–2), no headache was present; the right temporal artery pulse waves were of high amplitude, indicating vasodilation, and the EMG from the right temporal muscle was of low amplitude, indicating little activity. During the headache (middle of Figure 8–2), the pulse wave amplitude decreased, and muscle contraction increased. Both of these measures returned to baseline after about 20 minutes when the headache disappeared (right side of Figure 8–2). Case study data from a hypertensive patient also showed a strong correlation among head pain, vasoconstriction, and muscle contraction (Tunis & Wolff 1954, p. 431, Figure 5).

The state of the blood vessels in the conjunctiva of the eye and their reaction to levarterenol (a vasoconstricting drug) may be used as an index of vasoconstriction (Ostfeld and others 1957). Data were obtained from a total of 14 headaches in 11 people diagnosed as having tension headaches. During 12 of the 14 headaches, blood flow in the conjunctival blood vessels was reduced as indicated by increased arteriolar vasomotion and spasm, and increased sensitivity to levarterenol. The vasoconstriction of the conjunctival blood supply and the head pain of the headache termi-

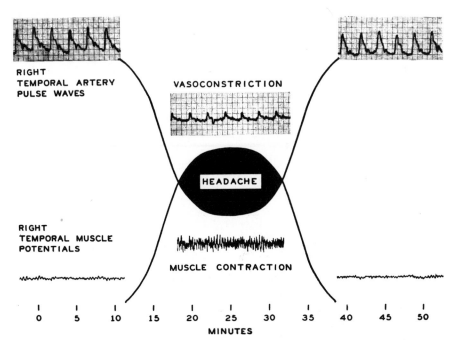

FIGURE 8-2   The Relationship Between Vasoconstriction in the Right Temporal Artery and the Head Pain of a Tension Headache.
During the headache, indicated in the center of the illustration, the magnitude of the pulse waves in the artery decreased, indicating vasoconstriction, while the amount of activity in the temporal muscles increased. These results suggest a vascular as well as a muscular component in tension headaches. *(From M. M. Tunis and H. G. Wolff, 1954. In* American Journal of the Medical Sciences, *224 (1952), p. 430. Reprinted by permission.)*

nated together. In another study, levarterenol was injected intravenously in five people during a total of 12 headaches; the head pain in ten of these headaches had a slight to moderate increase. Intravenous injections when the people did not have headaches did not produce head pain. Ergotamine (also a vasoconstricting drug) was injected intravenously during five headaches. The head pain intensity increased profoundly during one headache, increased moderately during two others, and did not change in the remaining two. When the induced vasoconstriction ceased, the head pain decreased. Five people inhaled amyl nitrate (a vasodilating drug) during a total of six headaches. Head pain intensity decreased on five of the six tests. When the induced vasodilation ceased, head pain increased. In summary, vasoconstriction accompanied spontaneous head pain, induced vasoconstriction increased already present head pain, and induced vasodilation decreased already present head pain in people diagnosed as having tension headaches.

Dalessio (1972, pp. 534 to 548) reviews these and other data collected by Wolff. He concludes (p. 548): "In short, increased skeletal muscle contraction about the head and humorally influenced extracranial vaso-constriction are parallel responses to certain life situations, and acting together in some persons they induce muscle contraction headache." Thus, the state of the vascular system may affect pain accompanying muscle contraction, suggesting that individuals with tension headaches may have a vascular disturbance manifesting itself as a chronic vasocon-striction, even without headache, and acute vasoconstriction during headache. If further research supports this idea, then biofeedback train-ing to produce vasodilation, particularly in the extracranial blood sup-ply, may become an appropriate treatment in addition to the muscle re-laxation techniques currently in use.

TREATMENT

If tension headaches are caused by excessive and/or sustained con-traction of muscles surrounding the head, then reduction of this activity should prevent headaches. The goal of biofeedback is to train the patient to reduce contraction of the involved muscles. Muscle activity is recorded from surface electrodes and some aspect of the resulting EMG is selected as feedback to indicate to the patient the degree of muscle contraction. Treatment has typically focused on the frontalis muscle. Recording elec-trodes can easily be placed over this muscle, and the person trained to relax it. Biofeedback training teaches the patient to sense the amount of activity in the frontalis muscle and to reduce it to minimal levels, elim-inating headaches that have already begun and preventing the appear-ance of new headaches.

Biofeedback training to reduce frontalis EMG levels is becoming a frequently used procedure for the treatment of tension headaches, es-pecially when combined with other training emphasizing physiological relaxation and/or with psychotherapeutic interventions. As indicated by the review below, such efforts have been successful. Within a relatively short time, people have reported a substantial decrease in the frequency, intensity, and/or duration of their headaches and a reduction in the amount of medication used. Reviews of both published reports and papers presented during scientific conventions indicate that biofeedback alone is faster than relaxation alone in achieving reductions in headache activity and is effective for more than 70% of the patients (Budzynski 1978). In some cases, individuals were able to eliminate headaches com-pletely and reported no additional problems during follow-up interviews.

The procedures and results from 18 published studies are summarized in Table 8–5. In addition to providing information about the specific studies, this table indicates the substantial success of biofeedback with a variety of different types of people ranging in age from 16 to 65. Fourteen of the studies used biofeedback to train relaxation of the frontalis muscle, and many of them included in their treatment package some form of home practice, relaxation training, or other behavioral procedures. Biofeedback treatment has produced a decrease in both the head pain symptoms and the levels of muscle activity.

Case Study A

This case illustrates a relatively simple application of biofeedback training in the clinic along with home practice of this skill to successfully eliminate persistent tension headaches. The patient was a 29-year-old female who had experienced tension headaches for 20 years (Budzynski and others 1970). Her headaches were dull and aching, appeared bilaterally, began in the morning, and lasted throughout the day. EMG from the frontalis muscle was approximately double that found in people without headaches in the same clinic.

Training sessions lasted 30 minutes each and took place two or three times a week. Surface electrodes recorded the EMG activity from the frontalis muscle. A tone provided analogue feedback; the lower the EMG, the lower the pitch of the tone. A shaping procedure was used so that during the first few training sessions, a slight decrease in muscle activity produced a large decrease in the pitch of the tone. As she became better at lowering muscle activity, greater decreases in muscle activity were required to produce a given decrease in pitch. She was instructed to practice at home once a day the same muscle relaxation skills she learned in the clinic. A daily record was kept of the intensity of headache activity, rated each hour on a scale from 0 (no headache) to 5 (intense headache). Formal treatment in the clinic lasted nine weeks, after which she was instructed to practice relaxing her frontalis muscle at home whenever needed.

After one week of treatment, headache frequency, intensity, and duration began to decrease slightly. Three weeks later, all three measures showed substantial decreases, and they continued to decline during the rest of treatment. She reported greater awareness of the amount of contraction of the forehead muscles, greater control of the level of contraction, and an improved ability to deal with stressful events. Three months later at the follow-up, ". . . headaches had virtually disappeared and the patient was in good spirits generally. There was no evidence of symptom substitution" (Budzynski and others 1970, p. 208).

This case study illustrates the diversity of approaches that may be integrated with biofeedback treatment (Reeves 1976). The patient was a female college student, 25 years old, with a five-year history of tension headaches. Neurological examinations failed to determine an organic basis for the headaches which had not been controlled with several types of medication such as Fiorinal and Valium. The procedure began with two weeks of pretreatment baseline during which frontalis EMG levels were monitored in the laboratory three times weekly. The next two weeks used "cognitive skills training" to identify and reverse negative self-statements regarding environmental stressors. Then biofeedback training took place for six weeks. She was instructed to practice "stress management" (Budzynski 1973) for 15 minutes each day. Headache intensity was rated on a scale from 0 to 5 and was recorded every hour. EMG from the frontalis muscle was measured in uV rms (root mean square). During the pretreatment baseline and the cognitive skills training, EMG remained constant at 9 uV rms. During biofeedback, it decreased more than 30% to 5.9 uV rms and decreased even further to 5.0 uV rms six months later. Headache activity decreased in a similar fashion. During the pretreatment baseline, the mean hourly headache activity was 1.9, a figure which decreased slightly to 1.2 during cognitive skills training. With biofeedback treatment, there was a further reduction to .6, a value which decreased only slightly more six months later. Thus, biofeedback preceded and accompanied by cognitive skills training reduced EMG activity by approximately 50% to normal levels and decreased headache activity by 75% during a period of two months.

Discussion of Treatments

Biofeedback Training and Home Practice.   Several studies have shown the therapeutic effectiveness of biofeedback training by itself. Patients were trained in the clinic to lower the level of activity in the frontalis muscle and instructed to practice this skill at home. No other treatment procedures were used. Two studies discussed here also incorporated an incorrect feedback condition (see Chapter 1) in which the information given to the person did not accurately reflect the state of the frontalis muscle. These control procedures were not effective in changing headache activity, showing that the specific training to lower muscle activity, rather than some other more general aspect of the treatment, was responsible for the therapeutic success.

One group of 18 people with tension headaches responded to advertisements in local papers (Budzynski and others 1973). They were between 22 and 44 years of age and had experienced tension headaches for an average of nine years. Headache intensity was recorded hourly on a six-point scale. Following two weeks of pretreatment baseline, during which time headache activity was recorded but no treatment took place, biofeedback training began. EMG was recorded from the frontalis muscle. Analogue feedback was provided by a tone, with decreases in muscle activity reflected by decreases in pitch. Each biofeedback session was 20 minutes long; 16 sessions took place in nine weeks. Patients were instructed to practice twice daily at home (without feedback) the muscle relaxation skills they had learned in the clinic; each home practice lasted 15 to 20 minutes. After biofeedback training was completed, the patients kept hourly records of headache activity for three months, and then returned to the laboratory for another EMG measurement. During the pretreatment baseline, frontalis EMG averaged 10 uV, peak-to-peak. This activity was reduced by biofeedback to 3.9 uV and it remained at that level at the follow-up. A composite measure of headache discomfort (the product of headache intensity and the number of hours at that intensity, divided by 24) was reduced from a mean of .5 during the pretreatment baseline to a mean of .2 during biofeedback and .1 at the follow-up. Thus both EMG and headache activity were substantially reduced by the combination of biofeedback training in the clinic and home practice of this skill.

The two studies to be discussed next support the conclusion that biofeedback by itself is an effective treatment for tension headaches and also demonstrate that a critical component for the success of biofeedback is accurate information about the state of muscle activity. Both studies compared the effectiveness of correct feedback with that from a control procedure in which people were given incorrect feedback. Accurate control in a feedback system can take place only with correct information (see Chapter 2). Thus, if the feedback portion of these treatments is the critical component responsible for their therapeutic effectiveness, reductions of headache activity should be seen only with the correct feedback procedure.

A group of five females whose symptoms had not been helped by a variety of other treatments participated in one study (Wickramasekera 1972). Psychological testing, a complete physical examination by a consulting internist, and an EEG examination by a consulting neurologist indicated no organic bases for the headaches. The experimental design included three weeks of pretreatment baseline during which headache activity was recorded, six sessions of incorrect feedback in three weeks, and six sessions of correct feedback in six weeks. Each biofeedback session lasted 30 minutes. Surface electrodes recorded the EMG from the frontalis muscle. The pitch of a tone provided auditory analogue feedback. For incorrect feedback, the pitch varied independently of muscle activity, while for correct feedback, it decreased as muscle activity decreased. Headache activity was recorded on a scale from 0 (no headache) to 5 (intense headache) during the entire 18-week period. The participants were asked to stop taking all medication for their headaches. During the baseline, EMG averaged 6.3 uV. It remained unchanged during incorrect feedback but decreased to 2.7 uV at the end of treatment. A similar pattern appeared for headache activity. During the pretreatment baseline, the mean headache intensity was 4.0, and the mean number of hours of headache activity during the week was 15. These values remained virtually the same during incorrect feedback (4.3 and 15 respectively) but dramatically decreased during correct feedback so that at the end of treatment the mean headache intensity was 1.7 and the mean number of hours of headache activity was 3.7.

The relative effects of correct and incorrect feedback have been compared both within a biofeedback session and across a number of sessions (Kondo & Canter 1977). The participants were 20 people with a history of tension headaches ranging from eight months to almost four years. During the study, each person recorded the number of headaches experienced. Following 10 days of pretreatment baseline, 10 biofeedback sessions took place within 17 to 21 days. Surface electrodes recorded the EMG from the frontalis muscle. A tone provided analogue feedback. Half the people were placed in a correct feedback procedure in which the pitch of the tone correctly reflected the level of muscle activity, while the other half were placed in an uncorrelated feedback procedure in which the pitch of the tone was not related to muscle activity. A follow-up interview took place 12 months later. In the uncorrelated feedback condition, there was little change in the EMG or the frequency of tension headaches either during the biofeedback sessions or at the follow-up. In the correct feedback condition, there was a substantial reduction in both EMG and headache frequency. At the first biofeedback session, the mean EMG was reduced from 27 uV during the first five minutes to 22 uV during the last five minutes. At the tenth session, EMG was further reduced from 15 uV at the beginning of the session to 10 uV at the end. The mean number of headaches declined from 1.1 per day during the pretreatment baseline to .7 during the first five days of biofeedback training and .2 during the last five days. At the follow-up interview, four of the five people contacted said that headache frequency had remained low, while the fifth said that headaches occurred less frequently than they had in the pretreatment baseline, but more frequently than they had during the biofeedback treatment.

Taken together, these studies make two important points. First, biofeedback training by itself can produce a significant reduction in headache activity and in frontalis EMG activity. The inclusion of a pretreatment baseline during which headache activity was recorded but no treatment was given and the long history of tension headaches in some of the individuals make these changes particularly dramatic. Second, the comparison of the results of correct feedback with those of incorrect feedback shows the relative ineffectiveness of the latter. Because all aspects of these treatment procedures were the same except for the type of feedback, the results indicate that the success of the biofeedback treatment was due to the specific training to reduce frontalis EMG, rather than to some placebo effect of the treatment procedure.

A similar conclusion comes from a comparison of the effectiveness of frontalis EMG biofeedback with that of a medication placebo (Cox and others 1975). The 18 participants had headaches at least three times weekly. Nine of them received auditory analogue feedback of frontalis EMG levels twice weekly for 30 minutes. The other nine received a placebo (green and white glucose capsule) dispensed during a weekly visit; they were told that the drug was a muscle relaxant with a proven effectiveness. A headache index (Budzynski and others 1973) reflecting the weighted average of intensity, frequency, and duration of head pain was used to assess changes in headache activity. The headache index for the biofeedback group decreased from 1.7 before treatment to .6 after treatment. The headache index in the placebo group began at a similar point, 1.6, but decreased only slightly to 1.3. These results indicate that biofeedback was more successful than the medication placebo in reducing headache activity.

Treatment of Severe and/or Persistent Headaches. Many people who have sought biofeedback treatment tried it as a last resort when other attempts had failed. As can be seen from the review of the treatment reports in Table 8–5, extensive histories of severe headaches are common. In the studies of Wickramasekera (1972, 1973a), biofeedback was successful with patients who experienced tension headaches for up to 20 years; the shortest headache history in that group of people was six years.

Patients with headache histories ranging from 11 years to 39 years have also been treated successfully (Cox and others 1975). The participants were 9 adults, 16 to 64 years of age, with tension headaches occurring at least 3 times a week. Two weeks of pretreatment baseline were followed by eight weeks of biofeedback treatment. Surface electrodes recorded the EMG from the frontalis muscle; analogue feedback was provided by the pitch of a tone. Two biofeedback sessions, each 30 minutes long, took place twice each week. The participants also practiced a cued relaxation procedure several times a day, using the word "relax" as the stimulus. There were two follow-up periods, one two weeks after treatment and another four months later. Although headache activity was not entirely eliminated, it was substantially reduced, indicating the effectiveness of biofeedback even with frequent headaches which had persisted for many years. The mean number of headache hours per week decreased from 95 in the pretreatment baseline to 33 and 31 respectively in the follow-up periods. During these same three periods, the number of headaches per week was 18, .1, and 8 respectively, while a composite headache score was 1.7, .6, and .6 respectively.

Headaches associated with chronic anxiety have been reduced by biofeedback (Raskin and others 1973). The patients were ten people, four of whom were diagnosed as troubled by tension headaches for at least one year. Training sessions took place five times weekly for 2 to 12 weeks. Surface electrodes recorded EMG from the frontalis muscle. Feedback was provided by the pitch of a tone. Each session was one hour unless muscle activity was reduced below a criterion of 2.5 uV per minute for 25 minutes, in which case the session was terminated. Frontal EMG activity for the group averaged 14.1 uV/min during the first three training sessions which served as a baseline measurement. From this level, EMG was reduced to the criterion of 2.5 uV in an average of six weeks of training. Headache activity also decreased. Three of the people were rated as "markedly improved" and the fourth as "moderately improved." The authors additionally reported that as the headache frequency and intensity decreased, the people learned to prevent the appearance of anticipated headaches and reduce the intensity of already established ones.

Permanence of Treatment Effects.   The reductions in headache activity produced by biofeedback are durable. In the study by Kondo and Canter (1977) discussed above, patients received biofeedback sessions every one or two days for a total of ten sessions. When contacted twelve months later, all patients who had received correct feedback reported that headaches occurred less frequently than they had during the pretreatment baseline; four patients had maintained the substantial reductions in headache activity they had achieved at the end of biofeedback training, while one had experienced an increase since then. Similar successes have been reported with follow-up periods of one month (Hutchings & Reinking 1976), three months (Budzynski and others 1973), four months (Cox and others 1975), seven months (Haynes and others 1975), and up to five years (Diamond and others 1979). Our experience at the Phipps Clinic has been that a person who is able to reduce headache activity as a result of biofeedback training maintains or continues to improve even when biofeedback is stopped. In most cases headache activity is virtually eliminated thereafter. These results show that successful treatment is usually permanent.

Biofeedback and Relaxation.   Some form of relaxation training is often used to treat tension headaches. This treatment by itself, or in conjunction with biofeedback training, can be effective in reducing headache activity. A major advantage of relaxation training is that it can be practiced without instruments and is easy to incorporate into a home practice schedule. The issue for the practicing clinician is not really one of "biofeedback versus relaxation," as if one treatment excludes the other, but rather the incorporation of both treatments where they can be maximally effective.

Comparable effects of biofeedback training and relaxation training were found in the treatment of college students (Haynes and others 1975). Eight students received biofeedback sessions, each 20 minutes long, twice a week for three weeks. Frontalis EMG was recorded with surface electrodes and feedback provided by a tone. Eight other students listened to relaxation instructions for equivalent periods of time. For the students receiving biofeedback, headache frequency decreased from 5.5 per week at the beginning of treatment to 1.5 per week one week following treatment; for students receiving relaxation instructions, headache frequency decreased from 5.2 per week to 1.4 per week. The same pattern of results was found with a composite measure of headache activity which included frequency, duration, and intensity. This measure decreased from 81 to 21 for the people receiving biofeedback, and from 102 to 19 for those receiving relaxation. Thus the changes in headache activity for both groups were similar, and significantly greater than those in a third group which received no treatment.

A second experiment comparing the effectiveness of biofeedback, relaxation, and a medication placebo came to the same conclusion (Cox and others 1975). Nine participants received biofeedback training while another nine received relaxation instructions. Both groups were given eight sessions, twice weekly, for four weeks. For those receiving biofeedback, EMG was recorded from the frontalis muscles and feedback was provided by a tone. The relaxation instructions were those outlined by Bernstein and Borkovec (1973). Following biofeedback and relaxation, respectively, headache frequency was reduced by 51% and 51%, headache duration by 65% and 53%, and a composite measure by 63% and 53%. The changes in both groups were substantially greater than those found with a group given a medication placebo.

One of the first comparisons of biofeedback and relaxation found relaxation ineffective in reducing headache activity (Wickramasekera 1973). The participants were five males "diagnosed by neurologists as chronic and almost daily tension headache cases" (p. 74). Three weeks of pretreatment baseline were followed by three weeks of relaxation training, three weeks of biofeedback training, and a nine-week follow-up period.

TABLE 8-5   Summary of Biofeedback Treatments for Tension Headaches

Study	Patients	Biofeedback Treatment	Other Treatment	Results Symptoms	Biological Function
Budzynski, Stoyva, & Adler, 1970	Female, age 29; female, age 33; female, "middle-aged"; female, "young high school teacher"; male, "middle-aged"	Auditory feedback of frontal EMG during 30-min sessions, 2 or 3 times weekly for at least 5 weeks	Daily home practice	Average hourly headache activity, subjectively rated from 0 to 5, was reduced from a baseline average of .84 to .30 after the 4th week of training	Average microvolt levels of EMG: baseline, 5.8; training week #1, 4.6; training week #2, 4.0; training week #3, 3.7; training week #4, 3.5
Budzynski, Stoyva, Adler, & Mullaney, 1973	2 males, 16 females; average age, 36; range, 22 to 44	Auditory feedback of frontal EMG during 30-min sessions, twice weekly for 9 weeks	Home practice twice daily for 15 to 20 min	Average hourly headache activity, subjectively rated from 0 to 5, decreased from .5 during the baseline to .2 at the end of training to .1 at 3-month follow-up	Average microvolt levels of EMG: baseline, 10; training, 3.9; 3-month follow-up, 3.9. Weekly headache activity was correlated (.90) with frontal EMG levels
Chesney & Shelton, 1976	22 females, 2 males	Auditory and visual feedback of frontal EMG during eight, 30-min feedback sessions twice weekly for 4 weeks	None reported	Average levels during first and fourth weeks: headache frequency, 4.8 and 2.8; duration, 5.3 and 6.3 hours; severity on a scale of 1 to 100, 52.3 and 32.5	Data Unavailable
Cox, Freundlich, & Meyer, 1975	20 females, 7 males; age range: 16 to 64; symptom duration, 1 to 39 yrs; average age, 11	Auditory analogue feedback of frontal EMG during 30-min sessions twice weekly for 4 weeks	Cue controlled breathing immediately following feedback and prior to each meal; relaxation as learned in biofeedback sessions twice daily; medication	Average levels during the baseline, 2-week follow-up, and 4-month follow-up: headache index, 1.7, .6, and .6; duration 95, 33, and 31; frequency, 18, .1, and 8; medication used, 34, 14, and 9; psychosomatic checklist scores, 32, 13, and 17	Correlation between reductions in EMG and changes in headache activity: .42

Diamond, Medina, Diamond-Falk, & DeVeno, 1979	19 with muscle contraction headaches; 265 with combined muscle contraction and vascular headache	Auditory analogue feedback of frontal EMG for 10 min and finger temperature for 20 min, 2 to 10 times weekly for up to 4 weeks	Relaxation exercises; home practice twice a day for up to 4 weeks	Percent stating that biofeedback helped their headaches: muscle contraction alone, 72; combined muscle contraction and vascular headache, 73	Data unavailable
Epstein, Hersen, & Hemphill, 1974	Male, age 39; symptom duration, 16 years	Experiment one: auditory feedback of patient-selected music contingent upon reductions in frontal EMG during 24, 10-min sessions; experiment two: 10-min auditory feedback and 10-min no-feedback segments in counter balanced order	While an inpatient in hospital (Exp. 1) Sinequan 25 mg. q.i.d., Phenobarbital 1.5 mg/day, Dilantin 300 mg/day; While an outpatient (Exp. 2) a placebo was administered with home relaxation instructions	Average in baseline #1, feedback #1, baseline #2, and feedback #2, in experiment one: headache intensity, 5.0, 3.5, 5.8, and 2.5; averages in baseline #1, feedback #1, and baseline #2 in experiment two: headache intensity, 6.2, 4.8, and 10.8; medication used, 3.2, 1.2, and 2.2; no headache was reported on 64 of 66 days during the follow-up	Number of seconds per minute below criterion of 10uV experiment one: baseline #1, 21; feedback #1, 37; baseline #2, 30; feedback #2, 45
Epstein & Abel, 1977	2 males, 4 females; average age, 32.8	Feedback of frontal EMG during 16, 20-min sessions	A 20-min "no-feedback" segment followed each feedback session	Average hourly headache activity (rated 0–5): baseline, 2.2; treatment, 1.7; follow-up, 1.5	Average uV level of frontal EMG: baseline, 19.4; feedback, 17.8; follow-up, 20.6
Feuerstein, Adams, & Beiman, 1976	Female, age 67 with combined migraine and tension headache	Feedback of frontal EMG for 20 min, once weekly for 6 weeks followed by feedback of cephalic vasomotor responses for 30 min, once weekly for 6 weeks	Home practice for 10 min, twice daily	Average weekly headache frequency: baseline, 4.4; EMG feedback, 1.8; baseline, 3.3; CVMR feedback, 1.3; 8-week follow-up, 2.5; average intensity (rated 1 to 4): baseline, 2.8; EMG feedback, 1.5; baseline 2.1; CVMR feedback, 2.6; 8-week follow-up, 1.3; average duration:	Frequency of vasospasm during baseline, feedback, and baseline of sessions 5 and 6: EMG feedback, 7.7, 5.3, and 2.9; CVMR feedback, .8 1.1, and .4

Study	Patients	Biofeedback Treatment	Other Treatment	Symptoms	Results Biological Function
				baseline 15.8; EMG feedback, 5.3; baseline, 9.9; CVMR feedback, 4.6; 8-week follow-up, 7.5; no headache reported for 3 weeks during CVMR feedback; use of tranquilizers was reduced from 3 to 1 during the study	
Fried, Lamberti, & Sneed, 1977	6 females; age range 31 to 47; 1 with tension headaches, 2 with mixed tension and vascular headaches	Home practice of skin temperature raising with a portable trainer twice daily	Autogenic phrases repeated twice daily for 2 weeks preceding temperature training	Number improved by more than 75%: 1 with tension headache, 1 with mixed tension and vascular headache; number improved very little or questionable: 1 with mixed tension and vascular headache	Data unavailable
Haynes, Griffin, Mooney, & Parise, 1975	7 males, 14 females; average age 20.9; average symptom duration, 5.2 years	Feedback of frontal EMG during 20-min sessions, twice weekly for 3 weeks	None reported	Average levels during baseline, 1-week follow-up, and 5- to 7-month follow-up: frequency, 5.5, 1.5, and 1.2; intensity, 3.4, 1.7, and 4.1; duration, 4.7, 2.9, and 2.3; headache index, 82.1, 20.9, and 11.4	Data unavailable
Hutchings & Reinking, 1976	14 females, 4 males; average age, 23	Auditory analogue feedback of frontal EMG during 10, 15-min sessions	Practice twice daily, especially when in "stress-producing situations"	By the end of a 28-day follow-up, 66% improved; composite headache scores (computed by multiplying the # of H.A. hours times the average intensity for that day) were reduced from 10 prior to treatment, to 6 during treatment, to 4 following treatment	Average level of EMG in microvolts/min: 19 prior to treatment, 8 during treatment, 5 during the follow-up

Study	Subjects	Procedure	Additional	Headache results	EMG levels
Kondo & Canter, 1977	18 females, 2 males; age range, 19 to 38; symptom duration, 8 to 45 months	Auditory analogue feedback of frontal EMG during 20-min sessions every 1 or 2 days for 10 sessions	None reported	Average number of headaches decreased from approx. 5.3 during the 10 days preceding training to approx. 1.9 during training	Average Mv levels of frontal EMG during the first and last 5 mins of session #1: 27 and 22; during session #10: 15 and 10
McKenzie, Ehrisman, Montgomery, & Barnes, 1974	6 females, 1 male; average age, 33; range, 28 to 42	Binary visual feedback of EEG activity twice weekly for 5 weeks	None reported	Average number of headache hours per week: 41 before treatment, 8 during treatment, 7 at 1-month follow-up, 2 at 2-month follow-up	Data unavailable
Philips, 1977b	15 with headaches at least twice weekly	Auditory feedback of frontal or temporal EMG during 20-min sessions twice weekly for 6 weeks	None reported	Average pretreatment, post-treatment, and follow-up levels: intensity, 1.1, .8, and .2; frequency, 5.4, 3.8, and 2.2; average number of medications used: 6.5, 8.5, and 2.6	Average microvolt levels: pretreatment, 5.6, posttreatment, 2.9 and follow-up, 3.6
Raskin, Johnson, & Rondestvedt, 1973	6 males, 4 females; average age, 27; 4 had tension headaches	Auditory feedback of frontal EMG levels during 1-hour sessions 5 times weekly until EMG activity averaged less than 2.5 Mv for 25 min	Instruction to relax specific muscle groups aided by feedback; training sessions without feedback interspersed; home relaxation once some progress was apparent; "pain medication for headache"	3 of 4 patients were rated as "markedly improved," and 1 as "moderately improved" in symptom intensity; "the 4 patients . . . experienced considerable reduction in the frequency and intensity . . . they learned to . . . abort anticipated or beginning headaches and even to diminish the pain of an established headache"	The group reduced EMG levels from an average of 14.1 mv/min during a 2-week baseline, to less than 2.5 mv/min during an average of 6 weeks of training (range 2 to 12 weeks)
Reeves, 1976	Female, age 20 with a 5-year history of headache	Auditory analogue feedback of frontal EMG during 20-min sessions, 3 times weekly for 6 weeks	"Stress management" 15 min daily; "cognitive skills training"	Average hourly headache activity: baseline, 1.9; cognitive skills training, 1.2; biofeedback, .6; follow-up, .5	Average levels of frontal EMG (Mv rms): baseline, 9; cognitive skills training, 9; biofeedback, 5.9; follow-up, 5

Study	Patients	Biofeedback Treatment	Other Treatment	Results	
				Symptoms	Biological Function
Wickramasekera, 1972	5 females with 6 to 20-year histories of headache	Feedback of frontal EMG during 6, 30-min sessions in 6 weeks	None reported; patients were instructed to cease taking medication	Average maximum headache intensity: baseline, 4.0; false feedback, 4.3; true feedback, 1.8; average number of hours of headache pain: baseline, 15; false feedback, 15; true feedback, 7.3	Frontal EMG activity averaged 6.2 uV during the baseline and during false feedback and 3.5 during true feedback
Wickramasekera, 1973a	5 females with 6 to 20-year histories of headache	Feedback of frontal EMG during 10-min sessions, 3 times weekly for 3 weeks; visual feedback was additionally provided during Session #1	Verbal relaxation instructions 40 min daily for three days preceding the feedback training; home relaxation sessions at least twice weekly during feedback	Average maximum headache intensity: baseline, 4.5; verbal relaxation instructions, 3.8; feedback, 1.9; follow-up, .5	Average microvolt levels of frontal EMG: baseline, 14; relaxation, 14; biofeedback, 6.5; 8-week follow-up, 5

Biofeedback sessions were 30 minutes each and took place three times weekly. Frontalis EMG levels averaged 14 uV peak-to-peak in the baseline period. This level remained unchanged during relaxation but decreased to 6.5 uV during biofeedback. Headache intensity, 4.5 (on a scale from 0 to 5) in the baseline period, decreased slightly to 3.8 during relaxation and dropped markedly to 1.9 during biofeedback. Thus clinically significant changes in both EMG and headache intensity were found during biofeedback, but not during relaxation. The failure of relaxation training to reduce headache activity in this study suggests that a short period of relaxation may not be effective for people who have severe and frequent tension headaches. However, this result does not allow us to conclude that more extended relaxation training would also have been ineffective, or that biofeedback by itself would have reduced headache activity more rapidly than relaxation by itself. To address these issues, the treatment periods would have to be extended, and the experimental design would have to include a group which received biofeedback treatment prior to relaxation.

Measures of Headache Activity. As can be seen in the summary of treatment reports in Table 8–5, several different measures of headache activity have been used to evaluate the clinical effectiveness of biofeedback. These include the intensity, duration, and frequency of the head pain, the amount of medication taken, and composite indices from several different measures. In most cases, all these measures of headache activity change during biofeedback treatment, reflecting a decrease in all aspects of the head pain. Occasionally, however, one or more measures appear to be relatively independent of the others. For example, measures of headache frequency and duration, along with a composite measure of headache activity, were all substantially decreased in a follow-up period after biofeedback, while headache intensity actually increased slightly (Haynes and others 1975). The participants were 21 undergraduate students suffering from "distinct, frequently occurring tension-headache syndromes" (p. 673). Following two weeks of pretreatment baseline, biofeedback training took place twice weekly for three weeks. From the baseline to the follow-up period, seven months later, three of the headache measures decreased: the number of headaches per week fell from 5.5 to 1.2, the number of hours per headache fell from 4.7 to 2.3, and the composite headache index fell from 82.1 to 11.3. The intensity of headaches, rated on a scale from 0 to 5, actually increased during the same time, going from 3.4 to 4.1. Consequently the students had fewer headaches which lasted for a shorter period of time, but when they had a headache it was just as severe as it had been prior to biofeedback treatment.

In another study, the frequency and intensity of headaches decreased while the duration increased (Chesney & Shelton 1976). Biofeedback sessions lasted 30 minutes each and took place twice weekly for four weeks. The participants received visual and auditory feedback of frontalis EMG levels. Headache activity was measured during the first and last week of treatment. Headache frequency fell from 4.8 to 2.8 headaches per week, and headache intensity (on a scale from 0 to 100) fell from 52 to 33. Headache duration, however, increased from 5.3 hours per week to 6.3 hours per week. Although none of these changes was significantly different from those in a control group which received no treatment, headache duration was obviously not closely linked with headache frequency or intensity because it moved in a direction opposite to the other two measures.

The implication of these findings is clear: multiple measures of headache activity should be obtained whenever possible (see Chapters 3 and 7). They are necessary to evaluate accurately the course of treatment and may be particularly useful in more closely defining the immediate goals of treatment. For example, a client might say that the major problem is that the headaches last for a long period of time and the constant low level of pain is most upsetting, rather than the brief moments of high intensity pain. For this person, therapy should start by reducing the duration of the headaches, rather than their intensity. At the beginning of treatment, multiple measures are particularly useful because a change may appear in one before appearing in others. This initial success can motivate the client to practice the biofeedback procedure and provide encouragement about the ultimate success of therapy.

CLINICAL PROGRAM

(We remind the reader that these sections should be read in conjunction with the relevant parts of Chapter 6 describing psychophysiological procedures, Chapter 7 describing clinical procedures in general, and the beginning of the treatment section in each appropriate chapter summarizing biofeedback applications.)

A medical examination is important before any biofeedback treatment, but with headaches it becomes critical. The organic and physiological stimuli that can cause headaches are numerous and diverse, ranging from malfunction of the jaw and teeth to brain tumors. There are three practical benefits of the medical examination, assuming it shows no physiological abnormalities. First, the therapist can proceed confidently with treatment, knowing that the client is in good health. Second, the client can approach the therapy optimistically and with a sense of relief, knowing that there is no disease producing the symptoms. Third, the elimination of a physical cause can often focus attention on psychological factors, providing the therapist with an opportunity to discuss these with the client.

The diagnosis of tension headaches is not clear-cut, and the complex of head pain symptoms supposedly diagnostic of tension headaches may not be as useful as once thought. Getting an accurate description of the head pain is necessary, particularly with respect to the adjectives commonly used to characterize tension headaches and separate them from migraine headaches. Here, an adjective checklist can be particularly beneficial. An important instruction to the client is to consider whether there are different types of headaches, each occurring independently and with different sets of symptoms (Sturgis, Tollison, & Adams 1978). Retrospective descriptions can be helpful but are inevitably prone to distortion. Thus, a means should be provided for the client to describe individual headaches at the time they occur, not only with respect to headache intensity, but also to the types of head pain experienced and their time course. An example of a headache questionnaire is presented in the following list (see also Bakal & Kaganov 1976; Thompson & Collins 1979; and list p. 91.)

An Example of a Headache Survey for Use in the Clinic

Place a check mark beside each symptom in the list if you experience that symptom during a headache.

_____band-like feeling

_____cold hands and feet

_____constriction around head

_____cramping of head muscles

_____nausea

_____pressure

_____soreness or dull pain

_____steady, nonpulsating pain

_____throbbing, pulsating pain

_____tightness around head

_____viselike feeling

_____vomiting

Answer each of the questions below.

1. What drugs have relieved the pain?
2. What drugs have not relieved the pain?
3. Who else in your family has headaches like yours?
4. Where does the pain occur?
5. When is the pain most likely to occur?
6. How long does the pain last?
7. How frequently does it appear?

8. Is it preceded by any types of sensations such as tingling in the hands, spots before the eyes, etc? If so, what sensations do you have?

9. Does the pain tend to come after you have eaten certain types of foods?

10. Have you consulted a physician about the pain? If so, what did the physician tell you about the pain?

Note: This survey may be used for a retrospective analysis of previous headaches, and adapted as a means of recording headaches as they occur. See also the symptom questionnaire in Chapter 7 (list p. 91).

A psychophysiological analysis will be useful both for diagnosis and for choosing the course of treatment. A chronic elevation of the EMG from the frontalis muscle suggests that excessive muscle activity may be at least a contributory, if not a major, mechanism of the headaches. EMG from other muscles can also be taken and are certainly appropriate if the patient indicates the site of the head pain in areas other than the forehead. Skin temperature of the hands and especially of the head regions containing the blood supply to the painful areas should be obtained to determine if there may be a chronic vasoconstriction in addition to the elevated muscle activity.

Decreasing frontalis EMG activity has been therapeutic, and approximately 80% of the individuals treated in this way have substantially reduced their headaches (Budzynski 1978). The general considerations of biofeedback training reviewed in the earlier chapters are relevant here too, and the therapist must set up an optimal training program for the client. Engel (1973) has suggested that learning to both increase and decrease the activity of a biological function may be beneficial in learning control in either direction, and Jacobson (1929, 1938) regularly incorporated a brief period of muscle tensing prior to initiation of muscle relaxation to assist the client in identifying the undesirable state. Consequently, short periods of increasing the EMG may be helpful to point out the sensations of tenseness that are to be eliminated in the subsequent biofeedback sessions. Biofeedback training to reduce muscle activity in other head muscles may also be indicated if the pain is situated in areas other than the forehead, and if muscles in these areas are abnormally contracted.

People who suffer from tension headaches may have a substantial vasoconstriction of the blood vessels supplying the head, and the ischemia from this vasoconstriction may be an important factor influencing the onset of head pain. Skin temperature raising, at least on an exploratory basis, is appropriate for any client with tension headaches and is especially applicable if a psychophysiological analysis indicates that there is excessive vasoconstriction, either during a headache or persisting throughout nonheadache periods. Increasing digital skin temperature is a standard biofeedback procedure and can result in a generalized peripheral vasodilation. The point of interest, of course, is the vascular supply to the head, and concentration on vasodilation here may be more appropriate.

Both EMG and skin temperature feedback can result in highly specific physiological changes, as described earlier. Such an outcome is often undesirable in therapy, and relaxation can help produce a generalized change in these physiological functions. Furthermore, the relaxation can be accomplished outside of the laboratory without any biofeedback equipment. Relaxation procedures were reviewed in Chapter 7.

If the headaches regularly appear in response to specific events in the client's life, some investigation of those events and modification of responses to them may be appropriate. As usual, both the client and the therapist need to be certain of the goals of the therapy, and intensive psychological analysis may be undesirable. But to the extent that the person's life style or personality structure is interfering with the elimination of headaches, these topics are appropriate for discussion.

The EMG is recorded from the skin over the frontalis muscle by surface electrodes. Details for preparation of the skin and recording the EMG were reviewed in Chapter 6 and will not be repeated here. Clinic sessions may be held once or twice weekly in the early stages of training. As a client develops the ability to control muscle activity, the interval between sessions may be increased to prepare for elimination of feedback. Each session can last 20 to 40 minutes with a short rest if needed. Home practice with a portable trainer or with a relaxation procedure may be scheduled daily or twice daily for about 15 minutes.

RESEARCH CONSIDERATIONS

As reviewed earlier, some individuals have a symptom complex classically associated with tension headaches: head pain that is bilateral, dull and constant, rather than throbbing, and described as tightness or constriction, without nausea and/or vomiting and not preceded by a prodrome. However, the general applicability of this diagnosis to the population of people suffering from headaches is questionable. Consequently, a sophisticated analysis of the manner in which the symptoms of head pain group themselves together is needed. Furthermore, most surveys to date have used a very restricted set of adjectives to describe the head pain. Melzak and Torgerson (1971) present a detailed analysis of pain related adjectives, and incorporation of their scheme (or some other equally exhaustive one) may help to clarify the situation. In any case, the usefulness of the diagnostic category "tension headache" is under considerable attack, and a better way of classifying headaches is needed than is currently available.

Traditionally, tension headaches have been associated with disturbance of the skeletal muscle system while migraine headaches have been associated with disturbance of the vascular system. This dissociation on the basis of vascular involvement may not be appropriate in the light of the data suggesting an excessive vasoconstriction in clients having tension headaches. Understanding the role of muscle ischemia in tension headaches will help describe the mechanism of head pain and design appropriate treatment. Another question about the mechanism of tension headaches is the variability of muscle activity. Although some individuals who have headaches do have a substantial elevation of frontalis EMG, such is frequently not the case. These data suggest that variables other than muscle activity interact to determine the amount of head pain, and an understanding of this interaction will help to explicate the headache mechanism.

An important and currently unresolved issue is the relationship between the site of head pain and the sites of physiological malfunction. Past research has focused almost exclusively on the frontalis muscle, even though the head pain of tension headaches is often located in the back of the head or the neck. If the frontalis muscle is not the best indicator of head pain or if control of the frontalis muscle is not the most effective way to alleviate head pain, then therapy ought to change its focus. But the necessary information cannot be obtained until the reactions of other head muscles is detailed.

MIGRAINE HEADACHES

9

Introduction

Symptoms

Mechanism

Treatment

Clinical Program

Research Considerations

INTRODUCTION

The word "migraine" comes to us via the French from the Greek. There are two important facts that are relevant to this etymology. First, migraine headaches have been known for a long time. Indeed, the descriptions of head pain in Greek and Roman writings are very similar to the contemporary definitions of migraine headaches and include reference to their unilateral nature, the accompanying symptoms of nausea, and the desire to avoid bright illumination (Sachs 1970; Wolff 1948, p. 255). Although migraines are often associated with the stress of modern life, there is no question that they have plagued people for at least 2,000 years, and some authors have suggested that there is evidence that they have been present for an even longer period of time (Kunkle 1959; Lance 1975). The second fact that is important in the etymology of the word migraine is its translation, "hemicrania" or "half-headed." One of the defining characteristics of migraines is that the pain is located on one side of the head, at least when the headache begins.

Estimates of the prevalence of migraine headaches suggest that up to about 10% of the population may experience them, depending on the type of sample obtained. Although fewer people have migraine headaches than have tension headaches, the impact of these headaches is greater. The head pain is intense and often associated with nausea and vomiting. *Migraineurs* (people who suffer from migraine headaches) are more likely to be incapacited when a headache strikes and are more likely to consult a physician for help (Henryk-Gutt & Rees 1973; see also Ekbom and others 1978).

The mechanism of migraine headaches includes the intracerebral vascular supply, the arteries that carry blood throughout the brain. Before the head pain begins, these arteries may be so constricted that the blood supply reaching nerve cells in the brain is insufficient to support normal function. As a result, various types of neurological symptoms appear. This period of excessive vasoconstriction is followed by a rebound vasodilation which stimulates stretch receptors surrounding the arteries and causes pain.

Biofeedback has trained people to raise the temperature of their hands. As discussed in Chapter 4, the blood vessels in the skin are innervated only by the sympathetic portion of the autonomic nervous system, which when stimulated causes vasoconstriction. Raising the temperature of the hands, then, should be accompanied by vasodilation of the vascular supply in the hand, which can only be accomplished by reducing sympathetic activity. How such treatment affects the blood supply in the head, which is the mechanism of the headaches, is unclear. None the less, biofeedback has been remarkably successful. Treatment periods are generally longer than those for tension headaches, presumably due to the difficulty of learning the skin temperature response and the severity of the headache. For about 80% of the people who seek treatment, however, headache activity is substantially reduced or eliminated after about two months of treatment.

Migraine headaches have often been defined in terms of both the symptoms of the head pain and the supposed mechanism underlying them (Ad Hoc Committee 1962). We have already discussed the difficulties of this dual definition in the introduction to Section III and in the discussion of tension headaches. Consequently, the different types of migraine headaches will be defined only on the basis of the symptoms associated with them; no implications about the mechanisms are intended.

Four different types of migraine headaches are often identified (Ad Hoc Committee 1962). In all cases, the symptoms associated with the head pain phase of the headache are similar, but other characteristics of the headache differ. A *classic migraine* is one which has a discrete prodrome preceding the head pain. The prodrome usually appears rapidly and fades as soon as the head pain begins. It may appear as a disturbance in any number of sensory, motor, or cognitive processes. Examples of prodromes include flashing lights or blind spots in the visual field, tingling or numbness in one or more limbs, loss of strength, and difficulty in speech. A *common migraine* has no prodrome; the head pain begins without any prior neurological signs. *Cluster headaches* are usually brief and appear in groups. The interval between the groups may be long, so that the headaches appear in clusters, giving them their name. Cluster headaches may be different from classic and common migraines in other characteristics as well, such as the age at which they first appear, the likelihood that close family relatives have similar headaches, and the influence of physical movement on the head pain (Ekbom 1970). A final category of migraines includes those having neurological signs that persist after the headache itself is gone. These headaches have received various names, including *complicated migraine* (Diamond & Dalessio 1978), and *hemiplegic* or *opthalmoplegic migraine* (Ad Hoc Committee 1962).

SYMPTOMS

Migraine attacks are not subtle. Descriptions of them emphasize the severe pain and their association with signs of substantial upset: nausea, vomiting, other gastrointestinal disorders, the desire for seclusion, the inability to work effectively, and the need to go to bed (Diamond & Dalessio 1978; Lance 1975; Sachs 1970; Wolff 1948, pp. 255–261). Four features of migraine attacks are often used to distinguish them from tension headaches:

1. The beginning of the head pain is usually unilateral and can be easily located by the person having the headache.
2. The head pain is relieved or prevented by vasoconstricting drugs, particularly ergotamine.
3. Gastrointestinal disorders, including nausea, vomiting, diarrhea, and constipation, usually accompany or follow the headache.
4. For all but the common migraine, neurological symptoms precede the head pain.

These features, along with several others, are summarized in Table 9–1. A comparison of the phrases here with those used to describe tension headaches (Table 8–1) highlights the ways in which these two are thought to differ from each other.

As discussed in the chapter on tension headaches, the real issue is not whether people have headaches that can be described with the adjectives listed in Table 9–1, but whether the headaches so described form a diagnostic category separate from other types of headaches. Some of the relevant data have already been presented in our discussion of tension headaches and suggest that a clear dichotomy between tension headaches and migraine headaches is difficult, if not impossible. Other data, dealing more selectively with the characteristics of migraine headaches support this conclusion.

The severity of the headache is closely correlated with the presence of migraine symptoms. An extensive survey of people with migraine headaches examined more than 9,000 males, 18 years old, as they presented themselves for conscription in Sweden (Ekbom and others 1978). Although the sample was homogeneous and restricted, the data are useful because they provide a quantitative analysis of migraine characteristics in a nonclinical population (Harrison 1975). The authors esti-

TABLE 9-1   Descriptions of Migraine Headaches and Their Sources

Description	Ad Hoc Committee, 1962, pp. 717–718	Beeson and McDermott, 1967, pp. 1476–1477	Cochrane, 1969, p. 181	Friedman and Merritt, 1959, p. 228	Sachs, 1970, pp. 35–53	Wolff, 1948, pp. 593–594
Unilateral in onset	X	X	X	X	X	X
Throbbing		X		X	X	
Vomiting, nausea	X	X	X	X	X	X
Prodromes	X		X	X		X
Cold hands and feet						X
Photophobia		X		X		X
Irritability		X				X
Relieved by ergotamine		X		X		X
Family history	X		X	X		

mate that 96% of the males of this age in their locale were included in their survey. If the person indicated that he had experienced headaches, he was given an additional questionnaire to fill out which asked about the characteristics of these headaches. Migraine headaches were defined as "paroxysmally occurring headaches separated by free intervals with at least two of the following four symptoms: nausea, visual aura, unilateral ache, and heredity, i.e., migraine in parents or siblings" (Ekbom and others 1978, p. 10). Approximately 2% of the population sampled had migraines by this definition. (This relatively low estimate of the prevalence of migraine headaches is probably due to the young age of the people in the sample.) The headaches occurred at least once a month for 90% of the people and several times a month for 60% of them. The headaches were generally short, lasting less than 6 hours. The first headaches had occurred early in life, 40% of the individuals having experienced them before the age of 13. Most headaches were severe, and 65% of the responders said that they were unbearable and prevented daily activities.

Another survey of a nonclinical population used a sample of almost 2,000 people in government jobs (Henryk-Gutt & Rees 1973). Four groups of 50 people each (25 women and 25 men) were constructed from the responders. One group had classic migraine headaches as defined by a neurological prodrome, unilateral headache, and nausea and/or vomiting. A second group had common migraine headaches; there was no prodrome, but the other criteria were met. A third group had headaches not meeting the criteria for common migraines, and a fourth group rarely experienced headaches, having two or less per year. There were no con-

161

sistent differences between the responses of males and females in any group, and consequently the results are pooled in the following discussion. The migraine headaches were much more severe than the nonmigraine ones. In both migraine groups, almost everyone experienced nausea; over half reported that they had to go to bed when the headache occurred and that they had consulted a doctor about the headache. In contrast, people in the nonmigraine headache group never experienced nausea or had to go to bed; fewer than 20% of them had consulted a doctor about their headaches.

All of the above data suggest that migraine headaches, defined as those preceded by a prodrome and having a unilateral onset, are generally more severe than tension headaches. The question, then, is whether the associated symptoms of nausea, vomiting, having to go to bed, neurological disorders, and consulting a physician are due to the difference in the type of headache (migraine vs. tension) or just to the intensity of the head pain (severe vs. moderate). Wolff (1948, p. 24) commented that head pain symptoms by themselves may not be good diagnostic signs for the type of headache because the quality of pain may be the same for different causes of headaches. A similar point of view has been expressed by Waters (1974) who conducted a survey of residents in Pontypridd, Wales. A total of 491 males and 741 females responded. Headache intensity was rated on a 7 point scale. There was a strong positive correlation between the severity of the headache and the symptoms of unilateral headache, preceded by a prodrome and accompanied by nausea and vomiting. For those with very mild headaches, 30% had unilateral headaches, 5% had a prodrome, and 20% experienced nausea. For those with almost unbearable headaches, 55% had unilateral headaches, 65% had a prodrome, and 75% experienced nausea. This correlation suggests a continuum of headache intensity, with tension headaches at one end and migraine headaches at the other, rather than a discrete division into two categories.

Furthermore, the individual symptoms thought to be characteristic of migraine headaches are not closely related to each other. The survey study of Waters (1974) just discussed provides some data relevant to this issue. If migraine headaches form a discrete category, then the symptoms characteristic of them should be highly correlated with each other. Such was not the case, however; 38% of the people who had unilateral head pain never had prodromes or nausea, 26% of those who had prodromes never had unilateral head pain or nausea, and 27% of those who had nausea never had unilateral head pain or prodromes. Thus, approximately one-third of those who had one of these symptoms did not have the other two, indicating that they were not highly correlated with each other, at least in the general population.

Even in a clinical setting, the symptoms of migraine headaches were not highly correlated when a factor analysis was used to examine their interrelationship (Ziegler and others 1972). Patients reporting to a clinic were given a self-administered questionnaire which listed different symptoms, asked whether each one was present, and requested some other specific information. A principal components analysis was conducted on the answers to the questionnaire to determine if particular sets of symptoms appeared in clusters. If migraine headaches constitute a homogeneous syndrome, then the symptoms of migraine headaches ought to be highly correlated with each other and not with those of tension headaches. This pattern of correlations should produce independent factors, one characterizing headaches of the tension type, the other characterizing headaches of the migraine type. The results of the principal components analysis produced five factors that were composed of different combinations of the symptoms on the questionnaire. One factor resulted from positive responses to the statements that the headache was of long duration and was present all the time. This factor had two of the characteristics often described for tension headaches and did not include any of the three symptoms characteristic of migraine headaches; it may be thought of as a tension headache factor because of this grouping. The symptoms of "pain in the neck" did not correlate with this factor, however. Three other factors appeared to be migraine factors. One included symptoms of unilateral head pain and pain above the eye, while another included nausea before and during the headache. These two factors were independent of each other, suggesting a separation of these two sets of symptoms (as was also seen in Friedman and others 1954). Both of these factors were significantly correlated with relief by ergotamine. In the sample at large, 15% of the patients had their head pain reduced by ergotamine; of the patients with these two clusters of symptoms, 26% of them had their head pain reduced by ergotamine. The third factor included symptoms of neurological disorders (sensory, motor, or speech disturbances) before, during, or after the headache. This factor may be thought of as a third migraine factor because of the prodromal symptoms, or it might be thought of as a factor indicating the general severity of the headache, independent of its other characteristics. In any case, the independence of these factors indicates that these three clusters of symptoms were not highly correlated with each other, as would be expected if migraine headaches formed a discrete diagnostic category.

Correlations among these three variables in a clinical setting may often appear to be greater than those reported above, but such a correlation may be a spurious result of the clinical bias of the sample. People with migraine headaches are more likely to consult a physician than those with other types of headaches. If severity is associated with gastrointestinal illness and neurological difficulties, then these will obviously be correlated with the head pain symptoms that brought the patient to the clinic. In short, sampling from a clinical population increases the likelihood of finding individuals with severe migraine headaches. The milder cases, in which only a single symptom occurs, are likely to be overlooked.

The variability of migraine headaches is reflected in the title of Friedman (1970): "The (infinite) variety of migraine." Current research emphasizes the need to state explicitly the criteria used to describe a headache as a migraine. Furthermore, the relative independence of the symptoms characterizing migraine has appeared in the operational definitions used to place a person in a migraine group. These definitions often specify a set of symptoms and then classify an individual on the basis of some subset of the symptoms. For example, Ekbom and others (1978) listed four symptoms characteristic of migraine headaches and placed an individual in the migraine group if the person had any two of them. A similar procedure was used by Price and Tursky (1976) who required the presence of any two of six migraine symptoms.

Taken together, the evidence reviewed above demonstrates that some people have severe headaches that meet the usual criteria for classical migraines: unilateral onset, preceded by a prodrome, associated with nausea and/or vomiting, and with a family history of similar symptoms. But the existence of a discrete diagnostic category based on the presence of these three symptoms remains to be demonstrated. If more data support this point of view, then speaking of migraine symptoms may be more useful than speaking of migraine headaches. For the present, however, we shall continue to use the term migraine headache to describe a headache with a particular subset of symptoms, realizing, however, that a better descriptive scheme may appear in the future.

MECHANISM

Both the prodromes and the head pain of migraine headaches are associated with pathological changes in the vascular system supplying blood to the brain. Prodromes follow a chain of events which begins with a massive constriction of the intracranial arteries. This in turn reduces the blood supply to nerve cells in the brain to such an extent that they become ischemic and unable to function normally. The symptoms of the prodrome reflect the areas of the brain in which the nerve cells are most severely impaired. The subsequent head pain begins with a rebound vasodilation. As the arteries expand, they stimulate stretch receptors surrounding them, which then produce the pain.

That vasodilation of the intracranial arteries can produce pain was demonstrated in patients who had their brains exposed for a surgical operation (Ray & Wolff 1940). The patients had sufficient anesthesia to control the pain associated with the operation itself but were still conscious and able to communicate with the surgeons about their sensations. Pain was reported when the brain arteries were dilated either by pulling on them with surgical threads or by injecting saline into them. The pain was described as deep, aching, and diffuse and was often accompanied by nausea. In contrast, no pain was reported when intracranial arteries were constricted by the application of drugs. These data indicate that vasodilation, but not vasoconstriction, of intracranial arteries is sufficient to produce pain.

The critical role of intracranial vasodilation in producing the head pain of a migraine was suggested by a variety of experiments which restricted the blood supply to the head and alleviated the head pain. A simple procedure was to use pressure on the carotid artery in the neck. If the carotid artery on the side of the head pain was occluded by this pressure, the head pain often decreased or disappeared; if the carotid artery on the side opposite from the head pain was occluded, the head pain was generally unaffected (Wolff 1948). Vasoconstriction produced by drugs, particularly ergotamine tartrate, often alleviated the head pain. Importantly, the time course of vasoconstriction and that of reduction of head pain closely paralleled each other. Also, supporting the idea that excessive vasodilation was the source of head pain was the presence of throbbing sensations accompanying the head pain. Each increase in head pain was associated with the contraction of the heart, producing an increase in blood pressure and further vasodilation. The throbbing characteristic by itself is not critical here, because it could be due to a variety of different mechanisms. What is important is that the throbbing is synchronized with the heart beat (Kunkle 1959). Thus, the idea that the head pain phase of migraine headaches was associated with vasodilation was supported by two pieces of data. First, production of vasodilation could generate head pain. Second, elimination of vasodilation could reduce the head pain.

Systematic data supporting the vascular hypothesis of migraine headaches have been gathered by studying the state of the arterial blood supply to the brain. Two approaches have been used. The first is indirect. It examines the state of the extracranial arteries, the ones that go to the scalp, and then makes inferences about the intracranial arteries, the ones that go to the brain. This analysis assumes that the extracranial and intracranial systems function together so that the state of the extracranial system accurately reflects the state of the intracranial system. Such an assumption may be incorrect (see Research Considerations later in this chapter), and the indirect approach to the measurement of intra-cranial blood flow may seem cumbersome, but until recently, direct measurement was possible only with neurosurgical procedures which exposed the brain, and these techniques could not be justified except in unusual cases. In any case, the extracranial measurements address some important questions about the reactions of the vascular system in people who have migraine headaches.

A second method of analyzing the intracranial blood flow is more direct. Radioactive substances are placed in the blood supply until the brain is uniformly saturated. The administration of radioactivity is stopped, and the rapidity with which the radioactivity leaves the brain is measured. This *clearance rate* is taken as a measure of blood flow; the faster the rate at which the radioactivity leaves, the greater the blood flow. There are two advantages of this technique. First, it avoids making an assumption about the relationship of the intracranial and extracranial blood supply. Second, it allows an examination of the blood flow in restricted portions of the brain. This regional analysis of blood flow is much more discrete than was ever possible with the extracranial approach and has been particularly useful because the areas in which there is the greatest change in blood flow can be related to the patient's sensory or motor symptoms during the prodrome.

Extracranial Blood Flow

Extracranial blood flow is measured indirectly, usually with a thermistor or photoplethysmograph as described earlier in Chapter 6. Both of these procedures assume that there is some quantitative relationship between blood flow on the one hand and the temperature of the skin or the volume of the body part on the other. The precise nature of this relationship remains to be established, but the assumption of its existence is probably correct.

Results from experiments using extracranial measurements provide support for the vascular hypothesis of migraine headaches. During the prodrome, the extracranial blood supply is relatively vasoconstricted and during the head pain it is relatively vasodilated. Furthermore, there is a general relationship between the side of the head on which these vascular changes take place and the side of the body on which the symptoms appear. A second contribution of these experiments is to describe the ways in which the vascular reactions of migraine patients differ from those of other people. First, there is a chronic vasoconstriction, reflected in cold hands and feet. Second, the response to events that produce vasoconstriction is normal or enhanced, while the response to events that produce vasodilation is attenuated. Third, the state of the vascular system is relatively unstable and may fluctuate widely between vasoconstriction and vasodilation.

One measure of the state of the extracranial vascular supply is the amplitude of the bulge in the temporal artery as the pulse of blood from a heart beat passes through the artery (Tunis and Wolff 1952). This *pulse wave amplitude* was measured in the right temporal artery of ten patients with symptoms characteristic of migraine headaches. During a two-week period in which no headaches occurred, the average pulse wave amplitude was 26 mm. During the head pain phase of a migraine, it increased 65% to 43 mm, indicating a substantial vasodilation. Other experiments pointing out the close relationship between head pain and vasodilation showed that head pain was enhanced by a variety of procedures which increased blood flow and was reduced by procedures that decreased blood flow. The pulse wave amplitudes of migraineurs were also more variable than those of the controls, particularly during the few days immediately prior to a migraine attack.

People who suffer from migraine headaches may have a general tendency to produce and/or maintain vasoconstriction when not having headaches. The anecdotal reports of migraine patients having cold hands and feet support this idea of a chronic vasoconstriction, at least in the extracranial blood supply (Wolff 1948, p. 593). Measurements of pulse wave amplitudes, however, have not always provided confirming evidence (Tunis & Wolff 1952).

The vascular system of migraine patients reacts differently from that of normal people to events producing vasoconstriction or vasodilation. Blood flow was measured in the right index finger and the right temporal artery of nine migraineurs (Appenzeller 1969). Two stimuli were presented. The first was heat on the chest, an event that would be expected to produce vasodilation. A group of unspecified control people responded to this stimulus within 40 seconds with vasodilation. Of seven migraine patients, only two showed normal vasodilation in the scalp, and only five showed increased blood flow in the finger. A second stimulus was designed to produce vasoconstriction. Here the person's feet were placed in an ice water bath, or the person was asked to carry out mental arithmetic or take a single deep breath. All these events produced the expected vasoconstriction, of similar magnitude in both groups, indicating that the vasoconstrictor mechanism in the migraine patients was operating normally. Taken together these results suggest a vasomotor disturbance so that migraine patients may vasoconstrict normally but then remain in the vasoconstricted state for an extended period of time because they do not vasodilate appropriately.

Another procedure measured reflex vasodilation to a heat stimulus (Elliott and others 1974). Females reporting a throbbing head pain on one side of the head accompanied by nausea and/or vomiting and preceded by visual disturbances were given a reflexive vasodilation test. One arm was placed in a water bath at 44°C. The heat elimination from the opposite arm was taken as a measure of the amount of vasodilation in response to the heat stimulus. The migraine patients consistently had a smaller response than normals, showing that their vasodilation in response to the heat stimulus was less than in normals.

Further data suggesting a hyperactive vasoconstricting reflex in migraine patients comes from an examination of the vascular response to posture changes (Wennerholm 1961). The patients were 28 individuals who reported a unilateral throbbing headache usually accompanied by vomiting and/or nausea and preceded by a prodrome. The control group was composed of 30 individuals who did not have headaches. The pulse wave amplitude of the frontotemporal branch of the temporal artery was recorded while the individuals were in a horizontal position and then after they moved to an upright position. Both groups had a reduction in the magnitude of the pulse wave amplitude when moving from horizontal to upright, as would be expected. But the decrease for the migraine patients was substantially greater than that for the control group, indicating that for the same stimulus the magnitude of vasoconstriction was greater in those who suffered headaches than in the controls.

A relative propensity towards vasoconstriction on the part of migraineurs was also found in a biofeedback study (Price & Tursky 1976). A group of people suffering from migraines was recruited by a newspaper ad. In order to qualify for the migraine group, a person had to have at least two of the following symptoms: unilateral headache, throbbing pain, prodrome of some kind, nausea and/or vomiting, cyclic vomiting in childhood, family history of migraine. Vascular changes were recorded with a photoelectric back scatter technique which used fiber optic light guides to detect relative changes in total blood volume and blood pulse volume. A reflectance photoplethysmograph was placed over the superficial temporal artery, on the painful side of those people with unilateral headaches and on the left side for all others. All participants were given analogue and binary visual feedback and instructed to increase the temperature of the left hand during a single biofeedback session consisting of 16 two-minute periods. The people in the control group raised their skin temperature slightly during the last part of the experiment, in contrast to those in the migraine group who actually had a slight decrease in skin temperature during the same time. Thus, the migraine group was unable to produce a vasodilation as readily as the control group. An additional finding was a positive correlation between blood flow in the hands and blood flow in the temporal artery. This correlation was .79 for the control group and .67 for the migraine group.

Thus whatever vasodilation was produced in the hand as a result of the biofeedback was accompanied by vasodilation of the temporal artery, and the magnitude of this effect was the same for both groups.

These experiments provide support for the constriction-dilation hypothesis of prodrome and head pain in migraineurs. During the prodrome, the extracranial blood supply was relatively vasoconstricted, and during the head pain it was relatively vasodilated. Furthermore, there was a general relationship between the side of the head on which these vascular changes took place and the side of the prodromal symptoms and the head pain, although this relationship was not perfect. The data also suggest that the vascular system of migraine patients is generally unstable and relatively prone to vasoconstriction (Atkinson 1976; Wolff 1948). This chronic vasoconstriction seems to result from two factors. First, stimuli that produce vasodilation in people without migraine headaches produce little if any change in people with migraine headaches. Second, stimuli that produce vasoconstriction are still effective. The result, of course, is that every time the vascular system moves towards a relatively vasoconstricted state, it tends to stay there until a migraine attack occurs.

Intracranial Blood Flow

Recent developments with radioactive materials allow direct measurement of intracranial blood flow. Radioactive material is placed in the blood stream either directly through an arterial injection or indirectly through respiration. Scintillation counters are placed on the outside of the head to measure the rapidity with which the radioactivity disappears; the more rapid the disappearance, the greater the blood flow. These techniques confirm the results previously described from extracranial techniques, indicating that there is decreased blood flow through the brain during the prodrome, and increased blood flow during the head pain. They also provide new information about the localization of changes in blood flow with respect to the various types of symptoms reported by the individual. For the reader who wishes to pursue this topic, there are two good general sources. One was published in *Scientific American* (Lassen and others 1978) and describes the inhalation procedure. The second is a symposium covering many aspects of both the inhalation and the injection procedures and appears in *Acta Neurologica Scandanavica, Supplementum 14,* 1965. A comprehensive bibliography may be found in Obrist, Thompson, King, and Wang (1967), and in Obrist, Thompson, Wang, and Wilkinson (1975).

The radioactive materials used are either ^{133}Xe or ^{85}Kr. These substances have a short half-life and can be used in doses small enough to minimize risks for the individual being examined. They produce some X-ray (25.5 to 38.5 kiloelectron volts) radiation and considerable soft gamma-ray (67.5 to 94.5 kiloelectron volts) radiation (Isbister and others 1966; Sakai & Meyer 1978). They may be injected directly into the blood stream or inhaled. For injection, about 5 microcuries of the radioactive substance are suspended in saline (or some other medium) and injected into an artery supplying the head. For inhalation, a cylinder of radio-active gas is attached to an inhalation device, usually one used for anesthesia. The amount of radioactivity received by the person in the experiment is controlled by the relative concentrations of the radioactive gas and room air in the mixture that is breathed and the length of time this mixture is breathed. The person usually breathes the radioactive gas for one or two minutes and then stops. The inhalation technique gives results that are correlated with those of the injection technique, but the clearance rates tend to be longer and the resulting estimates of blood flow lower than those found with injections (Jensen and others 1966).

The amount of radioactivity is measured by scintillation counters placed around the head. The counters are very thin disks sensitive to the amount of radiation striking them. They can be placed over different portions of the brain and focused so that each one receives activity from only a small area, sometimes no more than one cm^2, beneath it. By this means, the distribution of the radioactivity in different brain areas can be examined.

The analysis of clearance rates is somewhat complex. One variable that needs to be considered is the contribution from the extracranial blood supply (Mallett & Veall 1965; Oldendorf 1969; Sakai & Meyer 1978). A second factor has to do with the metabolic rates of different por-tions of the brain. Particularly important here is the difference between the gray matter, containing cell bodies, and the white matter, containing myelinated axons. Most of the cell's metabolism takes place in the cell body, rather than the axon, and *blood flow rates* in the gray matter, in-dicated as F_g, are considerably greater than those in the white matter, indicated as F_w. Typically, F_g is about 90 ml/100gm/min while F_w is about 20ml/100gm/min (Ingvar and others 1965; Mathew and others 1976; Obrist and others 1967; Obrist and others 1975).

Accurate determination of the blood flow in any particular region of the brain must consider the relative proportion of gray and white matter in that region. Overall, both the inhalation and injection procedures suggest that the brain is composed of about 55% gray matter, a figure compatible with that drawn from autopsy material (see Hoedt-Rasmus-sen and others 1966). The flow rate for any given brain area is indicated as rCBF, standing for *regional cerebral blood flow*. It is calculated by multiplying the F_g and F_w by the relative proportion of gray matter and white matter, respectively, in that area. Because rCBF is made up of both F_g and F_w components, its value is always less than that of F_g and greater than that of F_w and is usually about 50 ml/100gm/min. In the sections that follow, the flow rates will always be given as either F_g or rCBF, as is appropriate. The particular measure used by any one given study is of little importance, but comparisons between studies must be made carefully because F_g and rCBF have different values. In order to save space, only the numerical values will be presented; the units are always ml/100gm/min.

As predicted by the vascular hypothesis, intracranial blood flow during the prodrome of a migraine is generally reduced, often to critical levels. In one patient, the prodrome consisted of a tactile disturbance in the right hand and difficulty speaking (Skinhøj & Paulson 1969). The rCBF in the left parietal and temporal lobes was about 50% of that observed when the same individual did not have a headache. More extensive data come from a group of 32 females with unilateral head pain, usually on the left side, and a family history of migraine (Simard & Paulson 1973). An injection procedure was used and rCBF determined for the left side of the brain. When the migraineurs were not having headaches, the rCBF was 43, within normal limits. When a prodrome was present, however, rCBF decreased to 21, about 50% of the normal value. Similar results were found in another group of three migraineurs (Mathew and others 1976). When no headache was present, rCBF was about 47 and F_g about 75, values similar to those found for control patients who did not have headaches. During the prodromes experienced by these patients, rCBF decreased to 35 and F_g decreased to 54.

The vascular hypothesis also predicts vasodilation during the head pain phase of a migraine attack, and blood flow increases of about 50% are typically found at this time. Thirteen migraineurs, when without headaches, had a mean rCBF of 47 and a mean F_g of 76, values which were essentially normal (Mathew and others 1976). During the head pain of a migraine, rCBF increased to 57 and F_g to 108. These increases in blood flow were general and occurred over the entire brain. Similar increases were found in 39 people who had migraines as defined by the Ad Hoc Committee (1962). When without a headache, the migraineurs had an F_g of 81, a value only slightly less than that of 84 found for people who did not have headaches (Sakai & Meyer 1978). During the head pain of a migraine attack, F_g increased to 109 and remained elevated at 97 for up to 48 hours afterwards. For another patient, the rCBF without headaches was 55, while during the head pain phase it was 81, an increase of 50% (Skinhøj & Paulson 1969). Six patients with complicated migraines and four with common migraines had an increase of about 50% in rCBF during head pain to a value of 63 (Skinhøj 1973). Breathing rates also increased during the headache but not enough to produce the observed change in blood flow. In all these studies, cerebral blood flow increased substantially during the head pain phase of a migraine attack, demonstrating an intracranial vasodilation which parallels the extracranial vasodilation discussed earlier.

Because intracranial measures can determine blood flow in restricted areas of the cortex, they can be used to ask more detailed questions about the mechanism of migraine headaches than was possible with the extracranial measurements. The vascular hypothesis predicts that there ought to be a close correlation between the types of symptoms exhibited during a prodrome and the areas of the brain in which the greatest reductions in blood flow occur. For example, if an individual experiences a scotoma in the left visual field, then the greatest decrease in blood flow should be found in the right occipital cortex, an area of the brain which processes information from the left visual field. The available data support this type of correlation.

In one patient (Skinhøj & Paulson 1969), the prodromal symptoms were tactile and motor disturbances in the right hand, and speech and language difficulties, symptoms characteristically found after damage to the left parietal and temporal lobes. Cerebral blood flow was reduced throughout the brain during the prodrome, but the greatest reduction was in the parietal and temporal lobes. For two other patients, the prodrome was characterized by sensory and motor disturbances in the left arm. In one patient, there was a substantial reduction of F_g to 52 in the right post central gyrus. In the second patient, the greatest reduction in F_g (77) was not as large, but it was localized in the right parietal lobe. Both the right post central gyrus and the right parietal lobe are cortical areas normally functioning to provide information about the sense of touch in the left arm. Similar results were found with prodromes that included: (a) sensory and motor disturbances of the right hand and difficulty in speech, (b) visual disturbances, (c) abnormal tactile sensations in the right arm, and (d) visual disturbances accompanied by abnormal tactile sensations on the left side of the body (Skinhøj 1973). In each case, the author reports that the reduction of cerebral blood flow was greatest in the cortical area related to the symptoms, although no quantitative data are provided to evaluate his statement. These results show that during the prodrome, in addition to the generalized reduction in cerebral blood flow, there are highly localized changes of greater magnitude. The sites of the intense local ischemia correlate well with the behavioral symptoms observed during the prodrome, although there are a few exceptions to this rule (Mathew and others 1976).

The intracranial procedures can evaluate another prediction of the vascular hypothesis, this one concerning the head pain phase of the attack. Here, the side of the brain which has the greatest increase in blood flow ought to be the side of the head which hurts, assuming that the headache begins unilaterally as is usually the case. Few data are available on this point. For one group of patients with classic migraines, the greatest increase in blood flow usually occurred in the brain on the side of the body associated with the head pain (Sakai & Meyer 1978). However, this wasn't always the case, and the authors present no quantitative data to allow the extent of the correlation to be determined. Consequently, the data from the head pain phase of migraine headaches support the vascular hypothesis of migraines in a general way, showing that during the head pain, there is a substantial increase in blood flow. The specificity of the increases in blood flow and their relationship to the symptoms of the head pain remain to be demonstrated.

The intracranial blood flow studies can provide data relevant to other aspects of the mechanisms of migraine headaches. For example, a diagnostic distinction was drawn between classic migraines which are preceded by a prodrome and common migraines which are not. The vascular hypothesis of migraine headaches makes two predictions. First, common migraines should not be preceded by vasoconstriction, or if they are, the vasoconstriction should not be as great as that found during the prodrome of classic migraines. Second, during the head pain phase, which is similar for both types of headaches, there should be an equivalent increase in blood flow. Sakai and Meyer (1978) present data comparing the cerebral blood flows of patients with either common or classic migraines. No data are available from the preheadache phase of the people with common migraines, so the first prediction could not be tested. During the head pain phase, however, increases in cerebral blood flow were the same for both types of headaches, indicating that they do share a common mechanism at this point.

Another diagnostic distinction in migraine headaches is that between classic migraines and cluster headaches. The head pain of cluster headaches is similar to that of classic migraines, but the headaches are shorter than classic migraines and occur in groups. Patients with classic migraines and cluster headaches had substantial vasodilation during the head pain phase of the migraine (Sakai & Meyer 1978). However, the recovery from this vasodilation took place much faster in people with cluster headaches, reflecting the relatively shorter duration of the headache. A second difference between the cluster headaches and the migraine headaches was the degree to which the side of the head pain was correlated with the hemisphere having the greatest vasodilation. As described previously for classic migraines, the hemisphere associated with the head pain was usually the one in which the greatest increase in blood flow occurred. Such was not the case for cluster headaches; the most extensive increase in cerebral blood flow often took place in the hemisphere not associated with the head pain.

One other diagnostic category is that of complicated migraine. Unlike classic migraines, where the prodromal symptoms disappear as the head pain begins, complicated migraines are associated with neurological symptoms which persist throughout the headache and even after its termination. Cerebral blood flows should reflect this simultaneous occurrence of head pain and neurological symptoms with a general vasodilation throughout the brain intermixed with restricted sites of vasoconstriction, the particular site being predicted on the basis of the type of neurological symptoms. One patient with complicated migraine experienced both head pain and a loss of sensation in the left arm (Sakai & Meyer 1978). Blood flow throughout the brain was normal or increased with exception of the right parietal lobe, where the F_g was 59, reduced 14% below normal. Although this reduction was not as great as that found in the prodromes described previously, the pattern of the cerebral blood flow was that expected from the vascular hypothesis, and this pattern is important. Three other patients also exhibited simultaneous head pain and neurological symptoms (Mathew and others 1976). The cerebral blood flow in these individuals had marked increases of F_g to 459 in some areas and isolated areas of decreases to 7 in others. No comments were made about the relationship of the prodromal symptoms to the site of vasoconstriction.

Figure 9–1 illustrates the type of analysis that has been carried out with intracranial cerebral blood flow and demonstrates one of the patterns of blood flow found in a young woman with complicated migraine 18 hours after the head pain had subsided. The diagrams outline the left half and right half of the brain on the left and right sides of the figure, respectively. Each circle indicates an area of the brain from which F_g was measured, and the large figures within the circles give the results of that measurement in ml/100 g brain/min. Normal values were 84 ml/ 100 g brain/min for the left hemisphere and 82 ml/100 g brain/min for the right. In the left hemisphere F_g was slightly elevated throughout the brain. In the right hemisphere F_g was near normal with the exception of one area over the parietal lobe which was only 59 ml/100 g brain/min. At the time of the measurement, the patient said that she still did not have normal feelings in her left hand, a deficit commonly associated with damage to the right parietal lobe. Thus the localized change in F_g was highly correlated with the neurological symptoms persisting at the time of measurement (Sakai & Meyer 1978).

Overall, the studies examining intracranial blood flow provide important additions to the earlier work on extracranial blood flow. First, they offer direct and strong support for the vascular hypothesis that was derived largely from indirect measurements of extracranial blood flow.

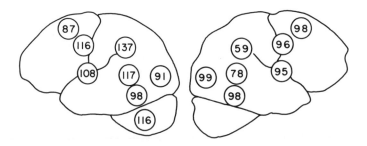

Left Hemisphere
Normal Mean = 84

Right Hemisphere
Normal Mean = 82

FIGURE 9–1   Intracerebral Blood Flow in a Woman with Complicated Migraine Who Had a Loss of Sensation in Her Left Hand 18 Hours After a Headache.

The site of the greatest decrease in intracerebral blood flow is the right parietal lobe, an area of the brain normally responsible for providing information about touch in the left hand. The drawing on the left represents the left hemisphere (with the front towards the left) while the drawing on the right represents the right hemisphere (with the front facing towards the right). The number in each circle describes the cerebral blood flow at that location in terms of Fg; the units are ml/100 g brain weight/minute. In the left hemisphere, Fg was slightly elevated from the normal value of 84 in all locations. In the right hemisphere, Fg was also slightly elevated with the exception of one spot in the parietal lobe where it was 59, a value significantly lower than that normally found. This localized reduction of blood flow was reflected in the specific symptoms of loss of sensation in the left hand. *(Adapted from F. Sakai and J. S. Meyer, 1978. In* Headache, *18 (1978), p. 126. Used by permission.)*

Second, and perhaps more important, the intracranial studies examine regional changes and address questions of localization that cannot be addressed by the extracranial approaches. Here, even though the data are limited, many specific points of the vascular hypothesis have received support:

1. The areas of the brain in which the greatest reduction of blood flow occurs during the prodrome are those associated with the symptoms of the prodrome.
2. The side of the hemisphere in which the greatest increase in blood flow occurs during the head pain is the one on which the head pain occurs.
3. The differentiation among types of migraines made on the basis of symptom patterns is generally supported by similarities and differences in the patterns of blood flow during the headache.

The one point on which the intracranial and extracranial studies do not seem to agree is the state of the vascular system when the individual is not experiencing a headache. The extracranial studies suggest that migraineurs have a chronic vasoconstriction, reflected in generally cold hands and feet and a relative refractoriness to vasodilatory stimuli. The intracranial studies, on the other hand, suggest that blood flow between headaches is relatively normal. This apparent contradiction is in need of resolution, which can easily be accomplished by obtaining intracranial and extracranial measurements of blood flow simultaneously. One outcome of such a study would be the demonstration that the two results are not mutually exclusive, and that between headaches the intracranial vasculature is normal while the extracranial vasculature is constricted. Other outcomes are also possible but are probably not worth debating because a little bit of data will go a long way in determining the actual state of affairs.

Diet

Many migraineurs say that some aspect of their diet triggers their headaches. For example, missing meals may be followed by headaches (Blau & Pyke 1970; Critchley 1933; Dexter and others 1978; Wilkinson 1949). One group of 12 people who had throbbing head pain associated with nausea and/or vomiting and photophobia followed their normal eating habits during a control period (Blau & Cummings 1966). During a fasting period, they were told to eat no food between 10 P.M. of the first day and 5:00 P.M. of the second; tea, coffee, and water were permitted. Headache intensity was rated from 0 to 4 each hour the person was awake. Six of the 12 people developed headaches. For five of them, the headache began before noon on the second day and grew to maximum intensity by 6:00 P.M. The sixth person did not have a headache until 7:00 P.M. but it grew to maximum intensity within the next two hours. The authors say that the headaches were typical of the ones the individuals normally experienced. Blood sugar levels, which were also examined, were not good predictors of headache activity.

Specific foods are often thought to elicit migraine headaches. Chocolate, red wine, and cheese are often mentioned, as well as idiosyncratic food items that appear to be important for a particular individual (Dalton 1975; Hanington 1967; Hanington & Harper 1968; Mathew and others 1976; Medina & Diamond 1978; Ryan 1974). Removing these food items from the diet helped alleviate migraines for people who were willing to try the diet and follow it for at least three months (Unger & Unger 1952). Complete relief was obtained for 65% of the participants, and partial relief, for an additional 20%.

One substance found in chocolate, red wine, and fermented cheese is tyramine. It produces vasoconstriction directly and through the release of norepinephrine, another substance which produces vasoconstriction (Ghose and others 1978). One of the first investigations of the role of tyramine in migraine headaches used both a placebo and a tyramine capsule to control for any effects of patient expectations (Hanington 1967; Hanington & Harper 1968). The participants in the study were 15 people with migraine headaches. They were selected from 240 people who were sent a questionnaire and replied that chocolate, cheese, fruits, and alcohol were among the items that precipitated a migraine attack. Capsules were sent by mail. One capsule contained lactose, a control substance, while the other contained 100 mg of tyramine. Each person took at least two capsules (some took more) and indicated whether or not a headache occurred afterwards. The data were convincing; 86% of the people had headaches following tyramine, while only 13% had headaches following the control capsule.

Subsequent tests of the ability of tyramine to elicit migraine headaches have not produced consistent results, and the number of people reporting headaches after tyramine is not as high as in the studies mentioned above, especially when the baseline frequency of headaches in control procedures is considered (Ghose and others 1978; Medina & Diamond 1978; Ryan 1974; Smith and others 1970; Zeigler and others 1976). There are two problems for the tyramine hypothesis. First, the effects of tyramine on headache activity have been small even for those people who say that headaches are triggered by substances containing tyramine. Second, orally ingested tyramine may have little or no metabolic effect, suggesting that it does not get absorbed in sufficient quantities to produce the required vascular changes (Shaw and others 1978). These experiments have by no means completely ruled out tyramine as a factor influencing migraine headaches, but further research is required to document its effects conclusively.

Although migraineurs reliably report that certain foods trigger their headaches, controlled studies suggest that the critical variable may not be the food itself. For example, consider chocolate, red wine, and cheese, three food items commonly mentioned as producing headaches. These are not commonly eaten at every meal but appear most frequently at dinner and especially on weekends and at parties. Consequently, a headache following the ingestion of these foods may be due more to the social activities associated with them than to the foods themselves. The expectations of the person eating the food may also influence headache activity (Jessup 1978). If on some previous occasion a headache occurred after a meal, the headache may be associated with the food eaten at that meal even though it occurred for reasons unrelated to the food. At subsequent meals the person may expect to have a headache after eating similar foods, and this expectation may increase the probability that a headache actually occurs. Evaluating the role of the food eaten, independently of the context in which it is eaten or the expectations of the eater, requires a well-controlled experimental design. Two types of meals are required, one having a great deal of the food thought to trigger the headache, one having very little. The food must be disguised in such a way that the person doesn't know what is being eaten. The pattern of meals and the circumstances in which they are eaten must be consistent.

When some of these controls are instituted, food appears to have little effect on headache activity (Moffett and others 1974). The participants were 25 patients with classic migraines who said that chocolate precipitated the migraine attacks. Two sets of candies were created, similar in appearance, texture, and taste. One set contained chocolate; the other did not. The participants were sent one type of candy and then the other. They were told to eat the candy (there was no check for compliance with this instruction) and to record headache activity for 48 hours. The data were analyzed in terms of the presence or absence of a headache (of unspecified intensity) during this time. Some people had headaches after eating the candy without chocolate (24% in Experiment 1, 29% in Experiment 2). These headaches may have been in response to eating the candy, or they may have been just at baseline frequency. In any case, the effect of chocolate (rather than just eating the candy or some other uncontrolled factor) must be measured by headache activity greater than that found in the control condition. In Experiment 1, 36% of the people had headaches in response to chocolate while 24% had headaches in response to the placebo, an increase of only 12%. In Experiment 2, a similar result was found: 43% had a headache following chocolate while 29% had a headache following the placebo, an increase of only 14%. Equally significant is the number of times that a headache did not appear following chocolate; all these people said that chocolate caused their headaches, but the majority of them (64% and 57%, respectively) had no headache following chocolate. These data provide little support for the idea that chocolate produces migraines, and question the ability of patients to identify what foods (if any) are associated with their migraines.

Similar results were found in an investigation of the influence of tyramine on headache activity in 31 migraineurs whose headaches were thought to be related to their diet, and in 35 migraineurs whose headaches were thought to be unrelated to their diet (Ryan 1974). The patients took two capsules. One contained tyramine; the other was a placebo. Headache activity was recorded during the following 24 hours. Tyramine had either a small effect (Experiment 1) or no effect at all (Experiments 2 and 3), even for those who said that chocolate and alcohol precipitated their headaches. Furthermore, headaches often followed the placebo capsule, and the percentage of people having headaches was greater for those who thought that food caused their headaches (52%) than for those who thought food was irrelevant (34%). The authors provided no information about headache frequency in a baseline condition in which the participants ate their normal diet, and this omission limits the interpretation of these data. However, the headache frequency following the placebo seems unusually high, and the greater frequency of headaches in the people who thought they had food-related migraines suggests that they were even more susceptible to expectations about food-related migraines than people in the other group.

The evidence reviewed here highlights the need for well-designed and well-controlled studies of the role of specific foods in producing migraines. Although patient reports may indicate a strong link between eating a specific food and having a headache, these reports are probably biased in at least three ways. First, the settings in which particular foods are eaten differ, so that the psychological circumstances surrounding the eating may be more important than the substance eaten. Second, the times when food was followed by a headache are likely to stand out to a much greater extent than the times when a headache did not occur, producing a consistent overestimation of the correlation between food and the headache. Third, once an individual has had a headache after eating a certain food, an expectation may develop increasing the likelihood of a headache whenever the food is eaten again. The positive results of uncontrolled studies may be influenced by a number of these and other factors. Some of them are relatively uninteresting, such as the unreliability of the patient's report. Others, however, may help identify nondietary factors that trigger headaches. Until additional experiments can provide further information on the relative influence of these and other factors, the additional contribution of specific foods must remain in question.

TREATMENT

Biofeedback treatment of migraine headaches has trained people to raise the skin temperature of a finger or increase the blood flow to a hand. A thermistor is used to record skin temperature, or a photoplethysmograph to record blood flow (see Chapter 5). Biofeedback sessions are held one or more times weekly along with daily home practice or relaxation. Headache activity has been markedly reduced, but the amount of time required for successful treatment is generally longer than that for tension headaches and may take up to several months.

The procedures and results of 16 published studies are summarized in

Table 9–2. The table indicates that substantial reductions in migraine activity have occurred within 3 to 14 weeks after biofeedback training was begun, even for people with a long history of severe headaches. Ten studies used skin temperature feedback, and most incorporated home practice into their treatment. Four included practice of the biofeedback skill at the first sign of a headache. Those studies reporting changes in skin temperature found an inverse relationship between skin temperature and headache activity; as skin temperature increased, headache activity decreased.

Case Study A

A female graduate student, 21 years of age, came to the clinic having had a history of increasingly severe and frequent migraines for a period of a year (Olton and others 1979). She was behind in her school work and had considered dropping out of school because of the disabling nature of the headaches. A previous examination by a physician indicated no neurological problems. Her hands were extremely cold, 74°F. She had tried ergotamine, but it produced severe side effects, as did some tranquilizers. Headaches occurred regularly, about one every two weeks, and lasted for about ten days. There were two principal components of treatment. First, she was given training to raise the skin temperature of her right index finger about once per week in the clinic. Skin temperature was recorded by a thermistor; analogue feedback was provided by the pitch of a tone which increased as skin temperature increased and by a visual display presenting absolute skin temperature, accurate to one tenth of a degree Farenheit. Two training trials, each 20 minutes long, usually occurred during each weekly visit, for 20 weeks. The second component of treatment was Benson's relaxation technique (Benson 1975) which she practiced once a day for about 20 minutes.

The results of treatment are presented in Figure 9–2. Maximum headache intensity for each day is plotted using a scale from 0 (no headache) to 5 (incapacitating headache). Each vertical mark on the abscissa indicates a Monday. The start of a new headache was defined as an increase in headache intensity to #2 or more following at least two days of intensity #1 or less. The beginning of each new headache is shown by a break in the line plotting headache intensity. The maximum skin temperature in degrees Farenheit during each biofeedback session is indicated by the numbers along the abscissa; their placement reflects the days she visited the clinic for biofeedback training. Thus on the second Tuesday of treatment, the maximum headache intensity was #1, and the highest skin temperature was 74°F.

The debilitating nature of the headaches at the start of treatment can

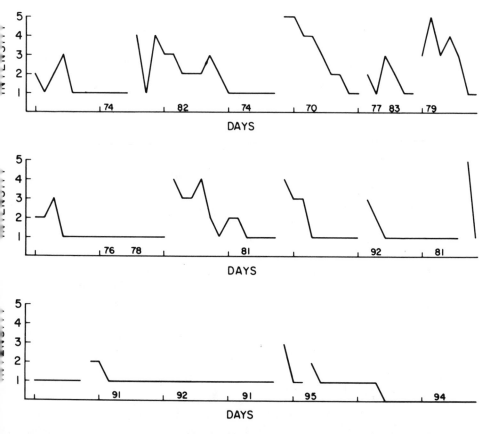

FIGURE 9–2   The Course of Treatment for the Client in Case Study A.
Headache intensity ranges from 0 indicating no headache to 5 indicating an incapacitating headache. The days are consecutive days with a Monday being indicated by a vertical hash mark. A "new" headache, reflected as a break in the chart, was defined as an increase in head pain to a level greater than 1 after two consecutive days of 1 or less. The numbers at the bottom of the graph indicate the maximum skin temperature obtained during a visit to the clinic. *(From Olton, Anderson, and Noonberg, 1979. Reprinted by permission.)*

be seen by their frequency, intensity, and duration. Indeed, most days were characterized by a score of 2 or more. Furthermore, skin temperature was uniformly low when she entered the clinic, and she was able to raise it only a few degrees. As treatment continued, skin temperature gradually increased and the frequency, intensity, and duration of headaches decreased. Critical periods were weekends and passing through a weekend without a headache almost inevitably meant that no migraine would develop during the following week. When this pattern of headaches became clear (after about six weeks of treatment), this weekly cycle of activities was examined. During the week, she lived a student's life, working long hours, staying mainly to herself, losing sleep, and skipping meals. When the weekend came, her life style changed dramatically; she spent almost all her time in social activities with friends, went to parties, and ate a great deal. Behavior therapy focused on smoothing out this cycle so that the week as a whole was more balanced, and emphasized the need for practicing relaxation during weekends, a period of time when one or more home sessions were often skipped.

As treatment continued, she became more sensitive to both the temperature of her hands and the appearance of a prodrome. In several instances, she had felt a headache beginning and had immediately practiced her hand-warming relaxation exercises, stopping the headache. At the end of treatment she said that her hands were generally warm and that many of her friends had asked "Where did your cold hands go?" She reported being more relaxed, contented, and energetic. Her baseline skin temperature had increased to about 90°F, and her ability to increase her skin temperature through feedback and through relaxation had developed so that she was able to produce a 5°F rise in about 10 minutes. She was discharged with instructions to keep practicing the relaxation procedure as necessary. At a follow-up one year later, her skin temperature reached 94°F, and she reported having had only two headaches since treatment stopped.

Case Study B

This person was trained to decrease the temperature of the hand before being trained to increase it. During the hand-cooling period, headache intensity increased slightly, while during the hand-warming period, it decreased substantially. These results again show the close relationship between skin temperature and headache activity and provide a control for the nonspecific or placebo effects of biofeedback treatment. Because all aspects of the hand-cooling and hand-warming procedures were the same except for the direction of skin temperature change, successful reduction of headache activity during hand warming is most reasonably attributed to the specific hand-warming skill rather than to other more general aspects of the treatment procedure.

The patient was a 27-year-old female nurse who had experienced increasingly severe migraines during the two years prior to treatment (Johnson & Turin 1975). She took ergotamine during treatment but was not given any additional medication. The treatment began with five weeks of baseline followed by six weeks of training to decrease skin temperature and then six weeks of training to increase skin temperature. She was told that both skin temperature decreases and skin temperature increases would help reduce her headache activity. Training sessions lasted 45 minutes and took place two times each week. Skin temperature was recorded from the index finger on the dominant hand. In each session, the first 25 minutes was a baseline period during which no feedback was given while the last 20 minutes was biofeedback training with continuous visual feedback. During the six weeks of hand cooling, the mean finger temperature decreased .7°F, and headache activity increased from the pretreatment baseline. During the subsequent six weeks of hand warming, the mean finger temperature increased 2°F and headache activity decreased. For the pretreatment baseline, hand-cooling, and hand-warming periods, respectively, the mean number of headaches each week was 1, 2, and .5, the mean duration of each headache was 6.6, 13.6, and 3.2 hours, and the mean number of pills taken each week was 3.0, 4.6, and 1.7.

Case Study C

Practice at home and in the clinic decreased the head pain of this 52-year-old woman and allowed her to eliminate medication which she had been taking (Drury and others 1979). She had experienced migraine headaches for 50 years, had not been able to control the headaches with Sansert or Ergotamine, and had been hospitalized because of the severity of the head pain. She read a magazine article which described the success of biofeedback in treating migraine headaches, learned to raise skin temperature in the clinic and at home, repeated autogenic phrases during the feedback sessions, and practiced muscle relaxation exercises for 20 minutes at least once a day at home.

For biofeedback, skin temperature was recorded from the middle finger of the dominant hand. Auditory and visual feedback were provided once each minute during sessions in the clinic. Each session included 10 minutes of baseline recording and 30 to 40 minutes of feedback during which she silently repeated the autogenic phrases. A shaping procedure eliminated feedback for about one minute in early sessions and systematically eliminated feedback for increasingly longer periods of time in subsequent sessions until feedback was present for about only 25% of the time. She had 18 sessions in the clinic.

Skin temperature increased and head pain and medication decreased. Skin temperature, which averaged 84°F during the pretreatment baseline, increased to more than 95°F within seven minutes of feedback in the clinic sessions. The severity of headaches, which averaged 2.5 without Sansert and 1.5 with Sansert during the pretreatment baseline, decreased to about 1.2 during feedback training even though she eliminated all medication at that time.

Discussion of Treatments

Skin Temperature Increases and Home Practice. Biofeedback training in the clinic, in conjunction with practice at home, has taught patients to increase the skin temperature of their hands and to reduce headache activity. Two of the studies discussed below suggest that the critical component of the biofeedback treatment was raising skin temperature. In both cases, prior to learning to raise skin temperature, patients learned some other biofeedback skill, either reducing the activity of the frontalis muscle or decreasing skin temperature. Headache activity was not reduced until the hand-warming procedure was instituted.

Two patients began biofeedback treatment by learning to reduce activity in the frontalis muscle (Wickramasekera 1973b). The man was 45 years old and had experienced headaches daily since adolescence; the woman was 46 years old and had experienced headaches for 16 years. Both had tried various medications, but these were all unable to control the headaches. EMG was recorded from the frontalis muscle, and feedback was provided to train decreases in muscle activity. Although training continued for at least 16 weeks, along with daily practice of relaxation for 20 minutes at home, headache activity was not reduced. Both patients initially resisted a suggestion to try skin temperature feedback but later accepted. Visual feedback of digital skin temperature was provided for an unspecified number of sessions during 10 or 11 weeks. Skin temperature increased by an average of 4°F during the feedback period. Headache activity decreased for both patients during this same time period. The mean number of hours of headache pain per week decreased from nine during the pretreatment baseline to four during treatment, and the average maximum headache intensity decreased from four to two. The use of analgesics did not change significantly during the baseline or feedback periods. Thus headache activity decreased as skin temperature increased, and skin temperature feedback proved effective after EMG feedback did not.

Other data indicating that skin temperature control is responsible for reductions in headache activity come from a comparison of the effects of increases and decreases in skin temperature (Turin & Johnson 1976). The patients were three men and four women between 20 and 58 years of age with histories of migraine headache ranging from two to 50 years. They had been taking ergotamine tartrate and agreed not to vary their medication during the study. All of them recorded headache activity during four to six weeks of pretreatment baseline. Biofeedback training followed, with sessions lasting 45 minutes and taking place twice each week. The first 25 minutes of each session was a baseline period during which no feedback was provided; the last 20 minutes were with feedback. Skin temperature was recorded from the index finger of the dominant hand. Three patients were trained to decrease skin temperature for six weeks and then to increase it for the next six weeks. The other four patients learned to increase skin temperature immediately following baseline and continued for 6 to 14 weeks. All patients were instructed to practice the technique they were learning in the clinic for ten minutes twice each day at home and at the first sign of a headache. While the three patients were being trained to decrease skin temperature, their mean skin temperature was slightly reduced and headache activity was unchanged. For all seven patients, by the tenth session of training to increase skin temperature, mean skin temperature rose .6°F and headache activity was significantly reduced. The mean number of headaches per week decreased from 2.2 during baseline to 1.3 during the final four to six weeks of training, the mean number of hours of headache activity each week decreased from 12.4 to 5.7, and the mean number of pills taken each week decreased from 2.2 to 1.3.

Treatment of Severe and/or Persistent Headaches. People have used biofeedback to reduce headache activity even after as many as 50 years of previously unsuccessful attempts with drugs or other treatments. In one instance, three men and three women had been unable to control their headaches for up to 40 years with a variety of drugs (Reading & Mohr 1976). Four to six weeks of pretreatment baseline were followed by a laboratory session in which the patients were asked to increase skin temperature but were not given feedback. The subsequent biofeedback sessions were each 21 minutes long. Skin temperature was recorded from the second finger on the right hand, and analogue visual feedback was provided. As the patients became able to increase skin temperature in the clinic, they were told to practice this skill at home for 15 minutes each day and whenever headaches began. After completion of an unspecified number of biofeedback sessions, each patient had one final session in which no feedback was given and returned for a follow-up one month and two months later. The ability to raise skin temperature progressively improved. The patients produced an average increase of 1.0°C at the final session (without feedback), and an average increase of .7°C during the follow-up period. Migraine activity was progressively reduced through treatment and remained low at both follow-up periods. An average of 4.1 headaches each week during baseline decreased to 1.9 during biofeedback treatment and 1.4 at the second follow-up period. The mean number of hours of headache was reduced from 25.3 each week to 10.4 and 5.1 during the same time periods, respectively, and a combined index of headache activity decreased from 9.0 to 5.4 and 3.0, respectively. Similar reports of improvement in migraine headaches following skin temperature biofeedback are available for patients with histories of migraines as long as 30 years (Wickramasekera 1973b) and 50 years (Turin & Johnson 1976). The data are consistent and demonstrate that patients with long histories of migraine headache may benefit from skin temperature biofeedback.

Skin Temperature Feedback, Relaxation, and Autogenic Training. Relaxation and autogenic exercises can increase skin temperature and, as shown below, can also be effective in reducing headache activity. Ten patients, between 21 and 77 years of age, received biofeedback training, autogenic training, or no treatment (Blanchard and others 1978). For those in the biofeedback group, skin temperature was recorded from the right index finger. Analogue visual feedback was provided by a needle on a meter; movement of the needle to one side indicated an increase in skin temperature; movement to the other side indicated a decrease. Feedback sessions were scheduled for 30 minutes twice weekly for six weeks; home practice of the hand-warming skill and the first two autogenic exercises (Schultz & Luthe 1969) lasted five to ten minutes, two or three times each day. Patients in the relaxation group were trained to relax 16 muscle groups with a variation (Paul 1966) of Jacobson's relaxation technique (Jacobson 1938) and practiced at home for 20 to 30 minutes each day. Those in the control group were told that two treatments were being tested and that they would receive the best one of them in about six weeks. Patients in both the relaxation and the biofeedback group substantially reduced their headache activity, and the two groups did not differ greatly from one another in the degree of improvement shown. For both groups, the average number of headaches per week decreased from 2.8 during the four weeks preceding training to 1.8 during training, and approximately 1.0 during a follow-up three months later. During the same periods, the average maximum intensity of head pain was reduced from 3.0 to 2.0 and 2.0, respectively, and the average number of headache hours per week was reduced from 14 to 8.0 and 1.0, respectively. Hence, both skin temperature biofeedback and progressive relaxation helped migraine patients to reduce headache activity.

A combination of biofeedback, autogenic training, and relaxation exercises produced a reduction in headache activity for a large number of patients with migraine headaches alone, or with both migraine headaches and tension headaches (Medina and others 1976; Diamond, Medina and others 1979). For biofeedback, skin temperature was measured from a finger and EMG was recorded from over the frontalis muscle. A tone provided analogue feedback. Training sessions were scheduled from two to ten times a week in the clinic, and the patients were instructed to practice twice a day at home. Treatment lasted for up to four weeks. Of 407 patients who responded to a questionnaire, 77% of those with migraine headaches only and 73% of those with both migraine and tension headaches said that biofeedback helped reduce their headaches.

Practice of biofeedback at home and in the clinic was successful in reducing head pain in four individuals who had experienced migraine headaches from 13 years to 50 years (Drury and others 1979). All had a family history of migraine and were taking medication; two had been hospitalized. The procedures for treatment were described previously in Case Study C. All patients raised their skin temperatures by 4°F in biofeedback sessions after three weeks of training. Headache severity, rated on a five-point scale (Budzynski and others 1973) decreased from 2.4 to 1.5. One patient eliminated medication entirely; the other three reduced medication by 40%.

Other Biofeedback Treatments for Migraine Headaches. The treatment procedures reviewed above all trained clients to increase the skin temperature of their hands to reduce headaches. They uniformly found that increases in digital skin temperature were accompanied by decreases in headache activity, and some of them found that decreases in digital skin temperature were accompanied by increases in headache activity. Surprisingly, in light of these findings, treatments that trained people to reduce blood flow have also reduced migraine activity.

Training to reduce blood flow in the temporal artery reduced migraine headache activity and blood flow in the hand (Friar & Beatty 1976). One photoplethysmograph measured blood flow in the temporal artery; a second measured blood flow in the finger. Nine people with migraine headaches received auditory and visual feedback about blood flow in the temporal artery during eight sessions in which they were trained to decrease that blood flow. After training, in a subsequent session, blood flow in the temporal artery was about 20% below the levels found during a pretreatment baseline. Blood flow in the finger also decreased, by 31%. The number of headaches at the end of treatment was 46% of that in the pretreatment baseline, and the headaches were slightly less intense. A second group was trained to decrease blood flow in the hands. They had the same treatment schedule as the first group of clients but were given feedback about blood flow from the finger photoplethysmograph. Following training, blood flow in the hands was reduced by 33% while that in the temporal artery was reduced by 5%. This training had little effect on headache activity; the frequency of headaches decreased by only 14% and the intensity of the headaches actually increased, by 17%. The finding that headache activity was not reduced by learning to lower the blood flow in the hands is consistent with the results of treatments reviewed earlier which showed that training to lower skin temperature in the hands did not have therapeutic effects. The success of decreasing blood flow in the temporal artery is difficult to explain, especially because it was accompanied by a decrease in the blood flow in the hands at the same time (see also Price & Tursky 1976).

Two case studies provide further support that decreasing temporal blood flow can reduce headache activity (Feuerstein & Adams 1977). Two family members, a father and his daughter, received biofeedback training to reduce frontalis EMG and to reduce blood flow in the temporal artery. The daughter was first trained to reduce EMG during six sessions and then trained to decrease blood flow during six sessions; the father was given the same treatments but in the opposite order. A tone provided binary feedback; the sessions lasted 20 minutes each. Both clients were instructed to practice at home for 10 minutes twice a day the skill they learned in the clinic. For the father, the number of headaches each week decreased from an average of 2.7 during the pretreatment baseline to 1.0 during blood flow feedback, .8 during EMG feedback, and 1.1 nine weeks after treatment was terminated. During the same time periods, the intensity of the headaches did not change appreciably, but the number of hours of head pain each week decreased from 12.7 to 4.9. A similar result was found for the daughter: during blood flow feedback the average number of headaches each week was 1.7, decreased from 2.8 during the pretreatment baseline and 3.8 during EMG feedback. Headache intensity did not change appreciably, but the average number of hours of headache pain per week decreased from 13.4 to 4.3. Thus, decreasing temporal blood flow decreased headache activity in both the father and the daughter.

Reductions of blood pulse volume in the temporal artery reduced headache activity for two women who had both migraine and tension headaches (Sturgis and others 1978). Both had experienced headaches since puberty; one was 34 years old at the time of treatment, the other was 54. The authors state that "both subjects could clearly discriminate between migraine and muscle-contraction headaches and viewed them as independent responses" (p. 218). Blood pulse volume was recorded from the left temporal artery where both participants reported unilateral head pain. EMG was recorded from over the frontalis muscle. Each patient received 15 sessions of binary feedback of blood pulse volume and 15 sessions of binary feedback of frontalis EMG. Feedback was provided for 20 minutes in each session. They were told to practice their new technique at home for 10 minutes each day. Both women decreased their average pulse volume during pulse volume feedback and decreased their average levels of frontalis EMG during EMG feedback. Headache activity decreased during both types of feedback for both women. The younger woman had an average of six hours of migraine headache pain during the baseline, two hours during blood pulse volume feedback training, and virtually none during EMG training or three weeks after treatment ended. The older woman had an average of eight hours of headache pain during the baseline, and almost none during EMG training, blood pulse volume training, and at the follow-up. By the end of the study, neither client took any medication to control headaches.

In another study, "temperature discrimination training" was used to treat migraine headache symptoms (Gainer 1978). The patient was 26 years old and had a ten-year history of headaches which occurred three to six times each week. She received eight one-hour sessions of assertiveness training and eight one-hour sessions of systematic desensitization (Paul 1966), but her headaches persisted. Biofeedback treatment was then initiated with auditory analogue feedback of hand skin temperature for 30 minutes in each of eight sessions. Her headaches continued. During biofeedback she was able to detect increases in hand temperature only 47% of the trials. "Temperature discrimination training" was then initiated. This consisted of three sessions during which she tried to increase the temperature of the hand as during the previous feedback period. Each session included 60 discrimination trials, each of which lasted 15 to 30 seconds and was followed by five seconds of rest. During the rests she was told what happened to skin temperature during the preceding trial. During feedback, hand skin temperature increased as much as 18°F by the fourth session and 20°F by the eighth. After two temperature discrimination sessions she correctly detected hand temperature increases on 79% of the trials. An average of 4.5 headaches per week was reported during the baseline and during feedback training. This level was reduced to one headache per week following temperature discrimination training. During these same three periods the average number of hours of headache pain was 5.5, 7.5, and 2.0, respectively, and the average intensity of headache pain was 2.8, 3.8, and 2.5, respectively. Within one week after temperature discrimination training, she had no headaches and stopped all medication.

CLINICAL PROGRAM

Some headaches are clearly psychogenic and related to the perceived stresses of daily life. Other headaches may arise for a variety of reasons, ranging from malfunctioning of the jaw and teeth to neurological disorders such as brain tumors or increased intracranial pressure. An adequate physical examination should be obtained before any biofeedback

TABLE 9–2   Summary of Biofeedback Treatments for Migraine Headaches

Study	Patients	Biofeedback Treatment	Other Treatment	Symptoms	Results	Biological Function
Andreychuk & Skriver, 1975	33 volunteers	Feedback of hand temperature for 45 min, once each week for 10 weeks	None reported	Average scores on a headache index for patients scoring high on a hypnotic induction profile: baseline, 156; last 5 weeks of training, 48; average scores for those scoring low on a hypnotic induction profile: baseline, 26; training, 17		Data unavailable
Blanchard, Theobald, Williamson, Silver, & Brown, 1978	25 females, 5 males; average age 39, range 21 to 77; average symptom duration 20 yrs, range 5 to 40	Visual feedback of finger temperature during 30-min sessions, twice weekly for six weeks	Autogenic training and home practice of handwarming for 5 to 10 minutes, 2 to 3 times each day	Average levels per week during the baseline, training, and 1 to 3 month follow-up: headache index, .74, .4, and .29; frequency, 3.2, 2.2, and 1.4; duration, 13.5, 7.6, and 2.0; medication index, 13, 7.6, and 6.7; intensity, 3.0, 1.9, and 1.4		Data unavailable
Diamond, Medina, Diamond-Falk, & DeVeno, 1979	123 with vascular headaches, 265 with combined vascular and muscle contraction headaches; age range 10 to 71	Auditory analogue feedback of frontal EMG activity for 10 min and finger temperature for 20 min, 2 to 10 times weekly for up to 4 weeks	Relaxation exercises; home practice twice a day for up to 4 weeks	Percent stating that biofeedback helped their headaches: vascular headache alone, 77; mixed vascular and muscle contraction, 73		Data unavailable
Drury, DeRisi, & Liberman, 1979	2 males, 2 females; age range 29 to 65	Auditory and visual feedback of finger skin temperature while silently repeating autogenic phrases for 30 to 40 min, once or twice weekly for 15 to 21 sessions	Reading an article to generate favorable expectations; relaxation training, imagery, and home practice	Scores on a headache severity index (from 1 to 5) decreased by .9 to 1.5; one patient eliminated all medication; 3 others decreased usage by about 40%		All patients raised finger skin temperature by at least 4°F within a session following 1 to 3 weeks of training

Study	Subjects	Procedure	Home practice	Results	Comments
Feuerstein & Adams, 1977	1 male, 1 female; average age 31	Auditory feedback of frontal EMG during six sessions and temporal blood flow feedback during 6 sessions, each 20 min long	Home practice for 10 min two times each day	Average levels per week during the baseline, training, and 9-week follow-up; frequency, 2.8, 1.4, and .8; duration, 13, 14, and 5; intensity, 1.9, 3.3, and 1.7	Data unavailable
Feuerstein, Adams, & Beiman, 1976	Female, age 67 with combined migraine and tension headache	Feedback of frontal EMG for 20 min, once weekly for 6 weeks followed by feedback of cephalic vasomotor responses for 30 min, once weekly for 6 weeks	Home practice for 10 min twice daily	Average weekly headache frequency: baseline, 4.4; EMG feedback, 1.8; baseline, 3.3; CVMR feedback, 1.3; 8-week follow-up, 2.5; average intensity (rated 1 to 4): baseline, 2.8; EMG feedback, 1.5; baseline 2.1; CVMR feedback, 2.6; 8-week follow-up, 1.3; average duration: baseline 15.8; EMG feedback, 5.3; baseline, 9.9; CVMR feedback, 4.6; 8-week follow-up, 7.5; no headache reported for 3 weeks during CVMR feedback; use of tranquilizers was reduced from 3 to 1 during the study	Frequency of vasospasm during baseline, feedback, and baseline of sessions 5 and 6: EMG feedback, 7.7, 5.3, and 2.9; CVMR feedback, .8, 1.1, and .4
Friar & Beatty, 1976	16 females, 3 males; average age 30	Auditory and visual feedback of skin temperature over the temporal artery during 8, 200-heartbeat trials in 3 weeks	None reported	Compared to average levels in a 30-day baseline, major attacks were reduced by 46%, number of episodes were reduced by 36%, intensity was reduced by 4%, and medication consumption was reduced by 45%	Average pulse amplitude decreased by 16% during training

Study	Patients	Biofeedback Treatment	Other Treatment	Symptoms / Results	Biological Function
Fried, Lamberti, & Sneed, 1977	6 females; age range 31 to 47; 3 with migraine headaches, 2 with mixed migraine and tension headaches	Home practice of skin temperature raising with a portable trainer twice daily	Autogenic phrases repeated twice daily for 2 weeks preceding temperature training	Number improved by more than 75%: 1 with migraine, 1 with mixed migraine and tension headaches; number improved very little or questionable: 2 with migraine, 1 with combined migraine and tension headache	Data unavailable
Gainer, 1978	Female, age 26; 10-year history of migraine	Auditory feedback of hand temperature during 8, 30-min sessions; "temperature discrimination training" for 3 sessions, each including 60 trials, 15 to 30 sec long	Home practice three times daily	Average levels per week during the baseline, feedback, and temperature discrimination training periods: frequency, 4.5, 4.5, and 1.0; duration, 5.5, 7.5, and 2.0; medication consumed 3, 2, and 1; intensity, 3.8, 3.8, and 2.5; degree of disability, 1.0, 2.0, and .7; one week after temp. disc. trng., frequency and medication consumption dropped to zero	Temperature increases to 18°F were produced by the 4th session; by the 8th session "changes of more than 20°F were reliably being produced"
Johnson & Turin, 1975	Female, age 27	Temperature feedback from the index finger on the dominant hand for 20 min, twice weekly for 12 weeks	10-min home practice sessions twice daily and at first sign of headache	Average levels per week during baseline, cooling, and warming: frequency, 1, 2, and .5; medication consumption, 3.0, 4.6, and .7; duration, 6.6, 13.6, and 3.2	Subject was able to cool hand by .7°F and to warm hand by 2°F

Study	Subjects	Feedback procedure	Additional treatment/home practice	Results	Temperature
Medina, Diamond, & Franklin, 1976	24 females, 3 males; average age 35; range 10 to 60	Auditory analogue feedback of frontal EMG of 10 min and finger temperature for 20 min, twice weekly for one month	Ergotamine	Three markedly improved (76–100%), 6 moderately improved (51–75%), 4 mildly improved (30–50%)	Data unavailable
Reading & Mohr, 1976	3 females, 3 males; average age 41; range 26 to 54	Feedback of finger temperature during sessions of approximately 30 min	15-min home practice sessions daily and as headache developed	Average levels per week during the baseline, training, 1-month follow-up, and 2-month follow-up: frequency, 4.1, 1.9, 1.4, and 1.0; duration, 25.3, 10.4, 5.4, and 5.1; headache index, 9.0, 5.4, 3.1, and 3.0	Subjects were able to produce average increases of 1.4°C during the final, no-feedback baseline and were able to produce increases of .7°C at two-month follow-up
Sargent, Green, & Walters, 1973; Solbach & Sargent, 1977	74 patients who received at least 270 days of training	Feedback of difference between finger and mid-forehead skin temperatures	None reported	Improvement ratings: 15 very good, 20 good, 16 moderate, 11 slight, 12 no improvement	Data unavailable
Sturgis, Tollison, & Adams, 1978	2 females, average age 44	Auditory analogue feedback of blood pulse volume and frontal EMG levels in 20-min sessions	Home practice 10 min daily and when expecting a headache	Average duration of headache decreased from 7.4 during baseline, to 1.4 during BVP feedback, to .75 during EMG feedback, to .75 at follow-up	Data unavailable
Turin & Johnson, 1976	3 males, 4 females	Feedback of finger temperature for 20 min, twice per week for 6 to 14 weeks	Home practice for 10 min twice daily and at first sign of headache	Average levels per week during the baseline and final 4 to 6 weeks of training: frequency, 2.2 and 1.3; medication consumption, 4.3 and 1.7; duration, 12.4 and 5.7	Skin temperature increased during the 10th session by .1°C to 1.7°C
Wickramasekera, 1973b	1 male, age 45; 1 female, age 46	Visual feedback of finger skin temperature	Home practice sessions	Average number of headache hours decreased from 9 during baseline to 4 during treatment; average maximum intensity decreased from 4 during baseline to 2 during treatment	Finger temperatures increased by an average of 4.3°F during training

treatment begins, but here it is most important, for the same reasons discussed in the preceding chapter on tension headaches. After a medical examination, information about the characteristics of the headache can be obtained, following the same guidelines as for tension headaches and using the same questionnaire (see list p. 92; list p. 153; Bakal & Kaganov, 1976; Thompson & Collins, 1979).

As indicated in the previous review, training to increase digital skin temperature is an effective way of alleviating migraine headaches. Information about the state of the hands and feet prior to treatment can be particularly valuable. Migraine patients often say they have cold hands especially in winter. The temperature of the hands during the first visit to the clinic may be obtained to provide objective data about skin temperature. These original measures are important for two reasons. First, they are necessary to establish a baseline against which future progress can be measured. Second, they can help provide the rationale for treatment and motivate the patient to participate in therapy. Changing skin temperature as a means of alleviating headaches often sounds suspicious to a patient and if this skepticism remains, treatment may progress slowly. Furthermore, if cold hands and feet have been a long-standing problem for the patient, just raising skin temperature may be an acceptable intermediate goal.

Skin temperature raising is often difficult and may take many sessions to be fully established. This is particularly true for migraine patients who tend to be relatively unreactive to manipulations that produce vasodilation. Therefore, considerable help and support must be offered to the client. Shaping the desired response is critical. The feedback instrument should be set to its most sensitive position and feedback given even for very slight increases in skin temperature. The temperature of the room is obviously important, and initial sessions should take place in a temperature that is at least comfortably warm. Baseline measurements must eventually be taken for a sufficiently long period to be certain that any resulting vasodilation comes from the feedback, rather than as a reflexive response to the room temperature. But at the beginning of treatment, any means of increasing the client's ability to raise skin temperature is important. As with any operant conditioning approach, this shaping process should be gradually removed as success with the desired response is achieved.

Support for the client is also important during this stage. We have seen clients who are so determined to raise their skin temperature to normal levels on the first attempt that the resulting sympathetic arousal actually lowers skin temperature. This event is instructive and can be used to demonstrate what should not be done. The reaction to this failure is often one of frustration. The therapist must be able to take these reactions, use them for beneficial instructive purposes, and support the client's confidence and optimism during the difficult periods. The records of progress made with respect to subjective symptoms (head pain) and objective symptoms (skin temperature) can also provide appropriate encouragement.

Normal people, when given skin temperature feedback, can learn to produce very specific changes in skin temperature, raising the temperature of only one finger while simultaneously lowering the temperature of some other part of the body (Taub 1977). Such a result is obviously not desirable in therapy. Relaxation training may help produce a generalized vasodilatory response throughout the periphery of the body. Because most relaxation techniques produce vasodilation, the particular technique can be chosen mainly on the basis of its suitability to the client and the therapist. Daily practice of the relaxation is important. This practice may take place in one or two relatively long sessions (10 to 20 minutes), and/or in many relatively short ones (one to five minutes). The short periods of relaxation are advantageous because they may be able to interrupt a vasoconstricting trend resulting from stress during daily life. The longer periods can be useful because they may be able to produce some vasodilation, changing the general set point of the system. The therapist should be certain that relaxation procedures are producing vasodilation by measuring skin temperature from several different portions of the body (hands, feet, temporal artery) during relaxation in the clinic. If not, specific training may have to take place to teach skin temperature increases in the deficient areas.

Most migraine clients also have tension headaches accompanied by an elevated state of muscle contraction of the muscles in the head. This result is not surprising because head muscles contract in response to pain, and the pain of migraines may be excruciating. Some of the highest levels of muscle contraction have been obtained with patients suffering primarily from migraine headaches. Relaxation of the frontalis muscle, or other head muscles that may be indicated by the client, should be carried out with typical surface EMG procedures as described in Chapter 6. This biofeedback training has several advantages. It is generally learned very rapidly, in contrast to skin temperature control, and can thus serve as an intermediate goal in treatment as well as a demonstration of the general principles of biofeedback. It can also help alleviate the possibility of a positive feedback system, where the pain of migraine generates increased muscle activity which in turn generates more head pain, and so on in a vicious circle. Indeed, EMG muscle relaxation may be one of the first steps taken with a migraine patient, and skin temperature feedback may be introduced after success is obtained here.

Migraine headaches typically occur when relaxation follows after stress

(Wolff 1948). The stress produces excessive vasoconstriction which when alleviated turns into vasodilation and head pain. In any case, one assumption underlying behavioral treatment of migraines is that there is at least some psychogenic component to them. As discussed in Chapter 7 on clinical procedures, several steps can be taken to obtain information about the role of stress in the production of headaches. Record keeping can be a useful way of determining the events in the client's life that trigger the headache attacks. Some migraineurs are often aware of these events, but others are not, at least until the therapist points them out at which time there may be an immediate realization of the relationship. Thus, the records should keep track not only of the headache activity, but also of the events that precede the headaches. A second reason to keep records is to document progress or the lack of it. If progress is occurring, demonstration of this to the client may be helpful in providing the necessary support until the headache problems are entirely alleviated. If progress is not occurring, the therapist must be able to redesign the treatment program in order to produce a more effective treatment. If the coldness of the hands and feet is substantial and the client indicates that it is of concern, records of subjective impressions of skin temperature may also be kept, coupled with objective measurements in the clinic.

Any client who comes to biofeedback treatment is likely to believe that psychological factors can produce physiological changes. But the magnitude of these interactions is often not appreciated. We have found that continuous physiological recording of skin temperature and/or frontalis EMG during an interview can be an effective and subtle means of showing the client the extent to which psychological variables can influence these physiological measurements. A minute by minute record of the general topics of conversation and the readings of the feedback monitors is kept, and sometimes feedback is provided to the client during the interview. Topics that are stressful to the client often produce rapid and marked increases in frontalis EMG and decreases in skin temperature. These can be reversed by a brief interlude spent on nonstressful, pleasant topics. Reviewing the relationship of the physiological variables and the topics of conversation after the end of the interview is instructive. It provides the therapist with some indication of the reactivity of the client's autonomic nervous system and provides the client with objective data concerning the way in which thoughts and feelings can influence physiology. The point to be made to the client, then, is that psychological variables do influence physiology, and that if the client is given the appropriate training, control of the psychological variables can produce a decrease in head pain.

The most widely used source of feedback has been the skin temperature of a finger or hand. As described in Chapter 6, a thermistor or photoplethysmograph can be attached to a finger with a porous tape. The finger should then be shielded from drafts and contact with extraneous objects, such as arms on chairs or other parts of the body. Room temperature and humidity should be held constant. The skin should be dried when the thermistor is attached. Analogue feedback is preferred because skin temperature may change very slowly. The feedback should be contingent on at most a one-tenth of a degree (Fahrenheit) change.

Laboratory sessions should be held once or twice weekly early in training. Because skin temperature is one of the more difficult physiological variables to control, the client should be forewarned that successful control of skin temperature may take considerable time. Each session should last about 40 minutes with small breaks if the client tires. Home practice is also useful with sessions lasting 10 to 20 minutes once or twice daily.

RESEARCH CONSIDERATIONS

Although there is general agreement about the types of symptoms that may appear with migraine headaches, there is substantial disagreement about the way in which these symptoms are associated together. The problem has to do with the defining characteristics of migraine headaches as presented by the client. Information about the way in which symptoms cluster together, their relationship with migraine headaches and other disorders, and the differences between clinical samples and the general population on these variables will help substantially in developing an accurate diagnosis and characterization of the migraine client. These are the same issues that were discussed earlier for tension headaches.

The cerebral blood flow studies have provided a substantial body of literature supporting the general outlines of the vascular hypothesis of migraines. Additional questions need to be answered. One is concerned with the different ways in which migraine headaches can be produced—psychological stress, hormone imbalance, diet, and so on. These events may be acting simply as triggers to set off a common mechanism, in which case the cerebral blood flow patterns in all the cases should be the same. Alternatively, these events may produce similar sets of symptoms through different mechanisms, in which case the cerebral blood flow patterns may be substantially different. Further details of the relationship between changes in cerebral blood flow, the prodromal symptoms, and the types of head pain in migraines will help to determine the details of the mechanism of migraine headaches. Already there have been some exceptions to the general picture. The reasons for these exceptions and the different mechanisms involved remain to be established. The regional cerebral blood flow studies have generated a remarkable amount of information in a short period of time, and developments in this field should be of particular interest in the future.

The data reviewed earlier in this chapter show that the mechanism of migraine headaches is a disorder in the cerebral vascular supply and that raising the temperature of the hands can alleviate migraine headaches. But how does raising the temperature of the hands (the therapy) influence the state of the cerebral vasculature (the mechanism)? Certainly the blood that goes to the hands must come from somewhere, but the likelihood of its coming from the brain is very small. The cerebral circulation is under tight homeostatic control, and only extreme physiological manipulations will alter it. This control has been called *autoregulation* (Mchedlishvili and others 1973; Scheinberg 1975) indicating that for every alteration in one variable, there is a compensatory alteration in some other variable resulting in constant blood flow through the brain.

Experimental data have been provided on this point by training people to raise skin temperature and then recording cerebral blood flow with the ^{133}Xe technique (Largen and others 1978). Nine college students (not suffering from migraine headaches) were trained with analogue auditory feedback to raise and lower finger temperature. They were then shown the procedures for the rCBF studies so they would be comfortable with them. During the critical test sessions, rCBF was measured with scintillation counters while the people altered blood flow. During the hand-warming period, digital skin temperature increased by an average of 3.1°; during the hand cooling, it decreased by 1.2°. There were few changes in rCBF, and the differences even for single scintillation counters were less than 10%. Thus, there was no evidence that the biofeedback had a consistent effect on rCBF.

As discussed earlier in this chapter, the peripheral vascular system of migraineurs is less stable than that of normals. Consequently, the failure to find changes in rCBF as a result of biofeedback with people who don't have migraine headaches may not accurately reflect the influence of biofeedback on the intracerebral blood flow of people who do have these headaches. The only way to address this issue is to examine the effects of biofeedback on rCBF of migraineurs. The available evidence suggests that for migraineurs, learning skin temperature control does have a significant influence on intracerebral blood flow (Mathew and others, in press). Eleven women with migraine headaches were trained to raise and lower skin temperature. A thermistor on the middle finger of the right hand provided analogue feedback. After two sessions of general relaxation training, each person learned to control skin temperature for 10 to 14 sessions during five weeks and practiced the biofeedback skill at home for

15 minutes each day. Then two measurements of rCBF were obtained with the ^{133}Xe inhalation technique. During one of these measurements, the person rested quietly. During the other, the person was given biofeedback and asked to either raise skin temperature or lower it. Recordings of Fg and changes in skin temperature were taken simultaneously.

The results showed that during biofeedback training Fg changed to a greater extent than during resting, and in a direction similar to the blood flow in the hand. This effect of biofeedback on cerebral blood flow was most obvious for F_g in the right hemisphere. For the individuals who practiced increasing their skin temperature, skin temperature during biofeedback was 2°F greater than skin temperature during resting. F_g, which had been 83 during resting, increased to 90 during biofeedback. For those who practiced decreasing their skin temperature, skin temperature during biofeedback was .5°F lower than during resting. F_g, which had been 84 during resting, decreased to 80 during biofeedback. Thus an increase in the skin temperature of the hands was accompanied by an increase in cerebral blood flow, while a decrease in the skin temperature of the hands was accompanied by a decrease in cerebral blood flow.

The effect of biofeedback on cerebral blood flow was less marked in the left hemisphere. For the individuals who practiced increasing their skin temperature, F_g during biofeedback was 83 as compared to 80 during resting. For those who practiced decreasing their skin temperature, F_g during biofeedback was 87 as compared to 86 during resting. In this last case, the change in cerebral blood flow was in a direction opposite to that in the hand. But even though F_g increased in the left hemisphere for people who lowered skin temperature, the magnitude of this increase (1°F) was less than that observed for the people who increased skin temperature during biofeedback (8°F) demonstrating that the biofeedback did have an influence on Fg in this hemisphere as well as in the right hemisphere.

These results demonstrate that the intracerebral blood flow of migraineurs is influenced by their control of peripheral skin temperature. Thus for migraineurs, the hand warming skills of biofeedback do have a direct relationship to the mechanisms of head pain. Furthermore, the intracerebral vasculature is less tightly controlled by the autoregulation mechanisms than in other people, a fact which reflects the abnormalities seen in the peripheral vasculature (reviewed early in this chapter). These results raise a set of questions about the factors responsible for the abnormal vascular reactions, and suggest that if a biofeedback technique can be developed to train directly the control of rCBF, this treatment might be even more successful than the currently used one which influences rCBF only indirectly.

A variety of means can be used to produce a general increase in peripheral skin temperature—biofeedback, relaxation, transcendental meditation, and so on. Is there any reason to prefer one of these methods to any of the others? Answering such a question requires a carefully controlled counterbalanced design so that extraneous variables do not influence the outcome. In reality, the question is not the overall efficiency in treatment of the general population, but the best choice for any individual client. The components of biofeedback that are important in producing the therapeutic effects need to be examined carefully. At present, the most effective way of dealing with a migraineur is to use all the procedures that appear to have been effective in past studies. But such an approach may be inefficient, because the marginal utility of additional procedures may be minimal and as more and more procedures are added, they may interfere with previous learned skills.

The most appropriate type of skin temperature control for treatment of migraine headaches still remains to be demonstrated. Certainly raising skin temperature has been effective. Lowering skin temperature or decreasing blood flow has reduced headache activity as well, but in some cases, this treatment has had the opposite effect, increasing headache activity. Thus the most important factor in controlling headache activity may not be increasing peripheral vasodilation, but stabilizing the peripheral (and perhaps intracranial) vascular system so that it doesn't fluctuate between extremes of vasoconstriction and vasodilation (Feuerstein and others 1976). Biofeedback studies systematically varying the type of training will be necessary to address this issue.

PERIPHERAL VASCULAR DISORDERS: RAYNAUD'S DISEASE

10

Introduction

Symptoms

Mechanism

Treatment

Clinical Program

INTRODUCTION

Cold hands and feet can arise for many different reasons. For most of us, this unpleasant condition appears only when we do not take adequate precautions to protect these extremities in cold weather, and the problems disappear as soon as we return to an appropriately warm environment. For some people, however, cold hands and feet are a chronic problem, and even relatively trivial events, such as removing a milk carton from a refrigerator, may cause the hands to become cold, white, insensitive to touch, and difficult to move. This condition may remain for many hours unless heat is applied directly to the affected area. For this group of individuals, biofeedback offers a possible means of alleviating the problems through skin temperature feedback.

In the late 1800s Maurice Raynaud described a series of patients who suffered from chronically cold hands and feet (Raynaud 1862, 1888). Because of this influential work, the term *Raynaud's disease* came to be used as a diagnostic category. As documented by a nice historical summary, "Raynaud's disease has been subject to more contradictory and conflicting reports than any other vascular disease entity" (Halpern and others 1960, p. 151; see also Allen & Brown 1932a, b; Lancet Editorial 1977). Indeed, Allen and Brown (1932b) point out that only six of Raynaud's original group of patients would now be classified as having Raynaud's disease. Because of these and other difficulties, Holling (1972) has suggested that the term *digital ischemia* be substituted for the various types of Raynaud's disorders. However, we have been unable to find consensus on a more appropriate diagnostic label and will continue to use the Raynaud's terminology, even though it may not be an optimal way of classifying symptoms arising from peripheral vascular disorders. Furthermore, there now seems to be considerable agreement as to the symptoms characteristic of Raynaud's disease. A symposium on Raynaud's disease, published in *Acta Chirurgica Scandinavica*, 1976 *Supplement 465*, provides excellent background information and a broad view of the knowledge about the area. An older but thorough review can be found in Holling (1972).

202

In one of the first attempts to develop a consistent terminology, Allen and Brown (1932a) briefly reviewed the case material provided by Raynaud (pp. 188–190) and suggested that primary Raynaud's disease be defined in the following way (p. 199):

1. intermittent attacks of discoloration of extremities
2. absence of evidence of organic arterial occlusion
3. symmetric or bilateral distribution
4. trophic changes, when present, limited to skin and never consisting of gross gangrene

They subsequently added two more criteria (Allen and Brown 1932b), p. 1471):

5. the disease must have been present for at least two years
6. there should be no evidence of any other disease that could produce the symptoms secondarily

This definition has been generally accepted and expanded. Holling (1972, p. 140) describes Raynaud's disease as ". . . a spasmodic contraction of arteries and small arteries of the fingers leading to slowing or cessation of the blood flow. It is provoked by exposure to cold and sometimes by emotion. The affected fingers are pallid or cyanosed when cold, and red and painful during the recovery phase." There should be no signs of underlying arterial or circulatory disorders; the symptoms should cease, and the pulse should appear with normal amplitude when the body parts are warmed by an external heat source.

If the cold hands and feet arise from an identifiable cause, then they are categorized as secondary rather than primary, and the term *phenomenon* is often (but not always) used in place of *disease*. Secondary Raynaud's phenomenon can result from vibrations, sclerodroma, vascular compression, atherosclerosis, reflex sympathetic dystrophy, drugs, and cold injury (Thulesius 1976). Distinguishing between primary and secondary Raynaud's disease can be complicated (see for example Kappert 1971). Diagnostic signs indicating secondary Raynaud's disease include: cold hands and feet even in a warm environment, first appearance in middle age, unilateral distribution, atrophy of the distal portions of the fingers, absence of pulse in the fingers, diminished response in a test of vasodilation (Holling 1972, p. 179). All of the above suggest a localized, permanent, and suddenly appearing difficulty which is usually caused by a particular physiological disorder. Further distinctions are presented by Duff (1956, p. 858) and include the age at which the first symptoms appeared, the sex of the patient, the distribution of the disease in the extremities, and the family history of similar problems. No data are offered to support the distinctions, so the categorization represents an idealized way of diagnosing patients, rather than an empirically based distinction. The distinctions of Duff (1956) are similar to those made by Thulesius (1976).

The typical patient is ". . . usually a middle-aged woman who has had cold fingers for many years. . . . The skin on the ends of her fingers is dry and hard and when compressed with the examiner's fingers gives a sensation described as an eggshell cracking. There may be small scars on the fingertips, cracks, and even ulceration alongside the fingernail. Symptoms disappear when the warmer weather occurs only to return the next winter" (Holling 1972, p. 140).

The coldness is found mainly in the hands and feet, appearing first at the extreme tips of the fingers and toes. In a group of 474 patients from the Mayo Clinic, the affected body parts were only the fingers for 55%, the fingers and toes for 43%, and the toes alone for 2% (Gifford & Hines 1957). Three factors predispose the extremities to these symptoms (Wilkins 1963a). First, the hands and feet are at the periphery of the circulatory system so that any problems arising from insufficient blood flow are likely to occur here before appearing elsewhere. Second, these body parts are usually exposed and are often not adequately protected from cold or from injury. Finally, the fingers have little muscle tissue, and the blood supply is almost all superficial (Graham 1955). Added together, these factors make the hands, and then the feet, the most likely candidates for problems arising from inadequate circulation.

SYMPTOMS

Cold hands and feet are associated with a variety of cardiovascular and other physiological malfunctions. To be classified as primary Raynaud's disease, these symptoms must appear as the primary problem and not as a response to any obvious precipitating cause, either pathological or environmental. Many of the symptoms listed in Table 10–1 result from this requirement. One of them, of course, is that a medical examination find no substantial pathology. The alleviation of the symptoms by heat and the recovery of the pulse in the affected extremities after an attack has passed both point to a fundamentally normal cardiovascular system. The intermittent, paroxysmal nature suggests a reaction to specific external stimuli, rather than the development of a pathological state, as does the failure of the disease to become progressively worse. The appearance early in life and the bilateral symmetry minimize the possibility of a specific arterial blockage because this event usually causes a discrete onset, rapid development, and a localized, asymmetrical problem.

Taken together, these characteristics indicate that Raynaud's disease,

TABLE 10-1   Symptoms of Primary Raynaud's Disease

	Abramson, 1974, pp. 222–223	Duff, 1956, p. 858	Holling, 1972, p. 140	Horowitz, 1971, pp. 1526–1530	Kappert, 1971, pp. 201–205	Thulesius, 1976, pp. 5–6	Wilkins, 1963b, p. 786
Begins early in life		X				X	
Bilateral and/or symmetrical		X					X
Mostly women are affected		X		X	X	X	X
No substantial pathology			X	X	X	X	X
Paroxysmal and/or intermittent	X				X		X
Provoked by: exposure to cold	X		X	X	X	X	X
emotion	X		X	X	X	X	X
Pulse normal in warm environment							
Relieved by heat		X	X	X	X		
Spasmodic			X				
Static and/or not progressive					X		X
When cold, hands are: pallid and/or white	X		X		X		X
cyanotic and/or blue	X		X		X		X
When recovering from cold, hands are: red	X		X		X	X	X
painful			X				
throbbing	X						X
tingling	X						X

properly diagnosed, is relatively benign (Hudson 1970) and not likely to lead to further complications. Indeed, common sense protection of the affected body parts is often the only treatment needed. For example, a group of 307 patients who were diagnosed as having primary Raynaud's disease using the criteria of Allen and Brown (1932b) were given conservative medical treatment—reassurance about the course of the disease and advice on how to take care of hands and feet (Gifford & Hines 1957). They were contacted again by a questionnaire after an average of 16 years. Only 16% of them reported that the symptoms had become worse. For 10%, the symptoms had gone, for 36%, the symptoms had improved, and for 38%, there had been no change. A similar pattern of results was found for men with primary Raynaud's disease (Hines & Christensen 1945). Most of the patients reported that the symptoms had improved (33%) or remained unchanged (44%); only 23% said they had gotten worse. Thus, primary Raynaud's disease tends to remain constant or improve over time (see also Morris 1968; Thulesius 1965).

Raynaud's patients almost always report that cold elicits their symptoms (Allen & Brown 1932b; Gifford & Hines 1957; Hines & Christensen 1945). Both environmental cold and local cooling are relevant. The effectiveness of cold localized to the involved hands was nicely documented in a series of case reports (Lewis 1929). Nine Raynaud's patients had their fingers dipped into cold water. For eight of them, this was followed by a typical Raynaud's attack with the usual pattern of color changes, even though the rest of their body was at normal room temperature. A more detailed study (Halpern and others 1960) tested five females with primary Raynaud's disease. One hand was placed in a 15°C water bath for ten minutes and then removed. For people without Raynaud's disease, skin temperature dropped to 20°C as a result of the immersion in the bath but recovered quickly and returned to normal levels (30°C) in 30 minutes. For the Raynaud's patients, the immersion produced the typical Raynaud's symptoms of pallor, tactile insensitivity, and cyanosis. Skin temperature at the end of the cooling period was 17°C and remained below 22°C for the next 50 minutes. Thus the reaction of the Raynaud's patients was more severe and of longer duration than that of the controls and also included the typical Raynaud's attack.

A variation on the local cooling procedure was a local warming one (Hyndman & Wolkin 1942). A very heroic patient with primary Raynaud's disease sat nude inside a refrigerator maintained at 4°C. The left arm was placed through a hole and into a warm box maintained at 40°C for 15 minutes and then 30°C for 15 minutes. The authors report that "two minutes after entering the refrigerator, the right index finger (sic) began to sting and became dead white" (p. 544), while the left hand remained pink and comfortable. Thus, local warming was as effective at preventing an attack as local cooling was in bringing it on.

Although provocation by stress is included in almost all of the definitions of Raynaud's disease, patients do not report stress as being as influential as cold (Gifford & Hines 1957). These questionnaire data may reflect a lack of perception on the part of the patients, but they certainly indicate that emotional factors are not perceived as important as cold. Stressful interviews may provoke a Raynaud's attack (Mittlemann & Wolff 1939). The interview was typically "a discussion dwelling on the difficulties in the individual's life situation to which he reacted with signs of distressing emotion" (p. 273), or which involved difficult mental problems during which time the experimenter distracted the person. After about 30 minutes of this stress, the patient was reassured, and encouraged to relax again. For people without Raynaud's disease, the interview produced a substantial drop in skin temperature to about 24°C, which recovered to the normal value of about 32°C within 30 minutes after the interview terminated. For patients with Raynaud's disease, the pattern of skin temperature change was the same as that for the controls, but a typical Raynaud's attack occurred, accompanied by pain, cyanosis, and pallor. The warmth of the patient influenced the course of the attack; patients in cool rooms and those wearing little clothing were more susceptible than patients in warm rooms and those wearing more clothing. Other data indicating that emotional stress is sufficient to provoke vasospastic attacks are reviewed by Sappington, Fiorito, and Brehony (1979).

A similar design was used by Graham (1955) but with substantially different results. Four patients with Raynaud's disease discussed disturbing topics for five to ten minutes while forearm skin temperature was measured. Skin temperature decreased during the interview, but only from 30.6°C to 29.7°C., and the author reports no cases of Raynaud's symptoms. The reasons for the discrepancy between these results and those of Mittlemann and Wolff (1939) are not clear. The stress may have been insufficient in either intensity or duration, or the location of the temperature recording may have been too far from the site of the symptoms.

During the course of an attack, the fingers go through a series of color changes vividly described by Raynaud (Allen & Brown 1932b, p. 401, taken in turn from Raynaud 1888). The classic Raynaud's attack has three major color changes: blue, white, and red (or cyanosis, pallor, and rubor, respectively) at least in patients with skin color that is not very heavily pigmented (Holling 1972). Not all patients have all three colors. In a group of 133 patients, 87% said they had all three phases, 22%

had two, and 13% had one (Gifford & Hines 1957). There may be some bias in these samples because patients who did not have distinct color changes may have been the least likely to report enough information to be included in the final sample. Thus, the presence of the three consecutive color changes provides evidence for Raynaud's disease, but their absence cannot be used to rule it out.

MECHANISM

The color changes in Raynaud's disease are thought to be due to a series of vascular changes affecting the amount of blood flow through the involved body area (Abramson 1974; deTakats & Fowler 1962; Hunt 1936). The pallor results from simultaneous stoppage of both venous and arterial blood flow, and the expelling of all remaining blood from the hand. During this stage, the finger does not bleed when it is pricked (deTakats & Fowler 1962). The cyanosis is caused from slight arterial inflow with no venous outflow, forming a pool of unoxygenated blood. The rubor follows as a reactive hyperemia with excessive vasodilation and a higher than normal blood flow.

Data supporting a decrease in blood flow in Raynaud's patients are abundant. They suggest an impairment while resting and when subjected to cold, either locally or generally. One patient with Raynaud's disease had a greater than normal decrease in blood flow in response to local cooling while sitting in a generally hot environment (Hillestad 1970). Room temperature was 32°C. The person's hand was placed in a water-filled plethysmograph at different temperatures ranging from 40°C to 6°C. The amount of blood flow at the lowest hand temperatures was substantially less than that in the hands of controls. Thus although the person was in a hot environment, local cooling produced a greater than normal decrease in blood flow in the affected extremity.

A comparison of the blood flow in hands maintained at different temperatures also shows the importance of the local temperature on blood flow (Jamieson and others 1971). The patients were lightly covered by a blanket in a room at 22°C. Each hand was placed in a plethysmograph and blood flow measured by venous occlusion. One hand was at 26°C; the other, at 36°C. One set of readings was taken while the person was under the blanket; then a second set was taken after an electric blanket had been turned on long enough to produce sweating. In each condition, the six patients with primary Raynaud's disease had lower blood flows than those of seven normal controls. The decrease in blood flow was minimal for the 36° hand (19% and 15% when the person was under an unheated and heated blanket, respectively) but was substantial for the 26° hand (57% and 47% for those two conditions, respectively).

Blood flow increased for both groups when the electric blanket was turned on, and the relative magnitude of this increase was about the same, indicating that the Raynaud's patients reacted to this test of vasodilation in a manner similar to that exhibited by controls.

When local cooling begins, it may produce a decrease in blood flow, not only in the hand that is cooled, but also in the other hand, even though it is maintained at a warm temperature (McGrath and others 1978). A venous-occlusion plethysmograph was used to measure blood flow. The participants in the study lay down in a room maintained at 23°C for 30 minutes and relaxed in order to stabilize blood flow rates. The right hand was a control and was placed in a plethysmograph at a constant 30°C. The left hand was placed in a similar plethysmograph which was first at 32°C, then at 27°C, 20°C, and 32°C. For normal controls, the blood flow in the cooled hand at 32°C, 27°C, and 20°C was 6, 4.7, and 2.1 ml/100ml/min, respectively. For 22 patients with primary Raynaud's disease as defined by Allen and Brown (1932b), blood flows were 3.3, 1.7, and .8 ml/100ml/min, respectively, a substantial reduction at all temperatures. For the people without Raynaud's symptoms, blood flow in the control hand did not change when the other hand was cooled; for Raynaud's patients, however, blood flow decreased 15% in that hand, even though it was maintained at a constant 32°C. These data suggest that localized cooling in one hand may make the other hand more susceptible to a Raynaud's attack.

Blood flow decreased more than usual in response to general cooling, both in people who had primary Raynaud's disease and in those with related disorders. The reactions of one group of patients with secondary Raynaud's phenomenon were compared to those of normals in both a warm (28°C) and a cool (20°C) room (Coffman & Cohen 1971). Blood flow in the finger was measured by venous-occlusion air plethysmography, and the cutaneous capillary blood flow by clearance rates of a radioisotope. The reactions of both groups of Raynaud's patients were similar. Blood flow in the finger and in the capillaries was about half that of the control patients in both rooms.

Another comparison included four groups of people: inpatients without Raynaud's disease, outpatients without Raynaud's disease, patients who had been diagnosed as having Raynaud's disease or primary acrocyanosis (a closely related problem), and students who suffered from pallor and cyanosis but had not reported to a clinic for treatment (Peacock 1959). Each person was lightly clothed in a 20°C environment and relaxed, lying down for 30 minutes. Skin temperature was taken from a thermistor on the finger, and blood flow was determined by a water-filled plethysmograph at the end of this period. Both skin temperature and blood flow were reduced for both groups of Raynaud's patients.

The control groups had an average skin temperature of 29°C, the Raynaud's patients averaged 22°C, and the students with mild Raynaud's averaged 24°C. Blood flow was 7.7 ml/100ml/min for the control groups and 2.9 ml/100ml/min for the Raynaud's patients.

The above studies demonstrate that the blood flow in the hands of patients with Raynaud's disease is generally less than that of normal people and is particularly sensitive to the local temperature of the hands. Thus one part of the mechanism underlying the pallor and/or cyanosis must be related to a decrease in blood flow. Further specification of the mechanism becomes difficult for two reasons. One is purely logical. By definition primary Raynaud's disease does not result secondarily due to some other disease. Thus, if a fundamental disorder in the cardiovascular system can be demonstrated in patients who are currently diagnosed as having primary Raynaud's disease, the diagnosis will have to be changed. The second problem is more substantial. Even those studies which have looked for physiological malfunctions accompanying primary Raynaud's disease have been unable to agree on a consistent pathophysiological state. Three general hypotheses have been suggested, and each of these will be reviewed briefly in turn.

Raynaud (1862, 1888) suggested that the major problem lay in an overreactivity of the sympathetic nervous system. This overreactivity would, of course, produce a vasoconstriction and subsequent reduction in blood flow. There are several problems with this argument, which according to Hunt (1936) even Raynaud recognized at the time. One body of evidence which at first glance is consistent with this theory concerns the effects of removal of the sympathetic ganglia innervating the involved extremities. Sympathectomy has been successful in the majority of cases. A review of seven studies (Gifford and others 1958) shows good to excellent results in 35% to 89% of the operations, with the success rate being higher for the feet than for the hands. There may be a reappearance of symptoms many years after surgery (Kinmonth & Hadfield 1952; Robertson & Smithwick 1951; Barcroft & Walker 1949), but some cases are successful even with follow-up periods as long as 10 years (Gifford and others 1958; Hall & Hillestad 1960).

Unfortunately these data do not provide support for the autonomic tone hypothesis of Raynaud because the mechanism of cure cannot be used to imply the mechanism of cause. The sympathectomy may have been beneficial simply because it reduced a normal influence which tended to exacerbate the symptoms and not because it removed a pathological one. The data on blood flow and skin temperature with local and general cooling just discussed are also incompatible with this theory because the temperature at the site of the hand is more important in determining the appearance of symptoms than the temperature of the body as a whole, which would have the greater influence on sympathetic tone. Thus pathological involvement of the sympathetic nervous system appears to be an unlikely mechanism.

An alternative explanation is the *local fault* hypothesis proposed by Lewis (1932, 1936, 1938a; Lewis & Kerr 1929; Lewis & Pickering 1934). According to this theory, Raynaud's patients have a problem localized to the involved extremity. The data describing the importance of local temperature on Raynaud's symptoms support this idea. Other support comes from six Raynaud's patients who had undergone sympathectomy (Lewis 1938a). In three of these, the attacks occurred spontaneously or could be induced. Thus although the sympathetic nervous system undoubtedly influenced the amount of blood flowing through the hand, something in the hand itself was important in determining the course of the symptoms. Although this formulation may be generally correct, it is little more than a restatement of the experimental data and does not help to specify the physiological mechanism.

A third hypothesis has suggested that the characteristics of the blood itself is altered in patients with Raynaud's symptoms (Goyle & Dormandy 1976; Pringle and others 1965; Tietjen and others 1975). According to this view, the blood of Raynaud's patients is different from that of normals and may be especially thick (see review by Goyle 1976). Unfortunately, these results have not been consistently replicated, and one study has demonstrated decreased blood flow in Raynaud's patients who had normal blood viscosity (McGrath and others 1978).

In summary, then, there is no question that patients with primary Raynaud's disease have a chronically decreased blood flow which is particularly susceptible to further reduction by localized or general cooling. The physiological mechanisms responsible for this decreased blood flow remain to be demonstrated, and in the final analysis a whole constellation of factors may be relevant, rather than just a single one.

TREATMENT

If Raynaud's attacks are caused by reduction of blood flow in the hands and feet, then procedures which increase blood flow to those areas should warm them and alleviate the attacks. Biofeedback treatment has used a thermistor to record skin temperature from the hands and provided feedback to train patients to increase their hand temperature. The results discussed here and summarized in Table 10–2 suggest that patients are able to reduce the frequency and severity of Raynaud's attacks by increasing skin temperature. These conclusions must be qualified by the limited number of people who have been treated and by the fact that biofeedback was most commonly used in conjunction with other procedures, such as counseling and autogenic training. Most of the studies report results from only a single individual, and these are presented in a series of four case studies. Other reviews, which include papers presented at scientific conventions, suggest that biofeedback can be used to treat Raynaud's disease even after other treatments have been unsatisfactory (Taub & Stroebel 1978; Sappington and others 1979).

Case Study A

This case illustrates the effectiveness of biofeedback alone, even for a person with a long history of Raynaud's disease. It also demonstrates a correlation between the ability to raise skin temperature and the decrease in symptoms. The patient was a woman, 28 years old, who said she had suffered from cold hands and feet for as long as she could remember (Blanchard & Haynes 1975). Her mother also had Raynaud's disease. Prior to biofeedback, she reported an average of one Raynaud's attack per month. The treatment began with four sessions of baseline. Then self-control sessions in which skin temperature was recorded but no feedback was provided were alternated with sessions during which she received analogue feedback. The order of the sessions was six self-control, six biofeedback, six self-control, and six biofeedback. Each session was 20 minutes long. Skin temperature was recorded from the hand and the forehead with thermistors, and analogue feedback provided information about the difference between the temperature of the hand and that of the forehead. Follow-up assessments were obtained at two, four, and seven months after treatment. The average temperature of the hand, which was 79°F in the pretreatment baseline period, rose to 92°F during feedback and remained between 87°F and 90°F at the three follow-up periods. During the feedback sessions she was able to raise her hand temperature by 3.6°F, an increase approximately double that demonstrated during the baseline and self-control sessions. Seven months after treatment, she was able to increase skin temperature by 2.2°F and reported that her symptoms had almost entirely disappeared.

Case Study B

Here, biofeedback was combined with relaxation and autogenic training to reduce Raynaud's symptoms which had persisted for 30 years (Peper, in Surwit 1973). The patient was a woman, 50 years old, who had experienced Raynaud's attacks since she was 20. For biofeedback, finger temperature was recorded with a thermistor. Feedback sessions were 10 minutes long and took place twice each day for 30 days. Relaxation instructions and autogenic training were also incorporated. The temperature of her finger, which was 75°F before training, increased to 85°F after training. She said she was able to hold on to the cold steering wheel of her car without gloves for the first time in 30 years.

Case Study C

Most people who seek treatment for Raynaud's disease are women. In this case, however, the patient was a man whose symptoms could not be treated by drugs due to undesirable side effects (Jacobson and others 1973). He was 31 years old with a three-year history of episodic coldness and tingling in the fingers. The Raynaud's attacks were triggered by cold temperatures, smoking, or anxiety at work. His aunt also had Raynaud's disease. Reserpine had been tried but was discontinued due to disturbing side effects. For biofeedback, skin temperature was recorded from the finger and forehead with thermistors. Feedback provided information about the difference between the skin temperature of the two areas, and he was asked to raise the temperature of his hand relative to that of his forehead in four sessions, each 15 minutes long. Training in autohypnosis and thermal suggestion was included and focused on feeling warmth in the limbs. The ability to raise skin temperature improved after training, and the Raynaud's symptoms decreased. During the final biofeedback session, he increased skin temperature by 4°C and said he could raise skin temperature and change the color of his hands by recalling his biofeedback training procedure. In addition, he was able to pick up cold objects without experiencing a Raynaud's attack. He retained the ability to increase skin temperature at a follow-up, seven months after treatment.

Case Study D

Although this treatment produced an improvement of Raynaud's symptoms for a short period of time, that improvement was temporary and lasted for only one year. The patient was a woman, 21 years old, with a five-year history of Raynaud's disease (Surwit 1973). She experienced attacks in the hands and feet, and her face was unusually sensitive to cold. Cervical and lumbar sympathectomies alleviated the symptoms in her feet, but pain continued in her hands and face. Her treatment included counseling, assertiveness training, relaxation, autogenic imagery, thermal suggestion, and biofeedback. Skin temperature was recorded with a thermistor. Biofeedback sessions were 30 minutes each and took place 14 times in three weeks. This was followed one month later by 20 minutes of feedback twice weekly for 16 weeks. Training was interrupted again for 30 days and then scheduled once weekly for six months. By the end of training, her finger temperature had increased to between 23°C and 26.6°C. The number of attacks "markedly decreased" (p. 126), and she was able to go outdoors during the Canadian winter without difficulty. Suddenly, one year after the training, she lost her ability to control skin temperature.

Discussion of Treatments

Biofeedback and Autogenic Training. The relative effectiveness of autogenic training alone and biofeedback in conjunction with autogenic training was examined with 32 women between 23 and 54 years of age (Surwit and others 1978). All of them were diagnosed as having Raynaud's disease but no other vasomotor irregularities. Half of them received modified autogenic training (Schultz & Luthe 1969) alone. The other half received both the autogenic training and biofeedback. For both groups, autogenic training took place with tape recordings, and they practiced both with and without the recordings. Training took place for 45 minutes, once every two weeks, for 11 weeks, either in the clinic or at home. For the patients who also received biofeedback, a thermistor or a crystal thermometer recorded skin temperature from the hand, and they practiced their autogenic exercises while getting feedback about hand temperature. All participants were told to practice the autogenic exercises at home, twice a day for 15 minutes each time and up to 30 times a day for 30 to 60 seconds each time. When practicing the autogenic training with the tape recordings, both groups of patients raised their skin temperature an average of .3°C. Without the tapes, however, neither group was able to significantly increase skin temperature. The patients had an average of 2.3 Raynaud's attacks each day during the four weeks prior to treatment but only 1.6 attacks per day during the training period. The authors report that at the end of training, patients could maintain approximately normal skin temperatures even with room temperatures as low as 17°C, and that the biofeedback procedure plus autogenic training was no more effective than autogenic training alone.

CLINICAL PROGRAM

As indicated in the introduction, cold hands and feet can arise from many different causes, some relatively benign, others threatening. A complete medical diagnosis is necessary to identify any physiological problems associated with the complaints of coldness and to make a prognosis about the future development of the disorder. A list of questions to obtain information about the symptoms of a Raynaud's patient is presented in List 10–1 (see also p. 92).

Some Questions About Symptoms for Patients Having Raynaud's Disease

What parts of your body are most often cold?

Describe the symptoms.

    Do your hands and/or feet turn different colors?

    If so,

        Do they become white?

        Do they become blue?

        Do they become red?

    Do your hands and/or feet hurt? If so, when?

    Do you have difficulty moving your hands and/or feet?

    Do you have difficulty feeling objects with your hands and feet?

When are the symptoms most likely to appear?

    Do they occur more frequently at certain times of the year?

    Do they occur more frequently before or after certain activities?

    Do you associate the symptoms with any kind of stress? If so, what kind?

Do you have other difficulties with your hands and feet?

    Do you have sores that don't heal?

    Is your skin hard or cracked?

    Do you have difficulties with your nails?

What do you do to help prevent or get rid of your symptoms?

    How do you dress?

    What do you do when you have an attack?

    What drugs have you taken and what has been their success?

    Have you tried any kind of relaxation or meditation?

Common sense should dictate clothing and life style. Primary Raynaud's disease is provoked by cold and prevented by warmth. Particularly important is protection of the hands, feet, and legs. Gloves should be worn when necessary and a means provided for an external source of heat whenever possible. Heavy socks and pants in winter are appropriate. The client should be made sensitive to the types of cold stimuli encountered in the normal course of life and told how to protect against the effects of those stimuli.

Nicotine is a potent vasoconstrictor. One or two cigarettes can decrease blood flow and increase peripheral resistance, resulting in a substantial drop of skin temperature (Coffman 1967; Eckstein and others 1957; Roth and others 1944). Furthermore, cessation of smoking may have a beneficial effect on blood flow (Janzon 1976). Medical treatment of Raynaud's disease almost always recommends abstinence of smoking as an important step in the control of the symptoms. A case report of a young woman with Raynaud's disease demonstrates the role of smoking in eliciting her symptoms (Hansteen 1965, p. 90). If she had not been smoking, having her hands placed in a 15°C water bath for 15 minutes produced a slight drop in hand temperature not accompanied by Raynaud's symptoms. The skin temperature recovered to normal in about

TABLE 10-2   Summary of Biofeedback Treatments for Raynaud's Disease

Study	Patients	Biofeedback Treatment	Other Treatment	Results	
				Symptoms	Biological Function
Blanchard & Haynes, 1975	Female, age 28	Feedback of changes in finger skin temperature during 12, 20-min sessions	None reported	Prior to treatment, episodes of "painful vasoconstriction" occurred once monthly; by the 7-month follow-up, "the clinical problem of Raynaud's disease was mostly abated"	Average hand temperature of 79°F rose to 91.1°F following training, and remained at 88.3°F at 7-month follow-up
Jacobson, Hackett, Surman, & Silverberg, 1973	Male, age 31	Feedback of changes in finger skin temperature during 4, 15-min sessions	Autohypnosis and thermal suggestions	Initial complaint was blueness and tingling of hands; "by the last session, the patient could induce changes in both the color and temperature of his hands," and could grasp cold objects without experiencing a vasospasmodic attack	Temperatures increased bilaterally from 3.9°C to 4.3°C during the final sessions; a 7½ month follow-up indicated that the subject was still as effective in controlling hand warmth as during training
Peper (in Surwit, 1973)	Female, age 50	Feedback of changes in finger skin temperature during 10-min sessions, twice daily for 30 days	Relaxation and autogenic training	Following treatment, the patient "reported that for the first time in 30 years she could hold on to the cold steering wheel of her car without gloves"	Basal finger temperature of 75°F increased to 85°F

| Surwit, 1973 | Female, age 21 | Feedback of left hand temperature for 30 min, 14 times during a three-week period; this was followed one month later with 20-min sessions twice weekly for 16 weeks and then at weekly intervals for six months | Relaxation, autogenic imagery, counseling, and assertiveness training | "Vasospasms in left hand and face" prior to training; "markedly decreased attacks" following training; at one year follow-up, patient complained of pain even when skin temperatures were normal and reported losing all ability to control skin temperature | After a year of training basal skin temperatures rose bilaterally from 23°C to an average of 26.6°C |
| Surwit, Pilon, & Fenton, 1978 | 32 females, age range 27 to 54 | Visual feedback of changes in finger skin temperature during six, 45-min sessions in 11 weeks while performing autogenic relaxation response | Autogenic training, home practice twice daily for 15 min, and a "response generalization" technique | Average number of attacks decreased from 2.3 per day during the four weeks preceding training, to 1.6 during training; severity ratings also decreased | Average increase of .3°C while listening to autogenic instructions; no other increases during the session; "the patients were able to maintain near normal levels of digital skin temperature after an hour's exposure to ambient temperatures down to 17°C" |

ten minutes. After a single cigarette, this same treatment produced a much greater drop in hand temperature which was accompanied by Raynaud's symptoms; skin temperature continued at a depressed level (22°C) for at least 20 minutes at which point it still showed no signs of recovery. Although the case for giving up smoking needs to be documented further, any vasoconstrictive substance should lower the threshold for Raynaud's symptoms and increase their severity and duration.

Relaxation procedures are important here, as with migraine headaches, and for the same reason. The relaxation can be practiced at home without equipment and should help induce a general peripheral vasodilation, rather than a localized change.

Exercise is a means of raising blood flow in the extremities. In treating clients with cold hands and feet, we have often incorporated a brief period of energetic exercise prior to a hand-warming session. This is particularly beneficial for clients who have difficulty raising skin temperature after about 10 to 15 minutes. A short break for running up and down three flights of stairs followed by biofeedback has had a marked effect, with skin temperatures increasing five to ten degrees Fahrenheit in the subsequent ten minutes. This procedure does not separate the individual components of exercise and biofeedback, but it does increase the hand temperature, which is the ultimate goal. It has been more effective than exercise alone.

The most widely used source of feedback has been skin temperature from an affected area such as the finger, toe, or face. Commercially available equipment is sufficient for most applications. The area should be shielded from drafts and contacts with extraneous sources, such as arms on chairs or other parts of the body. If the patient traps the thermistor between a finger and a leg, for example, the contact will create an abnormally high temperature. Room temperature and humidity should be held constant. The skin should be dry when the thermistor is attached. Analogue feedback is preferred because skin temperature changes very slowly in relation to many other physiological responses. The feedback should be contingent on at most a one-tenth of a degree (Fahrenheit) change.

Sessions should be held in the clinic, once or twice each week at the beginning of treatment, with each session composed of two trials lasting 20 minutes each, separated by a brief rest. As control is established and skin temperature rises, the interval between sessions can be increased to permit elimination of feedback. Home practice with or without a portable trainer should be included each day. Skin temperature may be relatively difficult to control so that many sessions may be required for success, particularly during cold weather. Because large temperature changes may be expected when a client enters the laboratory from a cold environment, and because only small changes in skin temperature might be seen initially during an early trial, we recommend a baseline period at the beginning of each session. Once the client's temperature stabilizes, such as plus or minus .3°F for three minutes, biofeedback training can begin.

ASTHMA

11

Introduction

Symptoms

Mechanism

Treatment

Clinical Program

Research Considerations

INTRODUCTION

During a typical asthmatic attack, there is a shortness of breath (dyspnea) and trouble breathing, particularly during expiration when considerable muscular effort is required and wheezing occurs. The attacks are intermittent and range in severity from a minor inconvenience to status asthmaticus, a life threatening condition in which so much effort is required to breathe and so little air is exchanged that hospitalization may be required and death may result (Thurlbeck 1978; also see Bocles 1970; Weiss 1978). In 1960, a health survey estimated that there were two million children in the United States with asthma and hay fever, and that of these about one-quarter of a million had chronic intractable asthma with pulmonary function subnormal, even between acute attacks (Peshkin 1967). Another survey interviewed all the 9,926 residents of a small town in Michigan (Broder and others 1974). Asthma was defined as the patient reporting a wheezing sound, a shortness of breath, and difficulty exhaling, along with an allergic response and a positive diagnosis for allergy by a physician. Four percent of the people were diagnosed as certainly having asthma, and an additional four percent were diagnosed as probably having asthma. The initial reports of almost half of the patients disagreed with their final diagnosis by the interviewers; 18% of the people who said they had asthma did not, and 25% of them who said they did not have asthma, did. A review of earlier surveys is presented in Broder, Barlow and Horton (1962).

A precise definition of asthma, and especially its distinction from other respiratory diseases, has remained elusive. In some cases, investigators have refused to come to a conclusion about a definition (Ciba Foundation 1971). In other cases, comprehensive classifications have been offered in an attempt to encompass all possibilities (Fraser & Paré 1970, Chapter 13; MacDonnell 1976, pp. 699–703; Murphy 1976, pp. 522–523; Scadding 1976, p. 23; Vaughn and others 1973) and to distinguish asthma from bronchitis and other pulmonary diseases (American Thoracic Society 1962; Lowell 1978; Petty 1978; Snider 1976;

Williams & McNicol 1969). The difficulty is exacerbated because the symptoms of asthma may appear following many different kinds of pathophysiologies (Fraser & Paré 1970, p. 971; Valentine 1976), leading to the view that asthma is a syndrome and not a disease, with wheezing as the only invariant characteristic.

There is a general agreement that asthma is characterized by shortness of breath, wheezing, and difficulty breathing, particularly during expiration. Furthermore, these symptoms are due to an obstruction of the airways that is at least partially reversible. Other characteristics of asthmatic patients vary widely. The presence or absence of allergies is indicated by the adjectives *atopic* and *nonatopic*, respectively. Atopic patients have allergies identifiable by skin tests and the presence of antibodies; they usually have a family history of allergy and develop their asthmatic symptoms at an early age (Fraser & Paré 1970, p. 971). Nonatopic patients do not have identifiable allergies. Another distinction is between patients for whom specific substances can be identified which provoke asthma and patients for whom this is not possible. The terms *extrinsic* and *intrinsic* are often used to describe these two groups, respectively. The permanence of the asthmatic symptoms may be differentiated with appropriate adjectives. *Intractable* asthma refers to symptoms that are not completely reversible, that persist for a long period of time (one year or longer), and require continued medical treatment (Peshkin & Friedman 1975, p. 166). The symptoms may vascillate in severity during this period, but they are always present in some degree. *Status asthmaticus* is an even more severe attack in which hospitalization may be required (Weiss 1978).

A number of specific factors are known to increase the susceptibility to asthma. Workers in some occupations develop specific reactions to substances with which they work, leading to the classification of *occupational* asthma (Karr and others 1978; Murphy 1976). The substances include: wood dust (carpenters), flour (bakers), tea (tea makers), coffee (coffee workers) and specific chemicals (hair dressers, plastic workers). Even the location of residence within a city can be associated with a substantial increase in the incidence of asthma (Goldstein & Arthur 1978). Air pollution and cigarette smoke are also relevant. Thus, the clinical symptoms of asthma may occur in response to a variety of stimuli.

Asthma is interesting to the psychophysiologically oriented clinician for three reasons. First, of course, it is a disorder that may be successfully treated with biofeedback. Second, psychological variables can enhance or suppress asthmatic attacks. The strong reactions of some asthmatic patients to stress and suggestion provide excellent examples of the extent to which these factors can alter the course of disease states and add an important dimension to the behavioral treatment of this disorder. Third, the mechanism of asthma attacks places heavy emphasis on the role of the parasympathetic portion of the autonomic nervous system. Stress related disorders are often linked to overreactivity of the sympathetic nervous system, but with asthma the symptoms are enhanced by parasympathetic activity and suppressed by sympathetic activity, providing further support for the ability of the autonomic nervous system to function discretely.

Two different types of biofeedback treatments have been used to reduce asthmatic symptoms. One teaches general relaxation. Surface electrodes are placed on the forehead over the frontalis muscle, and the person is taught to relax this muscle. The other treatment trains the person to increase the amount of air exhaled at each breath or to decrease the resistance of the airways to the passage of air. Because the respiratory functions of most asthmatic patients return to normal levels between attacks, mild asthmatic symptoms are induced before training begins. If the person is successful in reducing the severity of the symptoms with biofeedback, training continues. If not, then drugs are used to eliminate the attack. Biofeedback has increased respiratory function and decreased asthmatic attacks.

SYMPTOMS

Respiratory Function

The experience of an asthmatic person during an attack is often compared to that of a normal person breathing through a straw. Although this is obviously distressing and uncomfortable, it still doesn't capture the true difficulty because the asthmatic person has to breathe with the lungs constantly inflated in order to keep the airways open enough to breathe (Permutt 1973; Summer 1978). Thus a more accurate model is obtained by a person taking a deep breath, expanding the lungs as much as possible, and then exchanging only a small portion of the air in the lungs at each breath (while breathing through a straw) so that lungs remain hyperinflated even at the end of an exhalation. In this latter model, the air exchange is less efficient, producing a greater need for oxygen, and the accessory muscles for respiration are brought into use, requiring more effort to breathe.

Two measures of respiratory function, illustrated in Figure 11–1, reflect the asthmatic patient's respiratory difficulties. *Vital capacity,* abbreviated VC, is the volume of air measured in cubic centimeters (or liters) that can be exhaled beginning with a full inspiration. It is measured by having the person take as large a breath as possible and then exhale as much as possible. During an attack, vital capacity is reduced

FIGURE 11–1   A Comparison of Respiratory Function for a Normal Person Breathing Normally (Curve A), a Normal Person Breathing Through a Resistance (Curve B), and an Asthmatic Patient Breathing Freely During an Asthmatic Attack (Curve C).
Vital capacity is the volume of air which can be exhaled from the lungs beginning with a full inspiration. FEV_1 is the volume of air that can be exhaled from the lungs (beginning with a full inspiration) in one second. The asthmatic patient had a reduced vital capacity and a reduced FEV_1, showing that an asthmatic attack cannot be modelled by having a normal person simply breath through a straw because this reduced only FEV_1. *(From Earle B. Weiss, M.D., ed., Status Asthmaticus. Copyright © 1978 by University Park Press, Baltimore. Reprinted by permission.)*

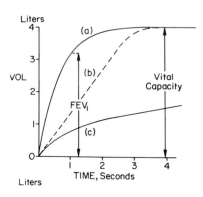

(curve *c* at 4 seconds), indicating that the normal lung volume is not fully available to the person. The *forced expiratory volume in one second*, abbreviated FEV_1, is the volume of air measured in cubic centimeters (or liters) that can be exhaled in one second following a full inspiration. Because the measure is one of volume per time, it provides an indication of the speed with which a person can eliminate air from the lungs. It too is markedly decreased (curve *c* at 1 second) during an asthma attack.

Figure 11–1 compares the respiratory function of an asthmatic patient with that of a normal person breathing normally, and breathing through a resistance, which decreases the FEV_1 but does not affect VC. As compared to the normal person breathing normally in curve *a*, the asthmatic person in curve *c* not only exhaled less air in one second, indicating a reduced FEV_1, but also exhaled less air irrespective of time, indicating a reduced vital capacity. The normal person breathing through a resistance in curve *b* had a reduced FEV_1 similar to that of the asthmatic patient but did not have a reduced vital capacity. Another example comes from an experiment in which five normal healthy volunteers breathed through a resistance valve that increased airway resistance from 2.3 cm $H_2O/L/sec$ to 31.9 cm $H_2O/L/sec$ (Kazemi & Kanarek 1978). This produced only a slight decrease in vital capacity and no differences in the oxygen or carbon dioxide content of the blood. Thus more than just increased airway resistance is needed to model an asthmatic attack, and this is a reduced vital capacity, which is highly correlated with the magnitude of the decrease in arterial oxygen (Kazemi & Kanarek 1978). The need to keep the lungs inflated to a greater than normal volume in order to exhale also forces the use of accessory muscles of respiration, which means that more effort is required to breathe. A whole constellation of cardiopulmonary changes follow: the partial pressure of arterial oxygen increases, the partial pressure of carbon dioxide decreases, oxygen consumption increases, and the cardiac index increases (Summer 1978, p. 91). Together, these measures point out the inefficiency of the person's respiration, reflecting the greater effort and decreased effectiveness of breathing, and the implications of this inefficiency for the entire body.

Even when not having an attack, asthmatic patients are more sensitive to pulmonary irritants than normals (see reviews by Nadel 1973; Widdicombe 1963). Indeed, this increased sensitivity may be the most important feature of asthma (Bouhuys 1974). Cold air, citric acid aerosols, chemicals, dust, mechanical stimulation, bronchoconstricting drugs—all these produce significant bronchoconstriction in asthmatic patients at concentrations that are usually ineffective for people with normal respiratory function (Townley and others 1975; Ryo & Townley 1976). Asthmatic patients may be more sensitive to stress as well (Khan & Olson 1977; Strauss and others 1977).

Psychological Variables

Family Interactions   For children with asthma, unsatisfactory interpersonal relationships with family members may be a major factor provoking attacks. Data supporting this view come from a variety of sources. For example, children with severe intractable asthma may leave their family home and enter a special residential treatment facility where they can receive comprehensive care. Of these children, about 40% show substantial improvement within a few days to a few weeks, even without any change in medication (Peshkin 1930, 1959, 1966, 1967, 1976; Peshkin & Friedman 1975; Rogerson 1934; Tuft 1957; Unger & Unger 1952). These children have been called *rapid remitters* (Purcell 1963, 1965; Purcell and others 1961; Purcell and others 1969) to emphasize the speed with which their symptoms disappear and to distinguish them from *corticosteroid dependent* children whose symptoms appear to be mainly a function of their medication regimen and are not particularly influenced by removal from the home. These two categories of children reflect the end points of a continuum, rather than mutually exclusive categories, emphasizing the consistent finding that about one-third of the asthmatic population is strongly influenced by psychological variables, while another one-third is influenced very little. (The remaining third is, of course, intermediate between these extremes.) Importantly, the rapid remitting and steroid dependent groups do not differ in terms of the physical characteristics of their asthmatic symptoms (Purcell and others 1961), so that these variables are unlikely to be responsible for the differences between the groups.

Entrance into a residential facility has been referred to as *parentectomy* suggesting that the critical change is separation of the child from its parents. But many variables, physical as well as psychological, change when a child moves away from home, so that additional data are necessary before the rapid remission of symptoms can be directly attributed to removal of parental influences. Environmental variables are not critical because rapid remitters appear among children who come from the same geographical location as the treatment facility (Tuft 1957). Likewise, medication cannot be the important factor because children often get better within a few days of admission, before any substantial changes have been made in their medication.

The most direct test of the role of the parents in producing asthmatic attack was carried out in an imaginative study in which the asthmatic children remained home while the rest of the family moved away (Purcell and others 1969). The participants in the study were 25 children, five to 13 years old. For four weeks prior to the separation, information was obtained about the characteristics of the asthmatic attacks and the role of emotion in precipitating them. The participants listed events that provoked asthma attacks and ordered these in their importance. The children were divided into two groups on the basis of a questionnaire given prior to separation. *Positive Responders* listed emotional events among the three most important events provoking asthma attacks, *Negative Responders* did not. The experimenters predicted that the subsequent separation from the family would alleviate asthmatic symptoms for the 13 children who were Positive Responders but not for the 12 children who were Negative Responders. During two weeks of separation, the family moved to a nearby hotel and was requested to avoid all contact with the child. A trained guardian came to live with the child at home, and the child maintained the usual daily routine of school, play, and so on. Four measures of asthma were obtained: peak expiratory flow in one second, the amount of wheezing at a clinical examination, the amount of medication taken, and reports of the guardian. These same measures were taken during a subsequent two-week period of reunion when the guardian left and the family returned. For the Positive Responders, the separation and reunion had a substantial effect on asthmatic symptoms. As compared to the two weeks prior to and following the separation, the two weeks of separation were accompanied by a greater peak flow (increased from 160 1/min to 180 1/min), fewer attacks (decreased from .8 per week to .4 per week), less medication (decreased from 2.4 units to 1.4), and lowered symptom scores during the clinical examination (4.1

units as compared to 5.5). Using a measure of clinical usefulness in which the symptoms had to improve significantly during separation and regress during the reunion, the authors concluded that the separation had a clinically significant effect for 7 of the 13 Positive Responders but only 3 of the 12 Negative Responders. These results are important for two reasons. First, family interactions can be pinpointed as the critical variable because the family was removed from the child, rather than the child from the family, thus minimizing extraneous physical and/or psychological changes that take place when a child is taken to an institution for care. Second, the difference in susceptibility of asthmatics to psychological variables is emphasized; the children for whom emotions were listed as important precipitating factors showed a substantial change while the children for whom emotions were not listed as important precipitating factors did not. The authors also report that some families realized the importance of their interactions as the study progressed, and those who changed their interpersonal relationships often produced significant reductions in the child's symptoms.

Retrospective questionnaires and interviews consistently identify emotional factors as being important for about half the children examined in treatment centers and in outpatient clinics. These may appear as the only influential variable for some children or as one of a set of variables for others. Examples of the types of events eliciting the attacks typically describe interpersonal interactions with members of the immediate family (Ford 1963; Rees 1964; Wright 1965). As might be expected, children who were rapid remitters reported being more influenced by emotional factors than children who were steroid dependent (Purcell 1963).

Interviews with the families of children admitted to residential treatment centers give the impression that the parents are often hostile towards the child and that the rapid remitters are aware they live in an unpleasant home (Bentley 1975; Miller & Baruch 1948). Identifying and quantifying the child-rearing practices that may be important has been difficult. Structured interviews and projective tests demonstrate slight differences between the interactions of families with asthmatic children and those with normal children, but these are often difficult to interpret (Rees 1963) and in most cases are very small (Fitzelle 1959; Sandler 1965a,b).

Taken together, these studies show that psychological factors, particularly family interactions, can have a significant influence on asthma. Both children and parents list interpersonal relations within the family as important precipitants of asthmatic attacks, and removal of the asthmatic child from the family may significantly improve respiratory function, even with no changes in medication. Not all children are equally affected by these factors, and the asthmatic attacks of 25% to 50% of asthmatic children appear to be unrelated to family stress. The families of children for whom family stress is an important precipitator of asthma attacks are not markedly different from the families of children for whom family stress is largely irrelevant. Consequently, the variables distinguishing between children whose asthma is affected mainly by family stress and children whose asthma is affected mainly by other variables must lie, not in the family interactions they experience, but rather in the child's reaction to them. These results in no way minimize the importance of family variables in provoking asthmatic attacks, they just make the identification of the critical conditions more difficult (see also the summary by Knapp and others 1976, p. 1064; Rees 1964).

Suggestion. For some people with asthma, an expectation about the effects of an inhaled substance may have a profound effect on pulmonary function. In these demonstrations, the person inhaled an aerosol spray after being given a suggestion as to the nature of the substance in the spray and/or the effects it should have on respiration. In some cases, of course, the suggestion was appropriate for the inhaled substances, while in other cases it was not. Some people consistently reacted to these suggestions. For any given substance, a suggestion that it was a bronchoconstrictor suppressed respiratory function, relative to a condition in which no suggestion was given. Some of the results were dramatic. Physiological saline, which normally has no effect on respiratory function, has produced asthmatic attacks when given with a suggestion that it is an allergen and has eliminated attacks when given along with a suggestion that it is *Isuprel,* a therapeutic bronchodilating drug used to reduce asthmatic symptoms. Likewise, the respiratory effects of bronchodilating and bronchoconstricting drugs have been enhanced or suppressed by appropriate suggestions. The experience of the people in the testing situation (Khan and others 1973; Strupp and others 1974) and the substance being inhaled may influence the magnitude of the results, but the overall pattern is remarkably consistent.

One of the first investigations of the effects of suggestion on airway reactivity studied the reactions of 40 patients with asthma, 15 with bronchitis, and 10 without respiratory disease (Luparello and others 1968). Each person took ten deep breaths of a physiological saline aerosol but was told that it was an allergen. Of the 40 asthmatics 12 had a typical asthma attack with dyspnea and wheezing. These 12 patients were then given another saline aerosol to inhale and told that it was Isuprel. The asthmatic symptoms were substantially alleviated, and respiratory function improved by 80%. The patients with bronchitis and the normal controls did not react to the suggestion, nor did the other asthmatics.

Emergency room patients also responded to suggestion (Luparello and others 1970). Each patient was given either 125 uG of *isoproteronol* (a bronchodilator) or 50 uG of *carbachol* (a bronchoconstrictor) and was told that the substance was a bronchodilator or that it was a broncho-constrictor, producing four groups (two substances $\times$ two suggestions). As was to be expected, the bronchodilator decreased the severity of the attack while the bronchoconstrictor enhanced it. The expectations of the patient were important too, and the suggestions had an effect half as great as the drugs themselves, significantly modifying the response to the drugs.

Correct and incorrect suggestions had similar effects on the reactions of asthmatic outpatients to saline and to *mecholyl*, a bronchoconstrictor (Philipp and others 1972). Half of the patients had identifiable allergies; the other half did not. Each substance was given with either the correct suggestion (neutral substance for saline, bronchoconstrictor for mecholyl) or the incorrect suggestion (neutral substance for mecholyl, bronchocon-strictor for saline). Both a drug effect and a suggestion effect occurred. Greater bronchoconstriction occurred to mecholyl (16% decrease from baseline) than to saline (5% reduction) and to the bronchoconstriction suggestion (13%) than to the saline suggestion (8%). The atopic and nonatopic patients reacted similarly except that the atopic ones failed to show an effect of the suggestion when inhaling saline.

Patients are usually consistent in their reactions to suggestion. One group of 29 patients was given a saline aerosol to inhale on two different tests (McFadden and others 1969). They were told they would be in-haling an agent which would produce an asthma attack and that it would be given five times, each one with a concentration greater than the last. Each person took ten deep breaths during 30 seconds; four minutes later, airway resistance was measured. The respiratory function of 15 of the patients was markedly reduced; 11 of these people had a typical asthmatic attack. In a second test, 13 of these 15 patients reacted again with de-creased respiratory function. Additional variations were carried out. After the second set of tests, if a person had an asthmatic attack, Isuprel was given along with the instructions that it was a bronchoconstrictor. Inhalation produced a slight bronchoconstriction instead of the usual bronchodilation.

There are two important results from this series of experiments. First, some people consistently react to suggestion, demonstrating an important role of psychological variables in pulmonary function for these indi-viduals. Second, only some people are reactors; about half of the people tested showed no reaction to suggestion, as used in these experimental pro-cedures. The magnitude of the change obviously depends on the relative strength of the suggestion and the inhaled substance. None the less, the observed effects have been dramatic; suggestions have produced and eliminated asthmatic attacks in response to saline and significantly influenced respiratory responses to both bronchodilating and bronchoconstricting drugs.

Panic-Fear.   Patients differ in their reactions to asthmatic attacks along a dimension that has been called *panic-fear*. High panic-fear patients exaggerate their problems and constantly seek treatment, even when it isn't needed. Low panic-fear patients deny the severity of their disorder and don't seek treatment, even when it is needed. In between these two extremes lies a group who are sensitive to their symptoms and behave appropriately with respect to them. Two measures of panic-fear have been obtained. One is the *asthmatic symptom checklist,* asking questions specifically about asthma. Items on the panic-fear scale include: statements about being scared, worried, panicky, frightened, worried about an asthmatic attack, worried about oneself, and afraid of dying (Kinsman and others 1973; Kinsman and others 1974). The second measure is with a group of items from the MMPI, a commonly used personality test. These items are taken from throughout the MMPI, and form a new scale (Dahlem and others 1977; Dirks, Jones, & Kinsman 1977). The correlates of these two scales may differ; a possible reason lies in the difference between them, the MMPI using very general items, the asthmatic symptom checklist using items closely related to asthma (Dirks, Kinsman and others 1977; Dirks, Kleiger and others 1978). In essence, the MMPI may be more sensitive to *trait* variables while the asthmatic symptoms checklist may be more sensitive to *state* variables (Dirks, Kinsman and others 1978).

High MMPI Panic-Fear patients describe themselves as fearful, highly emotional, sensitive to criticism, helpless, and inclined to give up easily in the face of difficulty. At the opposite extreme, *low MMPI Panic-Fear* patients describe themselves as experiencing very little discomfort or anxiety and as being unusually calm, stable, and self-controlled (Dahlem and others 1977, p. 295). This distinction is important because it interacts strongly with the way in which asthmatics treat their symptoms, and perhaps even the way in which they perceive the severity of their attacks. The asthmatic symptom checklist was used to separate 87 asthmatic patients into high panic-fear (at least .5 standard deviation greater than the mean), low panic-fear (at least .5 standard deviation below the mean), and moderate panic-fear (the rest). High panic-fear patients requested medication twice as often as low panic-fear patients, even though the respiratory functions of the two groups were essentially the same. In addition, neither of the groups varied the amount of medication with the severity of their attacks, taking the same amount of medication when pulmonary function was normal and when it was subnormal. Only the patients with moderate panic-fear varied the amount of medication with the severity of their attacks, taking more when pulmonary function was subnormal and less when it was normal. Patients who had either high or low panic-fear scores were more likely to be rehospitalized than patients who had moderates scores (Dirks, Kinsman and others 1978). The participants were 236 patients admitted to a hospital for treatment of asthma. Within the first year following discharge from the hospital, the percent of patients in each panic-fear group who sought readmission for treatment of an asthma attack was high, 58%; moderate, 32%; low, 57%. As usual, the amount of panic-fear was not correlated with the severity of asthma (Dirks, Kinsman and others 1978; Kinsman and others 1977; Kinsman and others 1974).

Together, these studies demonstrate that there is a major difference in the way in which asthmatic patients react to their symptoms. Both high and low panic-fear patients react inappropriately: the first group exaggerates the severity of their symptoms at all times; the second group minimizes them. Only the moderate panic-fear patients appear to be able to monitor their symptoms accurately and respond to them adaptively. Because panic-fear scores are independent of respiratory measures, this dimension describes the manner in which patients cope with their symptoms, and not the symptoms themselves. As emphasized by Dirks, Kinsman, Horton, Fross, and Jones (1978), these different personality styles call for different types of therapeutic treatment, a point which is considered again later.

Laboratory Studies of Stress. Although many people with asthma say their attacks are closely tied to stress and emotions, laboratory studies trying to demonstrate the influence of stress on asthma have had mixed results (Khan 1973; Leigh 1953; McDermott & Cobb 1939). Typical asthmatic attacks were elicited by stressful interviews (Wolf & Goodell 1968) and by stimuli associated with a disturbing dream (Dekker & Groen 1956). Slight but significant reductions in respiratory function were produced in college students carrying out mental arithmetic while being criticized (Mathe & Knapp 1971) and in children listening to a tape recording of an event which had produced fear or anger (Tal & Miklich 1976). No effect on respiratory function was found with children who listened to a tape recording of an asthmatic attack or waited for an unpredictable electric shock (Weiss and others 1976) or in children who carried out mental arithmetic while being given unexpected loud noises or electric shock (Hahn 1966; Hahn & Clark 1967).

Many factors may be responsible for this lack of consistency. For example, the stimuli used in the experiments may not have been sufficient to elicit the desired reactions (Tal & Miklich 1976). Other reasons include the person's familiarity with the types of stimuli usually eliciting an attack, sophistication with respect to experimental procedures, and relative insensitivity to suggestion. Finally, sufficient stress may suppress, rather than enhance, asthmatic symptoms, as indicated in both case reports (Hale 1966; McDermott & Cobb 1939) and experimental studies (Funkenstein 1953). These results are unexpected in light of the regularly reported importance of emotional factors in provoking asthmatic attacks, suggesting that more imaginative, convincing, and relevant stressful situations need to be tried.

MECHANISM

Respiratory Function

As described in Figure 11-1, the asthmatic patient has a decreased vital capacity and difficulty exhaling. These result from several fundamental changes in the respiratory system. First, the smooth muscles surrounding the airways contract, producing bronchoconstriction, so that at any given pressure the lung volume available for respiration is reduced. Second, there is a massive secretion of mucuous in the lungs, further reducing the useable lung volume. Third, other factors, such as pulmonary edema, further reduce the respiratory capacity of the individual. The asthmatic patient has to breathe at higher than normal lung volumes in order to keep the airways expanded sufficiently to allow air to pass through them. A severe asthmatic attack can be detected by almost any measure of pulmonary function, including forced expiration, lung volume, and airway resistance (Fraser & Paré 1970; McFadden 1976; Summer 1978; Swineford 1965).

Autonomic Nervous System

Both the sympathetic and parasympathetic nervous systems influence pulmonary functions (see Chapter 4). Activity in the sympathetic system produces bronchodilation. Thus, any drug which stimulates the sympathetic nervous system (isoproteronol, epinephrine) will produce bronchodilation and if given during an asthmatic attack, will help alleviate some of the symptoms. The parasympathetic nervous system produces the opposite effect, bronchoconstriction. Drugs that increase the activity of the parasympathetic nervous system (carbachol, acetyl-beta-methylcholine or mecholyl) produce bronchoconstriction, and drugs that block the activity of this system (atropine) produce bronchodilation. Some constriction is normally present at all times, so that blockage of the parasympathetic nervous system results in a slight dilation. Together, these two mutually antagonistic systems determine the size of the bronchioles, and excessive bronchoconstriction must reflect an imbalance between them (see reviews by Cabezas and others 1971; Nadel 1973).

This pattern of innervation is puzzling in light of the emphasis that has been put on the role of the sympathetic nervous system mediating the reactions to stressful conditions. As reviewed earlier in this chapter, the same stressful situations that usually produce physiological signs indicating sympathetic dominance in normals produce bronchoconstriction in asthmatic patients, demonstrating that at least in the pulmonary portion of the autonomic nervous system, the parasympathetic division has become relatively more active than the sympathetic division. The autonomic balance of asthmatic patients as compared to normals has received considerable attention, with the relative sympathetic and/or parasympathetic dominance being the main issue (Abbasy and others 1967; Hahn 1966; Hahn & Clark 1967; Kumar and others 1971; Masuda and others 1966; Mathé & Knapp 1969, 1971; Morris and others 1972; Wenger 1948, 1957; Widdicombe & Sterling 1970). These studies have not provided a consistent picture so that a full explanation of the paradox described above is not available. In any case, these results emphasize the point that the autonomic nervous system can function discretely, with a major parasympathetic activation at the lung, but not necessarily at other sites (see also Chapter 4).

Parasympathetic Nervous System. The vagus nerve and the parasympathetic nervous system mediate the reflexive bronchoconstriction occurring in response to many different stimuli. The data supporting this statement come from experiments with humans in which an anticholinergic drug, such as atropine, was used to pharmacologically block the action of the vagus, and from experiments with animals in which the vagus was surgically transected. In both cases, stimuli that produced bronchoconstriction before the intervention were ineffective after it, demonstrating the role of the vagus in the bronchoconstrictive reflex.

Bronchoconstriction in response to inhaled irritants was mediated by the vagus nerve. In one experiment, 13 patients with asthma inhaled aerosols of charcoal dust, citric acid, or cold air (Simonsson and others 1967). All three of these substances produced an increase in airway resistance which was about twice that seen in the baseline state. Atropine given prior to the inhalation completely blocked this response even though the patient's cough reflex was intact. Because the response of coughing was unaffected by atropine, the drug must have been acting on the motor side of the reflex rather than on the sensory side. Similar results were found in response to an aerosol of an antigen which provoked a positive skin test (Yu and others 1972). The antigen aerosol by itself produced a 79% increase in airway resistance corrected for thoracic gas volume. Atropine given intravenously after this increase in airway resistance reduced it to only 12% of baseline, and atropine given before the antigen aerosol completely blocked it. Bronchoconstriction following deep inhalations (Gayrard and others 1975) and in response to charcoal dust (Widdicombe and others 1962), was reduced by two drugs blocking the parasympathetic nervous system, Sch-1,000 (n-isopropyl-nortropine-tropate) and by atropine, respectively.

The bronchoconstriction in humans that occurs in response to suggestion involves the vagus (McFadden and others 1969). The experiments examining the mechanism of bronchoconstriction were carried out following the other experiments on suggestion described earlier. Five participants who reacted to the suggestions were given a few milligrams of atropine and then were presented the saline solution to inhale (while being told it was the same allergen that earlier had produced the bronchoconstriction). For all five people, no bronchoconstriction occurred. Tests were also carried out with potent doses of carbachol, a drug that stimulates the cholinergic system and produces bronchoconstriction. Following atropine, the patients did not react to the carbachol either. The importance of the pharmacological blockage is indicated by the results of a retest three hours later (when the drug was no longer active), at which time bronchoconstriction took place in response to both the suggestion of an allergen and to the carbachol. Drug-induced bronchoconstriction is also mediated by the vagus (Greico & Pierson 1970). Six patients with chronic asthma were given an aerosol containing the bronchoconstrictor, methacholine. When an atropine aerosol was given prior to the methacholine, the expected changes in FEV_1 did not occur.

Experimental preparations in animals also support the role of the vagus in bronchoconstriction. In one case, an aerosol of a worm antigen produced bronchoconstriction, resulting in a doubling of airway resistance (Gold and others 1972). Vagal blockade was produced in four ways: cooling of the entire vagus nerve, both afferents and efferents; cooling of the afferent fibers alone; cooling of the efferent fibers alone; and pharmacological blockade with an atropine aerosol. All these manipulations prevented the reflex bronchoconstriction normally seen to the antigen. The results of the cooling experiments are an important addition to the pharmacological ones because the cooling was restricted to the vagus alone while the drug injections inevitably produced effects throughout the body. Thus blockade by cooling specifically identifies the vagus as the nerve participating in both the afferent and the efferent component of the bronchoconstrictive reflex arc.

A similar experimental design was used to study the vagal mediation of bronchoconstriction in cats in response to charcoal dust (Widdicombe 1963). In the baseline condition, charcoal dust produced a 51% increase in airway resistance relative to thoracic gas volume, and the experimenters could measure nervous activity in both tracheal receptors and vagal efferents, demonstrating that these pathways were normally active during the bronchoconstrictive reflex. After nervous activity in the vagus nerve was blocked by cooling the nerve, inspiration of the charcoal dust was followed by an increase in airway resistance of only 3%. As before, this animal experiment provides information about the specificity of the bronchoconstrictive reflex that cannot be obtained with drug procedures and provides additional support for the selective involvement of the vagus nerve.

Not all bronchoconstriction is mediated by the activity of the vagus nerve. The bronchoconstriction produced by inhalation of histamine is independent of the vagus nerve (Woenne and others 1978). The potentiation of exercise induced bronchoconstriction by cold air (Deal and others 1978; Strauss and others 1977) is not affected by atropine (Deal and others 1978), indicating that it too is not vagally mediated, even though this may not be true in a similar reflex when the person is at rest (Simonsson and others 1967).

Together, these experiments provide a consistent demonstration of the importance of the vagus nerve in many bronchoconstrictive reflexes. When this nerve is intact, bronchoconstriction occurs. When the nerve is blocked either pharmacologically or surgically, bronchoconstriction no longer occurs. These data do not, of course, indicate that an abnormality of the vagus nerve is responsible for asthma. The nerve may function normally and the real problem may lie elsewhere—an excessive sensitivity to stimuli that activate the vagus nerve, a lack of activity in the sympathetic bronchodilators, and so on. Other reviews of experiments discussing the importance of the vagus in reflexive bronchoconstriction are provided by Mills, Sellick, and Widdicombe (1969), Nadel (1976), and Simmonson, Jacobs, and Nadel (1967).

Sympathetic Nervous System. The tone of the bronchial muscles is determined not just by the vagus, but by the interaction of the vagus and the sympathetic system so that the sympathetic nervous system may be involved in asthma too. The *beta-adrenergic theory* of asthma proposes that decreased sympathetic activity is the single common factor in asthma, which is seen as ". . . a unique pattern of bronchial hyperreactivity to a broad spectrum of immunological, psychic, infectious, chemical, and physical stimuli" (Szentivanyi 1968, p. 211). The beta-adrenergic theory has been discussed in detail in several review papers (Szentivanyi 1968; Szentivanyi & Fishel 1976) which provide an extensive review of the evidence supporting it. The data demonstrate that *beta blockers* (drugs that block the beta adrenergic portion of the sympathetic nervous system) enhance or provoke asthmatic attacks and sensitize the individual to many bronchoconstricting stimuli, while *beta stimulators* reduce bronchoconstriction and alleviate asthmatic symptoms. There are some difficulties with the beta-adrenergic theory (Cabezas and others 1971; see also Nadel 1976), and there is no physiological reason why asthma has to result from activity of only one portion of the autonomic nervous system. Together the data suggest that both sympathetic and parasympathetic divisions are important mediators of asthmatic symptoms.

TREATMENT

Biofeedback treatments have sought to increase pulmonary function and to decrease the frequency of asthmatic attacks. Two approaches have been used. The first is a direct one in which some measure of respiratory function is obtained, most commonly peak expiratory flow or forced expiratory volume. The person is given feedback about this respiratory function and trained to change it towards a more normal level. The second approach is an indirect one and uses biofeedback to help the person learn to relax. Here, frontalis muscle activity is measured by surface electrodes, feedback is provided, and the person trained to reduce frontalis EMG. Both these techniques have successfully increased pulmonary function and decreased asthmatic attacks.

Table 11–1 presents the procedures and results of nine studies. Five of them used a direct method of training changes in pulmonary function, and the other four used an indirect method to train general relaxation. In all cases, the patients were taking medication while receiving biofeedback. This fact prevents any conclusion about the effectiveness of biofeedback training alone. None the less, as biofeedback became effective in reducing the number of asthma attacks, medication was reduced as well. Consequently there is no reason to believe that patients must always be maintained on medication. Biofeedback has had clinically significant results, reducing asthmatic attacks, and physiologically significant results, returning pulmonary function to more normal levels. In general the data are promising and suggest that biofeedback training can produce substantial gains with a minimum of risk to the patient. Most impressive are the studies which produce bronchoconstriction and then train the patient to relieve the bronchoconstriction through biofeedback. As patients reduce asthmatic activity, they simultaneously reduce their sensitivity to those bronchoconstrictors which induce asthmatic activity.

Case Study A

Biofeedback was used to train a girl to improve respiratory function by decreasing total respiratory resistance. The study also illustrates the role of emotional turmoil in precipitating asthmatic activity and the failure of a simple rest to relieve an attack. Biofeedback training gave her a more normal state of pulmonary function and produced effects comparable to a major drug typically used to control asthmatic activity.

M. K., 16 years old, was a patient in a children's hospital (Feldman 1976). Her total lung capacity, residual lung volume, forced expiratory volume at one second, maximum midexpiratory volume, and peak expiratory flow were all substantially different from predicted normal values (Polgar & Promadhat 1971). She had developed asthma at age two along with multiple allergies. She was in otherwise stable medical condition. She required oral steroids and inhalation therapy, but these were unable to control her attacks. Partial relief was achieved by placing a nebulizer in her room although she developed a dependency on it and would wheeze in its absence. There was an emotional component to her illness indicated by predictable wheezing attacks following parental visits. Her drug treatment during the study included Ectasule Minus Sr., once every eight hours, and Quibron, once every six hours. Isoproterenol was administered as needed.

Total respiratory resistance was measured by the forced oscillation technique (Fisher and others 1968). A 3 Hz pressure variation was introduced into the airways while she was breathing. The resulting signal was passed through an active band-pass filter, amplified and rectified to produce a voltage varying directly with total respiratory resistance. Auditory analogue feedback of changes in total respiratory resistance was provided during sessions lasting five to ten minutes. She used a mouthpiece to breathe directly into the feedback trainer while she compressed her cheeks with her hands and blocked her nose with a nasal clip. She was instructed to match the pace of breathing cycles on a tape with 1.5 second inspirations and 1.75 second expirations. The feedback signal was louder than the recording of the breathing cycle so she could hear both. Peak flow, maximum midexpiratory flow, and total respiratory resistance were determined at the beginning and the end of each session.

M. K. improved on all measures of respiration. Prior to training her average peak flow was 42% of the predicted normal level; it increased to 45% following the feedback training. Similarly, her average maximum midexpiratory flow rate increased from 25% to 33% of the predicted normal level, and total respiratory resistance was reduced from an average of 332% to 231%. In contrast to biofeedback treatment, resting for 30 minutes failed to produce a decrease in total respiratory resistance and in fact increased the measure from 4.3 to 5.8 cm $H_2O/L/sec$. The changes produced by biofeedback were equivalent to those produced by isoproterenol therapy.

Case Study B

This case study illustrates the ability of biofeedback to reduce the sensitivity to events that produce bronchoconstriction (Khan and others 1973, patient #2). Bronchospasm was induced and the patient trained to increase the volume of air expired in one second (FEV_1). The procedure reduced the number of emergency room visits, hospitalizations, number of asthmatic attacks, and the amount of medication taken to control the asthmatic symptoms.

A highly allergic child, this 15-year-old girl was also susceptible to suggestion. When she inhaled a saline vapor after being told that it was an allergen, FEV_1 decreased by 20% and the resulting bronchoconstriction could be heard through a stethoscope. For biofeedback, FEV_1 was measured by an electronic pulmonary function analyzer. A red light provided visual feedback whenever FEV_1 was above a criterion level. For the first five sessions, she was trained to increase FEV_1. For the next ten sessions, bronchoconstriction was induced at the beginning of each training trial by having her recall previous asthmatic attacks, giving her saline vapor to inhale but telling her that it was an allergen, and by voluntary hyperventilation, exercise, or drugs such as carbachol. She then received feedback along with praise for increasing FEV_1 relative to previous levels. Five additional sessions were held one, two, three, and six months following the feedback training.

With biofeedback, she was able to reverse the induced bronchospasm within 10 minutes. The number of emergency room visits, number of hospitalizations, amount of medication, and number of asthmatic attacks during the nine months following the feedback training all decreased from the levels during the nine months before training began. There were a total of 35 emergency room visits before training and one afterwards; four hospitalizations before and none afterwards; 14 medications taken before and three afterwards; and 56 asthmatic attacks before and six afterwards.

Discussion of Treatments

Biofeedback for Changes in Respiratory Function. The treatments to be discussed all used biofeedback of respiratory function to teach asthmatic patients to reduce bronchoconstriction, and measured the effectiveness of this training with clinically relevant parameters. Biofeedback reduced the frequency, intensity, and duration of asthmatic attacks, the amount of medication needed to control them, the number of hospital visits made for treatment, and the pulmonary reaction to a variety of bronchoconstricting agents.

Visual and verbal feedback for increases in FEV_1 were used to treat 20 asthmatic children between 8 and 15 years of age (Khan and others 1973). All were randomly selected from an allergy clinic and had undergone hyposensitization treatment for at least one year before the biofeedback study began. Of the 20 children, 10 had at least a 20% reduction in FEV_1 when inhaling a saline vapor which they were told contained an allergen to which they knew they were sensitive. A treatment group and a control group were formed, each containing half of the children who reacted wih the 20% reduction in FEV_1 and half of those who did not. At the beginning of each training session, bronchoconstriction was induced by suggestion, hyperventilation, exercise, exposure to tape recordings of wheezing episodes, or a bronchoconstricting drug, such as carbachol. Feedback was then delivered for increases in FEV_1. Most children were able to increase FEV_1 and alleviate the bronchoconstriction within 10 minutes. Children unable to alleviate the induced bronchoconstriction within 10 minutes were given isoproterenol before additional trials. A total of 15 sessions were scheduled. All children received additional biofeedback sessions one month, three months, and six months after completion of the initial training. The children who received biofeedback had a marked decrease in all measures of asthma from the nine months preceding treatment to the nine months following treatment. The number of emergency room visits decreased from 88 to 13, the number of hospitalizations decreased from 5 to 0, the amount of medication decreased from 108 units to 39, and the number of attacks decreased from 413 to 193. All of these changes were substantially greater than those found for the children in the control group who did not receive biofeedback. In fact, the number of attacks for children in the control group actually increased from 477 before treatment to 588 after treatment. These results demonstrate that biofeedback can be effective, and that it is more influential than just the continuation of treatment not including biofeedback.

Similar procedures were later used with 80 asthmatic children between 8 and 15 years of age (Khan 1977). All were attending outpatient allergy clinics, and half reacted with at least a 15% reduction in FEV_1 when inhaling a saline vapor which they were told contained an allergen to which they knew they were sensitive. A treatment group and a control group were formed, each containing half of the children who reacted with the 15% reduction in FEV_1 and half of those who did not. The treatment had two phases. In the first, all children were trained to increase FEV_1. Sessions were 50 minutes long, and each child received between five and eight sessions. Isoproterenol was administered if a child failed to increase FEV_1 by at least six percent by the end of the third session of this phase. In phase two, bronchoconstriction was induced by suggestion, exposure to tape recordings of wheezing episodes, or a bronchoconstricting drug, such as mecholyl. Each child was then provided with feedback for increases in FEV_1 along with instructions to relax and return their physiological condition to baseline levels. This phase lasted 10 sessions. Children unable to reduce the induced bronchoconstriction within 10 minutes were given isoproterenol before additional trials. Each session was terminated when FEV_1 readings returned to levels observed at the beginning of the session. Children in the control group did not receive biofeedback. They reported for observation and recording of FEV_1 levels during five sessions in phase one and were seen once weekly during phase two. Children who received biofeedback showed a marked improvement; by the last quarter of training, the frequency, duration, and intensity of attacks were all reduced to approximately 50% of their values during the first quarter of training. Only slight differences were found for children in the control group which did not receive biofeedback and just continued their normal treatment. At the end of training, the group which received biofeedback had fewer attacks than the group which did not (11 as compared to 19). The attacks lasted for a shorter period of time (17 minutes as compared to 25) and were less severe (20 units as compared to 35 units).

These studies demonstrate that biofeedback can train children to increase pulmonary function following bronchoconstriction, and that this training can produce a clinically significant reduction in asthmatic attacks. These improvements lasted for at least six months following treatment (see also Scherr and others 1975).

Other reports did not state whether treatment had clinically significant effects on asthmatic activity. They are still of interest, however, because they show that biofeedback of respiratory function can markedly reduce bronchoconstriction. Furthermore, the improvement in respiration has been of sufficient magnitude to expect it to have clinical relevance. The data generally indicate that with biofeedback, asthmatic patients are able to increase airflow by reducing airway resistance.

The effectiveness of feedback training for decreases in total respiratory resistance was tested with 13 patients who responded to a newspaper advertisement about the training (Vachon & Rich 1976). They were between 18 and 30 years of age, had not used steroid medication for the past year, and had not taken any antiasthmatic medication for at least six hours prior to training. The biofeedback procedure had two phases. In the first, participants were provided with correct feedback for decreases in total respiratory resistance (Goldman and others 1970) during inhalation or exhalation and then during inhalation only. Subsequently, incorrect feedback was provided. In the second phase, patients were trained to reduce total respiratory resistance while maintaining thoracic gas volumes at the level found during a baseline. Trials in the three segments of phase one lasted about five minutes. As many as four trials were scheduled in each segment, and each trial was separated by five minutes of rest. Trials in phase two lasted three minutes and were separated by rests of one minute, which provided baseline measures for trials which followed them. A control group received incorrect feedback during the trials in phase two. The patients who received correct feedback in the second phase consistently decreased total respiratory resistance throughout training and had lower respiratory resistance during feedback than during rests. During the first phase of treatment, total respiratory resistance decreased from 6.1 cm $H_2O/L/sec$ in the baseline to 5.4 cm $H_2O/L/sec$ with feedback for inhalation and exhalation and decreased even further from 5.3 cm $H_2O/L/sec$ in the rest periods to 4.6 cm $H_2O/L/sec$ with feedback for inhalation only. Resistance increased slightly to 4.9 cm $H_2O/L/sec$ when the patients were given incorrect feedback. In the second part of the treatment, patients who were given correct feedback continued to improve respiratory function, decreasing total respiratory resistance to 3.9 cm $H_2O/L/sec$ by the end of training, a reduction to 64% of the pretreatment level. In contrast, patients who received incorrect feedback had a resistance of 5.1 cm $H_2O/L/sec$, a value very similar to the 5.4 cm $H_2O/L/sec$ at the beginning of this phase of the treatment. The average magnitude of change for patients receiving correct feedback was similar to that produced by a single administration of isoproterenol.

Total respiratory resistance was reduced through biofeedback for four severe asthmatics, one of whom was described in Case Study A (Feldman 1976). They were between 10 and 16 years of age with histories of asthma ranging from 7 to 14 years. All were hospitalized for their asthma and required oral medication and inhalation therapy. Total lung capacity, residual lung volume, forced expiratory volume at one second, maximum midexpiratory volume, and peak expiratory flow were all substantially different from predicted normal values (Polgar & Promadhat 1971). The feedback procedures were as described in Case Study A. The group of four children improved their total respiratory resistance by 64%, peak flow by 4%, and maximum midexpiratory flow by 8%.

Training to improve peak expiratory flow had only a small effect for six boys with moderately severe asthma who were residents in the National Asthma Center (Danker and others 1975). None showed any evidence of bronchoconstriction while their peak flow rates were measured, and all showed substantial differences between observed and predicted normal levels of pulmonary function. Each training session consisted of 10 consecutive blows, three to six of which were used as a baseline measure. One training session was scheduled each afternoon unless the child was wheezing. Feedback was delivered in each session if peak expiratory flow rates increased by at least 30%. The 30% requirement was increased across sessions if a child was successful, shaping the response. No evidence of any increase in peak expiratory flow rates was found, and the authors conducted a second study with five boys between eight and twelve years of age drawn from the same population with the same criteria. The study began with five to ten baseline sessions in two weeks, followed by five to 22 sessions in five weeks. No feedback was delivered during the first three blows of a session, and the average of these was used as the criterion for feedback during the session. The criterion for feedback was increased by five L/min if a child exceeded the previous criterion for three consecutive blows and was decreased by five L/min if a child failed to reach criterion for three successive blows. Improvement was defined as an increase in peak flow during the final three blows of a session as compared to the first three blows of that session. Three of the five children demonstrated a significantly higher proportion of "improvement sessions" during the feedback training than during the baseline period.

Biofeedback of Frontalis EMG and Relaxation. Asthma has been treated with procedures that do not provide feedback to the patient about pulmonary function. The two most common treatments have been biofeedback of frontalis EMG and relaxation. The success of these methods poses a paradox. As discussed earlier in the section on mechanisms, activity in the parasympathetic nervous system produces bronchoconstriction while activity in the sympathetic nervous system produces bronchodilation. Relaxation procedures are generally thought to increase parasympathetic dominance. If such were truly the case, then asthmatic symptoms would be enhanced rather than reduced. Thus at least in the case of the pulmonary system, relaxation should result in sympathetic dominance rather than parasympathetic dominance. In any case, these indirect methods provide an alternative means of altering pulmonary function in asthmatics and reducing asthmatic symptoms. Biofeedback plays an important role in teaching relaxation. Indeed, treatments without biofeedback have been generally ineffective.

Frontalis EMG biofeedback and Jacobsonian relaxation instructions helped asthmatic children reduce the frequency of infirmary visits, asthmatic attacks, and steroid dependency, and increase peak expiratory flow. The participants were 22 asthmatic children between 6 and 15 years of age (Scherr and others 1975). All were attending a summer camp which provided intensive care for their asthmatic conditions. Biofeedback trained reductions of frontalis EMG while the children followed tape recorded instructions for Jacobsonian relaxation. Each session lasted 30 minutes, three times weekly for six weeks. In the fourth week of training the children were asked to imagine an asthmatic attack while following the relaxation instructions. Peak expiratory flow rates were determined at breakfast, lunch, and dinner. One week before training began, the children had a peak expiratory flow rate which was 1100 ml below expected normal levels. Flow rates improved by 550 ml by the end of training. Children in a control group which did not receive biofeedback had a peak flow 1200 ml below predicted normal values before training; this increased by 300 ml at the end of their treatment. Thus the addition of biofeedback almost doubled the magnitude of improvement in pulmonary function. Biofeedback made a significant clinical difference as well. The control group had an average of .5 infirmary visits and 32 asthmatic attacks during the training period while the biofeedback group had an average of only .3 visits and 8 attacks.

One study compared the relative effectiveness of three different treatments on peak flow rates in 24 asthmatic children (Davis and others 1973). The participants were between 6 and 15 years of age, and were all residents in a treatment center for intractable asthma. Half of the participants in each of the three groups were maintained on corticosteroids (severe group), and half were not (less severe group). Participants receiving both biofeedback and Jacobsonian relaxation received analogue auditory feedback of changes in frontalis EMG levels while following Jacobsonian relaxation instructions. Children receiving only Jacobsonian relaxation followed the instructions without feedback, and those in the control group were told to relax while reading. The trained groups attended one session, 30 minutes long, each day for five days. Peak expiratory flow rates were determined before and after each session and at 8:00 A.M., 12 noon, and 8:00 P.M. each day. Children in the group receiving biofeedback and Jacobsonian relaxation increased peak flow rates by 5 L/min; children in the other two groups decreased flow rates by 3 and 10 L/min respectively. EMG levels were correlated with changes in flow rates. Thus the addition of biofeedback to Jacobsonian relaxation was critical to lower EMG levels and increased peak expiratory flow rates.

In a slightly different design, the influence of correct feedback of frontalis EMG levels on changes in peak expiratory flow rates was compared to that of incorrect feedback and no biofeedback treatment (Kotses and others 1976). The participants were 36 chronic asthmatic children between 8 and 16 years of age. All were attending a summer camp for the treatment of their condition. Children in the feedback groups received auditory analogue feedback of changes in frontalis EMG levels three times weekly for three weeks. Those receiving correct feedback decreased frontalis EMG levels during the three weeks and substantially increased peak expiratory flow. Figure 11–2 summarizes these data, presenting the results from the EMG in the top graph and those from the peak expiratory flow in the bottom. The EMG data are the activity levels observed during treatment; the peak expiratory flow data are the *changes* from pretreatment levels. The group receiving correct feedback (solid line and solid circles) began with an EMG of 16 uV in the first week which decreased to 12 uV by the last week. Peak expiratory flow was consistently elevated throughout training, ranging from an increase of 27 L/min to 30 L/min. In contrast, the group which received incorrect

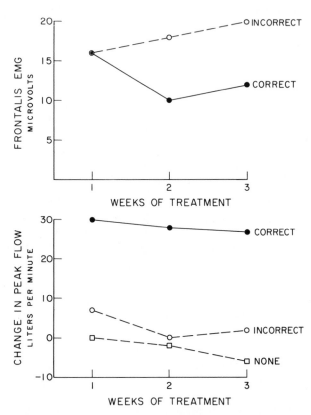

FIGURE 11–2   A Comparison of the Effects of Different Treatments on EMG Levels (Top Graph) and Changes in Peak Flow (Bottom Graph).

Children receiving feedback had the EMG recorded from the frontalis muscle. For those receiving correct feedback, the feedback accurately reflected the activity of the frontalis muscles; for those receiving incorrect feedback, it did not. A third group received no treatment. Children receiving correct feedback lowered their frontalis muscle activity and increased peak flow. Children receiving incorrect feedback or no treatment did not significantly change either during the course of treatment. Thus the success of correct feedback must have been due to the contingency between the activity of the muscle and the feedback, rather than to some nonspecific effects of treatment. *(The data are from Kotses, Glaus, Crawford, Edwards and Scherr, 1976.)*

feedback (open circles and dashed line) and the control group which had no biofeedback (open squares and dashed line) did not show a significant change in pulmonary function. The group having incorrect feedback did not decrease the frontalis EMG either.

A subsequent study in the same summer camp examined the effects of correct and incorrect feedback from frontalis and brachioradialis EMG on peak expiratory flow rates in 40 asthmatic children (Kotses and others 1978). Four groups were formed, each containing seven males and three females:

1. Correct feedback from the frontalis muscle
2. Incorrect feedback from the frontalis muscle
3. Correct feedback from the brachioradialis muscle
4. Incorrect feedback from the brachioradialis muscle

Feedback from the appropriate muscle was presented for 10 minutes, three times each week for three weeks. The group receiving correct feedback from the frontalis muscle demonstrated the largest decrease in EMG levels in both the first and last session of training and was the only one to have a substantial change in peak flow, increasing it by 11.1 L/min. All other groups had at most a 1.8 L/min change in peak flow. Again these data indicate the importance of correct feedback from the frontalis muscle.

CLINICAL PROGRAM

A program combining biofeedback to increase pulmonary function and produce relaxation should be the most effective. For direct training of pulmonary function, a mild asthmatic attack is usually induced through the most efficient means (suggestion, exercise, hyperventilation, inhalation of allergen, and so on). The client needs to be reassured that this procedure can be carried out without undue distress, and that the attacks can be reversed pharmacologically if the biofeedback is unsuccessful. Baseline measures of pulmonary function after induction of asthmatic symptoms should be taken, and a criterion of success set with respect to this level. Then training takes place to improve respiration. The simplest piece of equipment to be used here is a peak flow meter (see Polgar & Promadhat 1971, p. 25, for an example) which measures maximum flow rate during exhalation (Wright & McKerrow 1959), a measure which is highly correlated with forced expiratory volume in .75 seconds. A more complicated instrument is a spirometer (see Polgar & Promadhat 1971, pp. 12–17 for examples) which will provide measures of FEV_1, total lung

TABLE 11-1   Summary of Biofeedback Treatments for Asthma

Study	Patients	Biofeedback Treatment	Other Treatment	Symptoms	Results Biological Function
Danker, Miklich, Pratt, & Creer, 1975	Study one: 6 male inpatients; age range 9 to 12; Study two: 5 male inpatients; age range 8 to 12	Study one: visual feedback for increases in peak expiratory flow rates during sessions involving 10 consecutive blows; study two: same as study one with 20 blows per session and including 5 to 22 sessions in 5 weeks	Medication	Data Unavailable	No improvement in peak flow rates in study one; 3 of 5 children showed a significant number of "improvement sessions" during study two
Davis, Saunders, Creer, & Chai, 1973	24 children; age range 6 to 15	Auditory analogue feedback of frontal EMG levels during Jacobsonian relaxation; each session lasted 30 mins, once daily for 5 days	Medication	Data Unavailable	Levels of frontal EMG averaged 19 microamps during feedback; peak expiratory flow rates increased by an average of 5 L/min
Feldman, 1976	3 male and 1 female inpatients; age range 10 to 16	Auditory analogue feedback of changes in total respiratory resistance during 5- to 10-min sessions	Medication	Data Unavailable	Pre- to postfeedback changes expressed as a percent of the expected normal values: Peak flow, 63% to 66.8%; Maximum midexpiratory flow, 34.2% to 42%; Total respiratory resistance, 282% to 218%

Study	Subjects	Procedure	Control	Results	
Khan, 1977	80 children; age range 8 to 15	Visual feedback for increases in FEV_1 during 5 to 8, 50-min sessions in phase one; in phase two, the feedback was preceded by instigation of bronchoconstriction during 10 sessions	Medication	Average levels during the 1st, 2nd, 3rd, and 4th quarters of the year following completion of training: number of attacks, 23, 18, 12, and 11; duration of attacks, 34, 27, 17, and 17; severity, 42, 33, 21, and 20	Following instigation of bronchial constriction, FEV_1 level returned to basal averages
Khan, Staerk, & Bonk, 1973	20 children; age range 8 to 16	Visual and verbal feedback for increases in FEV_1 during 15 sessions lasting up to 10 mins; one additional session at 1, 3, and 6 months after completion of training; instigation of bronchial constriction preceded feedback during the final 10 sessions	Medication	Average levels before and after training: medication frequency, 108 and 39; hospital emergency room visits, 88 and 13; number of attacks, 413 and 193; number of hospitalizations, 5 and 0	Data Unavailable
Kotses, Glaus, Crawford, Edwards, & Scherr, 1976	27 male and 9 female asthmatic children in a summer treatment camp; age range 8 to 16	Auditory analogue feedback of frontal EMG levels during up to 20-min sessions, twice weekly for three weeks	Medication	Data Unavailable	Average uV levels of frontal EMG in weeks #1, 2, and 3: 16, 10, and 12; average increases in peak flow rates (L/min) during weeks #1, 2, and 3: 30, 28, and 27

TABLE 11–1   Summary of Biofeedback Treatments for Asthma

Study	Patients	Biofeedback Treatment	Other Treatment	Symptoms	Results Biological Function
Kotses, Glaus, Bricel, Edwards, & Crawford, 1978	28 male and 12 female asthmatic children in a summer treatment camp; average age 11	Analogue auditory and visual feedback of frontal EMG levels during up to 20-min sessions, twice weekly for 3 weeks	Corticosteroids and bronchodilators	Data Unavailable	Average microvolt decreases in frontal EMG levels during the first and last session: .9 and 3.0; peak flow rates increased 11.1 L/min by the end of training
Scherr, Crawford, Sergent, & Scherr, 1975	22 children, age range 6 to 15	Frontal EMG feedback-aided Jacobsonian relaxation during 30-min sessions three times weekly	Medication	Average levels for the experimental and control groups during training: frequency of infirmary visits, .3 and .5; number of attacks, 8.4 and 31.7; reduction in steroid dependency, 60% and 14%	The experimental group improved peak expiratory flow rates by 550 ml and the control group improved by 300 ml by the end of training
Vachon & Rich, 1976	13 asthmatics, age range 18 to 30	Visual feedback for decreases in total respiratory resistance in phase one; feedback was delivered in phase two only if such decreases were produced without accompanying changes in thoracic gas volume levels	Medication	Data Unavailable	Average changes in total respiratory resistance (cm $H_2O/L/sec$) during the three segments of phase one: −.7, −.7, and +.4; average changes in phase two: experimental group, −.6; control group, −.3

capacity, and midexpiratory flow rates. The most sophisticated option is a body plethysmograph (see Polgar & Promadhat 1971, p. 21 for an example) which will provide measures of resistance and capacitance. Other equipment and methods are reviewed by Cotes (1975, pp. 21–58). The studies reviewed here using biofeedback treatment do not indicate any advantage of one procedure over another, even though the pulmonary mechanisms being trained may be considerably different. Intervals between trials need to be sufficiently long to allow the person to recover because the effort of exhaling may be substantial, especially if procedures are used which require a maximal inhalation.

For relaxation training, measures of frontalis muscle activity may be used most easily. The procedures for recording frontalis EMG and providing feedback have been reviewed earlier in Chapters 6 and 7, respectively. Relaxation training using biofeedback should be effective for two reasons. First, the evidence reviewed here in the treatment reports shows that this type of treatment may have beneficial effects on pulmonary function, even though it is an indirect means of influencing respiration. Second, many asthmatic patients react with fear or anxiety when an attack begins, or when the prospect of attack appears, and this reaction may make the attack worse. Being able to control this emotional response may help to alleviate the symptoms of asthma even without explicit pulmonary training.

The most common events provoking asthma, especially in children, are unsatisfactory interpersonal relations with parents and/or siblings. An interview with each family member can be useful in uncovering any particularly inappropriate interrelations. Resolution of these difficulties through therapy may substantially decrease the amount of asthmatic activity. Another piece of information that should be obtained is the type of panic-fear reaction the person has. The data suggest that only those with moderate panic-fear are able to monitor their symptoms accurately and take appropriate action, and modifying excessively high or low panic-fear reactions can be helpful in keeping the symptoms under control. Thus both high panic-fear and low panic-fear clients need some counseling (Dirks, Kinsman and others 1978). Both groups need to be made more aware of the changes in their respiratory function and to be more accurate in evaluating the significance of these changes. In addition, the high panic-fear clients should benefit from procedures designed to increase their perception of self-control, while low panic-fear clients should be helped by procedures designed to decrease their denial of the importance of their symptoms.

For measures of total respiratory resistance, the nose is blocked with a noseclip while the client breathes directly into a breathing trainer. The trainer provides sounds of a fixed breathing cycle. A fixed interval should be used with approximately 1.5 second inspirations and 1.8 second expirations; these intervals can be adjusted to the needs of each individual client. The output of the unit is used to deliver an analogue auditory signal with a pitch varying directly with changes in airway resistance. The client's task is to decrease the pitch of the tone and hence respiratory resistance. Feedback trials should last about five to ten minutes if the client has no difficulty matching the pace of the breathing trainer. The trial should be terminated if the client becomes tired. One or two trials within each session, one to three times each week should be sufficient.

An alternate, although effort-dependent method for feedback training is forced expiratory volume in one second (FEV_1). The client is exposed to stimuli such as bronchoconstricting drugs or suggestion designed to instigate bronchoconstriction. Feedback is then provided for increases in FEV_1 following the instigation of bronchoconstriction. Clients unable to reduce the bronchoconstriction within 10 minutes are provided with isoproteronol inhalations before proceeding with training. Up to 15 FEV_1 trials within a feedback session are reasonable. Each trial should be separated by a period rest. Sessions are terminated when the FEV_1 readings return to about the baseline level.

RESEARCH CONSIDERATIONS

In the studies reviewed here, several different measures of pulmonary function were used for biofeedback. Some of them certainly depend on the amount of effort that is exerted by the person and should reflect the use of skeletal muscles, both normal and accessory, in exhalation. The amount of effort influences mainly the initial exhalation from a full inspiration. Thus measures such as FEV_1 and peak flow, which reflect the initial flow from a state of hyperinflation, are effort dependent (Lloyd & Wright 1963), as illustrated by flow-volume curves (Bates and others 1971, p. 35). The relationship between effort and flow is not linear, however, and excessively high effort may reduce flow at any given lung volume (Hyatt and others 1958: Lloyd & Wright 1963). These data suggest that FEV_1 and peak flow training are teaching the person to use optimal effort in respiration. This should increase the efficiency with which air is expelled from the lungs, improving pulmonary function and reducing the load on the cardiovascular system due to excessive muscle activity.

The measures of capacitance and resistance obtained from a body plethysmograph are independent of effort because they do not require hyperinflation or any particular increase in exhalation rate (DuBois and others 1956). Plethysmography measures may be independent of rate of flow measures (DuBois and others 1956; Fisher and others 1968). If biofeedback training with a body photoplethysmograph is also an effective means of reducing asthmatic symptoms, this procedure may be operating through a different mechanism. In any case, only treatment using a body plethysmograph will be able to determine the extent to which asthmatic patients can learn to control pulmonary functions independently of changes in effort.

EPILEPSY

12

Introduction

Symptoms

Mechanism

Treatment

Clinical Program

Research Considerations

INTRODUCTION

Epilepsy has had a long history and has been associated with mysticism as readily as with medicine (Temkin 1971). The behavioral disturbances manifest themselves in many forms, ranging from almost imperceptible motor movements or temporary loss of consciousness to the all-encompassing grand mal seizure. These symptoms arise from the abnormal activity of brain cells which can be recorded by placing electrodes on the scalp. The resulting *electroencephalogram*, or EEG, shows that during an epileptic seizure normal brain waves are suppressed and abnormal rhythms appear.

One striking characteristic of many epileptics is the absence of a 12 to 14 Hz rhythm normally recorded from the anterior portions of the brain, and the presence of a 4 Hz to 7Hz rhythm at the same location. Biofeedback has focused on these abnormalities and has sought to correct them both. The EEG is recorded from the scalp and the person given feedback about the presence of both the 12 Hz to 14 Hz activity and the 4 Hz to 7 Hz activity. Biofeedback trains the individual to increase the amount of 12 Hz to 14 Hz activity and to decrease the amount of 4 Hz to 7 Hz activity.

Control of brain waves is one of the most difficult skills learned through biofeedback. As will be seen in the following discussion, training sessions often last for more than an hour and take place several times a week for many months before significant changes take place in the pattern of seizures. This training has been successful, however. The biological function has changed, with increases in the amount of 12 Hz to 14 Hz activity and decreases in the amount of 4 Hz to 7 Hz activity. Clinically significant decreases in seizure activity have been found after biofeedback, even though the person has had epilepsy for many years and other treatments have been unsuccessful in controlling the seizures. Continued practice of the biofeedback skill may be necessary to maintain the therapeutic gains, and the extent to which biofeedback can eliminate the need for medication is not yet clear.

SYMPTOMS

Epileptic attacks range widely in their characteristics, from major seizures producing complete lack of consciousness and spasmodic contraction of muscles throughout the body, to almost imperceptible seizures, involving little change in consciousness and only a few twitches of an isolated muscle group. An extensive description of seizures has been provided in the case studies of Jackson (1931). Such diversity is expected given the wide range of brain tissue that can be involved, but it causes major problems in designing a diagnostic scheme to cover all the various ramifications.

This diversity of symptoms has led to considerable discussion about the appropriate diagnosis of epilepsy and the categories which should be used to classify seizures. Suggestions have ranged from a simple system with a few general categories (Marsden 1976) to elaborate ways of categorizing all types (Gastaut 1969a,b). At the present time, no single system appears to be completely successful, and about 20% of the epileptic cases are unclassifiable (Gastaut and others 1975; Joshi and others 1977). In light of these difficulties, the present section will focus on the description of seizures and the dimensions along which seizures can vary, emphasizing the types of symptoms that can appear rather than the names that ought to be attached to them.

Localization

Seizures vary with respect to the extent that they involve a discrete psychological or behavioral process. At one end of the continuum are generalized seizures which involve the entire body. The *grand mal* is one example. Here the seizure often begins with a peculiar cry, after which the person falls down and the entire body begins to shake and writhe as the muscles go through a tonic clonic cycle, first being completely contracted and then alternating in a rhythmical manner between contraction and relaxation. The seizure is usually accompanied by sweating, cyanosis, and autonomic changes such as urination. Consciousness is entirely lost so that when the person recovers from the seizure, there is no memory for the seizure itself or for the events that took place while the seizure was in progress. This type of generalized epilepsy is found in about 10% of people who have epilepsy (Gastaut and others 1975; Joshi and others 1977).

Less dramatic examples of generalized seizures include the *petit mal* or *absence* attacks. They account for the majority of the epilepsies (Gastaut and others 1975; Joshi and others 1977) and have a wide range of symptoms that are not described in terms of a single psychological function. The simple absence attack may be just a momentary loss of consciousness. If the person is having a conversation, talking ceases and any comments by others are not noticed. There is little postural change, just a cessation of movement. In other petit mal seizures, consciousness is lost, and motor changes occur. These may include mild muscle twitches as in the myoclonic absences, increases or decreases in postural tone, and even complex automatisms (Gastaut 1969a).

The focal or partial seizures stand in distinct contrast to the generalized ones just described. Here there is selective involvement of one or more psychological processes with the others remaining unaffected. Symptoms of focal epilepsy can appear in any of the sensory or motor systems. More complicated patterns may also appear. These may be associated with an impairment of consciousness and include integrated subjective experiences, such as changes in mood, the development of complex hallucinations, and automatisms. The important difference between these focal epilepsies and the generalized ones described earlier is the extent to which the entire body or just portions of it are involved in the seizure.

States of Consciousness

As already indicated in the above discussion, the state of consciousness may be altered during an epileptic attack, whether it is a generalized or a focal variety. In some cases, consciousness is entirely lost. During the seizure, the person does not react to any of the stimuli present in the immediate environment. Even after the attack is over, the person reports no memory for events that happened during the seizure. Indeed, one of the first indications that a seizure has taken place is the realization that the world has changed, time has passed, and the person has been unaware of it. Thus, there seems to be complete failure to remember any of the events associated with the attack.

During other seizures, consciousness may be normal. These are variations of the petit mal attacks which are restricted to sensory or motor systems. While the seizure is in progress, the person is aware of outside events and the seizure itself, and after the seizure is over, there is no evidence that anything has been forgotten.

Psychological Function Most Affected

This question is a logical outgrowth of the generalized-focal distinction already discussed and goes a little further, seeking to describe the psychological characteristics of the seizure in sufficient detail to attribute the events to particular behavioral processes and/or particular brain structures. In *generalized* seizures, of course, such an enterprise is of little interest because by definition these seizures involve the entire person. But in *focal* seizures, the symptoms may vary markedly. Consider, for example, a focal epilepsy with symptoms restricted to a particular sensory system. The seizure might appear in the visual system and manifest itself as flickering lights, or in the somatosensory system, as numbness or tingling in one arm. Restricted motor changes may occur, ranging from slight twitching in a few fingers through a general change in postural tone to a series of body movements, such as turning to the right, looking up, and reaching out with the right hand. Autonomic functions may be affected, and complex automatisms may appear, especially with temporal lobe dysfunction. In these and other instances of focal epilepsy, the psychological process that is disrupted usually reflects the function of a single brain area. Thus, the analysis is useful, not only for an adequate behavioral description, but also for a neurological assessment.

Stimulus-elicited Seizures

Some epilepsies appear to be triggered by specific sensory stimuli and have been called "reflex, triggered, stimulus-sensitive, evoked, (or) precipitated" (Bickford & Klass 1969). These evoked epilepsies are rare, accounting for perhaps only a few percent of all the cases (Gastaut & Tassinari 1966; Symonds 1959), but they are dramatic because the seizure is so closely tied to a particular stimulus. Flickering lights commonly evoke attacks; as the frequency becomes low enough to be perceptible and the intensity of the light increases, the likelihood of a seizure increases. Sounds are less important, but there are several well-documented cases of seizures caused by music. For example, one woman had attacks triggered by swing music (Daly & Barry 1957). A few minutes of listening to this type of music produced a feeling of fear and a series of motor movements including clasping of hands, rhythmic grimacing, and some automatic jive phrases. The attack lasted about a minute. These same authors provide a review of other musicogenic seizures concluding that at the time of their article, about 30 documented cases were available (see also Critchley, 1937).

Reviews of reflex epilepsies (Bickford & Klass 1969; Daube 1965; Gastaut & Tassinari 1966) list as important sensory events: intermittent light, reading and visual explorations, television, closing of the eyes, music, body movements or postures, and any unexpected stimulus producing a startle response. Seizures have been evoked by rubbing the face (Goldie & Green 1959), abdominal pain (Gastaut & Poirier 1964), touching of the right arm (Scollo-Lavizzari & Hess 1967), short periods of mathematical calculation (Ingvar & Nyman 1962), and eating food

(Cirignotta and others 1977). Forster (1977) provides information about other case studies and emphasizes the importance of making a distinction between conditioned and unconditioned reflexes (p. 301; also see Critchley, 1937; Chapter 3 of this book). Most of the evoked seizures appear to arise as an unconditioned response to an unconditioned stimulus; there is no history to indicate that the response resulted from learning, and there is no evidence that extinction can eliminate the response.

There is at least one example of a conditioned evoked epilepsy (Gastaut & Tassinari 1966, p. 132). The patient was a ten-year-old child who had seizures in response to family arguments. A regular pattern of behavior appeared so that her father would arrive home late and ring the bell; her mother would open the door, and a quarrel would ensue. Subsequently, the child began to develop seizures in response to the doorbell in anticipation of the quarrel. Here is an excellent example of a conditioned seizure, but it is probably an exception rather than the rule.

Stress

Convulsions may occur in response to lack of sleep, emotional stress, or overexertion and strain. Anticonvulsant medication is of little use in controlling these convulsions (Friis & Lund 1974), and the only effective treatment is avoidance of the precipitating event. These convulsions may be considered as a variant of the reflex seizure with the precipitating stimuli being general rather than specific.

A retrospective analysis was carried out with 37 patients admitted to a hospital for a seizure (Friis & Lund 1974). Of these, 29 listed lack of sleep as being important in eliciting their attack. Other items included: emotional stress (15 people), overexertion (16), intellectual stress (9), alcohol abuse (11), and drug abuse (2). In military personnel, the stress associated with combat missions (Bennett 1963) or leaving the battle site to return home (Gunderson and others 1973) increased the likelihood of seizures.

People have been deprived of sleep for extended periods of time to determine the effects on brain activity. In one study, patients who had a normal EEG between seizures were sleep deprived for 26 to 28 hours (Mattson and others 1965). In 34 of 89 patients, the EEG was abnormal; in 20 people who did not have epilepsy and were equivalently sleep deprived, no abnormalities were found. Similar results were found for a group of 114 patients (Pratt and others 1968). After the sleep deprivation, 47 of the 114 people had an abnormal EEG; 41 of the 114 reported that they thought lack of sleep brought on seizures.

An experimental study examining the role of emotional stress was carried out with 30 patients having a history of epilepsy (Stevens 1959). These patients had good relations with their interviewer, but on the test day the interviewer became hostile and accused each person of having some undesirable character trait (dishonesty, lack of cooperation, malingering) or discussed some life event that had been particularly disturbing to the individual. During the interview, nine patients developed EEG abnormalities usually seen during spontaneous seizures; 11 others had EEG abnormalities but of a type not usually found during their seizures. One person had a seizure, and two had an aura. In nine people without epilepsy, no EEG abnormalities were found.

Other data pointing out the role of stress in producing seizures show a decline in the rate of seizures when anxiety is reduced. Just admission to a treatment program in an understanding environment may result in a profound decrease in seizure frequency, even when there are no medical or pharmacological changes (Laidlaw & Laidlaw 1976). Better family relations and an understanding of the epileptic may reduce seizures substantially (Caveness 1955).

Animal experiments have provided experimental evidence demonstrating the importance of stress in producing epilepsy. Seizures were induced by physiological or pharmacological agents, and the frequency of the seizure or its threshold was measured. One set of experiments used aluminum hydroxide placed in the left precentral and postcentral gyrus of rhesus monkeys (Lockard & Barensten 1967). After four to six months, a characteristic seizure pattern developed with head turning and body movements (Barensten & Lockard 1969; Halpern & Ward 1969, p. 305). Eight monkeys were tested in an avoidance procedure in an operant box. When a light was turned on, the monkey had to make at least one response (pulling a lever) every 20 seconds to avoid shock. Throughout the test session, unavoidable shocks were given at random, and the lever was slightly electrified so that when the monkey pulled it to avoid the major shock he received a minor one. During the first week of this schedule, 7 of the 8 monkeys had more seizures than during the preceding baseline period; during the second week, 6 of them had more seizures than during baseline. Seizure frequency increased most in those monkeys who already had frequent seizures and was about twice that in the baseline. The seizures were not directly associated with the shock itself; they rarely occurred during the avoidance session and often appeared just before the testing began. The data indicate that the stress of the aversive test procedure increased the probability of seizures.

Another set of relevant experiments examined the susceptibility of mice to seizures produced by a pentylenetetrazol, a central nervous system stimulant (Swinyard and others 1961; Swinyard and others 1963). The drug was injected into the tail vein of mice at .005 ml/sec until the mouse developed a clonic seizure for three seconds. Various stressful events took place prior to the test, including intermittent foot shock for 20 minutes, being placed in the chamber in which foot shock had previously taken place but without shock present, being totally immobilized for 7 to 240 minutes, being placed in groups of three in small cages for 30 to 180 minutes. All of these manipulations lowered the amount of drug injected before a seizure occurred to about 80% of that in control groups. Thus, mice subjected to these stressful events were more likely to have a seizure than control mice who were taken directly from their cage to the drug injection.

MECHANISM

The electroencephalogram (EEG) of an epileptic may demonstrate a variety of abnormal patterns. During an attack, the EEG is commonly very synchronous with large amplitude spikes of very short duration occurring at very low frequencies, one to three per second. This hypersynchronization may completely dominate the EEG so that other wave forms are all but indistinguishable, and the appearance of these spikes has been described as the EEG abnormality most commonly associated with epilepsy (Driver & MacGillivray 1976).

Synchronization of brain activity is not abnormal. A variety of rhythmical patterns commonly occur, including *theta* (4 to 7 Hz) and *alpha* (12 to 14 Hz). The appearance of synchronous patterns implies that a group of nerve cells is acting together, producing the same potentials at the same time. The normal rhythms have relatively low amplitudes, and calculations suggest that only 1% of the total number of neurons is necessary to produce a wave of 100 uV (Driver & MacGillivray 1976, p. 111). This point is important, because it indicates that although theta, alpha, and other synchronous EEG patterns result from coordinated activity in different nerve cells, the vast majority of the cells are still firing independently. It is the recruitment of these normally independent cells that produces the high amplitude hypersynchronous response characteristic of epilepsy. Thus, the abnormality of the epileptic is not in the synchrony itself, but rather in the number of cells involved and their pattern of involvement (low frequency, short-duration spikes).

The susceptibility of the brain to stimuli producing epileptic attacks can be increased by a number of different procedures. Epilepsy with a known etiology is called *secondary* or *symptomatic* (Ford 1973). A review of 1,785 cases of epilepsy indicated that 44% had a cause that could be specified with a high degree of confidence, and that of these, trauma at birth was the most frequently cited event (Bergamini and others 1977).

The remaining cases were *essential* or *idiopathic,* that is, with unknown etiology.

TREATMENT

The EEG of epileptics typically shows more activity below 7 Hz and less activity between 12 Hz and 14 Hz than normal. Biofeedback training has focused on increasing the 12 Hz to 14 Hz activity, decreasing low frequency activity, or both. Some of the more recent studies have provided feedback for EEG rhythms within a specified frequency range only if they are of sufficient power. The rationale for this approach has been fully discussed by Sterman (1973; 1977a, pp. 63–68). Surface electrodes are placed on the scalp and used to record the EEG. Electronic circuits selectively process certain frequencies and filter out others. The amount of activity in each frequency and its duration determines the feedback. Patients are generally trained to increase the amount and/or duration of 12 Hz to 14 Hz activity and to decrease the amount and/or duration of 4 Hz to 7 Hz activity.

As indicated in Table 12–1, most patients received a substantial amount of training. Sessions typically lasted 40 to 60 minutes, up to six times weekly for as long as 18 months. Most patients increased the amount of desired higher frequency activity and reduced the amount of undesired lower frequency activity. As the characteristics of the EEG changed, the patients had a decrease in the frequency, intensity, and/or duration of seizures and were able to control their seizures with less medication.

Case Studies

The first case study is an early one describing a person who has been followed more than six years. The second case study is more recent and includes a more refined treatment procedure which we describe in detail. This comparison is not meant as a negative evaluation of the first case. On the contrary, the first case was one of the earliest using biofeedback and reflected the state of the science at that time. Biofeedback has advanced rapidly, and a comparison of the two procedures gives some indication of the types of changes that have taken place in the few years separating them. The two cases illustrate the relationship between biofeedback training, characteristics of the EEG, and seizure activity. During training, the EEG became more normal, and the frequency of seizures decreased. In addition, less medication was required to help control seizures as the 12 Hz to 14 Hz activity became more prevalent in the EEG.

M.F. was 27 years old with a seven-year history of epilepsy (Sterman & Friar 1972). One type of seizure was characterized by biting of the tongue and cheeks and occurred frequently, but only at night. Another type was characterized by strong motor movements and loss of consciousness and occurred about twice per month. Her EEG was basically normal, showed no evidence of focal brain damage, but did show some signs of spike and wave activity. At the beginning of training she was taking 200 mg of Mebarol and 200 mg of Dilantin each day.

The EEG was recorded by needle electrodes placed in the scalp over the lateral Rolandic cortex. The raw EEG activity was then amplified and fed into a filter which passed only activity in the range of 11 Hz to 13 Hz. The output of the filter was fed into a binary feedback relay which operated when the 11 Hz to 13 Hz activity was of sufficient power and duration. A light was used for feedback each time the EEG met criterion. Biofeedback training sessions lasted 30 to 60 minutes, once each week in the early stages and twice each week in later ones. M.F. was instructed to produce the 11 Hz to 13 Hz activity during each training session. Typical performance is illustrated in Figure 12–1. The bottom trace is the EEG. The middle trace is the action of the 11 Hz to 13 Hz filter. The top trace is the on-off action of the binary feedback relay. Notice the relationship between bursts of 11 Hz to 13 Hz activity and the binary feedback relay. Bursts of short duration failed to operate the relay while two longer ones did. Each movement of the relay illuminated the feedback light.

M.F.'s ability to increase the presence of 11 Hz to 13 Hz activity changed during training, as illustrated in Figure 12–2. During the second session (the left graph), she was not able to reliably increase the presence of 11 Hz to 13 Hz activity. By the fourth session (the middle graph), she doubled the amount of 11 Hz to 13 Hz activity within the session. By the 12th session (the right graph), three changes had occurred. First, in the five minutes of pretraining baseline, the amount of 11 Hz to 13 Hz activity was greater than that found during most of the previous sessions. Second, during the training, M.F. was able to double the amount of 11 Hz to 13 Hz activity, this time within 30 minutes. Third, after training the amount of 11 Hz to 13 Hz activity in the EEG session remained high; it was greater than that found during the baseline of this session and during previous sessions.

Biofeedback training had a marked effect on M.F.'s rate of seizures. As illustrated in Figure 12–3, they dropped from an average of 24 per year prior to biofeedback training (left column), to less than six per year in the five years after training. No seizures were reported in the first three

SMR RELAY

SMR FILTER
(11-13 Hz)

LATERAL
ROLANDIC AREA

40μV

FIGURE 12-1   The Relationship of Feedback to EEG Activity for the Client in Case Study A.
EEG from the Rolandic cortex (bottom trace) was processed by a filter (middle trace) which selectively passed the sensory motor rhythm (SMR) of 11 to 13 Hz. A relay (top trace) was operated when the amount of activity in this frequency range was of sufficient amplitude and duration; the relay turned on the next light in the feedback display. (From M. B. Sterman and L. Friar, 1972. In Electroencephalography and Clinical Neurophysiology, 33 (1972), p. 91, published by Elsevier/North-Holland Scientific Publishers Ltd. Reprinted by permission.)

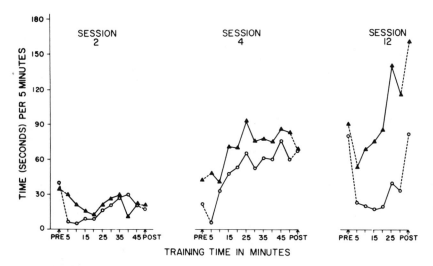

FIGURE 12–2   Increases in SMR as a Result of Biofeedback for the Client in Case Study A.
The length of time that SMR was present is indicated on the vertical axis; each five minute period is indicated on the horizontal axis. "PRE" is the five minutes of baseline before the treatment session began; "POST" is the five minutes of baseline following the session. In both baseline periods, no feedback was given. *(From M. B. Sterman and L. Friar, 1972. In Electroencephalography and Clinical Neurophysiology, 33 (1972), p. 91, published by Elsevier/North-Holland Scientific Publishers, Ltd. Reprinted by permission.)*

months of biofeedback training (second column) although they subsequently reappeared, but at a lower rate. Two years after training ended (last column), M.F. stopped taking Mebarol, and seizure frequency continued to decline. Substantial changes in M.F.'s personality took place during treatment. Initially she was a quiet and unobtrusive person. She became more confident, outgoing, and interested in her appearance as time went on. She reported that she went to sleep faster, had a more refreshing sleep, and woke up faster in the morning.

Case Study B

K.S. was a 14-year-old female with frequent seizure activity (Lubar 1977; Lubar & Bahler 1976, case E4; Seifert & Lubar 1975, case E4). Her EEG was very abnormal, characterized by slow alpha waves and spiking activity. Her seizures were generally myoclonic head jerks which occurred about 13 times each day. She was taking 1.5 grains of Phenobarbital each day. The EEG was recorded from the lateral Rolandic area of the sensorimotor cortex. The resulting signal was processed successively by: a filter which passed only activity in the 12 Hz to 14 Hz range; an ampli-

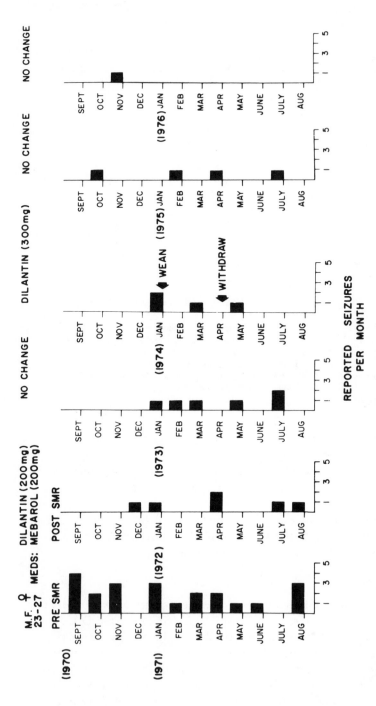

FIGURE 12-3   The Therapeutic Effectiveness of Biofeedback for the Client in Case Study A Showing Both the Decrease in the Frequency of Seizures and the Reduction in Medication.

The number of seizures per month is indicated on the horizontal axis; each month is indicated on the vertical axis. The first column summarizes the frequency of seizures before biofeedback training began (1970 to 1971). The subsequent columns summarize seizure frequency during treatment (September 1971 to April 1974) and after the cessation of therapy (May 1974 through 1976). *(From M. B. Sterman, "Effects of Sensorimotor EEG Feedback Training on Sleep and Clinical Manifestations of Epilepsy." In J. Beatty and H. Legewie (Eds.), Biofeedback and Behavior (1977), p. 176. Reprinted by permission of Plenum Publishing Corp., New York.)*

tude discriminator which passed only high amplitude activity; a window discriminator which distinguished 12, 13, and 14 Hz activity; a second amplitude discriminator which passed only activity which was above a certain amplitude at each of the three frequencies. The EEG was also taken through another set of amplifiers and filters to measure 4 Hz to 7 Hz activity. Feedback indicating success was based on two criteria. First, 12 Hz to 14 Hz activity had to be increased to a certain level of power and duration. Second, 4 Hz to 7 Hz activity had to be minimal. If 4 Hz to 7 Hz activity was present, an inhibit circuit blocked feedback to the patient, even if the 12 Hz to 14 Hz activity was of sufficient power and duration. In short, the system required both the presence of 12 Hz to 14 Hz activity and the absence of 4 Hz to 7 Hz waveforms. Auditory and visual feedback indicated success in satisfying the two contingencies. Sessions lasted 40 minutes, three times each week.

K.S. improved her EEG only slightly at first but was able to demonstrate a more normal EEG later on. Figure 12–4 illustrates the difference between an EEG record obtained early in training and one obtained three months later. In the early record, A on the left, the raw EEG (line one) was very irregular. Although some 12 Hz to 14 Hz activity was detected by the 12 Hz to 14 Hz filter (line two), a substantial amount of 4 Hz to 7 Hz activity was also present, detected by the 4 Hz to 7 Hz filter (line four), which prevented feedback (line three) to the patient. In fact, the inhibit circuit (line seven) was on more than it was off. The later record, B on the right, was obtained three months later and stands in marked contrast. The EEG (lines one and five) was more regular and of lower amplitude. The 12 Hz to 14 Hz activity (line two) was present while the 4 Hz to 7 Hz activity (line four) was generally absent so that the inhibit circuit was usually turned off (line seven).

K.S. reduced seizure activity with biofeedback training, although the course of this reduction was not smooth. A one-week interruption of training (after day 40), the beginning of school (day 100), and Christmas vacation (day 160) were all associated with a temporary increase in seizure frequency. At day 330, laboratory feedback was stopped, and K.S. was given a portable feedback device for home practice. Lubar (personal communication, June 30, 1978) reported that she was free from seizures during the week while at college but experienced seizures when she returned home on weekends.

Discussion of Treatments

Biofeedback without Medication. One study provided biofeedback training for a patient who was not taking any medication, and another treated a patient who began training with daily medication but elim-

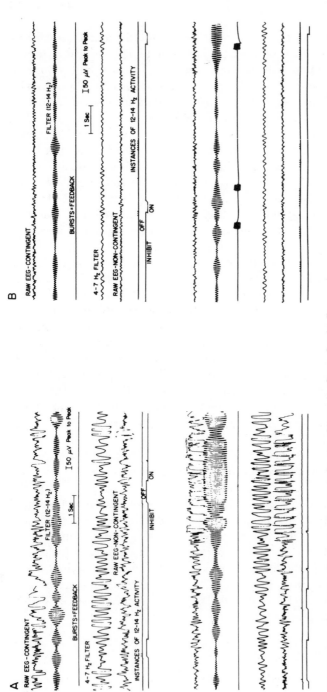

FIGURE 12–4   Two Records Taken from the Client in Case Study B.

The left half (A) is at the beginning of treatment; the right half (B) is three months later. In A, the raw EEG for both the contingent and the noncontingent hemispheres is markedly abnormal and although some 12 to 14 Hz activity is present, there is also a great deal of 4 to 7 Hz activity (line 4) so that the inhibit circuit (line 6) is on most of the time. In B, the raw EEG has become more normal (line 1), there is relatively little 4 Hz to 7 Hz activity (line 4), and the inhibit circuit (line 7) is off more than it is on, resulting in three periods of feedback indicating success in the bottom section. *(From J. F. Lubar and W. W. Bahler, "Behavioral Management of Epileptic Seizures Following EEG Biofeedback Training of the Sensorimotor Rhythm." In Biofeedback and Self Regulation, 1 (1976), p. 94. Reprinted by permission of Plenum Publishing Corp., New York.)*

266

inated it before training was complete. These studies show that biofeedback training without medication can make the EEG more normal and decrease the frequency and severity of seizures.

The patient who took no medication was one of eight epileptics who received feedback of central cortical EEG activity for treatment of various seizure disorders (Sterman & Macdonald 1978, patient six). She did not take drugs during the study, despite eight years of mixed psychomotor and tonic-clonic seizures. The remaining seven participants were taking anticonvulsant medications. Initial training in the laboratory was followed by training at home with a portable feedback unit. In the laboratory, EEG was recorded with surface electrodes over the left sensorimotor cortex, 10% and 30% lateral to vertex with reference electrodes near C_3 and T_3. At home, the EEG was recorded from electrodes in an elastic headband. Feedback was provided by two lights and a tone. When the desired EEG frequency was present and undesired ones were absent, a green light was turned on and the tone presented. When undesired EEG frequencies or high voltage transients were present, a red light was illuminated without the tone. Laboratory training lasted at least 10 sessions, after which home practice began. Each session at home lasted at least 30 minutes and took place six days per week for two weeks. Each patient then returned to the laboratory for one training session and waited two weeks to resume home practice. The cycle of practice for two weeks, rest for two weeks, lasted for three phases, each three months long, in an A-B-A design. During the first three months (first A), patient six was trained to increase the amount of activity in the 18 Hz to 23 Hz range while suppressing the amount of activity in the 6 Hz to 9 Hz range. During the second three months (B), these contingencies were reversed so that she was trained to increase the 6 Hz to 9 Hz activity and decrease the 18 Hz to 23 Hz activity. The final three months returned to the original training procedure (second A). The frequency of seizures steadily decreased during training. For patient number six, seizures decreased from an average of nine per month during the three months prior to treatment to 1.6, .2, and 0 seizures per month during the three phases of treatment, respectively. No seizures were reported during the three months following treatment. The remaining seven patients had similar training schedules with varying combinations of increases and decreases of 18 Hz to 23 Hz activity, 12 Hz to 15 Hz activity, and 6 Hz to 9 Hz activity. Their seizure rate decreased from an average of 5.2 seizures per month prior to training to an average of 3.1 after training.

Another patient began training while taking anticonvulsant medication but stopped taking the drug during treatment. She was 19 years old and had experienced 15 to 20 complex and generalized seizures per month, with an unspecified number of grand mal convulsions during the past four years (Seifert & Lubar 1975; patient El). Another five adolescents who experienced severe seizures not well controlled by high levels of anticonvulsant medication were treated in the same study. Patient El took Dilantin, 300 mg each day at the beginning of training but stopped the medication before training was complete. The other patients took drugs before and during the training. The EEG was recorded from the right and left Rolandic cortex 10% and 30% from vertex with the ear as the reference. Auditory and visual feedback were provided following at least six 12 Hz to 14 Hz waveforms of at least five microvolts in amplitude within .5 second, if 4 Hz to 7 Hz activity was absent. Training sessions lasted 40 minutes, three times each week. During the baseline period the EEG of El contained 8% of 12 Hz to 14 Hz activity; this increased to 14% within 54 training sessions. For the remaining five patients, 12 Hz to 14 Hz activity composed 9% of the EEG before training and 12% after 30 to 45 training sessions. High-voltage, slow-wave activity decreased while in later sessions the 12 Hz to 14 Hz activity increased to between 10 and 15 microvolts. Seizure frequencies were reduced during the feedback training. For patient El, complex and generalized seizures occurred 9 to 13 times per month, and grand mal convulsions did not occur at all by the end of training. The remaining five patients also had a more normal EEG and decreased seizure activity.

Treatment of Severe and/or Persistent Seizures. Epileptics who have had seizures for up to 32 years have been treated successfully with biofeedback. They decreased high-voltage, slow-wave activity, increased the presence of frequencies above 11 Hz, and reduced the frequency of seizures. Particularly striking is the fact that prior to biofeedback, most of the patients had tried many anticonvulsants, all of which were unable to control their seizures. Four epileptics had histories of seizures ranging from five to 32 years (Sterman and others 1974). They were between six and 46 years of age and had taken a variety of medications, none of which were able to control their disorders. All took anticonvulsants daily during the study. One patient had generalized tonic-clonic seizures, and the remaining three had mixed seizure disorders. The EEG was recorded over the left and right central cortex from 10% off vertex to 30% off vertex with surface electrodes. Each patient received auditory and visual feedback when 12 Hz to 14 Hz activity was present in the EEG for at least .75 seconds. Sessions lasted 20 to 40 minutes, three times weekly for at least six to 18 months. During training, 12 Hz to 14 Hz activity became more prevalent, while 5 Hz to 9 Hz activity and spike activity was reduced. The average number of seizures decreased from 80 per month before training to 38 per month following training.

Ten years of grand mal seizures were reported by a girl, 18 years old (Johnson & Meyer 1974). Even with anticonvulsant medications, she had seizures about three times per month. After she received two weeks of relaxation training (Wolpe 1958), she was taught to reduce muscle activity in forearm extensor and frontalis muscles during a total of seven sessions, each 30 minutes long. The EEG was recorded from electrodes at O_z and T_4 with the ground electrode on the right ear. She was first taught to increase alpha activity, then to increase both alpha and theta, and finally to increase only theta. Training took place for 36 sessions during 12 months. At the end of training, the frequency of seizures decreased to 1.5 per month, about one-half the rate before treatment. An average of less than one seizure per month occurred three months later. She also reported being able to prevent the occurrence of seizures once she experienced premonitory signs.

One person, 22 years old, had experienced focal motor seizures for 21 years (Sterman & Macdonald 1978, patient number five). Convulsions had begun at one year of age, and were poorly controlled by the combination of dilantin, valium, phenobarbital, and synthroid. The treatment procedures have been described earlier in the section discussing biofeedback without medication. The EEG was recorded from the left central cortex. An A-B-A design was used in which the patient was first trained to increase 18 Hz to 23 Hz activity in the absence of 6 Hz to 9 Hz waveforms, then to reverse this procedure and increase 6 Hz to 9 Hz activity in the absence of 18 Hz to 23 Hz waveforms, and finally to return to the original procedure. Each of these three phases lasted three months. Seizure activity decreased consistently across the training periods from an average of 46 seizures per month prior to training to 10 per month in the three months after training.

Another person, 30 years old at the time of treatment, began to have psychomotor seizures which began when he was six months old (Cott and others 1979). Auras were associated with the seizures which were not fully controlled by the combination of valium, dilantin, and mysolin. The EEG was recorded from scalp electrodes placed at C_3–T_3 or C_4–T_4 positions (Jasper 1958). He was trained to decrease the amount of 4 Hz to 7 Hz waveforms, spike activity, and EMG activity. Auditory and visual feedback were provided whenever the 4 Hz to 7 Hz activity or the spike activity was present. His task was to avoid feedback by reducing the presence of this undesired activity in the EEG. Training sessions lasted 40 minutes, twice each week for six months. The frequency of feedback decreased significantly during the training sessions indicating the reduction of the undesired EEG patterns, and the presence of 12 Hz to 14 Hz activity increased significantly (even though he was not given feedback about activity in the 12 Hz to 14 Hz range). During baseline, the undesired EEG patterns were present for an average of 16.1 sec/min, while during training they were present for an average 12.5 sec/min. The 12 Hz to 14 Hz activity increased from an average of 21.9 sec/min during the baseline to 23.3 during training. Seizures, which occurred at the rate of five per month before treatment, decreased to 3.5 per month during the six months of training.

Four epileptics between seven and 47 years of age had mixed seizure disorders which included motor disturbance (Sterman 1973). EEG activity was recorded from the Rolandic or central cortical regions with one electrode 10% of the vertex and another near C_3. Visual feedback was given when 12 Hz to 14 Hz activity was between three and six microvolts in amplitude. Training sessions lasted 20 to 40 minutes, three times weekly, for at least six and up to 20 months. The EEG and rate of seizures both improved during the feedback training. The amplitude, duration, and number of 12 Hz to 14 Hz waveforms increased within two weeks. Both grand mal and petit mal activity decreased during training, and the patients reported very low rates of seizures. Two patients improved their school performance. Many other treatments have reduced seizure activity for patients with severe and/or long lasting disorders (Finley and others 1975; 1976; 1977; Sterman 1977b; Sterman and others 1974; patient M.F.). These are discussed elsewhere in this chapter.

Enduring Nature of the Results. The longest follow-up in the studies reported here is five years (Sterman 1977b). A reduced seizure rate was maintained, even after anticonvulsant medication was stopped. Three months following treatment, seizure rates have been consistently reduced below those before training began (Cott and others 1979; Johnson & Meyer 1974; Sterman & Friar 1972; Sterman 1977b; Sterman & Macdonald 1978). Similar results were found one year following treatment (Kaplan 1975). Thus the reduction in seizures produced during biofeedback treatment continues even after that treatment is stopped.

Type of EEG Activity Recorded for Feedback. As is apparent from the treatments already reviewed, patients have been trained to alter several different components of the EEG, either separately or in conjunction with each other. One of the most common procedures has been to record EEG from the Rolandic or sensorimotor cortex and to train the patient to increase the amount of activity in the 12 Hz to 14 Hz range. In some procedures, the filtering and amplification system has produced a very narrow range of EEG frequencies so that feedback is based almost exclusively on the 12 Hz to 14 Hz band. In other cases, a much broader band of EEG has been used to provide feedback.

Examples of biofeedback treatments emphasizing only the increase in 12 Hz to 14 Hz activity have already been presented as Case Study A (Sterman & Friar 1972) and in the section on severe and persistent seizures (Sterman 1973). In both cases, the patients increased the amount of 12 Hz to 14 Hz activity in the EEG and reduced the severity of their seizures. Two other studies using a similar technique found little change in the EEG but a significant reduction in seizure activity. One of them provided feedback for the presence of 12 Hz to 14 Hz and then 6 Hz to 12 Hz activity (Kaplan 1975). The four patients had histories of either grand mal, akinetic, petit mal, or psychomotor seizures which were uncontrolled by anticonvulsant medication. The EEG was recorded from the Rolandic area on the right side just posterior to C_4 with the reference electrode at A_2. At first, auditory and visual feedback was given for increases in 12 Hz to 14 Hz activity during 30-minute sessions, three times weekly for three to four months. Then feedback was given for increases in 6 Hz to 12 Hz activity for five months. The EEG of the patients did not change significantly during training, but the number of seizures each month was markedly reduced from 207 before training to 202 during 12 Hz to 14 Hz training, and 132 during 6 Hz to 12 Hz training. When the patients were contacted eight weeks to one year later, seizure frequency had decreased even further to 60 per month.

Another treatment procedure which found no changes in EEG but reductions in seizures trained five females to increase the amount of 9 Hz to 12 Hz activity (Kuhlman & Allison 1977). All patients had either focal motor or psychomotor seizures which were poorly controlled by anticonvulsant medication. The EEG was recorded from the left central area around C_3. There were two phases in the training design. First, uncorrelated feedback (see Chapter 1), generated from the previous session, was presented for 30 minutes, three times weekly for about four weeks. Second, correct feedback was provided for 30 minutes, three times weekly for at least eight weeks. Although the EEG did not change significantly during either part of the treatment, the frequency of seizures did change. During uncorrelated feedback the frequency of seizures increased by 5% for three patients; long interruptions in training occurred for the other two patients making their data difficult to interpret. During correct feedback, seizure frequency was reduced by 40% in two of five patients within 14 weeks and by 25% in the remaining three patients after nine weeks. Medication levels were unchanged during these periods.

A second component of the EEG which patients have been trained to alter is 4 Hz to 7 Hz activity (Cott and others 1979). For therapeutic treatment, emphasis has been placed on decreasing the amount of activity in this range. The seven patients had a variety of seizures including psychomotor, grand mal, focal, and tonic-clonic. Two patients were mentally retarded. The EEG was alternately recorded from C_3–T_3 and C_4–T_4 positions (Jasper 1958). Four of the patients received auditory and visual feedback indicating the presence of 4 Hz to 7 Hz activity in the EEG. Feedback sessions lasted 40 minutes, twice each week for six months. For two of the four patients, the amount of 4 Hz to 7 Hz activity was reduced, and the frequency of seizures decreased from seven per month before training to three per month during training. For the third patient, the EEG did not change, but the frequency of seizures was reduced, while for the fourth just the opposite pattern was found, a decrease in 4 Hz to 7 Hz activity with no change in seizures.

The most common treatment procedure has been to arrange a double contingency, simultaneously training patients to both increase 12 Hz to 14 Hz activity and decrease 4 Hz to 7 Hz activity. An example of the effectiveness of this treatment has already been discussed as Case Study B (Lubar 1977; Lubar & Bahler 1976; Seifert & Lubar 1975) and in the section on biofeedback treatment without medication (Seifert & Lubar 1975). A similar treatment program was used to reduce seizures in a boy who was 13 years old at the start of treatment (Finley and others 1975; Finley 1976; 1977). His first convulsions had appeared when he was two years old. He had petit mal seizures with spike wave discharges at three per second when he was four years old. At age seven, his seizures were accompanied by loss of consciousness and muscle tone so that he fell down. EEG was recorded between C_3 and F_3 with the reference electrode at A_2. Auditory and visual feedback were provided for increases in 11 Hz to 13 Hz activity during the first 34 sessions and for either increases in 11 Hz to 13 Hz activity or decreases in 4 Hz to 7 Hz activity during sessions 35 to 80. Each session lasted 50 minutes, three times weekly. The presence of 11 Hz to 13 Hz activity, the presence of slow wave activity, and seizure frequency changed systematically during the 80 trials. Prior to training, the EEG contained about 10% of the 11 Hz to 13 Hz activity; this increased to 50% during training. At the same time, the amount of slow-wave activity decreased from 45% to 22% during training. The average rate of seizures was reduced from eight per hour to 1.6 per hour during training.

Treatment of this patient continued (Finley 1976). For five months, he was trained to produce at least three 12 Hz waveforms of at least five microvolts in the absence of 5.5 Hz activity. Then he was given 14 sessions of incorrect feedback, followed by more sessions of correct feedback. The 12 Hz waveforms increased with correct feedback, decreased during incorrect feedback, and increased again when correct feedback was reintroduced. At the end of training, they composed 70% of the EEG. Similarly, the slow-wave epileptiform activity decreased with correct feedback, increased during incorrect feedback, and decreased again when correct feedback was reintroduced so that by the end of training, it composed 14% of the EEG. The frequency of seizures decreased with the additional training before incorrect feedback, increased during incorrect feedback, and decreased again when correct feedback was reintroduced. By the end of training, seizures had decreased to less than one per hour. In a later report (Finley 1977), slow-wave epileptiform activity was present in only

15% of the EEG, and seizure frequency had decreased to less than one per three hours.

Less consistent success with combined training to increase 12 Hz to 14 Hz activity and decrease 4 Hz to 7 Hz activity was found with three epileptics (Cott and others 1979). The EEG was recorded from C_3–T_3. Auditory and visual feedback was provided when 12 Hz to 14 Hz activity was present and 4 Hz to 7 Hz activity was absent. One patient did reduce both 4 Hz to 7 Hz activity and the frequency of seizures. A second reduced the frequency of seizures but did not alter the EEG, while a third increased the rate of seizures even though 12 Hz to 14 Hz activity increased and 4 Hz to 7 Hz activity decreased. For the three people, the frequency of seizures during the 30 days prior to treatment was 72, 255, and 16, respectively, which changed to 60, 174, and 25 during the last 30 days of treatment (days 150 to 180), respectively.

Other types of EEG feedback have also been applied to the treatment of epilepsy. A combination of alpha and theta training successfully reduced grand mal seizures in one person (Johnson & Meyer 1974, discussed in the section on treatment of persistent and severe seizures). Various combinations of changes in 6 Hz to 9 Hz, 12 Hz to 15 Hz, and 18 Hz to 23 Hz have also been effective (Sterman & Macdonald 1978, discussed in the section on treatment without medication). Increases in the voltage of EEG frequencies above 14 Hz, increases in the percent contribution to the EEG by higher frequencies, and decreases in the amount of EEG below 14 Hz have also been used successfully in biofeedback (Wyler and others 1976). The patients were five adults over 18 years of age with seizures which were poorly controlled by anticonvulsant medications. They were not told that the procedure would necessarily help their conditions and were also informed that it might include incorrect feedback. The EEG was recorded from the areas nearest the epileptic focus and included F_3–C_3, T_4–F_8, and T_3–F_3. Auditory and visual feedback were provided to train increases in fast-wave activity or decreases in activity below 10 Hz, during 50-minute sessions, three to five times weekly. Synchronization of the EEG increased epileptic activity while desynchronization decreased such activity. Seizure frequency decreased in two patients, and seizure severity decreased in two others. The fifth patient received only EMG feedback to serve as a control; no change in the frequency of seizures occurred.

CLINICAL PROGRAM

Biofeedback treatment of epilepsy will most likely take place in association with a clinic that has already established appropriate neurological facilities. In any case, the equipment necessary to record the EEG and

TABLE 12-1   Summary of Biofeedback Treatments for Epilepsy

Study	Patients	Biofeedback Treatment	Other Treatment	Results Symptoms	Biological Function
Cott, Pavloski, & Black, 1979	4 females, 3 males; age range 15 to 30	Auditory and visual feedback for decreases in 4 to 7 Hz EEG activity for three people; feedback for decreases in 4 to 7 Hz activity and feedback for increases in 12 to 14 Hz for the remaining four; sessions lasted 40 mins, twice weekly for 6 weeks	Anticonvulsant medication	Seizure frequency decreased for five people	12 to 14 Hz activity increased in 3 people; 4 to 7 Hz activity decreased in five
Finley, Smith & Etherton, 1975	Male, age 13 with 11-year history of convulsions	EEG was recorded from approximately C_3 and F_3 with reference at A_2; auditory and visual feedback for increases in 11 to 13 Hz activity and for decreases in 4 to 7 Hz activity during 45 sessions; each session lasted 50 mins, 3 times weekly for about 6 months	Valium 30 mg t.i.d, Phenobarbital 60 mg t.i.d.	Seizure rate per hour: baseline, 8; sessions 1 to 34, 2.7; sessions 35 to 80, .7	Percent of 11 to 13 Hz activity in the EEG: baseline, 10; sessions 35 to 80, 55; percent of 4 to 7 Hz activity: baseline, 45; sessions 1 to 34, 25; sessions 35 to 80, 19
Finley, 1976	Male, age 15; same as studied by Finley, Smith, & Etherton, 1975	EEG was recorded from approximately C_3 and F_3 with reference at A_2; auditory and visual feedback for increases in 12 Hz activity in the absence of 5.5 Hz waveforms	Valium 30 mg t.i.d., Phenobarbital 60 mg t.i.d.	Seizure rate per hour: before false feedback, .30; false feedback, .46; after false feedback, .43; proportion of urine-loss events increased during false feedback	Percent of 12 Hz activity in the EEG: before false feedback, 70; false feedback, 63; after false feedback, 75; percent of 5.5 Hz activity in the EEG: before false feedback,

Finley, 1977	Male, age 15	EEG was recorded from approximately C₃ and F₈ with a reference at A₂; auditory and visual feedback for 11 to 13 Hz activity in the absence of 4 to 7 Hz waveforms during about another 80 sessions; false feedback during sessions 148 to 162; each session lasted 50 mins, 3 times weekly for (another) 5 months	Medication	Seizure frequency decreased to less than one per hour	Percent of 5.5 Hz activity in the EEG: 15; false feedback, 18; after false feedback, 14
Johnson & Meyer, 1974	Female, age 18; 10-year history of grand mal seizures	EEG was recorded from O_z and T_4 with ground on right ear; alpha feedback followed by training of 6.5 to 9.5 Hz activity	Two weeks of relaxation training; EMG training; medication	Seizure rate was reduced from three per month during the baseline to 1.5 per month following 12 months of training; no more than one seizure per month was reported during the 3-month follow-up	Data unavailable
Kaplan, 1975	3 females, 1 male; seizure histories ranging from 6 to 21 years	EEG was recorded from about C_4 with reference at A_2; Feedback for increases in 12 to 14 Hz activity during experiment one; feedback for increases in 6 to 12 Hz activity in experiment two; sessions lasted 30 mins, three times weekly for 3 to 4 months in experiment one and for 5 to 6 months in experiment two	Range of anticonvulsants	Average frequency of seizures: 207 prior to feedback, 202 during experiment one, 132 during experiment two, and 60 after termination	No change in the proportion of 12 to 14 Hz activity present during experiment one; no significant change in 6 to 12 Hz activity present during experiment two

TABLE 12–1   Summary of Biofeedback Treatments for Epilepsy

Study	Patients	Biofeedback Treatment	Other Treatment	Results	
				Symptoms	Biological Function
Kuhlman & Allison, 1977	Five females; age range 14 to 42	EEG was recorded from C_3 area; feedback of 9 to 14 Hz activity for 30 mins, three times weekly; false feedback (based on previous session EEG) for 30 mins, three times weekly for 4 weeks in phase one; feedback of 9 to 14 Hz activity for 30 mins, three times weekly for at least 8 weeks in phase two	Anticonvulsants	Seizure activity decreased by 40% for two of five patients in 14 weeks, and decreased by 25% for 3 patients in 9 weeks; seizure frequencies increased by 5% during false feedback	No change in 9 to 14 Hz activity or in 3 to 6 Hz activity
Lubar & Bahler, 1976	6 studied by Seifert & Lubar (1975) plus two additional patients	EEG was recorded from C_3–T_3 on the left hemisphere and C_4–T_4 on the right; auditory and visual feedback for increases in 12 to 14 Hz waveforms in the absence of 4 to 7 Hz activity; sessions lasted 40 mins, three times weekly for about 7 months	Anticonvulsants	Seizure frequency, duration and intensity decreased for some patients; two patients with multiple seizures per week have been seizure free for up to one month	12 to 14 Hz activity increased by 30% during the feedback sessions

Study	Subjects	Procedure	Medication	Seizure Outcome	EEG Outcome
Seifert & Lubar, 1975	3 females, 3 males	EEG was recorded from left and right Rolandic cortex 10% and 30% off vertex with reference to ear; auditory and visual feedback of 6, 12 to 14 Hz waveforms lasting .5 seconds in the absence of 4 to 7 Hz activity during 30-min sessions, 3 times weekly for 3 to 4 months	Anticonvulsants	Seizure frequency decreased from an average of 72 per month before training to 24 per month after training	Percent of 12 to 14 Hz activity in the EEG: baseline, 8.7; training, 12.7; slow wave activity decreased during training
Sterman, 1973	4 epileptics	EEG was recorded from approximately C_3; visual feedback for increases in 12 to 14 Hz activity during 30- to 60-min sessions up to 2 times weekly	Anticonvulsants	Lowest rates of seizure activity were achieved in all patients	Increases in 12 to 14 Hz activity was observed in all patients; decreases in abnormal low frequency discharge patterns
Sterman, 1977a	1 female, 2 males; age range 19 to 28	EEG was recorded from approximately C_3 and T_3, and at P_3 and O_1. Visual feedback for enhancement or suppression of either 12 to 15 Hz, 6 to 9 Hz, or 18 to 23 Hz activity (see text for discussion); lab sessions for 1 to 3 weeks followed by home training for 30 mins 6 times weekly	Anticonvulsants	By the end of training, seizures had ceased in two patients and decreased by 50% in the third	Training at both higher frequencies normalized the EEG, reducing abnormal low frequency paroxysms

TABLE 12-1   Summary of Biofeedback Treatments for Epilepsy

Study	Patients	Biofeedback Treatment	Other Treatment	Results Symptoms	Biological Function
Sterman, 1977b	Female, age 19; male, age 28 (same as studied by Sterman, 1977a)	Same as in Sterman, 1976	Anticonvulsants	Seizure frequency improved; see case study	Training at both higher frequencies reduced epileptiform activity and increased 12 to 15 Hz sleep spindles
Sterman & Friar, 1972	Female, age 23	EEG was recorded from about F_3 and C_3 and C_3 and P_3; auditory and visual feedback for large amplitude 11 to 13 Hz activity during 34 sessions, 30 to 60 min long	Anticonvulsants	An average of two seizures per month were reported prior to training; two seizures occurred six days after training began; no further seizures demonstrated for three months; medication decreased	Number of seconds of 11 to 13 Hz waveforms per 5 min: session two, 25; session four, 65; session 12, 100
Sterman & Macdonald, 1978	8 epileptics; age range 10 to 40 yrs	EEG was recorded from the left central cortex slightly medial to T_3 and C_3; visual feedback for enhancement or suppression of either 12 to 15 Hz, 6 to 9 Hz, or 18 to 23 Hz activity (see text for discussion); lab training for 2 to 3 weeks followed by home training	Anticonvulsants	Seizure frequency was reduced by an average of 56% within three months following training	Not reported

Sterman, Macdonald & Stone, 1974	4 epileptics	EEG was recorded from the left and right central cortical area 10% and 30% off vertex; auditory and visual feedback of 12 to 14 Hz activity during 20 to 40-min sessions, three times weekly for 6 to 18 months	Anticonvulsants	Seizure frequency decreased from 80 per month prior to treatment to 38 per month during treatment	12 to 14 Hz activity increased; trains of 12 to 16 Hz activity were demonstrated; gradual reduction in high voltage slow waves
Wyler and others, 1976	Five adults over age 18	EEG was recorded from the area nearest the focus, about F_3-C_3, T_4-F_8, T_3-F_3, and other places; auditory and visual feedback of either (1) increases in amplitude of filtered activity above 14 Hz, (2) increases in filtered activity's % contribution to the EEG or (3) decreases in the amount of EEG activity below 14 Hz; 50-min sessions were scheduled three to five times weekly	Anticonvulsants and an initial "EMG decrease" feedback session	Seizure frequency decreased in two patients, seizure severity decreased in two others; no change was reported in the fifth (control) subject who received only EMG feedback	Data unavailable

the procedures necessary to train people to alter brain waves will not be discussed in detail here because such a discussion would have to be more extensive than is appropriate for this book.

The most effective biofeedback treatment appears to be a combination of training for at least two waveforms. The first is the sensorimotor rhythm, 12 Hz to 14 Hz over Rolandic cortex, which the client should be trained to increase. The second waveform is of lower frequency, either the 4 Hz to 7 Hz theta activity, or the 1 Hz to 3 Hz epileptiform activity, which the client should be trained to decrease. This double contingency helps to ensure that the amount of desired waveforms will be increased while the amount of undesired waveforms will be reduced. Although separate feedback could be given for each waveform, most studies have provided feedback only when both of them have been changed appropriately.

An example of the procedures used by Lubar is presented in Figure 12–5. Electrodes record the brain waves from the client in the top left. Information is taken from both hemispheres of the brain and stored on an FM tape recorder, but feedback comes from only one half, the "contingent" hemisphere. The signal from the preamplifier for the contingent hemisphere produces the raw EEG in two places, on the top half of the oscilloscope monitor (represented by the circle in the top right of the illustration), and on the top trace of the polygraph record (represented by the rectangle on the right underneath the FM tape recorder).

The signal also goes through two filters, indicated on the left under the patient's head. The SMR filter selectively passes 12 Hz to 14 Hz activity. This activity is reproduced on the second channel of the polygraph and is further processed by an amplitude discriminator, frequency-to-amplitude converter, window discriminator, and burst detector (in the middle of the illustration). Bursts of SMR which meet the criterion for amplitude and duration result in feedback, which is represented on the third trace on the polygraph. A second filter (again just below the client's head) selectively passes 4 Hz to 7 Hz activity. This goes to the fourth trace on the polygraph and through an amplitude discriminator which is in the inhibit circuit. If the amount of 4 Hz to 7 Hz activity is too great, the inhibit circuit is activated as indicated in the bottom trace on the polygraph, and feedback is not given even though there may be SMR bursts present. The entire system is controlled from a master program, represented on the bottom left of the illustration, and many different types of feedback are available, including the digital display, colored lights, a tone, and slides, indicated at the bottom center of the figure.

EEG biofeedback is difficult to learn, and effective use of the shaping processes described earlier is critical to obtain success. Furthermore, interruption of training has lead to an increase in symptoms, even if the

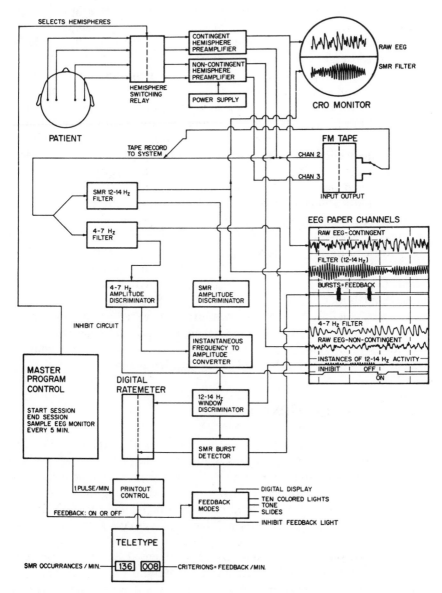

FIGURE 12–5   A Flow Chart Diagramming the Treatment Procedure Used by Lubar.

For explanation of the diagram, see text. *(From A. R. Seifert and J. F. Lubar, 1975. In Biological Psychology, 3 (1975), p. 166. Reprinted by permission.)*

period of time is only a week or two. The data reviewed here suggest that frequent (every day or every other day) sessions of substantial length (up to one hour) are important to produce the desired changes. Because of these findings, a home monitor may be useful for individuals who do not have convenient access to the clinic.

For most psychophysiological disorders, the client does not have to engage in conscious practice following treatment and can stop taking medication to control the symptoms. In the majority of cases of epilepsy, however, biofeedback has reduced seizure activity and/or the amount of medication taken but has not eliminated seizures or the need for some pharmacological control. The currently available data show that biofeedback for epilepsy is of therapeutic benefit, but that this benefit is limited, and continued practice may be necessary to maintain it.

For clients whose seizures are closely related to stressful events, behavioral intervention in the stress-seizure chain may be beneficial. Several options are available. One is relaxation training of some form, teaching the person to reduce the anxiety and/or fear reactions that arise in response to stressful stimuli. Another is dealing directly with the stressful events themselves. Many people are unfamiliar with epilepsy and do not understand how to deal with it. Education of the epileptic client, relatives, close friends, and fellow employees may reduce difficult interpersonal interactions that may affect an epileptic. Helping to resolve difficulties in the family may also reduce stress, especially for a younger person who has unsatisfactory relations with his parents.

RESEARCH CONSIDERATIONS

The EEG is a complicated and continuous series of waveforms. The distinction between different patterns is entirely arbitrary, making the association between particular patterns and psychological and/or behavioral functions difficult. Particularly puzzling is why the changing of one waveform (12 Hz to 14 Hz) in an area of the brain (lateral Rolandic cortex) which does not have an abnormal focus of activity should influence epileptic seizures that arise from a different form of activity in some other part of the brain. Most studies have focused on enhancement of 12 Hz to 14 Hz activity over Rolandic cortex and the suppression of 4 Hz to 7 Hz or epileptiform activity. The optimal waveforms to choose and the changes that are most appropriate to make remain to be demonstrated. Controlled studies examining the responsiveness of individuals to different types of EEG changes would be very beneficial in deciding which brain wave patterns should be changed and in what directions for the optimal treatment. A related question is the correlation between changes in EEG and changes in seizure rate. In the available studies, these have been relatively low, suggesting that there are other activities (either in the brain or elsewhere) that are not being measured which are important in therapy. Obtaining information about these other variables may indicate alterations in procedures which will produce a more effective form of treatment than is currently available.

For treatment, the therapist must decide the place from which the EEG will be recorded, the EEG frequencies that will be changed, and the direction in which they should be changed. A quick review of the treatments reported here indicates that success has often been achieved with treatments that record the EEG from the Rolandic cortex and teach the person to increase the amount of 12 Hz to 14 Hz activity, decrease the amount of 4 Hz to 7 Hz activity, or produce both changes. However, these results cannot determine if the success of these treatments was due specifically to these EEG changes, or whether they resulted from some other, more general alteration in brain function. This issue can be addressed only by a parametric comparison of the relative effectiveness of training to produce different types of EEG changes in different areas of the brain while recording from many different sites simultaneously. The available data suggest that almost any EEG change may be effective, which seems unlikely to be the case. However, training to *increase* frequencies of EEG that included the 4 Hz to 7 Hz range has been effective in reducing seizures; increasing 6 Hz to 12 Hz (Kaplan 1975) and increasing 6 Hz to 9 Hz (Sterman & Macdonald 1978, second phase of treatment) were both associated with decreased rates of seizures. Furthermore, changes in the EEG recorded from the posterior portions of the brain have also been effective; increasing 12 Hz to 14 Hz activity and increasing 4 Hz to 7 Hz activity either separately or together reduced seizure activity (Johnson & Meyer 1974). Part of the difficulty may lie in the fact that even though the person is being given feedback about a restricted portion of the EEG at a single site, learning to change these EEG frequencies at that site may be accompanied by other changes both at that and other sites (Cott and others 1979). Thus we need to know not only what happens at the site from which feedback is given, but what happens in other areas as well. Only in this fashion can we determine which changes in brain wave activity are responsible for the decreased seizure activity.

NEUROMUSCULAR REEDUCATION

13

INTRODUCTION

MUSCLES OF THE LIMBS AND TRUNK

Paralysis and Paresis

Peripheral Nerve Injury

Cerebral Palsy

Foot Drop Following Cerebral Stroke

MUSCLES OF THE HEAD AND NECK

Spasmodic Torticollis

Bell's Palsy

Facial Paralysis Following Traumatic
Damage to the Facial Nerve

Temporomandibular Joint Syndrome

Blepharospasm

Excessive Contraction of Throat Muscles

Parkinson's Disease

CLINICAL PROGRAM

INTRODUCTION

The types of abnormal muscle activity treated by biofeedback may be grouped into three broad classes. In the first, a muscle is contracted when it should not be, forcing limbs into unnatural positions, limiting the range of motion in one or more directions, and making coordinated movements very difficult. This contraction may be chronic. The muscle may grow excessively large and strong and as a result of this *hypertrophy* overwhelm all other muscles in the joint, drastically reducing their ability to move the joint. The contraction may also be phasic. Such a *spastic muscle* may have almost normal tone when at rest but contract inappropriately during voluntary or reflexive movement. In the second class of abnormal function, the problem is just the opposite. The muscle is not contracted when it ought to be. A chronic lack of use or exercise produces *atrophy*. This decrease in the bulk, tone, and strength of a muscle may be so great that even when it is contracted, it is not strong enough to counteract the other muscles around the joint. Finally, muscles may have the appropriate tone but not be sufficiently coordinated to produce an integrated movement. Here the activity of a single muscle is not in question, but rather the time dependent activity of many different muscles. Even if each muscle can be voluntarily controlled by itself, adaptive movements will not occur unless this control can be placed in a coordinated sequence.

Although each of the above problems can be described independently, in many disorders all three appear to some extent. Thus the general approach of biofeedback treatment is to measure the baseline of activity in all relevant muscles and then begin a sequence of treatment (DeBacher 1979). First the person is taught to relax excessively tight muscles, often beginning with an overall relaxation procedure. Then the person is trained to contract weak or flaccid muscles, with special attention being paid to maintaining relaxation in any previously overactive muscles at the same time. This stage may require feedback from two sets of muscles and a conjoint criterion of increasing activity in the weak muscle while decreasing activity in the strong muscle. Finally, the person is taught to produce coordinated movements, a process which may require recording from several muscles and organizing changes in activity over time. Here visual feedback from the joint movement itself may be most valuable.

Skeletal muscle disorders come in many forms and categorizing them is difficult. Various approaches have been tried, based on the etiology of the symptoms, the part of nervous system affected, the type of pathology, and the behavioral symptoms. None of these is entirely satisfactory, and all of the characteristics of muscle disorders described previously are interrelated. We have chosen to organize the following discussion into two major categories, determined on the basis of the body parts involved. The first section deals with muscles in the limbs and trunk; the second section, with muscles in the head and neck. Within each of these major sections, we have divided the disorders further on the basis of the clinical diagnosis given to them. Chapter 4 should be consulted if information is needed about the location of the muscles in the body and their function.

In most of the treatments to be described, other forms of therapy have also been included. The question of interest is not whether biofeedback should replace these, but whether it can add additional benefits. As will be seen, biofeedback has made major contributions in two ways. Following other types of therapy, it has produced significant and in many cases almost miraculous improvements that were not obtained previously, even after many years of other approaches. In conjunction with other therapy, it has produced greater and more rapid control over muscles than the other treatments without biofeedback. Biofeedback can be a more sensitive indicator of muscle contraction than visual observation of a limb, and can also be relatively inexpensive because the individual can practice without constant supervision (Johnson & Garton 1973). As a consequence, biofeedback deserves a place in virtually every program of neuromuscular rehabilitation (Basmajian 1979).

Biofeedback, as described in Chapter 2, usually obtains a direct biological measure of the system being controlled. In the context of neuromuscular reeducation, this measure is an electromyogram, or EMG. The majority of treatments described below have used an EMG. Some, however, have used a more indirect, but equally important, measure of muscle activity, namely the movement of a joint. In these cases, the transducer measures what happens to the limb, which reflects what the muscles are doing. All other aspects of the procedures are identical to those of biofeedback treatment, incorporating the principles of feedback systems discussed earlier. Because these approaches have been used successfully to correct muscle problems, and because they are so similar to the strictly defined biofeedback treatments, they have been included in the following sections where appropriate.

MUSCLES OF THE LIMBS AND TRUNK

The disorders considered here have major functional repercussions for the individual, severely impeding normal locomotion and/or manipulation. Disruption of coordinated movement in the extremities can arise for many reasons. Some of these are relatively circumscribed, as for example those resulting from a stroke. Others are more widespread, as those resulting from cerebral palsy. In all cases, despite the diversity of mechanisms underlying the disorder, the assumption is that the individual still has some voluntary control which is not being fully used. Thus the general procedure is as described before: train relaxation in hyperactive muscles, train contraction in hypoactive muscles, and then train coordination where necessary.

Paralysis and Paresis

SYMPTOMS AND MECHANISM

Paralysis describes a complete inability to move a limb while *paresis* describes a weakness and relative difficulty in moving a limb. Paralysis and paresis can arise from damage anywhere in the neuromuscular system. In the cases below, the problems have generally resulted from a traumatic injury to the spinal cord or cortical brain areas serving movement. These injuries have destroyed brain cells or axons which carry out voluntary movement. Although brain cells that are killed are not replaced, those that are damaged (but alive) may regrow and become functional again. Biofeedback teaches the person how to use these remaining cells to produce desired movements.

TREATMENT

Because the problem here is mainly lack of movement, the major emphasis is on training the individual to produce coordinated muscle contractions. If necessary, the person is first taught to relax spastic muscles. A baseline measurement of muscle activity and voluntary limb movement is obtained. Then the individual is given feedback about muscle contraction in the muscles to be strengthened. Because muscle activity may be at such a low level, proper positioning of the electrodes to pick up muscle activity and simple criteria for success are critical during the initial trials. Needle electrodes may be required for patients with severe symptoms. As limb movement becomes visible, the individual can practice with visual feedback from the movement itself as well as from the EMG. The results are encouraging, demonstrating that biofeedback can significantly improve function.

Case Study A: Hemiparesis

The patient was a young man who injured the right side of his head nine years earlier, resulting in left hemiparesis with spastic overlay (Amato and others 1973). In spite of physical therapy, muscle function remained severely impaired. He had good position sense, and his touch sensations were normal. However, the upper and lower left extensor muscles were hypertonic, and intense overflow into fingers and wrist flexor muscles prevented testing of forearm, wrist, and finger motion. Muscle strength was good during left shoulder motions and elbow flexion and was fair during elbow extension. Hip function was good, and the knee could be flexed actively to 90°. Gastrocnemius-soleus hypertonicity severely limited ankle motions, anterior tibialis function was largely absent, and foot evertors barely functioned. When he walked, the left foot inverted and dorsiflexed, contacting the floor on the lateral surface. Only limited weight could be placed on the foot, and knee flexion was minimal. Prior to treatment, dorsiflexion in the left ankle was zero with 10° inversion; plantar flexion was 35°. During the first treatment session, EMG was recorded from the region of the left medial gastrocnemius with surface electrodes. Visual feedback was provided. The patient was told to become familiar with the feeling of contracted and relaxed states of the muscles and to dorsiflex the left ankle while relaxing the gastrocnemius; constant gastrocnemius contraction prevented this motion. He was given a portable feedback device and told to practice at home twice daily for 30 minutes each time. The first 10 minutes were used to contract and then relax the gastrocnemius muscle; the final 20 minutes were spent dorsiflexing the left ankle with the hip and knee at 90°. After two months of feedback training, he had increased dorsiflexion in the left ankle to 15° and strengthened his muscles. His walking had improved so that he could place his foot flat on the floor from heel strike to mid-stance.

Case Study B: Hemiplegia

Thrombosis of the central cerebral artery in the right hemisphere had produced left hemiplegia in this 64-year-old man (Marinacci & Horande 1960). No motor unit activity was detected in the left upper extremity. A needle electrode was inserted into the normal right deltoid, and the patient was given auditory feedback of motor unit activity via a loudspeaker. After he was trained to increase muscle activity on this unaffected side, the electrode was inserted into the deltoid muscle on the injured side. He soon generated 10% to 15% of the expected motor units, and the electrode was then used with the triceps, extensors and flexors, and the muscles of the left hand. Within an hour he was able to develop 20% function in the muscles of the upper extremity; the same procedure produced a slight return of function in the left lower extremity.

Case Study C: Quadriparesis

A young man had a fracture dislocation of the upper spinal cord resulting in total paralysis of the lower extremities and nonfunctional movement in the upper ones (Brudny, Korein and others 1974). He had received physical therapy for three years, but the treatments were unable to restore functional movements. A laminectomy brought only limited improvement, and he remained a total care patient. Biofeedback treatment provided auditory and visual feedback of EMG activity recorded from the spastic right biceps. He was instructed to reduce the EMG and pronate the forearm for use with a wrist-driven splint. Sessions lasted approximately 30 minutes, three times weekly. Within two weeks he was able to relax the biceps in both arms and pronate both forearms even though the feedback had been produced from only the right side. Two years later, he continued to improve and could feed himself, type, and drive an electric wheelchair.

Discussion of Treatments

Two studies have compared the ability of biofeedback with that of conventional therapy to improve motor control. In both of them, the biofeedback produced significant gains in function. The relative effectiveness of physical therapy was compared to that of auditory EMG feedback to improve walking which was impaired by overactivity of the quadriceps (Swann and others 1974). The patients were between 17 and 77 years of age; four were hemiplegic and the remaining three had poliomyelitis. All had normal function in the quadriceps and peroneous longus muscles although contractions of the latter interfered with normal walking. Auditory feedback of peroneous longus EMG activity was presented for 10 minutes, three times weekly for two weeks. The patients also received conventional physical therapy for 10 minutes at each feedback session; the order of administration of the two types of treatment was alternated daily. The patients were instructed to stretch their legs while reducing the auditory feedback signal. Before and after each session, they were instructed to stretch their leg five times while relaxing the lower part of the leg. Knee-angle measurements during feedback and conventional therapy segments of the sessions increased 6.3° and 2.4°, respectively. Four of the seven patients performed better with feedback than with physical therapy, one patient performed equally well with both types of treatments, and one performed better during physical therapy than during feedback.

Another study comparing the effectiveness of biofeedback and physical therapy trained hemiplegic patients to increase the range of motion in the wrist and arm (Mroczek and others 1978). The patients were between 50 and 75 years of age; strokes had occurred one to 10 years earlier. Muscular contraction was trained in wrist extensors in seven patients and in the biceps in one; muscular relaxation was trained in the biceps in one. Baseline measurements of muscular function were obtained twice weekly for two weeks. Thereafter five patients received four weeks of biofeedback training followed by four weeks of physical therapy; four other patients were treated in the reverse order. The biofeedback sessions were 30 minutes long. Each patient was given auditory and visual feedback of EMG activity from the appropriate muscle along with instructions to increase or decrease activity as indicated. Feedback from muscles in the normal limb was provided during the first session in order to acquaint the patients with the relationship between EMG signals and muscle activity. A total of 12 sessions with the affected limb were administered three times weekly. The physical therapy sessions used a variety of conventional techniques to stress contraction and relaxation of muscles in both the affected and unaffected limbs. Both EMG and range of motion were improved by biofeedback, and the gains were similar to those obtained from physical therapy. However, those patients receiving biofeedback prior to physical therapy showed more improvement in EMG, but not range of motion, than did those who had physical therapy first.

The motor control of hemiparetic patients with spastic, flaccid or paretic muscular activity in the extremities was improved by biofeedback (Brudny and others 1976; Brudny, Korein and others 1974). The patients were between 13 and 81 years of age; motor impairments had been present from nine months to 35 years. Visual and auditory feedback was provided from selected muscle groups during sessions lasting up to 45 minutes, up to five times weekly for eight to 12 weeks. In addition, mirrors provided visual information about limb movement. The earlier study reported that of 13 patients, four demonstrated prehension, six developed assistive capacities, one developed control of spasticity, and two did not change motor function. The later study reported that 27 of 39 patients demonstrated either actual prehension or assistive capacity. Three to 36 months after treatment, 20 of the 39 patients who demonstrated prehension or assistive capacity used their extremity actively.

Three of six patients who were given feedback for leg movements achieved previously absent ankle dorsiflexion capability while sitting or standing and showed some improvement during walking.

Asymmetrical standing in patients with hemiparesis has been treated successfully (Wannstedt & Herman 1978). Here, muscle activity was not indicated directly by an EMG, but indirectly by a transducer which was placed in the shoe and measured the amount of weight being placed on each foot. As discussed earlier in this chapter, the procedure is not really an example of biofeedback because that term usually implies direct measurement of biological function. However, the general treatment program is identical to those used in biofeedback treatments, and the procedure is relevant to neuromuscular reeducation. The patients were between 32 and 75 years of age with histories of left or right hemiparesis ranging from six months to 15 years. All had completed a program of conventional physical therapy which was unable to restore normal motor function; they could stand without an assistive device but had an asymmetrical posture. All patients wore an ankle-foot orthosis. The percent of weight bearing on each limb was determined while the patients were instructed to stand as straight as possible. Thereafter, all 30 patients participated in an initial training session, and 20 of them had up to 28 more sessions with one follow-up assessment 30 days later. Each session lasted 20 minutes with alternating periods of feedback and rest, each one minute long. Sessions were held twice weekly in the laboratory and once daily at home. Auditory feedback was generated by a transducer worn in the shoe. During the session, the patient was instructed to reduce the loudness of the audio signal which decreased in volume as weight bearing on it approached preset levels. The signal was set to stop when load levels ranged between 43% and 57% of body weight. During the initial treatment session, 23 of the 30 patients achieved symmetrical standing. Of these, all with initial pressures above 30% of bodyweight were successful. The remaining seven patients improved their posture but could not put equal weight on both feet; all of them had initial pressures below 30% of bodyweight, and six of them used quad canes. After continued training for 20 patients, 16 achieved symmetrical standing. One month later, 14 of the 16 successful patients maintained their symmetrical weight bearing; the two patients who did not had both demonstrated initial weight bearings of less than 30% of body weight.

Deltoid muscle weakness following a stroke was improved by EMG biofeedback (Lee and others 1976). The patients were between 31 and 79 years of age. The hemiplegia had been present from six weeks to seven years. All had reduced strength in the deltoid muscle. EMG activity was recorded from the deltoid muscle. Auditory and visual analogue feedback were used to train the patients to increase deltoid muscle activity. Each session contained 20 five-second trials with ten seconds of rest between them. The feedback trials were followed each day by incorrect feedback and then no-feedback trials. The authors say that EMG decreased during correct feedback but not during incorrect or no-feedback trials.

Inactive biceps and triceps have been strengthened through biofeedback (Andrews 1964). The 20 patients had histories of hemiplegia ranging from one to 14 years and had no voluntary movement of the biceps and triceps muscles. Needle electrodes were inserted into normal muscles to acquaint the patients with the auditory output from the muscle groups. The electrodes were then moved to a paretic muscle, and the patient was instructed to contract it. If no EMG activity was found, the muscle was slowly manipulated through its range of motion, and then the patient was asked to voluntarily complete the procedure. Visual feedback was provided via an oscilloscope. Whenever the first action potentials appeared, the patient was instructed to watch them and to continue to influence muscle activity voluntarily. Patients were given up to five minutes to acquire voluntary control over muscle activity, after which the treatment was stopped. Seventeen of the 20 were able to produce action potentials sufficient for strong, voluntary, controlled action in the tested muscle. Of the three who failed to meet the criterion, one was later found to have sensory aphasia not detected at the time of training, a second obtained control in 15 minutes in a subsequent session, and the third was unmotivated.

Peripheral Nerve Injury

SYMPTOMS AND MECHANISM

The previous section has discussed paralysis and paresis due to damage to the central nervous system mechanisms, either in the spinal cord or in the cerebrum. Damage to peripheral nerves can produce similar symptoms because there is no way for the brain to order the muscles to move.

TREATMENT

Case Study

The patient was a young woman who injured the ulnar, median, and radial nerves of her right forearm (Marinacci & Horande 1960). Muscles of the right hand showed considerable atrophy, and she was unable to voluntarily contract her muscles, dorsiflex her wrist, or extend her fingers. Insertion of a needle electrode into the right extensor pollicus longus detected some motor unit activity which was used to generate auditory feedback via a loudspeaker attached to a polygraph. She was trained to increase the firing frequency of these units and became able to produce moderate dorsiflexion of the wrist. Motor units were recorded in the right thenar eminence and the first dorsal interossei, which she learned to contract. Training sessions were then scheduled once weekly for six months. After the first session, she had regained from 20% to 60% of normal function in the muscles innervated by the radial, median, and ulnar nerves. After six months of treatment, she had almost complete recovery of function for the muscles innervated by the radial and median nerves and about 50% recovery in the muscles innervated by the ulnar nerve. One year later, her coordination in the muscles of the hand continued to improve.

Cerebral Palsy

SYMPTOMS AND MECHANISM

Cerebral palsy, a disease appearing in young children, has a variety of symptoms, reflecting the brain area primarily involved in the disease (Walton 1977) and the severity of that involvement. At one extreme the symptoms may be slight and appear only as a muscular weakness. At the other extreme the child may be entirely unable to care for himself and may be severely retarded as well. The brain damage has a variety of etiologies including anoxia, ischemia, and metabolic disorders.

TREATMENT

Biofeedback has focused on the muscular disabilities of the person with cerebral palsy. As will be seen in the reports to be discussed, a variety of practical problems have been treated. These include teaching simple movements which had been a problem for the individual and suppressing the contorted and bizarre *athetoid* movements. The general strategy has been to pinpoint movements that are to be changed, examine the muscles responsible for these movements, and then train the muscles in the necessary way. Biofeedback is not a cure for cerebral palsy because it focuses on the motor symptoms of the disorder and not the central mechanism. The available literature, however, indicates that it can significantly improve the person's motor abilities.

Case Study A: Hemiparesis

Biofeedback improved hand and leg control for an 18-year-old female with left spastic hemiparesis caused by cerebral palsy in the first year of life (Brudny, Korein and others 1974). She had total paralysis of the lower extremities and nonfunctional movement in the upper ones. Earlier surgical treatments had brought only limited improvement. She complained of constant, painful contractions of the left peroneal muscles which failed to respond to the use of a cast and brace. Auditory and visual feedback were presented with instructions to increase EMG activity in atrophied and/or paretic muscles and to decrease activity in spastic or spasmodic muscles. Sessions were scheduled for 30 minutes, three times weekly for four weeks. Within the first two weeks of treatment, she was free of pain and discarded her leg brace. By the sixth week, she learned to control her left hand, which she had never used functionally and eventually used her hand to cut meat, tie shoelaces, and cook.

Discussion of Treatments

Unstable head and limb positions in 18 children with athetoid movements were improved by biofeedback (Harris and others 1974). Two feedback devices were used. Ten children used a head control device consisting of four piezoelectric elements mounted in a helmet worn on the head. Auditory feedback was provided by the rate of clicks which increased as the child's head position deviated from neutral. The child was instructed to bring the head to the neutral position from any starting point and to move the head through extreme ranges of motion, ending in the neutral position. The second device was a limb position monitor which used transducers to measure the angle of rotation about the axis of elbow and wrist joints. Feedback was an unpleasant noise which was delivered when arm movements exceeded criterion limits. The child was instructed to move the elbow and/or wrist over the entire range of motion possible, move the joint smoothly stopping at upper and lower limits, and then gradually diminish the range of motion. Each treatment session lasted 30 minutes, three to seven times weekly for two to 12 months. All children using the helmet increased their ability to maintain a neutral head position from a few seconds to more than five minutes. The tone of the neck muscles became more normal. Similarly, all children using the limb position monitor decreased or eliminated tremor, improved the smoothness and accuracy of movements of their arms, and increased the range of motion at the elbow joint. While practicing with the appropriate device, the children had fewer extraneous movements from other parts of the body and less drooling. Teachers of the children reported noticeable improvements, and in one dramatic case, a child who initially required crutches while walking became able to walk independently.

Relaxation of the frontalis muscle was used to improve speech and motor functions in six patients with cerebral palsy of the athetoid type (Finley and others 1976). The patients were four males and two females between 14 and 31 years old. Their IQ scores ranged from 49 to 171. Three could walk and talk, one could walk but not talk, and two could do neither. Two were not medicated during treatment, and the remaining four were using either valium, L-dopa, or dantrium. Auditory and visual feedback of frontal EMG levels were presented during sessions of up to 50 minutes, twice weekly for six weeks. Each patient's speech and fine and gross motor performance was assessed before and after therapy. Levels of frontal EMG activity decreased from 28.9 uV peak-to-peak before training to 13.0 uV following training. Four of six patients had a significant improvement in scores on speech tests with an average increase of 74%; two severely impaired patients showed an increase of 39%. Gross motor performance improved from 71% to 92%.

Frontal EMG biofeedback was later used to improve speech and motor function in four children with spastic cerebral palsy (Finley and others 1977). They were between six and ten years old with spasticity and speech impediments ranging from mild to severe. Speech function was assessed by the ability to initiate and sustain *ah, e,* and *s* sounds. Fine motor function was assessed by the length of time necessary to bring the hands together, touch the mouth with each hand, and grasp an object. Gross motor performance was assessed by having the children move across the floor on their backs and stomachs, roll, crawl, kneel, sit, and walk. Each child received two periods of biofeedback training. The first was six weeks long and the second, which followed after a period of six weeks without training, was four weeks long. The EMG was recorded from above the frontalis muscle and both auditory (clicks) and visual (a needle on a meter) feedback were provided. Explicit reinforcement consisting of money, candy, or toys was given each time the integrated EMG level remained below criterion for 60 seconds. A sliding criterion was used so that progressively lower levels of the EMG were necessary to earn the reinforcements. Biofeedback sessions took place weekly for 30 minutes. Frontal EMG levels were substantially reduced during the treatment, and speech and motor function improved during periods of feedback training, but deteriorated when training was stopped. The frontal EMG, which was 22 uV peak-to-peak before training was reduced to 14 uV peak-to-peak by the end of training. A combined measure of speech and motor performance decreased from 191 units during the first feedback period to 92 units by the end of training, indicating a substantial improvement.

Ranges of motion in the ankle were increased by biofeedback, but these improvements were lost after training was stopped (Skrotzky and others 1978). The patients were three males and one female between 11 and 29 years old. Feedback sessions were scheduled twice daily for 10 consecutive days. In each session the patient was positioned with the knee joint at a 70° angle and instructed to perform exercises contracting and then relaxing the spastic gastrocnemius and tibialis anterior muscles of one leg while paying attention to auditory and visual feedback. All patients increased their range of motion in the ankle joint to an average of 17°. Four weeks later, however, limb function had returned to pretreatment levels.

Foot Drop Following Cerebral Stroke

SYMPTOMS AND MECHANISM

In the normal person, walking is performed as a smooth coordinated action. One important component of walking is lifting the foot and pointing the toes up as the leg is brought forward. This movement is called *dorsiflexion* reflecting the fact that it requires flexion of a muscle and moving of the toes upward in a dorsal direction. The most important muscle for this movement is the *tibialis anterior,* the muscle in the front of the lower leg.

Following damage in the areas of the brain responsible for voluntary movement of the legs, the tibialis anterior may become paretic. The patient loses control of the dorsiflexion process and has trouble walking. The toes are dragged on the floor as the leg is moved forward, the foot may be planted on the ground in a flat position rather than with the heel first, and the entire rhythm of walking may be disrupted. The most prominent difficulty is raising the foot. Analysis of the walking pattern of patients by means of EMG (Peat and others 1976) and strobocinegraphic techniques (Takebe & Basmajian 1976) indicates that there is also a general problem in the phasic pattern or movement. The patients walk with a stiff knee and flexed hip, and the swing time of the leg is greatly increased. In addition, of course, the foot is generally pointed downward, even when it should be pointed up as the foot is placed forward for another step.

The problem of foot drop has been approached in a number of different ways. One of them is to provide a short leg brace which automatically makes the needed correction of foot angle. Another solution is a cane. Intensive physical therapy is incorporated into most treatments. A sequence of exercises includes passive movement of the joint, active movement with and without resistance, and finally exercises in walking. These therapeutic procedures restore function so that in most cases the person can at least walk alone, even if physical aids, such as a cane or leg brace, are required. Inclusion of biofeedback training into the therapeutic regimen can produce a faster and better restoration of function.

TREATMENT

Biofeedback has emphasized training the patient to have more control over the function of the tibialis anterior muscle both in a resting state and during walking. EMG recordings are taken from the muscle, and feedback is provided to the patient who is instructed to contract the tibialis anterior, in turn producing dorsiflexion.

Case Study

A man, 45 years old, had paresis on his left side as a result of a stroke which had occurred six months earlier (Takebe & Basmajian 1976, case 4, p. 308). He was able to walk with the assistance of a short leg brace, but he dragged his toes and put his foot flat on the ground instead of placing his heel first. When moved passively, his foot formed a right angle with the leg, indicating that the joints had the needed range of movement but that this movement could not be produced voluntarily. Surface electrodes were placed on the skin above the tibialis anterior. Feedback was provided visually, by digital numbers, and auditorily. Training took place three times a week for five weeks. Each session included 20 minutes of physical therapy and 20 minutes of EMG biofeedback. The 20-minute biofeedback session was composed of short trials with breaks between them to alleviate fatigue. A complex series of sliding criteria (see Chapters 3 and 7) were used to gradually shape the person into muscle control (see flow diagram on p. 199 of Kukulka & Basmajian 1975). The patient was first made aware of EMG activity in the muscle and then trained to increase it. At the end of training, the tibialis anterior on the side of the paresis had gained strength although it was still not as strong as the one on the unaffected side. The patient learned to walk without a short leg brace, was able to carry out dorsiflexion of the affected foot, and had a well-coordinated gait.

Discussion of Treatments

Biofeedback in conjunction with physical therapy was more effective than physical therapy alone (Basmajian and others 1975). All 20 patients had residual foot dorsiflexion paresis and at most, 90° of passive dorsiflexion from complete plantarflexion to neutral position but were able to walk with or without a cane. One group received 40 minutes of therapeutic exercise. The second group had 20 minutes of exercise followed by 20 minutes of auditory and visual feedback of EMG activity from the tibialis anterior. All were treated three times weekly for five weeks. Before and after training, measurements of dorsiflexion strength with the knee maintained at 30° flexion were obtained using a footpad attached to a spring dynamometer. Active ranges of motion were obtained with the patient in the sitting position. The group that received exercise alone increased their strength of dorsiflexion by 1.1 kg and their range of motion by 5.7°. The group that received the exercise plus biofeedback showed greater improvement in both measures, increasing the strength of dorsiflexion by 2.5 kg and the range of motion by 10.8°. Three of the patients in the biofeedback group dragged their toes prior to treatment; all were able to walk more normally after the treatment, and two were able to walk without leg braces. Four to 16 weeks later, both groups maintained their therapeutic effect.

Improved dorsiflexion and walking was learned by 10 hemiplegic patients who had foot dorsiflexion paralysis which had been present up to three years (Johnson & Garton 1973). They ranged in age from 27 to 73 years old. EMG was recorded from the paralyzed tibialis anterior, and the patient was instructed to contract the muscle. The patients practiced at home with a portable EMG unit twice daily for 30 minutes. Clinical follow-ups were scheduled every one or two weeks, and training was stopped when patients could walk without a short leg brace or when no improvement had been demonstrated during a one-month interval. Each patient's progress was rated on a five-point scale indicating zero, trace, poor, fair, or good improvement. Before training, nine of the ten patients required a short leg brace while walking, two of them had poor function, one had a trace of function, and six had none. By the end of treatment, three patients had eliminated their short leg brace and had developed good function and a safe gait. Of the remaining seven, one became able to walk for up to 10 minutes without the leg brace, two showed fair improvement without functional change, one developed fair improvement and then moved from the area, one had minimal improvement but practiced inconsistently due to a defective feedback unit, and two trained only briefly due to poor motivation.

Also relevant are the treatments discussed previously in the sections on paralysis and paresis and cerebral palsy. Foot drop was usually not included as a specific description of the patients' problems, but in light of the global impairment of walking for some of these people, dorsiflexion of the foot was certainly a problem. The results of these studies indicate that biofeedback can improve walking for individuals who have a relatively circumscribed motor deficit due to a localized cerebral stroke, and for individuals who have a more general problem following brain damage that is more wide spread.

MUSCLES OF THE HEAD AND NECK

This group of studies describe treatments for abnormalities which arose from muscles in the head or neck. The treatments involve the three principles discussed earlier: train relaxation in abnormally contracted muscles, train contraction in abnormally relaxed muscles, and train coordination to get integrated movements when needed. These treatments have been successful with a wide range of disorders, including flaccid paralysis as in Bell's palsy, muscle hypertrophy as in torticollis, and spasmodic twitching as in blepharospasm. The results are encouraging and indicate that biofeedback can significantly reduce the symptoms in all of these disorders.

Spasmodic Torticollis

SYMPTOMS

Torticollis is the combination of two terms meaning "twisted column." A person with torticollis typically has the head drawn to one side and continuously looks over one shoulder (DeMeyer 1977; Elliott 1971; Meares 1971; Podivinsky 1968; Walton 1977). The position of the head is generally sustained, although spasms or jerks may be superimposed on top of the head deviation. The head usually resists an outside force to turn it into the correct position. The symptoms may become worse when the person is under emotional stress (Bowman 1971), when attention is brought to the difficulty, or when voluntary movements of the head are attempted. The symptoms disappear when the individual falls asleep, only to return upon waking. The head may be brought around to the correct posture by paying attention to distant objects or by laying the finger gently on the chin or face. This latter maneuver does not work from the force applied. Indeed, it may be successful with the finger placed on either side of the face.

Torticollis may appear as an isolated problem in the absence of other obvious neurological signs. Alternatively, it may be associated with other disorders such as Huntington's chorea, athetosis, dystonia musculorum deformans, and Parkinsonism (Couch 1976; Podivinsky 1968). It often has a discernable onset from which it develops slowly over the course of several weeks to months and then becomes a stable state. The first symptoms commonly appear late in life, around the age of 40.

The prognosis of torticollis is poor. It generally shows little or no remission and becomes a permanent disability if left untreated. Drug treatment has been unsuccessful. Surgical treatment has attempted to cure the problem by placing lesions at various points in the neural system thought to underly torticollis, ranging from the peripheral nerves of the upper spinal cord to central nervous system structures, such as the basal ganglia and the thalamus. In addition to the risks and undesirable side effects of such procedures, their success rate has been very low (DeMyer 1977; Elliott 1971; Gilbert 1971; Podivinsky 1968; Sorensen & Hamby 1966; Walton 1977). Thus, although spasmodic torticollis is relatively rare and is not directly life threatening, it can disrupt the person's social and professional life and is not effectively controlled by drugs or surgery.

MECHANISM

The sternocleidomastoid, trapezius, and splenius muscles (see Chapter 4) are usually involved. The ones turning the head to its altered position are often hypertrophied, while the antagonists may be atrophied. However, the disorder does not arise from the activity of a single muscle. The head movement is a coordinated one, and all the muscles of rotation participate; occasionally the antagonists for the head movement will be active as well. Which muscles are most active is partly a function of the position of the head but is also due to other variables which cannot be specified at the moment. Particular attention has been paid to the sterno- cleidomastoid, however, because in most cases it is the most active and/or hypertrophied muscle. Because of the attachment of this muscle, the muscle on one side of the head swings the face in the opposite direction. Thus contraction of the left sternocleidomastoid causes the person to look over the right shoulder (DeMyer 1977; Elliott 1971; Podivinsky 1968; Smorto & Basmajian 1977).

The central nervous system mechanism responsible for spasmodic torticollis is presumed to involve the brain stem and basal ganglia. Such a description is made on the basis of knowledge about the general functions of the central nervous system and the assumption that spasmodic torticollis reflects an integrated movement which must be coordinated at a central nervous system level higher than the spinal cord. However, there are no data directly supporting this assumption, even though a few animal models have supported the idea. In any case, explanations are unlikely to lie in a very peripheral mechanism and will probably involve some aspects of the motor system responsible for integrated activity (DeMyer 1977; Podivinsky 1968; Tarlov 1970). The association of torticollis with a variety of other movement disorders, and its appearance due to many different etiologies complicates the analysis (Podivinsky 1968).

TREATMENT

Biofeedback treatment has sought to reduce the activity of the muscles responsible for head turning, particularly the sternocleidomastoid. The first step is to obtain baseline readings of both the head position and the EMG from the muscles of the head and neck. Next, the patient is given feedback to reduce the muscle activity of the hyperactive muscles. Measurements are taken of the reduction in muscle activity and the head position. This treatment assumes that irrespective of the central mechanism responsible for the initial problem, the individual can still learn to control the relevant skeletal muscles if given appropriate feedback. Some of these treatments have used an explicit reinforcer—a slight electric shock—to punish the individual for excessive muscle contraction. The shock was effective, which may have been due to its distracting qualities as well as its aversive ones. In any case, the use of explicit positive as well as negative reinforcers should enhance the effectiveness of biofeedback as discussed in Chapter 3.

Case Study

The patient was a 55-year-old male with a three-year history of torticollis (Brudny, Grynbaum & Korein 1974). His chin was pointed 90° to the right over his shoulder, he couldn't voluntarily move his head to look straight, and he was unable to work. The left sternocleidomastoid muscle was tense and enlarged while the one on the right was shrunken. EMG was recorded from the spasmodic left and the atrophied right muscle. Visual and auditory feedback were provided for decreasing the activity of the left and increasing the activity of the right sternocleidomastoid muscles. Sessions lasted 30 to 60 minutes, three to five times weekly. At the beginning of training the activity levels in the two muscles were markedly different. As training progressed, he learned to relax the spasmodic left muscle and increase activity in the atrophied right one. He became able to move his head to a central position and after eight weeks of therapy, developed a full range of motion. He returned to work, regained self-assurance, resumed social interactions, and reported being able to reduce or prevent spasms.

Discussion of Treatments

Following biofeedback, patients with torticollis had greater voluntary control over head movements and participated in more daily activities (Brudny and others 1976; Brudny, Korein, and others 1974). All patients were between 13 and 81 years of age with histories of torticollis ranging from nine months to 35 years. The EMG was recorded from selected muscles in the neck. Training sessions lasted up to 45 minutes, up to five times weekly for eight to 12 weeks. In the earlier report, prior to treatment, only three of the 13 patients could maintain a neutral head position (looking forward) for more than a few minutes. By the end of the treatment, all of the patients maintained the neutral position during feedback. Three patients maintained voluntary control without feedback for several months. The latter study reported that of 48 patients trained, 19 demonstrated either "meaningful" or "major" improvements in activities of daily living; some decreased their medication usage, and some easily controlled occasional spasmodic episodes.

Substantially greater success was reported in another study from the same clinic (Brudny, Grynbaum, & Korein 1974). The patients were between 20 and 58 years of age; torticollis had been present for up to 15 years. EMG activity was recorded from spasmodic muscles and from the atrophied contralateral muscles. Visual and auditory feedback were presented during sessions which lasted from 30 to 60 minutes and took place three to five times weekly for an average of 10 weeks. The frequency of treatment was reduced as patients gained voluntary control. By the end of therapy, all nine patients maintained a neutral head position. EMG activity in the hypertrophied sternocleidomastoid at rest was decreased from 95 units (on a calibrated scale) prior to treatment, to five units following treatment. EMG activity in the atrophied muscle during a maximal contraction was increased from 31 units prior to training to more than 120 units after training. Seven of the patients maintained a neutral head position with feedback for an indefinite period of time, one for hours, and one for 30 minutes during therapy. Following the treatment, three maintained voluntary control for months, three for hours, one for five to ten minutes, and two for two to five minutes. Seven patients were able to resume a neutral position without feedback, one could do so periodically, and one could not.

EMG feedback was combined with shock to reduce the frequency of spasms in nine patients with torticollis and one with retrocollis (Cleeland 1973). Symptom histories ranged from two to 60 months. EMG was recorded from the left and right sternocleidomastoid. Analogue feedback was provided by the pitch of a tone. All patients were instructed to lower the pitch of the auditory feedback and in so doing, relax spastic and/or hypertrophied muscles while attempting to reach a neutral head position. Shock was delivered continuously to two fingers whenever EMG levels increased above criterion values. Each session included six to eight trials, each five minutes long, separated by several minutes of rest; training was given once or twice daily for a total of six to 23 sessions. All patients except for one were reexamined at follow-up periods ranging from one to 40 months. The treatment was evaluated by measures of spasm frequency and by rating each patients' degree of improvement on a three-point scale. The frequency of spasm, which averaged 53.5 per five minutes before treatment, was reduced to 24.8 following treatment. All ten patients showed a decrease in muscle spasms, and two of them eliminated the spasms entirely. Three of the ten were rated as markedly improved, three moderately improved, and three minimally improved.

Bell's Palsy

SYMPTOMS

Bell's palsy is a facial paralysis which is almost always unilateral, affecting only one side of the face. It persists in spite of voluntary attempts to move the face, emotional events causing typical expressions (such as smiling or frowning), and stimuli that might produce reflexive changes. The onset of the symptoms is usually sudden, appearing almost complete within a few hours. It is most common in young adults, and produces a masklike face on the involved side with a drooping eyelid, expressionless face, and no wrinkle in the forehead. The disorder may spread to include paralysis of one side of the tongue and loss of taste (Bannister 1978; Jankel 1978; Miller 1967; Taverner 1955; Thomas 1978; Walton 1977).

For approximately 85% of the people who contract Bell's palsy, recovery of function begins to appear about three weeks after the appearance of the symptoms and is complete within 12 months. The facial muscles in the individuals who recover usually have no evidence of *fibrillation*, a sign of nervous degeneration (Taverner 1955). For the remaining 15%, however, the prognosis is poor (Granger 1976; Jankel 1978; Miller 1967; Thomas 1978). If there is fibrillation, little if any recovery occurs, presumably reflecting complete degeneration of the facial nerve (Taverner 1955). In general, the more extensive and more normal the muscle activity shortly after the onset of the disorder, the better the recovery (Granger 1976; Taverner 1955).

MECHANISM

The basic disorder in Bell's palsy lies in the seventh cranial nerve, the nerve which innervates the face and is responsible for muscle movement. Although this is the nerve that fails to function, the reason for its lack of function is not clear. The frequency of Bell's palsy does not appear to be random, suggesting that it may have an origin in some infectious process (Leibowitz 1969). Others have assumed a different precipitating cause such as trauma, cold, or injury (Walton 1977), with the ultimate outcome an inflammation of the facial nerve (Bannister 1978) or some form of a vascular or ischemic process causing disruption of the metabolic support of the facial nerve (see discussion in Leibowitz 1969). Direct evidence for a particular lesion, however, is generally lacking (Miller 1967), making further analysis of the mechanism difficult (Jankel 1978; Thomas 1978).

TREATMENT

The major problem in Bell's palsy is flaccid paralysis; there are few other complications. Biofeedback first trains the individual to regain control over muscle activity and then to coordinate the activity in the two sides of the face so there is normal symmetry. Baseline records are first obtained from all the muscles in the face. If activity is minimal, needle electrodes may be used initially to record muscle signals. Starting with the most active muscles, the patient seeks to increase the activity of these. As more control of a single muscle is obtained, therapy moves to other muscles as needed. When the patient is successful enough to produce readily observable facial movements, practice with a mirror can provide sufficient feedback for continued improvement. Such practice is also useful in obtaining symmetrical control over the movements in both sides of the face.

Case Study A

Facial paralysis on the right side had persisted for 15 years prior to biofeedback treatment in this 28-year-old woman (Jankel 1978). Right-sided smiling was impaired, the right eyelid was closed, the eye was rotated upward and laterally, and tears appeared in the eye while she was chewing. Both the zygomaticus and orbicularis oculi muscles showed fibrillation and conduction delays. In addition, the jaw was displaced laterally 1.3 cm to the left side. Electrical stimulation, massage, and heat therapy had failed to restore normal control. EMG was recorded from the masseter, zygomaticus, or orbicularis muscles. Sessions lasted 30 minutes daily for three weeks. Contraction of the masseter, zygomaticus, and orbicularis muscles increased. The patient's jaw position became more normal, her facial movements and smile were symmetrical, and the lateral rotation of her eye disappeared. Fibrillation was almost eliminated. Conduction delays were normalized in the nerves to the masseter and zygomaticus muscles but were borderline in the nerves to the orbicularis oculi.

Case Study B

At the beginning of biofeedback treatment, this young man had a severe facial paralysis and no motor unit activity in the right frontalis and orbicularis oris muscles when he attempted to move them (Marinacci & Horande 1960). The paralysis had persisted for six years and probably resulted from bulbar poliomyelitis. A needle electrode recorded muscle activity from the orbicularis oris muscles. Auditory feedback reflected motor unit activity. He was first instructed to increase the firing rate of the motor units in the muscles on the normal (left) side to familiarize himself with the procedure. The electrode was then moved to the muscles on the paralyzed right side. Within an hour, a reflex potential of 400 uV was detected with a firing rate of 10 per second. Several sessions were held during the next few days and were then scheduled twice a week for six months. Unit activity increased to about 15 per second and many more motor units appeared in the orbicularis oris as well as reflex ones in the right frontalis. Within a week he regained about 20% of the voluntary contraction of both the orbicularis oris and frontalis muscles. Voluntary control continued to improve with 40% of the function returning by the end of treatment. Another patient treated in the same laboratory was a woman with a 23-year history of Bell's palsy. After feedback training, she had regained 40% function of her right orbicularis oris although no function was regained in the right frontalis.

Facial Paralysis Following Traumatic Damage to the Facial Nerve

SYMPTOMS AND MECHANISM

As discussed in the preceding section on Bell's Palsy, the muscles of the face are innervated by the seventh (facial) nerve. Destruction of this nerve for any reason will cause paralysis. In the case below, a fracture of the skull damaged the nerve.

TREATMENT

Case Study

Following an automobile accident, this woman had facial paralysis (Booker and others 1969). The petrous portion of the left temporal bone was fractured, severing the left facial nerve. Surgery was performed to reinnervate the facial muscles with axons normally leading to the trapezius and sternocleidomastoid muscles. Subsequent physical therapy was not able to restore voluntary control over facial muscles. She was unable to use muscles on the left side of her face or blink her left eye.

An oscilloscope was used to present visual feedback of EMG activity from both sides of her face. She was instructed to alter the signal generated from the left (affected) side so that it matched the one produced by the right (unaffected side). Training sessions ranged from 17 to 60 minutes and took place up to four times weekly for three weeks. She also practiced at home in front of a mirror. During treatment, she strengthened the facial muscles with minimal shoulder movement, progressing to eye closure independent of activity in the lower half of the face. At the end of training, she produced facial movements without any shoulder activity. However, an asymmetry did remain during facial expressions, such as smiling, and during speech. A partial regression of therapeutic gains was evident four months later although three days of retraining were sufficient to reestablish previous control.

Temporomandibular Joint Syndrome

SYMPTOMS AND MECHANISM

The temporomandibular joint, or TMJ, is located just below and in front of the ear. It is primarily involved in chewing and is different from other joints in many ways (Sarnat 1964; Shapiro & Gorlin 1970; Sicher 1964; Walker 1978). First, there are two joints, one on either side of the head, and they function together to move the jaw. Second, the TMJ is complex with three directions of movement: up and down, left and right, and forward and backward. Third, it is morphologically different from other joints; there is a disc within the joint, and the load-bearing surfaces are composed of fibrous cartilage rather than the more usual hyaline cartilage.

The TMJ is moved by four different muscles, as illustrated in Figure 13–1. Three of the muscles move the jaw vertically. These include the

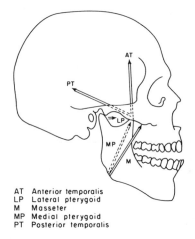

AT Anterior temporalis
LP Lateral pterygoid
M   Masseter
MP Medial pterygoid
PT Posterior temporalis

FIGURE 13-1   A Diagram of the Head Showing the Temporomandibular Joint (At the Arrow). The four muscles moving the joint and their direction of action are also illustrated: AT—anterior temporalis, PT—posterior temporalis, MP—medial pterygoid, LP—lateral pterygoid. *(Adapted from A. Walker, "Functional Anatomy of Oral Tissue: Mastication and Deglutition." In J. H. Shaw and E. A. Sweeney (Eds.),* Textbook of Oral Biology, *p. 284. Copyright © 1978 by W. B. Saunders Company, Reprinted by permission.)*

anterior and posterior branches of the temporal muscles (AT and PT in the diagram, respectively), the masseter (M), and the medial pterygoid (MP). One muscle, the lateral pterygoid (LP), moves the jaw laterally. The diagram also shows the position of the joint itself, at the arrow near where the ear would be located.

Pain may be associated with the TMJ, even though there is no obvious pathology of the joint or the jaw (Alderman 1975; Laskin 1969; Lehner 1978; Munro 1975; Shapiro & Gorlin 1970). This pain has been given a variety of names, including *temporomandibular joint syndrome, myofacial pain dysfunction,* and *temporomandibular joint pain dysfunction syndrome.* The primary symptoms are pain and tenderness, usually associated with movement of the jaw or pressure on the area surrounding the TMJ. The pain is most often on just one side of the face. It may be localized to the TMJ area, or it may radiate into adjacent areas. Another symptom is *crepitation* or clicking which occurs whenever the jaw is opened and closed. Movement of the jaw may be limited. *Tinnitus,* or ringing in the ear, and headaches may be present.

Pinpointing a single mechanism responsible for the TMJ syndrome is difficult and perhaps impossible due to the complex interactions that take place in the TMJ. Action of the joint is influenced by the characteristics of the joint itself, the muscles that move it, and the position of the teeth in the jaw. A change in any one of these variables is likely to produce changes in the others, which will in turn have further repercussions for the system as a whole (Alderman 1975). Thus abnormal function of one or more of the muscles moving the joint should exacerbate TMJ pain, and EMG recordings from these muscles support that view. Patients who have TMJ pain often have generally elevated EMGs. The muscles used to close the jaw may be more active than normal prior to jaw closing and continue to be active for a longer period of time after jaw closing (Munro 1975). These data do not answer the question of whether the abnormal muscle activity preceded or followed the pain, but they do suggest that continuation of the pain may in part be due to the inappropriate muscle contractions (Garliner 1976; Schwartz 1955; Travell 1960; Weinmann & Sicher 1964; but see Kydd 1959 for an exception).

Two other factors contribute to the TMJ syndrome. One is inappropriate oral habits, such as smoking a pipe, chewing gum, or biting objects. Between 30% (Garliner 1976) and 80% (Lupton 1966) of the patients with TMJ pain report having inappropriate oral habits, sometimes associated with their work: examples include a seamstress biting thread or a violin player practicing many hours a day with the violin pressing against her jaw (Alderman 1975). A second factor is emotional stress. Many patients who have the TMJ syndrome report that the pain is exacerbated when they are under stress (Moulton 1966). Two case reports document this relationship (Kydd 1959). In one, moving to a new neighborhood and concerns about occupational status preceded the TMJ syndrome. In another, worrying about performance on a chemistry exam was the critical stimulus. Furthermore, emotional support and reassurance of the patient may be all that is necessary to produce a profound reduction in the pain (Alderman 1975). Indeed, psychological counseling may be as effective as standard dental treatment in reducing TMJ pain providing, of course, that there are not pathological changes that require correction by dental surgery (Lupton 1969).

TREATMENT

Biofeedback treatment focuses on the muscles moving the joint and emphasizes relaxation of those muscles. One form of treatment has been a standard relaxation training procedure designed to produce a decrease in the activity of all muscles in the body. The other form has been specific relaxation of the muscles around the temporomandibular joint, particularly the masseter muscles. Baseline measures of EMG, pain, and range of movement of the jaw are obtained. Feedback is given about the level of activity in the masseter muscles, and the patient is trained to decrease this activity. The few reports reviewed here provide optimism about the effectiveness of biofeedback for this problem. Dental treatment may be necessary to eliminate abnormalities in the TMJ itself or in the teeth and jaw (Griffin 1975; Sarnat & Laskin 1969; Thompson 1964).

Pain in the right side of the lower jaw, the masseter and the right temporomandibular joint had been present for many years in this young woman (Carlsson and others 1975). Equilibration of the dentition, local anesthetics, nocturnal mouthguards, short-wave diathermy, and anti-epileptic medications had failed to alleviate the pain. Surgical denervation of the involved area was being considered when she sought biofeedback treatment. EMG was recorded from the masseter muscle. Visual feedback was provided during 18 sessions, once or twice weekly. Initially she alternately tensed and relaxed the muscle to become familiar with the correlation between EMG output and subjective tension. Thereafter, she was instructed only to relax the muscle. As she increased her ability to lower EMG activity with feedback, feedback was removed and at the end of each trial she was told the level of EMG attained. Finally, she was trained to achieve specified levels of EMG activity in progressively shorter periods of time. To increase further her sensitivity to daily fluctuations in muscular activity, she kept an hourly record of subjective muscle contraction one or two days each week.

At the beginning of training, she was reluctant to contract the masseter muscle because of the pain it produced, and in one session contraction caused a pain lasting several hours. During the first half of the treatment, she increased her awareness of muscular tension and its correlation with frustration. She became increasingly able to relax the masseter muscle during the last half of therapy and reported no attacks of pain after the twelfth session. Six months later, she reported only periodic muscle tension without pain and was able to eliminate it by voluntary relaxation. Some clicking in the right TMJ was the only remaining symptom.

Discussion of Treatments

Biofeedback reduced the pain associated with the TMJ syndrome in 11 patients, all of whom had not been successfully treated with standard dental procedures (Carlsson & Gale 1977). The pain had persisted for at least three years and up to 13 years. EMG was recorded from the masseter muscle and visual feedback provided. Six to 18 training sessions took place in one to four months. Training was terminated for each patient when there was no evidence of improved ability to relax the masseter muscle or when there was no additional reduction in pain during six consecutive sessions. At the end of training, two patients had no pain, two were "practically symptom-free," and six showed some improvement. Four to 15 months later, nine of the 11 patients were rated as improved.

SYMPTOMS, MECHANISM, AND TREATMENT

Blepharospasm is an involuntary, bilateral blinking of the eyes and usually appears in older people. The muscles responsible for the blinking are the orbicularis oculi surrounding the eyes. The reason for the excessive, spasmodic activity of these muscles is not clear. The inappropriate contraction of the eye muscles responsible for normal blinking should be confirmed by EMG records from around the eye. After baseline records are obtained, the individual is given EMG biofeedback to reduce the activity of these muscles and to increase the length of time between blinks. Recordings are taken of both EMG and the frequency of eye blinks, and reductions are sought in both.

Case Study

The patient was a 50-year-old woman who recently developed spasmodic winking around both eyes (Peck 1977). Her condition included a general allergic reaction, minor optic pathology, and lack of tear secretion. Ophthalmologic, neurologic, and psychiatric treatments reduced all but the spasms which produced deep facial furrows and disrupted her domestic, social, and professional life. EMG activity in the left frontal and lower obicularis oculi areas was integrated and used to provide an analogue auditory feedback signal varying directly in pitch with changes in muscle tension. The training included two sessions with incorrect feedback followed by 17 sessions with correct feedback, each 20 minutes long, two to three times weekly. She was instructed to reduce the loudness of the feedback signal. Both EMG levels and blinking decreased with treatment. The EMG, which was 30 uV during baseline, decreased to 20 uV during incorrect feedback, to 15 uV during the first three correct feedback sessions, and to 7.2 uV during the last three. The number of blinking spasms during each session decreased from 1,300 during baseline to 14 in the last half of training. All progress made with the left eye generalized to the right eye and was maintained at home. She was free of spasms for about an hour each day by the ninth session and for a week by the 17th. Overall, the spasm was reduced from a massive muscular contraction to "a rather pronounced wink" (p. 277) by session seven and to "nothing more than an ordinary blink" (p. 277) during the last three sessions. These improvements were maintained four months later.

Excessive Contraction of Throat Muscles

SYMPTOMS, MECHANISM, AND TREATMENT

Case Study A

The patient was a male woodwind musician who during the past 19 years experienced increasing tightness in lip, cheek, and throat muscles which severely jeopardized his music career (Levee and others 1976). Visual feedback was generated from the frontalis, right and left orbicularis oris, infrahoid (alongside the trachea and larynx), and genioglossus muscle areas. Training included four phases totalling 20 sessions. Each session lasted up to 40 minutes. Phase one acquainted the patient with the equipment and trained him to reduce frontal EMG from an average of 70 uV to 15 uV. The second phase of the treatment was tailored more closely to his particular complaints and recorded EMG from areas near the infrahoid and genioglossus muscles. EMG levels were reduced from 78 uV to 55 uV. The third phase included counterconditioning. He generated low EMG levels, then played his flute in an acoustical chamber, and then returned as rapidly as possible with feedback to the EMG levels prior to playing. The average levels of EMG activity in this phase were 10 uV before and 5 uV after flute playing. The last phase was basically the same as the third without the acoustical chamber. EMG levels averaged 35 uV at the beginning of the sessions and were reduced to 8 uV at the end. Following the fourth phase, the patient advanced from the third chair position to first chair position for three instruments, performed solo, and had no other symptoms. During the follow-up sessions, his EMG was consistently between 5 uV and 10 uV.

Case Study B

Prolonged constriction of the pharyngeal and esophageal throat muscles made swallowing difficult for this 25-year-old woman (Haynes 1976). During stress, her swallowing difficulties frequently prevented her from eating; relaxation therapy and minor tranquilizers were unable to control her condition. The training used auditory feedback of frontal EMG levels. Each of 20 sessions lasted 30 minutes, three times weekly for four weeks, twice weekly for two weeks, and once every other week for three weeks. She practiced at home when she felt her throat becoming tense or tight. Frontal EMG levels decreased from 7.7 uV/min during the first and last block of four trials in the first session, to 4.4 uV/min during the same period in the last session. Swallowing difficulty, rated from zero to 10 during meals each day, decreased from 2.7 before treatment to .5 during treatment and .3 at follow-up. She also reported better ability to relax her throat during meals.

Parkinson's Disease

SYMPTOMS AND MECHANISM

Parkinson's disease is a progressive disorder which appears late in life, usually beginning when the person is about 60 years old. The symptoms change as the disease progresses and involves more body systems. Some of the most characteristic symptoms are a tremor in the hands, rigidity in movements, a masklike face with almost no expression, drooling, reduction of postural reflexes, and difficulty initiating movements (Fahn 1977; Fahn & Duffy 1977; Selby 1968). Parkinson's disease is due to a selective loss of a particular transmitter, dopamine, in the substantia nigra. The changes in the substantia nigra of a Parkinson's patient are so severe that at autopsy they can be seen even without the aid of a microscope. A substantial literature (see review in Fahn & Duffy 1977) has documented the involvement of this biochemical-neuroanatomical system, and the mechanism of Parkinson's disease can be considered well established. The etiology of the disease is unclear, but it may be due to viral infections.

TREATMENT

The standard treatment for Parkinson's disease is L-dopa, a precursor to the missing transmitter, dopamine. When taken by mouth, L-dopa is converted into dopamine and in conjunction with other drugs is capable of restoring normal body movement in many patients. However, L-dopa has substantial side effects including general loss of muscle tone, gastrointestinal upset, psychotic episodes, and choreiform movements. As a result of these side effects and other toxic processes, about 25% of the people with Parkinson's disease cannot use L-dopa effectively. Thus biofeedback can be used to advantage with these patients, and might be able to reduce the dose of L-dopa necessary to control the symptoms in other patients.

Case Study

A woman, 64 years old, had a 15-year history of Parkinsonism (Netsell & Cleeland 1973). Following two surgeries, she developed a complete bilateral retraction of the upper lip, exposing the upper gum and precluding normal lip closure for *p, b,* and *m* sounds. This development was accompanied by extreme eye squinting, wrinkling of the forehead, reduced loudness and imprecise pronunciation of consonants. Biofeedback training was used to improve her speech. The EMG was recorded from the area of the levator labii superioris and produced auditory analogue feedback. Training sessions were 30 minutes long. She was instructed to vary the pitch of the auditory feedback which corresponded to a range of lip postures. During the first session she was able to relax the upper lip until it lightly contacted the lower lip in the absence of EMG activity from the levator labii superioris. This was accompanied by a decrease in eye squinting and wrinkling of the forehead. By the end of treatment, she no longer retracted her upper lip above her gum and ". . . demonstrated complete control of the lip in nonspeech activities" (p. 137). Although her conversational speech was accompanied by some lip retraction, she showed much more normal activity and demonstrated several bilabial closures which were absent in the first session. One objective measure of changes in EMG levels indicated that orbicularis oris activity, which was above 100 uV while speaking in session one, was reduced to 20 uV during session two when she was not speaking.

CLINICAL PROGRAM

The amount of voluntary control over muscles can be assessed by asking the person to move the affected parts of the body and by recording the EMG from the involved muscles with surface electrodes. For extremely flaccid muscles, subcutaneous electrodes may be necessary to determine if any motor units are present. Neuromuscular reeducation can always be assisted by physical therapy exercises, and these should be incorporated into the treatment program.

The exact nature of the treatment will vary depending on the nature of the problem and its location in the body. The general sequence of treatment is the same. First, hypertrophic muscles should be trained to relax. Recording from these with standard surface electrodes presents no problem because of their excessive activity. Next, atrophied muscles should be trained to contract. Initial training may have to use subcutaneous electrodes and an oscilloscope display if unit activity is extremely low or if activity from neighboring muscles provides too much noise. Electrodes must be placed to record from only the desired muscles; individual electrodes are usually the most easy to use.

Training trials should be determined by the client's ability and energy. Short periods scheduled several times a day, are more appropriate

TABLE 13–1 Summary of Biofeedback Treatments for Neuromuscular Reeducation

Study	Patients	Biofeedback Treatment	Other Treatment	Results	
				Symptoms	Biological Function
Amato, Hermsmeyer, & Kleinman, 1973	Male, age 22	Visual feedback of changes in EMG activity in the left medial gastrocnemius muscle area during 30-min sessions, twice daily at home	Data unavailable	Gait improved and foot remained flat on floor from heel-strike to mid-stance	Dorsiflexion in the left ankle increased from zero with 10° inversion to 15° following training
Andrews, 1964	20 hemiplegics	Feedback of EMG activity from the previously inactive biceps or triceps for 5 min	Data unavailable	17 of 20 patients were able to generate EMG activity capable of producing "strong, voluntary, controlled action of the tested muscle"	Data unavailable
Basmajian, Kukulka, Narayan, & Takebe, 1975	10 males, 10 females; age range 30 to 63	Auditory and visual feedback of EMG activity during 20-min sessions, 3 times weekly for 5 weeks	Physical therapy prior to each feedback session	2 of 3 patients were able to walk without their leg braces following training	Dorsiflexion strength increased by an average of 2.5 kg; range of motion increased by 10.8°
Booker, Rubow, & Coleman, 1969	Female, age 36	Visual feedback of affected and unaffected muscular activity during 17- to 60-min sessions up to 4 times weekly	Home practice with a mirror	Increased ability to voluntarily facilitate muscular activity on the affected side; symmetry in appearance of the two sides of the face was achieved	Data unavailable
Brudny, Grynbaum, & Korein, 1974	7 males, 3 females with torticollis; age range 20 to 58	Visual and auditory feedback of spasmodic and atrophied EMG activity during 30- to 60-min sessions, 3 to 5 times weekly for an average of 10 weeks	Data unavailable	7 became able to maintain a neutral head position with feedback for an indefinite period of time, one could do so for hours, and one for 30 mins; following treatment, 7 patients could resume a disturbed normal position without feedback, 1 could do so periodically, and 1 could not	Levels of hypertrophied sternocleidomastoid EMG activity decreased from 95 to 5 (arbitrary) units; ipsilateral activity increased from 31 to 120 units

Levidow, Grynbaum, Lieberman, & Friedmann, 1974	range 13 to 68	activity from spastic and/or atrophied muscles during 30-min sessions, 3 times weekly for 8 to 12 weeks		demonstrated by 1 quadriparetic, 10 hemiparetics, 8 patients with torticollis, 2 with hemifacial spasms, and 1 with dystonia	Data unavailable
Brudny, Korein, Grynbaum, Friedmann, Weinstein, Sachs-Frankel & Belandres, 1976	114 patients; age range 13 to 81	Feedback of EMG activity from spastic and/or atrophied muscles during 30- to 45-min sessions, 3 to 5 times weekly for 8 to 12 weeks	Medication	23 of 45 hemiparetics partially improved; 19 of 48 with torticollis demonstrated "meaningful" or "major" improvement and decreased medication usage; 2 quadriparetics achieved prehension; 2 of 4 patients with facial spasms improved; 3 with dystonia improved; 2 nonwalking patients with quadriceps muscle atrophy were able to walk	
Carlsson & Gale, 1977	6 males, 5 females with temporomandibular joint pain	Visual feedback of masseter muscle activity during 6 to 18 sessions in 1.5 to 4 months	Data unavailable	3 showed some and 3 showed major improvement; 2 practically symptom-free, three slightly better or totally symptom-free, one slightly better, and 2 practically unchanged	Lowest uV level of EMG activity at the end of treatment ranged from 4 to 11
Carlsson, Gale, & Öhman, 1975	Female, age 21	Visual feedback of masseter muscle activity during 10, one-min trials once or twice weekly for 18 trials	Data unavailable	Pain attacks were eliminated by the 12th session, and 1-year follow-up; episodic tension reduced	Data unavailable
Cleeland, 1973	4 males, 6 females with torticollis or retrocollis; age range 15 to 64	Auditory feedback of sternocleidomastoid activity during 6 to 8 five-min trials, once or twice daily	Shock contingent on increases in EMG activity	Frequency of spasm per 5 minutes averaged 53.5 and was reduced to 24.8 after treatment; 3 of 10 patients rated as markedly improved, 3 moderately, 3 minimal or none, and 1 lost at follow-up	Data unavailable

TABLE 13–1 Summary of Biofeedback Treatments for Neuromuscular Reeducation

Study	Patients	Biofeedback Treatment	Other Treatment	Results Symptoms	Biological Function
Finley, Niman, Standley, & Ender, 1976	4 males, 2 females with athetoid cerebral palsy; age range 14 to 31	Auditory and visual feedback of frontal EMG levels during 12 sessions of up to 50 min	Medication	Performance on speech tests improved by 74% in 4 of 6 patients; all improved by 82% on measures of fine and gross motor performance	Frontal EMG levels decreased from 29 to 13 uV peak-to-peak
Finley, Niman, Standley, & Wansley, 1977	2 males, 2 females with spastic cerebral palsy; age range 6 to 10	Auditory and visual feedback of frontal EMG levels during 20 sessions lasting 30 min	None reported	On a scale ranging from 1 (best performance) to 4 (poorest performance), a combined measure of speech and motor function improved from 190.5 to 91.5 by the end of training	Frontal EMG levels decreased from 21.6 to 13.9 uV p-p
Gessel, 1975	22 females, 1 male with myofacial pain-dysfunction syndrome	Auditory feedback of masseter and temporalis EMG activity during 30-min sessions once or twice weekly	Home practice	15 of 23 patients reported relief after 3 to 10 sessions	Data unavailable
Harris, Spelman, & Hymer, 1974	18 athetoid cerebral palsied children, age range 7 to 18	Auditory and visual feedback of head position, and visual feedback of arm position, during 30-min sessions, 3 to 7 times weekly for 2 to 12 months	Data unavailable	Children improved ability to maintain neutral head position and normalization of neck muscle tone; decreases in tremor in, and increases in smoothness of arm movements; ranges of motion in elbow joints increased; extraneous body movements reduced; drooling decreased; one patient shed crutches and could walk independently	Data unavailable

Study	Subjects	Feedback	Practice		Results
Harrison & Connolly, 1971	4 patients with spasticity	Auditory feedback of EMG spikes from the forearm flexors	Data unavailable	Data unavailable	Patients produced "spike" activity 88.3% of the time requested within an average of 71, 100-sec intervals; "nonspike" activity (inhibition) was demonstrated 190 times during the first training segment and 130 times during the final segment
Haynes, 1976	Female, age 25 with dysphagia spastica	Feedback of frontal EMG levels during 20, 30-min sessions	Home practice	Better ability to relax throat muscles while eating; self reports of discomfort (ranging from 0–10) decreased from an average of 3.0 to 0.5 during feedback and at follow-up	Frontal EMG levels averaged 7.7 uV/min during the first four sessions and 4.4 uV/min during the last four
Jacobs & Felton, 1969	14 adults, age range 21 to 57	Visual feedback of upper trapezius muscle activity during 10, 15-min trials	10, 15-min relaxation trials	Data unavailable	Trapezius EMG levels were reduced from 5.6 to .79 millimeters (measured on an oscilloscope)
Jankel, 1978	Female, age 28 with Bell's Palsy	Feedback of either masseter, zygomaticus, or orbicularis oculi muscle activity during 30-min sessions, daily for 3 weeks	Data unavailable	Displacement of jaw position normalized; facial movements and smile characteristics symmetrical; lateral rotation of the eye eliminated; fibrillation in muscles largely reduced; conduction delays normalized in the zygomaticus and masseter muscles and was borderline in the orbicularis oculi	Changes in EMG activity: masseter, 10.4; zygomaticus, 10.4; orbicularis, 9.1

TABLE 13-1 Summary of Biofeedback Treatments for Neuromuscular Reeducation

Study	Patients	Biofeedback Treatment	Other Treatment	Results Symptoms	Biological Function
Johnson & Garton, 1973	6 males, 4 females; age range 27 to 73	Auditory and visual feedback of tibialis anterior muscle activity during 30-min sessions, 3 times weekly for 1 week in the laboratory and twice daily at home	Home practice	4 patients (40%) became able to walk without a leg brace; 3 demonstrated "fair" improvement, 1 minimal improvement and two failed to improve	Data unavailable
Kukulka & Basmajian, 1975	2 males, 1 female; age range 42 to 48	Auditory and visual EMG feedback for 20 mins 3 times weekly for 3 weeks	Whirlpool bath, physical therapy	Data unavailable	6 of 17 joints in 6 fingers acquired normal ranges of motion; increases in the remaining 11 averaged 48°
Lee, Hill, Johnston, & Smiehorowski, 1976	18 adults, age range 31 to 79	Auditory and visual analogue feedback of deltoid EMG activity during 20, 5-sec contraction trials, once daily for 3 days	Data unavailable	Data unavailable	EMG levels did not change significantly during the trials
Levee, Cohen, & Rickles, 1976	Male, age 52 with facial and throat tension	Visual feedback of frontalis, orbicularis oris, infrahoid, and genioglossus EMG activity during four phases with 17 sessions, each lasting up to 40 mins	Data unavailable	Tension decreased progressively during treatment and the patient became able to resume playing woodwind instruments without difficulty	EMG levels decreased from an average of 50 uV to 20 uV; follow-up levels consistently averaged 5 to 10 uV
Macpherson, 1967	Female, age 60	Auditory feedback of EMG activity from various muscle groups	Relaxation (Jacobsonian), counter-conditioning, and home relaxation practice	Involuntary muscular activity was reduced by 50% by the end of treatment and was practically absent at 1-year follow-up; the patient became able to wear dentures without difficulty	Data unavailable

Study	Subjects	Feedback procedure	Comparison treatment	Outcome measure 1	Outcome measure 2
Mroczek, Halpern, & McHugh, 1978	2 females, 7 males with hemiparesis	Auditory and visual feedback of EMG levels in wrist extensors or biceps during 12, 30-min sessions in 4 weeks	Physical therapy	Data unavailable	In group with sequence biofeedback (BF) then physical therapy (PT): EMG activity increased 23.4 uV during BF and 21.1 during PT; increases in range of motion averaged 14.4% during BF and 18.3% during PT; in group with sequence PT then BF: EMG activity increased 14.6 uV during PT and 29.6 during BF, increases in range of motion averaged 7.9% during PT and 6.7% during BF
Netsell & Cleeland, 1973	Female, age 64 with 15-year history of Parkinsonism	Auditory feedback of EMG activity from the levator labii superioris during 5, 30-min sessions	Data unavailable	Upper lip was relaxed so that upper gum did not show during nonspeech periods; retraction occurred only during speech; bilabial closures became evident; eye squinting and wrinkling of the forehead disappeared	Orbicularis oris EMG activity was greater than 100 uV during speech in session #1, and ranged between 10 and 20 uV during silences in speech in session #2
Peck, 1977	Female, age 50 with blepharospasm	Feedback of frontal and orbicularis oculi activity during 17, 20-min sessions	Data unavailable	Blinking and/or spasm frequencies per 20 min: baseline 1300; false feedback, 1600; first 3 feedback sessions, 1062; last 3 feedback sessions, 14	Integrated EMG levels uV (peak-to-peak): baseline, 30; false feedback, 20; first 3 feedback sessions, 15.3; last 3 feedback sessions, 7.2
Sachs, Martin, & Fitch, 1972	Female, age 11	Visual feedback of finger-to-thumb touches during 20 trials in each of 36 sessions	Data unavailable	Average response time for the finger-to-thumb touches: baseline, 17.7; random feedback, 13.9; contingent visual feedback, 5.2	Data unavailable

TABLE 13–1 Summary of Biofeedback Treatments for Neuromuscular Reeducation

Study	Patients	Biofeedback Treatment	Other Treatment	Symptoms	Results	
					Biological Function	
Skrotsky, Gallenstein, & Osternig, 1978	3 males, 1 female with spastic cerebral palsy	Feedback of gastrocnemius EMG activity during 20 sessions in 10 consecutive days	Data unavailable	Data unavailable	Range of motion increased by 4.3° to 17°; gastrocnemius EMG activity decreased by 90% to 99% in about 5 seconds for some patients during feedback	
Spearing & Poppen, 1974	Male, age 23 with athetoid-type cerebral palsy	Auditory feedback of foot dragging during 3, 10-min trials each day for 19 days	Data unavailable	Incidence of foot dragging: baseline, 71%; feedback, 33%; baseline, 68%; feedback, 20%; effect maintained at 3-month follow-up	Data unavailable	
Swann, van Wieringen, & Fokkema, 1974	4 males, 3 females; age range 17 to 77	Feedback of EMG activity in the peroneus longus area for 10 mins, 3 times weekly for 2 weeks	Physical therapy; relaxation	Data unavailable	Increases in range of motion; EMG feedback, 6.3°; physical therapy 2.4°	
Wannstedt & Herman, 1978	Right and left hemiparetics; age range 32 to 75	Auditory feedback of weight placed on affected limb during 20-min sessions, 1 to 28 times daily	Data unavailable	During an initial session 23 of 30 patients achieved symmetrical standing; the remaining 7 corrected postures somewhat; 16 of 20 patients who continued training for 3 to 28 sessions achieved symmetrical standing, 4 did not; 14 of 16 maintained symmetrical standing at 1-month follow-up	Data unavailable	

than longer periods because fatigue can reduce motor control. In all cases, the client should understand that even though the EMG changes at the beginning of training may not be accompanied by perceptible movement, they are a necessary step to obtain that movement. Often just finding out that the muscle is indeed alive, even though it can't produce joint movement, will provide strong encouragement for a client to work with feedback (Baker and others 1977). When movement appears, appropriate physical therapy exercises can be instituted either with or without feedback. For some motor problems, such as torticollis, these can be effectively carried out by the client after minimal instruction. For others, such as those following cerebral palsy or a stroke, a formal physical therapy program should also be included.

The procedures for using and applying surface electrodes have been discussed elsewhere (Chapter 6) and won't be repeated here. The first training session may teach the client to control unimpaired muscles. Preferably, these will be the same muscles that are to be subsequently treated but located on the opposite side of the body which is not affected by the disorder. Alternatively, any muscle which the client can voluntarily control may be used. This training explains the principles of feedback and the client begins treatment with a successful session.

Analogue feedback is preferred over binary feedback because it provides continuous information about smaller changes in muscle activity. Because the use of muscles which have previously been inactive can by itself be very reinforcing, the therapist may wish to videotape a session or, where practical, provide feedback via closed circuit television. In this case the biological function serves as a source of both feedback and reinforcement.

Initially, feedback sessions should be held as frequently as possible, perhaps three times weekly. Each session may last up to 40 minutes with rests as needed. Home practice each day and specific exercises to involve the muscles being trained should also be developed.

EMG biofeedback teaches the person how to control muscle activity but not how to produce coordinated movements. Biofeedback can both increase and decrease muscle activity, which is necessary for movements to occur. But learning how to make the actual movements themselves is more effectively carried out with physical therapy, perhaps aided by biofeedback, rather than by biofeedback alone (Mroczek and others 1978).

GASTROINTESTINAL DISORDERS

14

INTRODUCTION

Peptic Ulcers

Fecal Incontinence

OTHER GASTROINTESTINAL DISORDERS

Functional Diarrhea

Urinary Retention and Incontinence

CLINICAL PROGRAM

INTRODUCTION

The present chapter focuses on two disorders that have been treated with biofeedback, peptic ulcers and fecal incontinence. Although these differ in terms of their symptoms, mechanisms, type of treatment, and success of treatment, they are placed together here for two reasons. First, they are both related to the gastrointestinal system. Peptic ulcers occur near the beginning of it, in the stomach and duodenum, while fecal incontinence is due to problems with the very end of it, at the rectum. Second, both have required sophisticated technology to make biofeedback appropriate. In the preceding chapters, the biological function measured has been reached from the surface of the body, but here the functions can be measured most effectively only in the interior, making access to them very difficult. For both ulcers and fecal incontinence, engineering and imagination have made biofeedback possible. These treatments provide examples of the ways in which complex internal biological functions can be monitored and suggest the ways in which biofeedback may be developed in the future.

Peptic Ulcers

SYMPTOMS

The chief complaint of a person with peptic ulcers is usually some type of *dyspepsia* or indigestion. Although attempts have been made to distinguish between gastric and duodenal ulcers on the basis of these subjective symptoms, a differential diagnosis has been difficult, and the following discussion considers both types of ulcers together unless otherwise indicated. Some symptoms are highly characteristic of peptic ulcers. One is the temporal pattern of the pain. In a 24 hour cycle, the pain is least about 8:00 A.M. and greatest about 2:00 A.M., following the circadian rhythm of acid secretion (Moore & Motoki 1979). Pain is often eliminated after eating food but may reappear several hours later. A similar pattern may be found after antacid medication. Symptoms typically appear for several days or weeks and then disappear for a longer period of time, months or years (Bockus 1974a,b; Isenberg and others 1978; Krag 1966; Krause 1963; Richardson 1973; Smith 1954; Spiro 1977; Veselý and others 1968; Walker 1973; Walsh 1975).

The physical location of the pain from the ulcer is also predictable. It is found in the *epigastrum,* along the midline below the rib cage and above the umbilicus. It is deep visceral pain, radiating to the back in some cases. With gastric ulcers, the pain may appear to the left of the midline and with duodenal ulcers, it may appear to the right of the midline. These asymmetric patterns are more likely when perforation occurs, but they are complicated in other cases by the confusing patterns that may arise due to involvement of other organs of the body (Bockus 1974a; Richardson 1973; Rivers 1935; Smith 1954; Way 1976).

The adjectives used to describe the more subtle characteristics of the pain are highly variable. Descriptions often include: dull ache, gnawing feeling, hunger sensations (Bockus 1974b); gnawing, burning, pressing, aching like a hunger pain (Spiro 1977); dull, cramping, hot, burning, sore (Richardson 1973); burning, gnawing, cramping, boring, aching, pressure, heaviness, or hunger (Walsh 1975). However, other descriptions have emphasized the diffuse and elusive nature of the pain (Rivers 1935; Walker 1973). Quantitative analyses of the pain descriptions suggest that the above adjectives apply to only a small portion of the cases (Edwards & Coghill 1968), and up to 30% of the patients with peptic ulcers may report no pain at all (Spiro 1977). Nausea, vomiting, and loss of appetite may also be associated with the pain (Smith 1954; Richardson 1973; Veselý and others 1968; Walker 1973).

A quantitive study of the types of pain arising from dyspepsia used information from interviews with 84 patients having gastric ulcers, 119 patients having duodenal ulcers, and 221 patients not having ulcers but still reporting dyspepsia (Edwards & Coghill 1968). No substantial differences were found in the pain descriptions of patients having gastric ulcers and those having duodenal ulcers. The most common symptom was some form of dyspepsia located in the epigastrum (52%) and relieved by eating food (57%) or taking antacid medication (84%). Relatively few of the patients reported the pain as having the characteristics commonly attributed to peptic ulcers: boring or gnawing (15%); aching, cramplike, or dull (30%); or hot, burning, or sore (7%).

The incidence of ulcers increases systematically with age, being almost negligible prior to 20 years of age and reaching a peak in both males and females at about 50 years of age (Niwayama & Terplan 1959; Portis & Jaffé 1938; Walker 1973; Watkinson 1960; Weir & Backett 1968). Approximately 10% of people in Western civilizations can expect to have an ulcer during their lifetime (Langman 1974; Spiro 1977). Estimating the number of people who have ulcers is difficult because people who have ulcers but experience no pain (Brettschneider and others 1965; Spiro 1977; Sturdevant & Walsh 1978) are unlikely to seek medical help, and because the frequency and distribution of ulcers in the population has changed markedly during the past 150 years. In the late 1800s, ulcers were less prevalent than they are now and appeared equally in both sexes (Jennings 1940; Spiro 1977). Since that time, the incidence of ulcers has increased in general, and males are afflicted more often than females, at least with duodenal ulcers (Sun 1974). In the past 20 years, the incidence may have decreased slightly.

MECHANISM

Peptic ulcers are small areas of the digestive tract which have been destroyed. They are distinguished from *erosions,* which are shallower and don't extend into the deep layers of the gastrointestinal wall, and from *perforations,* which are deeper and penetrate completely through the wall. Two types of peptic ulcers are distinguished based on their location within the gastrointestinal system. *Gastric ulcers* are located in the stomach just above the pyloris, while *duodenal ulcers* are located in the duodenum just below the pyloris.

Ulcers have four distinct layers (Eigenbrodt 1973; Spiro 1977). Beginning with the superficial layer in the stomach, these are (a) an inflammatory reaction with leukocytes and erythrocytes, (b) fibrinoid necrosis, (c) a layer of granular tissue and fibroblasts, rich blood vessels, and (d) very fibrous scar tissue. Pictures of ulcers obtained with an endoscope (Belber 1979; Colcher 1974) show a clean base, small regular size, and radiating folds of mucosa around the top. The diameter of the ulcer is only a few millimeters (Isenberg 1975; Niwayama & Terplan 1959). Thus only a very small portion of the gastrointestinal system has an ulcer at any given time, even though the magnitude of the pain may make the patient feel otherwise.

The gastrointestinal system is in a constant battle between aggressive events that tend to destroy the wall and defensive events that tend to preserve it and build it back up. The acid and the pepsin within the stomach constitute the major aggressive factors, while the layer of mucosal cells lining the interior of the stomach cavity is the major defensive system. This *mucosal barrier* is composed of cells with tight junctions between them forming an effective barrier holding the acid within the stomach and preventing its diffusion into the muscle layers surrounding the stomach where it would destroy them. Mucosal cells secrete a layer of mucus which covers them and lines the interior of the stomach, but this mucus is not an effective barrier to the diffusion of acid and has only a weak buffering effect on acid. Thus the mucus provides lubrication aiding the passage of material through the gastrointestinal tract, rather than defending against the acid (Grossman 1978; Rudick & Janowitz 1974; Sun 1974; Walsh 1973).

Acid is secreted from the *parietal* or *oxyntic cells* in the fundic area of the stomach. Activity in the parasympathetic portion of the autonomic nervous system stimulates acid secretion in two ways. The first is through a direct route to the parietal cells. The second is through an indirect route to the pyloric glands. Stimulation of these glands produces the release of gastrin, a hormone which then moves through the stomach and stimulates the parietal cells, causing them to secrete acid (Rudick & Janowitz 1974).

A number of different procedures have been developed for measuring acid secretion (see Isenberg 1973, for a review; Sun & Roth 1974). A *basal* or *resting level* is obtained following a fast of about 12 hours and without any stimulation that might increase acid secretion. Resting levels are approximately 3 milliequivalents of acid per hour (mEq/h). A *maximal* or *peak level* is obtained following an injection of a drug such as histamine acid phosphate, betazole, pentagastrin, or gastrin in a dose appropriate to stimulate acid secretion. Measurements are taken periodically following the injection, and the maximum rate of secretion is determined. Peak acid secretion is approximately 10 mEq/h in individuals without ulcers, but it ranges widely.

In a review of the role of acid secretion in peptic ulcers, Fordtran (1973a) emphasizes the marked overlap of acid secretion rates in normals and ulcer patients, but concludes that ". . . an active (uncomplicated) duodenal ulcer requires a peak secretory capacity of greater than 12–15 mEq per hour" (p. 177). Sun and Roth (1974) reach a similar conclusion. The population from which comparisons are made influences the overall levels; individuals who are inpatients or participants in a gastrointestinal clinic will generally have acid levels much higher than those found in the general population. Gastric ulcers, however, are not usually associated with excessive acid.

Increased peak acid secretion may arise in at least two different ways. The parietal cells might be more sensitive to stimulation, so that in response to a stimulus, they secrete more acid than normal. Alternatively, each parietal cell might be normally sensitive, but there may be more of them so that a given stimulus produces a normal amount of acid from each cell, but an overall increase in the amount of acid secreted. The data support the latter point of view. For example, a group of patients undergoing surgery for ulcers was given an augmented histamine test for peak acid secretion before the surgery. The number of parietal cells present in the stomach was estimated on the basis of a portion of the stomach removed during surgery. The correlation between the density of the parietal cells and the peak acid flow was .89, and between the total number of parietal cells and the peak acid flow was .95 (Myren & Semb 1967). Other studies have compared the maximum acid secretion in response to histamine with the number of parietal cells and determined that approximately 40 million parietal cells are necessary to produce 1 mEq/h of acid, and that this production is the same in normal patients and those with ulcers (Card & Marks 1960; Sun 1974). Thus any increase in acid secretion is due not to an increase in the sensitivity of the acid secreting system, but to an increase in the number of cells secreting acid.

Further evidence that excess acid is not due to hyperactivity in the vagus-parietal cell system comes from a study in which the activity of the vagus nerve was blocked with an anticolinergic drug, hexamethonium bromide (Singh and others 1968). Prior to administration of the drug, the maximum acid secretion in response to histamine acid phosphate was 14 mEq/h for the normal controls and 29 mEq/h in the patients with duodenal ulcers. Following the drug, the maximum rates for the two groups were 4.8 mEq/h and 9.9 mEq/h, respectively. The percentage decrease for the controls was 67% while for the ulcer patients, it was 64%. This similarity suggests that the sensitivity of the vagal system in both the normals and ulcer patients was equivalent so that the excess acid secretion must have been due to some other cause, presumably an excess number of parietal cells.

Acid along with pepsin, which is active only at very high levels of acid (Fordtran 1973b), are undoubtedly responsible for the destruction of the gastrointestinal wall and the pain associated with the ulcer. Yet excess acid cannot be the only variable responsible for the ulcer. Several lines of data support this conclusion. One is the simple fact that an ulcer is a discrete, localized disruption in the gastrointestinal wall, even though large sections of the digestive system are exposed to the same levels of acid. Thus there is a need to explain how one particular segment of the gastrointestinal wall succumbs to the acid while the majority of the wall remains perfectly intact. A further need for considering variables other than acid arises from the fact that there is a tremendous range of acid secretion both in people who do not have ulcers and people who do. Consequently, many individuals without ulcers have levels of acid secretion higher than other individuals with ulcers. People with gastric ulcers are particularly notable on this point, and most studies have suggested that the level of acid secretion in gastric ulcer patients is not markedly different from that in normals (Christensen 1971; see review in Wormsley & Grossman 1965).

The anatomical pattern of ulcers in the stomach and duodenum has led Oi and his colleagues to postulate a dual mechanism determining the site of the ulcer (Oi and others 1969; Oi and others 1959; Oi and others 1966; see also Marks & Shay 1959). One variable determining the position of the ulcer is a change in mucosa so that ulcers occur near the boundary between two different mucosae, opposite the acid secreting area. Thus gastric ulcers should always occur in the pyloric mucosa; duodenal ulcers should lie in the fundic gland area in the duodenum. Surgical specimens of ulcers obtained from 640 patients with ulcers support this description (Oi and others 1969; Study 1). Ulcers were classified as *adjacent* if they were within 2 cm of the mucosal boundary, and *distant* if they were further than 2 cm from this boundary. Of 499 gastric ulcers and 355 duodenal ulcers, 97% were adjacent to the boundary and in the pyloric area, opposite the acid secreting mucosa. A second component of the dual control mechanism is the pattern of muscles surrounding the gastrointestinal tract. Of 327 specimens of the gastrointestinal system removed in surgery, 94% of 158 gastric ulcers were found in an area specified by the intersection of three muscle bands, and 100% of the duodenal ulcers were found in an area specified by one muscle band.

Oi's studies suggest that both the mucosa and the pattern of muscles surrounding the gastrointestinal system determine the susceptibility of the gastric lining to ulceration. The interaction between these two variables was nicely demonstrated in the same 327 surgical specimens described earlier by determining the probability of a gastric ulcer if the area of susceptibility as defined by the junction between the mucosa overlapped with the area of susceptibility as defined by the muscle pattern. Where this overlap occurred, the probability of a gastric ulcer alone or in conjunction with a duodenal ulcer was 99% and 100%, respectively, while in specimens where these two areas did not overlap, the probabilities were 1% and 0%, respectively (Oi and others 1969).

TREATMENT

If excess acid is necessary for pain and destruction of the gastrointestinal lining, reducing acid levels should reduce pain and protect the stomach lining, even if the person does not have higher than normal acid levels at the time. Determining the amount of acid in the stomach is difficult and cannot easily be accomplished from the outside of the body. Two techniques have been developed. In one, a *nasogastric tube* is inserted through the nose and swallowed by the person. Liquid is removed from the stomach through the tube and analyzed for its acidity. Alternatively, a small *pH meter* may be swallowed; the pH of the stomach is detected by the meter and transmitted to a receiver outside the person. The studies to be reviewed demonstrate that people are able to reduce stomach acidity through biofeedback. These changes are large enough to be therapeutic, but more data are needed to determine if they will be useful enough for biofeedback to be included as a standard treatment of ulcers.

Discussion of Treatments

Ten people with duodenal ulcers reduced acid concentration with biofeedback (Welgan 1974). All had a pH less than 3.6 and stomach secretions of at least 10 cc/min in baseline conditions. Prior to biofeedback, they fasted for 12 hours and took no anticholinergic drugs. Stomach contents were aspirated with a nasogastric tube. Analogue visual feedback was provided each time the pH increased by .1. Three training trials, each 15 minutes long, were separated by rest intervals of the same length in a single session. During at least one 15-minute period, acid concentrations and the rate of stomach secretions decreased while pH increased. For the whole session, however, the changes found during biofeedback were not significantly greater than those found during rest, questioning the importance of biofeedback in producing these changes. However, the within-subjects A-B-A reversal procedure is not the best way to address the importance of biofeedback as compared to rest because the therapeutic gains resulting from treatment often persist after treatment is stopped.

A subsequent study using a between-subjects procedure found that biofeedback produced a significantly greater reduction in acid concentration than an equivalent period of rest. The participants were five men with duodenal ulcers and a stomach pH of less than 3.6; they were divided into two groups. Both groups began with a baseline period of 30 minutes and then had alternating 15-minute periods of rest and biofeedback. The order of these periods varied for the two groups. People in the one group received biofeedback first, followed by rest and then biofeedback again. People in the second group received a rest period first, followed by biofeedback and then rest. As before, stomach contents were removed by suction through a nasogastric tube, and during biofeedback analogue visual and auditory feedback were provided for each .1 increase in pH. The results for the group which received rest first are summarized in the top graph of Figure 14–1, while the results from those who received biofeedback first are in the bottom graph. During the baseline period, both groups had substantially elevated acid concentrations. For the group that rested for 15 minutes, these levels increased slightly as indicated by the second point in the top graph. For the group that received biofeedback first, they dropped dramatically, decreasing to about 20% of the original value. Clearly, biofeedback reduced acid concentration more effectively than rest. Two other points are also of interest. When the group which received rest first was subsequently given biofeedback, their acid levels dropped too, as indicated by the third point in the top graph. When the group which received biofeedback first sub-

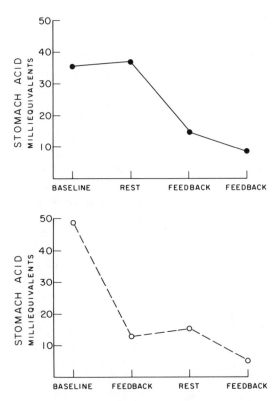

FIGURE 14–1   The Effects of Biofeedback and an Equivalent Period of Rest on Stomach Acid.

The clients in the group illustrated in the top graph had 15 minutes of rest prior to biofeedback; stomach acid decreased only after biofeedback. Clients in the group illustrated in the bottom graph had biofeedback immediately after the baseline period; stomach acid decreased during biofeedback and remained low for the rest of the treatment. Thus biofeedback effectively reduced stomach acid, while rest did not. *(Data taken from Welgan, 1974.)*

sequently rested for 15 minutes, their level of acid increased only slightly. This latter finding confirms the suggestion made earlier that the therapeutic gains made during treatment are often carried over to periods when treatment is stopped, making between-subjects comparisons, as in the present case, a better procedure to compare the effectiveness of different forms of treatment than within-subjects comparisons.

Increasing the number of biofeedback sessions can increase the amount of control over stomach acid (Welgan 1977). The patients received three biofeedback trials, each 15 minutes long. Liquid was continuously aspirated from the stomach by a nasogastric tube with its tip in the atrium of the stomach. Analogue visual feedback was provided by a polygraph pen which reflected the pH of the aspirated liquid. Nine patients received correct feedback and were trained to increase stomach pH. Eighteen other patients received incorrect feedback, being told that movement of the pen in one direction indicated an increased pH when in reality it indicated a decrease; thus these patients were trained to decrease pH. During the three biofeedback trials, the group which received correct feedback reduced the volume of stomach secretions, but not the pH measures, as compared to the patients who received incorrect feedback.

A subsequent experiment used the same procedures as just described but gave the participants, who had already had ten sessions of biofeedback, ten more sessions scheduled twice weekly. The group receiving correct feedback increased pH and decreased volumes to a greater extent than the groups receiving incorrect feedback in six and seven of the ten sessions, respectively. These results demonstrate the importance of the feedback component of this treatment and suggest that many trials may be required to gain voluntary control of acid secretions.

Fecal Incontinence

For most adults, fecal continence is not difficult. We are sensitive to the need to defecate, can inhibit defecation when the setting is inappropriate, and initiate it later at a more convenient time. Fecal continence can be lost for many reasons, including surgery, degenerative neural diseases, and accidents. The loss of the ability to control defecation usually has a profound impact on all aspects of a person's life. Traditional treatment has included regular meals, time schedules for defecation, enemas, and surgery, but these have often been unsuccessful in returning continence (Whitehead 1978). Biofeedback, in just a few hours of training, has been able to provide voluntary control over defecation even though such control had been resistant to other treatments for many years. The procedure has two steps. First the person is taught to become aware of the sensations that indicate a full rectum and an impending bowel movement. Then the person is trained to control both the internal and external anal sphincters. The procedures have been so successful that a recent task force concluded that they "should be used routinely" as the treatment of choice for fecal incontinence (Whitehead 1978, p. 382).

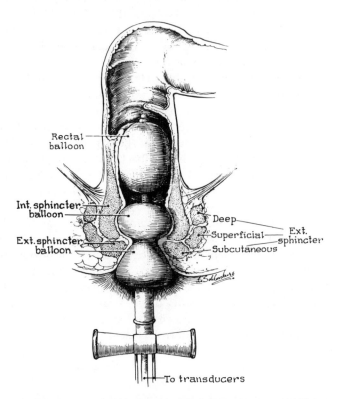

FIGURE 14–2 The Balloon Recording System Used by Schuster for the Treatment of Fecal Incontinence.

The drawing is of a side view of the rectum. The three components of the external sphincter are identified on the right; the internal sphincter is identified on the left. The rectal balloon is placed in the rectum; when inflated it simulates the movement of fecal matter into the rectum and is the stimulus for the rectosphincteric reflex. The middle balloon is placed next to the internal sphincter; the most external balloon is placed next to the external sphincter. These two balloons are slightly inflated and connected to pressure recording devices; contraction of a sphincter produces an increase in pressure in the balloon lying next to it. *(From Schuster, Hookman, Hendrix, and Mendeloff, 1965. In* Bulletin of the Johns Hopkins Hospital, 116, *p. 79. Reprinted by permission.)*

A critical step in the application of biofeedback to fecal incontinence was the development of a means of recording the activity of the anal sphincters and simulating the passage of fecal matter into the rectum. Because of the location and complexity of the muscles making up the two sphincters, standard electromyographic techniques are not applicable. The problem was solved by the development of a triple balloon system (Schuster and others 1965) illustrated in Figure 14–2. Three balloons were mounted on a shaft and connected to tubes which ran down the middle of the shaft. When deflated, the balloons were inserted through the anus. When located appropriately, the internal balloon was inflated in the rectum, simulating the passage of fecal material. The other two balloons were located just beside the internal and external sphincters, respectively. These were inflated just enough to become pressed up against the two muscles. When the appropriate muscle contracted, it increased the pressure in the balloon which was registered by a manometer attached to the other end of the tube leading from the balloon through the shaft. Information about the activity of both the internal and external anal sphincters is useful because they must be carefully coordinated for normal defecation (Schuster 1979).

SYMPTOMS AND MECHANISM

The symptoms of fecal incontinence appear ultimately as an inability to control bowel movements. The person may be entirely unaware of the urge to defecate and surprised when feces appear, or may know that defecation is about to take place but be unable to control it. Rectosphincter reflexes (see below) are usually absent.

After food has passed through the small intestine, it enters the colon, where it may remain for a substantial period of time before being eliminated. Waves of muscular activity pass the material through the colon towards the anus (Connel 1968), where there are two sets of sphincters formed by muscle bands (Schuster & Mendeloff 1968; Sleisenger 1973a, 1973b). As illustrated in Figure 14–2, the internal anal sphincter is a thickening of the smooth muscle at the junction between the anus and rectum. The muscles are about 3 cm long, 2 cm to 5 cm thick, and are innervated by the autonomic nervous system coming from the most ventral portions of the spinal cord. The sympathetic nerves are excitatory and cause contraction of the muscles, while the parasympathetic nerves are inhibitory and cause relaxation (see Chapter 4). The external anal sphincter is composed of three bundles of striated muscle and lies around and more peripheral to the internal anal sphincter. It also receives a nerve supply from the most ventral portions of the spinal cord, but this is from the somatic, rather than the autonomic, nervous system. In addition, the nervous supply is only excitatory; relaxation of the external anal sphincter takes place only by decreasing activity in the nerve supplying it.

Both the internal and external sphincters have a role in fecal continence as shown by studies of rectosphincteric reflexes (Schuster & Mendeloff 1968; Alva and others 1967). The stimulus for this reflex is distension of the rectum, as might be produced by the movement of feces into the rectum. The response appears in both the internal and external anal sphincters. When the rectum is distended, the internal anal sphincter relaxes, allowing material to pass towards the anus and producing sensations of the need to defecate. At the same time, the external anal sphincter contracts, containing the material in the colon. The resulting urge to defecate usually passes within a minute or so, at which time the sphincter tone returns to normal, unless the rectum is very full. Subsequent defecation takes place, then, by voluntarily relaxing the external anal sphincter and increasing intra-abdominal pressure.

Documentation of rectosphincteric reflexes has taken place using the triple balloon system (Schuster and others 1965). The stimulus for this reflex is the rapid inflation and deflation of the balloon in the rectum. This is followed by two responses. First, the internal anal sphincter relaxes and then returns to baseline, as indicated by a rapid but transient decrease in the pressure of the middle balloon. Second, the external anal sphincter contracts and then returns to baseline, as indicated by a rapid but transient increase in the pressure of the most external balloon.

TREATMENT

Biofeedback teaches a person to become more sensitive to bowel movements and to gain control over them. The rationale and general procedure are explained to the patient, and feedback is provided about the pressure in each of the three balloons. During the first part of training, the balloon in the rectum is rapidly inflated and deflated while the person watches the feedback from this balloon and learns to become sensitive to the changes in pressure in the rectum. During the second part of training, inflation of the balloon in the rectum is used as the stimulus to train the rectosphincteric reflex. The person uses feedback from the other two balloons to learn to relax the internal anal sphincter and contract the external anal sphincter in response to inflation of the balloon in the rectum.

The patient was a six-year-old girl who had been incontinent since birth due to myelomeningocele (Engel and others 1974). She was incontinent two to eight times per month, and impactions had to be removed manually or by enemas. She_was first trained to control each sphincter independently—to relax the internal sphincter and to contract the external sphincter. Finally, she was trained to synchronize contractions of the external sphincter with relaxatión of the internal sphincter. Insertion and inflation of rectal balloons permitted the measurement and feedback of sphincteric activity as previously described. Polygraph tracings provided visual feedback. When she succeeded in controlling the muscles, she was given positive reinforcers in the form of praise and felt tip pens. Each training session had about 50 training trials, each about 50 seconds long. Four sessions were given, separated by about three months. To teach her to become sensitive to distension of the rectum, the balloon in the rectum was initially inflated with 30 ml of air. When she became sensitive to this degree of inflation, the amount of air was gradually reduced making the discrimination more difficult until she was no longer able to detect the stimulus. A level of inflation sufficient to produce a sensation was used in subsequent sessions to train rectosphincteric reflexes. As she gained control over the reflexes, feedback was gradually eliminated by preventing her from seeing the polygraph tracings. Home practice of the sphincteric reflexes was encouraged. Bowel movements became normal during the training period, and six months later she was still continent.

Case Study B

A slightly different procedure was used to reduce fecal incontinence in a boy who had been incontinent for all of his life (Kohlenberg 1973). Surgical removal of a section of his colon had not helped his condition, and a colostomy was being considered. He was hospitalized at the time of the study, and his attendants reported that his bed clothes were constantly soiled, confirming comments made by his parents. Inadequate sphincter tone was found during a digital examination of the rectum. Sphincter pressures were measured by a tube which was inserted into the rectum. The tube contained water and contraction of the sphincter increased the height of the water in a column connected to the tube, providing visual feedback about sphincter tone. Three biofeedback sessions, each 15 minutes long, failed to produce a significant increase in sphincter pressure. In subsequent sessions, each 15 minutes long, successful sphincter control was followed by just the feedback, as in the initial sessions, or by nickels dropped into a glass jar. This explicit reinforcement was given at 10-second intervals if sphincter pressure exceeded a criterion. By the end of three sessions, he kept sphincter pressure above criterion for at least 10 minutes, a value double that seen in the initial sessions without the money. He had a tendency to increase the sphincter pressure just prior to when a nickel was dropped in the jar and to reduce it slightly just afterwards. In subsequent sessions, money was obtained only if sphincter pressure was maintained above criterion for gradually longer periods of time, beginning with 14 seconds and ending with 58 seconds. The duration of time that pressure exceeded criterion steadily increased and by the last session, one response lasted for almost the entire 15 minutes. Resting pressures increased from 35 to 50 mm Hg. The colostomy was postponed. Nurses reported that he did not soil his bed clothes once during the final three days of hospitalization. He was discharged without a colostomy. One month later, his parents said that he did not soil his bed clothes for periods of approximately eight hours.

Discussion of Treatments

Biofeedback successfully restored continence for five adults (Engel and others 1974). They had experienced incontinence daily for up to eight years. The procedures were as described in Case Study A except that initial training to decrease contractions of the internal sphincter was omitted. Briefly, the triple balloon device was inserted as illustrated in Figure 14–2. The patients were first trained to become sensitive to distensions of the rectum by inflating the balloon in the rectum and by providing feedback through movements of a polygraph pen reflecting that pressure. Then they were trained to increase external sphincter pressure and decrease internal sphincter pressure synchronously in response to balloon inflation. Each biofeedback session lasted two hours and contained fifty trials, each 50 seconds long. Up to four sessions were scheduled with three weeks between sessions. The patients were contacted regularly for up to five years. Four of the five patients remained completely continent; the remaining one was continent at night but had occasional problems during the day.

A later report summarized the results from 50 patients between six and ninety-seven years old (Cerulli and others 1979). All patients had daily, intractable incontinence; for 35 people it resulted from surgery, for the other 15 it resulted from a localized or systemic physiological disturbance. The triple balloon system as described earlier (Engel and others 1974) was used to determine the threshold for sensation. Then biofeedback training was begun as described previously. Prior to training, 40 cc's of air was required in the rectal balloon to produce an external sphincter response. Following training, this threshold was reduced to 16 cc's for 72% of the patients and to about 33 cc's for the remaining patients. Incontinence was markedly reduced and was only 10% of that in the pretreatment baseline condition for 72% of the patients. Learning was rapid, and successful control of sphincter contraction was learned in a single session by half of the people. Continence was maintained for the longest follow-up periods, which were nine years.

OTHER GASTROINTESTINAL DISORDERS

Biofeedback has been used to treat several other gastrointestinal disorders. Only a few examples are presented here. Because each one has been examined in less detail than the two problems already discussed, they are summarized only briefly. They are important, not only because they suggest that biofeedback can be effective in treating these problems as well, but also because they point to the ways in which biofeedback may develop to treat a variety of different problems in the future.

Functional Diarrhea

SYMPTOMS, MECHANISM, AND TREATMENT

Case Study

This woman had never had normal bowel function and received daily enemas for the first six months of life (Furman 1973). When she came for treatment at the age of 24, she had cramping with diarrhea up to 15 times daily. No blood was found in her stools although some mucus was noticed; barium enemas and sigmoidoscopic examinations found no abnormalities. Her condition was exacerbated by emotional stress, and uncontrolled by a variety of drugs and diets. Peristaltic activity was recorded from the lower gastrointestinal tract. Feedback was provided by a tone. Biofeedback sessions, each 30 minutes long, were held once a week. In each session she tried to increase and then decrease peristaltic activity four times and was praised for success. After three sessions, she both increased and decreased peristaltic activity. She had only three mild attacks during training and then attained complete continence for the following three months.

Discussion of Treatments

The effects of feedback of bowel sounds recorded from the lower gastrointestinal tract on diarrhea were tested with five females between 15 and 62 years of age (Furman 1973). One of these patients was described in the previous case study. None had normal bowel function. They reported four to 15 bowel movements daily with an exacerbation of symptoms during stress. The procedures were as described in the case study. Sessions were 30 minutes long and took place once a week. Within five sessions, all patients had some control of intestinal mobility and the magnitude of this control was correlated with symptomatic improvement. These results suggest that intestinal activity may be influenced by biofeedback training and that such procedures may help normalize bowel function in individuals with diarrhea.

Urinary Retention and Incontinence

SYMPTOMS, MECHANISM, AND TREATMENT

Case Study

This 27-year-old woman had learned to control her bowel movements but did not have control over urination (Pearne and others 1977). She typically withheld urine until several drops passed involuntarily at which time she hurried to a toilet to release the remainder. She had never experienced the feeling of a full bladder and severe urinary retention led to kidney infections by age eight; a urethrostomy was performed at age 23. Incontinence then developed with several incidents each week. At age 25 she had a partial cystectomy which reduced incidents to once weekly but did not control her condition. Residual urine readings ranged between 200 and 300 cc. Urine losses during weekly episodes averaged more than one liter. Eventual kidney failure and ileal loop surgery were predicted. Feedback training began three months later using an indirect approach which taught her to relax the frontalis muscle. Auditory analogue feedback of frontalis EMG levels was delivered for 30 minutes, twice weekly for two months, once weekly for the next two months, and once every other week for the next four months. She practiced at home for 10 or 15 minutes each day and was asked to urinate after each feedback and home practice session. Frontalis EMG levels declined progressively from 4 uV to 1 uV by the last session. Following a 17 uV decrease in the first session, the patient voluntarily passed urine for the first time she could remember. Major problems resulting from incontinence ceased by the second week of treatment, and voluntary urination occurred twice daily. After three months of treatment, she could voluntarily urinate five to six times daily. Residual urine levels declined progressively from 300 to 60 cc during the feedback training. Four months later, she continued home practice, had no major incidents of incontinence, urinated five to six times daily, and had sensations of bladder fullness.

CLINICAL PROGRAM

FECAL INCONTINENCE

Treatment of fecal incontinence uses the three balloon system described earlier in this section. The patient should lie on one side with the balloons inserted so that the most interior one is in the rectum, the middle one lies next to the internal sphincter, and the exterior one is by the external sphincter. Tubing connects the balloons to pressure transducers which produce an electrical signal that can be amplified and recorded on a polygraph. The rectal balloon should be inflated to approximately 50 ml of air and the client directed to observe any sphincter responses which normally occur. The person is then trained to decrease internal sphincter contractions and increase external sphincter contractions. This is accomplished by inflating the balloon to approximately 30 ml of air. As the patient learns to produce the sphincteric responses, the magnitude of air in the rectal balloon is decreased gradually. This serves to increase the proficiency of the sphincteric responses and sensitize the client to the simulation of the arrival of smaller and smaller stools.

Sessions can include about 50 training trials lasting about one minute each. One or two brief breaks may also be included so each session will last about two hours. Scheduling sessions once every one to three weeks should be sufficient. Home practice of the sphincteric responses should be encouraged.

GASTRIC ACID ACTIVITY

As indicated in the review here, the clinical efficacy of feedback to reduce stomach acid remains to be demonstrated. None the less, the results suggest that it deserves to be undertaken in an exploratory manner whenever it might be appropriate. Changes of the pH of acid secretions can be used for feedback. Clients should fast for about 12 hours before beginning a session. A nasogastric tube should be swallowed so that the

TABLE 14–1 Summary of Biofeedback Treatments for Gastrointestinal Disorders

Study	Patients	Biofeedback Treatment	Other Treatment	Results Symptoms	Biological Function
Engel, Nickoomanesh, & Schuster, 1974	4 females, 2 males; age range 6 to 54	Analogue visual feedback of sphincter activity during fifty, 50-sec trials every 3 weeks	Data unavailable	Four of six patients became continent; one had rare episodes of soiling; one soiled during waking hours only	Data unavailable
Furman, 1973	5 females; age range 15 to 62	Bowel-sound feedback during 30-min sessions once weekly	Data unavailable	No normal bowel function; varying degrees of incapacity; pretreatment frequencies of bowel movements ranged from 4 to 15 daily	Control of intestinal mobility demonstrated within five sessions
Kohlenberg, 1973	Male, age 13	Visual feedback of resting yield sphincter pressure during 1-hour sessions in three phases	Hospitalization	Daily soiling was eliminated by the final 3 days of treatment and for up to 8-hour periods at 1-month follow-up	Resting yield pressure increased from 35 to 50 mm Hg
Pearne, Zigelbaum, & Peyser, 1977	Female, age 27	Analogue auditory feedback of frontal EMG levels for 30 mins 2 to 8 times weekly	Home practice 10 or 15 mins daily	No sensations of bladder fullness; daily urine incontinence; voluntary urination occurred twice daily by the second week of treatment, five to six times daily by the third month of treatment, and was maintained at 4-month follow-up	Residual urine readings declined from 300 to 60 cc's; end-of-session frontal EMG levels decreased from 4 to 1 uV by the last session

Study	Subjects	Procedure			Results
Schuster, 1974	6, 2 of whom had hiatal hernias	Analogue visual feedback of lower esophageal activity during 50-sec trials	Data unavailable	Data unavailable	Most patients increased esophageal pressures up to 2.5 mm Hg within 3 to 6 trials; intragastric pressure did not change significantly
Welgan, 1974	Study #1: 8 males, 2 females; Study #2 10 males	Analogue visual feedback of pH levels during three, 15-min trials in both studies	Data unavailable	Data unavailable	Study #1: levels of pH increased and acid concentration and volume decreased; study #2: levels of pH increased, acid concentration and volume decreases were significantly greater during feedback than during rest periods
Welgan, 1977	Experiment #1: 27 patients with peptic ulcers; Experiment #2: eight patients with peptic ulcers	Analogue visual feedback of pH levels during three, 15-min trials in experiment #1; experiment #2 involved 2 training sessions each week for 5 weeks	Data unavailable	Data unavailable	Experiment #1: the experimental group significantly decreased its volume of acid secretions; Experiment #2: levels of pH increased and acid volume decreased significantly

tip rests in the stomach. Stomach secretions can be aspirated by connecting the nasogastric tube to a thermotic drainage pump and finally
a collection vessel. Stomach contents are analyzed outside the body with
a pH meter connected to a pH recorder. Auditory or visual feedback
can be delivered for approximately .1 pH changes in acidity. Sessions
should last about 90 minutes with two to three trials lasting about 15
minutes each and one or two rests as needed. Sessions should be scheduled once each week.

CARDIOVASCULAR DISORDERS

15

INTRODUCTION

HYPERTENSION

CARDIAC ARRHYTHMIAS

Wolff-Parkinson-White Syndrome

Premature Ventricular Contractions

Tachycardia and Fibrillation

OTHER CARDIAC ABNORMALITIES

Postural Hypotension

CLINICAL PROGRAM

INTRODUCTION

In this chapter we consider two types of cardiovascular problems. The first is *essential hypertension,* an increase in blood pressure of unknown etiology. Hypertension is one of the major health problems in the world today. Effective treatment could provide a major breakthrough in health care, and biofeedback has been used as one treatment to lower blood pressure. The second problem is that of *cardiac arrhythmias,* abnormal heart beats. These may arise for a number of reasons but have in common the fact that they can lead to cardiac failure.

Treatment of these two disorders provides an interesting comparison of different approaches. The treatment of hypertension is a direct one; biofeedback is used to train the individual to lower blood pressure, the symptom that needs changing. In contrast, treatment of arrhythmias is indirect; the patient receives no feedback about the arrhythmia itself, but about heart rate. Both of these treatments have been successful, producing clinically significant changes which are maintained even when treatment is stopped.

HYPERTENSION

The circulatory system is extensive, and its terminal branches, the capillaries, have a small diameter. Both of these factors increase friction which slows the movement of blood. Sufficient force must be applied by the heart to overcome this friction, and the result is blood pressure which fluctuates with the heart beat.

Patients are often grouped into three classes on the basis of their blood pressure. *Normotensive* patients have blood pressure within the expected range and are not likely to be treated. *Hypertensive* patients have blood pressure at the far end of the range and require immediate treatment. *Borderline hypertensive* patients have blood pressure in between the above two classes; it is not high enough to demand immediate medical attention, but it is not low enough to be completely ignored because the risk of becoming hypertensive is increased about two times above normal (Julius 1977a; Julius and Schork 1971).

Epidemiological studies suggest that about 20% of the population in the United States and about 10% of the population world wide have blood pressures in the hypertensive range, above 150/90 mm Hg (Kannel 1977; Paul 1977; Silber & Katz 1975). A variety of factors influence blood pressure, including age, sex, family history, body weight, use of oral contraceptives, and perhaps salt.

As blood pressure increases, life expectancy decreases (Pickering 1974a, Society of Actuaries 1959). At every age for both sexes, increases in blood pressure were associated with decreases in life expectancy. This effect was most marked for men at age 35 where an increase in blood pressure to 150/100 mm Hg was accompanied by a decrease in life expectancy from 41.5 years to 25 years, a change of almost 40% (Pickering 1974a). Of the individuals with high blood pressure who go untreated, about one-third die of heart failure, presumably due to the extra effort the heart must exert to overcome the excessively high pressure. Another large group will die of a stroke, a rupturing of the blood supply to the brain, again as a result of the excessive pressure. Even if an individual lives, substantial complications can arise with high blood pressure, so the disorder is indeed a medically important one (Pickering 1968, 1974a). If high blood pressure can be reduced through appropriate treatment, this reduction can substantially increase life expectancy (Fries 1970).

What is hypertension? Figures have varied markedly, ranging from 120/80 mm Hg to 180/110 mm Hg (Pickering 1974a). There are two difficulties in defining hypertension and differentiating it from normal blood pressure. First, blood pressure is distributed in a smooth fashion across the population; there is no obvious break point with one group having blood pressure considerably below this level and another group having blood pressure above it. Second, the risks associated with blood pressure appear to increase as blood pressure increases even at very low levels of blood pressure; every increase in blood pressure is accompanied by a slightly decreased life expectancy. In short, blood pressure appears to have a smooth continuous distribution both in terms of the general population and in terms of its risks. Because of these findings, Pickering (1968, 1974a, 1974b) has argued that hypertension is not a well-differentiated disease state, but rather the end point of a continuum (see also Weiner 1977). Some levels of blood pressure may be in more drastic need of treatment than others, but any increase in blood pressure carries with it increased risks of medical complications.

Similar results have been found from the Framingham study, reviewed recently by Kannel (1975, 1977). In 1949, the study began by recording the blood pressures of virtually all the citizens of this community. Approximately 5,000 individuals had their blood pressure taken every two years. About 20% of them had blood pressures above 160/95 mm Hg, confirming the results of other epidemiological studies (Paul 1977). The people who had blood pressures this high were found to be more susceptible to a variety of medical problems. The probability of a coronary attack increased three times, of a brain infarction (stroke) eight times, of congestive heart failure six times, and of cardiovascular disease three times. Borderline hypertension increased the risks of these diseases as well, but not as much. Thus, the general finding is that any increase in blood pressure increases the risk of illness.

SYMPTOMS AND MECHANISM

The primary characteristic of hypertension is an increase in blood pressure. But a variety of other changes appear as well, not only in the peripheral circulation, but also in the heart and kidney (Silber & Katz 1975, p. 189). Initially, the increased blood pressure fluctuates above and below an arbitrary cut off point for hypertension. At this stage, it is often referred to as *labile* (Conn & Horwitz 1971) or *borderline* (Julius 1977a) hypertension. As the disorder progresses, however, the blood pressure generally increases so that even when there are temporary decreases, these do not bring blood pressure below the criterion for the upper bound of normal blood pressure. At this point, the hypertension is often referred to as *fixed* or *essential* (Conn & Horwitz 1971). Even though blood pressure still fluctuates, it does not drop sufficiently low to be considered normal.

Many factors can produce increases in blood pressure. These include the kidney and its hormones, the adrenal gland and its hormones, pregnancy, size of the bladder, posture, exercise, pain, emotions such as anger, sexual intercourse, a visit to a physician for a checkup, and age, at least in Western civilization (Peart 1971; Pickering 1974a; Shapiro and others 1977). The type of hypertension considered here in treatment with biofeedback is usually *idiopathic* hypertension, a disease which appears without any apparent extrinsic cause. Approximately 90% of the cases of hypertension are idiopathic (Silber & Katz 1975). The increase in blood pressure reflects an increase in peripheral resistance. Because of this resistance, the heart must work harder to circulate the blood, producing hypertrophy of the ventricular muscles which in turn increase the risk of coronary artery disease, cerebral vascular accidents, and uremia (Conn & Horwitz 1971).

Blood pressure is usually measured with the constant cuff method (Shapiro and others 1969) described in Chapter 6. A blood pressure cuff is inflated by a device which can set the pressure at any given point and raise or lower it in increments of 2 mm Hg. A microphone is attached to the cuff and placed directly over the brachial artery in the arm. The pressure of the cuff is set at the mean level of systolic blood pressure during the immediately preceding time period. If blood pressure goes above cuff pressure, a Korotkoff sound is picked up by the microphone. If blood pressure goes below cuff pressure, no sound is heard. A logic system is used to specify the time period in which a Korotkoff sound might appear. The time between the contraction of the heart as measured by the R wave on the EKG and the appearance of the Korotkoff sound in the arm is approximately 30 milliseconds. Consequently, an EKG is taken from the person as well. Thirty milliseconds after the appearance of an R wave, the system looks for a Korotkoff sound from the microphone. If a sound is present, blood pressure has increased; if a sound is absent, blood pressure has decreased.

In order to maintain adequate circulation in the arm of the person, the cuff must be deflated periodically to allow blood to flow freely through the arm. Training consists of a number of brief trials, each about one minute long. At the beginning of a trial, the cuff is inflated to the appropriate pressure. Feedback begins and continues for about 45 seconds after which the cuff is rapidly deflated. Training emphasizes lowering of systolic blood pressure. A sliding criterion is used to shape blood pressure control. The criterion pressure for feedback on any given trial is the average blood pressure on the preceding trial. If the average blood pressure on the current trial is about the same as on the preceding one, the criterion remains the same for the next trial. If the person produces the desired change in blood pressure on 75% or more of the heart beats, the criterion is changed a few mm Hg to make the task more difficult. If the person produces the desired change in blood pressure on 25% or fewer of the heart beats, the criterion is changed a few mm Hg to make the task more easy. In this way, the criterion is adjusted up and down, always providing the person with useful feedback and some success, but at the same time trying to maximize the level of performance attained.

An evaluation of the success of biofeedback must keep in mind the evidence reviewed earlier in this section showing that any increase in blood pressure increases the risks of cardiovascular diseases and decreases life expectancy. Consequently, any decrease in blood pressure should reduce the risks of cardiovascular diseases and increase life expectancy. Biofeedback treatment will be most useful if it can reduce blood pressure to the lower end of the normal range. But any decrease should be therapeutic, even if it still leaves the individual with generally elevated pressures.

The treatment reports reviewed below and summarized in Table 15–1 indicate that biofeedback can have clinically significant results which are enduring. Even people with severe cases of hypertension which were uncontrolled by drugs and which had been present for many years were able to reduce both systolic and diastolic pressures. Other literature reviews of both published reports and papers presented during scientific conventions indicate that normotensive and hypertensive people exhibit a great deal of variability in their response to biofeedback training but are usually able to increase and decrease blood pressure by as much as 10 mm Hg (Williamson & Blanchard 1979).

Case Study

A woman had blood pressure of about 170/120 mm Hg which was still rising in spite of drug treatment (Kristt & Engel 1975). For five weeks prior to the biofeedback training, she took her blood pressure at home where it averaged 168/117 mm Hg. She entered a research ward of a hospital where she was an inpatient for three weeks. The constant cuff procedure (Shapiro and others 1969) was used to measure systolic blood pressure; binary information about the level of blood pressure was presented. She received approximately 14 training sessions each week. Each session was composed of a baseline period of about 30 minutes; during this time the necessary connections and adjustments to the biofeedback apparatus were made, and she was asked to rest quietly. Three blocks of ten trials followed. Each trial began with 17 seconds for inflation of the cuff, feedback about blood pressure for 24 heart beats, and then 15 seconds of cuff deflation and rest. A sliding criterion for shaping blood pressure was used as described earlier.

She was trained to increase blood pressure during the first week, decrease it during the second week, and alternately increase and decrease it during the third. In the last four training sessions in each condition, she demonstrated successful control. During sessions in which she was trained to increase blood pressure, systolic blood pressure rose from 163 mm Hg to 180 mm Hg, and during sessions in which she was trained to decrease blood pressure, it fell from 143 mm Hg to 115 mm Hg. During the alternating sessions she changed blood pressure by about 8 mm Hg on 70% to 95% of the trials; these changes were less than those in the previous sessions but were still significant. She left the hospital and three months later returned for another training session. She again succeeded but not as well as at the end of biofeedback treatment. Her blood pressure, which was originally 168/117 mm Hg, dropped to 132/97 mm Hg, an absolute decline of 36/20 mm Hg. In addition, she had reduced one of her drug dosages by 50%.

Discussion of Treatments

Use of Biofeedback Alone To Treat Hypertension. Some studies have used biofeedback by itself to treat hypertension. Prior to treatment, the patients had blood pressures of about 150/90 mm Hg. The studies reviewed here include some of the first attempts to produce changes in blood pressure with biofeedback, and the results are mixed. A few treatments made only slight, short-lived changes in blood pressure that probably had little clinical significance. Most, however, resulted in changes of up to 20 mm Hg in both systolic and diastolic pressures that were enduring. An important variable is the amount of training an individual received. Significant reductions of blood pressure have required intensive training, and failures to change blood pressure appear to result mainly from insufficient training in the clinic and/or practice at home.

Both systolic and diastolic blood pressure were reduced in seven hypertensive patients who received feedback about median systolic pressure (Benson and others 1971). Six of them took antihypertensive medication at constant doses during treatment. Blood pressure was determined with the automated constant cuff system. When Korotkoff sounds disappeared indicating that systolic pressure had been reduced, the patient received feedback via a flashing light, a tone, slides of scenic pictures, and money. Five to 16 baseline recording sessions were followed by 8 to 34 training sessions scheduled on consecutive weekdays. Each session included 30 trials of 50 consecutive heartbeats. Rest periods, 30 to 45 seconds long, separated trials. Median systolic pressure did not change during the pretreatment baseline and averaged 165 mm Hg during the last five baseline sessions. By the last five training sessions, it decreased significantly to 148 mm Hg. The average decrease in systolic blood pressure within sessions was 5 mm Hg. No consistent changes in heart rate occurred in any of the patients while blood pressure was changing. Generally, patients with higher baseline levels showed the greatest reductions during training. For the six patients whose pressure decreased, changes during training were significantly correlated with baseline levels, indicating that biofeedback was most successful with those who had the highest blood pressures.

Biofeedback successfully reduced blood pressure in five people who decreased their medication levels before treatment began (Kristt and Engel 1975). Elevated blood pressures had been present between 10 and 20 years, and at the beginning of treatment the average blood pressure for the group was 153/88 mm Hg. All patients were trained to record their own blood pressure four times daily for five weeks. They were then hospitalized on a research ward, and their medication levels were reduced but not eliminated. Training lasted three weeks: one week of feedback to increase systolic blood pressure, one week of feedback to reduce systolic blood pressure, and one week of feedback to lower, raise, and then lower systolic blood pressure within each session. Feedback of median systolic blood pressure (Tursky and others 1972) was provided during about 14 sessions per week, each with three blocks of ten trials separated by two-minute rest periods. Each trial lasted 24 heart beats, followed by 15 seconds of rest when the pressure cuff was deflated. The patients left the hospital and returned home. For 12 weeks they practiced lowering systolic blood pressure between 4 and 30 times a day, using a pressure cuff and a procedure similar to that used in the hospital. Their ability to control blood pressure was evaluated in the hospital twice during this period. During the initial training sessions in the hospital, the patients were able to increase blood pressure (by about 15%) and decrease it when given feedback. By the end of training in the hospital, blood pressure had been substantially reduced from an average of 162/95 mm Hg to an average of 144/87 mm Hg for four of the five patients, a decrease of 18/8 mm Hg. (No baseline data were presented for the fifth patient.) No reliable changes were found in heart rate, respiration rate, EMG activity from the triceps brachii, or the EEG. Practice at home continued to reduce systolic blood pressure from 141 mm Hg to 125 mm Hg, even though medication was reduced at the same time.

Training to decrease systolic blood pressure was more effective in reducing blood pressure than an equivalent period of general relaxation (Blanchard and others 1975). The six participants had average systolic pressures ranging from 141 mm Hg to 182 mm Hg prior to treatment. Blood pressure was determined once each minute with an automated pressure cuff connected to a polygraph which recorded the occurrence of Korotkoff sounds along with a tracing of the blood pressure changes. A closed circuit television monitor allowed the patient to watch the polygraph tracings for feedback. Training sessions were 40 minutes long and took place once a day. Each session began with 20 minutes of baseline. Then biofeedback training took place for 20 minutes, or the patient relaxed and watched television for 20 minutes. An A-B-A-B design was used with watching television as the *A* procedure and biofeedback as the *B* procedure. The number of sessions with each procedure ranged between four and eight. Blood pressure measured during the baseline period at the start of each session was consistently lower when the patients were learning biofeedback than when they were watching television. The average systolic blood pressure was 154 mm Hg and

137 mm Hg during the first and second television (*A*) periods, respectively, but it was reduced to 128 mm Hg and 122 mm Hg during the first and second biofeedback (*B*) periods, respectively. Two patients who were contacted several weeks following treatment maintained reduced systolic blood pressures of 127 mm Hg.

The effectiveness of the biofeedback treatment as compared to general relaxation is supported by the results of another study treating 11 men whose blood pressures were at least 140/95 mm Hg at the beginning of treatment (Goldman and others 1975). Those who received biofeedback treatment had sessions lasting two hours once a week for nine weeks. Feedback of systolic pressure was produced by the constant cuff method (Tursky and others 1972). Each training session had 25 to 30 trials, each of which lasted for about 30 heart beats and was followed by one minute of rest during which time the cuff was deflated. Those who were in the control group came to the clinic for the same length of time. They were told to relax as much as possible, and blood pressure was recorded, but no feedback was given. For patients in the control group neither systolic, nor diastolic blood pressure changed significantly, starting at 155/99 mm Hg and ending at 157/95 mm Hg. For patients in the biofeedback group, systolic, but not diastolic, blood pressure decreased, from 161/94 mm Hg at the beginning of training to 157/95 mm Hg. Although the absolute changes in blood pressure produced by biofeedback in this treatment were not as great as those in the preceding report, biofeedback was still more effective than just relaxation.

Biofeedback and praise from the therapist were more effective in teaching people to reduce blood pressure than either biofeedback alone or no treatment at all (Elder and others 1973). The participants were 18 men whose blood pressures averaged about 155/100 mm Hg before treatment. Three groups were formed. People in the control group had their blood pressure taken but did not receive feedback. Those receiving only visual feedback watched a red light which was illuminated when diastolic blood pressure decreased. Those receiving visual feedback and praise watched the same light but were also told "good" when blood pressure first fell below criterion, "very good" if it decreased 5 mm Hg below criterion, and "wonderful" if it decreased 10 mm Hg. Blood pressure was measured every two minutes for 40 minutes in each session. Sessions were held once in the morning and once in the afternoon for four consecutive days. One week following treatment, blood pressure had decreased 11/0 mm Hg for those in the control group, 5/9 mm Hg for those who received only visual feedback and 23/19 mm Hg for those who had visual feedback and praise.

Reductions in blood pressure learned in a clinic have been maintained both at home and at work (Kleinman and others 1977). The patients were eight men between 26 and 63 years of age with blood pressures of at least 140/95 mm Hg; none were taking any medication. Treatment sessions were two hours long, held once weekly for 12 weeks. The first three sessions were used as a control period without feedback. During the subsequent nine sessions, auditory and visual feedback were provided for changes in systolic blood pressure measured by the automated constant cuff method (Tursky and others 1972). Each session had 25 to 30 trials, each 30 heart beats long, followed by one minute of rest. After the last feedback session, patients recorded their own blood pressures daily for four months. Blood pressure in the clinic decreased from 151/94 mm Hg during the pretreatment control sessions to 143/85 mm Hg during the last feedback session. Blood pressure at home and at work decreased from 155/97 mm Hg one day before the last two control sessions to 147/89 mm Hg two days before the last two feedback sessions. Four months later, blood pressure in three patients who were representative of the group remained low.

Biofeedback in Conjunction with Relaxation.   One treatment program has combined biofeedback with relaxation training (Patel 1973, 1975; Patel & North 1975). Both procedures took place while the patients reclined on a couch. The biofeedback treatment was indirect. Galvanic skin resistance or muscle activity was recorded. An auditory signal provided feedback, and the patients were trained to increase skin resistance or decrease muscle activity. At the same time, they concentrated on smooth breathing, repeated the word "relax" with each expiration, and used autogenic phrases if they wished.

This treatment program decreased both systolic and diastolic blood pressure by about 15 mm Hg (Patel 1973, 1975). The participants were 20 people with hypertension that had been present for up to 19 years. Two groups were formed. Both came to the clinic three times a week for three months. Patients in one group received the treatment just described. Patients in the other group were told to lie on the couch and rest; they did not receive biofeedback training or the relaxation instructions. Blood pressure for the patients who received treatment was initially 159/100 mm Hg. It decreased to 139/86 mm Hg in the final four sessions of treatment and remained steady at about 145/88 mm Hg when the patients were examined 3 months, 6 months, and 12 months later. Blood pressure for the patients who just rested was initially 163/99 mm Hg; it remained within 5 mm Hg of that value while the patients came to the clinic and at the subsequent follow-up examinations. Patients who received treatment reduced their medication levels by 41%, and five of them stopped all hypertensive medication. Heart rate, respiration rate, and body weight did not change during treatment.

The consistency of the blood pressure in the group which did not receive treatment confirms the results of studies reviewed in the previous section showing that periods of rest without explicit relaxation instructions are ineffective in changing blood pressure.

Further support for the effectiveness of this treatment program as compared to simply resting was found in a subsequent study varying the order in which the treatment and rest conditions were given (Patel & North 1975). Two groups of 17 patients were formed. Both came to the clinic for 30 minutes twice a week for six weeks. Patients in the treatment group received the combination of biofeedback and relaxation described earlier, while those in the other group were told to rest on the couch. Patients in the treatment group were also encouraged to practice the relaxation at home. During the subsequent three months, blood pressure was measured every two weeks. Then both groups of patients returned to the clinic once again for 30 minutes twice a week for six weeks. However, the procedures for the two groups were reversed; the patients who had originally received treatment now rested, while those who had originally rested received treatment. Six months later, blood pressures were measured again.

The treatment was effective while the equivalent period of rest was not, as summarized in Figure 15–1. For patients who received treatment first (top graph), both systolic (top part of the top graph) and diastolic (bottom part of the top graph) blood pressure decreased from the beginning of treatment to the end of treatment. Furthermore, these reductions were maintained throughout the subsequent period when the patients rested. For patients who just rested at first (bottom graph), neither systolic (top part of the bottom graph) nor diastolic (bottom part of the graph) blood pressure changed during that time. When they subsequently began biofeedback treatment, however, blood pressure decreased and at the examination six months later, it was very similar to that in the other group. Thus treatment was effective while resting was not, and reductions obtained through treatment persisted when treatment was terminated.

In one study, biofeedback treatment had little effect on blood pressure (Elder & Eustis 1975). The 23 patients were all diagnosed as having essential hypertension by a physician. A massed practice procedure was used with 4 clients; they had one treatment session daily for ten days. A spaced practice procedure was used for the other 19; they received their ten sessions during three months. Diastolic blood pressure was measured every minute. Training sessions had two blocks of ten trials, each one minute long. A green light was illuminated when diastolic blood pressure fell below criterion; a red light was illuminated at the end of a trial if diastolic blood pressure remained above criterion. Although blood pressure decreased from the first to the second block of ten training trials

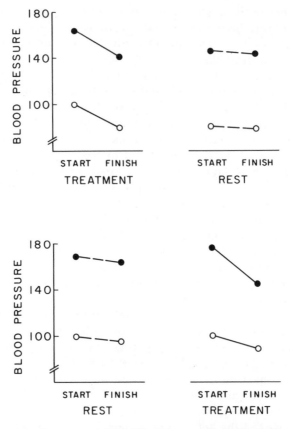

FIGURE 15–1 The Effectiveness of Biofeedback Compared to that of Rest for Treatment of Hypertension.

In the top graphs are the results from clients who received six weeks of biofeedback treatment and then six weeks in which they came to the clinic and just rested (without feedback). Both systolic blood pressure (solid circles) and diastolic blood pressure (open circles) decreased during treatment (the left half of the figure) and remained low during the subsequent rest (the right half of the figure). In the bottom graphs are the results from clients who came to the clinic and rested for a period of time equivalent to that spent by clients who received biofeedback treatment in the first group; neither systolic nor diastolic blood pressure decreased during rest (the left half of the graph). When biofeedback treatment was initiated (the right half of the graph), both systolic and diastolic blood pressure decreased. Thus biofeedback, but not an equivalent period of rest, significantly lowered blood pressure. *(Data are from Patel and North, 1975.)*

in the treatment sessions, one month following the end of treatment diastolic blood pressure was virtually the same as it was before treatment.

A Comparison of the Effectiveness of Biofeedback and Relaxation Procedures. As reviewed in the previous two sections, biofeedback treatment by itself or in conjunction with trained relaxation procedures can reduce blood pressure. The studies discussed here compared the effectiveness of biofeedback alone with that of relaxation procedures alone. The results of these do not provide definitive support for either procedure being more effective than the other. Part of the problem is that blood pressure changes in the relevant studies were generally small, so that they are not readily comparable to the results of the more effective treatments reviewed earlier. A second difficulty is the inconsistency of the results, with biofeedback being more effective in some cases and not as effective in others.

Biofeedback, but not progressive relaxation, reduced blood pressure levels in one study (Walsh and others 1977). Unfortunately, the blood pressure of the group which received biofeedback first was higher than that of the group which received progressive relaxation first. The results of previous studies have shown that success at lowering blood pressure is positively correlated with initial blood pressure. Thus the people with higher blood pressure might have been more successful with any treatment. The participants were 24 people between 24 and 69 years of age with blood pressures averaging 143/93 mm Hg at the start of training. They were divided into two groups: one had biofeedback training and then learned progressive relaxation; the other learned progressive relaxation and then had biofeedback. For biofeedback, pulse wave velocity (see Chapter 6) was recorded. Analogue feedback was provided by a tone and by an oscilloscope which indicated the length of the pulse transit time. One biofeedback session, with seven trials each three minutes long, took place each week for five weeks. For progressive relaxation, the patients learned the procedures outlined by Wolpe (1958) in group sessions, each 90 minutes long, held once a week for five weeks. They were instructed to practice the relaxation procedure in their home. Blood pressure for those who received biofeedback decreased from 147/94 mm Hg at the start of training to 133/84 mm Hg by the fifth session, while blood pressure for those who received relaxation remained essentially unchanged, beginning at 138/92 mm Hg and decreasing only slightly to 137/89 mm Hg by the fifth session. The procedures for the two groups were then reversed. Those who received biofeedback first practiced progressive relaxation, and those who received relaxation first learned biofeedback. Blood pressure for both groups remained virtually unchanged at 135/87 mm Hg and 137/89 mm Hg, respectively. Twelve months later the blood pressures were still the same, representing a significant decrease for the group which received biofeedback first (and initially had higher blood pressures) but not for the group which received relaxation first. No change in heart rate or respiration rate took place during the treatments.

Hypnosis produced a greater reduction of blood pressure than biofeedback for a group of 48 people who had blood pressures of about 145/95 mm Hg (Friedman & Taub 1977, 1978). One group of patients received biofeedback only. Systolic and diastolic blood pressures were measured, feedback was provided about both, and the patients were instructed to concentrate on reducing diastolic levels. A second group of patients received hypnosis only. They were hypnotized and instructed to relax as much as possible; blood pressure was recorded, but no feedback was given. Both groups received treatment for seven sessions, after which the people in the hypnosis group were instructed to hypnotize themselves for three minutes twice a day and practice what they had learned in the clinic. For the group that received biofeedback, blood pressure declined from 147/96 mm Hg in the pretreatment baseline to 137/94 mm Hg and 140/88 mm Hg three months and six months later, respectively. For the patients who received hypnosis, blood pressures declined from 143/93 mm Hg to 132/86 mm Hg and 127/85 mm Hg in the same time periods, respectively. The final levels of blood pressure following hypnosis were lower than those following biofeedback and were significantly different from those for a group of patients who received no treatment.

Two studies found that neither biofeedback nor relaxation produced substantial changes in blood pressure. In one, the participants had blood pressures of at least 140/99 mm Hg with no obvious organic bases (Surwit & Shapiro 1977). Eight patients were assigned to one of three treatment groups. Treatment sessions were held twice a week for four weeks; a follow-up session was held six weeks later. One group of patients received biofeedback training to lower both blood pressure and heart rate; auditory and visual feedback were provided whenever blood pressure dropped by 2 mm Hg and heart rate decreased at the same time. A second group received biofeedback training to reduce the EMG in the extensor muscles of the forearm and the frontalis muscle of the forehead. A third group was trained to relax using the procedures of Benson, Rosen, Marzetta, and Klemchuk (1974). All patients were shown cumulative graphs of their blood pressure following each session and were told to practice lowering blood pressure at home. Both during treatment and six months following treatment, neither systolic nor diastolic blood pressure had decreased substantially; the final blood pressure averaged 138/86 mm Hg as compared to their initial values of 143/88 mm Hg.

Similar results were found in a subsequent study treating 18 adult hypertensives between 27 and 59 years of age (Surwit and others 1978). The cardiovascular biofeedback group received visual and auditory feedback following simultaneous decreases in median systolic blood pressure and heart rate. Each session had 20 trials, one minute long, followed by 30 seconds of rest. The EMG biofeedback group was asked to meditate according to the instructions of Benson (1975). All patients attended two sessions each week for four weeks, plus a follow-up session six months after treatment. Training sessions lasted 60 to 90 minutes. Patients were also told to practice their learned strategy at home as often as possible after the first session. Six months following treatment, each patient was instructed to lower blood pressure using the strategy learned during training. Systolic blood pressure did not change significantly, averaging about 138 mm Hg during the baseline for all three groups, 138 mm Hg during the training sessions, and about 135 mm Hg at follow-up.

CARDIAC ARRHYTHMIAS

As reviewed earlier in Chapter 6, the heart normally beats in a very regular manner. Excitation begins at the sinus node, travels to the atrioventricular node, and produces a patterned contraction of the ventricles. Occasionally, this pattern is disrupted, and an arrhythmia results. This abnormal pattern of the heart beat is reflected in the EKG and may have serious consequences. The arrhythmia is less efficient than the normal heart beat, meaning that less blood is circulated for the work being done. More importantly, the arrhythmia may lead to flutter or fibrillation, rates of contraction which are so high that cardiac insufficiency and death may result.

In most of the cases discussed here, an indirect approach was taken; the person was given information only about heart rate and not about the arrhythmia itself. The most common treatment (Bleecker & Engel 1973a,b; Weiss & Engel 1973) has used the procedure that was outlined in the beginning of Chapter 2. The patient reclined on a couch, and EKG electrodes were placed on the chest. A green light on the display panel was an instruction to raise heart rate; a red light was an instruction to lower it. A yellow light indicated success and was illuminated when the heart rate change exceeded criterion in the desired direction. The first biofeedback sessions were *slowing* sessions in which the patient was asked to decrease heart rate. These were followed by *speeding* sessions in which the patient was asked to increase the heart rate and then by *slowing and speeding* sessions in which the patient was asked to decrease heart rate for four minutes and then to increase it for the same length of time.

Three results of these treatments are of particular interest. First, heart rate training reduced the arrhythmias. Second, success took place even when individuals were unable to speed or slow heart rate (Weiss & Engel 1973). Thus just the effort made to control heart rate (rather than the actual control itself) must have been sufficient to eliminate the arrhythmia. Finally, the results of pharmacological experiments carried out with these patients have identified the component of the autonomic nervous system which was responsible for eliciting the arrhythmia and which was used by the patient to control it. Heart rate increases have been produced by both increasing sympathetic activity and decreasing parasympathetic activity, while heart rate decreases have been produced by both decreasing sympathetic activity and increasing parasympathetic activity (Bleecker & Engel 1973a,b; Williamson & Blanchard 1979).

Wolff-Parkinson-White Syndrome

SYMPTOMS AND MECHANISM

The Wolff-Parkinson-White syndrome (Wolff and others 1930) is an example of an arrhythmia also called preexcitation (Silber & Katz 1975). The EKG is characterized by two main changes (see Chapter 6). First, the PR interval is shortened. Second, the QRS complex is abnormal and usually shows a delta wave (Silber & Katz 1975, p. 153; Zipes & McIntosh 1971, p. 363). The Wolff-Parkinson-White syndrome is due to abnormal conduction, leading to the early activation of the ventricular musculature (Wolff and others 1930; Silber & Katz 1975; Zipes & McIntosh 1971). The short PR interval reflects the excessively rapid conduction from the sinus node to the atrioventricular node, and the abnormal QRS complex indicates that the resulting ventricular contraction is inefficient. There are several pathways which may be responsible for the anomalous conduction, and each of these may be associated with a particular variant of the syndrome (Silber & Katz 1975, p. 138).

TREATMENT

Case Study

Ten years of episodic tachycardia associated with dyspnea, syncope, and chest pain were reported by this young woman (Bleecker & Engel 1973b). During the last three years she had a conduction pattern typical of the Wolff-Parkinson-White syndrome with sinus tachycardia and supraventricular tachycardias of 200 bpm to 400 bpm. PR and QRS intervals were .18 and .07 seconds, respectively, during normal conduction, and .10 and .12, respectively, during Wolff-Parkinson-White conduction. Treatment began with heart rate slowing, speeding, and alternate slowing and speeding as described earlier. Each slowing and speeding session had a baseline period, eight minutes long, followed by feedback for about 17 minutes. The slowing and speeding sessions had four consecutive periods, each four minutes long, in an A-B-A-B sequence. She was then trained to control cardiac conduction. A heart beat with a normal QRS complex was followed by an auditory signal. She was instructed to increase the frequency of the signal during eight sessions and to decrease it during three sessions, indicating an increase and decrease in abnormal heart beats, respectively. Finally, she was trained to increase the frequency of normal heart beats, without feedback. In the slowing sessions, heart rate decreased by an average of 3.4 bpm; in the speeding sessions it increased by an average of 2.5 bpm. In the alternate slowing and speeding session of the third treatment period, the average difference between heart rate during speeding and slowing was 5.5 bpm. During training in QRS control, she increased the number of normal heart beats in four of eight sessions when instructed to do so and increased Wolff-Parkinson-White conduction significantly in two of three sessions when instructed to do so. Overall, she increased the number of heart beats with normal conduction by an average of 14.5% and the number of heart beats with Wolff-Parkinson-White conduction by an average of 6.7%. When instructed in the final stage of training to increase normal conduction with alternating periods of feedback and no feedback, she increased normal conduction by an average of 13%. She retained the ability to differentially modify cardiac conduction ten weeks later.

Premature Ventricular Contractions

SYMPTOMS AND MECHANISM

A *premature ventricular contraction* (abbreviated PVC) comes from a contraction of the ventricle that is too early in the heart beat sequence. The PVCs result from a focus of stimulation that is *ectopic,* or out of place. There are a number of different places this ectopic focus can be located, but they all serve to interrupt the normal heart beat sequence and to produce contractions of the ventricles that are too early in the heart beat cycle. Consequently, the name premature ventricular contraction (Bellet 1972; Kay 1971).

As might be expected, a PVC changes the form of the EKG substantially. Instead of a normal PQRST complex with a well-defined R peak, as described in Chapter 6, the QRS complex is bizarre, often with a duration substantially longer than normal. Figure 15–2 illustrates a run of PVCs following a normal heart beat. Note the rapidity with which the PVCs appeared.

PVCs occur in about 5% of the population (Bellet 1972). A single isolated PVC is probably of little consequence. But as illustrated in Figure 15–2, they often come in runs in which many successive heart beats are abnormal, a condition called *ventricular paroxysmal tachycardia*: ventricular, because the difficulty lies in contraction of the ventricles of the heart, paroxysmal, because it has a very sudden onset, and tachycardia, because it is an excessively rapid beating of the heart. Unlike the single PVC, the tachycardia has important and dramatic medical consequences. As the rate increases, the heart becomes less efficient in moving blood, and the person may die from cardiac arrest (Kay 1971). Consequently, the concern is not with the individual PVC, but rather with the fact that they often become more frequent over time and develop into long runs resulting in paroxysmal tachycardia and death.

Subjectively, the patient may or may not be sensitive to the occurrence of PVCs. If the individual does sense them, they may be described as a palpitation, heart turning over, or heart stopping. With a run of PVCs and ventricular paroxysmal tachycardia, sweating, anxiety, and breathlessness may appear, all of which are usually very obvious to the individual (Bellet 1972). Training in biofeedback usually increases an individual's awareness of the PVCs (Weiss & Engel 1973), as well as the ability to control them.

TREATMENT

Biofeedback treatment of PVCs has used the same indirect method as was described earlier. The symptoms to be controlled are PVCs, but the person is taught to control heart rate itself. Information about heart rate is given to the patient who is trained to control it. Attempting to increase heart rate decreases the rate of PVCs.

Case Study A

Five myocardial infarctions in 13 years had led to persistent PVCs in this woman who was 52 years old at the start of treatment (Weiss & Engel 1973, p. 82). Continuous drug therapy was not successful and produced undesirable side effects. Biofeedback training sessions were 80 minutes long and took place one to three times daily while she was a

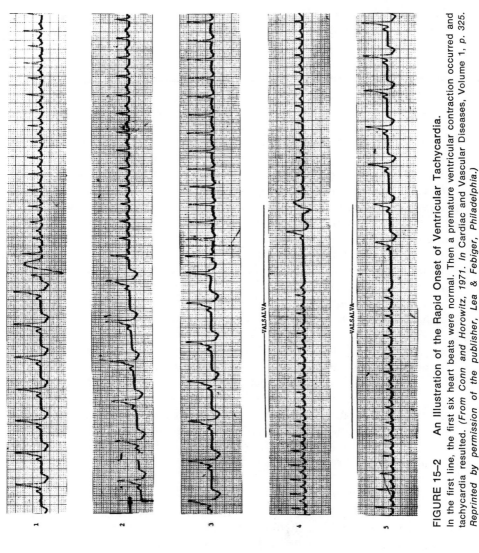

FIGURE 15–2   An Illustration of the Rapid Onset of Ventricular Tachycardia.
In the first line, the first six heart beats were normal. Then a premature ventricular contraction occurred and tachycardia resulted. *(From Conn and Horowitz, 1971. In Cardiac and Vascular Diseases, Volume 1, p. 325. Reprinted by permission of the publisher, Lea & Febiger, Philadelphia.)*

patient on a research ward. Each session began with a baseline period during which she relaxed and lay quietly in a bed. There followed 34 minutes of biofeedback training in which she was asked to increase or decrease heart rate.

Heart rate was recorded through a standard set of EKG leads. Information was given to the patient through three lights, as described in the introduction to this section. All the records from the experiment were made available to the patient. Biofeedback training began with slowing, speeding, and then alternately slowing and speeding. Finally, she was asked to hold heart rate within a certain range. This last training differed from the slowing or speeding instructions because it specified end points, rather than just a direction.

At first, she had little control over heart rate and could not produce consistent changes in either direction. During training, she gradually learned some control, although the magnitude of this control was small, especially in the third condition where she had to alternately increase and decrease heart rate. When she was asked to increase heart rate, the rate of PVCs increased from about two per minute to about 10 per minute. When she was asked to decrease heart rate, PVCs almost disappeared, a result also found when she was asked to keep her heart rate within a certain range. These data suggest two conclusions. First, the mechanism responsible for the PVCs was associated with a heart rate speeding mechanism. Second, by attempting to slow heart rate, she could reduce the frequency of PVCs even though heart rate did not change.

Following training, she was released from the hospital and was gradually taken off all drugs. The rate of PVCs was low, about one every ten minutes, for several months, and then it gradually increased to about one per minute. She reported being able to detect PVCs at home when they occurred, at which time she would sit down and rest. The attacks of PVCs were rare, and she was able to eliminate them successfully through this resting procedure. At the time of this report, she had been followed for 21 months after release from the hospital, and her condition appeared to be stable.

Case Study B

An irregular heart rhythm in the absence of other evidence of heart disease had been present for at least eight years in this woman, who was 31 years old at the start of treatment (Pickering & Gorham 1975). Her EKG had up to 15 PVCs per minute but was otherwise normal; exercise increased the rate to 37 PVCs per minute. The arrhythmia was always present when heart rate exceeded 106 bpm and was always absent below

72 bpm. Continuous visual feedback of heart rate was provided during 16 sessions, each one hour long, that took place during six weeks. Each session included some combination of rest, speeding heart rate with feedback, slowing heart rate with feedback, or speeding and slowing heart rate without feedback, followed by graded exercise on a bicycle ergometer which increased her heart rate above 120 bpm. Initially she could increase her heart rate without feedback by an average of 3.8 bpm but could not decrease it. After six sessions, the parasystolic rhythm appeared above an average of 79 bpm. She increased her heart rate progressively from the seventh session to the 16th session with increases of 12 and 25 bpm, respectively. Changes in heart rate with and without feedback were comparable throughout training. As her ability to raise heart rate improved, her threshold for the occurrence of the parasystolic rhythm increased significantly to an average of 94 bpm during both heart rate speeding and during exercise-stimulated increases in heart rate.

Discussion of Treatments

Alternately increasing and decreasing heart rate consistently reduced the rate of PVCs in a group of eight patients who had been diagnosed as having abnormal heart beats up to eight years prior to treatment (Weiss & Engel 1973). Other cardiovascular abnormalities included cardiomegaly, congestive heart failure, a 27-year history of hypertension, and up to five myocardial infarctions. All patients were hospitalized for the study and received one to three 80-minute sessions each day. A 10-minute baseline (without feedback) preceded either one 34-minute training trial or two 17-minute trials within each session. Heart rate speeding took place for approximately 10 sessions, heart rate slowing for 10 sessions, and alternate speeding and slowing for periods of one to four minutes for the next 10 sessions. Finally feedback was provided for the maintenance of heart rate within predetermined upper and lower limits for about 11 sessions. The range for each individual was the one that had the lowest frequency of PVCs. In the last period, feedback was eliminated for increasingly longer intervals within each session to train control without feedback. Patients were progressively successful in changing heart rate as instructed, and the incidence of PVCs during these periods decreased progressively from 11.9 per session to 4.8 per session. Five patients showed a decrease in PVCs associated with the feedback training. Approximately two years after treatment, the rate of PVCs in the group of eight patients ranged from .3 to 17.1 per minute. Four patients had very low rates of PVCs.

SYMPTOMS

Tachycardia is an abnormally high heart rate. It may lead to *fibrillation*, a heart beat so rapid that the heart does not pump blood efficiently and the person may die from cardiac arrest. Tachycardia is caused by a variety of abnormalities. Biofeedback has trained patients to reduce heart rate and thus reduce the tachycardia and fibrillation.

Case Study A

Tachycardia, which had been present for 20 years, eventually developed to such an extent that this man had been unable to work for the previous 14 months (Scott and others 1973). Heart rate was recorded during four baseline sessions. Treatment began with 26 sessions of biofeedback, each 20 minutes long, in which he was instructed to decrease heart rate. Visual feedback was provided by running time meters which recorded the total number of seconds that heart rate was below a criterion. He was reinforced with one cent for every ten seconds of successful performance. During these initial training sessions, the criterion for success was held constant throughout the session. Training failed to teach him to lower heart rate which remained at about 90 bpm, the same rate as in the baseline sessions.

The procedure was then changed so that a sliding criterion was used. If he decreased heart rate below the initial criterion during the first minute of a trial, the criterion level was lowered so that he had to decrease heart rate further to be successful. If he failed to reach criterion during a trial, the criterion was either left unchanged, or it was raised one or two bpm for the next trial. During 18 sessions with this sliding criterion, he decreased heart rate by 17 bpm so that it averaged 72 bpm during the last six sessions. During six subsequent baseline sessions, heart rate increased slightly to 77 bpm but still remained below the 89 bpm at the beginning of training. He reported feeling less anxious and returned to work. Eighteen months later, he was still employed and had decreased the amount of a minor tranquilizer that he had been taking regularly for over a year to one-fourth of his initial level.

Case Study B

An inpatient in a psychiatric ward, this 50-year-old man had been diagnosed as an anxiety neurotic and reported feelings of anxiety and weakness (Scott and others 1973). He had complained of various problems, including tachycardia for 26 years and had not worked for the last two years. Four baseline sessions were followed by 10 biofeedback sessions which used the sliding criterion as described above. Heart rate, which was 96 bpm during baseline, decreased to 83 bpm in the last biofeedback session. In the subsequent eight baseline sessions without feedback, heart rate decreased further to 78 bpm.

Discussion of Treatments

Increasing and decreasing heart rate reduced atrial fibrillation in six patients with a history of rheumatic valvular heart disease (Bleecker & Engel 1973a). The patients were three men and three women between 28 and 62 years of age, all of whom had had congestive heart failure. They took stable doses of digitalis for at least three months and then were hospitalized on a research ward. They were trained to decrease heart rate for 12 to 24 slowing sessions, increase heart rate for 10 to 12 speeding sessions, and alternately speed and slow heart rate for 12 to 31 sessions. Half of the patients were trained to speed and then slow heart rate; the other three were trained in the reverse order. Each session with only speeding or slowing had 17 minutes of feedback, while each session with both speeding and slowing had four consecutive trials of eight minutes each. The percentage of sessions in which heart rate was changed in the appropriate direction ranged from 67% to 86%. Heart rate increased from −.5 bpm to 9.5 bpm during the speeding sessions, and decreased from .8 to 3.5 bpm during the slowing sessions. The difference in heart rate between the speeding trials and the slowing trials of the sessions in which heart rate was alternately increased and decreased was 7.2 bpm. The percentage of trials in which heart rate was changed successfully in these last sessions was 30%, 50%, 70%, and 90% for each of four patients, respectively, and 100% for the other two.

OTHER CARDIAC ABNORMALITIES

Postural Hypotension

SYMPTOMS AND MECHANISM

A person who suffers from postural hypotension has difficulties when moving from a prone position to a sitting or standing position. This movement is accompanied by dizziness, fading of vision, sweating, and sometimes lack of consciousness. Putting the head lower than the heart (by bending over, for example), can often reverse these symptoms, and moving very slowly from the prone position to the standing one may help alleviate them. The hydrostatic pressure of the blood when an

TABLE 15-1   Summary of Biofeedback Treatments for Cardiovascular Disorders

Study	Patients	Biofeedback Treatment	Other Treatment	Symptoms	Results Biological Function
Benson, Shapiro, Tursky, & Schwartz, 1971	7 hypertensive patients; age range 30 to 54	8 to 34 sessions with auditory and visual feedback for decreases in median systolic pressure during 30 trials of 50 heartbeats	Medication for some	Data unavailable	Median systolic pressure averaged 165 mmHg during the last five baseline sessions and decreased to 148 in the last five training sessions; average within-session decrease was 5 mmHg; heart rate did not change consistently
Blanchard & Abel, 1976	Female, age 30 with sinus tachycardia	Binary visual feedback of heart rate levels during 33, 20-min trials in 8 to 17 weeks	Dilantin, 100 mg. twice daily	By the last phase, listening to a tape of a raping incident failed to evoke tachycardia as before treatment; spells which occurred once weekly before treatment disappeared	Heart rate increased over 150 bpm during rape tape in phase two; heart rate decreased during the same tape after feedback training in 23 of 25 sessions by an average of 3 bpm; effect maintained at follow-up
Blanchard, Young & Haynes, 1975	3 males, 1 female with elevated blood pressure; age range 25 to 50	Visual feedback of changes in systolic blood pressure and occurrence of Korotkoff sounds during eight, 20-min sessions in the first treatment period and during 4 sessions in the second; sessions were generally scheduled each day	Hospitalization and diazepam, 5 mg. t.i.d for two patients	Data unavailable	Systolic pressure averaged 154, 128, 137, 122, and 127 mmHg during the first baseline, first feedback, second baseline, second feedback, and follow-up periods, respectively

| Bleecker & Engel, 1973a | 3 males, 3 females with atrial fibrillation; age range 28 to 62 | Visual feedback for increases and decreases in ventricular rate during 16 to 22 sessions lasting from 4 to 17 mins | Medication, Hospitalization | Data Unavailable | Ventricular rates increased by an average of −.5 to 9.5 bpm during speeding, decreased by an average of .8 to 3.5 bpm during slowing, and differed by an average of 7.2 bpm during the alternately-speed-and-slow phase; success rates in the sessions averaged 67%, 47%, and 86%, respectively |
| Bleecker & Engel, 1973b | Female, age 29 with Wolff-Parkinson-White syndrome | Auditory and visual feedback for increases and decreases in heart rate and for increases and decreases in normal cardiac conduction during 4- to 17-min trials for 3 to 26 sessions | Medication | Data Unavailable | Heart rate decreased by an average of 3.4 bpm during slowing, increased by an average of 2.5 bpm during speeding, and differed by an average of 5.5 bpm during the alternate-slowing-and-speeding segment; normal cardiac conduction increased by an average of 14.5% and decreased by an average of 6.7% during the appropriate period; normal cardiac conduction increased during alternated feedback and no feedback periods by an average of 13%; ability to differentially modify cardiac conduction maintained at 10 week follow-up |

TABLE 15-1 Summary of Biofeedback Treatments for Cardiovascular Disorders

Study	Patients	Biofeedback Treatment	Other Treatment	Symptoms	Results Biological Function
Brucker & Ince, 1977	Male, age 31 with postural hypotension	Auditory feedback of blood pressure during 60-min training sessions four times weekly for a total of 11 sessions	Home practice	Patient became able to stand and walk for up to 4 hours following training	Systolic and diastolic blood pressure increased by 17 mmHg during the first two sessions and by 48 mmHg during the last two; one-month follow-up session produced 48 mmHg increases in systolic and diastolic levels; blood pressure decreased from 110 to 50 mmHg when standing without prior attempt to increase pressure; with prior increase of 35 mmHg, pressure decreased from 145 to 100 mmHg in the same two-min interval
Elder & Eustis, 1975	14 males, 8 females reporting a diagnosis of essential hypertension; age range 23 to 80	Visual feedback of relative changes in diastolic blood pressure during either 10 days with feedback sessions once per day (massed practice), or with sessions scheduled in decreasing weekly frequency (spaced practice) for 80 days; sessions included 10 one-min trials	Medication	Data Unavailable	Baseline pressure of 147/85 mmHg was significantly reduced to 139/82 mmHg in the last training session; massed-practice group reduced diastolic pressure in 88% of the sessions; 30-day follow-up of spaced-practice group indicated a return of systolic pressure to baseline levels while diastolic pressure remained approximately 1% below such values

Study	Subjects	Feedback Procedure	Additional Treatment		Results
Elder, Ruiz, Deabler, & Dillenkoffer, 1973	18 male hypertensive patients; age range 23 to 59	Visual or visual plus verbal feedback for decreases in systolic blood pressure during 40-min sessions, twice daily for 4 days	Hospitalization	Data Unavailable	Blood pressure averaged 156/112 mmHg during baseline and decreased 5/9 mmHg by follow-up in the visual feedback group; visual feedback plus verbal reinforcement group averaged 154/102 mmHg in the baseline and decreased blood pressure levels by 23/19 mmHg at follow-up
Friedman & Taub, 1977, 1978	39 male, 9 female hypertensive patients; age range 23 to 60	Visual feedback of diastolic pressure during 7 sessions	Medication	Data Unavailable	Blood pressure averaged 147/96 mmHg, 137/94 mmHg, and 140/88 mmHg during baseline, 1-month follow-up, and 6-month follow-up periods, respectively
Goldman, Kleinman, Snow, Bidus, & Korol, 1975	7 male hypertensive patients; age range 35 to 68	Auditory and visual feedback of changes in mean systolic blood pressure during 2-hour sessions, once weekly for 3 weeks	Home Practice	Data Unavailable	Baseline blood pressure averaged 167/109 mmHg and was reduced to 161/94 mmHg in the last feedback session
Kleinman, Goldman, Snow, & Korol, 1977	8 male hypertensive patients; age range 26 to 63	Auditory and visual feedback of mean systolic pressure during 25 to 30, 30-heartbeat trials during each of 9 sessions	None	Data Unavailable	Laboratory-measured blood pressure averaged 149/95 mmHg, 152/92 mmHg, and 142/85 mmHg during the first control session, last control session, and last feedback session, respectively; blood pressure determined by the patient at home and work averaged 155/97 mmHg during the control period and 147/89 mmHg before the last two feedback sessions

TABLE 15-1 Summary of Biofeedback Treatments for Cardiovascular Disorders

Study	Patients	Biofeedback Treatment	Other Treatment	Symptoms	Results Biological Function
Kristt & Engel, 1975	4 females, 1 male with hypertension; age range 46 to 70	Visual feedback of relative changes in average systolic blood pressure during about 14 sessions per week for 3 weeks	Medication and hospitalization during the 3-week study which was followed by home practice with a pressure cuff for 12 weeks	Data Unavailable	Pre- and posttraining blood pressure (systolic/diastolic): 162/95 mmHg and 144/87 mmHg respectively; no reliable change in heart rate, respiration rate, triceps brachii EMG activity, or alpha EEG activity; systolic blood pressure averaged 141 mmHg before, and 125 mmHg after 12-week home training; 3 patients reduced their medication levels while maintaining the treatment effect at 12-week follow-up
Patel, 1973, 1975	11 females, 9 males with hypertension	Auditory feedback of changes in skin resistance during 30-min sessions, 3 times weekly for 3 months	Autogenic and yogic instructions; medication	Data Unavailable	Blood pressure averaged 159/100 mmHg, 139/86 mmHg, 145/86 mmHg, 147/88 mmHg, and 144/87 mmHg in the baseline, posttreatment, three-month follow-up, six-month follow-up, and 9- to 12-month follow-up, periods, respectively
Patel & North, 1975	13 male, 21 female hypertensive patients; age range 34 to 75	30-min feedback-relaxation sessions twice weekly for 6 weeks	Medication and home practice	Data Unavailable	Blood pressure averaged 168/100 mmHg during the baseline and decreased to 141/84 mmHg after treatment; blood pressure in a control group which was later treated averaged 177/104 mmHg before and 149/89 mmHg after treatment

Study	Subjects	Procedure			Results
Pickering & Gorham, 1975	Female, age 31 with ventricular parasystolic rhythm	Instruction with and without visual feedback to increase and decrease heart rate during 4 one-min trials in each of 16 sessions	Exercise on bicycle ergometer following the 4 trials	Pinching in chest	Initial increases in heart rate averaged 3.8 bpm and were averaging 12 bpm in session seven, and 25 bpm in session 16; arrhythmias occurred at rest with heart rates above 72 bpm and the threshold was increased to 85 bpm in session 16; parasystolic rhythm threshold was 79 bpm in session six; 94 bpm in session 16, and was unchanged by an intraveneous injection of propanolol
Scott, Blanchard, Edmunson, & Young, 1973	2 males with chronic tachycardia; ages 46 and 50	One patient received visual feedback during constant-criterion and during variable-criterion phases; the second patient received only variable-criterion sessions with visual feedback; each of 19 sessions lasted 20 mins	Medication	Data Unavailable	Patient #1's heart rate averaged 89, 89, 72, and 77 bpm during the baseline, constant criterion, variable-criterion, and baseline segments respectively; patient #2's heart rate averaged 96, 82, and 78 bpm during baseline, variable-criterion, and baseline segments respectively
Surwit & Shapiro, 1977	8 hypertensive patients under age 60	Auditory and visual feedback of simultaneous changes in median systolic blood pressure and heart rate during 8, 60 to 90 min sessions in 5 weeks; each session included 20, one-min trials alternated with 10 second rests	Medication	Data Unavailable	No significant change in median systolic pressure across sessions or at follow-up; baseline levels averaged 142 mmHg systolic and 90 mmHg diastolic and were reduced to 139 mmHg and 84 mmHg respectively at follow-up; heart rate decreased by 3 bpm

TABLE 15-1 Summary of Biofeedback Treatments for Cardiovascular Disorders

Study	Patients	Biofeedback Treatment	Other Treatment	Symptoms	Results Biological Function
Surwit, Shapiro, & Good, 1978	18 adult hypertensive patients; age range 27 to 59	Auditory and visual feedback of either EMG activity from the frontalis and forearm extensor areas, or integrated (patterned) heart rate and median systolic blood pressure during eight; 60 to 90 min sessions held twice weekly	Medication and home practice	Data Unavailable	Systolic pressure in the cardiovascular group averaged 137 mmHg during the baseline and 139 mmHg during the training sessions; EMG group averaged 137 mmHg and 140 mmHg respectively; within-session (first-to-last-trial) changes decreased from 139 mmHg to 128 mmHg for the cardiovascular group and from 142 mmHg to 139 mmHg for the EMG group
Walsh, Dale, & Anderson, 1977	9 female, 15 male hypertensive patients; age range 24 to 69	In phase one, 7 three-min trials to reduce pulse transit time with auditory and visual feedback once weekly for 5 weeks; in phase two, 90-min session once weekly for 5 weeks	Medication for some; progressive relaxation in study two	Data Unavailable	Blood pressure (systolic/diastolic) averaged 147/94, 133/84, 135/87, and 133/86, and 135/84 mmHg during the first session of phase one, last session of phase two, 3-month follow-up, and 12-month follow-up respectively; heart and respiration rates did not change significantly across the sessions
Weiss & Engel, 1973	5 males, 3 females with premature ventricular contractions	Visual feedback for heart rate speeding, slowing, alternate speeding and slowing, and maintenance within specified limits during approximately 10, 10, 10, and 11 sessions respectively; each session included 34 min of feedback	Medication and hospitalization	Some patients became aware of heart beat abnormalities as they occurred in the environment	Frequency of PVC's averaged 12.9, 11.9, 9.9, 5.1, 4.8, and 5.9/min during pretreatment, speeding, slowing, alternate speeding and slowing, maintenance within specified range, and follow-up periods, respectively; 5 patients showed a decrease in PVC's associated with feedback training

individual is erect is substantial. The mean arterial pressure at the wrist (with the hand held over the head) is about 44 mm Hg, while that at the ankle is about 170 mm Hg (Rushmer 1976). The fact that the head is above the heart means that the heart must work particularly hard to send blood to the head. When an individual changes posture, from lying down to standing up, there is usually an automatic change in blood pressure to compensate for change in the relative position of the head and the heart. If this change does not take place, the blood flow to the head may be reduced to such an extent that the brain cells do not receive adequate circulation.

TREATMENT

Case Study

The patient was a young man with a spinal cord lesion at T_3 (Brucker & Ince 1977). When he attempted to stand, diastolic blood pressure decreased sharply to less than 30 mm Hg, and syncope developed. He was trained to increase and decrease blood pressure during biofeedback sessions which lasted one hour each and took place four times a week. One to three training trials, each five minutes long were separated by three minutes of rest. Feedback was provided verbally by telling the patient his blood pressure every 60 seconds during the training trials. One month later he had four more trials. Thereafter, he practiced increasing blood pressure at home prior to and during periods of standing and walking. Increases in systolic and diastolic blood pressure averaged six mm Hg during the first two sessions and 17 mm Hg during the last two. One month later, he increased both systolic and diastolic pressure by 48 mm Hg. In the ninth training session, when he stood up from a sitting position without attempting to raise blood pressure, systolic pressure fell from 110 mm Hg to 50 mm Hg within two minutes. When he raised systolic pressure from 110 mm Hg to 145 mm Hg prior to standing, systolic pressure remained above 88 mm Hg after five minutes of standing. Following additional practice, he was able to stand and walk for periods of up to four hours while maintaining normal blood pressure.

CLINICAL PROGRAM

HYPERTENSION

Changes in median systolic blood pressure are used for feedback. An inflatable pressure cuff is wrapped around the upper part of the client's arm as described earlier in this chapter. The pressure cuff is connected to an air pump. A brachial artery microphone is inserted in the pressure cuff which is wrapped around the client's arm. The pressure cuff is then inflated to a point at which only half of the heartbeats are followed by a Korotkoff sound. This marks the point of median systolic blood pressure. The cuff pressure is held constant during a trial lasting about 50 heartbeats or about 60 to 90 seconds. The client is provided with feedback of increases or decreases in median systolic pressure with each beat of the heart. This is accomplished by informing the client whether each beat was followed by a Korotkoff sound. Appearance of Korotkoff sounds indicate that blood pressure has risen while the disappearance of Korotkoff sounds indicate that blood pressure has decreased. Cuff pressure should be raised by about 2 mm Hg after each trial during which Korotkoff sounds followed 75% of the heartbeats and should be lowered by about 2 mm Hg following trials during which Korotkoff sounds occurred after fewer than 25% of the heartbeats.

Each session should last about 45 minutes with up to 20 trials lasting about 50 heartbeats. A few short breaks may be interspersed with the trials. Sessions can be scheduled about three times weekly in the early stages of training and about one or two times weekly in the later stages. Home practice of the technique should be included for about 20 minutes, twice each day.

CARDIAC ARRHYTHMIAS

The procedure as used by Engel and described earlier is appropriate. The heart rate itself is used for feedback. The R wave of the EKG provides a sufficient amplitude signal for feedback purposes. Surface electrodes are attached to the skin, one about the heart, one below the heart, and one for a ground. Of the other two electrodes which will be used for the actual recording of the signal, one should be placed on the right side of the body and one on the left side.

The client is trained to speed and slow heart rate by using feedback about heart rate. Treatment sessions are about one hour long, with baseline recording and several periods of training to control heart rate. As heart rate control is learned, the effect of changing heart rate on cardiac abnormalities can be assessed. Once an optimal range or direction of change is found, the client is trained to control the heart within the appropriate limits.

GLOSSARY

Here are a set of technical terms used throughout the book. Each one is followed by a brief definition and then the chapter number (and sometimes a figure number) in which the term is first discussed.

ACTION POTENTIAL: The change in membrane potential that is responsible for transmission of nerve impulse in an axon. Chap. 4, Fig. 4–1.

ANALOGUE FEEDBACK: Feedback that has many states; it changes in proportion to the state of the biological system. Chap. 2, Fig. 2–3.

APPETITIVE CONDITIONING: Classical conditioning procedures that use a desirable event for the unconditioned stimulus. Chap. 3.

ARRHYTHMIA: An abnormal rhythm, particularly of the heart. Chap. 15.

ATOPIC ASTHMA: Asthma associated with allergies. Chap. 11.

ATRIOVENTRICULAR NODE: One of the nodes of the heart; it is responsible for organization of the heart beat. Chap. 4.

ATROPINE: A drug that blocks the parasympathetic nervous system. It produces bronchodilation, reducing the symptoms of an asthmatic attack (Chap. 11), and blocks the vagus nerve, increasing the heart rate (Chap. 15).

ATROPINE: A drug that produces bronchodilation and reduces the symptoms of an asthmatic attack. Chap. 11.

AUTOGENIC TRAINING: A procedure designed to produce relaxation. Chap. 7, Table 7–6.

AUTONOMIC NERVOUS SYSTEM: The portion of the nervous system connected to the viscera. Chap. 4, Fig. 4–2.

AUTOREGULATION: The homeostatic control of blood flow in the brain. Chap. 9.

AVERSIVE CONDITIONING: Classical conditioning procedures that use an undesirable event for the unconditioned stimulus. Chap. 3.

AXON: An extension of a nerve cell specialized for transmission. Chap. 4, Fig. 4–1.

BELL'S PALSY: Unilateral facial paralysis. Chap. 13.

BICEPS: Muscles that bring the arm towards the body. Chap. 4.

BIDIRECTIONAL DISCRIMINATED CONTROL DESIGN: An experimental procedure that demonstrates voluntary control of an autonomic function. Chap. 5, Table 5-1.

BILATERAL: On both sides. Chap. 8.

BINARY FEEDBACK: Feedback that has only two states. Chap. 2, Fig. 2-3.

BLEPHAROSPASM: Involuntary blinking of the eyes. Chap. 13

BRONCHOCONSTRICTION: Contraction of the bronchioles of the lungs, impairing respiration. Chap. 11.

BROCHODILATION: Expansion of the bronchioles of the lungs, allowing better respiration. Chap. 11.

CARBACHOL: A drug that produces bronchoconstriction and makes the symptoms of an asthmatic attack worse. Chap. 11.

CLASSIC MIGRAINE: A migraine headache preceded by a prodrome. Chap. 9.

CLEARANCE RATE: The rate at which radioactivity leaves the brain, a measure of intracranial blood flow. Chap. 9.

CLUSTER HEADACHE: A variation of migraine headaches in which the periods of head pain are relatively short but occur in groups. Chap. 9.

CONDITIONED RESPONSE: The response produced by a conditioned stimulus in a classical conditioning procedure. Chap. 3.

CONDITIONED STIMULUS: The stimulus that produces a response similar to that following an unconditioned stimulus because of association with the unconditioned stimulus in a classical conditioning procedure. Chap. 3.

COMMON MIGRAINE: A migraine headache not preceded by a prodrome. Chap. 9.

COMPLICATED MIGRAINE: A migraine headache in which neurological symptoms occur during periods other than just the prodrome. Chap. 9.

CONSTANT CUFF METHOD: An automated means of recording blood pressure changes. Chap. 6.

CONTINGENCY: The relationship between a response and a reinforcer. Chap. 3.

CORRELATIONAL EXPERIMENT: A procedure that trains an individual to control an autonomic function while monitoring other autonomic functions at the same time. Chap. 5.

CORRECT FEEDBACK: Information about the state of a biological function that accurately reflects the state of that function and is therapeutically appropriate. Chap. 1.

COUNTERCONDITIONING: The elimination of a phobia through classical conditioning of relaxation to the stimulus that initially elicited the phobia. Chap. 3.

CYANOSIS: Blue color, the second stage of Raynaud's attack. Chap. 10.

DELAY OF REINFORCEMENT: The period of time between the response and the reinforcement. Chap. 3.

DESENSITIZATION: The elimination of a phobia through classical conditioning of relaxation to the stimulus that initially elicited the phobia. Chap. 3.

DIASTOLIC BLOOD PRESSURE: The blood pressure at diastole, when the heart is relaxed. Chap. 6.

DIFFERENTIATION: A procedure that trains a person to control two or more autonomic functions simultaneously. Chap. 5.

DIRECT MEDIATION: A process that occurs in a middle position between the controller and the function being controlled. Chap. 5., Fig. 5–1.

DISSOCIATIVE CONDITIONING: A procedure that trains a person to control two or more autonomic functions simultaneously. Chap. 5.

DORSIFLEXION: Movement of the foot in an upward direction. Chap. 13.

DUODENAL ULCER: An ulcer located in the duodenum just below the pylorus. Chap. 14.

DYPEPSIA: Indigestion. Chap. 14.

ECTOPIC: Out of place; an ectopic focus of stimulation in the heart produces an abnormal heart beat. Chap. 15.

EKG: Electrocardiogram, a recording of the heart's activity. Chap. 6, Fig. 6–4.

ELECTROCARDIOGRAM: A recording of the heart's activity. Chap. 6, Fig. 6–4.

ELECTROENCEPHALOGRAM: A recording of the electrical activity of the brain. Chap. 6, Fig. 6–5.

ELECTROMYOGRAM: The recording of the electrical activity of the muscles. Chap. 6, Fig. 6–3.

EMG: Electromyogram, the recording of the electrical activity of the muscles. Chap. 6, Fig. 6–3.

ERGOTAMINE: A vasoconstricting drug used to treat migraine headaches. Chap. 9.

ESSENTIAL DISEASE: One that does not have an obvious organic basis, as in essential epilepsy. Chap. 12.

ESSENTIAL HYPERTENSION: Hypertension that remains high and has no obvious organic basis. Chap. 15.

EVOKED EPILEPTIC SEIZURES: Epileptic seizures that occur in response to a particular stimulus. Chap. 11.

EXCITATORY POSTSYNAPTIC POTENTIAL: A change in the membrane potential that takes place in the dendrites of a nerve cell and makes the cell more likely to produce an action potential. Chap. 4, Fig. 4–1.

EXTERNAL SPHINCTER: One of the sphincters involved in defecation. Chap. 14, Fig. 14–1.

EXTINCTION: The procedure in which responses are no longer followed by reinforcement. Chap. 3.

EXTRINSIC ASTHMA: Asthma resulting from specific substances. Chap. 11.

FECAL INCONTINENCE: The inability to voluntarily control defecation. Chap. 14.

FEEDBACK: Information about the state of a system given to the controller of that system in order to improve the control of the system. Chap. 2, Fig. 2–2.

FEV_1: Forced expiratory volume in one second; the amount of air that can be exhaled in one second beginning with a full inspiration Chap. 11, Fig. 11–1.

FIBRILLATION: An excessively rapid heart beat. Chap. 15.

FOOT DROP: The difficulty a person has raising the toes of the foot when walking, due to a stroke. Chap. 13.

FORCED EXPIRATORY VOLUME IN ONE SECOND: The volume of air that can be exhaled in one second beginning with a full inspiration. Chap. 11, Fig. 11–1.

FRONTALIS MUSCLE: A muscle in the forehead. Chap. 4, Fig. 4–4.

GASTRIC ULCER: An ulcer located in the stomach just above the pylorus. Chap. 14.

GENERALIZATION GRADIENT: The tendency of a response conditioned to one stimulus to occur following similar stimuli. Chap. 3.

GRAND MAL SEIZURE: An epileptic seizure that involves loss of consciousness and produces major physical convulsions. Chap. 12.

GSR: Galvinc skin resistance (or response). Chap. 3.

HEMI: Half, as in hemiparesis, involving one half of the body. Chap. 13.

HOMEOSTATIC MECHANISM: A mechanism that uses negative feedback to maintain the same state. Chap. 2, Fig. 2–4.

HYPERTENSION: Excessive blood pressure. Chap. 15.

HYPERTROPHY: An increase in the size of tissue, as in excessively large and strong muscles. Chap. 13.

HZ: Hertz, or cycles per second. Chap. 4.

IDIOPATHIC: A disease that appears with no obvious organic cause, as in idiopathic hypertension. Chap. 15.

INCORRECT FEEDBACK: Uncorrelated feedback or therapeutically inappropriate feedback. Chap. 1.

INDIRECT MEDIATION: A process that the controller must manipulate in order to control the system. Chap. 5, Fig. 5–1.

INDWELLING ELECTRODES: Those that are inserted into a muscle in order to record from it. Chap. 6.

INHIBITORY POSTSYNAPTIC POTENTIAL: A change in the membrane potential of a nerve cell that makes the cell less likely to produce an action potential. Chap. 4, Fig. 4–1.

INTERNAL SPHINCTER: One of the sphincters in the rectosphincteric reflex; it is involved in defecation. Chap. 14, Fig. 14–1.

INTERVENTION EXPERIMENT: A procedure that trains an individual to control one autonomic function while other autonomic functions are also controlled, either by drugs or by some other means. Chap. 5.

INTRACTABLE ASTHMA: Asthmatic symptoms that persist in between attacks. Chap. 11.

INTRINSIC ASTHMA: Asthma that does not result from specific substances. Chap. 11.

INVASIVE RECORDING PROCEDURES: Those that require surgery to record from the biological system. Chap. 6.

ISCHEMIA: Inadequate blood supply. Chap. 13.

ISOPROTERENOL: A bronchodilating drug used to treat asthma. Chap. 11.

ISUPREL: Isoproterenol, a bronchodilating drug used to treat asthma. Chap. 11.

KOROTKOFF SOUNDS The sound heard through a stethoscope when recording blood pressure. Chap. 6.

LABILE HYPERTENSION: Hypertension that is generally high, but fluctuates, returning to normal levels. Chap. 15.

LEVARTERENOL: A drug that produces vasoconstriction. Chap. 8.

LOCALIZATION OF FUNCTION: The hypothesis that different areas of the brain are responsible for different behavioral functions. Chap. 4.

MEDIATION: The processes between the individual doing the controlling and the system being controlled. Chap. 5, Fig. 5–1.

MECHOLYL: A drug that produces bronchoconstriction and makes the symptoms of an asthmatic attack worse.

MIGRAINE: Half-headed; a headache in which the head pain usually begins on one side of the head. Chap. 9.

MIGRAINEUR: A person who has migraine headaches. Chap. 9.

MYELOMENINGOCELE: A failure of the spinal cord to fuse with the result that the nervous system protrudes from the spinal cord. Chap. 14.

NASOGASTRIC TUBE: A tube inserted through the nose into the stomach; it is used for measuring the acid content of the stomach. Chap. 14.

NEGATIVE FEEDBACK: The type of control present in a homeostatic mechanism to maintain the same state. Chap. 2, Fig. 2–4.

NEGATIVE REINFORCEMENT: The presentation of a negative reinforcer following a response. Chap. 3, Table 3–1.

NEGATIVE REINFORCERS: Events that are undesireable; these decrease the probability of a response that preceded them. Chap. 3.

NEGATIVE RESPONDERS: Children who do not list emotional factors as being important precipitators of their asthmatic attacks. Chap. 11.

NEURON: A nerve cell. Chap. 4, Fig. 4–1.

NONATOPIC ASTHMA: Asthmatic symptoms that occur without demonstrable allergies. Chap. 11.

NONINVASIVE RECORDING PROCEDURES: Those that can be obtained from outside the individual's body and do not require surgery. Chap. 6.

OCCUPATIONAL ASTHMA: Asthma resulting from substances associated with specific occupations. Chap. 11.

OXYNTIC CELL: A cell in the fundic area of the stomach; it secretes acid. Chap. 14.

PALLOR: White color, the first stage of a Raynaud's attack. Chap. 10.

PANIC-FEAR: A measure of the reaction of asthmatic patients to their asthmatic attacks. Chap. 11.

PARALYSIS: Inability to move a limb. Chap. 13.

PARASYMPATHETIC NERVOUS SYSTEM: Part of the autonomic nervous system. Chap. 4, Fig. 4–2.

PARENTECTOMY: Removal of the parents from a child, a factor often helping to reduce asthmatic attacks. Chap. 11.

PARESIS: Difficulty in moving a limb. Chap. 13.

PARIETAL CELL: A cell in the fundic area of the stomach; it secretes acid. Chap. 14.

PEAK FLOW: The greatest flow of air from the lungs beginning with a full inspiration. Chap. 11.

PETIT MAL SEIZURE: A seizure that may be accompanied by some loss of consciousness and some motor convulsions, but these are less than those found in a grand mal seizure. Chap. 11.

PHOTOPHOBIA: Desire to avoid light; one of the symptoms of migraine headaches. Chap. 9.

PHOTOPLETHYSMOGRAPH: A device for measuring changes in the volume of a finger to record blood flow. Chap. 6, Fig. 6–6.

PLACEBO: An experimental procedure to control for the expectations of the individual about the effects of treatment. Chap. 8.

POSITIVE REINFORCEMENT: The presentation of a positive reinforcer following a response. Chap. 3, Table 3–1.

POSITIVE REINFORCERS: Events that are desireable; these increase the probability of a response that preceded them. Chap. 3.

POSITIVE RESPONDERS: Children who list emotional factors as being important precipitators of their asthmatic attacks. Chap. 11.

PQRST COMPLEX: The shape of the electrocardiogram reflecting the heart beat. Chap. 4.

PREMATURE VENTRICULAR CONTRACTION: A type of cardiac arrhythmia in which the ventricle contracts too early in the cardiac cycle. Chap. 15 .

PRIMARY DISEASE: A disease or set of symptoms that occurs for no obvious organic reason, as in primary Raynaud's disease. Chap. 10.

PRIMARY REINFORCERS: Events which have their influence over behavior because their desireable or undesireable characteristics are inherent in them. Chap. 3.

PRODROME: The neurological signs that precede a classic migraine headache due to excessive vasoconstriction of the blood supply to the brain. Chap. 9.

PROGRESSIVE RELAXATION: A procedure designed to produce relaxation. Chap. 7.

PULSE WAVE AMPLITUDE: The amplitude of the bulge in an artery as the blood is forced through it. Chap. 9.

PUNISHMENT: The removal of a positive reinforcer or the presentation of a negative reinforcer following a response. Chap. 3, Table 3–1.

PVC. Premature ventricular contraction; a type of cardiac arrhythmia in which the ventricle contracts too early in the cardiac cycle. Chap. 15.

PYLORUS: The part of the gastrointestinal system separating the stomach and the duodenum. Chap. 14.

QUADRI-: Involving all four limbs, as in quadriparesis Chap. 13.

RAYNAUD'S DISEASE: A set of symptoms with the primary problem being cold hands and feet. Chap. 10.

rCBF: Regional cerebral blood flow: the rate of blood flow through a given area of the brain. Chap. 9.

RECTOSPHINCTERIC REFLEX: The stimulus for this reflex is distension of the rectum, the response is relaxation of the internal sphincter and contraction of the external sphincter. Chap. 14, Fig. 14–1.

REFERENCE INPUT: The desired state of a system in a control systems analysis. Chap. 2.

REGIONAL CEREBRAL BLOOD FLOW: The rate of flood flow through a given area of the brain. Chap. 9.

REINFORCERS: Events following a response and influencing the probability of that response being made on subsequent occasions. Chap. 3.

RELAXATION RESPONSE: A procedure used to produce relaxation. Chap. 7, Table 7–7.

RESPONSE AMPLITUDE: The size of a response. Chap. 3.

RESPONSE FREQUENCE: The number of responses in a particular period of time. Chap. 3.

RESPONSE LATENCY: The length of time between the beginning of a trial and the occurrence of a response. Chap. 3.

RESPONSE PROBABILITY: The probability that an individual will make a response when given the opportunity to do so. Chap. 3.

RESPONSE RATE: The number of responses in a particular period of time Chap. 3.

RESPONSE SPEED: The length of time between the start of a response and its completion. Chap. 3.

RESPONSE STRENGTH: Measures of probability, rate, latency, speed, and amplitude of a response; an intervening variable that describes how likely an individual is to make that response. Chap. 3.

ROLANDIC CORTEX: The part of the brain from which sensorimotor rhythm is recorded and information obtained for the feedback for treatment of epileptics. Chap. 12.

RUBOR: Red color, the third stage of a Raynaud's attack. Chap. 10.

SECONDARY DISEASE: A disease or set of symptoms that occurs as a result of some organic pathology, as in secondary Raynaud's disease. Chap. 10.

SECONDARY REINFORCERS: Events that have their influence over behavior because their desirable or undesirable characteristics have developed through learning. Chap. 3.

SENSORIMOTOR RHYTHM: 12 to 14 Hz activity recorded from the Rolandic cortex, increases of which are associated with decreases in the frequency of epileptic attacks. Chap. 12.

SET POINT: The desired state of a system in a control systems analysis. Chap. 2, Fig. 2-2.

SHAPING: The procedure whereby the desired response is gradually developed. Chap. 3.

SIGNAL-TO-NOISE RATIO: The ratio of the relative amplitude of the desired electrical activity (the signal) to the undesired electrical activity (the noise) expressed in decibels. Chap. 6.

SINOATRIAL NODE: One of the nodes of the heart; it is responsible for organization of the heart beat. Chap. 4.

SLIDING CRITERION: The criterion used for feedback is changed depending on previous success. Chap. 7.

SMR: Sensorimotor rhythm: 12 to 14 Hz activity recorded from the Rolandic cortex, increases of which are associated with decreases in the frequency of epileptic attacks. Chap. 12.

SPASMODIC TORTICOLLIS: Turning of the head towards one side. Chap. 13.

SPLENIUS MUSCLE: Turns head to one side. Chap. 4, Fig. 4-4.

STATUS ASTHMATICUS: A severe asthmatic attack requiring hospitalization. Chap. 11.

STERNOCLEIDOMASTOID MUSCLE: Turns head to one side. Chap. 4, Fig. 4-4.

STIMULUS HIERARCHY: A generalization gradient of the amount of fear appearing in response to stimuli similar to the one responsible for a phobia. Chap. 3.

SURFACE ELECTRODES: Those that are placed on the surface of the skin in order to record from the muscles underneath them. Chap. 6.

SYMPATHETIC NERVOUS SYSTEM: Part of the autonomic nervous system. Chap. 4, Fig. 4-2.

SYNAPSE: The gap between two cells where chemical transmission takes place. Chap. 4, Fig. 4-1.

SYSTOLIC BLOOD PRESSURE: The blood pressure at systole, when the heart contracts. Chap. 6.

TACHYCARDIA: A heart beat that is too rapid. Chap. 15.

TEMPORAL ARTERY: The artery on the side of the head supplying the scalp; it lies along side of the forehead. Chap. 9.

TEMPOROMANDIBULAR JOINT: The joint between the temporal and mandibular bones; it is primarily involved in chewing. Chap. 13, Fig. 13-1.

THERAPEUTICALLY INCORRECT FEEDBACK: Information about the state of the biological function that accurately reflects the state of that function, but which is used to train the person to change the function in a direction opposite to that which will reduce the symptoms. Chap. 1.

THERMISTOR: A transducer placed on the surface of the skin to record skin temperature. Chap. 6.

TRICEPS: Muscles that extend the arm from the body. Chap. 4, Fig. 4–5.

TRAPEZIUS MUSCLE: Turns head to one side. Chap. 4, Fig. 4–4.

TYRAMINE: A vasoconstricting substance in foods thought to be related to migraine headaches. Chap. 9.

ULCER: A small area of the digestive tract which has been destroyed. Chap. 14.

UNCONDITIONED RESPONSE: The response produced by an unconditioned stimulus in a classical conditioning procedure. Chap. 3.

UNCONDITIONED STIMULUS: A stimulus that naturally elicits a response in a classical conditioning procedure. Chap. 3.

UNCORRELATED FEEDBACK: Information about the state of the biological function that does not reflect the state of that function. Chap. 1.

UNILATERAL: On one side.

VAGUS NERVE: The tenth cranial nerve; part of the parasympathetic nervous system. Chap. 4, figs. 4–2, 4–3.

VC: Vital capacity, the volume of air that can be exhaled beginning with a full inspiration. Chap. 11. Fig. 11–1.

VASOCONSTRICTION: Constriction of the blood vesels causing less blood to flow through them. Chap. 9.

VASODILATION: Expansion of the blood vessels allowing more blood to flow through them. Chap. 9.

VENTRICULAR PAROXYSMAL TACHYCARDIA: A cardiac arrhythmia in which the heart beats too rapidly. Chap. 15.

VITAL CAPACITY: The volume of air measured in cubic centimeters that can be exhaled from a full inspiration. Chap. 11, Fig. 11–1.

VOLUNTARY RESPONSE: A response that is systematically influenced by instructions from an individual other than the one making the response. Chap. 5.

WOLFF-PARKINSON-WHITE SYNDROME: A type of cardiac arrhythmia. Chap. 15.

REFERENCES

ABBASY, A. S., FAHMY, M. S., & KANTOUSH, M. M. 1967. The adrenal cortical gluco-corticoid function in asthmatic children. *Acta Paediatrica Scandinavica, 56,* 593–600.

ABRAMSON, D. I., 1974. *Vascular Disorders of the Extremeties (2nd. ed.).* Harper & Row Publishers, Inc., New York.

Ad Hoc Committee on Classification of Headache. 1962. *Journal of the American Medical Association, 179,* 717–718.

ADOLPH, E. F. 1967. The Heart's Pacemaker. *Scientific American, 216* (3), 32–37.

ALDERMAN, M. M. 1975. Disorders of the temporomandibular joint and related structures. In M. A. Lynch (Ed.), *Burkett's oral medicine: Diagnosis and treatment* (7th ed.). J. P. Lippincott Co., Philadelphia, pp. 235–274.

ALLEN, E. V., & BROWN, G. E. 1932a. Raynaud's disease: A critical review of minimal requisites for diagnosis. *American Journal of the Medical Sciences, 183,* 187–200.

ALLEN, E. V., & BROWN, G. E. 1932b. Raynaud's disease. A clinical study of one hundred and forty-seven cases. *Journal of the American Medical Association, 99,* 1472–1478.

ALVA, J., MENDELOFF, A. I., & SCHUSTER, M. M. 1967. Reflex and electromyographic abnormalities associated with fecal incontinence. *Gastroenterology, 53,* 101–106.

AMATO, A., HERMSMEYER, C. A., & KLEINMAN, K. M. 1973. Use of electromyographic feedback to increase inhibitory control of spastic muscles. *Physical Therapy, 53,* 1063–1066.

American Thoracic Society. A statement by the Committee on Diagnostic Standards for Nontuberculous Respiratory Diseases. 1962. Definitions and classification of chronic bronchitis, asthma, and pulmonary emphysema. *American Review of Respiratory Diseases, 85,* 762–768.

ANDERSON, D. E., & BRADY, J. V. 1971. Preavoidance blood pressure elevations accompanied by heart rate decreases in the dog. *Science, 172,* 595–597.

ANDERSON, D. E., & BRADY, J. V. 1972. Differential preparatory cardiovascular responses to aversive and appetitive behavioral conditioning. *Conditional Reflex, 7,* 82–96.

ANDREWS, J. M. 1964. Neuromuscular re-education of the hemiplegic with the aid of the electromyograph. *Archives of Physical Medicine and Rehabilitation, 45,* 530–532.

ANDREYCHUK, T., & SKRIVER, C. 1975. Hypnosis and biofeedback in the treatment of migraine headache. *The International Journal of Clinical and Experimental Hypnosis, 23,* 172–183.

ANLIKER, J. 1977. Biofeedback from the perspectives of cybernetics and systems science. In J. Beatty and H. Legewie (Eds.), *Biofeedback and behavior.* Plenum Publishing Corporation, New York, pp. 21–45.

ANREP, G. V. 1960. *Conditioned reflexes: An investigation of the physiological activity of the cerebral cortex by I. P. Pavlov.* Dover Publications, Inc., New York.

APPENZELLER, O. 1969. Vasomotor function in migraine. *Headache, 9,* 147–155.

ATKINSON, R. A. 1976. Hemicrania and Raynaud's phenomenon; Manifestations of the same disease? *Headache, 16,* 1–3.

BAKAL, D. A. 1979. *Psychology and medicine. Psychobiological dimensions of health and illness.* Springer Publishing Company, Inc., New York.

BAKAL, D. A., & KAGANOV, J. A. 1976. A simple method for self-observation of headache frequency, intensity, and location. *Headache, 16,* 123–124.

BAKAL, D. A., & KAGANOV, J. A. 1977. Muscle contraction and migraine headache: Psychophysiologic comparison. *Headache, 17,* 208–215.

BAKER, M., REGENOS, E., WOLF, S. L., & BASMAJIAN, J. V. 1977. Developing strategies for biofeedback. Applications in neurologically handicapped patients. *Physical Therapy, 57,* 402–408.

BANNISTER, R. 1978. *Brain's clinical neurology* (5th ed.). Oxford University Press, London.

BARCROFT, H., & WALKER, A. J. 1949. Return of tone in blood-vessels of the upper limb after sympathectomy. *Lancet, 1,* 1035–1039.

BARENSTEN, R. I., & LOCKARD, J. S. 1969. Behavioral experimental epilepsy in monkeys II. Video-tape control gate for detection and recording of motor seizures. *Electroencephalography and Clinical Neurophysiology, 27,* 89–92.

BASMAJIAN, J. V. 1976. Facts vs. myths in EMG biofeedback. *Biofeedback and Self-Regulation, 1,* 369–371. (Editorial)

BASMAJIAN, J. V. 1978. *Muscles alive: Their functions revealed by electromyography* (4th ed.). The Williams & Wilkins Co., Baltimore.

BASMAJIAN, J. V. (ed.). 1979. *Biofeedback—Principles and practice for clinicians.* The Williams & Wilkins Co., Baltimore.

BASMAJIAN, J. V., KUKULKA, C. G., NARAYAN, M. G., & TAKEBE, K. 1975. Biofeedback treatment of foot-drop after stroke compared with standard rehabilitation technique: Effects on voluntary control and strength. *Archives of Physical Medicine and Rehabilitation, 56,* 231–236.

BATES, D. V., MACKLEM, P. T., & CHRISTIE, R. V. 1971. *Respiratory function in disease: An introduction to the integrated study of the lung.* W. B. Saunders Company, Philadelphia.

BEARY, F., & BENSON, H. 1974. A simple psychophysiologic technique which elicits the hypometabolic changes of the relaxation response. *Psychosomatic Medicine, 36,* 115–120.

BELBER, J. P. 1973. Gastroscopy and duodenoscopy. In M. H. Sleisenger & J. S. Fordtran (Eds.), *Gastrointestinal disease: Pathophysiology, diagnosis, management.* W. B. Saunders Company, Philadelphia, pp. 521–535.

BELBER, J. P. 1979. Gastroscopy and duodenoscopy. In M. H. Sleisenger & J. S. Fordtran (Eds.), *Gastrointestinal disease: Pathophysiology, diagnosis, management* (2nd. ed.). W. B. Saunders Company, Philadelphia, pp. 691–713.

BELLET, S. 1972. *Essentials of cardiac arrythmias. Diagnosis and management.* W. B. Saunders Company, Philadelphia.

BENNETT, D. R. 1963. Sleep deprivation and major motor convulsions. *Neurology, 13,* 953–958.

BENSON, H. 1975. *The relaxation response.* William Morrow & Company, Inc., New York.

BENSON, H., ROSNER, B. A., MARZETTA, B. R., & KLEMCHUK, H. M. 1974. Decreased blood-pressure in pharmacologically treated hypertensive patients who regularly elicited the relaxation response. *Lancet, 1,* 289–291.

BENSON, H., SHAPIRO, D., TURSKY, B., & SCHWARTZ, G. E. 1971. Decreased systolic blood pressure through operant conditioning techniques in patients with essential hypertension. *Science, 173,* 740–742.

BENTLEY, J. 1975. Asthmatic children away from home: A comparative psychological study. *Journal of Asthma Research, 13,* 17–25.

BERGAMINI, L., BERGAMASCO, B., BENNA, P., & GILLI, M. 1977. Acquired etiological factors in 1,785 epileptic subjects: Clinical-anamnestic research. *Epilpesia, 18,* 437–444.

BERNSTEIN, D. A., & BORKOVEC, T. D. 1973. *Progressive relaxation training: A manual for the helping professions.* Research Press, Chicago.

BICKFORD, R. G., & KLASS, D. W. 1969. Sensory precipitation and reflex mechanisms. In H. H. Jasper, A. A. Ward Jr., & A. Pope (Eds.), *Basic mechanisms of the epilepsies.* Little, Brown & Company, Boston, pp. 543–564.

BILODEAU, E. A. 1966. *Acquisition of skill.* Academic Press, Inc., New York.

BILODEAU, E. A. (Ed.). 1969. *Principles of skill acquisition.* Academic Press, Inc., New York.

BIRK, L. 1973. Biofeedback—Furor therapeuticus. In L. Birk (Ed.), *Biofeedback: Behavioral medicine.* Grune and Stratton, Inc., New York, pp. 1–4.

BLACK, A. H. 1967. Operant conditioning of heart rate under curare. *Technical Report No. 12,* Department of Psychology, McMaster University, Hamilton, Ontario.

BLACK, A. H. 1974. Operant autonomic conditioning: The analysis of response mechanisms. In P. A. Obrist, A. H. Black, J. Brener, & L. V. DiCara (Eds.), *Cardiovascular psychophysiology: Current issues in response mechanisms, biofeedback, and methodology.* Aldine Publishing Company, Chicago, pp. 229–250.

BLACK, A. H., COTT, A., & PAVLOSKI, R. 1977. The operant learning theory approach to biofeedback training. In G. E. Schwartz and J. Beatty (Eds.), *Biofeedback theory and research.* Academic Press, Inc., New York, pp. 89–127.

BLANCHARD, E. B., & ABEL, G. G. 1976. An experimental case study of the biofeedback treatment of a rape-induced psychophysiological cardiovascular disorder. *Behavior Therapy, 7,* 113–119.

BLANCHARD, E. B., & HAYNES, M. R. 1975. Biofeedback treatment of a case of Raynaud's disease. *Journal of Behavior Therapy and Experimental Psychiatry, 6,* 230–234.

BLANCHARD, E. B., THEOBALD, D. E., WILLIAMSON, D. A., SILVER, B. V., & BROWN, D. A. 1978. Temperature biofeedback in the treatment of migraine headaches. *Archives of General Psychiatry, 35,* 581–588.

BLANCHARD, E. B., & YOUNG, L. D. 1974. Clinical applications of biofeedback training: A review of evidence. *Archives of General Psychiatry, 30,* 573–589.

BLANCHARD, E. B., YOUNG, L. D., & HAYNES, M. R. 1975. A simple feedback system for the treatment of elevated blood pressure. *Behavior Therapy, 6,* 241–245.

BLAU, J. N., & CUMMINGS, J. N. 1966. Method of precipitating and preventing some migraine attacks. *British Medical Journal, 2,* 1242–1243.

BLAU, J. N., & PYKE, D. A. 1970. Effect of diabetes on migraine. *Lancet, 2,* 241–243.

BLEECKER, E. R., & ENGEL, B. T. 1973a. Learned control of ventricular rate in patients with atrial fibrillation. *Psychosomatic Medicine, 35,* 161–175.

BLEECKER, E. R., & ENGEL, B. T. 1973b. Learned control of cardiac rate and cardiac conduction in the Wolff-Parkinson-White Syndrome. *New England Journal of Medicine, 288,* 560–562.

Bockus, H. L. 1974a. Part I: Clinical and diagnostic aspects of uncomplicated peptic ulcer. In H. L. Bockus (Ed.), *Gastroenterology*. W. B. Saunders Company, Philadelphia, pp. 619–649.

Bockus, H. L. 1974b. Part I. Management of uncomplicated peptic ulcer. In H. L. Bockus (Ed.), *Gastroenterology* (Vol. I, 3rd ed.). W. B. Saunders Company, Philadelphia, pp. 674–710.

Bocles, J. S. 1970. Status asthmaticus. *Medical Clinics of North America, 54,* (2), 493–509.

Booker, H. E., Rubow, R. T., & Coleman, P. J. 1969. Simplified feedback in neuromuscular retraining: An automated approach using electromyographic signals. *Archives of Physical Medicine and Rehabilitation, 50,* 621–625.

Bouhuys, A. 1974. *Breathing. Physiology, environment, and lung disease.* Grune and Stratton, Inc., New York.

Bowman, K. 1971. Effect of emotional stress on spasticity and rigidity. *Journal of Psychosomatic Research, 15,* 107–112.

Brazier, M. A. B. 1958. The development of concepts relating to the electrical activity of the brain. *Journal of Nervous and Mental Disease, 126,* 303–321.

Brener, J. 1977. Sensory and perceptual determinants of voluntary visceral control. In G. E. Schwartz & J. Beatty (Eds.), *Biofeedback theory and research.* Academic Press, Inc., New York, pp. 29–66.

Brener, J., Eissenberg, E., & Middaugh, S. 1974. Respiratory and somatomotor factors associated with operant conditioning of cardiovascular responses in curarized rats. In P. A. Obrist, A. H. Black, J. Brener, & L. V. DiCara (Eds.), *Cardiovascular psychophysiology,* Aldine Publishing Co., Chicago, pp. 251–275.

Brettschneider, L., Monafo, W., Osborn, D. P. 1965. Intestinal obstruction due to antacid gels. Complication of medical therapy for gastrointestinal bleeding. *Gastroenterology, 49,* 291–294.

Broadhurst, P. L. 1957. Emotionality and the Yerkes-Dodson law. *Journal of Experimental Psychology, 54,* 345–352.

Broder, I., Barlow, P. P., & Horton, R. J. M. 1962. The epidemiology of asthma and hay fever in a total community, Tecumseh, Michigan. I. Description of study and general findings. *The Journal of Allergy, 33,* 513–523.

Broder, I., Higgins, M. W., Mathews, K. P., & Keller, J. B. 1974. Epidemiology of asthma and allergic rhinitis in a total community, Tecumseh, Michigan, III. Second survey of the community. *The Journal of Allergy and Clinical Immunology, 53,* 127–138.

Brolund, J. W., & Schallow, J. R. 1976. The effects of reward on occipital alpha facilitation by biofeedback. *Psychophysiology, 13,* 236–241.

Brown, B. 1977. *Stress and the art of biofeedback.* Harper & Row Publishers, Inc., New York.

Brown, C. C. (Ed.). 1967. *Methods in psychophysiology.* The Williams & Wilkins Co., Baltimore.

Brown, C. C. 1972. Instruments in psychophysiology. In R. S. Greenfield & R. A. Sterbach (Eds.), *Handbook of psychophysiology.* Holt, Rinehart & Winston, Inc., New York, pp. 159–195.

Brucker, B. S., & Ince, L. P. 1977. Biofeedback as an experimental treatment for postural hypotension in a patient with a spinal cord lesion. *Archives of Physical Medicine and Rehabilitation, 58,* 49–53.

Brudny, J., Grynbaum, B. B., & Korein, J. 1974. Spasmodic torticollis: Treatment by feedback display of the EMG. *Archives of Physical Medicine and Rehabilitation, 55,* 403–408.

Brudny, J., Korein, J., Grynbaum, B. B., Friedmann, L. W., Weinstein, S., Sachs-Fran-

KEL, G., & BELANDRES, P. V. 1976. EMG feedback therapy: Review of treatment of 114 patients. *Archives of Physical Medicine and Rehabilitation, 57,* 55–61.

BRUDNY, J., KOREIN, J., LEVIDOW, L., GRYNBAUM, B. B., LIEBERMAN, A., & FREIDMANN, L. W. 1974. Sensory feedback therapy as a modality of treatment in central nervous system disorders of voluntary movement. *Neurology, 24,* 925–932.

BUDZYNSKI, T. 1978. Biofeedback in the treatment of muscle-contraction (tension) headache. *Biofeedback and Self-Regulation, 3,* 409–434.

BUDZYNSKI, T., STOYVA, J., & ADLER, C. 1970. Feedback-induced muscle relaxation: Application to tension headache. *Journal of Behavior Therapy and Experimental Psychiatry, 1,* 205–211.

BUDZYNSKI, T. H. 1973. Biofeedback procedures in the clinic. *Seminars in Psychiatry, 5,* 537–547.

BUDZYNSKI, T. H., STOYVA, J. M., ADLER, C. S., & MULLANEY, D. J. 1973. EMG biofeedback and tension headache: A controlled outcome study. *Psychosomatic Medicine, 35,* 484–496.

CABEZAS, G. A., GRAF, P. D., & NADEL, J. A. 1971. Sympathetic versus parasympathetic nervous regulation of airways in dogs. *Journal of Applied Physiology, 31,* 651–655.

CAMPBELL, B. A., & CHURCH, R. M. 1969. *Punishment and aversive behavior.* Meredith Corporation, New York.

CARD, W. I., & MARKS, I. N. 1960. The relationship between the acid output of the stomach following "maximal" histamine stimulation and the parietal cell mass. *Clinical Science, 19,* 147–163.

CARLSSON, S. G., & GALE, E. N. 1977. Biofeedback in the treatment of long-term temporomandibular joint pain. An outcome study. *Biofeedback and Self-Regulation, 2,* 161–171.

CARLSSON, S. G., GALE, E. N., & ÖHMAN, A. 1975. Treatment of temporomandibular joint syndrome with biofeedback training. *Journal of the American Dental Association, 91,* 602–605.

CAVENESS, W. F. 1955. Emotional and psychological factors in epilepsy. General clinical and neurological considerations. *American Journal of Psychiatry, 112,* 190–193.

CERULLI, M. A., NIKOOMANESH, P., & SCHUSTER, M. M. 1979. Progress in biofeedback conditioning for fecal incontinence. *Gastroenterology, 76,* 742–746.

CHESNEY, M. A., & SHELTON, J. L. 1976. A comparison of muscle relaxation and electromyogram biofeedback treatments for muscle contraction headache. *Journal of Behavior Therapy and Experimental Psychiatry, 7,* 221–225.

CHRISTENSEN, J. 1971. The controls of gastrointestinal movements: Some old and new views. *New England Journal of Medicine, 285,* 85–98.

Ciba Foundation Study Group No. 38. 1971. *Identification of asthma.* Churchill Livingstone, Edinburgh and London.

CIRIGNOTTA, F., MARCACCI, G., & LUGARESI, E. 1977. Epileptic seizures precipitated by eating. *Epilepsia, 18,* 445–449.

CLEELAND, C. S. 1973. Behavioral technics in the modification of spasmodic torticollis. *Neurology, 23,* 1241–1247.

CLIFTON, R. K. 1974. Cardiac conditioning and orienting in the infant. In P. A. Obrist, A. H. Black, J. Brener, & L. V. DiCara (Eds.), *Cardiovascular psychophysiology: Current issues in response mechanisms, biofeedback, and methodology.* Aldine Publishing Company, Chicago, pp. 479–504.

COFFMAN, J. D. 1967. The attenuation by reserpine or guanethidine of the cutaneous vasoconstriction caused by tobacco smoking. *American Heart Journal, 74,* 229–234.

COFFMAN, J. D., & COHEN, A. S. 1971. Total and capillary fingertip blood flow in Raynaud's phenomenon. *New England Journal of Medicine, 285,* 259–263.

COHEN, B. A. 1979. Basic biofeedback electronics for the clinician. In J. V. Basmajian

(Ed.), *Biofeedback—Principles and practice for clinicians.* The Williams & Wilkins Co., Baltimore, pp. 243–256.

COHEN, M. J. 1978. Psychophysiological studies of headache: Is there a similarity between migraine and muscle contraction headaches? *Headache, 18,* 189–196.

COLCHER, H. 1974. Endoscopy of the stomach and duodenum. In H. L. Bockus (Ed.), *Gastroenterology* (Vol. I, 3rd ed.). W. B. Saunders Company, Philadelphia, pp. 454–474.

CONN, H. L. JR., & HORWITZ, O. 1971. *Cardiac and vascular diseases* (Vol. 2). Lea & Febiger, Philadelphia.

CONNEL, A. M. 1968. Motor action of the large bowel. In C. F. Code (Ed.), *Handbook of physiology: A critical comprehensive presentation of physiological knowledge and concepts* (Sec. 6, Vol. 4). American Physiological Society, Washington, pp. 2075–2091.

COTES, J. E. 1975. *Lung Function. Assessment and application in medicine.* Blackwell Scientific Publications, Oxford.

COTT, A., PAVLOSKI, R. P., & BLACK, A. H. 1979. Reducing epileptic seizures through operant conditioning of central nervous system activity: Procedural variables. *Science, 203,* 73–75.

COUCH, J. R. 1976. Dystonia and tremor in spasmodic torticollis. In R. Eldridge & S. Fahn (Eds.), *Advances in neurology* (Vol. 14). Raven Press Books, Ltd., New York, pp. 245–258.

COX, D. J., FREUNDLICH, A., & MEYER, R. G. 1975. Differential effectiveness of electromyograph feedback, verbal relaxation instructions, and medication placebo with tension headaches. *Journal of Consulting and Clinical Psychology, 43,* 892–898.

CRIDER, A., SCHWARTZ, G. E., & SHNIDMAN, S. 1969. On the criteria for instrumental autonomic conditioning: A reply to Katkin and Murray. *Psychological Bulletin, 71,* 455–461.

CRITCHLEY, M. 1933. Migraine. *Lancet, 1,* 123–126.

CRITCHLEY, M. 1937. Musicogenic epilepsy. *Brain, 60,* 13–27.

DAHLEM, N. W., KINSMAN, R. A., & HORTON, D. J. 1977. Panic-fear in asthma: Requests for as-needed medications in relation to pulmonary function measurements. *The Journal of Allergy and Clinical Immunology, 60,* 295–300.

DALESSIO, D. J. 1972. *Wolff's headache and other head pain.* Oxford University Press, Inc., New York.

DALTON, K. 1975. Food intake prior to a migraine attack—Study of 2,313 spontaneous attacks. *Headache, 15,* 188–193.

DALY, D. D., & BARRY, M. J. JR. 1957. Musicogenic epilepsy: Report of three cases. *Psychosomatic Medicine, 19,* 399–408.

DANKER, P. S., MIKLICH, D. R., PRATT, C., & CREER, T. L. 1975. An unsuccessful attempt to instrumentally condition peak expiratory flow rates in asthmatic children. *Journal of Psychosomatic Research, 19,* 209–213.

DARWIN, C. 1965. *The expression of the emotions in man and animals.* The University of Chicago, Chicago.

DAUBE, J. R. 1965. Sensory precipitated seizures: A review. *Journal of Nervous and Mental Disease, 141,* 524–539.

DAVIS, J. F. 1959. *Manual of surface electromyography.* Allan Memorial Institute of Psychiatry, McGill University. Republished at Wright-Patterson Air Force Base, Ohio. WADC technical Report 59–184, United States Air Force.

DAVIS, M. H., SAUNDERS, D. R., CREER, T. L., & CHAI, H. 1973. Relaxation training facilitated by biofeedback apparatus as a supplemental treatment in bronchial asthma. *Journal of Psychosomatic Research, 17,* 121–128.

DAVIS, R. C. 1942. Methods of measuring muscular tension. *Psychological Bulletin, 39,* 329–346.

DEAL, E. C. JR., MCFADDEN, E. R. JR., INGRAM, R. H. JR., & JAEGER, J. J. 1978. Effects of atropine on potentiation of exercise-induced bronchospasm by cold air. *Journal of Applied Physiology: Respiratory, Environmental and Exercise Physiology, 45,* 238–243.

DEBACHER, G. 1979. Biofeedback in spasticity control. In J. V. Basmajian (Ed.), *Biofeedback—Principles and practice for clinicians*. The Williams & Wilkins Co., Baltimore, pp. 61–80.

DEESE, J., & HULSE, S. H. 1967. *The psychology of learning* (3rd ed.). McGraw-Hill, Inc., New York.

DEKKER, E., & GROEN, J. 1956. Reproducible psychogenic attacks of asthma. A laboratory study. *Journal of Psychosomatic Research, 1,* 58–67.

DEKKER, E., PELSER, H. E., & GROEN, J. 1957. Conditioning as a cause of asthmatic attacks: A laboratory study. *Journal of Psychosomatic Research, 2,* 97–108.

DEMYER, W. 1977. Spasmodic torticollis, status marmoratus, and status dysmyelinatus. In E. L. Goldensohn & S. H. Appel (Eds), *Scientific approaches to clinical neurology* (Vol. 11). Lea & Febiger, Philadelphia, pp. 1234–1247.

DETAKATS, G., & FOWLER, E. F. 1962. Raynaud's phenomenon. *Journal of the American Medical Association, 179,* 1–8.

DEXTER, J. D., ROBERTS, J., & BYER, J. A. 1978. The five-hour glucose tolerance test and effect of low sucrose diet in migraine. *Headache, 18,* 91–94.

DIAMOND, S., & DALESSIO, D. J. 1978. *The practicing physician's approach to headache* (2nd ed.). The Williams & Wilkins Company, Baltimore.

DIAMOND, S., MEDINA, J., DIAMOND-FALK, J., & DEVENO, T. 1979. The value of biofeedback in the treatment of chronic headache: A five-year retrospective study. *Headache, 19,* 90–96.

DIRKS, J. F., JONES, N. F., & KINSMAN, R. A. 1977. Panic-fear: A personality dimension related to intractability in asthma. *Psychosomatic Medicine, 39,* 120–126.

DIRKS, J. F., KINSMAN, R. A., HORTON, D. J., FROSS, K. H., & JONES, N. F. 1978. Panic-fear in asthma: Rehospitalization following intensive long-term treatment. *Psychosomatic Medicine, 40,* 5–13.

DIRKS, J. F., KINSMAN, R. A., JONES, N. F., SPECTOR, S. L., DAVIDSON, P. T., & EVANS, N. W. 1977. Panic-fear: A personality dimension related to length of hospitalization in respiratory illness. *Journal of Asthma Research, 14,* 61–71.

DIRKS, J. F., KLEIGER, J. H., EVANS, N. W. 1978. ASC panic-fear and length of hospitalization in asthma. *Journal of Asthma Research, 15,* 95–97.

DIXON, H. H., & DICKEL, H. A. 1967. Tension headache. *Northwest Medicine, 66,* 817–820.

DORPAT, T. L., & HOLMES, T. H. 1955. Mechanisms of skeletal muscle pain and fatigue. *Archives of Neurology and Psychiatry, 74,* 628–640.

DRIVER, M. V., & MACGILLIVRAY, B. B. 1976. Electroencephalography. In J. Laidlaw & A. Richens (Eds.), *A textbook of epilepsy*. Churchill Livingstone, Edinburgh, pp. 109–144.

DRURY, R. L., DERISI, W. J., & LIBERMAN, R. P. 1979. Temperature biofeedback treatment for migraine headache: A controlled multiple baseline study. *Headache, 19,* 278–284.

DUBOIS, A. B., BOTELHO, S. Y., & COMROE, J. H. JR. 1956. A new method for measuring airway resistance in man using a body plethysmograph: Values in normal subjects and in patients with respiratory disease. *Journal of Clinical Investigation, 35,* 327–335.

DUFF, R. S. 1956. The diagnosis and treatment of Raynaud's disease. *British Journal of Clinical Practice, 10,* 855–867.

DWORKIN, B. R., & MILLER, N. E. 1977. Visceral learning in the curarized rat. In G. E. Schwartz & J. Beatty (Eds.), *Biofeedback theory and research*. Academic Press, Inc., New York, pp. 221–242.

ECCLES, J. C. 1959. Neuron physiology—Introduction. In J. Field, H. W. Magoun, & V. E. Hall (Eds.), *Handbook of physiology. A critical, comprehensive presentation of physiological knowledge and concepts* (Sec. 1, Vol. 1). American Physiological Society, Washington, pp. 59–74.

ECKSTEIN, J. W., WOOD, J. E., & WILKINS, R. W. 1957. Comparative vasoconstrictor effects of inhaling tobacco smoke in warm and cool environments and before and after abstinence from tobacco. *American Heart Journal, 53,* 455–462.

EDWARDS, F. C., & COGHILL, N. F. 1968. Clinical manifestations in patients with chronic atrophic gastritis, gastric ulcer, and duodenal ulcer. *Quarterly Journal of Medicine, 37,* 337–360.

EIGENBRODT, E. H. 1973. The pathology of peptic ulcer. In M. H. Sleisenger & J. S. Fordtran (Eds.), *Gastrointestinal disease: Pathophysiology, diagnosis, management.* W. B. Saunders Company, Philadelphia, pp. 621–627.

EKBOM, K. 1970. A clinical comparison of cluster headache and migraine. *Acta Neurologica Scandinavica Supplementum, 41,* 5–48.

EKBOM, K., AHLBORG, B., & SCHÉLE, R. 1978. Prevalence of migraine and cluster headache in Swedish men of 18. *Headache, 18,* 9–19.

ELDER, S. T., & EUSTIS, N. K. 1975. Instrumental blood pressure conditioning in outpatient hypertensives. *Behaviour Research and Therapy, 13,* 185–188.

ELDER, S. T., RUIZ, Z. R., DEABLER, H. L., & DILLENKOFFER, R. L. 1973. Instrumental conditioning of diastolic blood pressure in essential hypertensive patients. *Journal of Applied Behavior Analysis, 6,* 377–382.

ELLIOTT, F. A. 1971. *Clinical neurology* (2nd ed.). W. B. Saunders Company, Philadelphia.

ELLIOTT, K., FREWIN, D. B., & DOWNEY, J. A. 1974. Reflex vasomotor responses in the hands of patients suffering from migraine. *Headache, 13,* 188–196.

ENGEL, B. T. 1973. Clinical applications of operant conditioning techniques in the control of the cardiac arrythmias. In L. Birk (Ed.), *Biofeedback: Behavioral medicine.* Grune and Stratton, Inc., New York, pp. 73–78.

ENGEL, B. T., NIKOOMANESH, P., & SCHUSTER, M. M. 1974. Operant conditioning of rectosphincteric responses in the treatment of fecal incontinence. *New England Journal of Medicine, 290,* 646–649.

EPSTEIN, L. H., & ABEL, G. G. 1977. An analysis of biofeedback training effects for tension headache patients. *Behavior Therapy, 8,* 37–47.

EPSTEIN, L. H., HERSEN, M., & HEMPHILL, D. P. 1974. Music feedback in the treatment of tension headache: An experimental case study. *Journal of Behavior Therapy and Experimental Psychiatry, 5,* 59–63.

EYSENCK, H. J., & BEECH, H. R. 1971. Counter conditioning and related methods. In A. E. Bergin & S. L. Garfield (Eds.), *Handbook of psychotherapy and behavior change: An empirical analysis.* John Wiley & Sons, Inc., New York, pp. 543–611.

FAHN, S. 1977. Secondary Parkinsonism. In E. L. Goldensohn & S. H. Appel (Eds.), *Scientific approaches to clinical neurology* (Vol. II). Lea & Febiger, Philadelphia, pp. 1159–1189.

FAHN, S., & DUFFY, P. 1977. Parkinson's Disease. In E. L. Goldensohn & S. H. Appel (Eds.), *Scientific approaches to clinical neurology* (Vol. II). Lea & Febiger, Philadelphia, pp. 1119–1158.

FELDMAN, G. M. 1976. The effect of biofeedback training on respiratory resistance of asthmatic children. *Psychosomatic Medicine, 38,* 27–34.

FERSTER, C. B., & SKINNER, B. F., 1957. *Schedules of reinforcement.* Prentice-Hall, Inc., Englewood Cliffs, New Jersey.

FEUERSTEIN, M., & ADAMS, H. E. 1977. Cephalic vasomotor feedback in the modification of migraine headache. *Biofeedback and Self-Regulation, 2,* 241–254.

FEUERSTEIN, M., ADAMS, H. E., & BEIMAN, I. 1976. Cephalic vasomotor and electromyographic feedback in the treatment of combined muscle contraction and migraine headaches in a geriatric case. *Headache, 16,* 232–237.

FINLEY, W. W. 1976. Effects of sham feedback following successful SMR training in an epileptic. Follow-up study. *Biofeedback and Self-Regulation, 1,* 227–235.

FINLEY, W. W. 1977. Operant conditioning of the EEG in two patients with epilepsy: Methodologic and clinical considerations. *Pavlovian Journal of Biological Science, 12,* 93–111.

FINLEY, W. W., NIMAN, C., STANDLEY, J., & ENDER, P. 1976. Frontal EMG–Biofeedback training of athetoid cerebral palsy patients: A report of six cases. *Biofeedback and Self-Regulation, 1,* 169–182.

FINLEY, W. W., NIMAN, C. A., STANDLEY, J., & WANSLEY, R. A. 1977. Electrophysiologic behavior modification of frontal EMG in cerebral-palsied children. *Biofeedback and Self-Regulation, 2,* 59–79.

FINLEY, W. W., SMITH, H. A., & ETHERTON, M. D. 1975. Reduction of seizures and normalization of the EEG in a severe epileptic following sensorimotor biofeedback training: Preliminary study. *Biological Psychology, 2,* 189–203.

FISHER, A. B., DuBOIS, A. B., & HYDE, R. W. 1968. Evaluation of the forced oscillation technique for the determination of resistance to breathing. *Journal of Clinical Investigation, 47,* 2045–2057.

FITZELLE, G. T. 1959. Personality factors and certain attitudes toward child rearing among parents of asthmatic children. *Psychosomatic Medicine, 21,* 209–217.

FORD, F. R. 1973. *Diseases of the nervous system in infancy, childhood, and adolescence* (6th ed.), Charles C Thomas, Publisher, Springfield, pp. 1332–1373.

FORD, R. M. 1963. The causes of childhood asthma: An assessment of the relative importance of the allergic, infective, and emotional factors in childhood asthma. *The Medical Journal of Australia, 2,* 128–130.

FORDTRAN, J. S. 1973a. Acid secretion in peptic ulcer. In M. H. Sleisenger & J. S. Fordtran (Eds.), *Gastrointestinal disease: Pathophysiology, diagnosis, management.* W. B. Saunders Company, Philadelphia, pp. 174–188.

FORDTRAN, J. S. 1973b. Pepsinogens and pepsins in peptic ulcer. In M. H. Sleisenger & J. S. Fordtran (Eds.), *Gastrointestinal disease: Pathophysiology, diagnosis, management.* W. B. Saunders Company, Philadelphia, pp. 189–194.

FORDTRAN, J. S. 1973c. The pathogenesis of peptic ulcer. In M. H. Sleisenger & J. S. Fordtran (Eds.), *Gastrointestinal disease: Pathophysiology, diagnosis, management.* W. B. Saunders Company, Philadelphia, pp. 628–641.

FORSTER, F. M. 1977. *Reflex epilepsy, behavioral therapy and conditional reflexes.* Charles C Thomas, Publisher, Springfield.

FOTOPOULOS, S. S., & SUNDERLAND, W. P. 1978. Biofeedback in the treatment of psychophysiologic disorders. *Biofeedback and Self-Regulation, 3,* 331–361.

FRASER, R. G., & PARÉ, J. A. P. 1970. *Diagnosis of diseases of the chest: An integrated study based on the abnormal roentgenogram* (Vol. 2). W. B. Saunders Company, Philadelphia, pp. 966–1067.

FRIAR, L. R., & BEATTY, J. 1976. Migraine: Management by trained control of vasoconstriction. *Journal of Consulting and Clinical Psychology, 44,* 46–53.

FRIED, F. E., LAMBERTI, J., & SNEED, P. 1977. Treatment of tension and migraine headaches with biofeedback techniques. *Missouri Medicine, 74,* 253–255.

FRIEDMAN, A. P. 1970. The (infinite) variety of migraine: Sandoz Foundation lecture. In A. L. Cochrane (Ed.), *Background to migraine* (Vol. 3). Springer-Verlag, Inc., New York, pp. 165–180.

FRIEDMAN, A. P., DE SOLO POOL, N., & VON STORCH, T. J. C. 1953. Tension headache. *Journal of the American Medical Association, 151,* 174–177.

FRIEDMAN, A. P., & MERRITT, H. H. 1959. *Headache: Diagnosis and treatment.* F. A. Davis Company, Philadelphia.

FRIEDMAN, A. P., & VON STORCH, T. J. C. 1953. Studies on vascular headache: One thousand cases of migraine and tension headache. *Southern Medical Journal, 46,* 1127–1132.

FRIEDMAN, A. P., VON STORCH, T. J. C., & MERRITT, H. H. 1954. Migraine and tension headaches: A clinical study of two thousand cases. *Neurology, 4,* 773–788.

FRIEDMAN, H., & TAUB, H. A. 1977. The use of hypnosis and biofeedback procedures for essential hypertension. *The International Journal of Clinical and Experimental Hypnosis, 25,* 335–347.

FRIEDMAN, H., & TAUB, H. A. 1978. A six-month follow-up of the use of hypnosis and biofeedback procedures in essential hypertension. *American Journal of Clinical Hypnosis, 20,* 184–188.

FRIES, E. D. 1970. Effects of treatment on morbidity in hypertension. II. Results in patients with diastolic blood pressure averaging 90 through 114 mm Hg. Veterans Administration Cooperative Study Group on Antihypertensive Agents, *Journal of the American Medical Association, 213,* 1143–1152.

FRIES, E. D. 1974. The clinical spectrum of essential hypertension. *Archives of Internal Medicine, 133,* 982–987.

FRIIS, M. L., & LUND, M. 1974. Stress convulsions. *Archives of Neurology, 31,* 155–159.

FUNKENSTEIN, D. H. 1953. The relationship of experimentally produced asthmatic attacks to certain acute life stresses. *The Journal of Allergy, 24,* 11–17.

FURMAN, S. 1973. Intestinal biofeedback in functional diarrhea: A preliminary report. *Journal of Behavior Therapy and Experimental Psychiatry, 4,* 317–321.

GAARDER, K. R., & MONTGOMERY, P. S. 1977. *Clinical biofeedback: A procedural manual.* The Williams & Wilkins Co., Baltimore.

GAINER, J. C. 1978. Temperature discrimination training in the biofeedback treatment of migraine headache. *Journal of Behavior Therapy and Experimental Psychiatry, 9,* 185–188.

GALAMBOS, R. 1962. *Nerves and muscles.* Doubleday and Co., Inc., Garden City, New York.

GAMBRILL, E. D. 1977. *Behavior modification: Handbook of assessment, intervention, and evaluation.* Jossey-Bass Inc., Publishers, San Francisco.

GANONG, W. F. 1977. *The nervous system.* Lange Medical Publications, Los Altos.

GARLINER, D. 1976. *Myofunctional therapy.* W. B. Saunders Company, Philadelphia.

GASTAUT, H. 1969a. Clinical and electroencephalographical classification of epileptic seizures. *Epilepsia, 10,* S2–S13.

GASTAUT, H. 1969b. Classification of the epilepsies. Proposal for an international classification. *Epilepsia, 10,* S14–S21.

GASTAUT, H., GASTAUT, J. L., GONCALVES E SILVA, G. E., & FERNANDEZ SANCHEZ, G. R. 1975. Relative frequency of different types of epilepsy: A study employing the classification of the International League Against Epilepsy. *Epilepsia, 16,* 457–461.

GASTAUT, H., & POIRIER, F. 1964. Experimental, or "reflex," induction of seizures: Report of a case of abnominal (enteric) epilepsy. *Epilepsia, 5,* 256–270.

GASTAUT, H., & TASSINARI, C. A. 1966. Triggering mechanisms in epilepsy: The electroclinical point of view. *Epilepsia, 7,* 85–138.

GAYRARD, P., OREHEK, J., GRIMAUD, C., & CHARPIN, J. 1975. Bronchoconstrictor effects of a deep inspiration in patients with asthma. *American Review of Respiratory Disease, 111,* 433–439.

GESCHWIND, N. 1965a. Disconnexion syndromes in animals and man. Part I. *Brain, 88,* 237–294.

GESCHWIND, N. 1965b. Disconnexion syndromes in animals and man. Part II. *Brain, 88,* 585–644.

GESSEL, A. H. 1975. Electromyographic biofeedback and tricyclic antidepressants in myofascial pain-dysfunction syndrome: Psychological predictors of outcome. *Journal of the American Dental Association, 91,* 1048–1052.

GHOSE, K., COPPEN, A., & CARROLL, D. 1978. Studies of the interaction of tyramine in migraine patients. In R. Greene (Ed.), *Current concepts in migraine research.* Raven Press Books, Ltd., pp. 89–95.

GIFFORD, R. W. JR., & HINES, E. A. JR. 1957. Raynaud's disease among women and girls. *Circulation, 16,* 1012–1021.

GIFFORD, R. W. JR., HINES, E. A. JR., & CRAIG, W. M. 1958. Sympathectomy for Raynaud's phenomenon. Follow-up study of 70 women with Raynaud's disease and 54 women with secondary Raynaud's phenomenon. *Circulation, 17,* 5–13.

GILBERT, G. I. 1971. The medical treatment of spasmodic torticollis and effect of surgery. *Lancet, 2,* 503–506.

GOLD, W. M., KESSLER, G. F., & YU, D. Y. C. 1972. Role of the vagus nerves in experimental asthma in allergic dogs. *Journal of Applied Physiology, 33,* 719–725.

GOLDIE, L., & GREEN, J. M. 1959. A study of the psychological factors in a case of sensory reflex epilepsy. *Brain, 82,* 505–524.

GOLDMAN, H., KLEINMAN, K. M., SNOW, M. Y., BIDUS, D. R., & KOROL, B. 1975. Relationship between essential hypertension and cognitive functioning: Effects of biofeedback. *Psychophysiology, 12,* 569–573.

GOLDMAN, M., KNUDSON, R. J., MEAD, J., PETERSON, N., SCHWABER, J. R., & WOHL, M. E. 1970. A simplified measurement of respiratory resistance by forced oscillation. *Journal of Applied Physiology, 28,* 113–116.

GOLDSTEIN, D. S., ROSS, R. S., & BRADY, J. V. 1977. Biofeedback heart rate training during exercise. *Biofeedback and Self-Regulation, 2,* 107–125.

GOLDSTEIN, I. B. 1972. Electromyography: A measure of skeletal muscle response. In R. S. Greenfield & R. A. Sternbach (Eds.), *Handbook of psychophysiology,* Holt, Rinehart & Winston, Inc., New York, pp. 329–365.

GOLDSTEIN, I. F., & ARTHUR, S. P. 1978. "Asthma Alley": A space clustering study of asthma in Brooklyn, New York City. *Journal of Asthma Research, 15,* 81–93.

GOODGOLD, J., & EBERSTEIN, A. 1972. *Electrodiagnosis of neuromuscular diseases.* The Williams & Wilkins Company, Baltimore.

GOYLE, K. B., & DORMANDY, J. A. 1976. Abnormal blood viscosity in Raynaud's phenomenon. *Lancet, 1,* 1317–1318.

GRAHAM, D. T. 1955. Cutaneous vascular reactions in Raynaud's disease and its state of hostility, anxiety, and depression. *Psychosomatic Medicine, 17,* 200–207.

GRANGER, C. V. 1976. Prognosis in Bell's Palsy. *Archives of Physical Medicine and Rehabilitation, 57,* 33–35.

GREENFIELD, R. S., & STERNBACH, R. A. (Eds.). 1972. *Handbook of psychophysiology.* Holt, Rinehart and Winston, Inc., New York.

GRIBBIN, B., STEPTOE, A., & SLEIGHT, P. 1976. Pulse wave velocity as a measure of blood pressure change. *Psychophysiology, 13,* 86–90.

GRIECO, M. H., & PIERSON, R. N. JR. 1970. Cardiopulmonary effects of methacholine in asthmatic and normal subjects. *Journal of Allergy, 45,* 195–207.

GRIFFIN, C. J. 1975. The treatment of the temporomandibular joint syndrome. *Monographs in Oral Medicine, 4,* 170–187.

GROSSMAN, M. I. 1978. Control of gastric secretion. In M. H. Sleisenger & J. S. Fordtran (Eds.), *Gastrointestinal disease: Pathophysiology, diagnosis, management.* W. B. Saunders Company, Philadelphia, pp. 640–659.

GUNDERSON, C. H., DUNNE, P. B., & FEYER, T. L. 1973. Sleep deprivation seizures. *Neurology, 23,* 678–686.

HAHN, W. W. 1966. Autonomic responses of asthmatic children. *Psychosomatic Medicine, 28,* 323–332.

HAHN, W. W., & CLARK, J. A. 1967. Psychophysiological reactivity of asthmatic children. *Psychosomatic Medicine, 29,* 526–536.

HAINES, R. W. 1932. The laws of muscle and tendon growth. *Journal of Anatomy, 66,* 578–585.

HAINES, R. W. 1934. On muscles of full and of short action. *Journal of Anatomy, 69,* 20–24.

HALE, R. 1966. Observations concerning the effects of emotional stress on asthma. *Annals of Allergy, 24,* 183–184. (Editoral)

HALL, K. V., & HILLESTAD, L. K. 1960. Raynaud's phenomenon treated with sympathectomy. A follow-up study of 28 patients. *Angiology, 11,* 186–189.

HALPERN, A., KUHN, P. H., SHAFTEL, H. E., SAMUELS, S. S., SHAFTEL, N., SELMAN, D., & BIRCH, H. G. 1960. Raynaud's disease, Raynaud's phenomenon, and serotonin. *Angiology, 11,* 151–167.

HALPERN, L. M., & WARD, A. A. Jr. 1969. The hyperexcitable neuron as a model for the laboratory analysis of anticonvulsant drugs. *Epilepsia, 10,* 281–314.

HANINGTON, E. 1967. Preliminary report on tyramine headache. *British Medical Journal, 2,* 550–551.

HANINGTON, E., & HARPER, M. A. 1968. The role of tyramine in the aetiology of migraine, and related studies on the cerebral and extracerebral circulations. *Headache, 8,* 84–97.

HANSTEEN, V. 1976. Medical treatment in Raynaud's disease. *Acta Chirurgica Scandinavica Supplementum, 465,* 87–91.

HARPER, R. G., and STEGER, J. C. 1978. Psychological correlates of frontalis EMG and pain in tension headache. *Headache, 18,* 215–218.

HARRIS, A. H., and BRADY, J. V. 1977. Long-term studies of cardiovascular control in primates. In G. E. Schwartz & J. Beatty (Eds.), *Biofeedback theory and research.* Academic Press, Inc., New York, pp. 243–264.

HARRIS, A. H., GILLIAM, W. J., FINDLEY, J. D., & BRADY, J. V. 1973. Instrumental conditioning of large-magnitude, daily, 12-hour blood pressure elevations in the baboon. *Science, 182,* 175–177.

HARRIS, F. A., SPELMAN, F. A., & HYMER, J. W. 1974. Electronic sensory aids as treatment for cerebral-palsied children. Inapproprioception: Part II. *Physical Therapy, 54,* 354–365.

HARRISON, A., & CONNOLLY, K. 1971. The conscious control of fine levels of neuromuscular firing in spastic and normal subjects. *Developmental Medicine and Child Neurology, 13,* 762–771.

HARRISON, R. H. 1975. Psychological testing in headache: A review. *Headache, 14,* 177–185.

HASSETT, J. 1978. *A primer of psychophysiology.* W. H. Freeman & Co., Publishers, San Francisco.

HAYNES, S. N. 1976. Electromyographic biofeedback treatment of a woman with chronic dysphagia. *Biofeedback and Self-Regulation, 1,* 121–126.

HAYNES, S. N., GRIFFIN, P., MOONEY, D., & PARISE, M. 1975. Electromyographic biofeedback and relaxation instructions in the treatment of muscle contraction headaches. *Behavior Therapy, 6,* 672–678.

HENRYK-GUTT, R., & REES, W. L. 1973. Psychological aspects of migraine. *Journal of Psychosomatic Research, 17,* 141–153.

HERTZMAN, A. B. 1953. Some relations between skin temperature and blood flow. *American Journal of Physical Medicine, 32,* 233–251.

HILLESTAD, L. 1970. Blood flow in vascular disorders: A plethysmographic study. *Acta Medica Scandinavica, 188,* 185–189.

HINES, E. A. JR., & CHRISTENSEN, N. A. 1945. Raynaud's disease among men. *Journal of the American Medical Association, 129,* 1–4.

HØEDT-RASMUSSEN, K., SVEINSDOTTIR, E., & LASSEN, N. A. 1966. Regional cerebral blood flow in man determined by intra-arterial injection of radioactive inert gas. *Circulation Research, 18,* 237–247.

HOLLING, H. E., 1972. *Perpheral vascular diseases: Diagnosis and management.* J. B. Lippincott Company, Philadelphia.

HOLMES, T. H., & RAHE, R. H. 1967. The social readjustment rating scale. *Journal of Psychosomatic Research, 11,* 213–218.

HOLMES, T. S., & HOLMES, T. H. 1967. Short-term intrusions into the life style routine. *Journal of Psychosomatic Research, 14,* 121–132.

HONIG, W. K., & STADDON, J. E. R. (Eds.). 1977. *Handbook of operant behavior.* Prentice-Hall, Inc., Englewood Cliffs.

HOREL, J. A., & KEATING, E. G. 1969. Partial Kluver-Bucy syndrome produced by cortical disconnection. *Brain Research, Amsterdam, 16,* 281–284.

HORWITZ, O. 1971. Diseases of the arteries of the extremities. In *Cardiac and vascular disease,* H. L. Conn Jr. & O. Horwitz (Eds.). Lea & Febiger, Philadelphia, pp. 1517–1543.

HUDSON, R. E. B. 1970. *Cardiovascular pathology.* The Williams & Wilkins Company, Baltimore.

HULSE, S. H., DEESE, J., & EGETH, H. 1975. *The psychology of learning.* McGraw-Hill Inc., New York.

HUNT, J. H. 1936. The Raynaud phenomena: A critical review. *Quarterly Journal of Medicine, 5,* 399–444.

HUTCHINGS, D. F., & REINKING, R. H. 1976. Tension headaches: What form of therapy is most effective? *Biofeedback and Self-Regulation, 1,* 183–190.

HYATT, R. E., SCHILDER, D. P., & FRY, D. L. 1958. Relationship between maximum expiratory flow and degree of lung inflation. *Journal of Applied Physiology, 13,* 331–336.

HYNDMAN, O. R., & WOLKIN, J. 1942. Raynaud's disease: A review of its mechanism with evidence that it is primarily a vascular disease. *American Heart Journal, 23,* 535–554.

INGVAR, D. H., CRONQVIST, S., EKBERG, R., RISBERG, J., & HØEDT-RASMUSSEN, K. 1965. Normal values of regional cerebral blood flow in man, including flow and weight estimates of grey and white matter. *Acta Neurologica Scandinavica Supplementum, 14,* 72–78.

INGVAR, D. H., & NYMAN, G. E. 1962. Epilepsia arithmetices. *Neurology, 12,* 282–287.

ISBISTER, W. H., SCHOFIELD, P. F., & TORRANCE, H. B. 1966. Cerebral blood flow estimated by 133Xe clearance technique. *Archives of Neurology, 14,* 512–521.

ISENBERG, J., RICHARDSON, C. T., & FORDTRAN, J. S. 1978. Pathogenesis of peptic ulcer. In M. H. Sleisenger & J. S. Fordtran (Eds.), *Gastrointestinal disease: Pathophysiology, diagnosis, management* (2nd ed.). W. B. Saunders Company, Philadelphia, pp. 792–806.

ISENBERG, J. I. 1973. Gastric secretory testing. In M. H. Sleisenger & J. S. Fordtran (Eds.), *Gastrointestinal disease: Pathophysiology, diagnosis, management.* W. B. Saunders Company, Philadelphia, pp. 536–554.

ISENBERG, J. I. 1975. Diagnostic studies and medical treatment. In P. B. Beeson & W. McDermott (Eds.), *Textbook of medicine* (14th ed.). W. B. Saunders Company, Philadelphia, pp. 1202–1208.

JACKSON, J. 1931. *Selected writings of John Hughlings Jackson* (Vol. One). *On epilepsy and epileptiform convulsions,* J. Taylor (Ed.). Hodder and Stoughton Limited, London.

JACOBS, A., & FELTON, G. S. 1969. Visual feedback of myoelectric output to facilitate muscle relaxation in normal persons and patients with neck injuries. *Archives of Physical Medicine and Rehabilitation, 50,* 34–39.

JACOBSON, A. M., HACKETT, T. P., SURMAN, O. S., & SILVERBERG, E. L. 1973. Raynaud phenomenon: Treatment with hypnotic and operant technique. *Journal of the American Medical Association, 225,* 739–741.

JACOBSON, E. 1929. *Progressive relaxation.* The University of Chicago Press, Chicago.

JACOBSON, E. 1938. *Progressive relaxation.* The University of Chicago Press, Chicago.

JACOBSON, E. 1964. *Anxiety and tension control:* A physiologic approach. J. B. Lippincott Company, Philadelphia.

JACOBSON, E. 1978. *You must relax.* McGraw-Hill, Inc., New York.

JAMIESON, G. G., LUDBROOK, J., & WILSON, A. 1971. Cold hypersensitivity in Raynaud's phenomenon. *Circulation, 44,* 254–264.

JANKEL, W. R. 1978. Bell Palsy: Muscle reeducation by electromyograph feedback. *Archives of Physical Medicine and Rehabilitation, 59,* 240–242.

JANZON, L. 1976. Smoking cessation and peripheral circulation: A population study in 59-year-old men with plethysmography and segmental measurements of systolic blood pressure. In A. Kappert, H. J. Lev, & P. Waibel (Eds.), *Recent advances in vascular diseases.* Hans Huber Publishers, Bern, pp. 54–59.

JASPER, H. H. 1958. Then ten twenty electrode system of the International Federation. *Electroencephalography and Clinical Neurophysiology, 10,* 371–375.

JAVEL, A. F., & DENHOLTZ, M. S. 1975. Audible GSR feedback and systematic desensitization: A case report. *Behavior Therapy, 6,* 251–253.

JENNINGS, D. 1940. Perforated peptic ulcer: Changes in age-incidence and sex-distribution in the last 150 years. *Lancet, 1,* 444–447.

JENSEN, K. B., HØEDT-RASMUSSEN, K., SVEINSDOTTIR, E., STEWART, B. M., & LASSEN, N. A. 1966. Cerebral blood flow evaluated by inhalation of ^{133}Xe and extracranial recording: A methodological study. *Clinical Science, 30,* 485–494.

JESSUP, B. 1978. The role of diet in migraine: Conditioned taste aversion. *Headache, 18,* 229. (Letter to the editor)

JOHNSON, H. E., & GARTON, W. H. 1973. Muscle re-education in hemiplegia by use of electromyographic device. *Archives of Physical Medicine and Rehabilitation, 54,* 320–322, 325.

JOHNSON, R. K., & MEYER, R. G. 1974. Phased biofeedback approach for epileptic seizure control. *Journal of Behavior Therapy and Experimental Psychiatry, 5,* 185–187.

JOHNSON, W. G., & TURIN, A. 1975. Biofeedback treatment of migraine headache: A systematic case study. *Behavior Therapy, 6,* 394–397.

JOHNSTON, D. 1977. Biofeedback, verbal instructions, and the motor skills analogy. In J. Beatty and H. Legewie (Eds.), *Biofeedback and behavior.* Plenum Publishing Corporation, New York, pp. 331–341.

JONES, B., & MISHKIN, M. 1972. Limbic lesions and the problem of stimulus-reinforcement associations. *Experimental Neurology, 36,* 362–377.

JOSHI, V., KATIYAR, B. C., MOHAN, P. K., MISRA, S., & SHUKLA, G. D. 1977. Profile of epilepsy in a developing country: A study of 1,000 patients based on the international classification. *Epilepsia, 18,* 549–554.

JULIUS, S. 1977a. Borderline hypertension: Epidemiologic and clinical implications. In J. Genest, K. Koiw, & O. Kuchel (Eds.), *Hypertension physiopathology and treatment.* McGraw-Hill, Inc., New York, pp. 630–640.

JULIUS, S. 1977b. Classification of hypertension. In J. Genest, E. Koiw, & O. Kuchel (Eds.), *Hypertension physiopathology and treatment.* McGraw-Hill Book Company, Inc., New York, pp. 9–12.

JULIUS, S., & SCHORK, M. A. 1971. Borderline hypertension—A critical review. *Journal of Chronic Diseases, 23,* 723–754.

KANNEL, W. B. 1975. Role of blood pressure in cardiovascular disease: The Framingham study. *Angiology, 26,* 1–14.

KANNEL, W. B. 1977. Importance of hypertension as a major risk factor in cardiovascular disease. In J. Genest, E. Koiw, & O. Kuchel (Eds.), *Hypertension physiopathology and treatment*. McGraw-Hill, Inc., New York, pp. 888–910.

KAPLAN, B. J. 1975. Biofeedback in epileptics: Equivocal relationship of reinforced EEG frequency to seizure reduction. *Epilepsia, 16*, 477–485.

KAPPERT, A. 1971. *Diagnosis of peripheral vascular diseases*. Hans Huber Publishers, Bern.

KARR, R. M., LEHRER, S. B., BUTCHER, B. T., & SALVAGGIO, J. E. 1978. Coffee worker's asthma: A clinical appraisal using the radioallergosorbent test. *Journal of Allergy and Clinical Immunology, 62*, 143–148.

KATKIN, E. S. 1971. *Instrumental autonomic conditioning*. General Learning Corporation, New York.

KATKIN, E. S., & MURRAY, E. N. 1968. Instrumental conditioning of autonomically mediated behavior: Theoretical and methodological issues. *Psychological Bulletin, 70*, 52–68.

KATKIN, E. S., MURRAY, E. N., & LACHMAN, R. 1969. Concerning instrumental autonomic conditioning: A rejoinder. *Psychological Bulletin, 71*, 462–466.

KATZ, B. 1966. *Nerve, muscle, and synapse*. McGraw-Hill, Inc., New York.

KAY, C. F. 1971. Clinical principles. Disorders of impulse formation. Disorders arising from the sinus node. In P. B. Beeson & W. McDermott (Eds.), *Cecil-Loeb Textbook of Medicine* (13th ed.). W. B. Saunders Company, Philadelphia, pp. 1066–1083.

KAZEMI, H., & KANAREK, D. J. 1978. Gas exchange in asthma. In E. B. Weiss (Ed.), *Status asthmaticus*. University Park Press, Baltimore, pp. 101–113.

KHAN, A. U. 1973. Present status of psychosomatic aspects of asthma. *Psychosomatics, 14*, 195–200.

KHAN, A. U. 1977. Effectiveness of biofeedback and counter-conditioning in the treatment of bronchial asthma. *Journal of Psychosomatic Research, 21*, 97–104.

KHAN, A. U., & OLSON, D. L. 1977. Deconditioning of exercise-induced asthma. *Psychosomatic Medicine, 39*, 382–392.

KHAN, A. U., STAERK, M., & BONK, C. 1973. Role of counter-conditioning in the treatment of asthma. *Journal of Psychosomatic Research, 17*, 389–392.

KIMBLE, G. A. 1961. *Hilgard and Marquis' conditioning and learning*. Prentice-Hall, Inc., New Jersey.

KIMMEL, H. D. 1967. Instrumental conditioning of autonomically mediated behavior. *Psychological Bulletin, 67*, 337–345.

KINMONTH, J. B., & HADFIELD, G. J. 1952. Sympathectomy for Raynaud's disease. Results of ganglionectomy and preganglionic section compared. *British Medical Journal, 1*, 1377–1379.

KINSMAN, R. A., DAHLEM, N. W., SPECTOR, S., & STAUDENMAYER, H. 1977. Observations on subjective symptomatology, coping behavior, and medical decisions in asthma. *Psychosomatic Medicine, 39*, 102–119.

KINSMAN, R. A., LUPARELLO, T., O'BANION, K., & SPECTOR, S. 1973. Multidimensional analysis of the subjective symptomatology of asthma. *Psychosomatic Medicine, 35*, 250–267.

KINSMAN, R. A., SPECTOR, S. L., SHUCARD, D. W., & LUPARELLO, T. J. 1974. Observations on patterns of subjective symptomatology of acute asthma. *Psychosomatic Medicine, 36*, 129–143.

KLEINMAN, K. M., GOLDMAN, H., SNOW, M. Y., & KOROL, B. 1977. Relationship between essential hypertension and cognitive functioning II: Effects of biofeedback training generalize to non-laboratory environment. *Psychophysiology, 14*, 192–197.

KNAPP, P. H., MATHÉ, A. A., & VACHON, L. 1976. Psychosomatic aspects of bronchial asthma. In E. B. Weiss & M. S. Segal (Eds.), *Bronchial asthma: Mechanisms and therapeutics*. Little, Brown & Company, Boston, pp. 1055–1080.

KOELLE, G. B. 1975. Neuromuscular blocking agents. In L. S. Goodman & A. Gilman (Eds.), *The pharmacological basis of therapeutics.* Macmillan, Inc., New York, pp. 575–588.

KOHLENBERG, R. J., 1973. Operant conditioning of human anal sphincter pressure. *Journal of Applied Behavior Analysis, 6,* 201–208.

KOIZUMI, K., & BROOKS, C. McC. 1974. The autonomic nervous system and its role in controlling visceral activities. In V. B. Mountcastle (Ed.), *Medical physiology* (Vol. 1). C. V. Mosby Company, Saint Louis, pp. 783–812.

KONDO, C., & CANTER, A. 1977. True and false electromyographic feedback: Effect on tension headache. *Journal of Abnormal Psychology, 86,* 93–95.

KOTSES, H., GLAUS, K. D., BRICEL, S. K., EDWARDS, J. E., & CRAWFORD, P. L. 1978. Operant muscular relaxation and peak expiratory flow rate in asthmatic children. *Journal of Psychosomatic Research, 22,* 17–23.

KOTSES, H., GLAUS, K. D., CRAWFORD, P. L., EDWARDS, J. E., & SCHERR, M. S. 1976. Operant reduction of frontalis EMG activity in the treatment of asthma in children. *Journal of Psychosomatic Research, 20,* 453–459.

KRAG, E. 1966. Long-term prognosis in medically treated peptic ulcer. A clinical, radiographical, and statistical follow-up study. *Acta Medica Scandinavica, 180,* 657–670.

KRAUSE, U. 1963. Long-term results of medical and surgical treatment of peptic ulcer. A follow-up investigation of patients initially treated conservatively between 1925–34. *Acta Chirurgica Scandinavica Supplementum, 310,* 3–111.

KRISTT, D. A., & ENGEL, B. T. 1975. Learned control of blood pressure in patients with high blood pressure. *Circulation, 51,* 370–378.

KUHLMAN, W. N., & ALLISON, T. 1977. EEG feedback training in the treatment of epilepsy: Some questions and some answers. *Pavlovian Journal of Biological Science, 12,* 112–122.

KUKULKA, C. G., & BASMAJIAN, J. V. 1975. Assessment of an audio-visual feedback device used in motor training. *American Journal of Physical Medicine, 54,* 194–208.

KUMAR, L., MIKLICH, D. R., & MORRIS, H. G. 1971. Plasma 17–OH corticosteroid concentrations in children with asthma. *The Journal of Pediatrics, 79,* 955–962.

KUNKLE, E. C. 1959. Mechanisms of headache. In A. P. Friedman & H. H. Merritt (Eds.), *Headache: Diagnosis and treatment.* F. A. Davis Co., Philadelphia, pp. 3–22.

KYDD, W. L. 1959. Psychosomatic aspects of temporomandibular joint dysfunction. *Journal of the American Dental Association, 59,* 31–44.

LACEY, J. I., BATEMAN, D. E., and VANLEHN, R. 1953. Autonomic response specificity: An experimental study. *Psychosomatic Medicine, 15,* 8–21.

LAIDLAW, J., & LAIDLAW, M. V. 1976. People with epilepsy—Living with epilepsy. In J. Laidlaw & A. Richens (Eds.), *A textbook of epilepsy.* Churchill Livingstone, Edinburgh, pp. 355–382.

LANCE, J. W. 1975. *Headache: Understanding, alleviation.* Charles Scribner's Sons, New York.

Lancet Editorial. 1977. Episodic digital vasospasm—The legacy of Maurice Raynaud. *Lancet, 1,* 1039–1040.

LANGMAN, M. J. S. 1974. Epidemiology of peptic ulcer. In H. L. Bockus (Ed.), *Gastroenterology,* (Vol. 1). W. B. Saunders Company, Philadelphia, 611–618.

LARGEN, J. W., MATHEW, R. J., DOBBINS, K., MEYER, J. S., & CLAGHORN, J. L. 1978. Skin temperature self-regulation and non-invasive regional cerebral blood flow. *Headache, 18,* 203–210.

LASKIN, D. M. 1969. Etiology of the pain-dysfunction syndrome. *Journal of the American Dental Association, 79,* 147–153.

LASSEN, N. A., INGVAR, D. H., & SKINHØJ, E. 1978. Brain function and blood flow. *Scientific American, 239, (4)* 62–71.

LEE, K., HILL, E., JOHNSTON, R., & SMIEHOROWSKI, T. 1976. Myofeedback for muscle retraining in hemiphlegic patients. *Archives of Physical Medicine and Rehabilitation, 57,* 588–591.

LEHNER, T. 1978. The mouth and salivary glands. In R. B. Scott (Ed.), *Price's textbook of the practice of medicine.* Oxford University Press, Oxford, pp. 597–610.

LEIBOWITZ, U. 1969. Epidemic incidence of Bell's palsy. *Brain, 92,* 109–114.

LEIGH, D. 1953. Asthma and the psychiatrist. A critical review. *International Archives of Allergy and Applied Immunology, 4,* 227–246.

LEVEE, J. R., COHEN, M. J., & RICKLES, W. H. 1976. Electromyographic biofeedback for relief of tension in the facial and throat muscles of a woodwind musician. *Biofeedback and Self-Regulation, 1,* 113–120.

LEWIS, T. 1929. Experiments relating to the peripheral mechanism involved in spasmodic arrest of the circulation in the fingers, a variety of Raynaud's disease. *Heart, 15,* 7–101.

LEWIS, T. 1932. Raynaud's disease. *New England Journal of Medicine, 206,* 1192–1198.

LEWIS, T. 1936. *Vascular disorders of the limbs. Described for practititioners and students.* Macmillan, Inc., New York.

LEWIS, T. 1938a. Raynaud's disease and preganglionic sympathectomy. *Clinical Science, 3,* 321–336.

LEWIS, T. 1938b. The pathological changes in the arteries supplying the fingers in warm-handed people and in cases of so-called Raynaud's disease. *Clinical Science, 3,* 287–319.

LEWIS, T. 1942. *Pain.* Macmillan Inc., New York.

LEWIS, T., & KERR, W. J. 1929. Experiments relating to the peripheral mechanism involved in spasmodic arrest of the circulation in the fingers, a variety of Raynaud's disease. *Heart, 15,* 7–101.

LEWIS, T., & PICKERING, G. W. 1934. Observations upon maladies in which the blood supply to the digits ceases intermittently or permanently, and upon bilateral gangrene of digits; observations relevant to so-called "Raynaud's disease." *Clinical Science, 1,* 327–366.

LEWIS, T., PICKERING, G. W., & ROTHSCHILD, P. 1931. Observations upon muscular pain in intermittent claudication. *Heart, 15,* 359–383.

LIPOWSKI, Z. J., LIPSITT, D. R., & WHYBROW, P. C. (Eds.), 1977. *Psychosomatic medicine: Current trends and clinical applications.* Oxford University Press, New York.

LLOYD, T. C. JR., & WRIGHT, G. W. 1963. Evaluation of methods used in detecting changes of airway resistance in man. *American Review of Respiratory Diseases, 87,* 529–537.

LOCKARD, J. S., & BARENSTEN, R. I. 1967. Behavioral experimental epilepsy in monkeys 1. Clinical seizure recording apparatus and initial data. *Electroencephalography and Clinical Neurophysiology, 22,* 482–486.

LOWELL, F. C. 1978. Chronic bronchitis and asthma-poor terms for two common diseases. *The Journal of Allergy and Clinical Immunology, 62,* 325–326.

LUBAR, J. F. 1977. Electroencephalographic biofeedback methodology and the management of epilepsy. *Pavlovian Journal of Biological Science, 12,* 147–185.

LUBAR, J. F., & BAHLER, W. W. 1976. Behavioral management of epileptic seizures following EEG biofeedback training of the sensorimotor rhythm. *Biofeedback and Self-Regulation, 1,* 77–104.

LUPARELLO, T. J., LEIST, N., LOURIE, C. H., & SWEET, P. 1970. The interaction of psychologic stimuli and pharmacologie agents on airway reactivity in asthmatic subjects. *Psychosomatic Medicine, 32,* 509–513.

LUPARELLO, T., LYONS, H. A., BLEECKER, E. R., & McFADDEN, E. R. JR. 1968. Influences of suggestion on airway reactivity in asthmatic subjects. *Psychosomatic Medicine, 30,* 819–825.

LUPTON, D. E. 1966. A preliminary investigation of the personality of female temporomandibular joint dysfunction patients. *Psychotherapy and Psychosomatics, 14,* 199–216.

LYNCH, J. J. 1973. Biofeedback: Some reflections on modern behavioral science. In L. Birk (Ed.), *Biofeedback: Behavioral medicine.* Grune & Stratton, Inc., New York, pp. 191–202.

MACCORQUODALE, K., & MEEHL, P. E. 1948. On a distinction between hypothetical constructs and intervening variables. *Psychological Review, 55,* 95–107.

MACDONNELL, K. F. 1976. Differential diagnosis of asthma. In E. B. Weiss & M. S. Segal (Eds.), *Bronchial asthma: Mechanisms and therapeutics,* Little, Brown & Company, Boston, pp. 679–705.

MACPHERSON, E. L. R. 1967. Control of involuntary movement. *Behaviour Research and Therapy, 5,* 143–145.

MALLETT, B. L., & VEALL, N. 1965. The measurement of regional cerebral clearance rates in man using Xenon-133 inhalation and extracranial recording. *Clinical Science, 29,* 179–191.

MALMO, R. B., & SHAGASS, C. 1949a. Physiologic studies of reaction to stress in anxiety and early schizophrenia. *Psychosomatic Medicine, 11,* 9–24.

MALMO, R. B., & SHAGASS, C. 1949b. Physiologic study of symptom mechanisms in patients under stress. *Psychosomatic Medicine, 11,* 25–29.

MALMO, R. B., SHAGASS, C., & DAVIS, F. H. 1950. Symptom specificity and bodily reactions during psychiatric interview. *Psychosomatic Medicine, 12,* 362–376.

MALMO, R. B., & SMITH, A. A. 1954. Forehead tension and motor irregularities in psychoneurotic patients under stress. *Journal of Personality, 23,* 391–406.

MALMO, R. B., WALLERSTEIN, H., & SHAGASS, C. 1953. Headache proneness and mechanisms of motor conflict in psychiatric patients. *Journal of Personality, 22,* 163–187.

MARINACCI, A. A., & HORANDE, M. 1960. Electromyogram in neuromuscular re-education. *Bulletin of the Los Angeles Neurological Society, 25,* 57–71.

MARKS, I. N., & SHAY, H. 1959. Observations on the pathogenesis of gastric ulcer. *Lancet, 1,* 1107–1111.

MARSDEN, C. D. 1976. Neurology. In J. Laidlaw & A. Richens (Eds.), *A textbook of epilepsy.* Churchill Livingstone, Edinburgh, pp. 15–55.

MASUDA, M., NOTSKE, R. N., & HOLMES, T. H. 1966. Catecholamine excretion and asthmatic behavior. *Journal of Psychosomatic Research, 10,* 255–262.

MATHÉ, A. A., & KNAPP, P. H. 1969. Decreased plasma free fatty acids and urinary epinephrine in bronchial asthma. *New England Journal of Medicine, 281,* 234–238.

MATHÉ, A. A., & KNAPP, P. H. 1971. Emotional and adrenal reactions to stress in bronchial asthma. *Psychosomatic Medicine, 33,* 323–340.

MATHEW, N. T., HRASTNIK, F., & MEYER, J. S. 1976. Regional cerebral blood flow in the diagnosis of vascular headache. *Headache, 15,* 252–260.

MATHEW, R. J., LARGEN, J. W., DOBBINS, K., MEYER, J. S., SAKAI, F., & CLAGHORN, J. L. Biofeedback control of skin temperature and cerebral blood flow in migraine. *Headache.* (In press)

MATTSON, R. H., PRATT, K. L., & C(LVERLEY, J. R. 1965. Electroencephalograms of epileptics following sleep deprivation. *Archives of Neurology, 13,* 310–315.

MAYR, O. 1970. The origins of feedback control. *Scientific American, 223, (4)* 111–118.

MCDERMOTT, N. T., & COBB, S. 1939. A psychiatric study of fifty cases of bronchial asthma. *Psychosomatic Medicine, 1,* pp. 203–244.

MCFADDEN, E. R. JR. 1976. Respiratory mechanics in asthma. In E. B. Weiss and M. S. Segal (Eds.), *Bronchial asthma: Mechanisms and therapeutics.* Little, Brown & Company, pp. 259–278.

MCFADDEN, E. R., JR., LUPARELLO, T., LYONS, H. A., & BLEECKER, E. 1969. The mechanism of action of suggestion in the induction of acute asthma attacks. *Psychosomatic Medicine, 31,* 134–143.

McGrath, M. A., Peek, R., & Penny, R. 1978. Raynaud's disease: Reduced hand blood flows with normal blood viscosity. *Australian and New Zealand Journal of Medicine,* 8, 126–131.

Mchedlishvili, G. I., Mitagvaria, N. P., & Ormotsadze, L. G. 1973. Vascular mechanisms controlling a constant blood supply to the brain ("autoregulation"). *Stroke,* 4, 742–750.

McKenzie, R. E., Ehrisman, W. J., Montgomery, P. S., & Barnes, R. H. 1974. The treatment of headache by means of electroencephalographic biofeedback. *Headache,* 13, 164–172.

Meares, R. 1971. Features which distinguish groups of spasmodic torticollis. *Journal of Psychosomatic Research,* 15, 1–11.

Medina, J. L., & Diamond, S. 1978. The role of diet in migraine. *Headache,* 18, 31–34.

Medina, J. L., Diamond, S., & Franklin, M. A. 1976. Biofeedback therapy for migraine. *Headache,* 16, 115–118.

Melzak, R., & Torgerson, W. S. 1971. On the language of pain. *Anesthesiology,* 34, 50–59.

Mikulas, W. L. 1974. *Concepts in learning.* W. B. Saunders Company, Philadelphia.

Miller, H. 1967. Facial paralysis. *British Medical Journal,* 3, 815–819.

Miller, H., & Baruch, D. W. 1948. Psychosomatic studies of children with allergic manifestations. I. Maternal rejection: A study of sixty-three cases. *Psychosomatic Medicine,* 10, 275–278.

Miller, N. E. 1969. Learning of visceral and glandular responses. *Science,* 163, 434–445.

Miller, N. E. 1975. Clinical applications of biofeedback: Voluntary control of heart rate, rhythm, and blood pressure. In H. I. Russek (Ed.), *New horizons in cardiovascular practice.* University Park Press, Baltimore, pp. 239–249.

Miller, N. E. 1978. Biofeedback and visceral learning. *Annual Review of Psychology,* 29, 373–404.

Miller, N. E., & DiCara, L. 1967. Instrumental learning of heart rate changes in curarized rats: Shaping, and specificity to discriminative stimulus. *Journal of Comparative and Physiological Psychology,* 63, 12–19.

Miller, N. E., & Dworkin, B. R. 1974. Visceral learning: Recent difficulties with curarized rats and significant problems for human research. In P. A. Obrist, A. H. Black, J. Brener, & L. V. DiCara (Eds.), *Cardiovascular psychophysiology.* Aldine Publishing Company, Chicago, pp. 312–331.

Mills, J. E., Sellick, H., & Widdicombe, J. G. 1969. Activity of lung irritant receptors in pulmonary microembolism, anaphylaxis, and drug-induced bronchoconstrictions. *Journal of Physiology,* 203, 337–357.

Mishkin, M. 1958. Visual discrimination impairment after cutting cortical connections between the inferotemporal and striate areas in monkeys. *American Psychologist,* 13, 414–423.

Mishkin, M. 1966. Visual mechanisms beyond the striate cortex. In *Frontiers of physiological psychology,* Academic Press, New York, pp. 93–119.

Mishkin, M. 1972. Cortical visual areas and their interactions. In A. G. Karczmar & J. C. Eccles (Eds.), *Brain and human behavior.* Springer-Verlag, Berlin, pp. 187–208.

Mittlemann, B., & Wolff, H. G. 1939. Affective states and skin temperature: Experimental study of subjects with "cold hands" and Raynaud's syndrome. *Psychosomatic Medicine,* 1, 271–292.

Moffett, A., Swash, M., & Scott, D. F. 1972. Effect of tyramine in migraine: A double-blind study. *Journal of Neurology, Neurosurgery, and Psychiatry,* 35, 496–499.

Moffett, A. M., Swash, M., & Scott, D. F. 1974. Effect of chocolate in migraine: A double-blind study. *Journal of Neurology, Neurosurgery, and Psychiatry,* 37, 445–448.

Moore, J. G., & Englert, E. 1970. Circadian rhythm of gastric acid secretion in man. *Nature,* 226, 1261–1262.

MOORE, J. G., & MOTOKI, D. 1979. Gastric secretory and humoral responses to antici-pated feeding in five men. *Gastroenterology, 76,* 71–75.

MORRIS, H. G., DeROCHE, G., & EARLE, M. R. 1972. Urinary excretion of epinephrine and norepinephrine in asthmatic children. *The Journal of Allergy and Clinical Immunology, 50,* 138–145.

MORRIS, L. E. 1968. Diagnosis and treatment for Raynaud's phenomenon. *The Heart Bulletin, 17,* 81–85.

MOULTON, R. E. 1966. Emotional factors in non-organic temporomandibular joint pain. *Dental Clinics of North America, November,* 609–620.

MROCZEK, N., HALPERN, D., & McHUGH, R. 1978. Electromyographic feedback and physical therapy for neuromuscular retraining in hemiplegia. *Archives of Physical Medicine and Rehabilitation, 59,* 258–267.

MULHOLLAND, T. B. 1977. Biofeedback as scientific method. In G. E. Schwartz & J. Beatty (Eds.), *Biofeedback theory and research.* Academic Press, Inc., New York, pp. 9–28.

MUNRO, R. R. 1975. Electromyography of the masseter and anterior temporalis mus-cles in the open-close-clench cycle in temporomandibular joint dysfunction. *Mono-graphs in Oral Science, 4,* 117–125.

MURPHY, R. L. H. JR. 1976. Industrial disease with asthma. In E. B. Weiss & M. S. Segal (Eds.), *Bronchial asthma: Mechanisms and therapeutics.* Little, Brown & Company, Boston, 517–536.

MURRAY, K. 1967. Operant conditioning. In C. C. Brown (Ed.), *Methods in psycho-physiology.* The Williams & Wilkins Co., Baltimore, pp. 291–310.

MYREN, J., & SEMB, L. S. 1967. Relationship between the number of parietal cells and gastric secretion of acid. In M. H. Sleisenger & J. S. Fordtran (Eds.), *Gastrointestinal disease.* W. B. Saunders Company, Philadelphia.

NADEL, J. A. 1973. Neurophysiologic aspects of asthma. In K. F. Austen and L. M. Lichtenstein (Eds.), *Asthma: Physiology, immunopharmacology, and treatment.* Academic Press, Inc., New York, pp. 29–38.

NADEL, J. A. 1976. Airways: Autonomic regulation and airway responsiveness. In E. B. Weiss & M. S. Segal (Eds.), *Bronchial asthma: Mechanisms and therapeutics.* Little, Brown & Company, Boston, pp. 155–162.

NETSELL, R., & CLEELAND, C. S. 1973. Modification of lip hypertonia in dysarthria using EMG feedback. *Journal of Speech and Hearing Disorders, 38,* 131–140.

NIWAYAMA, G., & TERPLAN, K. 1959. A study of peptic ulcer based on necropsy records. *Gastroenterology, 36,* 409–422.

OBRIST, P. A., LIGHT, K. C., McCUBBIN, J. A., HUTCHESON, J. S., & HOFFLER, J. L. 1979. Pulse transit time: relationship to blood pressure and myocardial performance. *Psychophysiology 16,* 292–301.

OBRIST, W. D., THOMPSON, H. K. JR., KING, C. H., & WANG, H. S. 1967. Determination of regional cerebral blood flow by inhalation of ^{133}-Xenon. *Circulation Research, 20,* 124–135.

OBRIST, W. D., THOMPSON, H. K. JR., WANG, H. S., & WILKINSON, W. E. 1975. Regional cerebral blood flow estimated by ^{133}Xe inhalation. *Stroke, 6,* 245–256.

OI, M., ITO, Y., KUMAGAI, F., YOSHIDA, K., TANAKA, Y., YOSHIKAWA, K., MIHO, O., & KIJIMA, A. 1969. A possible dual control mechanism in the origin of peptic ulcer. A study on ulcer location as affected by mucosa and musculature. *Gastroenterology, 57,* 280–293.

OI, M., OSHIDA, K., & SUGIMURA, S. 1959. The location of gastric ulcer. *Gastroenterology, 36,* 45–56.

OI, M., TANAKA, Y., YOSHIDA, K., & YOSHIKAWA, K. 1966. Dual control of peptic ulcers by both the gastric mucosa and musculature. *Review of Surgery, 23,* 373–374.

OLDENDORF, W. H. 1969. Utilization of characteristic X-radiation to identify gamma radiation originating external to skull. *Journal of Nuclear Medicine, 10,* 740–742.

OLTON, D. S., ANDERSON, D. E., & NOONBERG, A. R. 1979. Behavioral medicine treatment of migraine headaches. (Unpublished manuscript)

OSTFELD, A. M., REIS, D. J., & WOLFF, H. G. 1957. Studies in headache. Bulbar conjunctival ischemia and muscle contraction headache. *Archives of Neurology and Psychiatry, 77,* 113–119.

PATEL, C. H. 1973. Yoga and bio-feedback in the management of hypertension. *Lancet, 2,* 1053–1055.

PATEL, C. 1975. 12-month follow-up of yoga and bio-feedback in the management of hypertension. *Lancet, 1,* 62–64.

PATEL, C., & NORTH, W. R. S. 1975. Randomised controlled trial of yoga and bio-feedback in management of hypertension. *Lancet, 2,* 93–95.

PAUL, G. L. 1966. *Insight vs. desensitization in psychotherapy: An experiment in anxiety reduction.* Stanford University Press, Stanford.

PAUL, O. 1977. Epidemiology of hypertension. In J. Genest, E. Koiw, & O. Kuchel (Eds.), *Hypertension physiopathology and treatment.* McGraw-Hill Inc., New York, pp. 613–630.

PEACOCK, J. H. 1959. A comparative study of the digital cutaneous temperatures and hand blood flows in the normal hand, primary Raynaud's disease, and primary acrocyanosis. *Clinical Science, 18,* 25–33.

PEARNE, D. H., ZIGELBAUM, S. D., & PEYSER, W. P. 1977. Biofeedback-assisted EMG relaxation for urinary retention and incontinence. A case report. *Biofeedback and Self-Regulation, 2,* 213–217.

PEART, W. S. 1971. Arterial Hypertension. In P. B. Beeson & W. McDermott (Eds.), *Cecil-Loeb textbook of medicine* (13th ed.), W. B. Saunders Company, Philadelphia, pp. 1050–1062.

PEAT, M., DUBO, H. I. C., WINTER, D. A., QUANBURY, A. O., STEINKE, T., & GRAHAME, R. 1976. Electromyographic temporal analysis of gait: Hemiplegic locomotion. *Archives of Physical Medicine and Rehabilitation, 57,* 421–425.

PECK, D. F. 1977. The use of EMG feedback in the treatment of a severe case of blepharospasm. *Biofeedback and Self-Regulation, 2,* 273–277.

PEFFER, K. E. 1979. Equipment needs for the psychotherapist. In J. V. Basmajian (Ed.), *Biofeedback—Principles and practice for clinicians.* The Williams & Wilkins Co., Baltimore, pp. 257–268.

PERMUTT, S. 1973. Physiologic changes in the acute asthmatic attack. In K. F. Austen & L. M. Lichtenstein (Eds.), *Asthma: Physiology, immunopharmacology, and treatment.* Academic Press Inc., New York, pp. 15–27.

PESHKIN, M. M. 1930. Asthma in children IX. Role of environment in the treatment of a selected group of cases: A plea for a "home" as a restorative measure. *American Journal of Diseases of Children, 39,* 774–781.

PESHKIN, M. M. 1959. Intractable asthma of childhood. Rehabilitation at the institutional level with a follow-up of 150 cases. *International Archives of Allergy and Applied Immunology, 15,* 91–112.

PESHKIN, M. M. 1966. The emotional aspects of allergy in childhood. *Journal of Asthma Research, 3,* 265–277.

PESHKIN, M. M. 1967. The evolution of allergies in childhood. *Journal of Asthma Research, 4,* 253–258.

PESHKIN, M. M. 1968. Analysis of the role of residential asthma centers for children with intractable asthma. *Journal of Asthma Research, 6,* 59–92.

PESHKIN, M. M. 1976. Intractable asthma in children. In E. B. Weiss & M. S. Segal

(Eds.), *Bronchial asthma: Mechanisms and therapeutics.* Little, Brown & Company, Boston, pp. 957–970.

PESHKIN, M. M., & FRIEDMAN, I. 1975. Residential asthma treatment centers in the United States and problems in relation to them. *Journal of Asthma Research, 12,* 129–175.

PETTY, T. L. 1978. Chronic bronchitis versus asthma—Or what's in a name? *The Journal of Allergy and Clinical Immunology, 62,* 323–324.

PHILIPP, R. L., WILDE, G. J. S., & DAY, J. H. 1972. Suggestion and relaxation in asthmatics. *Journal of Psychosomatic Research, 16,* 193–204.

PHILIPS, C. 1977a. Headache in general practice. *Headache, 16,* 322–329.

PHILIPS, C. 1977b. The modification of tension headache pain using EMG biofeedback. *Behaviour Research and Therapy, 15,* 119–129.

PHILIPS, C. 1978a. A psychological analysis of tension headache. In S. Rachman (Ed.), *Contributions to medical psychology.* Pergamon Press, Ltd., Oxford, pp. 91–113.

PHILIPS, C. 1978b. Tension headache: Theoretical problems. *Behavior Research and Therapy, 16,* 249–261.

PICKERING, G. W. 1968. *High blood pressure* (2nd ed.). J. & A. Churchill Ltd., London.

PICKERING, G. W. 1974a. *Hypertension: Causes, consequences management* (2nd ed.). Churchill Livingstone, Edinburgh.

PICKERING, G. W. 1974b. Hypertension: Definitions, natural histories, and consequences. In J. H. Laragh (Ed.), *Hypertension manual: Mechanisms, methods, management.* Dun-Donnelly Publishing Corporation, New York, pp. 3–30.

PICKERING, T., & GORHAM, G. 1975. Learned heart-rate control by a patient with a ventricular parasystolic rhythm. *Lancet, 1,* 252–253.

PODIVINSKY, F. 1968. Torticollis. In P. J. Vinken & G. W. Bruyn (Eds.), *Handbook of clinical neurology* (Vol. 6). North-Holland Publishing Company, Amsterdam, pp. 567–603.

POLGAR, G., & PROMADHAT, V. 1971. *Pulmonary function testing in children: Techniques and standards.* W. B. Saunders Company, Philadelphia.

PORTIS, S. A., & JAFFÉ, R. H. 1938. A study of peptic ulcer based on necropsy records. *Journal of the American Medical Association, 110,* pp. 6–13.

PRATT, K. L., MATTSON, R. H., WEIKERS, N. J., & WILLIAMS, R. 1968. EEG activation of epileptics following sleep deprivation: A prospective study of 114 cases. *Electroencephalography and Clinical Neurophysiology, 24,* 11–15.

PRICE, K. P., & TURSKY, B. 1976. Vascular reactivity of migraineurs and non-migraineurs: A comparison of responses to self-control procedures. *Headache, 16,* 210–217.

PRINGLE, R., WALDER, D. N., & WEAVER, J. P. A. 1965. Blood viscosity and Raynaud's disease. *Lancet, 1,* 1086–1089.

PURCELL, K. 1963. Distinctions between subgroups of asthmatic children. Children's perceptions of events associated with asthma. *Pediatrics, 31,* 486–494.

PURCELL, K. 1965. Critical appraisal of psychosomatic studies of asthma. *New York State Journal of Medicine, 65,* (Pt. 2), 2103–2109.

PURCELL, K., BERSTEIN, L., BUKANTZ, S. C. 1961. A preliminary comparison of rapidly remitting and persistently "steroid-dependent" asthmatic children. *Psychosomatic Medicine, 23,* 305–310.

PURCELL, K., BRADY, K., CHAI, H., MUSER, J., MOLK, L., GORDON, N., & MEANS, J. 1969. The effect on asthma in children of experimental separation from the family. *Psychosomatic Medicine, 31,* 144–164.

RACHMAN, S. J., & PHILIPS, C. 1975. *Psychology and Medicine.* Temple Smith, London.

RAHE, R. H. 1975. Life changes and near-future illness reports. In L. Levi (Ed.), *Emotions—Their parameters and measurement.* Raven Press Books, Ltd., New York, pp. 511–529.

RASKIN, M., JOHNSON, G., & RONDESTVEDT, J. W. 1973. Chronic anxiety treated by feedback-induced muscle relaxation. A pilot study. *Archives of General Psychiatry, 28,* 263–267.

RAY, B. S., & WOLFF, H. G. 1940. Experimental studies on headache. Pain-sensitive structures of the head and their significance in headache. *Archives of Surgery, 41,* 813–856.

RAYNAUD, A. G. M. 1862. *L'Asphyxia locale et de la gangrene symetrique des extremites.* Rignoux, Paris.

RAYNAUD, A. G. M. 1888. On local asphyxia and symmetrical gangrene of the extremities. In T. Barlow (trans.), *Selected Monographs.* New Syndenham Society, London.

READING, C., & MOHR, P. D. 1976. Biofeedback control of migraine: A pilot study. *British Journal of Social and Clinical Psychology, 15,* 429–433.

REES, L. 1956. Physical and emotional factors in bronchial asthma. *Journal of Psychosomatic Research, 1,* 98–114.

REES, L. 1963. The significance of parental attitudes in childhood asthma. *Journal of Psychosomatic Research, 7,* 181–190.

REES, L. 1964. The importance of psychological, allergic, and infective factors in childhood asthma. *Journal of Psychosomatic Research, 7,* 253–262.

REEVES, J. L. 1976. EMG-Biofeedback reduction of tension headache: A cognitive skills training approach. *Biofeedback and Self-Regulation, 1,* 217–225.

REEVES, J. L., & MEALIEA, W. L. 1975. Biofeedback-assisted cue-controlled relaxation for the treatment of flight phobias. *Journal of Behavior Therapy and Experimental Psychiatry, 6,* 105–109.

RESCORLA, R. A., & SOLOMON, R. L. 1967. Two-process learning theory: Relationships between Pavlovian conditioning and instrumental learning. *Psychological Review, 74,* 151–182.

RICHARDSON, C. T. 1973. Chronic gastric ulcer. In M. H. Sleisenger & J. S. Fordtran (Eds.), *Gastrointestinal disease: Pathophysiology, diagnosis, management.* W. B. Saunders Company, Philadelphia, pp. 692–713.

RIVERS, A. B. 1935. Pain in benign ulcers of the esophagus, stomach, and small intestine. *Journal of the American Medical Association, 104,* 169–174.

ROBERTSON, C. W., & SMITHWICK, R. H. 1951. The recurrence of vasoconstrictor activity after limb sympathectomy in Raynaud's disease and allied vasomotor states. *New England Journal of Medicine, 245,* 317–320.

RODBARD, S. 1970. Muscle pain. In B. L. Crue, Jr. (Ed.), *Pain and suffering: Selected aspects.* Charles C Thomas, Publisher, Philadelphia, pp. 154–167.

RODBARD, S. 1975. Pain in contracting muscle. In B. L. Crue, Jr. (Ed.), *Pain research and treatment.* Academic Press, Inc., New York, pp. 183–196.

ROGERSON, C. H. 1934. The role of psychotherapy in the treatment of the asthma-eczema-prurigo complex in children. *British Journal of Dermatology and Syphilis, 46,* 368–378.

ROTH, G. M., McDONALD, J. B., & SHEARD, C. 1944. The effect of smoking cigarets and of intravenous administration of nicotine on the electrocardiogram, basal metabolic rate, cutaneous temperature, blood pressure, and pulse rate of normal persons. *Journal of the American Medical Association, 125,* 761–767.

RUDICK, J., & JANOWITZ, H. D. 1974. Gastric physiology. In H. L. Bockus (Ed.), *Gastroenterology* (Vol. 1, 3rd ed.). W. B. Saunders Company, Philadelphia, pp. 405–418.

RUSHMER, R. F. 1976. *Cardiovascular Dynamics* (4th ed.). W. B. Saunders Company, Philadelphia.

RYAN, R. E. 1974. A clinical study of tyramine as an etiological factor in migraine. *Headache, 14,* 43–48.

RYO, U. Y., & TOWNLEY, R. G. 1976. Comparison of respiratory and cardiovascular effects of isoproterenol, propranolol, and practolol in asthmatic and normal subjects. *The Journal of Allergy and Clinical Immunology, 57,* 12–24.

SACHS, D. A., MARTIN, J. E., & FITCH, J. L. 1972. The effect of visual feedback on a digital exercise in a functionally deaf cerebral palsied child. *Journal of Behavior Therapy and Experimental Psychiatry, 3,* 217–222.

SACHS, O. W. 1970. *Migraine: The evolution of a common disorder.* University of California Press, Berkeley and Los Angeles.

SAINSBURY, P., & GIBSON, J. G. 1954. Symptoms of anxiety and tension and the accompanying physiological changes in the muscular system. *Journal of Neurology, Neurosurgery, and Psychiatry, 17,* 216–224.

SAKAI, F., & MEYER, J. S. 1978. Regional cerebral hemodynamics during migraine and cluster headaches measured by the 133Xe inhalation method. *Headache, 18,* 122–132.

SANDLER, L. 1965a. Child-rearing practices of mothers of asthmatic children. Part 1. *Journal of Asthma Research, 2,* 109–142.

SANDLER, L. 1965b. Child-rearing practices of mothers of asthmatic children. Part 2. *Journal of Asthma Research, 2,* 215–256.

SAPPINGTON, J. T., FIORITO, E. M., & BREHONY, K. A. 1979. Biofeedback as therapy in Raynaud's disease. *Biofeedback and Self-Regulation, 4,* 155–169.

SARGENT, J. D., GREEN, E. E., & WALTERS, E. D. 1973. Preliminary report on the use of autogenic feedback training in the treatment of migraine and tension headaches. *Psychosomatic Medicine, 35,* 129–135.

SARNAT, B. G. 1964. Preface to the second edition. In B. G. Sarnat (Ed.), *The temporomandibular joint* (2nd ed.). Charles C Thomas, Publisher, Springfield, p. ix.

SARNAT, B. G., & LASKIN, D. M. 1964. Surgery of the temporomandibular joint. In B. G. Sarnat (Ed.), *The temporomandibular joint* (2nd ed.). Charles C Thomas, Publisher, Springfield, pp. 185–238.

SCADDING, J. G. 1976. Definition and clinical categorization. In E. B. Weiss & M. S. Segal (Eds.), *Bronchial asthma: Mechanisms and therapeutics.* Little, Brown & Company, Boston, pp. 19–30.

SCHEINBERG, P. 1975. The cerebral circulation. In R. Zelis (Ed.), *The peripheral circulations.* Grune and Stratton, Inc., New York, pp. 151–162.

SCHERR, M. S., CRAWFORD, P. L., SERGENT, C. B., & SCHERR, C. A. 1975. Effect of biofeedback techniques on chronic asthma in a summer camp environment. *Annals of Allergy, 35,* 289–295.

SCHULTZ, J. H., & LUTHE, W. 1969. *Autogenic Therapy.* Vol. 1, *Autogenic Methods.* Grune and Stratton Inc., New York.

SCHUSTER, M. M. 1974. Operant conditioning in gastrointestinal dysfunctions. *Hospital Practice, 9,* 135–143.

SCHUSTER, M. M. 1979. Biofeedback control of gastrointestinal motility. In J. V. Basmajian (Ed.), *Biofeedback—Principles and practice for clinicians.* The Williams & Wilkins Co., Baltimore, pp. 230–237.

SCHUSTER, M. M., HOOKMAN, P., HENDRIX, T. R., & MENDELOFF, A. I. 1965. Simultaneous manometric recording of internal and external anal sphincteric reflexes. *Bulletin of the Johns Hopkins Hospital, 116,* 79–88.

SCHUSTER, M. M., & MENDELOFF, A. I. 1968. Motor action of rectum and anal sphincters in continence and defecation. In C. F. Code (Ed.), *Handbook of physiology: A critical, comprehensive presentation of physiological knowledge and concepts* (Sec. 6, Vol. 4). American Physiological Society, Washington, pp. 2121–2146.

SCHWARTZ, G. E. 1972. Voluntary control of human cardiovascular integration and differentiation through feedback and reward. *Science, 175,* 90–93.

SCHWARTZ, G. E. 1974. Toward a theory of voluntary control of response patterns in the cardiovascular system. In P. A. Obrist, A. H. Black, J. Brener, & L. V. DiCara

(Eds.), *Cardiovascular psychophysiology*. Aldine Publishing Company, Chicago, pp. 406–440.

SCHWARTZ, G. E. 1977. Biofeedback and patterning of autonomic and central processes: CNS-cardiovascular interactions. In G. E. Schwartz & J. Beatty (Eds.), *Biofeedback Theory and Research*. Academic Press Inc., New York, pp. 183–219.

SCHWARTZ, G. E., & BEATTY, J. 1977. Introduction. In G. E. Schwartz & J. Beatty (Eds.), *Biofeedback theory and research*. Academic Press Inc., New York, pp. 1–6.

SCHWARTZ, G. E., SHAPIRO, D., & TURSKY, B. 1972. Self-control of patterns of human diastolic blood pressure and heart rate through feedback and reward. *Psychophysiology, 9*, 270. Reported in Schwartz, G. E. 1977. Biofeedback and patterning of autonomic and central processes: CNS-cardiovascular interactions. In G. E. Schwartz & J. Beatty (Eds.), *Biofeedback Theory and Research*. Academic Press Inc., New York, pp. 183–219.

SCHWARTZ, L. L. 1955. Pain associated with the temporomandibular joint. *Journal of the American Dental Association, 51*, 394–397.

SCHWARTZ, R. P., HEATH, A. L., & HUDSON, F. W. 1949a. Instrumentation in relation to electromyography. I. factors influencing recording and interpretation of electromyograms. *Archives of Physical Medicine, 30*, 383–394.

SCHWARTZ, R. P., HEATH, A. L., & HUDSON, F. W. 1949b. Instrumentation in relation to electromyography. II. a discussion of instrumentation requirements for high fidelity electromyographic recording using skin electrodes. *Archives of Physical Medicine, 30*, 394–400.

SCOLLO-LAVIZZARI, G., & HESS, R. 1967. Sensory precipitation of epileptic seizures. Report on two unusual cases. *Epilepsia, 8*, 157–161.

SCOTT, R. W., BLANCHARD, E. B., EDMUNSON, E. D., & YOUNG, L. D. 1973. A shaping procedure for heart-rate control in chronic tachycardia. *Perceptual and Motor Skills, 37*, 327–338.

SEIFERT, A. R., & LUBAR, J. F. 1975. Reduction of epileptic seizures through EEG biofeedback training. *Biological Psychology, 3*, 157–184.

SELBY, G. 1968. Parkinson's disease. In P. J. Vinken and G. W. Bruyn (Eds.), *Diseases of nerves*. North-Holland Publishing Company, Amsterdam, pp. 173–211.

SHAGASS, C. 1972. Electrical activity of the brain. In N. S. Greenfield & R. A. Sternbach (Eds.), *Handbook of psychophysiology*. Holt, Rinehart and Winston, Inc., New York, pp. 263–328.

SHAPIRO, B. L., & GORLIN, R. J. 1970. Disorders of the temporomandibular joint. In R. J. Gorlin & H. M. Goldman (Eds.), *Thoma's oral pathology* (Vol. 2). C. V. Mosby, St. Louis, pp. 577–606.

SHAPIRO, D. 1974. Operant-feedback control of human blood pressure: Some clinical issues. In P. A. Obrist, A. H. Black, J. Brener, & L. V. DiCara (Eds.), *Cardiovascular psychophysiology: Current issues in response mechanisms, biofeedback, and methodology*. Aldine Publishing Company, Chicago, pp. 441–455.

SHAPIRO, D., MAINARDI, J. A., & SURWIT, R. S. 1977. Biofeedback and self-regulation in essential hypertension. In G. E. Schwartz & J. Beatty (Eds.), *Biofeedback theory and research*. Academic Press Inc., New York, pp. 313–347.

SHAPIRO, D., & SURWIT, R. S. 1976. Learned control of physiological function and disease. In H. Leitenberg (Ed.), *Handbook of behavior modification and behavior therapy*. Prentice-Hall, Inc., Englewood Cliffs, pp. 74–123.

SHAPIRO, D., TURSKY, B., GERSHON, E., & STERN, M. 1969. Effects of feedback and reinforcement on the control of human systolic blood pressure. *Science, 163*, 588–590.

SHAW, J. C. 1967. Quantification of biological signals using integration techniques. In P. H. Venables & I. Martin (Eds.), *A manual of psychophysiological methods*. North-Holland Publishing Company, Amsterdam, pp. 403–465.

SHAW, S. W. J., JOHNSON, R. H., & KEOGH, H. J. 1978. Oral tyramine in dietary migraine sufferers. In R. Greene (Ed.), *Current concepts in migraine research,* Raven Press Books, Ltd, pp. 31–39.

SICHER, H. 1964. Functional anatomy of the temporomandibular joint. In B. G. Sarnat (Ed.), *The temporomandibular joint* (2nd ed.). Charles C Thomas, Publisher, Springfield, pp. 28–58.

SILBER, E. N., & KATZ, L. N. 1975. *Heart disease.* Macmillan, Inc., New York.

SIMARD, D., & PAULSON, O. B. 1973. Cerebral vasomotor paralysis during migraine attack. *Archives of Neurology, 29,* 207–209.

SIMONS, D. J., DAY, E., GOODELL, H., & WOLFF, H. G. 1943. Experimental studies on headache: Muscles of the scalp and neck as sources of pain. *Research Publications of the Association for Research in Nervous and Mental Disease, 23,* 228–244.

SIMONS, D. J., & WOLFF, H. G. 1946. Studies on headache: Mechanisms of chronic posttraumatic headache. *Psychosomatic Medicine, 8,* 227–242.

SIMONSSON, B. G., JACOBS, F. M., & NADEL, J. A. 1967. Role of autonomic nervous system and the cough reflex in the increased responsiveness of airways in patients with obstructive airway disease. *Journal of Clinical Investigation, 46,* 1812–1818.

SINGH, H., GOYAL, R. K., AHLUWALIA, D. S., & CHUTTANI, H. K. 1968. Vagal influence in gastric acid secretion in normals and in duodenal ulcer patients. *Gut, 9,* 604–608.

SKINHØJ, E. 1973. Hemodynamic studies within the brain during migraine. *Archives of Neurology, 29,* 95–98.

SKINHØJ, E., & PAULSON, O. B. 1969. Regional blood flow in internal carotid distribution during migraine attack. *British Medical Journal, 3,* 569–570.

SKROTZKY, K., GALLENSTEIN, J. S., & OSTERNIG, L. R. 1978. Effects of electromyographic feedback training on motor control in spastic cerebral palsy. *Physical Therapy, 58,* 547–551.

SLEISENGER, M. H. 1973a. Physiology of the colon. In M. H. Sleisenger & J. S. Fordtran (Eds.), *Gastrointestinal disease: Pathophysiology, diagnosis, management.* W. B. Saunders Company, Philadelphia, pp. 229–249.

SLEISENGER, M. H. 1973b. Anatomy. In M. H. Sleisenger & J. S. Fordtran (Eds.), *Gastrointestinal disease: Pathophysiology, diagnosis, management.* W. B. Saunders Company, Philadelphia, pp. 1234–1248.

SMITH, I., KELLOW, A. H., & HANINGTON, E. 1970. A clinical and biochemical correlation between tyramine and migraine headache. *Headache, 10,* 43–52.

SMITH, L. A. 1954. The pattern of pain in the diagnosis of upper abdominal disorders. *Journal of the American Medical Association, 156,* pp. 1566–1573.

SMORTO, M. P., & BASMAJIAN, J. V. 1977. *Electrodiagnosis: A Handbook for neurologists.* Harper & Row, Publishers, Inc., New York.

SNIDER, G. L. 1976. The interrelationship of asthma, chronic bronchitis, and emphysema. In E. B. Weiss & M. S. Segal (Eds.), *Bronchial asthma: Mechanisms and therapeutics.* Little, Brown & Company, Boston, pp. 31–41.

Society of Actuaries. 1959. *Build and blood pressure study* (Vol. I). Society of Actuaries, Chicago.

Society of Actuaries. 1960. *Build and blood pressure study* (Vol. II). Society of Actuaries, Chicago.

SOLBACH, P., & SARGENT, J. D. 1977. A follow-up evaluation of the Menninger pilot migraine study using thermal training. *Headache, 17,* 198–202.

SOLOMON, R. L., & WYNNE, L. C. 1954. Traumatic avoidance learning: The principles of anxiety conservation and partial irreversibility. *Psychology Review, 61,* 353–385.

SORENSEN, B. F., & HAMBY, W. B. 1966. Spasmodic torticollis. Results in 71 surgically treated patients. *Neurology, 16,* 867–878.

SPEARING, D. L., & POPPEN, R. 1974. Single case study. The use of feedback in the reduction of foot dragging in a cerebral palsied client. *Journal of Nervous and Mental Disease, 159*, 148–151.

SPERRY, R. W. 1952. Neurology and the mind-brain problem. *American Scientist, 40*, 291–312.

SPERRY, R. W. 1961. Cerebral organization and behavior. *Science, 133*, 1749–1757.

SPERRY, R. W., & GAZZANIGA, M. S. 1967. Language following surgical disconnection of the hemispheres. In F. L. Darley (Ed.), *Brain mechanisms underlying speech and language*. Grune and Stratton, Inc., New York, pp. 108–121.

SPIRO, H. M. 1977. *Clinical gastroenterology* (2nd ed.). Macmillan, Inc., New York.

STEPTOE, A., SMULYAN, H., & GRIBBIN, B. 1976. Pulse wave velocity and blood pressure change: Calibration and applications. *Psychophysiology, 13*, 488–493.

STERMAN, M. B. 1973. Neurophysiologic and clinical studies of sensorimotor EEG biofeedback training: Some effects on epilepsy. In L. Birk (Ed.), *Biofeedback: Behavioral medicine*. Grune and Stratton, Inc., New York, pp. 147–165.

STERMAN, M. B. 1977a. Sensorimotor EEG operant conditioning: Experimental and clinical effects. *Pavlovian Journal of Biological Science, 12*, 63–92.

STERMAN, M. B. 1977b. Effects of sensorimotor EEG feedback training on sleep and clinical manifestations of epilepsy. In J. Beatty & H. Legewie (Eds.), *Biofeedback and behavior*. Plenum Publishing Corporation, New York, pp. 167–200.

STERMAN, M. B., & FRIAR, L. 1972. Suppression of seizures in an epileptic following sensorimotor EEG feedback training. *Electroencephalography and Clinical Neurophysiology, 33*, 89–95.

STERMAN, M. B., & MACDONALD, L. R. 1978. Effects of central cortical EEG feedback training on incidence of poorly controlled seizures. *Epilepsia, 19*, 207–222.

STERMAN, M. B., MACDONALD, L. R., & STONE, R. K. 1974. Biofeedback training of the sensorimotor EEG rhythm in man: Effects on epilepsy. *Epilepsia, 15*, 395–416.

STEVENS, J. R. 1959. Emotional activation of the electroencephalogram in patients with convulsive disorders. *Journal of Nervous and Mental Disease, 128*, 339–351.

STOUT, A. P. 1947. Tumours of the stomach. *Bulletin of the New York Academy of Medicine, 23*, 101–108.

STRAUSS, R. H., HAYNES, R. L., INGRAM, R. H. JR., & MCFADDEN, E. R. JR. 1977. Comparison of arm versus leg work in induction of acute episodes of asthma. *American Journal of Physiology: Respiratory, Environmental and Exercise Physiology, 42*, 565–570.

STRAUSS, R. H., MCFADDEN, E. R. JR., INGRAM, R. H. JR., & JAEGER, J. J. 1977. Enhancement of exercise-induced asthma by cold air. *New England Journal of Medicine, 297*, 743–747.

STROEBEL, C. F., & GLUECK, B. C. 1973. Biofeedback treatment in medicine and psychiatry: An ultimate placebo? In L. Birk (Ed.), *Biofeedback: Behavioral medicine*. Grune and Stratton, Inc., New York, pp. 19–33.

STRUPP, H. H., LEVENSON, R. W., MANUCK, S. B., SNELL, J. D., HINRICHSEN, J. J., & BOYD, S. 1974. Effects of suggestion on total respiratory resistance in mild asthmatics. *Journal of Psychosomatic Research, 18*, 337–346.

STURDEVANT, R. A. L., & WALSH, J. H. 1978. Duodenal ulcer. In M. H. Sleisenger & J. S. Fordtran (Eds.), *Gastrointestinal disease: Pathophysiology, diagnosis, management* (2nd ed.). W. B. Saunders Company, Philadelphia, pp. 840–860.

STURGIS, E. T., TOLLISON, C. D., & ADAMS, H. E. 1978. Modification of combined migraine-muscle contraction headaches using BVP and EMG feedback. *Journal of Applied Behavior Analysis, 11*, 215–223.

SUMMER, W. R. 1978. Physiological changes in the acute asthmatic attack. In E. B. Weiss (Ed.), *Status asthmaticus*. Unversity Park Press, Baltimore, pp. 81–99.

SUN, D. C. H. 1974. Etiology and pathology of peptic ulcer. In H. L. Bockus (Ed.),

Gastroenterology (Vol. 1, 3rd ed.). W. B. Saunders Company, Philadelphia, pp. 579–610.

SUN, D. C. H., & ROTH, J. L. A. 1974. Tests employed in analysis of the stomach contents and their clinical application. In H. L. Bockus (Ed.), *Gastroenterology* (Vol. 1, 3rd ed.). W. B. Saunders Company, Philadelphia, pp. 419–453.

SURWIT, R. S. 1973. Biofeedback: A possible treatment for Raynaud's disease. In L. Birk (Ed.), *Biofeedback: Behavioral medicine*. Grune and Stratton, Inc., New York, pp. 123–130.

SURWIT, R. S., PILON, R. N., & FENTON, C. H. 1978. Behavioral treatment of Raynaud's disease. *Journal of Behavioral Medicine, 1,* 323–335.

SURWIT, R. S., & SHAPIRO, D. 1977. Biofeedback and meditation in the treatment of borderline hypertension. In J. Beatty & H. Legewie (Eds.), *Biofeedback and behavior*. Plenum Publishing Corporation, New York, pp. 403–412.

SURWIT, R. S., SHAPIRO, D., & FELD, J. L. 1976. Digital temperature autoregulation and associated cardiovascular changes. *Psychophysiology, 13,* 242–248.

SURWIT, R. S., SHAPIRO, D., & GOOD, M. I. 1978. Comparison of cardiovascular biofeedback, neuromuscular biofeedback, and meditation in the treatment of borderline essential hypertension. *Journal of Consulting and Clinical Psychology, 46,* 252–263.

SWANN, D., VAN WIERINGEN, P. C. W., & FOKKEMA, S. D. 1974. Auditory electromyographic feedback therapy to inhibit undesired motor activity. *Archives of Physical Medicine and Rehabilitation, 55,* 251–254.

SWETS, J. A., PICKETT, R. M., WHITEHEAD, S. F., GETTY, D. J., SCHNUR, J. A., SWETS, J. B., & FREEMAN, B. A. 1979. Assessment of diagnostic technologies. *Science, 205,* 753–759.

SWINEFORD, O. JR. 1962. The asthma problem. A critical analysis. *Annals of Internal Medicine, 57,* 144–163.

SWINEFORD, O. JR. 1965. Definition of asthma. A critical review. One brief and one comprehensive definition. *Journal of Asthma Research, 2,* 283–292.

SWINYARD, E. A., CLARK, L. D., MIYAHARA, J. T., & WOLF, H. H. 1961. Studies on the mechanism of amphetamine toxicity in aggregated mice. *Journal of Pharmacology and Experimental Therapeutics, 132,* 97–102.

SWINYARD, E. A., MIYAHARA, J. T., CLARK, L. D., & GOODMAN, L. S. 1963. The effects of experimentally-induced stress on pentylenetetrazol seizure threshold in mice. *Psychopharmacologia, 4,* 343–353.

SYMONDS, C. 1959. Excitation and inhibition in epilepsy. *Brain, 82,* 133–146.

SZENTIVANYI, A. 1968. The beta adrenergic theory of the atopic abnormality in bronchial asthma. *The Journal of Allergy, 42,* 203–232.

SZENTIVANYI, A., & FISHEL, C. W. 1976. The beta-adrenergic theory and cyclic AMP-mediated control mechanisms in human asthma. In E. B. Weiss & M. S. Segal (Eds.), *Bronchial asthma: Mechanisms and therapeutics*. Little, Brown & Company, Boston, pp. 137–153.

TAKEBE, K., & BASMAJIAN, J. V. 1976. Gait analysis in stroke patients to assess treatments of foot-drop. *Archives of Physical Medicine and Rehabilitation, 57,* 305–310.

TAL, A., & MIKLICH, D. R. 1976. Emotionally induced decreases in pulmonary flow rates in asthmatic children. *Psychosomatic Medicine, 38,* 190–200.

TARLOV, E. 1970. On the problem of the pathology of spasmodic torticollis in man. *Journal of Neurology, Neurosurgery, and Psychiatry, 33,* 457–463.

TAUB, E. 1977. Self-regulation of human tissue temperature. In G. E. Schwartz & J. Beatty (Eds.), *Biofeedback theory and research*. Academic Press Inc., New York, pp. 265–300.

TAUB, E., & STROEBEL, C. F. 1978. Biofeedback in the treatment of vasoconstrictive syndromes. *Biofeedback and Self-Regulation, 3,* 363–373.

TAVERNER, D. 1955. Bell's palsy. A clinical and electromyographic study. *Brain, 78,* 209–228.

TEMKIN, O. 1971. *The falling sickness.* The Johns Hopkins Press, Baltimore.

THOMAS, P. K. 1978. Third, fourth, and sixth cranial nerves. In R. B. Scott (Ed.), *Price's textbook of the practice of medicine.* Oxford University Press, Oxford, pp. 1306–1312.

THOMPSON, J. K., & COLLINS, F. L. JR. 1979. Reliability of headache questionnaire data. *Headache, 19,* 97–101.

THOMPSON, J. R. 1964. Temporomandibular disorders: Diagnosis and dental treatment. In B. G. Sarnat (Ed.), *The temporomandibular joint.* Charles C Thomas, Publisher, Philadelphia, pp. 146–184.

THULESIUS, O. 1976. Primary and secondary Raynaud phenomena. *Acta Chirurgica Scandinavica Supplementum, 465,* 5–6.

THURLBECK, W. M. 1978. Pathology of status asthmaticus. In E. B. Weiss (Ed.), *Status asthmaticus.* University Park Press, Baltimore, pp. 19–31.

TIETJEN, G. W., CHIEN, S., LEROY, E. C., GAVRAS, I., GAVRAS, H., & GUMP, F. E. 1975. Blood viscosity, plasma proteins, & Raynaud syndrome. *Archives of Surgery, 110,* 1343–1346.

TOWNLEY, R. G., RYO, U. Y., KOLOTKIN, B. M., & KANG, B. 1975. Bronchial sensitivity to methacholine in current and former asthmatic and allergic rhinitis patients and control subjects. *Journal of Allergy and Clinical Immunology, 56,* 429–442.

TRAVELL, J. 1960. Temporomandibular joint pain referred from muscles of the head and neck. *Journal of Prosthetic Dentistry, 10,* 745–763.

TUFT, H. S. 1957. The development and management of intractable asthma of childhood. *American Journal of Diseases of Children, 93,* 251–254.

TUNIS, M. M., & WOLFF, H. G. 1952. Analysis of cranial artery pulse waves in patients with vascular headache of the migraine type. *American Journal of the Medical Sciences, 224,* 565–568.

TUNIS, M. M., & WOLFF, H. G. 1954. Studies on headache. Cranial artery vasoconstriction and muscle contraction headache. *Archives of Neurology and Psychiatry, 71,* 425–434.

TURIN, A., & JOHNSON, W. G. 1976. Biofeedback therapy for migraine headaches. *Archives of General Psychiatry, 33,* 517–519.

TURSKY, B. 1974. The indirect recording of human blood pressure. In P. A. Obrist, A. H. Black, J. Brener, & L. V. DiCara (Eds.), *Cardiovascular psychophysiology: Current issues in response mechanisms, biofeedback, and methodology.* Aldine Publishing Company, Chicago, pp. 93–105.

TURSKY, B., SHAPIRO, D., & SCHWARTZ, G. E. 1972. Automated constant cuff-pressure system to measure average systolic and diastolic blood pressure in man. *IEEE Transactions on Bio-medical Engineering, 19,* 271–276.

UNGER, A. H., & UNGER, L. 1952. Migraine is an allergic disease. *The Journal of Allergy, 23,* 429–440.

UNGER, L., & UNGER, A. H. 1952. Treatment of bronchial asthma. *Journal of the American Medical Association, 150,* 562–569.

VACHON, L., & RICH, E. S. JR. 1976. Visceral learning in asthma. *Psychosomatic Medicine, 38,* 122–130.

VALENTINE, M. D. 1976. Chemical mediators in asthma. In E. B. Weiss & M. S. Segal (Eds.), *Bronchial asthma: Mechanisms and therapeutics.* Little, Brown & Company, Boston, pp. 181–190.

VAUGHN, J. H., TAN, E. M., MATHISON, D. A., STEVENSON, D. D., BERMAN, S. Z., & BRAUDE, A. I. 1973. In K. F. Austen & L. M. Lichtenstein (Eds.). *Asthma: Physiology, immunopharmacology, and treatment.* Academic Press Inc., New York, pp. 1–13.

VAUGHN, R., PALL, M. L., & HAYNES, S. N. 1977. Frontalis EMG response to stress in subjects with frequent muscle-contraction headaches. *Headache, 16,* 313–317.

VENABLES, P. H., & MARTIN, I. (Eds.). 1967. A manual of psychophysiological methods. North-Holland Publishing Company, Amsterdam.

VESELÝ, K. T., KUBICKOVA, A., DVORAKOVA, M., & ZVOLÁNKOVÁ, K. 1968. Clinical data and characteristics differentiating types of peptic ulcers. *Gut, 9,* 57–68.

WALKER, A. 1978. Functional anatomy of oral tissues: Mastication and deglutition. In J. H. Shaw, E. A. Sweeny, C. C. Capuccino, & S. M. Meller (Eds), *Textbook of oral biology.* W. B. Saunders Company, Philadelphia, pp. 277–296.

WALKER, C. O. 1973. Chronic duodenal ulcer. In M. H. Sleisenger & J. S. Fordtran (Eds.), *Gastrointestinal disease: Pathophysiology, diagnosis, management.* W. B. Saunders Company, Philadelphia, pp. 665–691.

WALSH, J. H. 1973. Control of gastric secretion. In M. H. Sleisenger & J. S. Fordtran (Eds.), *Gastrointestinal disease: Pathophysiology, diagnosis, management.* W. B. Saunders Company, Philadelphia, pp. 144–162.

WALSH, J. H. 1975. Clinical and endocrine aspects. In P. B. Beeson & W. McDermott (Eds.), *Textbook of medicine* (14th ed.). W. B. Saunders Company, Philadelphia, pp. 1208–1210.

WALSH, P., DALE, A., & ANDERSON, D. E. 1977. Comparison of biofeedback pulse wave velocity and progressive relaxation in essential hypertensives. *Perceptual and Motor Skills, 44,* (Pt. 2), 839–843.

WALTON, J. N. 1977. *Brain's diseases of the nervous system* (8th ed.). Oxford University Press, Oxford.

WANNSTEDT, G. T., & HERMAN, R. M. 1978. Use of augmented sensory feedback to achieve symmetrical standing. *Physical Therapy, 58,* 553–559.

WARD, A. A. JR. 1969. The epileptic neuron: Chronic foci in animals and man. In H. H. Jasper, A. A. Ward Jr., & A. Pope (Eds.), *Basic mechanisms of the epilepsies.* Little, Brown & Company, Boston, pp. 263–298.

WATERS, W. E. 1970. Community studies of the prevalence of headache. *Headache, 9,* 178–186.

WATERS, W. E. 1974. The Pontypridd headache survey. *Headache, 14,* 81–90.

WATKINSON, G. 1960. The incidence of chronic peptic ulcer found at necropsy. A study of 20,000 examinations performed in Leeds in 1930–49 and in England and Scotland in 1956. *Gut, 1,* 14–30.

WATSON, J. B., & RAYNER, R. 1920. Conditioned emotional reactions. *Journal of Experimental Psychology, 3,* 1–14.

WAY, L. W. 1976. Abdominal pain and the acute abdomen. In M. H. Sleisenger & J. S. Fordtran (Eds.), *Gastrointestinal disease: Pathophysiology, diagnosis, management* (2nd ed.). W. B. Saunders Company, Philadelphia, pp. 394–410.

Webster's New Collegiate Dictionary. 1973. G. & C. Merriam Co., Springfield.

WEINER, H. 1977. Personality factors and the importance of emotional stresses in hypertension. In J. Genest, E. Koiw, & O. Kuchel (Eds.), *Hypertension physiopathology and treatment.* McGraw-Hill, Inc., New York, pp. 661–673.

WEINER, N. 1948. *Cybernetics: Or control and communication in the animal and the machine.* John Wiley & Sons, Inc., New York.

WEINMANN, J. P., & SICHER, H. 1964. Pathology of the temporomandibular joint. In B. G. Sarnat (Ed.), *The temporomandibular joint* (2nd ed.). Charles C Thomas, Publisher, Springfield, pp. 89–101.

WEIR, R. D., & BACKETT, E. M. 1968. Studies of the epidemiology of peptic ulcer in a rural community: Prevalence and natural history of dyspepsia and peptic ulcer. *Gastroenterology, 9,* 75–83.

WEISS, E. B. (Ed.). 1978. *Status asthmaticus.* University Park Press, Baltimore.

WEISS, J. H., LYNESS, J., MOLK, L., & RILEY, J. 1976. Induced respiratory change in asthmatic children. *Journal of Psychosomatic Research, 20,* 115–123.

WEISS, T., & ENGEL, B. T. 1973. Operant conditioning of heart rate in patients with premature ventricular contractions. In L. Birk (Ed.), *Biofeedback: Behavioral medicine.* Grune and Stratton Inc., New York, pp. 79–100.

WELGAN, P. R. 1974. Learned control of gastric acid secretions in ulcer patients. *Psychosomatic Medicine, 36,* 411–419.

WELGAN, P. R. 1977. Biofeedback control of stomach acid secretions and gastrointestinal reactions. In J. Beatty & H. Legewie (Eds.), *Biofeedback and behavior.* Plenum Publishing Corporation, New York, pp. 385–393.

WENGER, M. A. 1948. Studies of autonomic balance in Army Air Forces personnel. *Comparative Psychology Monographs, 19,* 1–111.

WENGER, M. A. 1957. Pattern analyses of autonomic variables during rest. *Psychosomatic Medicine, 19,* 240–244.

WENNERHOLM, M. 1961. Postural vascular reactions in cases of migraine and related vascular headaches. *Acta Medica Scandinavica, 169,* 131–139.

WHITEHEAD, W. E. 1978. Biofeedback in the treatment of gastrointestinal disorders. *Biofeedback and Self-Regulation, 3,* 375–384.

WHITFIELD, I. C. 1953. *An introduction to electronics for physiological workers.* Macmillan, Inc., Ltd., London.

WHITTERIDGE, D., & WALSH, E. G. 1963. The physiological basis of the electroencephalogram. In D. Hill & G. Parr (Eds.), *Electroencephalography: A symposium on its various aspects.* Macdonald & Co., Ltd., pp. 99–146.

WICKRAMASEKERA, I. 1972. Electromyographic feedback training and tension headache: Preliminary observations. *American Journal of Clinical Hypnosis, 15,* 83–85.

WICKRAMASEKERA, I. 1973a. The application of verbal instructions and EMG feedback training to the management of tension headache—Preliminary observations. *Headache, 13,* 74–76.

WICKRAMASEKERA, I. 1973b. Temperature feedback for the control of migraine. *Journal of Behavior Therapy and Experimental Psychiatry, 4,* 343–345.

WIDDICOMBE, J. G. 1963. Regulation of tracheobronchial smooth muscle. *Physiological Reviews, 43,* 1–37.

WIDDICOMBE, J. G., KENT, D. C., & NADEL, J. A. 1962. Mechanism of bronchoconstriction during inhalation of dust. *Journal of Applied Physiology, 17,* 613–616.

WIDDICOMBE, J. G., & STERLING, G. M. 1970. The autonomic nervous system and breathing. *Archives of Internal Medicine, 126,* 311–329.

WILDER, J. 1957. The law of initial values in neurology and psychiatry. Facts and problems. *Journal of Nervous and Mental Disease, 125,* 73–86.

WILKINS, R. W. 1963a. Diseases of the peripheral vessels. In P. B. Beeson & W. McDermott (Eds.), *Cecil-Loeb textbook of medicine* (11th ed.). W. B. Saunders Company, Philadelphia, pp. 777–781.

WILKINS, R. W. 1963b. Peripheral vascular diseases due to abnormal vasoconstriction or vasodilatation. In P. B. Beeson & W. McDermott (Eds.), *Cecil-Loeb textbook of medicine,* (11th ed.). W. B. Saunders Company, Philadelphia, pp. 786–790.

WILKINSON, C. F. 1949. Recurrent migrainoid headaches associated with spontaneous hypoglycemia. *American Journal of the Medical Sciences, 218,* 209–212.

WILLIAMS, D. 1976. Foreword. In J. Laidlaw & A. Richens (Eds.), *A Textbook of Epilepsy.* Churchill Livingstone, Edinburgh, pp. v–vi.

WILLIAMS, H., & McNICOL, K. N. 1969. Prevalence, natural history, and relationship of wheezy bronchitis and asthma in children. An epidemiological study. *British Medical Journal, 4,* 321–325.

WILLIAMSON, D. A., & BLANCHARD, E. B. 1979. Heart rate and blood pressure biofeedback. I. a review of the recent experimental literature. *Biofeedback and Self-Regulation, 4,* 1–34.

WOENNE, R., KATTAN, M., ORANGE, R. P., & LEVISON, H. 1978. Bronchial hyperreactivity to histamine and methacholine in asthmatic children after inhalation of SCH 1000 and chlorpheniramine maleate. *The Journal of Allergy and Clinical Immunology, 62,* 119–124.

WOLF, S. 1956. Life Stress and allergy. *American Journal of Medicine, 20,* 919–928.

WOLF, S., & GOODELL, H. 1968. *Harold G. Wolff's stress and disease* (2nd ed.). Charles C Thomas, Publisher, Springfield.

WOLF, S. L. 1978. Essential considerations in the use of EMG biofeedback. *Physical Therapy, 58,* 25–31.

WOLF, S. L. 1979. Anatomical and physiological basis for biofeedback. In J. V. Basmajian (Ed.), *Biofeedback—Principles and practice for clinicians.* The Williams & Wilkins Co., Baltimore, pp. 31–42.

WOLFF, H. G. 1948. *Headache and other head pain.* Oxford University Press, Inc., New York.

WOLFF, H. G. 1963. *Headache and other head pain* (2nd ed.). Oxford University Press, Inc., New York.

WOLFF, H. G. 1968. *Stress and disease* (2nd ed.), S. Wolf & H. Goodell (Eds.). Charles C Thomas, Publisher, Springfield.

WOLFF, L., PARKINSON, J., & WHITE, P. D. 1930. Bundle-branch block with short P–R interval in healthy young people prone to paroxysmal tachycardia. *American Heart Journal, 5,* 685–704.

WOLPE, J. 1958. *Psychotherapy by reciprocal inhibition.* Stanford University Press, Stanford.

WOODBURY, J. W. 1965. Action potential: Properties of excitable membranes. In T. C. Ruch & H. D. Patton (Eds.), *Physiology and Biophysics.* W. B. Saunders Company, Philadelphia, pp. 26–58.

WORMSLEY, K. G., & GROSSMAN, M. I. 1965. Maximal histalog test in control subjects and patients with peptic ulcer. *Gastroenterology, 6,* 427–435.

WRIGHT, B. M., & McKERROW, C. B. 1959. Maximum forced expiratory flow rate as a measure of ventilatory capacity with a description of a new portable instrument for measuring it. *British Medical Journal, 2,* 1041–1047.

WRIGHT, G. L. T. 1965. Asthma and the emotions: Aetiology and treatment. *The Medical Journal of Australia, 1,* 961–967.

WYLER, A. R., LOCKARD, J. S., WARD, A. A. JR., & FINCH, C. A. 1976. Conditioned EEG desynchronization and seizure occurrence in patients. *Electroencephalography and Clinical Neurophysiology, 41,* 501–512.

YU, D. Y. C., GALANT, S. P., & GOLD, W. M. 1972. Inhibition of antigen-induced bronchoconstriction by atropine in asthmatic patients. *Journal of Applied Physiology, 32,* 823–828.

ZIEGLER, D. K., HASSANEIN, R., & HASSANEIN, K. 1972. Headache syndromes suggested by factor analysis of symptom variables in a headache prone population. *Journal of Chronic Diseases, 25,* 353–363.

ZIEGLER, D. K., HASSANEIN, R. S., & WARD, D. F. 1976. Migraine, tyramine, and blood serotonin. *Headache, 16,* 53–57.

ZIPES, D. P., & McINTOSH, H. D. 1971. Cardiac arrhythmias. In H. L. Conn, Jr., & O. Horwitz (Eds.), *Cardiac and vascular diseases.* Lea & Febiger, Philadelphia, pp. 301–395.

AUTHOR INDEX

Abbasy, A. S., 233
Abel, G. G., 38, 40, 147, 366
Abramson, D. I., 205, 208
Adams, H. E., 147, 153, 188, 191, 193, 200
Ad Hoc Committee on Classification of Headache, 115, 118, 119, 120, 122, 123, 134, 159, 160, 161, 171
Adler, C. S., 119, 127, 129, 130, 139, 140, 143, 144, 146, 187
Adolph, E. F., 81
Ahlborg, B., 158, 160, 161, 164
Ahluwalia, D. S., 327
Alderman, M. M., 307, 308
Allen, E. V., 202, 203, 206, 207, 209
Allison, T., 271, 276
Alva, J., 334
Amato, A., 288, 314
American Thoracic Society, 221
Anderson, D. E., 65, 180, 181, 355, 372
Andrews, J. M., 292, 314
Andreychuk, T., 190
Anliker, J., 10, 12, 13, 18
Anrep, G. V., 35
Appenzeller, O., 167
Arthur, S. P., 222
Atkinson, R. A., 169

Backett, E. M., 324
Bahler, W. W., 263, 272, 276
Bakal, D. A., 92, 120, 122, 123, 153, 194
Baker, M., 321
Bannister, R., 303, 304
Barcroft, H., 210
Barensten, R. I., 258
Barnes, R. H., 149
Barry, M. J. Jr., 256
Basmajian, J. V., 75, 77, 78, 286, 296, 297, 300, 314, 318, 321
Bateman, D. E., 94, 95
Bates, D. V., 250
Beary, F., 109
Beatty, J., 14, 187, 192
Beech, H. R., 39
Beiman, I., 147, 191, 200
Belandres, P. V., 290, 302, 315
Belber, J. P., 325
Bellet, S., 359, 360
Benna, P., 259
Bennett, D. R., 257
Benson, H., 32, 103, 107, 108, 109, 180, 349, 356, 366
Bentley, J., 227
Bergamasco, B., 259
Bergamini, L., 259
Berman, S. Z., 221
Bernstein, D. A., 145
Bernstein, L., 225, 226
Bickford, R. G., 256
Bidus, D. R., 351, 369

Bilodeau, E. A., 13, 17
Birch, H. G., 202, 206
Birk, L., 14
Black, A. H., 62, 64, 68, 69, 269, 270, 271, 273, 274, 283
Blanchard, E. B., 6, 38, 40, 103, 186, 190, 212, 216, 348, 350, 358, 364, 366, 371
Blau, J. N., 176
Bleecker, E. R., 21, 47, 228, 229, 234, 357, 358, 365, 367
Bockus, H. L., 324
Bocles, J. S., 221
Bonk, C., 228, 237, 238, 247
Booker, H. E., 306, 314
Borkovec, T. D., 145
Botelho, S. Y., 250, 251
Bouhuys, A., 225
Bowman, K., 299
Boyd, S., 228
Brady, B. A., 226, 227
Brady, J. V., 65, 106
Brady, K., 225
Braude, A. I., 221
Brazier, M. A. B., 83
Brehony, K. A., 207, 212
Brener, J., 59, 62
Brettschneider, L., 325
Bricel, S. K., 245, 248
Broadhurst, P. L., 31
Broder, I., 221
Brolund, J. W., 32
Brooks, C. McC., 50
Brown, B., 31, 32
Brown, C. C., 72
Brown, D. A., 186, 190
Brown, G. E., 202, 203, 206, 207, 209
Brucker, B. S., 368, 373
Brudny, J., 289, 290, 293, 301, 302, 314, 315
Budzynski, T. H., 119, 127, 129, 130, 138, 139, 140, 143, 144, 146, 187
Bukantz, S. C., 225, 226
Butcher, B. T., 222
Byer, J. A., 176

Cabezas, G. A., 232, 235
Calverley, J. R., 257
Campbell, B. A., 25, 26
Canter, A., 142, 144, 149
Card, W. I., 327
Carlsson, S. G., 309, 315
Carroll, D., 177
Caveness, W. F., 258
Cerulli, M. A., 336
Chai, H., 225, 226, 227, 243, 246
Charpin, J., 233
Chesney, M. A., 127, 146, 152
Chien, S., 211
Christensen, J., 328
Christensen, N. A., 206

Christie, R. V., 250
Church, R. M., 25, 26
Chuttani, H. K., 327
Ciba Foundation Study Group No. 38, 221
Cirignotta, F., 257
Claghorn, J. L., 198, 199
Clark, J. A., 231, 233
Clark, L. D., 258
Cleeland, C. S., 302, 312, 315, 319
Clifton, R. K., 68
Cobb, S., 231, 232
Coffman, J. D., 209, 215
Coghill, N. F., 324
Cohen, A. S., 209
Cohen, B. A., 73
Cohen, M. J., 40, 120, 311, 318
Colcher, H., 325
Coleman, P. J., 306, 314
Collins, F. L. Jr., 91, 153, 194
Comroe, J. H. Jr., 250, 251
Conn, H. L. Jr., 346
Connel, A. M., 333
Connolly, K., 317
Coppen, A., 177
Cotes, J. E., 249
Cott, A., 69, 269, 270, 271, 273, 274, 283
Couch, J. R., 299
Cox, D. J., 143, 144, 145, 146
Crawford, P. L., 240, 243, 245, 247, 248
Creer, T. L., 241, 243, 246
Crider, A., 67
Critchley, M., 176, 256, 257
Cronqvist, S., 170
Cummings, J. N., 176

Dahlem, N. W., 230, 231
Dale, A., 355, 372
Dalessio, D. J., 119, 124, 138, 160
Dalton, K., 176
Daly, D. D., 256
Danker, P. S., 241, 246
Darwin, C., 36
Daube, J. R., 256
Davidson, P. T., 230
Davis, F. H., 133
Davis, J. F., 79
Davis, M. H., 243, 246
Davis, R. C., 79
Day, E., 124, 125
Day, J. H., 229
Deabler, H. L., 103, 351, 369
Deal, E. C. Jr., 235
DeBacher, G., 285
Deeker, E., 38, 231
Deese, J., 27, 33
DeMyer, W., 114, 115, 119, 299, 300, 301
Denholtz, M. S., 38, 39
DeRisi, W. J., 183, 187, 190
DeRoche, G., 233
de Solo Pool, N., 120, 121
de Takats, G., 208
DeVeno, T., 144, 147, 186, 190
Dexter, J. D., 176
Diamond, S., 144, 147, 160, 176, 177, 186, 190, 193
Diamond-Falk, J., 144, 147, 186, 190

Dickel, H. A., 128
Dillenkoffer, R. L., 103, 351, 369
Dirks, J. F., 230, 231, 249
Dixon, H. H., 128
Dobbins, K., 198, 199
Dormandy, J. A., 211
Dorpat, T. L., 135
Downey, J. A., 167
Driver, M. V., 259
Drury, R. L., 183, 187, 190
Dubo, H. I. C., 296
DuBois, A. B., 237, 250, 251
Duff, R. S., 203, 204, 205
Duffy, P., 312
Dvorakova, M., 324
Dworkin, B. R., 65

Earle, M. R., 233
Eberstein, A., 78, 79
Eccles, J. C., 75
Eckstein, J. W., 215
Edmunson, E. D., 103, 364, 371
Edwards, F. C., 324
Edwards, J. E., 243, 245, 247, 248
Egeth, H., 27
Ehrisman, W. J., 149
Eigenbrodt, E. H., 325
Eissenberg, E., 62
Ekberg, R., 170
Ekbom, K., 158, 159, 160, 161, 164
Elder, S. T., 103, 351, 353, 368, 369
Elliott, F. A., 299, 300
Elliott, K., 167
Ender, P., 295, 316
Engel, B. T., 10, 20, 21, 47, 103, 106, 154, 335, 336, 340, 348, 349, 357, 358, 365, 367, 370
Englert, E., 323
Epstein, L. H., 147
Etherton, M. D., 270, 272, 274
Eustis, N. K., 353, 368
Evans, N. W., 230
Eysenck, H. J., 39

Fahmy, M. S., 233
Fahn, S., 312
Feld, J. L., 84
Feldman, G. M., 237, 241, 246
Felton, G. S., 317
Fenton, C. H., 214, 217
Fernandez Sanchez, G. R., 254
Ferster, C. B., 25
Feuerstein, M., 147, 188, 191, 200
Finch, C. A., 273, 279
Findley, J. D., 65
Finley, W. W., 270, 272, 274, 275, 295, 316
Fiorito, E. M., 207, 212
Fishel, C. W., 235
Fisher, A. B., 237, 251
Fitch, J. L., 319
Fitzelle, G. T., 227
Fokkema, S. D., 77, 289, 320
Ford, R. M., 227, 259
Fordtran, J. S., 324, 326, 327
Forster, F. M., 257
Fotopoulos, S. S., 4

Fowler, E. F., 208
Franklin, M. A., 186, 193
Fraser, R. G., 221, 222, 232
Freeman, B. A., 123
Freundlich, A., 143, 144, 145, 146
Frewin, D. B., 167
Friar, L. R., 187, 192, 261, 262, 263, 270, 278
Fried, F. E., 148, 191
Friedman, A. P., 118, 120, 121, 161, 163, 164
Friedman, H., 356, 369
Friedman, I., 222, 225
Friedmann, L. W., 289, 290, 293, 302, 315
Fries, E. D., 345
Friis, M. L., 257
Fross, K. H., 231, 249
Fry, D. L., 250
Funkenstein, D. H., 232
Furman, S., 337, 338, 340

Gaarder, K. R., 110
Gainer, J. C., 189, 192
Galambos, R., 75
Galant, S. P., 233
Gale, E. N., 309, 315
Gallenstein, J. S., 295, 320
Gambrill, E. D., 99
Ganong, W. F., 48
Garliner, D., 308
Garton, W. H., 286, 298, 318
Gastaut, H., 254, 255, 256, 257
Gastaut, J. L., 254
Gavras, H., 211
Gavras, I., 211
Gayrard, P., 233
Gazzaniga, M. S., 51
Gershon, E., 81, 346, 348
Geschwind, N., 51, 53
Gessel, A. H., 316
Getty, D. J., 123
Ghose, K., 177
Gibson, J. G., 126, 127, 131, 132
Gifford, R. W. Jr., 204, 206, 207, 210
Gilbert, G. I., 300
Gilli, M., 259
Gilliam, W. J., 65
Glaus, K. D., 243, 245, 247, 248
Glueck, B. C., 6, 31
Gold, W. M., 233, 234
Goldie, L., 256
Goldman, H., 351, 369
Goldman, M., 240
Goldstein, D. S., 106
Goldstein, I. B., 75, 78
Goldstein, I. F., 222
Goncalves e Silva, G. E., 254
Good, M. I., 357, 372
Goodell, H., 124, 125, 231
Goodgold, J., 78, 79
Goodman, L. S., 258
Gordon, N., 225, 226, 227
Gorham, G., 362, 371
Gorlin, R. J., 306, 307
Goyal, R. K., 327
Goyle, K. B., 211

Graf, P. D., 232, 235
Graham, D. T., 204, 206, 206
Graheme, R., 296
Granger, C. V., 303
Green, E. E., 193
Green, J. M., 256
Greenfield, R. S., 72
Gribbin, B., 81
Grieco, M. H., 234
Griffin, C. J., 308
Griffin, P., 127, 130, 131, 144, 145, 148, 151
Grimaud, C., 233
Groen, J., 38, 231
Grossman, M. I., 326, 328
Grynbaum, B. B., 289, 290, 293, 301, 302, 314, 315
Gump, F. E., 211
Gunderson, C. H., 257

Hackett, T. P., 213, 216
Hadfield, G. J., 210
Hahn, W. W., 231, 233
Haines, R. W., 75
Hale, R., 232
Hall, K. V., 210
Halpern, A., 202, 206
Halpern, D., 290, 319, 321
Halpern, L. M., 258
Hamby, W. B., 300
Hanington, E., 176, 177
Hansteen, V., 215
Harper, M. A., 176, 177
Harper, R. G., 128
Harris, A. H., 65
Harris, F. A., 294, 316
Harrison, A., 317
Harrison, R. H., 160
Hassanein, K., 163
Hassanein, R., 163, 177
Hassett, J., 75, 79, 83
Haynes, M. R., 212, 216, 350, 366
Haynes, R. L., 225
Haynes, S. N., 127, 130, 131, 133, 134, 144, 145, 148, 151, 311, 317
Heath, A. L., 79
Hemphill, D. P., 147
Hendrix, T. R., 334
Henryk-Gutt, R., 158, 161
Herman, R. M., 291, 320
Hermsmeyer, C. A., 288, 314
Hersen, M., 147
Hertzman, A. B., 84
Hess, R., 256
Higgins, M. W., 221
Hill, E., 291, 318
Hillestad, L., 208, 210
Hines, E. A. Jr., 204, 206, 207, 210
Hinrichsen, J. J., 228
Hoedt-Rasmussen, K., 170
Hoffler, J. L., 81
Holling, H. E., 202, 203, 204, 205, 207
Holmes, T. H., 6, 135, 233
Honig, W. K., 25
Hookman, P., 334
Horande, M., 289, 292, 305
Horel, J. A., 51, 53

Horton, D. J., 230, 231, 249
Horwitz, O., 205, 346
Hrastnik, F., 170, 171, 172, 174, 176
Hudson, F. W., 79
Hudson, R. E. B., 206
Hulse, S. H., 27, 33
Hunt, J. H., 208, 210
Hutcheson, J. S., 81
Hutchings, D. F., 144, 148
Hyatt, R. E., 250
Hyde, R. W., 237, 251
Hymer, J. W., 294, 316
Hyndman, O. R., 206

Ince, L. P., 368, 373
Ingram, R. H. Jr., 225, 235
Ingvar, D. H., 169, 170, 256
Isbister, W. H., 170
Isenberg, J., 324, 325, 326
Ito, Y., 328

Jackson, J., 254
Jacobs, A., 317
Jacobs, F. M., 233, 235
Jacobson, A. M., 213, 216
Jacobson, E., 67, 107, 108, 154, 186
Jaeger, J. J., 225, 235
Jaffe, R. H., 324
Jamieson, G. G., 208
Jankel, W. R., 303, 304, 317
Janowitz, H. D., 326
Janzon, L., 215
Jasper, H. H., 83, 269, 271
Javel, A. F., 38, 39
Jennings, D., 325
Jensen, K. B., 170
Jessup, B., 177
Johnson, G., 144, 149
Johnson, H. E., 286, 298, 318
Johnson, R. H., 177
Johnson, R. K., 268, 270, 273, 275, 283
Johnson, W. G., 182, 184, 186, 192, 193
Johnston, D., 13, 17
Johnston, R., 291, 318
Jones, B., 51
Jones, N. F., 230, 231, 249
Joshi, V., 254
Julius, S., 345

Kaganov, J. A., 120, 122, 123, 153, 194
Kanarek, D. J., 224, 225
Kang, B., 225
Kannel, W. B., 345
Kantoush, M. M., 233
Kaplan, B. J., 270, 271, 275, 283
Kappert, A., 203, 205
Karr, R. M., 222
Katiyar, B. C., 254
Katkin, E. S., 62, 64, 66, 67
Kattan, M., 235
Katz, B., 75
Katz, L. N., 345, 346, 358
Kay, C. F., 359, 360
Kazemi, H., 224, 225
Keating, E. G., 51, 53
Keller, J. B., 221

Kellow, A. H., 177
Kent, D. C., 234
Keough, H. J., 177
Kerr, W. J., 211
Kessler, G. F., 234
Khan, A. U., 225, 228, 231, 237, 238, 239, 247
Kijima, M., 328
Kimble, G. A., 28, 31, 35, 58
Kimmel, H. D., 58
King, C. H., 169, 170
Kinmonth, J. B., 210
Kinsman, R. A., 230, 231, 249
Klass, D. W., 256
Kleiger, J. H., 230
Kleinman, K. M., 288, 314, 351, 369
Klemchuk, H. M., 356
Knapp, P. H., 228, 231, 233
Knudson, R. J., 240
Koelle, G. B., 63
Kohlenberg, R. J., 103, 335, 340
Koizumi, K., 50
Kolotkin, B. M., 225
Kondo, C., 142, 144, 149
Korein, J., 289, 290, 293, 301, 302, 314, 315
Korol, B., 351, 369
Kotses, H., 243, 245, 247, 248
Kragg, E., 324
Krause, U., 324
Kristt, D. A., 348, 349, 370
Kubickova, A., 324
Kuhlman, W. N., 271, 276
Kuhn, P. H., 202, 206
Kukulka, C. G., 297, 314, 318
Kumagai, F., 328
Kumar, L., 233
Kunkle, E. C., 158, 166
Kydd, W. L., 308

Lacey, J. I., 94, 95
Lachman, R., 67
Laidlaw, J., 258
Laidlaw, M. V., 258
Lamberti, J., 148, 191
Lance, J. W., 158, 160
Lancet Editorial, 202
Langman, M. J. S., 325
Largen, J. W., 198, 199
Laskin, D. M., 307, 308
Lassen, N. A., 169, 170
Lee, K., 291, 318
Lehner, T., 307
Lehrer, S. B., 222
Leibowitz, U., 304
Leigh, D., 231
Leist, N., 228
Leroy, E. C., 211
Levee, J. R., 40, 311, 318
Levenson, R. W., 228
Levidow, L., 289, 290, 293, 302, 315
Levison, H., 235
Lewis, T., 135, 206, 211
Liberman, A., 289, 290, 293, 302, 315
Liberman, R. P., 183, 187, 190
Light, K. C., 81
Lipowski, Z. J., 6

Lipsitt, D. R., 6
Lloyd, T. C. Jr., 250
Lockard, J. S., 258, 273, 279
Lourie, C. H., 228
Lowell, F. C., 221
Lubar, J. F., 263, 268, 272, 276, 277, 281
Ludbrook, J., 208
Lugaresi, E., 257
Lund, M., 257
Luparello, T. J., 228, 229, 230, 231, 234
Lupton, D. E., 308
Luthe, W., 67, 107, 108, 109, 186, 214
Lynch, J. J., 67
Lyness, J., 231
Lyons, H. A., 228, 229, 234
MacCorquodale, K., 27
Macdonald, L. R., 267, 268, 269, 270, 273, 278, 279, 283
MacDonnell, K. F., 221
MacGillivray, B. B., 259
Macklem, P. T., 250
Macpherson, E. L. R., 318
Mainardi, J. A., 346
Mallett, B. L., 170
Malmo, R. B., 130, 131, 133, 134
Manuck, S. B., 228
Marcacci, G., 257
Marinacci, A. A., 289, 292, 305
Marks, I. N., 327, 328
Marsden, C. D., 254
Martin, I., 72
Martin, J. E., 319
Marzetta, B. R., 356
Masuda, M., 233
Mathe, A. A., 228, 231, 233
Mathew, N. T., 170, 171, 172, 174, 176
Mathew, R. J., 198, 199
Mathews, K. P., 221
Mathison, D. A., 221
Mattson, R. H., 257
McCubbin, J. A., 81
McDermott, N. T., 231, 232
McDonald, J. B., 215
McFadden, E. R. Jr., 225, 228, 232, 234, 235
McGrath, M. A., 209, 211
Mchedlishvili, G. I., 198
McHugh, R., 290, 319, 321
McIntosh, H. D., 358
McKenzie, R. E., 149
McKerrow, C. B., 245
McNicol, K. N., 222
Mead, J., 240
Mealiea, W. L., 40
Means, J., 225, 226, 227
Meares, R., 299
Medina, J. L., 144, 147, 176, 177, 186, 190, 193
Meehl, P. E., 27
Melzak, R., 123, 155
Mendeloff, A. I., 333, 334
Merritt, H. H., 118, 121, 161, 163
Meyer, J. S., 170, 171, 172, 173, 174, 175, 176, 198, 199
Meyer, R. G., 143, 144, 145, 146, 268, 270, 273, 275, 283

Middaugh, S., 62
Miho, O., 328
Miklich, D. R., 231, 233, 241, 246
Mikulas, W. L., 26, 28
Miller, N. E., 5, 14, 30, 58, 65, 69, 227, 303, 304
Mills, J. E., 235
Mishkin, M., 51, 53
Misra, S., 254
Mitagvaria, N. P., 198
Mittlemann, B., 207
Miyahara, J. T., 258
Moffett, A. M., 178
Mohan, P. K., 254
Mohr, P. D., 185, 193
Molk, L., 225, 226, 227, 231
Monafo, W., 325
Montgomery, P. S., 110, 149
Mooney, D., 127, 130, 131, 144, 145, 148, 151
Moore, J. G., 323
Morris, H. G., 233
Morris, L. E., 206
Motoki, D., 323
Moulton, R. E., 308
Mroczek, N., 290, 319, 321
Mulholland, T. B., 13
Mullaney, D. J., 119, 127, 129, 130, 140, 143, 144, 146, 187
Munro, R. R., 307, 308
Murphy, R. L. H. Jr., 221, 222
Murray, E. N., 67
Murray, K., 31
Muser, J., 225, 226, 227
Myren, J., 326

Nadel, J. A., 225, 232, 233, 234, 235
Narayan, M. G., 297, 314
Netsell, R., 312, 319
Nikoomanesh, P., 103, 106, 335, 336, 340
Niman, C., 295, 316
Niwayama, G., 324, 325
Noonberg, A. R., 180, 181
North, W. R. S., 352, 353, 354, 370
Notske, R. N., 233
Nyman, G. E., 256

O'Banion, K., 230
Obrist, P. A., 81
Obrist, W. D., 169, 170
Ohman, A., 309, 315
Oi, M., 328
Oldendorf, W. H., 170
Olson, D. L., 225
Olton, D. S., 180, 181
Orange, R. P., 235
Orehek, J., 233
Ormotsadze, L. G., 198
Osborn, D. P., 325
Oshida, K., 328
Osternig, L. R., 295, 320
Ostfeld, A. M., 136

Pall, M. L., 130, 133, 134
Pare, J. A. P., 221, 222, 232

Parise, M., 127, 130, 131, 144, 145, 148, 151
Parkinson, J., 358
Patel, C. H., 352, 353, 354, 370
Paul, G. L., 186, 189
Paul, O., 345, 346
Paulson, O. B., 171, 172
Pavloski, R. P., 69, 269, 270, 271, 273, 274, 283
Peacock, J. H., 209
Pearne, D. H., 338, 340
Peart, W. S., 346
Peat, M., 296
Peck, D. F., 310, 319
Peek, R., 209, 211
Peffer, K. E., 73
Pelser, H. E., 38
Penny, R., 209, 211
Permutt, S., 223
Peshkin, M. M., 221, 222, 225
Peterson, N., 240
Petty, T. L., 221
Peyser, W. P., 338, 340
Philipp, R. L., 229
Philips, C., 118, 120, 121, 122, 128, 129, 130, 149
Pickering, G. W., 135, 211, 345, 346
Pickering, T., 362, 371
Pickett, R. M., 123
Pierson, R. N. Jr., 234
Pilon, R. N., 214, 217
Podivinsky, F., 299, 300, 301
Poirier, F., 256
Polgar, G., 237, 241, 245, 249
Poppen, R., 320
Portis, S. A., 324
Pratt, C., 241, 246
Pratt, K. L., 257
Price, K. P., 164, 166, 188
Pringle, R., 211
Promadhat, V., 237, 241, 245, 249
Purcell, K., 226, 227
Pyke, D. A., 176

Quanbury, A. O., 296

Rachman, S. J., 118
Rahe, R. H., 6
Raskin, M., 144, 149
Ray, B. S., 165
Raynaud, A. G. M., 202, 210
Rayner, R., 38
Reading, C., 185, 193
Rees, L., 227, 228
Rees, W. L., 158, 161
Reeves, J. L., 40, 140, 149
Regenos, E., 321
Reinking, R. H., 144, 148
Reis, D. J., 136
Rescorla, R. A., 35
Richardson, C. T., 324
Rickles, W. H., 40, 311, 318
Riley, J., 231
Risberg, J., 170
Rivers, A. B., 324
Roberts, J., 176
Robertson, C. W., 210

Rodbard, S., 135
Rogerson, C. H., 225
Rondestvedt, J. W., 144, 149
Rosner, B. A., 356
Ross, R. S., 106
Roth, G. M., 215
Roth, J. L. A., 326
Rothschild, P., 135
Rubow, R. T., 306, 314
Rudick, J., 326
Ruiz, Z. R., 103, 351, 369
Rushmer, R. F., 373
Ryan, R. E., 176, 177, 178
Ryo, U. Y., 225

Sachs, D. A., 319
Sachs, O. W., 158, 160, 161
Sachs-Frankel, G., 290, 302, 315
Sainsbury, P., 126, 127, 131, 132
Sakai, F., 170, 171, 173, 174, 175, 199
Salvaggio, J. E., 222
Samuels, S. S., 202, 206
Sandler, L., 227
Sappington, J. T., 207, 212
Sargent, J. D., 193
Sarnat, B. G., 306, 308
Saunders, D. R., 243, 246
Scadding, J. G., 221
Schallow, J. R., 32
Scheinberg, P., 198
Schele, R., 158, 160, 161, 164
Scherr, C. A., 240, 248
Scherr, M. S., 240, 243, 247, 248
Schilder, D. P., 250
Schnur, J. A., 123
Schofield, P. F., 170
Schork, M. A., 345
Schultz, J. H., 67, 107, 108, 109, 186, 214
Schuster, M. M., 103, 106, 333, 334, 335, 336, 340, 341
Schwaber, J. R., 240
Schwartz, G. E., 14, 62, 64, 65, 67, 81, 103, 349, 350, 351, 352, 366
Schwartz, L. L., 308
Schwartz, R. P., 79
Scollo-Lavizzari, G., 256
Scott, D. F., 178
Scott, R. W., 103, 364, 371
Seifert, A. R., 263, 268, 272, 277, 281
Selby, G., 312
Sellick, H., 235
Selman, D., 202, 206
Semb, L. S., 326
Sergent, C. B., 240, 248
Shaftel, H. E., 202, 206
Shaftel, N., 202, 206
Shagass, C., 130, 131, 133, 134
Shapiro, B. L., 306, 307
Shapiro, D., 5, 65, 81, 84, 103, 346, 348, 349, 350, 351, 352, 356, 357, 366, 371, 372
Shaw, J. C., 80
Shaw, S. W. J., 177
Shay, H., 328
Sheard, C., 215
Shelton, J. L., 127, 146, 152

Shnidman, S., 67
Shucard, D. W., 230, 231
Shukla, G. D., 254
Sicher, H., 306, 308
Silber, E. N., 345, 346, 358
Silver, B. V., 186, 190
Silverberg, E. L., 213, 216
Simard, D., 171
Simons, D. J., 124, 125
Simonsson, B. G., 233, 235
Singh, H., 327
Skinhoj, E., 169, 171, 172
Skinner, B. F., 25
Skriver, C., 190
Skrotzky, K., 295, 320
Sleight, P., 81
Sleisenger, M. H., 333
Smiehorowski, T., 291, 318
Smith, A. A., 134
Smith, H. A., 270, 272, 274
Smith, I., 177
Smith, L. A., 324
Smithwick, R. H., 210
Smorto, M. P., 300
Smulyan, H., 81
Sneed, P., 148, 191
Snell, J. D., 228
Snider, G. L., 221
Snow, M. Y., 351, 369
Society of Actuaries, 345
Solbach, P., 193
Solomon, R. L., 35, 38
Sorensen, B. F., 300
Spearing, D. L., 320
Spector, S. L., 230, 231
Spelman, F. A., 294, 316
Sperry, R. W., 51
Spiro, H. M., 324, 325
Staddon, J. E. R., 25
Staerk, M., 228, 237, 238, 247
Standley, J., 295, 316
Staudenmayer, H., 231
Steger, J. C., 128
Steinke, T., 296
Steptoe, A., 81
Sterling, G. M., 233
Sterman, M. B., 260, 261, 262, 263, 264,
    267, 268, 269, 270, 273, 277, 278, 279, 283
Stern, M., 81, 346, 348
Sternbach, R. A., 72
Stevens, J. R., 257
Stevenson, D. D., 221
Stewart, B. M., 170
Stone, R. K., 268, 270, 279
Stoyva, J. M., 119, 127, 129, 130, 139, 140,
    143, 144, 146, 187
Strauss, R. H., 225, 235
Stroebel, C. F., 6, 31
Strupp, H. H., 228
Sturdevant, R. A. L., 325
Sturgis, E. T., 153, 188, 193
Sugimura, S., 328
Summer, W. R., 223, 225, 232
Sun, D. C. H., 325, 326, 327
Sunderland, W. P., 4
Surman, O. S., 213, 216

Surwit, R. S., 5, 84, 212, 213, 214, 216, 217,
    346, 356, 357, 371, 372
Sveinsdottir, E., 170
Swann, D., 77, 289, 320
Swash, M., 178
Sweet, P., 228
Swets, J. A., 123
Swets, J. B., 123
Swineford, O. Jr., 221, 232
Swinyard, E. A., 258
Symonds, C., 256
Szentivanyi, A., 235

Takebe, K., 296, 297, 314
Tal, A., 231
Tanaka, Y., 328
Tarlov, E., 301
Tarr, E. M., 221
Tassinari, C. A., 256, 257
Taub, E., 195, 212
Taub, H. A., 356, 369
Taverner, D., 303
Temkin, O., 253
Theobald, D. E., 186, 190
Thomas, P. K., 303, 304
Thompson, H. K. Jr., 169, 170
Thompson, J. K., 91, 153, 194
Thompson, J. R., 308
Thulesius, O., 203, 204, 205, 206
Thurlbeck, W. M., 221
Tietjen, G. W., 211
Tollison, C. D., 153, 188, 193
Torgerson, W. S., 123, 155
Torrance, H. B., 170
Townley, R. G., 225
Travell, J., 308
Tuft, H. S., 225, 226
Tunis, M. M., 119, 127, 135, 136, 137, 167
Turin, A., 182, 184, 186, 192, 193
Tursky, B., 65, 80, 81, 103, 164, 166, 188,
    346, 348, 349, 350, 351, 352, 366

Ungar, A. H., 176, 225
Ungar, L., 176, 225

Vachon, L., 228
Valentine, M. D., 222
VanLehn, R., 94, 95
van Wieringen, P. C. W., 77, 289, 320
Vaughn, J. H., 221
Vaughn, R., 130, 133, 134
Veall, N., 170
Venables, P. H., 72
Vesely, K. T., 324
von Storch, T. J. C., 120, 121, 163

Walder, D. N., 211
Walker, A., 306, 307
Walker, A. J., 210
Walker, C. O., 324
Wallerstein, H., 130, 131, 134
Walsh, E. G., 83
Walsh, J. H., 324, 325, 326
Walsh, P., 355, 372
Walters, E. D., 193
Walton, J. N., 293, 299, 300, 303, 304

Wang, H. S., 169, 170
Wannstedt, G. T., 291, 320
Wansley, R. A., 295, 316
Ward, A. A. Jr., 258, 259, 273, 279
Ward, D. F., 177
Waters, W. E., 118, 162
Watkinson, G., 324
Watson, J. B., 38
Way, L. W., 324
Weaver, J. P. A., 211
Webster's New Collegiate Dictionary, 60
Weikers, N. J., 257
Weiner, H., 345
Weiner, N., 10
Weinmann, J. P., 308
Weinstein, S., 290, 302, 315
Weir, R. D., 324
Weiss, E. B., 221, 222
Weiss, J. H., 231
Welgan, P. R., 329, 330, 341
Wenger, M. A., 233
Wennerholm, M., 168
White, P. D., 358
Whitehead, S. F., 123
Whitehead, W. E., 331, 332
Whitfield, I. C., 79
Whitteridge, D., 83
Whybrow, P. C., 6
Wickramasekera, I., 141, 143, 145, 150, 184, 186, 193
Widdicombe, J. G., 225, 234, 235
Wilde, G. J. S., 229
Wilder, J., 29
Wilkins, R. W., 204, 205, 215
Wilkinson, C. F., 176
Wilkinson, W. E., 169, 170

Williams, D., 344
Williams, H., 222
Williams, R., 257
Williamson, D. A., 186, 190, 348, 358
Wilson, A., 208
Winter, D. A., 296
Woenne, R., 235
Wohl, M. E., 240
Wolf, S., 231
Wolf, S. L., 21, 76, 321
Wolff, H. G., 95, 119, 120, 124, 125, 127, 129, 135, 136, 137, 158, 160, 161, 162, 165, 167, 196, 207
Wolff, H. H., 258
Wolff, L., 358
Wolkin, J., 206
Wolpe, J., 269, 355
Wood, J. E., 215
Woodbury, J. W., 75
Wormsley, K. G., 328
Wright, B. M., 245
Wright, G. L. T., 227
Wright, G. W., 250
Wyler, A. R., 273, 279
Wynne, L. C., 38

Yoshida, K., 328
Yoshikawa, K., 328
Young, L. D., 6, 350, 364, 366, 371
Yu, D. Y. C., 233, 234

Ziegler, D. K., 163, 177
Zigelbaum, S. D., 338, 340
Zipes, D. P., 358
Zvolankova, K., 324

SUBJECT INDEX

Note: Many of the major headings in the index are the same as in the text, that is, the subheadings under "Migraine headaches" are "clinical program," "mechanisms," "research considerations," "symptoms," and "treatments." A particular characteristic of migraine headaches, then, will appear under one or more of these subheadings.

A-B-A experimental design:
  epilepsy, 267, 269
  hypertension, 350–351
  ulcers, 329–331
Absence attack, 255 (*see also* Epilepsy)
Acetylcholine, 47
Acid and ulcers, 323, 326–328
Action potential, 44
Adrenalin, 47 (*see also* Epinephrine, Isoprel, Isoproterenol)
Afferent nerve:
  control systems diagram, 19–21
  spinal cord, 50
Alpha, 259

Aluminum hydroxide and epilepsy, 258
Amyl nitrate and tension headaches, 137
Analogue feedback:
  definition, 14–15
  example, 16
ANS (*see* Autonomic nervous system)
Anterior temporal muscle:
  anatomy, 307
  temporomandibular joint syndrome, 306–309
Arrhythmia (*see* Cardiac arrhythmias)
Assymetrical standing, 291
Asthma, 221–251
  clinical program, 245, 249–250

biofeedback, 245, 249
  family interactions, 249
  relaxation, 249
definitions, 221–222
mechanism, 232–236
  autonomic nervous system, 232–236
  beta-adrenergic theory, 235–236
  body plethysmograph, 249
  parasympathetic nervous system, 233–235
  vagus nerve, 233–234
research considerations, 250–251
symptoms, 221–225
  antigens, 233
  atopic, 222, 229
  corticosteroid dependent children, 225
  definitions, 221–222
  dyspnea, 221
  extrinsic, 222
  epidemiology, 221
  family interactions, 225–228, 237, 249
  forced expiratory volume, 223–224
  hospital readmission, 230–231
  intrinsic, 222
  laboratory studies of stress, 231–232
  negative responder, 226–227
  occupational, 222
  panic-fear, 230–231
  parentectomy, 226
  positive responder, 226–227
  psychological variables, 225–232
  rapid remitters, 225
  respiratory function, 223–225
  steroid dependent children, 225
  stress, 225–228, 230–232, 237, 249
  suggestion, 228–230
  vital capacity, 223–225
treatment, 236–248
  biofeedback for respiratory function, 238–242
  case studies, 236–238
  forced expiratory volume, 238–240, 250–251
  forced oscillation technique, 237, 241, 250–251
  frontalis electromyogram, 242–245
  incorrect feedback, 240–241, 243–245
  panic-fear, 230–231, 249
  peak expiratory flow, 241–242
  progressive relaxation, 242–243
  relaxation, 242–245, 249
  severe symptoms, 241
  total respiratory resistance, 236–237, 240–241, 250–251
Athetoid movements, 293–296
Atopic asthma, 222
Atrophy:
  muscle, 285
  Raynaud's disease, 203
Atropine, 232–233
Autogenic training:
  clinical procedures, 107–109
  mediation, 67
  migraine headaches, 183, 186–189
  practice, 107–109
  Raynaud's disease, 212–214

relaxation, 67
  skin temperatures, 199–200
Autonomic nervous system (see also Parasympathetic nervous system, Sympathetic nervous system)
  actions of, 48–49
  "fight-or-flight," 47
  heart rate, 81–82
  Raynaud's disease, 210–211
  anatomy, 48
  asthma, 233–236
  epilepsy, 256
  fecal incontinence, 333–334
  mediation, 60–67
  voluntary control, 58–70
Autoregulation, 198
Axon, 43–44

Band-pass filter, 73
Behavioral medicine, 4–8
  biofeedback as an example, 3–8
  patient's role, 5–6
Bell's palsy, 303–305
  clinical program, 285–287, 313, 321
  mechanism, 304
  symptoms, 303
  treatment, 304–305
Benson's relaxation response, 107–110 (see also Relaxation)
Beta-adrenergic theory, 235–236
Biceps:
  anatomy, 53
  neuromuscular reeducation, 288–290, 292
Biological mediation, 60–64
Blepharospasm, 310
Blood flow (see also Migraine headaches, Raynaud's disease)
  extracranial:
    migraine headaches, 161, 166–169, 175–176, 180–182, 187–189, 194
    Raynaud's disease, 208–210
    temporal artery, 136, 167, 187–189
    tension headaches, 134–138, 154–156
  intracranial, 169–176
    biofeedback, 197–199
    head pain, 165, 169–171
    migraine headaches, 165–166, 169–176
    prodrome, 165–166, 171–173
  migraine headaches, 165–176, 197–199
  muscle pain, 134–138
  photoplethysmograph, 84
  physiological basis, 84
  psychophysiology, 84–85
  Raynaud's disease, 208–210
  signal detection and processing, 84–85
  thermistor, 84
Blood pressure (see also Hypertension)
  borderline, 344, 346
  constant cuff, 80–81, 347, 373–374
  diastolic, 80–81
  heart rate changes during control of, 65, 349
  Korotkoff sounds, 80
  normotensive, 344
  physiological basis, 80
  psychophysiology, 80–81

Blood pressure (*continued*)
  signal detection and processing, 80–81
  systolic, 80–81
Blood sugar and migraine headaches, 176
Blood viscosity and Raynaud's disease, 211
Body plethysmograph, 249
Borderline hypertension, 344 (*see also* Hypertension)
Bowel control, 331–337 (*see also* Fecal incontinence)
Brachioradialis muscle, 245
Bronchoconstriction:
  antigen, 233–235
  asthma, 232–236
  autonomic nervous system, 233–236
  beta-adrenergic theory, 235–236
  carbachol, 229, 232
  pulmonary irritants, 225–226
  sensitivity of asthmatic patients, 225
  suggestion, 228–230
  vagus nerve, 47–50, 233–235

Carbachol, 229, 232
Cardiac arrhythmias, 357–365 (*see also* each arrhythmia)
  clinical program, 357–358, 374
  fibrillation, 364–365
  premature ventricular contractions, 359–363
  tachycardia, 364–365
  Wolff-Parkinson-White syndrome, 358–359
Cardiovascular disorders, 344–374 (*see also* each disorder)
  arrhythmia (*see* Cardiac arrhythmias)
  cardiac arrhythmia, 357–365
  clinical program, 357–358, 373–374
    cardiac arrhythmias, 357–358, 374
    hypertension, 357–358, 374
  fibrillation, 364–365
  hypertension, 344–357
  postural hypotension, 365, 373
  premature ventricular contractions, 359–365
  tachycardia, 364–365
  treatment tables, 366–372
  Wolff-Parkinson-White syndrome, 358–359
Central nervous system:
  control systems diagram, 19–21
  disconnection analysis, 51
  dissociation, 50–53
  localization of function, 50–53
Cerebral palsy, 293–296
  clinical program, 285–287, 313, 321
  mechanism, 293
  symptoms, 293
  treatment, 293–296
    case studies, 293–294
    speech, 295
Chocolate and migraine headaches, 176–179
Circadian rhythm of pain of peptic ulcers, 323
Classical conditioning, 34–40
  appetitive, 36
  aversive, 36
  conditioned response, 35–36, 38–40, 66, 257
  conditioned stimulus, 35–36, 38–40, 66, 257
  emotional reactions to CS, 36, 38–40
  epilepsy, 256–257
  extinction, 37–38
  food and migraine headaches, 177–178
  generalization, 36–37
  mediation, 66
  migraine headaches and food, 177–178
  phobia, 38–40
  secondary reinforcer, 27, 32, 102–103
  stimulus hierarchy, 39
  unconditioned response, 35–36, 38–40, 66, 257
  unconditioned stimulus, 35–36, 38–40, 66, 257
Classic migraine headaches (*see also* Migraine headaches)
  definition, 159
  intracranial blood flow, 173–174
Clearance rate:
  extracranial blood flow, 209
  intracranial blood flow, 170–171
  migraine headaches, 170–171
  Raynaud's disease, 209
Clinical procedures, 90–111 (*see also* each disorder treated by biofeedback)
  autogenic training, 107–109
  Benson's relaxation response, 107–110
  classical conditioning, 27
  contracts and goals, 99–102, 104–105
  counterconditioning, 38–40
  demonstration of biofeedback, 92–93
  description of client's complaint, 91–92
  desensitization, 38–40
  elimination of feedback, 94, 105–107
  failure to learn biofeedback skill, 105, 194–195
  generalization, 39–40, 103–107
  goals and contracts, 99–102, 104–105
  home practice, 107–110
    autogenic training, 107–109
    Benson's relaxation response, 108–110
    biofeedback skill, 107–108
    evaluation of, 110
    Jacobson's muscle relaxation, 108
    progressive relaxation, 108
    relaxation, 108–110
  medical history, 90–92
  negative reinforcer, 24–26, 302–303
  positive reinforcer, 24–26, 103, 295, 335–337, 349, 351
  practice of biofeedback, 101–106
    elimination of feedback, 94, 105–107
    feedback environment, 102
    generalization, 103–104
    praise from therapist, 30, 103, 335, 337, 351
    shaping, 29–30, 102
    sliding criterion, 81, 102, 104
  progressive relaxation, 107–108
  psychological history, 90–92
  psychophysiological profile, 92–96

relaxed, 95–96
stressed, 94–95
rationale for biofeedback, 93–95
record keeping, 28–29, 96–101, 215
relaxation, 107–110
reinforcers (*see* Clinical procedures, negative reinforcer; Clinical procedures, positive reinforcer)
response strength, 27–34
measures of, 27–29
variables affecting, 29–34
secondary reinforcer, 102
shaping, 29–30, 102
sliding criterion, 81, 102, 104
stimulus hierarchy, 39
trial length, 33–34, 104–105
Cluster headache (*see also* Migraine headaches)
definition, 159
intracranial blood flow, 173–174
Cold hands:
migraine headaches, 161, 166–169, 180–182, 194
Raynaud's disease, 202–219
Common migraine headache (*see also* Migraine headaches)
definition, 159
intracranial blood flow, 173
Complicated migraine headache (*see also* Migraine headaches)
definition, 160
intracranial blood flow, 174–175
Conditioned response (*see also* Classical conditioning)
definition, 35–36
food and migraine headaches, 177–178
mediation, 66
migraine headaches and food, 177–178
phobia, 38–40
Conditioned stimulus (*see also* Classical conditioning)
definition, 35–36
emotional reactions to, 36
food and migraine headaches, 177–178
generalization, 36–37
mediation, 66
migraine headaches and food, 177–178
phobia, 38–40
secondary reinforcer, 26–27
Conditioning (*see also* each type of conditioning)
classical, 34–40
control, 67–70
operant, 24–34
Consistent feedback, 16
Contingent reinforcers, 25–26
Contracts and goals, 99–102, 104–105
Control systems, 10–22
central nervous system, 19–21
diagrams:
advantages of, 18–19
examples of, 11, 12, 16, 19, 20, 281
epilepsy, treatment of, 280–281
feedback, 10, 14
feedforward, 12–13
homeostasis, 17–19

mediation, 21–22, 60–63
negative feedback, 17–19
reference input, 11–12
set point, 11–12
Corpus callosum, 50–52
Correct feedback, 7
Correlational experiment, 62
Counter conditioning, 39–40, 311
CR (*see* Conditioned response)
Crepitation, 307
CS (*see* Conditioned stimulus)
Curare:
biological mediation, 62–65
intervention procedure, 62–65
Cyanosis and Raynaud's disease, 205, 207–209 (*see also* Raynaud's disease)

Defecation (*see* Fecal incontinence)
Delayed reinforcement, 32–33 (*see also* Reinforcer)
Deltoid muscle:
anatomy, 53
neuromuscular reeducation, 288–289, 291–292
Dendrite, 43, 45–46
Diarrhea, 337–338
Diastolic blood pressure (*see* Blood pressure, Hypertension)
Diet and migraine headaches, 176–179
Differentiation, 64
Disconnection analysis, 51
Dissociation, 50
Dissociative conditioning, 64, 349
Dual mechanism of ulcers, 328
Duodenal ulcers, 324–328 (*see also* Peptic ulcers)
Dyspepsia, 323 (*see also* Peptic ulcers)
Dyspnea, 221

Ectopic focus, 359
EEG, 82–84 (*see also* Electroencephalogram)
Efferent nerve:
autonomic nervous system, 47–50
control systems, 19–21
spinal cord, 50
Electrocardiogram (EKG), 80–82
diagram, 82
physiological basis, 81–82
R wave, 81–82
signal detection and processing, 82
Electrodes, 76–78
brain waves, 83
electromyogram, 74–78
indwelling, 76
neuromuscular reeducation, 285–287, 313, 321
surface, 76
Electroencephalogram (EEG):
alpha, 259
diagram of examples, 82
epilepsy, 253–283
physiological basis, 82–84
signal detection and processing, 83–84

Electroencephalogram (EEG) (*continued*)
  tension headaches, (*see also* Tension
    headaches)
  theta, 259
Electromyogram (*see also* disorder treated
  by biofeedback)
  clinical procedures, 75–79, 92–94, 285–
    287, 313, 321
  demonstration of, 92–94
  electrodes, 76–78
  migraine headaches, 184, 188, 195
  neuromuscular reeducation, 283–321
  paralysis, 287–293
  paresis, 287–293
  phobia treatment, 40
  physiological basis, 75
  recordings, 79–80
  signal detection and processing, 76–80
  tension headaches, 126–134, 138–156
Elimination of feedback, 93–94, 105–107,
    111, 335 (*see also* Generalization,
    Shaping)
EKG (*see* Electrocardiogram)
EMG (*see* Electromyogram)
Epigastrum, 324
Epilepsy, 253–283
  clinical program, 273, 280–282
  control systems diagram, 281
  mechanism, 259–260
    secondary epilepsy, 259
  research considerations, 282–283
  symptoms, 254–259
    absence attack, 254–255
    consciousness, 255
    electroencephalogram, 259–260
    essential, 260
    focal seizure, 256
    generalized seizure, 255–256
    grand mal seizure, 254
    idiopathic, 260
    localization, 254–255
    petit mal seizure, 254–255
    secondary, 259
    stimulus-elicited seizures, 256–257
    stress, 257–259, 282
  treatment, 260–279
    4 Hz to 7 Hz, 253, 263–266, 268–269,
      271–273, 280, 283
    6 Hz to 9 Hz, 267, 269, 271, 273
    9 Hz to 12 Hz, 271
    11 Hz to 13 Hz, 261–263, 272
    12 Hz to 14 Hz, 253, 260, 263–266,
      268–273, 280, 283
    12 Hz to 15 Hz, 267, 273
    18 Hz to 23 Hz, 267, 269, 273
    biofeedback without medication, 265,
      267–268
    case studies, 260–265
    control systems diagram, 280–281
    incorrect feedback, 271–272
    persistent symptoms, 268–270, 272
    tables, 274–279
Epileptic seizures (*see* Epilepsy)
Epinephrine, 47
EPSP, 45 (*see also* Excitatory postsynaptic
  potential)

Equipment:
  functions of, 72–74
  mediation, 65–66
  role in biofeedback, 14, 17, 65–66
  suppliers of, 85–88
Ergotamine:
  migraine headaches, 160–161, 163, 182–
    183
  tension headaches, 137
Ergotrophic process, 47
Erosion, 325 (*see also* Peptic ulcers)
Esophogeal muscle, 311
Essential disease:
  epilepsy, 260
  hypertension, 346
Ethylmorphine hydrochloride, 124
Excitatory postsynaptic potential, 43, 45–
  46
Exercise:
  asthma, 225, 235
  Raynaud's disease, 218
External sphincter, 332–334
Extinction:
  classical conditioning, 37–38
  operant conditioning, 34
  phobia, 38–40
Extracranial blood flow:
  autonomic nervous system, 47–50
  migraine headache:
    symptoms, 166–169, 175–176, 180–182
    treatment, 180–187
  pulse wave amplitude, 135–136, 167
  temporal artery, 136, 167, 187–189
  tension headache, 134–138, 154–156
Extrinsic asthma, 222

Facial nerve, 305–306
Facial paralysis, 305–306 (*see also* Paralysis)
Family interactions and asthma, 225–228,
  249
Fecal incontinence, 331–337
  clinical program, 332–333, 339
  mechanism, 333–334
    external anal sphincter, 332–334
    internal anal sphincter, 332–334
    parasympathetic nervous system, 333–
      334
    sympathetic nervous system, 333–334
  symptoms, 333–334
  treatment, 334–337
    case studies, 335–336
    triple balloon system, 332
Feedback:
  analogue, 14–16
  binary, 14–16
  clinical procedures, 93–94, 104
  consistent, 16
  control systems analysis, 9–22
  correct, 7
  definition, 3, 7, 10–11, 14
  delayed, 15–16, 32–33
  environment, 102
  equipment:
    role in treatment, 14, 17, 93–94
    suppliers of, 85–88

feedforward control, 13–14, 15–16
homeostasis, 17–19
incorrect:
    definition, 7
    migraine headaches, 180–185
    tension headaches, 141–143
    therapeutically inappropriate, 7
    uncorrelated, 7
information, 4
instruments, 17
knowledge of results, 15–16
motor skills, 15–17
negative, 17–19
positive feedback and migraine headaches, 195
precise feedback, 16
reference input, 12
secondary reinforcer, 27
sensory modality, 14, 73
set point, 12
therapeutically inappropriate:
    definition, 7
uncorrelated incorrect:
    definition, 7
Feedforward:
    definition, 13
    diagram in controls systems analysis, 13
    goal of biofeedback, 13
    rationale for biofeedback treatment, 92–93
FEV (see Forced expiratory volume)
F_g (see Intracranial blood flow)
Fibrillation:
    cardiac, 357, 364–365
    muscle, 303
Fight-or-flight, 47
Filter:
    band pass, 73
    epilepsy, 260, 280–282
Fixed hypertension, 346
Flow gray (see Intracranial blood flow)
Flow white (see Intracranial blood flow)
Focal seizure, 255
Foot drop, 296–299
    clinical program, 285–287, 313, 321
    mechanism, 296–297
    symptoms, 296–297
    treatment, 297–299
Forced expiratory volume (FEV):
    asthmatic symptoms, 223–224
    treatment for asthma, 236–245, 248, 250–251
Forced oscillation technique, 237
Forearm extensor muscle:
    anatomy, 53
    tension headaches, 126
Frontalis electromyogram (EMG) (see also Frontalis muscle)
    asthma, 242–245
        incorrect feedback, 243–245
    Bell's palsy, 305
    cerebral palsy, 295
    hypertension, 352
    migraine headaches, 184, 195
    tension headaches:
        clinical program, 152–154

mechanism, 119, 126–134
    research considerations, 155–156
    stress, 132–134
    treatment, 138–150
    throat spasms, 311–312
Frontalis muscle (see also Frontalis electromyogram (EMG)
    anatomy, 52
    migraine headaches, 184, 188, 195
    stress, 132–134
    tension headaches, 123–138
F_w (see Intracranial blood flow)

Galvanic skin resistance (GSR), 39–40
Gastric ulcer, 324–338 (see also Peptic ulcers)
Gastrocnemius muscle:
    anatomy, 54
    neuromuscular reeducation, 296
Gastrointestinal disorders, 323–342 (see also each disorder)
    clinical program, 339, 342
    diarrhea, 337–338
    fecal incontinence, 331–336
    peptic ulcers, 323–331
    treatment tables, 340–341
    urinary retention and incontinence, 338–339
Generalization (see also Shaping, Sliding criterion, Stimulus hierarchy)
    classical conditioning, 36–37
    clinical procedures, 103–107
    elimination of feedback, 105–107
    phobia, 39–40
    stimulus hierarchy, 39
Generalized epileptic seizure, 255–256
Glossary, 375
Goals and contracts, 99–102, 104–105
GSR (see Galvanic skin resistance)

Headache (see Tension headaches, Migraine headaches)
Head pain:
    extracranial vasoconstriction and tension headaches, 134–138, 155–156
    frontalis muscle, 123–134
    intracranial vasoconstriction and prodromes, 171–173
    intracranial vasodilation and migraine headaches, 137–138, 165, 169, 171–173
    measures of, 27–29, 151–152
    migraine headaches:
        cluster headache, 173–174
        common migraine headache, 173
        complicated migraine headache, 174–175
        intracranial vasoconstriction, 171–175
        intracranial vasodilation, 137–138, 165, 169, 171–173
        symptoms, 155–156, 160–164
    principal components analysis of, 163
    records for, 97–98, 153–154, 181
    tension headaches:
        mechanism, 123–138
        symptoms, 118–123

Heart rate:
  biofeedback treatment, 357–365
  blood pressure changes during control of, 65, 349–350
  cardiac arrhythmia, 357–365
  psychophysiology, 81–82
  R wave, 81–82
Hemiparesis, 288–294
Hemiplegia, 288–292
Hemisphere of brain, 51–52
History of symptoms, 90–92
Homeostasis, 17–19
Home practice, 107–111
  autogenic training, 107–109
  Benson's relaxation response, 108–110
  biofeedback skill, 107–108
  evaluation of, 110–111
  progressive relaxation, 108
  relaxation, 109–110
Hypertension, 344–357
  clinical program, 347–348, 373–374
  symptoms, 344–346
    borderline, 344, 346
    definition of hypertension, 344–345
    epidemiology, 345
    essential, 346
    fixed, 346
    labile, 346
    normotensive blood pressure, 344
  treatment, 347–357
    biofeedback alone, 349–352
    case study, 348–349
    constant cuff method, 347
    hypnosis, 356
    progressive relaxation, 355
    relaxation, 355–357
Hypertrophy, 285
Hypnosis:
  hypertension, 356
  Raynaud's disease, 213

Idiopathic disease:
  epilepsy, 260
  hypertension, 346
Incontinence:
  fecal, 331–337
  urinary, 338–339
Incorrect feedback:
  asthma, 240–241, 243–245
  definition, 7
  epilepsy, 271–272
  migraine headaches, 182–185
  peptic ulcer, 331
  tension headaches, 141–143
  therapeutically inappropriate, 7
  uncorrelated, 7
Indexes:
  Author index, 417
  Glossary, 375
  Subject index, 424
Internal anal sphincter, 332–334
Intervention procedure, 62–65
Intracranial blood flow, 164–166, 169–176, 197–199
  autoregulation, 198

biofeedback treatment for migraine headaches, 197–199
cluster headache, 173–174
common migraine headache, 173
complicated migraine headache, 174–175
F_g, 170–171 (see also Flow gray)
flow gray, 169–176
flow white, 169–176
F_w, 170–171 (see also Flow white)
head pain, 137–138, 165, 169, 171–173
migraine headache, 169–176
procedures, 165–166, 169–170
prodrome, 165–166, 171–173
rCBF, 170–171 (see also Regional cerebral blood flow)
regional cerebral blood flow, 169–176
skin temperature control, effects of, 198–199
techniques for measuring, 165–166, 169–171
vasoconstriction and prodromes of migraine headaches, 165–166, 171–173
vasodilation and head pain of migraine headaches, 165, 169–171
Intractable asthma, 222
Intrinsic asthma, 222
IPSP (Inhibitory postsynaptic potential), 46
Ischemia:
  Bell's palsy, 304
  migraine headaches, 169–176
  muscles, 134–138
  pain in muscles, 134–135
  prodrome, 165–166, 171–173
  tension headaches, 135–138, 156
Isoprel (see also Isoproterenol)
  asthmatic symptoms and suggestion, 228–229
  treatment for asthma, 237
Isoproterenol, 229, 237

Jacobson's progressive muscle relaxation, 66–67, 107–108

Knowledge of results (KR), 15–16 (see also Feedback)
Korotkoff sounds, 80–81, 373–374

Labile hypertension, 346
Lateral pterygoid muscle:
  anatomy, 307
  temporomandibular joint syndrome, 306–309
L-dopa, 312
Learning, 23–40 (see also Classical conditioning, Operant conditioning, Performance, Response strength)
  baseline measures, 29
  classical conditioning, 34–40
  extinction, 33
  knowledge of results, 15–16
  operant conditioning, 24–34
  performance, 33
  response measures, 27–29

response strength, 27–29, 151–152
variables affecting strength of, 29–34
Levarterenol and tension headache, 136–137
Levator labii superioris muscle, 313
Life change units, 6
Local fault hypothesis of Raynaud's disease, 211
Localization of function, 50–52

Massed practice, 33
Masseter muscle:
  anatomy, 307
  Bell's palsy, 304–305
  temporomandibular joint syndrome, 306–309
Mechanism (see also each disorder)
  definition, 113–115
  independent of symptoms, 113–115, 118–119
Mecholyl:
  asthmatic symptoms and suggestion, 229
  biofeedback treatment and asthma, 239
Medial pterygoid muscle:
  anatomy, 307
  temporomandibular joint syndrome, 306–309
Mediating process, 59
Mediation, 21–22, 60–67
  autogenic training, 67
  biological, 60–64
  classical conditioning, 66
  control systems, 21–22
  correlational experiment, 62
  curare, 63–64
  differentiation, 64–65
  direct, 60–61
  dissociative conditioning, 64–65
  examples of, 21–22
  feelings, 21–22, 65–67
  images, 21–22, 65–67
  indirect, 60–61
  intervention procedure, 62–65
  Jacobson's relaxation, 66–67
  psychological, 21–22, 65–67
  relaxation, 66–67
  thoughts, 21–22, 65–67
  types used in learning biofeedback, 21–22
Medical history, 90–92
Meditation (see Relaxation)
Migraine headaches, 157–200
  clinical program, 189, 194–196
    check list for symptoms, 153–154
    relaxation, 199–200
  mechanism:
    blood sugar, 176
    diet, 176–179
    extracranial blood flow, 166–169
    foods, 176–179
    head pain, 164–165, 169–171, 173
    intracranial blood flow, 169–176, 197–199
      vasoconstriction and prodrome, 164–165, 171

vasodilation and head pain, 164–165, 169–171, 173
    peripheral vascular system, 166–169
    prodrome, 164–165, 171
    pulse wave amplitude, 167
    tyramine, 176–179
  research considerations, 197–200
  symptoms, 160–164
    adjectives used to describe headache, 161
    classical migraine headache, 159–164
    cluster headache, 159
    cold hands and feet, 161, 166–169, 181, 194
    common migraine headache, 159
    complicated migraine headache, 159–160
    diet, 176–179
    entymology of name, 160–161
    epidemiology, 160–161
    principal components analysis, 163
    pulse wave amplitude, 167–169
    records for, 92, 96–98, 151–154, 181
    severity, 162–163
    stress, 194–196
    tension headaches associated with migraine headaches, 195
    types of headaches, 159–160
  treatment, 179–189
    autogenic training, 183, 186–189
    biofeedback alone, 184–185
    blood flow reduction, 187–189
    case studies, 180–183
    cold hands and feet, 194
    electromyogram, 184, 188
    ergotamine, 183
    incorrect feedback, 182–185
    intracranial blood flow, 198–199
    persistent headaches, 185–186
    relaxation, 180, 183, 186–187, 195, 199–200
    severe symptoms, 185–186
    skin temperature lowering, 182–183
    skin temperature raising, 180–186
    stress, 195–196
    tables, 190–193
    temporal artery, 187–189
Motivation:
  behavioral effect, 30–32
  optimal level, 30–32
  PATI (Placebo-Active Therapeutic Index), 31
  Placebo-Active Therapeutic Index, 31
  Yerkes-Dodson law, 30–31
Motorneuron, 75
Motor skills analogy, 17
Motor unit, 75
Mucosal barrier, 325–326 (see also Peptic ulcers)
Muscle (see also each individual muscle, Electromyogram, Neuromuscular reeducation)
  arm:
    anatomy, 53
    biofeedback treatment, 287–299
  atrophy, 75

Muscle (*continued*)
  fiber, 75
  head:
    anatomy, 52
    biofeedback treatment, 299–313
  hypertrophy, 285
  leg:
    anatomy, 54
    biofeedback treatment, 287–299
  neck:
    anatomy, 52
    biofeedback treatment, 299–313
  neuromuscular reeducation, 284–321
  psychophysiology, 74–80
Muscle contraction headache (*see* 114–115, 118–119, Tension headaches)

Negative reinforcement (*see* Negative reinforcer)
Negative reinforcer (*see also* Reinforcer)
  behavioral effect, 24–26, 302–303
  clinical use, 24–26, 29, 32, 302–303
  definition, 24–25
Negative responder, 226
Nerve cell, 19–21, 43–47 (*see also* Neuron)
Nervous system (*see also* each type)
  autonomic, 47–50
  biofeedback and, 19–21
  control systems, 19–21
  parasympathetic, 47–50
  skeletal:
    control systems, 63
    muscles activated, 52–54
  sympathetic, 47–50
Neuromuscular reeducation, 284–321 (*see also* each disorder and each muscle treated by biofeedback)
  asymmetrical standing, 291
  Bell's palsy, 303–305
  biofeedback treatment, general plan of, 285–287, 313, 321
  biofeedback treatment compared to physical therapy, 286, 289–290, 297–298, 321
  blepharospasm, 310
  cerebral palsy, 293–296
  clinical program, 285–287, 313, 321
  facial paralysis following damage to facial nerve, 305–306
  footdrop following cerebral stroke, 296–299
  paralysis and paresis, 287–294
  Parkinson's disease, 299, 312–313
  peripheral nerve injury, 292–293
  physical therapy, 286, 289–290, 297–298, 321
  spasmodic torticollis, 299–303
  temporomandibular joint syndrome, 306–309
  throat muscles, 311–312
  torticollis (*see* Spasmodic torticollis)
  treatment tables, 314–320
Neuron, 43–47
  action potential, 44
  afferent, 20–21
  communication, 44–45

control systems, 19–21
dendrite, 43, 45–46
efferent, 20–21
EPSP, 45
excitatory postsynaptic potential, 43, 45–46
inhibitory postsynaptic potential, 43, 46
integration, 45–46
IPSP, 43–46
metabolic support, 47
perikaryon, 43, 46
synapse, 43–45
threshold for action potential, 44
transmission:
  autonomic nervous system, 47
  synaptic, 42–44
Nicotine and Raynaud's disease, 215
Noise and signal, 73
Nonatopic asthma, 222
Normotensive blood pressure, 344 (*see also* Hypertension)

Occupational asthma, 222
Operant conditioning, 24–34 (*see also* Learning, Performance)
  delay of reinforcement, 32–33
  extinction, 33
  massed practice, 33–34
  motivation, 30–32 (*see also* Motivation)
  negative reinforcer, 24–26
  partial reinforcement extinction effect, 34
  positive reinforcer, 24–26
  primary reinforcer, 26–27, 102
  punishment, 24–26
  reinforcement, 24–26
  reinforcers, 24–26
    clinical examples, 24–26, 30, 103, 295, 302–303, 335–337, 349, 351
  response strength, 27–29
  secondary reinforcer, 26–27, 102
  shaping, 30 (*see also* Clinical procedures, Sliding criterion)
  spaced practice, 33–34
  variables affecting response strength, 29–34
Orbicularis oculi muscle:
  anatomy, 52
  Bell's palsy, 304–305
  blepharospasm, 309
Orbicularis oris:
  anatomy, 52
  Bell's palsy, 304–305
  Parkinson's disease, 313
  throat spasms, 311
Oxyntic cells, 325–328

Pallor and Raynaud's disease, 205, 207–209
Panic-fear and asthma, 230–231, 249
Paralysis, 287–293
  clinical program, 285–287, 313, 321
  mechanism, 287
  symptoms, 287

432

treatment, 287–294
case studies, 288–289
Parasympathetic nervous system:
actions of, 47–50
anal sphincter, 333
anatomy, 48
asthma, 233–235
heart rate, 81–82
vagus nerve, 48–49
Parentectomy, 226
Paresis (see Paralysis)
Parietal cells, 325–328
Parkinson's disease, 285–287, 299, 312–313, 321
Partial reinforcement:
classical conditioning, 38
operant conditioning, 34
Partial reinforcement extinction effect, 34
Partial seizure, 255 (see also Epilepsy)
PATI (Placebo-Active-Therapeutic-Index), 31
Pavlovian conditioning (see Classical conditioning)
Peak acid flow, 326–328
Peak expiratory flow rate:
biofeedback treatment of asthma, 241–242
peak flow meter, 245
Pentylenetetrazol and epileptic seizures, 258–259
Pepsin, 327
Peptic ulcers, 323–331
clinical program, 328, 339, 342
mechanism, 325–328
acid, 326–328
dual mechanism, 328
mucosal barrier, 325–326
mucus, 325–326
pepsin, 327
symptoms, 323–325
treatment, 32–331
Perforation, 325 (see also Peptic ulcers)
Performance (see also Classical conditioning, Learning, Operant conditioning)
distinguished from learning, 33
variables affecting, 15–16, 29–34
Perikaryon, 43, 46
Peripheral nerve injury, 292–293
Permanence of treatment effects:
epilepsy, 265
fecal incontinence, 337
tension headaches, 149
Peroneus longus muscle, 289
Persistent symptoms:
Bell's palsy, 305
epilepsy, 268–270
fecal incontinence, 336
hypertension, 349–350
migraine headaches, 185–186
Raynaud's disease, 212
spasmodic torticollis, 302
tension headaches, 143–144
Petit mal seizure, 254–255 (see also Epilepsy)
pH and peptic ulcers, 329–331

Pharyngeal muscle, 311
Phobia:
biofeedback treatment, 38–40
classical conditioning, 38
Photophobia, 161, 176
Photoplethysmograph, 85–86
Physical therapy:
footdrop, 297–298
general, 286, 321
paralysis, 289–290
Placebo-Active-Therapeutic-Index (PATI), 31
Plethysmograph:
asthma, 249
blood flow, 84–85, 187–189, 208–210
body, 249
migraine headaches, 187–192
Raynaud's disease, 208–210
water, 208–210
Policus longus muscle, 292–293
Positive feedback and migraine headache, 195
Positive reinforcer, 24–26, 103, 295, 335–337, 349, 351 (see also Reinforcer)
Positive responder, 226
Posterior temporal muscle:
anatomy, 307
temporomandibular joint syndrome, 306–309
PQRST complex:
electrocardiogram, 81–82
premature ventricular contractions, 360
Practice (see also Clinical procedures)
autogenic training, 107–109
biofeedback skill, 101–108
equipment, 14, 17, 65–66, 85–88
feedback environment, 102
generalization, 103–104
reinforcers, 26, 29–30, 32, 102–103
shaping, 29–30, 94, 102, 105–107
sliding criterion, 81, 104
trials, length, 33–34, 104–105
progressive muscle relaxation, 107–109
relaxation, 107–110
Precise feedback, 16
Premature ventricular contraction:
mechanism, 359–360
ectopic focus, 359
symptoms, 359–360
treatment, 360–363
Primary reinforcer, 26–27
Prodrome:
intracranial blood flow, 165–166, 171–172
migraine headaches, 159–176
mechanism, 164–176
symptoms, 159–164
principal components analysis of headache symptoms, 163
tension headaches, 120–123
Progressive muscle relaxation, 66–67, 107–108 (see also Relaxation)
asthma, 242–243
clinical procedures, 107–108
hypertension, 355
migraine headache, 183

Progressive muscle relaxation (*continued*)
  practice of, 107–108
  relaxation, 66–67
Psychological history, 90–92
Psychological mediation, 21–22, 65–67
Psychophysiological profile, 94–96 (*see also* each disorder treated by biofeedback)
  relaxed, 94–95
  stressed, 95–96
Psychophysiology, 71–84 (*see also* each physiological function)
  blood flow, 84–85
  blood pressure, 80–81
  brain waves, 82–84
  equipment suppliers, 85–88
  heart rate, 81–82
  muscle activity, 74–80
  signals, 72–74
  skin temperature, 84–85
Pulse transit time, 355
Pulse wave amplitude:
  migraine headaches, 167, 187–189
  tension headaches, 135–137
Pulse wave velocity, 81
Punishment:
  behavioral effect, 24–26
  definition, 24–25
PVC, 359–363 (*see also* Premature ventricular contraction)
Pyloris, 325–328

Quadriceps muscle:
  anatomy, 54
  neuromuscular reeducation, 289
Quadriparesis, 289

Rapid remitters, 225
Raynaud's disease:
  clinical program, 214–215, 218–219
    exercise, 218
    protection of hands and feet, 206, 215
    questionnaire for symptoms, 215
  definition, 202–204
  mechanism, 208–211
    blood flow, 208–210
    cooling produces vasoconstriction, 208–210
    local fault hypothesis, 211
  primary disease, 203–205
  symptoms, 202–208
    cold hands and feet, 202–208
    color changes, 203, 205, 207–209
    cooling produces symptoms, 206–207
    cyanosis, 203, 205, 207–209
    pallor, 203, 205, 207–209
    primary, 203–205
    rubor, 203, 205, 207–209
    secondary, 203–206
    smoking, 215
    stress, 207
    table of, 205
  treatment, 211–214
    autogenic training, 212–214
    case studies, 212–214

    persistent symptoms, 212
    protection of hands and feet, 206, 215
    relaxation, 212–213, 218
    smoking, 215
    tables, 215–217
Raynaud's phenomenon, 203 (*see also* Raynaud's disease)
rCBF (*see* Intracranial blood flow, Regional cerebral blood flow)
Record keeping:
  measures of symptoms, 92, 96–98, 151–154, 181
  migraine headache symptoms, 92, 96–98, 151–154, 181
  Raynaud's disease, 215
  review during clinic visit, 100–101
  symptom history, 92
Rectosphincteric reflex, 334
Reference input:
  definition, 12
  diagram as part of control systems analysis, 11
  voluntary control, 59
Regional cerebral blood flow, 169–176 (*see also* Intracranial blood flow)
Reinforcement (*see* Reinforcer)
Reinforcer:
  clinical procedures, 26, 29–30, 32, 102–103
    candy, 295
    felt tip pens, 103, 335
    money, 103, 295, 336, 349
    muscle is alive, 321
    photographic slides, 103, 349
    praise, 30, 103, 335, 337, 351
    shock, 302–303
  contingent, 25
  delayed, 32–33
  magnitude, 32
  negative:
    behavioral effects, 24–26
    definition, 24–25
    examples in the clinic (*see* Reinforcer, clinical procedures)
  positive:
    behavioral effect, 24–26
    definition, 24–25
    examples in the clinic (*see* Reinforcer, clinical procedures)
  presentation of, 25
  primary, 26–27, 102
  punishment:
    behavioral effect, 24–26
    definition, 24–25
  removal of, 25
  secondary, 26–27, 102
  types, 24–26, 103
Relaxation:
  asthma, 242–245, 249
  autogenic training, 107–110
  Benson's relaxation response, 107–110
  clinical procedures, 107–110
  epilepsy, 269
  hypertension, 352–357
  Jacobson's progressive muscle relaxation, 66–67, 107–108

migraine headaches, 180–183, 195, 199–200
motivation, 31–32
neuromuscular reeducation, 285
premature ventricular contraction, 360–362
progressive muscle relaxation, 66–67, 107–108
psychophysiological profile, 95–96
Raynaud's disease, 212–215, 218
relaxation response of Benson, 107–110
tension headaches, 145, 151
Relaxation response of Benson, 107–110 (see also Relaxation)
Response latency, 27–29
Response magnitude, 27–29
Response probability, 27–29
Response speed, 27–29
Response strength (see also Learning, Performance)
definition, 27
measures of, 27–29
tension headaches, 151–152
variables affecting, 29–34
Rest:
hypertension, 353
peptic ulcer, 329–330
Retrocollis, 302–303
Rolandic cortex, 261, 263, 268, 270, 280, 283
Rubor and Raynaud's disease, 205, 207–209
R wave, 81–82

Saline and suggestion in asthma, 228–230
Secondary epilepsy, 259
Secondary Raynaud's disease, 203–206
Secondary reinforcer, 26–27, 102–103
Seizures (see Epilepsy)
Sensorimotor cortex, 267
Set point:
definition, 12
diagram as part of control systems analysis, 11
voluntary control, 59
Severe symptoms:
asthma, 241
epilepsy, 268–270
fecal incontinence, 336
migraine headaches, 185–186
neuromuscular reeducation, 295, 297
premature ventricular contractions, 360–362
tension headaches, 143–144
Shaping (see also Generalization, Learning, Performance, Sliding Criterion)
clinical procedures, 29–30, 94, 102, 105–107
blood pressure, 81, 347
elimination of feedback, 93–94, 105–107, 335
fecal incontinence, 335
goals and contracts, 99–100
migraine headaches, 194
motor skills, 13–14
neuromuscular reeducation, 295, 297

skin temperature control, 104, 194
temporomandibular joint syndrome, 309
general, 14, 29–30, 102
practice of biofeedback, 94, 102, 105–107
Signals, 72–74
Signal-to-noise ratio, 73
Sinoatrial node, 81, 357
Skeletal nervous system:
electromyogram, 74–78
mediation, 62–64
motor unit, 75
muscles controlled, 52–54
Rolandic cortex, 261, 263, 268, 270, 280, 283
sensorimotor cortex, 267
Skin temperature (see also Blood flow)
discrimination training, 189
migraine headaches:
symptoms, 161, 166–169, 180–182, 194
treatment, 179–198
photoplethysmograph, 84–85
physiological basis, 84
psychophysiology, 84–86
Raynaud's disease:
symptoms, 202–206
treatment, 211–214, 218
relaxation, 194–195
shaping, 194
stress, 207
thermistor, 84
Sleep and epilepsy, 257
Sliding criterion (see also Generalization, Shaping)
clinical procedures, 104
cerebral palsy, 295
constant cuff, 81, 347, 374
foot drop, 297
neuromuscular reeducation, 295, 297
tachycardia, 363
Spasmodic torticollis, 300
Speech:
biofeedback treatment:
Bell's palsy, 303–305
cerebral palsy, 295
Parkinson's disease, 312–313
corpus callosum, 51–52
hemispheric specialization, 51–52
intracranial blood flow, 171
localization of function, 51–52
migraine headache prodrome, 171–172
prodrome, 171–172
Spinal cord, 50, 75
Spirometer, 245–246
Splenius muscle:
anatomy, 52
spasmodic torticollis, 300
Status asthmaticus, 222
Sternocleidomastoid muscle:
anatomy, 52
spasmodic torticollis, 300
Steroid dependent children, 225
Stimulus hierarchy, 39–40
Stress:
asthma:
family interactions, 225–228, 237, 249

Stress: asthma (*continued*)
    laboratory studies, 231–232
      panic-fear, 230–231, 249
  clinical procedures for, 94–95
  electromyogram, 132–134
  epilepsy, 257–259, 265, 282
  frontalis muscle activity, 132–134
  life change units, 6
  migraine headaches, 194–196
  psychological history, 91
  psychophysiological profile in clinic, 94–95
  psychosomatic disease, 207
  rationale for biofeedback, 93
  Raynaud's disease, 4–6
  reactions to, in clinic, 94–95
  temporomandibular joint syndrome, 308
  tension headaches, 132–134
Suggestion and asthmatic symptoms, 228–230
Suppliers of biofeedback equipment, 85–88
Sympathetic nervous system (*see also* Autonomic nervous system)
  action of, 47–50
  anal sphincter, 333
  anatomy, 48
  asthma, 235–236
  heart rate, 82
  Raynaud's disease, 210–211
Symptoms (*see also* each disorder treated by biofeedback)
  definition of, 113–115, 118–119
  description of, 90–92
  history of, 90–92
  independent of mechanisms, 114–115, 118–119
  records for, 92–93, 96–101, 151–152, 215
Symptom substitution, 139
Synapse, 43–45
Synaptic transmitter, 45, 47, 63

Tachycardia, 360, 364–365
Temporal artery:
  migraine headache:
    symptoms, 167
    treatment, 187–189
  tension headache, 136
Temporal muscle:
  anatomy, 52
  tension headache, 127, 136
Temporomandibular joint syndrome, 306–309
  clinical program, 285–287, 313, 321
  mechanism, 306–308
  muscles, 307
  symptoms, 306–308
  treatment, 308–309
Tension, definition of, 118
Tension headaches, 118–156
  clinical program, 152–155
  measures of headache activity, 92, 96–98, 151–154, 181
  mechanism, 123–138
    electromyogram (*see* Tension headaches, muscle contraction)

EMG (*see* Tension headaches, muscle contraction)
    extracranial blood flow, 134–138, 154–156
    frontalis muscle contraction, 123–138
    head pain caused by muscle contraction, 123–125
    ischemic muscles, 134–138, 154–156
    muscle contraction causes head pain, 123–125
    muscle contraction increased in people with severe/frequent headaches, 129–132
    muscle contraction increased when an individual is having a headache, 125–129
    muscle ischemia, 134–138, 154–156
    stress, 132–134
    vasoconstriction, 134–138, 156
  research considerations, 155–156
  symptoms, 119–123, 155–156
    adjectives describing, 119–120
    check list for clinic, 153
    compared to those of migraine headaches, 120–123
    diagnosis, 118–123, 155–156
    epidemiology, 118
    principal components analysis, 163
    prodrome, 120–123
    records for, 92, 96–98, 151–154, 181
  treatment:
    biofeedback alone, 140–143
    case studies, 139–140
    electromyogram reduction, 138–152
    EMG reduction, 138–152 (*see also* Electromyogram)
    incorrect feedback, 141–143
    measures of headache activity, 151–152
    medication placebo, 143, 150
    permanence of effects, 149
    persistent headaches, 143–144
    records for, 92, 97–98, 151–154, 181
    relaxation, 145, 151
    severe headaches, 143–144
    skin temperature feedback, 154–155
    symptom substitution, 139
    tables, 146–150
    temperature discrimination training, 189
Thermistor:
  migraine headaches, 179–196
  psychophysiology, 84
  Raynaud's disease, 209–219
Theta, 259
Throat muscles, 285–287, 311–312, 313, 321
Tibialis anterior muscle:
  anatomy, 54
  cerebral palsy, 296
  foot drop, 296–299
  neuromuscular reeducation, 288, 296–299
  paresis, 288
Tinnitus, 307
Torticollis (*see* Spasmodic torticollis)

Total respiratory resistance, 236–237, 241–242
Transmission:
  autonomic nervous system, 47
  control systems diagram, 20–21
  curare, 62–65
  neuron, 42–44
  parasympathetic nervous system, 47
  sympathetic nervous system, 47
  synapse, 44–45
Trapezius muscle:
  anatomy, 52
  spastic torticollis, 300
Trial length, 32–34, 101, 104–105 (see also each disorder treated by biofeedback)
Trials, distribution of, 33, 104–105
Triceps:
  anatomy, 53
  neuromuscular reeducation, 289, 292
Triple balloon system:
  diagram, 332
  fecal incontinence, 332–337, 339
  rectosphincteric reflexes, 334
Trophotropic process, 47
Tyramine and migraine headaches, 176–179

UCR (see Unconditioned response)
UCS (see Unconditioned stimulus)
Ulcer, 323–331 (see also Peptic ulcers)
Unconditioned response (UCR):
  definition, 35–36
  mediation, 66
  phobia, 38–40
Unconditioned stimulus (UCS):
  appetitive, 36
  aversive, 36
  definition, 35–36
  mediation, 66
  phobia, 38–40
Unilateral head pain:
  intracranial blood flow, 164–166, 172–173
  migraine headaches, 160–164
  tension headaches, 118–123
Urinary incontinence, 338–339
Urinary retention, 338–339

Vagus nerve:
  acid secretion, 327
  anatomy, 47–50
  asthma, 233–235
  ulcers, 327

Vascular system (see also Extracranial blood flow, Intracranial blood flow)
  autonomic nervous system, 47–50
  conjunctiva of eye, 136–137
  extracranial:
    migraine headaches, 166–169, 175–176, 180–182
    parasympathetic nervous system, 48–50
    Raynaud's disease, 208–211
    sympathetic nervous system, 47–50, 210–211
    tension headaches, 134–138, 154–156
  intracranial:
    head pain, 137–138, 165, 169, 171–173
    migraine headache, 169–176
    prodrome, 164–166, 171–173
  migraine headaches, 166–169, 175–176, 180–182
  Raynaud's disease, 208–211
  tension headaches, 134–138, 154–156
Vasoconstriction:
  extracranial blood supply:
    migraine headaches, 164–169, 175–176, 180–187
    Raynaud's disease, 208–211
    tension headaches, 134–138, 154–156
  intracranial blood supply:
    migraine headaches, 164–166, 171–173
    prodrome, 164–165, 171–173
Vasodilation:
  extracranial blood supply:
    autonomic nervous system, 47–50
    head pain, 134–138, 154–156
    Raynaud's disease, 208–211
    tension headache, 134–139, 154–156
  intracranial blood supply:
    head pain, 137–138, 165, 169–173
    migraine headaches, 147–148, 165, 169–171
VC (see Vital capacity)
Ventricular paroxysmal tachycardia, 360
Vital capacity:
  asthmatic symptom, 221–223
  treatment for asthma, 236–245, 248
Voluntary control, 58–67
  mediation, 22
Voluntary response, 58–59

Water plethysmograph, 208–211
Wolff-Parkinson-White syndrome, 358–359

Zygomaticus muscle and Bell's palsy, 305